The Arc of the Universe Is Long

The Arc of the Universe Is Long

Unitarian Universalists, Anti-Racism and the Journey from Calgary

Leslie Takahashi Morris

Chip Roush

Leon Spencer

Skinner House Books

Boston

Printed in the United States

Cover design by Suzanne Morgan
Text design by Jeff Miller

ISBN 1-55896-548-3
978-1-55896-548-5

10 09
6 5 4 3 2 1

Morris, Leslie Takahashi.
    The arc of the universe is long : Unitarian Universalists, anti-racism, and the journey from Calgary / Leslie Takahashi Morris, Chip Roush, and Leon Spencer.
        p. cm.
    Includes bibliographical references and index.
    ISBN-13: 978-1-55896-548-5 (pbk. : alk. paper)
    ISBN-10: 1-55896-548-3 (pbk. : alk. paper)   1. Unitarian-Universalist Association—History—20th century.   2. Unitarian-Universalist Association—History—21st century. 3. Race relations—Religious aspects—Unitarian-Universalist Association.   4. United States—Race relations. 5. Anti-racism. 6. Church work. I. Roush, Chip. II. Spencer, Leon E.   III. Title.
    BX9933.M67 2009
    289.1'32089—dc22

                                                          2008047546

We gratefully acknowledge permission to use the following copyrighted materials:

"Principles of Organizing to Dismantle Institutional Racism" © Crossroads Anti-Racism Organizing & Training, Used with permission.

"Continuum on Becoming an Anti-Racist, Multicultural Institution," edited for use in the UUA by Jacqui James; © Crossroads Anti-Racism Organizing & Training. Adapted from original concept by Baily Jackson and Rita Hardiman, and further developed by Andrea Avazian and Ronice Branding. Used with permission.

We dedicate this book to all those who have walked ahead to forge a path that others may follow—whether they are elders, youth, or leaders with a particular courageous moment to contribute. We want to offer special honor and tribute to those who have left Unitarian Universalism, disillusioned by its seeming inability to "walk its talk" with regards to racial inclusiveness and those who died without sure knowledge that the efforts they put forth to build a more inclusive, more authentic faith would flower. We also dedicate this to the more than one hundred people who gave of their time and attention, often raising painful memories, so that all of us could learn from our history. All of them have passed the chalice flame to us—and it is up to us to keep it lit.

Acknowledgments

Leon: I wish to acknowledge my partner, Inge Spencer, for her love and support throughout this project. I also want to express my gratitude, respect, and deep appreciation to my colleagues, Leslie Takahashi Morris and Chip Roush, for their support, their challenges, and their ministry as they worked to be faithful to those who shared their experience with them.

Chip: To Becky Roush, my touchstone, who makes my professional ministry (especially this volume) possible; to Melissa Carvill-Ziemer, my pastor and my prophet; to Thandeka, my inspiration and guide, for her intellect, commitment, and unfailing compassion for all persons; to Jon Rice, for his historical analysis and willingness to share; to Purple Rodela, for her vision and pursuit of multiculturalism; and to my coauthors, Leslie Takahashi Morris and Leon Spencer, for their patience with me, their candor, and their willingness to engage at a very deep level.

Leslie: I wish to acknowledge Leon Spencer and Rev. Danielle DiBona, whose care and often "tough love" kept me as a Unitarian Universalist; Chip Roush for having the crazy idea to work on this book; Rev. David Takahashi Morris for hours of rekeying documents in the wee hours of summer mornings in 2006 and for his ceaseless support and comfort. Also, my children, Garner and Liam, who gave up so many holiday and vacation hours with their mom during the completion of this project. I also wish to honor the many colleagues and fellow Unitarian Universalists who gave of their time in interviews and conversations and exemplary service.

Special thanks are due to Rev. Joseph Santos-Lyons for his assistance in locating names and for his remarkable thesis for Harvard Divinity School; to Catie Chi Olson for transcribing, without reimbursement, the General Assembly sessions from 2005 and 2006 related to transracial adoption; to Mary Benard, our initial editor on this project, as well as the initial review committee; to Elandria Williams for her help with youth and young adult outreach. Thanks also to Nancy Lawrence, Susan Leslie, Kay Montgomery, Simona Munson, and Tracey Robinson-Harris of the Unitarian Universalist Association staff for their help in obtaining materials as well as to Jannette Lallier, administrator of the Unitarian Universalist Ministers Association. Also, to Margaret Smith, member extraordinaire of the Thomas Jefferson Memorial Church-Unitarian Universalist in Charlottesville, Virginia, for her above-and-beyond transcription work in summer 2006 and her layout assistance in 2007.

Our last and yet truly heartfelt thanks goes to Tom Stites, our editor, coach, and fellow traveler: We are deeply grateful that you were willing to walk awhile on this journey with us. And to Joni McDonald and Suzanne Morgan for their dedication to seeing this project to completion.

Contents

Foreword

As I write, Barack Obama, the first African-American president of the United States, has been in office just days. Some commentators are already talking about our nation moving into a "post-racial" era. How I wish that Obama's election had the potential for that kind of magic. I can tell you, with certainty, that my election as the first African-American president of the Unitarian Universalist Association in 2001 did not complete our faith's work on race and racism.

Our successes and our failures with issues of race, our challenges and our great opportunities, are the subject of this book. The story it tells begins with the passage of a "Resolution on Racial and Cultural Diversity" at the 1992 General Assembly in Calgary, Alberta, Canada, and recounts events and reactions through the middle years of the first decade of this century.

The book can be an excellent resource for personal study or congregational reflection, but for me this is a personal story. The 1992 Calgary General Assembly was my first since the tumultuous 1969 GA and what is called the "Black Empowerment Controversy." Like many others who journeyed to Calgary, I was a part of the networking and coalition-building that made the resolution's overwhelming passage possible. As UUA president I've probably spent more time thinking about, worrying about, and praying about Unitarian Universalism and race, and more time sitting in committee and task force meetings on race, than any other subject. I know that my decisions to modify our strategy have been a source of both pain and hope to our community.

In 2004, I became acutely aware that we do not have a collective narrative or story about our engagement and that, with the passage of time, we were in danger of losing memory of critical parts of our history. James Cone is quoted in the text as saying, "There is no justice without memory." We were in need of a telling of our story. Hence, this book was commissioned.

The authors, Leslie, Chip, and Leon, have my profound thanks for their willingness to take on this task. They volunteered to be sure. But as you will read in the first section of the book, their experience of creating this work has forced them to be present to all of the frustration, anger, and hope of the transformation we are attempting.

I hoped that this book could offer a cohesive narrative about our efforts to re-create ourselves as a diverse, anti-racist, multicultural faith. I hoped we might find inspiration in our successes and lessons in our failures. Indeed this book offers both. But history is best written after a passage of time. The transformation we are attempting is very much in process. Indeed, I can argue that we have only begun the journey.

So the authors have, I think wisely, chosen to step back from the usual role of historians and let many voices tell this story. Those voices speak out of their own vision and experience of our story and often the voices are contradictory. They have done an admirable job of allowing, perhaps even forcing, the readers to construct their own truths out of the rich body of information and opinion assembled and presented here.

It will be much easier to write a "history" of this period if and when we reach the promised land. In the interim, as we wander in the wilderness, this book provides an invaluable service. By offering the experience of those most involved, in their own words, *The Arc of the Universe Is Long* presents the complex and often conflicting versions of the story we will tell our children of our struggle to address the racism that we know is endemic not only to our society but to our congregations as well. Will ours be a story of triumph in which we can hold up our faith as a model of the Beloved Community? That would please us, of course, and give reality to our often overly grand self-assessment. Or will ours be a story of failure, in which our inertia wins out over our theological commitments? Or some middle ground? It is far too early to tell.

I would be less than honest to pretend that I don't appreciate the approval of my leadership that is contained in this book. And I would be lying to say that the criticisms of my decisions, often from people I consider good friends, do not hurt. A part of me wants to point to the success of Association initiatives such as the JUUST Change consultancy, the Diversity of Ministry Initiative, the Truth and Reconciliation invitation, and the openness of more of our congregational leaders to engage this work in my defense. But I have to be, as we all do, content to let the passage of time tell the final tale.

There are, however, a few comments I would make by way of introducing this text.

First, the early and critical decision to focus staff and volunteer energy on transformation of the Association's national structure was intentional. This strategy has been significantly successful and its consequences far reaching. The Association's Board of Trustees, key volunteer leaders, and staff all received anti-racism training early and have answered the call by modifying policies and procedures. But there has always been a disconnect between that national leadership structure and congregational life. In our life together, we elevate ecclesiology above theology. It will always be the lived experience of congregational life that defines who we are.

Second, we have shied away from addressing the question of measurement. How will we know if we have been successful? Five years after Calgary, the 1997 General Assembly adopted the Journey Toward Wholeness resolution, which shifted the focus from diversity (which can be measured numerically) to anti-racism. That shift was appropriate, in my view. The last thing we wanted congregations to do was to find a few more dark faces so that they would feel better about themselves. But it leaves the question of how you can measure anti-racist transformation. Do you count the number of workshops held? The number of committees formed? The number of resolutions passed? When we are talking about personal and institutional identity the changes we say we desire are far more difficult to assess.

Third, and really a corollary of my comments above, do we not ultimately want our faith to look like the world in which we live?

Racial and cultural diversity may not have been appropriate as a first objective, I agree completely. But ultimately if we do not find a way to minister to diverse congregations we will have failed. It is a tricky line to walk. But walk it we must.

Fourth, the engagement of the UU youth and young adult communities with anti-racism should be our pride, as it is theirs. The question is whether we older adults are willing to follow their leadership, to share our honest concerns about their approach, and accept that they are shaping the world in which they, not we, will live. We, those of us in my age group, need to cultivate the discipline of being elders; elders who share what we have learned but resist the temptation to impose our solutions on those who follow us.

Fifth, there is a great gulf between our understanding of anti-racism and of multiculturalism. One of the successes of the last fifteen years in Unitarian Universalism has been the emergence of voices from communities and experiences other than those of African Americans, my community. We must honor and celebrate the presence of those voices, those persons. But we cannot ignore the formative nature of the black-white paradigm that informs so much of our conversation about race, ethnicity, and culture. There is knowing and healing about our national and personal history that is long overdue.

This book is a great resource. Because we do not have the distance to tell a simple narrative, this work shines a light on the actual process of change—and shows how complex and "messy" change almost always is. Anti-racism consultants we have worked with, including Crossroads Ministry, tell us that the Unitarian Universalist Association has committed more energy and resources more consistently than almost any other institution. Viewed from the outside we fare pretty well. Viewed from the inside, as this book does, disagreements often seem to dominate.

What is true is that for Unitarian Universalism to move into a vibrant future, we will need to mine our past for stories of resistance to oppression, stories of openness to new ways of being religious, stories of transformation that have built new understandings into our narrative of who we are. The fact of a multicultural present and future for our world is undeniable. The only question for us is how we will respond. There can be no stronger motive, no greater sense of urgency to help us face our demons and claim a future that is worthy of the legacy we have received.

In faith,

Rev. William G. Sinkford
President, Unitarian Universalist Association
2001–2009

About the Authors

This project has been a group effort, representing our deep commitment that no one perspective can begin to grasp the complexities of race and culture. By way of introducing ourselves, our experiences, and the biases inherent in them, we offer a brief introduction of ourselves as individuals and as a working partnership. None of us is a professional historian. Two are ministers just years from seminary and the one with the most extensive experience is a psychologist. None of us has the distance from this material to sift it with the perspective necessary to separate all wheat from chaff. What we can say is that we have tried as much as possible to let as many voices as possible have their say.

Rev. Leslie Takahashi Morris has been active as a Unitarian Universalist since the mid-1980s and was ordained as a Unitarian Universalist minister in 2005. Identifying as a heterosexual, multi-racial woman with European-American and Japanese-American heritage, she has been involved in conversations about race and our faith since the mid-1990s. A writer by avocation, she has participated in anti-racism trainings and other events at the district, associational, and congregational levels as well as campaigns for marriage equality and work to address the impacts of homelessness and to champion the rights of the mentally ill.

Rev. Chip Roush serves as the senior minister to the Unitarian Universalist Congregation of Grand Traverse, in Traverse City, Michigan. He was born in 1963, in central Ohio, in a working-class family of mostly German and Irish heritage. He discovered Unitarian Universalism while working as a database administrator and entered divinity school five years later in 2001. He was a co-founder of "Undoing Racism at Meadville Lombard: a Committee for Honesty, Education and Reconciliation" at the Unitarian Universalist seminary in Chicago.

Dr. Leon Spencer's work on anti-racism and anti-oppression efforts for Unitarian Universalist congregations began in 1985, when he helped establish the Black Concerns Working Group. He was instrumental in the success of subsequent anti-oppression and racial identity task forces, including the Jubilee Working Group, the Journey Toward Wholeness Transformation Team, and the Diverse and Revolutionary Unitarian Universalist Multicultural Ministries (DRUUMM). He was also a founding member of the Thomas Jefferson District Anti-Racist Transformation Team. He has also served on the Board of Trustees of the Unitarian Universalist Association and as president of the Thomas Jefferson District Board; in 2007 he was honored with the Award for Distinguished Service to the Cause of Unitarian Universalism. He is a professor of counseling and psychology and a counselor educator at Georgia Southern University. He and his wife, Inge, are members of the UU Fellowship of Statesboro, Georgia. He is also a proud father and devoted grandfather.

Our journey as a team of three began in February 2005 and in May we asked ourselves to do what we knew we had to ask others to do. We began a conversation, a conversation around difference. We differed in our identities: one African-American male, one white male, one multiracial female. We also came with different experiences and different views of what works and doesn't in interracial dialogue. So we began by listening to ourselves. That we have stayed in this conversation in the intervening years is rooted in the fact that our conversation across difference was united in one larger hope—that the Unitarian Universalism that we share as a faith would stay on the path to realize the promise of racial reconciliation.

Here is an excerpt condensed from our initial conversation:

LESLIE: Perhaps the easier place to start is why we are undertaking this daunting effort?

LEON: Why I chose to help write this book—why I chose to be involved in hard work—this is a question I have been asked for thirty-six years. The fight against racism is part of the day-to-day of my existence as a person of color. And yet, I have a need to know. I have a need to know the history and the events that shape me and my faith community. As a counselor and a psychologist, frequently when we deal with clients, we talk about not starting at the past, and not living in the past, but really knowing it, before we can do anything to change the present and shape the future. I have a need to know and it is a spiritual need to know.

CHIP: That is why I am part of this effort as well. Leon lived through many of the events on timelines for the period we are studying. I came to Unitarian Universalism about ten years ago, after the General Assembly voted [the 1992 resolution to become more racially and culturally inclusive] at Calgary to become an anti-racist Association and so it is important to understand. Part of what I did was challenge myself to work with Leon and Leslie and to learn where I can go and to see how much I can change and grow and to find a place for white men in anti-racism dialogues. That is why I have chosen to be a part.

LESLIE: When Chip called and asked whether I might be interested in working with him on writing this history, my initial reaction was not positive. And yet, as I began to reflect on it, the reason I eventually said yes was that it was within Unitarian Universalism that I found my voice as a leader, it was within this faith that I found my identity as a deeply religious person. And it was also, in part, through the work of the Journey Toward Wholeness within Unitarian Universalism that I began to claim my identity as a multiracial person, to begin to wrestle with the tangles in my own personal history of what it means to be the product of a white mother and a Japanese-American father. It was also within the context of getting more involved in anti-racism efforts that I had my own wilderness journey, my own crisis of faith, my own time of questioning whether Unitarian Universalism can live its faith and whether I could be part of its efforts. In many ways for me this book has been a continued spiritual quest to understand the journey we all have been on.

CHIP: And we have different levels of experience. I have not been involved in efforts to address racism except more recently with this dialogue at Meadville Lombard Theological School. My impressions have been that there was an original program and that Rev. Dr. Thandeka responded and her criticisms seemed valid to me, because my view of the Association's efforts was that they starting by saying "all whites are racists," which seemed like a hard place to start. Recently I have been working with a group at Meadville to think about what is wholeness. I think it is much more a question of walking and talking together.

LEON: For me the discovery has been that everything is about identity. We as a movement have missed some real opportunities and issues of oppression.

LESLIE: For me what has come forward as an unknown is, How do we continue to challenge the racial and cultural assumptions inherent in the way we are as Unitarian Universalists and do so from a faith perspective? I was part of the initial movement to train teams from the districts of the Unitarian Universalist Association to implement anti-racism programs, and I realize now that was not a piece I got.

LEON: Where I am developmentally is as an older person of color. I don't want to be an older, bitter person living in despair with no sense of integrity. I think the work on anti-racism has personal, religious, racial, and cultural contexts.

LESLIE: So if we each had a question we hope to answer in looking at this history—for me it is simply a question of how we will embody what we say we believe. Can we find ways to have unity and diversity—in that paradox? I don't think there can be unity without divisiveness.

CHIP: Is there a place for me in efforts to build a more inclusive Unitarian Universalist Association? It is easy to make the white male the bad guy in the whole conversation. Can we do this together?

LEON: Will this be a place for me or for my children or grandchildren?

Notes on Language and Sources

What does "anti-racism" mean? What does "wholeness" mean and how does one journey toward it? What is a "historically marginalized group?" The very intellectualism that marks us as Unitarian Universalists—itself an example of a bias toward a particular educational, racial, and cultural context—has dictated the nature of our walk together through issues of race and heritage, for we have spent a great deal of energy debating how to use language and what language to use. Language is important, for it is what allows us to speak the truth to one another. So, offering our own disclaimers, here are some terms we have chosen to use:

- *People of color* is the term initially used to describe those who are not of European descent or those who would not be considered white by legal and other standards. A number of people who are not of European descent pointed out that this term does not include them and a new terminology emerged, referring to "historically marginalized groups" and "people of color or Latina/o and Hispanic origin." None of these is uniformly satisfactory and for the purposes of this book; we will use the term that seems to best fit the context and that seems to offer the most respectful inclusion.
- *Anti-racism* and *racism* are terms chosen with intention by those leading the charge in the Racial and Cultural Diversity Initiative and later the Journey Toward Wholeness. Some raised objections, saying the word "racism" was negative and guilt-producing and thus unproductive. Other terms offered included "anti-oppressive" and "multicultural," which people

on the other side of this discussion saw as not specific and descriptive enough. Knowing these caveats, we use these terms in certain contexts because they were part of the shape of the dialogue.

- *Anti-oppressive* has been used more frequently in later years to acknowledge that many forms of oppression exist and that they are interlocking. It also has its fans and its detractors—and again, because it is a term commonly put forward, we will use it in the context of those times.

- *Multiculturalism* describes the syncretistic process of creating something new that honors elements of many cultures. Beyond surface diversity, it is an iterative and evolving process that requires those involved to continue to be learners. We use it knowing that it is sometimes suspect, for as was noted in one meeting, "blacks are inevitably left out when groups submerge diversity into terms like multiculturalism."

The work is often used to refer to efforts to raise awareness about issues of racism or other oppressions. In the 1990s and into the new millennium, advocates of anti-racism, anti-oppression, and multiculturalism would often refer to their efforts as "the work." As we collected material for this book, we saw clear proof that what one person meant by "the work" was different from the next person's definition. Still, in particular quotes, that term is used—though some heard it as exclusionary and so it remains, for them, a source of pain.

And finally, a note on sources. Throughout this text, we use original source documents and materials from the times discussed as well as more contemporary interviews. The date of a particular comment may be helpful to understanding its context; this material is available in the endnotes.

The racial and cultural identity of various interview sources is also relevant. We had hoped to have photographs to help present the faces of the many voices here. Where people shared their own assessment of their identity, we presented it here. Otherwise it did not seem our place to do so.

Introduction

This book traces a dialogue about race and racism and Unitarian Universalism that began formally with a 1992 resolution adopted by the delegates at the General Assembly to increase the racial and cultural diversity of the Unitarian Universalist Association of Congregations.

The story this book tells can be seen from many vantage points. No one voice can describe the events in the period we are trying to present here. Our approach, in trying to be true to many perspectives, is to try to let many voices tell it as much as possible. At the same time though, through our reflections and dialogues, we will give you a sense of where we are coming from in shaping the words contained here, for shape them we inevitably did.

In 1997, General Assembly delegates adopted another resolution that launched the Unitarian Universalist Association of Congregations on a "Journey Toward Wholeness." Even the name—a phrase intended to express our desire to become a more racially and culturally diverse religious association—became controversial. Putting the criticisms aside for a moment, we would ask you to envision this book as the story of a journey, one taken by our Association. As with many journeys, this one was informed by earlier journeys and trips (as in the old joke that defines a trip as an accidental fall) and it will inform other traveling that might happen in the future. As we set out to map our account of this journey, we found ourselves overwhelmed from trying to embrace the pain and triumph, progress and setback that characterize these chapters in our Association's history. As we found our bearings, we also identified three threads woven through the chapters that follow:

Identity.   This journey has been one about identity and identities, the multiple ones that shape us as Unitarian Universalists and the various truths we hold each to ourselves. Our search for identity as a religious people—as individuals, as groups with shared characteristics, as congregations, and as an Association—seems also caught up in our identity searches around issues of race. Our identities as Unitarian Universalists, as liberal religionists, as justice-seeking people, are all intertwined here.

Faith.   As an Association, we are a religious body and, as such, this has been a journey of faith—faith in the sense that process theologian Henry Nelson Wieman defines it, faith as an act and a series of actions. It has also been about faith in the sense that the efforts to address racism within our Association have caused deep conversations about the nature of our faith, not only what is fitting for us to do together but also what we believe together and what vision we share for our collective future.

Relationship.   How we are in covenant and how we are in conflict are vital threads of the collective story you are about to read. A series of relationships sets the parameters of these narratives: relationships between the majority culture in our Association and those historically marginalized; between blacks and whites, much marked by residual emotions from the controversies of previous decades; within multicultural complexities as other races and ethnicities entered the dialogue; between the rights of individuals and the dream of a collective that is more representative of the communities we serve and better embodies our deepest values; between action and reaction; between time and money; between congregations and the Association staff; and on and on.

We began this work with a simple and obvious premise: that we do not believe there is one "right" story about the journey. A countless number of stories cry out to be told, and each is powerful. Rev. Dr. Mark Morrison-Reed wrote in his landmark book, *Black Pioneers in a White Denomination* (Boston: Skinner House, 1989), that the story is "politically instructive, intellectually challenging and spiritually broadening. It connects us to each other despite differences of sex and race, time and space. The story forces us to expand and correct our self-understanding.

"Story puts us in somebody else's world. It holds up their struggles and therein helps us to look at our own. This forces us to reappraise ourselves, to look more carefully at the assumptions of middle-classness, the assumptions of whiteness. In this process, one is 'liberated into particularity.' One's own existence becomes relative and distinctive. This is essentially an event that affirms the self."

To hear the many versions of this journey, one must listen to the stories, and that is what we have tried to do. The listening has not been easy, for often we were trying to interpret the pulsing of great silences. The legacies of the history of race relations and efforts at racial reconciliation in our Association include pain, divisiveness, distrust, and deep fears. Silence was often what greeted our multiple pleas for information.

So we begin with gratitude that, through repeated efforts, and with assistance from others, many found the compassion and the courage to answer our invitation. Some answered it with justifiable anger; some with a tentative relief; others with weariness so great that we had to question whether we had a right to ask those who had already given so much to contribute still more of their heart's energy.

We also begin by honoring all those who were too busy to respond to our appeals and requests, or who did not trust that we would or could treat their voices respectfully as well as those whose leadership we discovered too late in our process. Many who remain silent are people whose efforts deserve recognition, and we are saddened by the losses of relationship that have occurred through the years. As religious people, we must mourn these deep losses and we must be challenged to remember how high the cost of loss of relationship is to our religious life.

We were also stymied by the lack of written resources to inform us on many of the key events of this time. In more ways than we had anticipated or desired, this became an "oral" history of a time, subject to the vagaries of memory. In that sense, what you have before you is less a "history" than a collection of incomparable voices of those who forged paths for themselves and our Association, a collection of priceless lessons about what it means to struggle with the disconnection between what we aim to be and what we are as a religious movement. In these pages, personal exploration and institutional gaffes are witnessed. The intersections of intention and human limits are depicted.

What we present is assembled from stories that are often incomplete—after all, racial issues are far from resolved, both in our Association and in the wider world. So it is no surprise that many of the stories here are devoid of the satisfying conclusion, the proverbial "moral." Yet we have tried to honor the many voices. They speak to the multiplicity of truths that must be embraced in an expanding view of the world, many offer shards of perspective and understanding like haiku or stories from an oral tradition. In these voices, one can discover the affirmations of self that Morrison-Reed describes.

We were told by many that they did not wish to contribute to this work, that they did not trust that their voices would be heard or honored, that they did not want to lend credence to an account of a series of events about which they remain deeply disturbed. We were able to persuade some to allow their invaluable perspectives to be used, but we also respected the choice of others to abstain—and yet with this respect comes the acknowledgment of another way this account is incomplete.

Some voices are presented at length, often those of people who shaped the discussions and initiatives described within these pages. Many reflect the struggles of those who have been "chalice bearers," a term given to us by Janice Marie Johnson, a woman of African and Caribbean descent who used it in an interview to indicate those who had blazed a way for the rest of us to follow. Janice applied the term to those who had inspired her noting that she felt we are all "chalice bearers" when we take the unrewarding and unwelcoming positions as leaders in times of uncertainty.

Though we were not able to capture all the voices we sought, what is clear is that the initiatives of this time were guided by those of the trail-blazers from earlier periods, for each generation of leaders is indebted to those who came before. Chalice bearers are thus, in Janice's words, "those who believed in the worth of all races and who plodded along, making the inroads they could." During our more than three years of work on this project, we came to believe that we have many chalice bearers among us.

In 1961, Martin Luther King paraphrased nineteenth-century Unitarian preacher Theodore Parker, who once said, "The arc of the universe is long but it bends towards justice." In this sense, we offer this account of an arc that is too long to be seen completely at the time of this writing—yet appears to be bending toward justice. How do you tell a story that is still in progress, a story that is about, more than anything else, identity, relationship and faith, and about the ongoing dialogue that shapes each? In the chapters that follow, the reader will find a common structure.

The book is divided into six parts that correspond to a period of time, followed by a seventh that offers our concluding observations and the observations of a number of those with whom we were privileged to speak. In the beginning of the first six parts, a timeline sums up some of the period's key events, markers along the journey. Narrative chapters follow, based on the many voices who have offered their experiences and their truths. Each of these parts ends with a section on "learnings" from its period. You will also find examples of these voices set off for you to read outside the narrative; we believe that when working with differences specifics are illustrated best by examples that capture the spirit of dialogue at a given point. Wherever possible, we have attempted to provide multiple points of view, for that very much captures the character of this journey. These sections include personal perspectives shared either in some sort of public way or with us in interviews as a direct response to our many requests for information. They also include excerpts from published and unpublished writings and from official documents.

In the throes of this book's difficult birth process, we were asked by one astute observer of our Association if it was too early to attempt a history of this time. In fact, as we selected content, we wrestled with whether to include events that were literally unfolding as we wrote. Is it too early to write a definitive "history"? Yes. Will it always be impossible to write one version that will encompass all truths about this time? Yes. Can we afford to wait, to leave the learnings unexplored? We believe the answer to this is no. And so we have proceeded in faith.

We have been lauded for taking on important work; we have also been attacked by those who feel that we cannot and will not do justice to an important time, or, conversely, who believe that this is all best left under the rug. This has been a heavy, almost paralyzing burden at times, and yet the more we were wearied by the responsibilities of completing this book the more our commitment to present an open and uncensored account of this time increased. If the stories collected here have any lesson, it is the power of the untold, the hidden and held-back, to break relations. If we, as a faith community, are to pass the truth of our lives through the fire of thought, as Ralph Waldo Emerson once instructed Unitarian seminarians, we must be willing to look with frank and candid eyes at our most difficult times.

We acknowledge that despite our best efforts and true intention to use any information in the spirit in which it is offered, we have no doubt left out something that someone will feel is vital, overemphasized something someone will see as trivial, and neglected events that others will see as essential. We know that limits on our time and energy and knowledge—this was a very part-time endeavor—will have inevitable impact. In other words, we know that portions of this work will disappoint. And yet we hope that having this collected to the best of our ability will be useful, not only to those who were directly involved in shaping this time by placing their viewpoints in relationship to those of others, but also to the much greater number of people who were not involved, who only heard rumors of this time and who perhaps are interested in continuing to work in a Unitarian Universalist Association that more fully embodies its ideals. We celebrate this intention.

Just as one story cannot capture the nuances and complexities of the Association's struggle with these pervasive and difficult issues, one book cannot capture the full range of perspectives. Our intention has been to design a form that is consistent enough to allow a more measured walk through these events as well as the opportunity to delve deeper for those who have that need. Many points of entry are available in this text and through the index to this work. We invite you to find your own way into what is offered here.

—Leslie Takahashi Morris, Chip Roush, and Leon Spencer
January 2009

The Past That Did Not Pass

"Black Empowerment," "walkout," "racist" . . . the words we use, the language we have to describe the period of the late 1960s and early 1970s, are loaded. Why, for example, do we use the term "Black Empowerment Controversy?" It seems to make the anguish of that period the fault of a relatively small group of African-American Unitarian Universalists rather than the result of the white Unitarian Universalists' encounter with race and racism. The term "White Power Controversy" would be more accurate in many ways and would direct attention to the broad Unitarian Universalist movement, and its need for healing and transformation, rather than to the small, marginalized group of "black" people and their allies.

—Rev. William Sinkford, President of the
Unitarian Universalist Association

1963	**1965**	**1968**
Viola Liuzzo is killed in Alabama while participating in civil rights activities.	Unitarian Universalist ministers answer Rev. Dr. Martin Luther King Jr.'s call to come to Selma and stand in solidarity to protest the violence there. Rev. James Reeb is killed.	The General Assembly of the Unitarian Universalist Association passes a business resolution to recognize and finance a black empowerment group, the Black Affairs Council, at $250,000 a year for four years.

At the end of the 1980s, Unitarian Universalists were beginning to speak again about race relations and its relationship with the principles and history of their faith. Yet those conversations were marked by a legacy of relationships interrupted by events more than a decade earlier and left unresolved.

Being actors for social justice was a deep part of the Unitarian Universalist identity. As the Civil Rights struggle unfolded, Unitarian Universalists took a leadership position that earned them recognition by activists in many denominations and that attracted a number of African Americans to our congregations.

Yet integrating these new perspectives and life experiences into the predominantly white, middle-class culture of the Unitarian Universalist Association proved tricky. As the 1960s ended and the 1970s began, the Unitarian Universalist Association's members found themselves mired in a debate about how much self-

1969	1978	1980s
General Assembly delegates vote to reaffirm funding the Black Affairs Council and to not fund an integrationist group, Black and White Alternative, beginning the "Empowerment Controversy."	The City Center Church Advisory Committee was created in response to a General Assembly resolution seeking to monitor efforts to support urban churches.	The Unitarian Universalist Association's Board of Trustees undertakes an Institutional Racism Audit in 1980 to identify practices and policies that impede good race relations.
		New urban ministries are begun in seven cities.

determination blacks should have and what part Unitarian Universalist support, including financial help, should play. These decisions, referred to as the "Empowerment Controversies" in these pages, marked one of the most divisive and bitter chapters in the UUA's history. For Unitarian Universalism, the unresolved pain and anger, broken trust, and unrealized hopes from this period made this the past that did not pass.

More than two decades later, race was still a subject not easily discussed within the Association. Instead, those interested in promoting greater racial justice worked on "urban concerns" and focused on race by addressing places were the demographics were more diverse. Yet for some, these diffuse approaches had outlived their usefulness and, in the mid-1980s, new groups such as the Black Concerns Working Group were formed by the Association's leadership and asked to look again at issues of race and the Unitarian Universalist faith.

1982	1983	1984
UUA Board creates the Whitney M. Young Jr. Urban Ministry Fund to foster urban and multicultural/multiracial congregations.	*Empowerment: One Denomination's Quest for Racial Justice 1967–1982:* The 1983 study of the Unitarian Universalist Association by the Commission on Appraisal is released.	The Task Force on Racism publishes its findings, urging the creation of a group to work toward ending racism in our movement and in the larger society.
The Network of Black Unitarian Universalists forms.	The UUA Board appoints a Task Force on Racism as suggested by the Commission on Appraisal's report.	The UUA Board appoints an Anti-Racism Monitoring and Assessment Team.
LRY (Liberal Religious Youth) dissolves and YRUU (Young Religious UUs) is created during a conference known as Common Ground II.		The UUA Extension Department launches the first Racial Ethnic New Start congregations to create places where African Americans can minister.

Through their work, an Institutional Racial Audit was commissioned by the Association's Board of Trustees, who wished to determine what practices and policies might be unintentionally undercutting race relations within the Association of Congregations. As the work of the audit was completed, the desire to once again address issues of race head-on seemed to be building, becoming the force for change that would prepare the Association to enter into a new era around racial justice.

1985	1986	1988
The General Assembly establishes the Black Concerns Working Group to implement the Task Force on Racism's suggestions.	The Black Concerns Working Group holds its first meeting in Boston.	African-American ministers and religious professionals organize the African American Unitarian Universalist Ministry (AAUUM).
		The UUA's Department of Ministry Task Force on African American Ministers creates the *Beyond Categorical Thinking* program to help congregations envision hiring ministers from historically marginalized groups.
		The C*UUYAN (Continental UU Young Adult Network) is formed when bylaws are adopted and approved.

CHAPTER 1

Unitarian Universalists in the Civil Rights Era

From the beginning, the identity of the Unitarian Universalist Association was linked to social justice issues, expanding a legacy of our religious ancestors, both Unitarians and Universalists, who were often ahead of their contemporaries in discussing and expanding the grasp of who should be given rights—and often not. In no time in our religious history as a people of faith have these issues not been present.

In the earliest days of Unitarianism and Universalism, the issue of slavery lurked unresolved and the issue of race was a perpetual tension. As the Association's Commission on Appraisal noted in 1983,

> For a century and a half, there have been numerous stirrings of examples of devoted and effective individuals in the forefront of action, first to abolish slavery and then to level caste differences among free and supposedly equal citizens. But the institutions themselves, constrained by their principle of congregational polity and by wide differences of view and perspective among the congregants, struggled with the same paralyzing uncertainties that beset the whole society.
>
> One need not dig deep into history to find this dichotomy. Probably an overwhelming preponderance of Unitarian Universalists were proud of the national media pictures showing the President of their Association marching in the very front of a crucial civil rights demonstration in Alabama, and took solemn inspiration in the death of a UU minister senselessly murdered in Selma, Alabama. The goal,

a just society, was clear. But when it came time for a denominational march toward that goal, seemingly irreconcilable
divisions about the means to organize that march arose, and
the movement lurched and sputtered.

And the controversy around the role of liberal religionists in the
1960s era of black empowerment rocked the Unitarian Universalist
Association in its infancy—the Association was founded in 1961,
when the American Unitarian Association and the Universalist
Church of America consolidated—leaving developmental issues
that survive today. This was a period when basic issues of *identity*
were not worked out—for while the consolidation of the Unitarians
and Universalists was achieved at one level, at the level of identifying core beliefs, many believe the work was never done. As Rev.
Dr. Gordon B. McKeeman, past president of the Starr King School
for the Ministry, observed in an address at the 2004 General Assembly, "In our passion for freedom, we have accepted the association of
independent units, a kind of institutionalized individualism, and
we attempt to confront the excesses of a society which has placed
individual freedom, individual initiative and individual responsibility on the top of its hierarchy of values, and are puzzled at the impo-
tence of such arrangements to encourage group activity on behalf
of the entire human family." From the beginning of our shared
identity as Unitarian Universalists, in some sense, torn and divided
when we were still young, we became a people whose experience
foretold that discussion of differences was dangerous and divisive.

Unitarian Universalism came out of the 1970s with a painful
legacy around race. In addition to the Empowerment Controversy,
other histories informed this time, including the roles Unitarians
and Universalists played in colonization, in slavery, and in the
usurping of territories held by those of Hispanic and Latino
heritage.

Being actors for social justice was a deep part of the Unitarian
Universalist identity. Rev. Joseph Barndt of Crossroads Ministry, a
nonprofit group that helped shape the Unitarian Universalist Association's anti-racism work in the 1990s, recalled,

The wonderful thing about the UUA is . . . its commitment to justice is a given. . . . No white denomination, no white Christian denomination, and no white religious group in this country was really deeply involved in the Civil Rights movement until [Rev. Dr. Martin Luther King Jr. was assassinated on] April 4, 1968, when guilt got us all and everybody became in favor of racial justice and that includes my denomination, the Lutherans. Exceptions to that are the Quakers and Unitarian Universalists. In 1965, when Dr. King put out a call for people to come to Selma, there were a lot—all the denominations had individuals who responded, but none of them in the name of their denomination. The UUs were in the middle of a national board meeting, and they voted to go as a board to Selma.

"Looking back over our history, both the Unitarians and the Universalists have not always been progressive," Rev. Dr. Jerome Stone, adjunct professor at Meadville Lombard Theological School, observed. "Russell Miller, in his history of Universalism, points out how mixed was the Universalist response to the struggles of both women and blacks. . . . Criticisms of our ambiguous efforts might be easier to take and to respond to creatively if we realize that our actions have always been a mixed bag."

For the fledgling Unitarian Universalist Association of Congregations, the difficulties came in trying to respond to the black empowerment movement. The majority white and middle-class Association found itself tangled in a snarl of relationships that could not easily be understood or navigated. A desire to ally with a minority group's call for justice conflicted with a strong commitment to honoring decisions made through established process and by majority rule. All this came at a time when the shared faith of the young Association was still embryonic.

The Commission on Appraisal, which reexamined how the Association was affected by the Empowerment Controversy more than a decade after its key events occurred, wrote,

Religious liberals at the onset of the black empowerment movement were placed on the horns of a dilemma. Their profound commitment to tolerance and to integration and to democratic process was challenged to match the demands of those who, even more vehemently than Dr. King, saw these articles of faith as stumbling blocks to racial justice. For some, there could be no compromising any of these principles; the ends do not justify abhorrent means, they argued. It was, for them, clearly a matter of right and wrong. For others, the wrongs they suffered would wait upon no such argument; too long they had waited while "good means" were turned to indefinite or bad ends. It was, for them, clearly a matter of wrong against wrong.

Selma—Sacrifice and Pride

To understand the history of efforts around race in the Unitarian Universalist Association, one has to study how our history is entwined with the Civil Rights Movement. Unitarians and Universalists supported Rev. Dr. Martin Luther King, Jr., in Selma. Inspired by these actions, many people—including many blacks—joined Unitarian Universalism in the 1960s. A defining moment was the murder of Rev. James Reeb, a young, white UU minister who worked with poor people in Boston, and who died on March 11, 1965. As a newspaper account retold it, "He and two other Unitarians, the Rev. Clark Olsen and the Rev. Orloff Miller, were attacked in Selma, Ala. They had gone there, to the epicenter of the struggle for black voting rights, two days after state troopers had violently turned back a column of marchers, an event known as 'Bloody Sunday.'" Reeb's death became a rallying cry and point of pride for Unitarian Universalists, for it was critical in galvanizing the white support that led to the Voting Rights Act of 1965, though other lives were also lost, including African-American rights advocates and Viola Liuzzo, a Unitarian Universalist protester. Rev. Dr. Victor Carpenter recalled the Selma events this way: "It was a great defining moment for certainly my generation of ministers and the generation before mine. The moment had finally come when the sermons we had preached and the demonstrations we had, if not led, participated in—finally the moment had come."

EXCERPT
Empowerment

The following excerpt is from the Commission on Appraisal's 1983 report to the General Assembly on the Empowerment Controversies.

"What is proclaimed and practiced as tolerance today," wrote Herbert Marcuse, "is in many of its most effective manifestations serving the cause of oppression." It is difficult for even the most conscientious person to accept the extent to which he or she is fallible. Tolerance has long been an article of faith for religious liberals, who do not take kindly to the possibility that it, and more especially the practice of it, may serve ends they do not approve.

Unitarian Universalist commitment to racial integration was, has been, and is, a function of an institutionalized belief in tolerance, even as it is part and parcel of a desire to be generous. What are Unitarian Universalists to think, then, when it is announced that racial integration means racial disintegration, that what Unitarian Universalists have been serving is not the cause of tolerance but the cause of intolerance, not generosity but selfishness?

To what extent, of course, Unitarian Universalists were able to identify the "oppressed" within their midst—and, thence, to identify with them—was and still is problematic. The question of color to a religious association that aspired to be color-blind rankled. A large number of black and white religious liberals found the accusation that their high-minded commitment to tolerance, integration, and the democratic process was "sinful," that it "missed the mark," that it served the cause of oppression, specious and self-serving. They rejected it and deplored the attempts made to establish a separate caucus of the "oppressed" within the Association, arguing that such action was, for all its claims on behalf of justice, merely a resort to sectarianism. . . .

So the debate continued. And continues. After fifteen years, the UUA is, with the same issue still unresolved, a house divided. On the surface, the controversy seems to have subsided; Unitarian Universalists are again what they were before the upheaval and acrimony of the late sixties and early seventies; they are again, if not comfortable, at least settled in their principles—those regarding tolerance, integration, and the democratic process. And yet, what are Unitarian Universalists to make of the retreat religious liberals have made from their earlier overt commitment to racial equality and social justice, the disillusionment of many members of color within their midst, the perceived apathy of many toward the persistence of institutional racism in the Association, the all-too-evident failure of Unitarian Universalist churches and fellowships to attract persons outside of the white middle class?

Pride ran high in that era, as Carpenter recalled:

One of the things I've expressed, and this is a feeling that I share with a number of the people who were involved, is the excitement of it all. It was a buzz! We were really doing something! Suddenly some people actually thought we were dangerous. . . . Our phones were tapped. Moles were in our congregations. Very few UU ministers can complain about moles being in their congregations these days. We were on the cusp. When those of us who were involved meet at General Assemblies and this kind of thing, it still generates excitement. I still get excited when I talk about it, when I talk with these kids who've never heard of it. I mean they look at me in astonishment. You mean, we UUs did *that*? Yes, we did.

That sense of pride around the roles they played in Selma left them ill-prepared for what happened only a few years later. "It was basking in [the role at Selma] that I think really did not prepare us for the advent of black empowerment," Carpenter noted. "That was not on anybody's screen."

Empowerment Controversies
Yet on the heels of these sad, but proud, moments were to come the scarring and divisive events known as the "'Black Empowerment'/ 'White Power' Controversies." These events are outside the scope of this narrative and yet related. A succinct summary is difficult. At its most basic, the sequence of events goes thus: The 1968 General Assembly, in Cleveland, committed $1 million over four years to a UU black self-determination group, the Black Affairs Council (BAC), which sought to develop black-controlled projects to aid black people. No support was granted to an integrationist group, Black and White Alternative (BAWA, later Black and White Action). Almost immediately after the General Assembly votes, the Association's Board of Trustees discovered the Association lacked the money to fund its existing programs. Despite the financial strain, the Board voted in May 1969 not to reduce the promised funds, and further voted to grant $50,000 to BAWA.

The BAWA funding was controversial, as was the timing of the scheduled debate—at the end of the GA agenda. When several close votes failed to change the agenda, many blacks and more than 400 whites (of 1,379 total voting delegates) walked out of the GA. They were persuaded to return the next day, and a narrow majority voted to fund BAC and not BAWA. Carpenter recalled that it was an unprecedented level of controversy. "Nothing like this had happened before," he said. "Oh, yeah, individual churches had caused a GA rumpus every now and again, such as when Community Church [of New York City] left the Association under [Rev.] John Haynes Holmes, but nothing in my time equaled it before and nothing since."

In January 1970, the UUA Board voted to restructure its commitment to BAC, spreading the payments over five years instead of four. Angered and hurt, BAC disaffiliated from the UUA in April 1970. Disillusioned by these events, many people then left Unitarian Universalism.

The Racial and Cultural Diversity Task Force summarized this period:

> Unitarians and Universalists have a history that is intertwined with the abolitionist, suffragist, and anti-war movements of our country. While historically UUs have been on the cutting edge of social justice advocacy, many have been ill-prepared to recognize and acknowledge institutional racism within Unitarian Universalism. In 1968 when African American involvement in the UUA was at its height, African Americans numbered less than one percent. . . .
>
> After much debate and controversy the 1968 General Assembly voted to create the Black Affairs Council (BAC). Despite strong commitment by some individuals and congregations, suspicion, misunderstanding, and lack of funds contributed to the ultimate demise of BAC. The majority of white Unitarian Universalists did not accept the responsibility to understand and nurture the program they had dared to embrace in 1968. In spite of the dismay of many, this lack of support for the program became a source of division

EXCERPT

The More Things Change

The following excerpt is from the Commission on Appraisal's 1983 report to the General Assembly on the Empowerment Controversies.

The history of institutional racism in the Unitarian Universalist Association and its predecessors, the Unitarians and the Universalists, can be summarized succinctly: The more things change, the more they stay the same. It is true that the pages of American history are full of the courageous and inspired acts of individual Unitarians and Universalists who opposed the slave trade, supported the abolitionist movement, played daring and effective roles in the Underground Railroad, worked to better the lot of former slaves and gave their all to the civil rights struggles of recent times. Yet the institution—the denomination and its Unitarian and Universalist predecessors—has been unable to act effectively and frequently has been unable even to condemn injustice through an official stand. Those peculiarities of institutional character that exist today are historic: the emphasis on individual belief as opposed to corporate credos and the widely touted tolerance for the opinions of others, these tenets have made institutional action impossible in many situations. As [Rev. Dr.] Mark Morrison-Reed observes, "We do not stand above the social attitudes of our times, as we are prone to believe, but rather, flounder about in their midst with everyone else."

between those persons committed to cultural assimilation and those who advocated self-empowerment. Events came to a head at the 1969 General Assembly in Boston, and in 1970 funding for the BAC was eliminated. These actions resulted for some people in feelings of disenfranchisement, and unfortunately, in the eventual departure of a significant number of African American as well as white Unitarian Universalists. What has become clear, in retrospect, is that our painful experiences were once again those of pioneers. We confronted new problems of race before other religious groups did. How could we have known at the time that the model of racial assimilation and integration for which we had fought so long was inadequate to address the newly felt needs for empowerment?

Legacy of Distrust Persists

This promise made to BAC remains as an unpaid debt in some eyes. In 1981, a team conducting an institutional racism audit uncovered a range of strong emotions relating to the events of the 1960s and 1970s. "There is a concern that these leftover feelings from the past might block relationships and hinder constructive conflict in the future," its report noted.

In 2003, Rev. William Sinkford, president of the Unitarian Universalist Association, wrote,

Why . . . do we use the term "Black Empowerment Controversy"? It seems to make the anguish of that period the fault of the relatively small group of African-American Unitarian Universalists rather than the result of the white Unitarian Universalist encounter with race and racism. The term "White Power Controversy" would be more accurate in many ways and would direct attention to the broad Unitarian Universalist movement and its need for healing and transformation.

As the new millennium dawned, strong feelings remained. Rev. William (Chester) McCall, stating a position still heard, said in

2005, "The UUA owes people of color $750,000 to fund the continuation of the movement." Rev. Dr. Robert Nelson West, who was elected president of the Unitarian Universalist Association in 1969, at the same General Assembly that approved the money for the Black Affairs Council, presents a detailed account in his 2007 book, *Crisis and Change: My Years as President of the Unitarian Universalist Association, 1969–1977* (Skinner House, Boston). The book traces the factors that led to his administration and the Association's Board of Trustees altering the terms of what the 1969 General Assembly delegates voted. These included deficit spending, which came to a critical point as West was elected, and a desire to honor "the pluralism of the honestly held divergent beliefs of those who advocated the 'Blacks only' position, as well as those who favored the 'blacks and whites' approach." As to the funds dispersed, West said that the UUA paid $450,000 in direct allocation to the Black Affairs Council. He also said additional money that was raised through the sale of bonds to congregations must be added to the total. West wrote,

> I have been told there are some people today who are still bitter about how BAC was funded. They say they were defeated in their effort to prevent our denomination from turning its back on black people. I say what was defeated was the particular tactic they advocated for our denomination to employ in combating racial injustice. The UUA chose to follow a different approach in trying to help the cause of blacks: one that was within its means and in accord with the pluralism that is essential in our democratic denomination; one that resulted in our denomination giving in excess of $1.5 million to blacks-only organizations and programs as well as more than an additional $220 thousand to blacks-and-whites programs. BAC received $630 thousand directly from the UUA.

For some, the tragedy in the aftermath of the Empowerment Controversies was that it caused changes in the way Unitarian Universalists practiced their democratic procedures as changes were

VOICE
Dr. Norma Poinsett

These are Poinsett's words from General Assembly 2001. She is a former member of the Black Concerns Working Group.

I was not shocked by the angry black rebellion which finally ignited the UUA in 1968, echoing dramatic events in the larger society. For example, President Lyndon Johnson's National Advisory Commission on Civil Disorders had warned, "Our nation is moving toward two societies, one black, one white—separate and unequal." Perhaps, more accurately, the Commission could have reminded the nation that it had never in its history been one society. The Commission blamed mounting urban riots on "white racism" and urged massive aid to the black community.

This was only part of the social ambiance that triggered a rash of black caucuses around the nation, including the rise of the Black Unitarian Universalist Caucus (BUUC) in 1967. It emerged out of an emergency call for Unitarian Universalists to respond relevantly to mounting urban rebellions. Stressing the words "empowerment" and "self-determination," we argued that black people should take charge of affairs affecting black people. We argued that only we could determine what our values should be and what was good for our communities. We were experts on our chaotic condition, we contended, because we faced racism daily both north and south.

The Black Caucus urged the UUA to establish a Black Affairs Council (BAC) and called for increased Black representation on all of the UUA's policy-making boards and committees. We also urged the UUA to commit $250,000 a year to BAC for four years to fund community and economic development projects in Black America.

Out of the ensuing debate came FULLBAC, a white group which teamed with us to secure full funding for BAC. Concurrently, a more conventional, integrationist oriented group called BAWA (Black and White Action) emerged to compete with BUUC.

The black empowerment conflict reached a fever pitch at the 1968 General Assembly in the Renaissance Hotel here in Cleveland when delegates voted an unprecedented 836 to 326 to form and fund BAC. They also voted not to give BAWA funding or affiliate status. However, when the 1969 GA in Boston proposed to allocate a quarter million to BAC and $50,000 to BAWA, BAC insisted that either the UUA should or should not support Black empowerment. Once again, the delegates voted to fund BAC solely. Even so, the Cleveland GA vote to fund BAC for four years was modified by a UUA board ruling that BAC appropriations would have to be re-affirmed annually. When delegates in Boston were unable to reinstate the Cleveland GA's intent, BUUC walked out, followed later by FULLBAC and other BUUC supporters.

By 1971, not only BAC but FULLBAC and BAWA ceased to function. Hence, an estimated thousand disappointed African Americans left the UUA. I remained—not because I disagreed with them—but to continue addressing covert and overt racism within the UUA. . . .

I spoke up at my first GA in this city thirty-three years ago. Today, I am still here—taking a stand and standing.

made to ensure that General Assembly delegates could not make that type of financial commitment again. "In my view, when the GA stopped being actively involved in budget matters, it consigned racial justice initiatives and, indeed, all justice initiatives to being top/down by definition," said Denise Davidoff, known as Denny, who was the Association's moderator—chair of its Board—from 1993 to 2001. "The annual budget hearing, mandated by the UUA bylaws, is, on a good night, sparsely attended at best," she said of current General Assemblies. "Moreover, a passive General Assembly is always going to feel disempowered and disgruntled. That's organizational development 101. But passivity, disempowerment, and disgruntlement are not helpful when we as a religious movement need to feel, and be, brave."

For many young people, the Empowerment Controversies were disillusioning. Many left, including a young William Sinkford, who would return and, eventually, become the Association's first African-American president. Rev. Wayne Arnason, active as a youth in the 1960s, said the events that unfolded afterward served to cement the connection between youth and discussions of racial justice:

There were two things going on. . . . One was the role that youth played in directly supporting the Black Affairs Council membership, who either actively seized microphones on the floor, or who lined up behind the microphones in such a way that it wasn't possible for other people to speak, and shut down the Assembly at the point where they were deciding that they would not move the Black Affairs Council issues up to the front of the agenda—that's fairly well documented in other places. The youth caucus at that GA was a very active part of the group that left the GA at the Statler-Hilton Hotel [in Boston] and went over to Arlington Street Church and spent the next two days in debate about what do to, and whether to come back. . . .

The youth leaders were included essentially as equals and as partners in that negotiation process. . . .

All that experience led to the second connection that was built, as the Liberal Religious Youth executive committees continued to be deeply involved in working as partners in the FULLBAC coalition and the Fellowship for Renewal, the two white allies organizations that were supporting the Black Affairs Council.

Youth leaders were partners in the organization of the witness against the January 1970 UUA Board of Trustees meeting where they decided they would not follow through on the resolution that was passed by the 1969 GA. When that decision was made and the Black Affairs Council decided to go directly to UU congregations and seek support of the economic empowerment projects that they had planned to fund with UUA money, which they were not going to get, Liberal Religious Youth was the first organization to take its resources and invest them in Black Affairs Council bonds. That's probably the best short summary of what the precedent relationship was of LRY to those dramatic events in our anti-racist, anti-oppression history.

The connection between the controversy and the Journey Toward Wholeness was clear to those who experienced both. Betty Bobo Seiden, who had been active as a member of the Black and White Alternative (BAWA), recalled,

The most significant event of the Unitarian Universalist Association's efforts toward anti-racism and multiculturalism was the 1968 General Assembly in Cleveland. It was my first GA. I was actively involved in the religious education program at my local congregation, teaching the children to sing "This Little Light of Mine," "Go Tell It On the Mountain," and "Go Down, Moses" when I was delegated to go to Cleveland. That General Assembly changed my life and served as a catalyst that subsequently evolved into a journey towards wholeness for the UUA. If it had not been for the main event at GA in Cleveland I would most likely not have attended the General Assembly in Calgary in 1992, and the UUA probably would not have been ready to embark on a Journey Toward Wholeness.

VOICE

Rev. Melvin Hoover

Hoover served as the Unitarian Universalist Association's director for Racial and Cultural Diversity and, later, as the director of the Faith in Action Department. Ordained in 1971 as an Episcopal minister, Hoover formally became a Unitarian Universalist in 1980. His wide range of experience included ministry, education, human resource development, community organizing, administration, and policy development. The following is excerpted from his article, "The African American Experience and Unitarian Universalism," published in World *in 1993.*

African Americans have been involved with Unitarianism and Universalism from their beginnings. Gloster Dalton, a former slave, was one of the twelve founding members of the first Universalist church, the Independent Christian Church of Gloucester, MA. Both free men and escapees from slavery are recorded as attending Unitarian congregations in the Boston and Philadelphia areas.

In terms of slavery there were Unitarians and Universalists who were on both sides of the issue and there was a spectrum of resistance from non-violent to pro-active efforts to abolish slavery. Universalists such as Benjamin Rush, president of the Pennsylvania Society for Promoting the Abolition of Slavery, were among the first persons to call for the abolition of slavery. Many Universalists found slavery inconsistent with the religious call that all God's children are part of the same family. A number of Unitarians were followers of William Lloyd Garrison, editor of *The Liberator*, the leading anti-slavery newspaper. Among them were Samuel Jay May, Lydia Maria Child, William Ellery Channing, and Theodore Parker. One of the classic stories of anti-slavery times is that of the Rev. Theodore Parker, who provided sanctuary for several blacks in his church. A noted preacher, Parker always kept a loaded pistol on the pulpit and publicly declared that he would shoot anyone who tried to forcibly remove blacks from his congregation.

A prominent African-American Unitarian of this era was Frances Ellen Watkins Harper. Born in Baltimore on September 24, 1825, she lived in Philadelphia most of her adult life. Poet, novelist, essayist, she was a tireless abolitionist, stalwart supporter of the underground railroad and dedicated worker for women's rights. She excelled as a public speaker and was considered on a par with Frederick Douglass. A member of First Unitarian Church Philadelphia, she worked with the African Methodist Episcopal denomination and developed their religious education curriculum.

Not only were Unitarian Universalists important in the abolitionist movement and the success of the underground railroad, but they were among the first to call for education and health care for freed slaves and to assist in establishing schools and medical facilities.

After Reconstruction, as the country became resegregated under Jim Crow laws, Unitarians and Universalists were leaders in the fight to defeat discriminatory laws and promote equal rights for all people. Unitarian Universalists introduced legislation within the political arena and actively supported legislation and court decisions that promoted equality and justice.

The Civil Rights Era produced many leaders, among them Whitney M. Young, Jr., a prominent civil rights leader and active Unitarian Universalist. As the executive director of the National Urban League from 1961–1971, he brought the League into the civil rights movement and made it a force in the major events and debates of that tumultuous decade. He was also a leader of the 1963 March on Washington. Young's work produced historic breakthroughs for people of color in employment, education, and entrepreneurship. He was the author of two books, *To Be Equal* [McGraw Hill, 1964] and *Beyond Racism* [McGraw Hill, 1969] in which he developed his vision of an open society. What he envisioned was a pluralistic society (not simply an integrated one) that would thrive on ethnic and cultural diversity and ensure economic and racial justice.

The Unitarian Universalist Association became deeply immersed in and provided leadership in the civil rights

continues on page 16

movement after the death of Viola Liuzzo and the Rev. James Reeb. [Liuzzo], a homemaker and lay member of First Unitarian [Church in] Detroit, was brutally murdered for serving as a driver for voter registration efforts in the south. Jim Reeb, like hundreds of other clergymen, had responded to the Rev. Dr. Martin Luther King Jr.'s call to participate on the first march on Selma in March of 1965. After the march, the Rev. Clark Olsen, the Rev. Orloff Miller, and Jim [all Unitarian Universalists] were attacked by whites as they were walking back to their rooms after dining at a black restaurant. Jim was struck on the back of the head and was killed. The UUA Board of Trustees, upon hearing of Jim's death, adjourned their meeting to reconvene in Selma where they and half the ministers in the Association participated in a successful march.

After Selma, Unitarian Universalists throughout the country stepped up their efforts to open closed doors that denied basic human rights to African Americans in North America. The Association was among the first predominantly white religious organizations to positively respond to the new directions of the Black Empowerment Movement and established a significant program with dollars administered by blacks.

Although progressive in dealing with racism within society, Unitarian Universalism has been slower in addressing it internally. There are only a handful of African-American ministers in parish ministry and in denominational leadership positions. The history of Unitarian Universalist African-American religious professionals has most often been that of being a pioneer. Issues of race and class within the Association have until recently hindered the development of black religious professionals and the creation of appropriate resources to speak to and serve African-American needs. The first major history of the black minister's experience in Unitarian Universalism, *Black Pioneers in a White Denomination*, was produced in 1980 by the Rev. Dr. Mark Morrison-Reed. In his book Mark states, "The quandary I face is twofold. First, given my chosen vocation as a minister in a white denomination, how can I serve the black community? And, second, how can I inform the Unitarian Universalist tradition through the black experience?" Mark lifts up a reality that most African Americans experience in Unitarian Universalism, the sense of living in two worlds. The challenge historically has been to find a common ground in which both our heritage and our faith can be congruent.

CHAPTER 2

Urban Ministry and an Anti-Racism Audit

Proponents of racial justice efforts during the 1960s and 1970s had viewed the articulation of beliefs as an impediment to doing justice, rather than as a base for power since the new Association had little consensus around beliefs. After the pain of the Empowerment Controversies, Unitarian Universalist efforts to address racial justice issues became coded, embedded into less controversial initiatives around "urban concerns." Between the 1960s and the 1980s direct efforts to address race relations within Unitarian Universalism were few. The focus on urban concerns was real and powerful and while it kept the issue of race alive, it did it in a covert way.

Rev. Melvin Hoover, who is of African descent, called our congregations the "living lab of human interaction and relationship," observing, "That's where I've seen our faith. . . . That's part of our identity, to be diverse, our hope even for some, even though that diversity to them was more like be colorful and be like me—that would look good to other folks. That's what, shorthand, you know. To have Asians and Latinos and blacks that were UUs. So everybody looking at it would say, 'Aren't they diverse!'—but leave your culture at home."

In 1980, the UUA Board of Trustees contracted with Community Change, Inc., a Boston-based organization, to conduct an "Institutional Racism Audit." That audit, which contained more than thirty recommendations, said of the climate, "We have discovered that most UUs love to talk—and debate—perhaps endlessly. . . . There is something wrong when people delay by waiting for detail, more debate over issues which affect others so urgently. . . . Another behavioral characteristic which is related perhaps to the 'endless debate syndrome' is the propensity towards intellectualism and the reluctance to deal with 'difficult' emotions. . . . In our collective interviews, often questions about feelings of interviewers elicited "thought" responses. To get to some feelings about racial issues demanded a skill that could be referred to as 'verbal dentistry.'"

This was a period when steps to promote and value women's leadership and the inclusion and leadership of gays and lesbians were bearing fruit. Whether it was important to delve into the pain of addressing issues around race depended on whether one saw it as essential to our faith or not. With a radically open theology, this also became a matter of contention.

Urban Ministry (1970s)

Still smarting from the Empowerment Controversies, and wary even of the word "race," Unitarian Universalists could still focus on "urban" ministry. The 1978 General Assembly called for creation of a committee to monitor efforts to support urban churches. The City Center Church Advisory Committee (later renamed Urban Concerns and Ministry) was for a time the nexus of Unitarian Universalist work on race and multicultural diversity. Its focus shifted from urban to primarily racial concerns in the mid-1980s. During that time, urban extension ministries were planned for seven cities (Detroit, Michigan; Jamaica Plain, Massachusetts; Norfolk, Virginia; Oakland, California; Palisades, New Jersey; San Jose, California; and Tulsa, Oklahoma) and support given to eleven intentionally ethnic congregations (five of which survive, in Chicago, Illinois; Los Angeles, California; Durham, North Carolina; Tahlequah, Oklahoma; and Washington, D.C.).

Rev. William Schulz, the Association president, had a personal interest in urban areas, having grown up in the church in Pittsburgh, Pennsylvania. Hoover recalled that the urban ministry efforts were a way to begin a dialogue about race. "The Urban Church Coalition, which was a mixture of lay people and ministers, was an affiliate group that was challenging the UUA at that time to pay attention to urban ministry, which also was a way we could talk about race, because we had difficulty talking about race in that era," he said. "There was all this angst about well, we can't, we have to be nice and not talk about race because of black power, and it split us before. But there was no way you could talk about the urban agenda without having to talk about race and racial issues. That became the umbrella for trying to really address and begin to work with racial justice concerns." Several coalition members, including Rev. Nannene Gowdy, were credited with trying to keep the issue of race on the table.

In April 1982, the UUA Board of Trustees created the Whitney M. Young, Jr. Urban Ministry Fund, to foster urban and multicultural/multiracial congregations. (Now known as the Journey Toward Wholeness Sunday Whitney M. Young, Jr. Urban Ministry Fund, it supports the JUUST Change Anti-Oppression Consultancy and awards grants of up to $3,000 for local urban ministry projects and partnerships.) "Lots of folks told [UUA president William] Schulz, we must do something," said Rev. William Gardiner, who served on the staff of the UUA's Faith in Action Department. "'Urban Concerns' was code for race and racial justice. People say it is 'top-down' or 'imposed' but it was called from the grass roots."

Yet the explicit and articulated focus on race and race relations was missing. The Racial and Cultural Diversity Task Force later noted about this period,

> During the 1970s and 80s, Unitarian Universalists were very active in opposing the Vietnam War and in fighting for women's and gay and lesbian rights, all of which was positive, but the issue of race was put on the back burner. This lack of focus hindered the development of effective programs and initiatives for African Americans and other people of color at the very time, ironically, when the number of people of color who were open to liberal agendas was increasing.

Institutional Racism Audit (1980–81)
In 1980, the UUA Board authorized the Institutional Racism Audit. The audit report, prepared by a five-member team appointed by Community Change, Inc., defined racism as "attitudes, beliefs, norms, and values reflected in institutional policies, practices and procedures which deny to members of racial minority groups access to goods, services, and resources on the basis of race." Defining was

important because the word "racism" was itself controversial. Perhaps the most significant finding of the audit was about what Horace Seldon, Community Change's executive director, called "climate": "In one meeting I heard the word 'black' used in an all-white group with negative connotations. Phrases like 'Black Sunday' correlate black with gloomy. If I had been a black person sitting there, I don't think I would have been very comfortable. This creates an organizational climate that says to people of color, 'This is not for me.'"

The report made thirty-two recommendations and also identified a cultural phenomenon in the UUA:

> We have labeled factors which seem to block our efforts towards racial justice as the Liberal Syndrome. Although some of the institutional symptoms can seem inclusive, the behaviors and attitudes indicative of the Liberal Syndrome are exclusive: they exclude progress. For instance, while talking about racism, many UUs assumed the liberal church to be enlightened and therefore, not needing to do anymore in the way of action. Several people reported that liberals "welcome all views . . . all people" and then assumed that "we don't have to think about 'color' or 'group' . . . or inclusion." This sense of "openness or enlightenment makes people feel comfortable with the situation as it currently exists."

Finally, it called for an imperative:

> An imperative . . . expresses a command, is mandatory, is obligatory, is compulsory, is authoritative, is peremptory. Those words might sound strange in the context of Unitarian Universalism. . . . still the word imperative is used here to express a stance which it is suggested that the UUA take for its institutional efforts against racism. The word is intended to convey a sense of urgency . . . it is a word which will keep the UUA restless until the vision is actualized. . . . The imperative is not a matter of semantics. An imperative says that work against racism is not just one more program priority among many. . . . An imperative says that in addressing racism we are talking about an issue which pervades

every aspect of our institutional life. Consideration of that imperative cuts across the entire institution, affects every decision the institution makes, every position it takes, every expression of its being.

The Board adopted the following imperative in 1981:

Recognizing the fact that institutional racism is still embedded in American society in 1981, the Unitarian Universalist Association shall seek to eliminate racism in all its institutional structures, policies, practices, and patterns of behavior so that it will become a racially equitable institution and can make an effective contribution toward achieving a similarly equitable society.

The Board chose twenty-five of the audit's thirty-two recommendations to try to implement. One of the major recommendations was around the state of affirmative action in the Unitarian Universalist Association staffing. Rev. Joseph Santos-Lyon noted in 2006 as part of his seminary thesis,

The UUA was slow to react around establishing affirmative action policies and goals, the top recommendation of the 1981 UUA Institutional Racism Audit. Of concern to the auditors was the tension within the UUA, making it difficult to effectively implement affirmative action policies for People of Color given the UUA philosophy and White culture. They wrote: "The twin concepts of meritocracy and democracy seem at the core of the UUA philosophy. Developing human potential and enhancing production in culture, politics, society and morality, appear as artifacts of UUA actions and worship ideals. Imagine then our dismay to hear that when the questions of people of color and the ministry were at one time put before the Ministerial Fellowship Committee, a response was characterized with the following words: Do "they" fit the mold? Are "their" backgrounds, and experience typical of our usual placement requirements? Will we have to lower the standards?"

That this recommendation was adopted at all was significant as the Board was able to initially implement only a few of the audit's thirty-two recommendations and a series of task forces for monitoring racism was subsequently established.

The residual concerns about race relations spurred a new focus. "It took us over a decade to heal our wounds from the black empowerment controversy—to acknowledge our mistakes, renew our commitment, and sharpen our understanding about the 'new racism' of the 1980s," the Racial and Cultural Diversity Task Force was to note in 1993.

The Task Force described its origins: "At the beginning of the 1980s, recognizing that the problem of racism had not gone away and in fact had gotten even worse in society, the UUA commissioned an Institutional Racism Audit . . . which dealt with issues of race at UUA headquarters."

As a result of this audit, one other piece of history came to light, one mentioned in the twenty-third recommendation:

> The reference is to a years-long, monumental (1,000-page manuscript) curriculum project on racism, of which most UUs are quite unaware. It was commissioned just after the Cleveland General Assembly in 1968 by the UUA Department of Education and Social Concerns with the Black Unitarian Universalist Caucus. A curriculum team was appointed. The Reverend Hugo Hollerorth, Curriculum Editor for the Department, represented the UUA staff. BUUC members included Sandra Dillard, Clayton Flowers, Hayward Henry, Dr. Norma Poinsett, Robert Small, Margaret Williams, and Mary Luins Small. All engaged in writing units at first, but Mary L. Small was commissioned as the major writer, and it was she who labored, literally for a decade and more, on the subject.

The author, who had worked for more than a decade on the project, much of it unpaid, was given the rights to the manuscript, which was never published and which remains at the UUA offices along with a "voluminous file" on the subject.

VOICE
Rev. Dr. Mark Morrison-Reed

This reflection appeared in a 2000 issue of World, *when Morrison-Reed was serving as co-minister of the First Unitarian Congregation of Toronto, Ontario. Institutional religion is always a marriage of religion with culture.*

We like to think otherwise about ourselves, but our UU faith communities are also as much a product of our culture as of our religious perspective. UU norms—our style of worship, principles, attitudes, and social concerns—are shaped by our upper-middle-class, North American values. We don't see how strongly these influence us because we live inside that particular cultural box.

This points to a problem. In continental surveys, many UUs express a desire to embrace diversity and are frustrated by the slow pace of diversification. But is it really diversity we desire? And do we want it even if it means cultural upheaval? Or do we actually want to attract people of diverse ethnicity only if they fit into our culture—a culture we don't even recognize as one?

The temptation is to lie to ourselves. In 1967 the UUA Report of the Committee on Goals found that in regard to "Negro" ministers, 27 percent of UUs agreed that such a person's "race might hamper his effectiveness," while 47 percent said the same thing of women ministers and their gender. What then transpired calls our survey results into question. The number of women in our ministry grew from [21] in that year to 199 in 1987, and 431 out of the 853 in active ministry today. Meanwhile, the number of ministers of color, which in 1967 was [8], increased to 17 in 1987. It currently stands at 45, at least seven of whom are not in active ministry or haven't been involved in the UUA in a decade or more. Now compare the number of ministers of color to the number of openly lesbian, gay, bisexual, and transgender ministers, which stands at approximately 5 percent. Similar, but take note: the first openly gay minister was granted fellowship less than 25 years ago. The first minister of color, the Rev. Joseph Jordan, was licensed by the Universalists in 1888 and ordained in 1889.

We've chosen a path, and these numbers tell us which. Culture has prevailed. Diversity advances more quickly when the primary barrier to inclusivity is not culture but gender or sexual orientation. The people of color who have become UUs are those who already operate within our cultural norms. Examine the résumés of UU ministers, and it's often hard to tell who is of color and who not.

There are good reasons for us to become more inclusive—the survival and revitalization of Unitarian Universalism being foremost. But let's not fool ourselves about what such a change entails, for to misjudge what is possible is to set ourselves up for frustration and failure.

Controversies Revisited (1983–84)

In 1983, the General Assembly received a report by the Commission on Appraisal that unpacked the Empowerment Controversies of the late 1960s and early 1970s. This provided a way to reopen a conversation around these events. A series of pieces in the Association's *UU World* of March 1984 showed the range of perspectives still present on these issues. Hilda H.M. Mason, who had served as chair of the Greater Washington Black UU Caucus, noted that the Black Unitarian Universalist Caucus and the Unitarian Universalist Black Affairs Council "put the UUA on the cutting edge of response to Black demands for equality in the late 1960s." Rev. Dr. Donald Harrington, minister emeritus of Community Church of New York and active in Black and White Action, wrote from his perspective as a white participant that "the call for separation on racial grounds was offensive to a denomination which had just recently battled on the issue of requiring that all of its societies should be open racially." The founding co-chair of BAWA, Dr. Glover W. Barnes, then a black member of the East Shore Unitarian Church in Bellevue, Washington, wrote that "the great interest of our UUA white leaders seemed to be directed toward 'containing' the rebellion, particularly its monetary aspects." Rev. Charlotte Cowtan-Holm, then minister of the Unitarian Universalist Church of Flint, Michigan, noted the interplay of race and class, a theme that would be important again in the 1980s and 1990s. Rev. W. Frederick Wooden, then minister of the First Congregational Parish, Unitarian, in Petersham, Massachusetts, noted that the report was particularly important for white people under thirty-five who did not understand these events while "for many older than I, it may still be too soon." And Robert Hohler, a Vermont Unitarian Universalist who was active in FULLBAC (Full Recognition and Funding for the Black Affairs Council), an organization of white supporters of the Council, wrote, "What pain. It still hurts. After all these years I found to my surprise that it still hurts."

The Task Force published its findings—urging the creation of a body to work toward ending racism in our movement and in the larger society—at the 1984 General Assembly in Columbus, Ohio.

CHAPTER 3

Re-examining Issues of Race

As the 1980s got under way, new structures emerged designed to validate the particular identity of those who were black or African American and Unitarian Universalist, such as the Task Force on Racism, the Black Concerns Working Group, and the African American Unitarian Universalist Ministry. These groups forged relationships among those who shared a particular experience in their travels through Unitarian Universalism. Also, at this time, the Sanctuary movement with its call to offer shelter to refugees from Central America raised awareness of Latina/o/Hispanic people.

The question of what our faith compels us to do arose. Dr. Leon Spencer, who was appointed to the Black Concerns Working Group in 1985, noted that issues around theology came up as the Working Group looked for models it could use. "I borrowed from the United Methodists a little piece that they had about Jubilee," he recalled, continuing,

> I think that was the earliest point of us starting to think that the United Methodists had more or less a theological base from which they were moving. We tried to take and borrow the concept of Jubilee, not that it belonged to United Methodists, it belongs to all of us in a sense, but we took the concept of Jubilee and . . . worked on how we might put this into a UU perspective. What would be the meaning of Jubilee. . . . The thing that was striking to me in looking at the United Methodist piece was the fact that they did have a theology to tie it to. We didn't really sit and use the term theology at that early point, we just said they had something that they could tie this to. And I can remember conversations

about how you can do that with a Christian church, but how can you do that with UUs? We have such varied beliefs. And then we started thinking about we have the Principles and Purposes. There were discussions that went on early about this, that you can't really ignore that piece. You had people in the group who were humanists, people who were Christian, people who were from a variety of backgrounds: deists, theists, whatever. There was a real mix of folks on the Committee.

Black Concerns Working Group Forms (1985)

A Task Force on Racism was appointed by the UUA Board in 1983, in response to the Commission on Appraisal's report, *Empowerment: One Denomination's Quest for Racial Justice 1967–1982*, which discussed the need to have a body to "begin a fresh response to the issues of racism as a major priority for the UUA."

To implement its recommendations, the Task Force recommended a continuing body, establishing the Black Concerns Working Group of the Social Responsibility Section of the Unitarian Universalist Association at the 1985 General Assembly. Dr. Spencer, a member of the initial group, noted that the advocacy and groundwork for the group was initiated by the North Shore Unitarian Universalist Society in Plandome, New York, which had a group working on issues of race at the congregational level. At the time it was formed, only informal lists existed of African-American Unitarian Universalists. Dr. Spencer understood that he was brought on as a new member because they intentionally sought new perspectives.

The resolution to establish the Working Group acknowledged the need for a focused effort to address chronic problems. The goals of the Working Group, which did not meet until 1986, were to promote and encourage racial inclusivity at all levels in the Unitarian Universalist Association; to serve as an educational resource for professional religious leaders (ministers, religious educators, seminarians, etc.); to advocate for the issues surrounding racial inclusivity and urban development at General Assemblies; and to research and to share the efforts of other denominations and organizations.

The first meeting of the group took place as Hurricane Gloria was pummeling the East Coast. Rev. Melvin Hoover remembers that the beginning was less than auspicious:

> [They] told us we'd been appointed officially to the Black Concerns Working Group movement, and that our charge was . . . to eliminate racism within the Unitarian Universalist Association, and we had a budget of $5,000 to do it. And basically we laughed, then we cried, and basically I can remember saying, "I have two questions. The first is what is the most expensive restaurant in town. The second is what time is the train for me to get out of town." And that was virtually where everybody was. Fortunately, however, we couldn't get out of town.

Dr. Spencer agreed. "We were sort of stunned with the charge. I think all of us had read it before and probably secretly in our minds, or whatever, had said this is really quite a charge for $5,000! . . . The one thing we all really agreed on when we looked at each other and verbalized our reactions to what we had read in private was that the charge in itself was one that was unreal."

The funding issue touched a wound, for it echoed back to the money aspect of the Empowerment Controversies. "We started to really work at that point to build some group cohesion, but the one thing we were all on the same page with was the underfunding piece," Dr. Spencer recalled. "I think it was a sore piece for people who had been around a long time and had a history of remembering the whole piece around Empowerment. There were some initial kinds of tension that we didn't talk about for a while, and the tension was the urgency that one white member of the group had for getting this done now. I can remember conversations where we weren't feeling—it was important, but we weren't feeling the urgency that it had to be done now, because as people of color we knew it was an ongoing process. It was an ongoing process, and it was going to last. It's not something that you're going to make the change and it's done."

The Working Group was established after a significant grass-roots effort by laypeople and clergy who sought a serious effort to

---

RESOLUTION

Establishing the Black Concerns Working Group

WHEREAS, racism against Blacks is a pervasive social problem; and

WHEREAS, our denomination believes in the inherent worth and dignity of every person, in the democratic process based on equality and freedom, and in the individual right to enjoy all of our constitutional and other legal rights; and

WHEREAS, the Board of Trustees of the Unitarian Universalist Association has recognized the presence of racism in our denomination, as evidenced in conclusions of the Institutional Racism Audit; and

WHEREAS, our religious beliefs and our faith in the democratic principles impose upon us an obligation to oppose racism wherever we find it, and we recognize that our efforts to end racism against Blacks are also means of ending racism against all oppressed people in our society;

BE IT RESOLVED: That the 1985 General Assembly of the Unitarian Universalist Association recommends that there be established a Black Concerns Working Group of the Social Responsibility Section to assist in the implementation of the Report of the Task Force on Racism as approved by the 1984 General Assembly whose tasks shall be:

1. Helping Unitarian Universalist societies increase their awareness of racism and showing them how to reach out to minority groups by:
   a. providing educational material on the nature, causes, and consequences of racism to be made available to individual members of every congregation; and
   b. encouraging our societies, area councils and districts to establish Black Concerns Subcommittees or to appoint individuals to deal with the issue of racism as it pertains to individual societies both as a moral imperative and as a means of creating an environment within our association more inclusive of diverse races, cultures, and classes;
   c. drawing upon and publicizing the experience and knowledge of individual members of Unitarian Universalist societies who can contribute special insights into the issue of racism;
2. Initiating and suggesting activities designed to influence our political leaders at every level of government to eradicate racism whether imbedded in law or in social custom or practice; and

BE IT FURTHER RESOLVED: That this Assembly urges that an adequate budget be established for the realization of the intent of this resolution.

once again address racial discrimination and racial justice issues. Despite the anger, all Working Group members were committed to Unitarian Universalism and talk soon turned to what could be done and to the development of a more realistic plan. "We drafted a letter to the Board saying that we did not accept that charge, and we were not willing to accept that charge as stated, that it needed more than that," Hoover recalled. The group then wrote a charge that it felt more accurately and honestly represented what was possible. The fact that outside financial support from the Plandome, New York, congregation was available allowed the efforts to go forward.

In fact, no new dollars were allocated and no funds would have been available except that Dr. Loretta Williams, then Director of the Social Justice Department, anticipated this and set aside $5,000.

The Working Group formed a real new presence and watchdog. Working with its new charge, the group set out to get a dialogue started where it had stopped almost two decades before. Members began visiting congregations and groups to listen to their stories. The goal was to begin the discussion where people really were. "We went around and actively listened to people's pain and concerns and then lifted up their hopes and wishes," Hoover said.

"We began to work immediately," Dr. Spencer said. "We looked at how we could look at systemic change, how we could also do some of the educational pieces. There was always that need for education." The Working Group developed a workshop, "To Be Equal Beyond Racism" with the title formed by combining the titles of two books written by African American Whitney Young, who went on to be Director of the National Urban League: "To Be Equal" and "Beyond Racism." The annual General Assembly became a gathering place for the Working Group and others interested in racial justice issues. "We literally built ourselves an alternative General Assembly, and then over time that alternative became a new vision for GAs," Hoover said.

Working Group members brought models from their congregations: First Unitarian Society in Chicago; Community Church of New York; the North Shore Unitarian Universalist Society in Plandome, New York; the Unitarian Universalist Church in Asheville, North Carolina; and the Unitarian Universalist Fellowship

28

VOICE

Dr. Leon Spencer

This excerpt is from an address delivered around 1989, when Spencer was a UUA Board of Trustees member and chair emeritus of the Black Concerns Working Group.

Frequently I am asked, "Why should the Unitarian Universalist Association spend money, time, and resources on racial and cultural diversity?" I sometimes feel burdened with the expectation that I should have an answer because I am a psychologist by profession and because I happen to be an African American.

Often the person asking the question points out that not many African Americans would be interested in Unitarian Universalism or that we will never get a large number of them to come. Once, someone even invited me to leave and go back to whatever church I came from if it was so bad at the UUA.

The reason I want racial and cultural diversity in the UUA extends beyond issues of numbers, theology, or money. It has to do with the fact that this is the right thing to do. The religious challenge of our time moves us to open our doors to all and to promote wholeness in the midst of diversity. At times I don't understand why anyone challenges the value of this vision. Why all the fuss? Yet I also understand why. I understand all too well. Racism is powerful and it impedes our realization of a vision of a racially and culturally diverse community. Our understanding of this dichotomy can be an empowering experience. Many people seem to want racial diversity up to a point. I believe that true inclusivity removes that point.

Learning how to develop, value, and appreciate cross-cultural relationships is to everyone's benefit. Statistics are sometimes used to scare whites into being racially and cul-

turally diverse. They usually focus on the year 2000 when we will have a new "minority" in our country. The underlying message is that "you'd better change" because of a need for survival rather than it being the right and rewarding thing to do.

But there are more powerful reasons. A while back I was in Billings, Montana, co-leading a "Creating a Jubilee World" workshop. The small Unitarian Universalist fellowship in Billings gathered 40 people for this workshop. Even though there are few minority members in the fellowship, Native Americans, African Americans, Hispanics, Mexican Americans, people of different sexual orientations, youth, European Americans, people dealing with physical and emotional limitations, women and men—all came to examine themselves and to reach out to the community seeking wholeness and diversity.

Benjamin Pease, a Native American Unitarian Universalist, blessed each of us and our work. An African-American woman from the local African Methodist Episcopal Church led us in singing gospels and spirituals; a Catholic nun shared her journey; a youth of Hispanic and European descent challenged us with his pain of trying to find himself in a racist world. Everybody was included and empowered by what is sometimes referred to as "walking your talk."

Billings had recently been victimized by groups of skin heads and the Ku Klux Klan. The workshop empowered people to continue to speak up and stand unified across racial, cultural, and faith lines to do the right thing. The weekend did not focus on questions about the *number* of minorities who might be attracted to Unitarian Universalism, theological differences, or what minority group we should attract first. There were differences of opinion and yet no one was ignored, belittled, or asked to leave. We all brought gifts to the table to be shared. All were honored. All were enriched.

in Columbia, South Carolina. All had been experimenting with approaches to discussing race. Different experiences brought diverse opinions and relationships within the group were sometimes strained, especially when members became impatient at the pace of change— a theme that continues. Dr. Spencer remembered the poignancy of discovering that George Squier, a member of the group who was often a prod toward quicker change, was dying. "He just wanted to see something change and see this move before he wouldn't be around," Spencer recalled. "I think that had some impact."

The challenge in this era, given the unaddressed pain of previous ones, was speaking about the unspeakable. In 1987 Rev. William Schulz, the Association president, invited Hoover to join the UUA staff, in part to reopen a dialogue on race. Schulz recalled that Hoover, who had recently entered the Unitarian Universalist ministry, had strong ideas about how to begin diversity work within the Association: "I hired him on the staff in 1987 because . . . I wanted to make a symbolic gesture that these issues were worthy of a full position."

Hoover said a lot of energy in the late 1980s went into reopening a conversation and elevating Unitarian Universalism's social justice identity. "When I came in I said I wasn't even sure I wanted to do the racism route," Hoover recalled. "I said, 'We're not ready.' We clearly have a commitment to justice-making, but we don't have that at the heart of our congregations, necessarily, and not all of them are equipped to do that. So what we need to do is to bring part of our identity of Unitarian Universalists back to building back and lifting up the kind of creative and proactive justice-making as a critical aspect of our institutional identity at the congregational level and make it more national."

After Hoover joined the staff in 1987, he used his portfolio, which included both urban and international concerns, to bring diverse faces before the General Assembly: "When I agreed to join the UUA staff, it was with the understanding that I was hired to be an internal change agent and to assist our faith in its effort to become more effective in our urban and international ministries as part of our extension and growth efforts as well as to support efforts for racial inclusion and justice."

The Black Concerns Working Group built on the work of other groups, including the Task Force on Affirmative Action for African American Ministers, which had been meeting in late 1982 and was chaired by Rev. Dr. Mark Morrison-Reed. The Working Group's efforts included monitoring efforts of the various departments to be more inclusive, including religious education and ministerial development, publications, and communications. Reactions were mixed as noted in this excerpt from the March 1987 minutes:

> Judith Worth from the UUA Religious Education Department spoke to our group about the questionnaire which she devised and sent to 14 members of the Department. She asked them what had been accomplished in raising the consciousness level concerning Black concerns in the work which the Department does. The question "threw them" (Judith's words); they felt overwhelmed by it. . . . Judith felt her department was "sympathetic but needs provocation" but that changes are occurring. Norma [Poinsett] expressed a sense of déjà vu with: "Here we go again!"

The group also explored patterns in people's emotional reactions to conversations about race. Its response to those patterns became a training that evolved into the program known as Building a Jubilee World. Dr. Poinsett recalled, "As an original member of the UUA's Black Concerns Working Group organized in 1986 to develop and to conduct workshops in churches and General Assembly, our committee developed the 'Jubilee World Anti-Racism Workshop,' a weekend workshop that is still in great demand by congregations and for conferences throughout the continent."

The Working Group also sponsored programming at General Assemblies and programs coordinated with the urban church coalition. It also worked with the UUA Committee on Committees to identify people of color within the UUA movement who might be encouraged to become ministers to expand the pool of ministers of color and also to reach out to people of color no longer active in UU congregations.

ROSTER

Black Concerns Working Group 1994–1997

Members

Carole Baraka
Rev. W.D. (Don) Beaudreault
Rev. Nannene Gowdy
Sandy Decker
Rev. W. James Eller
Doris Edwards
Rev. Anne Hines
Lyle Hayes
Betty Holcomb
Rev. Larry Hutchison
Rev. Melvin Hoover
Rev. Kurt Kuhwald
Susan Leslie
Margaret Ann Link
Winifred Latimer Norman
Tamara Payne
Dr. Norma Poinsett
Rev. Lindi Ramsden
Layla Rivera
Rev. James Robinson
Dr. Leon Spencer
George Squier
Rev. Melanie Morel Sullivan
Harvey Thomas
Carole Walker
Sherry Weston

Staff Members: Hyh'nes Bakri and Mary Andrus-Overley

Interns: Paige Getty, Rev. Carol Jackson

continues on page 31

Why mention their names? Because those who have labored to address issues of racial intolerance in the Unitarian Universalist Association are largely invisible. Many of them, disillusioned, left our faith community. Others have ceased this advocacy for change. A few have died and their passing makes remembering their names more important.

Sanctuary Resolution of the General Assembly

While largely focused on the attraction and retention of African Americans within their congregations, Unitarian Universalists also dabbled with issues of concern to other racial and ethnic groups historically marginalized in our ranks. These included the Sanctuary movement, which offered shelter to refugees from Central American political violence and, in this country, inspired federal surveillance of movement supporters. In 1985, a resolution on "Sanctuary and Government Surveillance" was passed by the General Assembly in 1985, which read, in part:

> WHEREAS, the federal government of the United States has sent government agents and paid informers with tape recorders and wireless equipment to spy on church services where refugees have been in attendance and been ministered to, and has used the information thus gained to testify against those attending and the leaders of those church services, and has arrested and brought indictments against sixteen church workers including two priests, four nuns, a Protestant minister and several lay church workers, including Wendy LeWin, a Unitarian Universalist; and

> WHEREAS, this calculated invasion of the sanctity of the church has caused a serious disruption of the church life of the congregants and ministers in the churches so invaded; and . . .

> BE IT RESOLVED: That the 1985 General Assembly of the Unitarian Universalist Association commends Dr. Pickett for this timely leadership and commends the more than thirty Unitarian Universalist congregations and the many individual Unitarian Universalists involved in the Sanctuary Movement, including our sister, Wendy LeWin.

African American Unitarian Universalist Ministry (1988)

The African American Unitarian Universalist Ministry (AAUUM) was formed as a continental organization for African-American ministers and religious professionals in 1988. Among the founders was Rev. Marjorie Bowens-Wheatley. AAUUM reached its membership peak in the early 1990s, at more than one hundred, then helped to found Unitarian Universalist Religious Professionals of Color in 1997, and Diverse and Revolutionary Unitarian Universalist Multicultural Ministries (DRUUMM), in 1998. Rev. Wayne Arnason recalled that even before AAUUM existed, religious leaders of African descent had tried to approach the Unitarian Universalist Ministers Association leadership for assistance: "I remember that meeting very vividly, at least the emotional impact of it, and the effort to make that meeting happen," Arnason recalled. "I think they were trying very hard as well to have it be a confrontational meeting that was done in love. They wanted the UUMA exec to be leaders in this effort to bring antiracism training to the Association."

Rev. William Sinkford, who left Unitarian Universalism in response to the Empowerment Controversies and who returned to the fold in the 1980s, said AAUUM "was enormously important in my call and movement to ministry, just knowing that it was there. . . . I think my first meeting, which was in Boston in 1990 maybe, there may have been a dozen people, and that included non-ministers on the UUA staff. It was a tiny group, and struggling with these grand visions that everyone was called to for transformation and the reality that the human energy was so limited and everyone was struggling in their own right." A group for African-American laypeople called the Network was also in place at this time, Sinkford said.

In the Congregations
In 1965, Rev. Dr. Kenneth Torquil MacLean, then minister of Knoxville, Tennessee, wrote, "After a minister or layman has answered a call to go to Selma, Alabama, or McComb, Mississippi, or has otherwise participated directly in our new American Revolution, these questions arise: How are the depth and impelling quality of this kind of experience to be communicated to the church at home? And how are they to be translated into effective witness in one's own community?"

This problem, no doubt one of the complicating factors in the Empowerment era, also was true in terms of the efforts in the 1980s to draw attention to the concerns of African-American Unitarian Universalists. So few people had an opportunity for direct contact since so many congregations did not have a single African-American member and only a handful had experienced first-hand the challenges around leadership by African Americans in the overwhelmingly white Unitarian Universalist culture.

At the congregational level, multiracial involvement remained elusive, with a few exceptions, All Souls Church Unitarian in Washington, D.C.; Community Church of New York; First Unitarian Society of Chicago; and First Unitarian Universalist Church of Detroit. Meanwhile, a number of initiatives were launched to try to support ministers who were not white and in true Unitarian Universalist style, congregations began experimenting with their own initiatives around race, often focused on building relationships. For example, First Unitarian Church of Dallas had been engaged in conversations around race since the 1950s, when they had helped integrate a preschool; the congregation became more active in racial issues in the 1960s.

A number of congregations were working to foster dialogues around issues of race, including First Unitarian Society of Chicago, which had decided to become welcoming to all races in the 1940s. Rev. Dr. Fredric Muir came to the Unitarian Church of Anne Arundel County, Maryland, in the mid-1980s and began holding classes around the Commission on Appraisal's *Empowerment* report.

In the late 1980s, Rev. Dr. Lee Barker was minister at the Unitarian Church of Montclair, New Jersey, which had a growing population of African-American and biracial attendees. As seemed a common story, the efforts began out of a service. "I always felt I had a real gift at the Unitarian church in Montclair in being able to really learn from some people that had a lot of knowledge and experience, both as persons of color and as people who were trying to move our congregation from one place to another place," he recalled:

> I think one of the most pivotal experiences that I had was in
> some ways one of my own shaping, but it was only a shaping.
> It was a day when I decided I would invite three persons of

color, each from different generations and different lifetime experiences. One was a man who had been a Black Panther. Another was a young mother of six, a stay-at-home mother. The third was a woman who was a professional woman who had come up through the civil rights movements of the 40s and 50s. This was in the mid- to late 1980s. During a Sunday service we had a dialogue in the chancel about race and what it meant to be an African American in a congregation that kind of prided itself on being biracial—not multiracial, biracial—but at the same time was predominantly white. I think at the time that it was, the congregation was maybe 20 to 25 percent African-American and the rest Euro Americans. You know, there was an incredible amount of honesty that occurred in that dialogue, and it was honesty that came from different perspectives, so there wasn't the ability for anyone in the congregation or myself to say, "Oh, here's how black people think and feel in this church." It showed the complexity of the experiences that people had as African Americans in our congregation. Lots of it good, some of it painful, and all of it meaning that we needed to take some next steps for ourselves as a congregation.

The congregation hired the People's Institute for Survival and Beyond, a group providing training around race relations and racism. "It was a congregational workshop we did with the People's Institute for our congregation that allowed me as a minister, and as a white male, to see the structures of racism in different ways than I had ever seen it before," Barker recalled. "What it allowed me to do was to begin to have the kind of relationships in the larger community that were much deeper and much richer than they had been before. And it allowed me to have a leadership role, a ministerial leadership role, not just to the community's white congregations, but also to the African-American congregations in town."

In the mid-1980s, the Thomas Jefferson Memorial Church, Unitarian Universalist, in Charlottesville, Virginia, brought the People's Institute for Survival and Beyond to Charlottesville, Virginia, to assist a local effort that started around the Martin Luther

VOICE
Rev. Dr. William Jones

Rev. Dr. Jones is the director of black studies at Florida State University and a former UUA trustee.

The model I work with is an oppression-centric model where the understanding of the virus of oppression sets up the parameters within which you develop the therapy, the social policy, the RE curriculum, and so forth. I've come to understand that we start off with some myths about oppression that have to be corrected. I've also reached the understanding that oppression is a much more foundational human behavior than we had thought.

I argue that oppression is the primary human activity, and that we should not regard it as evil as we normally do. If we start off labeling oppression as evil, we're able to show that you set up a condition where you perpetuate it and allow it to prosper. But my foundational position is this: at the organic level of life in order to survive, you have to feed on something other than yourself. You cannot give me an exception to that. That's the primary premise I start with and read into, make the basis of all my analysis. . . . Everybody alive has rejected suicide. They have chosen to enhance their survival and their well-being, or at least their survival, at the expense of whatever it is that they eat. We all set up this two-category system of superior and inferior, establish ourselves as the superior, and justify consuming or eating whatever it is that we eat. Vegetarians to me don't get off the table any easier than the carnivores. But we do it at the expense of whatever it is that we eat.

To me, we operate on this "any means necessary" morality. So my whole approach is to show that we do what we do, we make what we make in order to enhance our survival and our well-being. If that's true, the only way you're going to be able to show someone, or convince them that they should stop oppression, is to show them that if they don't do this, their self-interest is at stake.

I operate on this principle of enlightened self-interest as a consequence of this analysis of oppression. Everything is oppression-centric. That to me is the foundational human activity and when everything falls right into place, I want you to pick out any issue that you had difficulty handling before and take an oppression-centric approach to it, and tell me whether or not you get a better understanding of it.

King holiday and led to formation of a group concerned with race at the church. "The King holiday made an occasion for there to be interfaith, interracial planning for a King event, and out of that came an antiracism group in Charlottesville," said Rev. Wayne Arnason, then the church's minister. "We brought People's Institute trainers into Charlottesville and had our own training. . . . We actually brought [civil rights leader Rev.] Ralph Abernathy to Charlottesville and had a march from the steps of the Albemarle County office building all the way down Preston Avenue, down Rugby Avenue, past the church to [the University of Virginia campus]. We got three hundred or four hundred people to march with us. It was related to a particular incident that had occurred in Charlottesville where an African-American man had been beaten in an overt act of racism. That's what prompted it."

During this period, many congregations sought to involve themselves in projects with African-American organizations and congregations, in response to awareness raised by the Black Concerns Working Group, Morrison-Reed's *How Open the Door?* curriculum, and other events such as the creation of Martin Luther King Day. An article the Unitarian Universalist Service Committee published in a supplement to *UU World* in 1981 noted that "[a] number of UU congregations are joining together with church congregations of a different denomination, ethnic background, color or theological emphasis for joint services, family celebrations and potlucks. Such interchanges are one small way to foster interracial harmony and to counter the breakdown in human relations that appears pervasive in general society." In the same supplement, Unitarian Universalist Service Committee director Loretta Williams noted the inter-racial nature of congregational justice-making and the front page of the issue displayed a picture of members of Liberal Religious Youth marching as part of Boston's 350th birthday parade carrying a banner reading "Unitarian Universalists for Racial Justice."

The Eno River Unitarian Universalist Fellowship in Durham, North Carolina, built a Habitat for Humanity house in partnership with The Links, an African-American women's service sorority. In the late 1980s, The First Church in Belmont, Massachusetts, an affluent Boston suburb, started a community group called Belmont Against Racism in response to a racist incident. The group began a breakfast on Martin Luther King Day that outgrew the church and had to be held in the high school. This involvement led the congregation to get involved in other efforts such as a program that brings inner-city youth to Belmont High School. The congregation also worked on issues of affordable housing, which led to a town commitment to have a human rights committee hear complaints of discrimination.

The focus was not only on relationships with African Americans. In Miami, Florida, First Unitarian Church worked with a coalition that included blacks, whites, and Latinos in efforts to address common problems and to revisit the legacy of the Civil Rights era. "Ignorance is the root of all evil," said Rev. Dr. Linnea Pearson, then the church's minister. "Our joint services were a time to be together." First Unitarian Church of Los Angeles also had a multiracial strategy, this one for its congregation. In 1980, Rev. Philip Zwerling reported that about twenty out of the three hundred parishioners were racial minorities. "To eliminate barriers to non-white attendance, we have set up a Racial Growth Committee with members from each ethnic and racial group . . . but we need to be more open to other cultures." The church planned a multilingual brochure and also was investigating the cost of simultaneous-translation technologies. Their doxology was translated into Spanish and Korean. It also made an effort to provide "visible presence of non-white persons" in the ranks of speakers, musicians, ushers, greeters, and singers.

To help congregations conceive of what it might be like to accept a new form of leadership, the *Beyond Categorical Thinking* (BCT) program was created by the UUA's Department of Ministry in 1988. Congregations searching for new ministers were encouraged to take a BCT training, to promote inclusive thinking and to prevent discrimination. More than fifteen years later the Association's Identity-Based Ministries Staff Group determined that congregations that took the BCT training "were nearly twice as likely to call a minister from one of the three areas the program addresses (race/ethnicity; sexual orientation/gender identity; physical/mental disability) than those that did not."

Dr. Leon Spencer recalls that members of the Black Concerns Working Group expressed fear as the program was being developed that if all oppressions were put under a common umbrella, the conversation on black-white issues that had just been revived might be lost. This fear would resurface again and again in the years to come.

CHAPTER 4

Racial and Ethnic New Congregations Pilot Project

Some of the experiments of the 1980s designed to broaden the inclusion of people of color and Latino/a/Hispanic people added to the legacies of broken trust. Of particular note were new congregations started by the Association to be intentionally racially or ethnically diverse.

At the 1985 General Assembly, Rev. Dr. Eugene Pickett announced a new initiative to increase the "racial/ethnic diversity of [the UUA's] membership through the development of new congregations." He went on to announce,

> While we have succeeded in reaching people of diverse beliefs, we have failed to connect with women and men of diverse color and backgrounds. It is clear that the challenge simply goes beyond the reach and resources of most local congregations. In most cases, one Unitarian Universalist society cannot serve the range of needs summoned up by the wide variation in cultural, social and economic levels represented by potential UUs in a given area. While we should continually strive for diversity within each congregation, we need not stop there. The struggle to achieve inclusiveness should not be circumscribed by the four walls of an existing church or fellowship. Fresh initiatives are needed for reaching out to new Unitarian Universalists and organizing with them. Our Association should intentionally organize new congregations for people not presently served by existing societies.

The reasons for starting these were stated by the Association's Extension Department, headed by Rev. Dr. Charles Gaines: "The congregation that sponsors a Martin Luther King, Jr., Sunday each January or offers special programs during Black History Month in February will not serve African Americans who need to see their racial identity expressed every week in song, story, history, language, and the enduring struggle against racism which is a daily occurrence in their lives."

Archene Turner, who later became a minister, served as a board member for the Sojourner Truth Congregation, Unitarian Universalist, in Washington, D.C., which was named for the former slave who became an abolitionist and crusader for women's rights. Turner observed that the fledgling congregation was hampered by an inadequate level of Associational funds and ended before it was given a chance to rise. "I think we pulled the plug too soon," she said. "There is a huge learning curve. We knew that if we followed the expectations, we would end up as a smaller, white congregation. . . . If we had [the] resources, Sojourner Truth would still be there."

"They didn't give us the tools we need," said Rev. Dr. Michelle Bentley, who led two new intentionally multiracial start-up congregations in the Chicago area. She said that these congregations, which were urban, allowed people of color such as herself to "stop by-passing their communities on the way to church." Within them, ministers of color could be engaged with the community, the desire to do so having often been their initial motivation for ministry. Since financial support for "community" ministries that were not congregationally based was very limited, these new congregations were a potential avenue for those who wished to be engaged in the real issues of those communities historically marginalized economically.

In these comments, one hears the deep sadness of those who touched a dream and then lost hold of it.

Growth vs. Multiculturalism (1980s)

Described as an attempt to "respond to pluralism," the effort began small. The Department of Extension established two intentionally racially diverse new congregations in 1984, in Washington, D.C., and in Tulsa, Oklahoma. The planning documents note, "Instead of a European-centric congregation, which is reflected in 99 percent of our Unitarian Universalist congregations, these two new congregations were planned to focus on African Americans. The services, theological perspectives, programs and ministry of the congregation are African American."

The founding minister of the Church of the Restoration, Unitarian Universalist, in Tulsa, Oklahoma, Rev. Charles Johnson, said his objectives were "the opportunity to minister to a significantly African-American population" while at the same time being a "radically open congregation," which he defined as "the willingness to deal with the tension of being open in an African-American setting." Johnson said he felt it was important to challenge Unitarian Universalists, stating, "As timid as UUs are about matters dealing with race, somebody has got to have more encouragement than rationality in the beginning, then do something."

In a 1993 assessment, the Department of Extension noted,

It is not just a coincidence that the congregation with the largest number of African Americans is one that had been served for twenty years by the late African American Senior Minister [Rev. Dr. David Eaton]. This congregation has more than three times the number of African Americans of any other congregation in the Unitarian Universalist Association. This was not so twenty years ago. This congregation, All Souls of Washington, DC, with leadership, resources and the will to move itself into the multicultural arena, has accomplished a great deal for the Unitarian Universalist Association. More than 15 percent of all African American Unitarian Universalists belong to this single congregation.

It may be impossible to expect that the Unitarian Universalist Association will ever attract thousands of African American, Hispanic, Asian or Native Americans to its membership. A more realistic mission might be to bring about a future where each district and metropolitan area where a multicultural constituency is present, there might be at least one multicultural model (an institutional presence) to raise our consciousness and provide an experience not easily available to most of our congregations.

One analogy is to the fact that so many Unitarian Universalists who visit Boston make a point to attend King's Chapel, a liturgical Christian Unitarian Universalist congregation. This experience cannot be found elsewhere. Is it not possible to bring a similar multicultural experience closer to home for every Unitarian Universalist? Is it not possible to provide a place where racial and ethnic diversity expressed through programs and worship could be shared by larger numbers of people from other congregations?

Rev. Melvin Hoover, an active lay leader in the Metro New York District before joining the Association staff, recalled some of the motivations for starting these congregations. "We had four or five ministers of color that were in seminary," he said. "Many of them at that time felt they didn't want to serve a traditional white UU congregation, that they wanted to have contact and support and try and bring . . . mostly black UUs into, and try and regrow that connection that had been broken." He also recalled conversations with colleagues about how to construct new congregations that could support these ministries, which had not been thriving in other congregations.

The focus on this extension ministry contained a big caveat:

The concern that must be addressed is whether or not the Unitarian Universalist Association is prepared to accept the possible slower rate of membership growth because of this transfer of resources [to intentionally multicultural congregations]. From the beginning, it must be acknowledged that multicultural initiatives might not result in the same membership numbers as those provided by our more traditional programs.

The new congregation effort was overseen by the Task Force on Affirmative Action for African American Ministers. At its October

CONGREGATIONAL STORIES
Racial and Ethnic New Congregations

In 1993–94, Rev. Marjorie Bowens-Wheatley was asked to undertake an assessment of the racial and ethnic new start congregations. These excerpts are from self-descriptions congregational leaders submitted to her.

From Sojourner Truth Congregation, Washington, D.C.
The Sojourner Truth Congregation is located in Capital Hill, a racially and economically mixed neighborhood [of Washington, D.C.] that is polarized in several ways. We are located on a commercial strip that is within six blocks of three low-income housing projects, one block from a Metro station that has two lines, one block from an intersection of crosstown buses and nine blocks from the Capital building. Thirty-eight percent of our community are persons of color and 37 percent are gay or lesbian. We have 49 members and 7 children. We are an open, refreshingly honest, intentionally diverse community of ministers, social workers, engineers, teachers, therapists, students, volunteers, lawyers, librarians, a court clerk, a management analyst, a personnel training manager, a gallery administrator and a nanny. We are atheists, witches, theists, Christians and pagans. . . .

Our congregation will celebrate the seventh anniversary of its charter in May. We were founded by the Rev. Dr. Yvonne Seon Chappelle Wood, supported by a mandate from the UUA to form congregations in urban areas to attract African Americans and other people who have not been adequately represented in our faith. . . . Our goal is to be a beacon of faith in the community and to be a model of diversity, to love each other and to make this world better for future generations.

From the Church of the Restoration, Tulsa, Oklahoma
Church of the Restoration was born in November of 1987. Charles Johnson was the founding minister and has been with the church since that time. Charles Johnson is now the called minister. . . . Restoration Church lists 77 members, some of which are dual members of Restoration and All Souls. These figures do not include the children, who certainly "count" in every other way! The vast majority of members are active in the church. Approximately half of the active members are African-American. The Church has many "active friends" who participate in activities and services on a regular basis, joining us and our over thirty children (at current count). We have members and friends of Hispanic and Native American heritage.

Given the current size of our membership (smaller than we want) and our aspirations (very large) many members should be very active in the church, and much work is shouldered by a few. However, the involvement of the members has grown very quickly since we began to "camp out" in our new space. We are still struggling with the rebirth of a working organization which we will hammer out soon.

The members want the Church to grow for many reasons. We enjoy the fellowship of people who find themselves attracted to an intentionally multicultural church. We also want to see our dreams for service to the community realized in the impact we hope to have—on harmony between people of diverse backgrounds—on our predominantly African American children in our immediate community who are in need of our help. We believe that spiritually based, committed organizations like Restoration are essential to progress toward the goals of racial justice and understanding. There are no major problems facing Restoration but many big challenges.

1989 meeting, the group heard reports on the new congregations, including a new one that was organizing in Decatur, Georgia, outside Atlanta—the Thurmer-Hamer-Ellington Congregation—under the leadership of Rev. Daniel Aldridge. But many had already encountered the difficulties that would lead to their dissolution:

> At the end of the third year [Sojourner Truth Congregation in Washington] has 50 members (20 of whom have assumed leadership positions). Average attendance is 30 adults and 10 children. They are on the cutting edge of youth ministry and are active in their community. They have been helping to develop the "Welcoming Congregation" model. There followed a detailed conversation about the fiscal status of the church. There was some breakdown of communications evident between Sojourner Truth and the Arlington [Virginia] church as to the specific commitments inherent in being a sponsoring church for the start-up phase.
> Tulsa: Church of the Restoration is also on shaky financial ground. All Souls has not delivered fully on their financial commitments. . . . This congregation has been very effective in serving both their surrounding community and in developing their worship life. Every effort should be made to support its continuation.
> Chicago: North River [UU Church] and South Loop [UU Church]. [Rev. Dr.] Michelle Bentley will be leaving North River in the near future. It should be noted that this was a District effort not directly under the sponsorship of the UUA. The congregation will likely survive but as a fellowship without ministerial leadership. . . .

The Task Force was interested in the congregations as the best strategy for reversing a history within the Association of unsuccessful ministries for ministers of African-American descent and was also working actively on a strategy to recruit ministers from other denominations. Aldridge, the Thurman-Hamer-Ellington Congregation's organizing minister in Atlanta, helped them identify issues to consider in establishing Afrocentric UU congregations.

The growth of these congregations was slow and the patterns were different from other congregations. Rev. Dr. Robert Eller-Isaacs, who observed them as a leader in the urban concerns efforts, said that it was hard to get away from the idea that "our current demographics would determine our future demographics." He noted that the bulk of the effort rested on the shoulders of a small number of ministers of color doing "entrepreneurial ministry." And when it failed, he said, "the ministers were then held responsible."

Rev. William (Chester) McCall, organizing minister for All Souls Church, Unitarian Universalist, in Durham, North Carolina, said his congregation was working with $50,000 of annual support at a time that a similar effort was seeded in the same small city with a $250,000 investment by the Methodists. "The financial resources were not there from the denomination," he observed. He also said the growth projections were not realistic, including the idea that the congregations would double every year. He said the reality was that intentionally anti-racist multicultural congregations need to grow at a slower rate.

PART 1

LEARNINGS

From the beginning, the identity of the Unitarian Universalist Association was linked to social justice issues, for both Unitarians and Universalists were often ahead of their contemporaries on social justice issues, starting with slavery, in discussing and expanding the grasp of who should be given rights. And because Unitarian Universalists come from two traditions with concern for real social issues—though each often faltered in how to honor these concerns day-to-day—there is no time in our religious history when these issues have not been present. These dynamics persisted and grew as centuries passed until, in the twentieth century, the broader question about how to resolve inequities based on race was a strain on relationships and a test of Unitarian Universalist faith.

The controversy around the role of liberal religionists in the 1960s era of black empowerment rocked the Unitarian Universalist Association when its new identity was still in its infancy—the Association was founded in 1961, when the American Unitarian Association and the Universalist Church of America consolidated—leaving developmental issues that survive today. The close timing between the consolidation of the Universalists and the Unitarians into the Unitarian Universalist Association and the Empowerment Controversies meant that the young religious movement was hit by difficult and divisive dynamics even before a clear sense of religious identity was worked out. Rev. William Sinkford, who became the first African-American president of the Unitarian Universalist Association in 2001, noted,

> I'm sure it became a central identity element for us, which made the struggles of the late '60s and early '70s period all the more painful because it felt like a giving up of identity. For those of us who are people of color, it felt like a betrayal, but I bet it felt like a giving up of identity for the majority culture. . . . The meta-blended family of the Unitarians and

the Universalists was incredibly new, and had not really even begun to solidify, so there was not that kind of confident understanding of who we were religiously.

Basic identity issues were not worked out—for while the consolidation of the Unitarians and Universalists was achieved at one level, at the level of identifying core beliefs, many believe the work was never done. As Rev. Gordon B. McKeeman, past president of the Starr King School for the Ministry, observed in an address at the 2004 General Assembly,

> In our passion for freedom, we have accepted the association of independent units, a kind of institutionalized individualism, and we attempt to confront the excesses of a society which has placed individual freedom, individual initiative and individual responsibility on the top of its hierarchy of values, and are puzzled at the impotence of such arrangements to encourage group activity on behalf of the entire human family.

From the beginning of our shared identity as Unitarian Universalists, in some sense, torn and divided when we were still young, we became a people whose experience foretold that discussion of differences was dangerous and divisive.

Unitarian Universalism came out of the 1970s with a painful legacy around race. In addition to the Empowerment Controversies, other histories informed this time, including the roles Unitarians and Universalists played in colonization, in slavery, and in the usurping of territories held by those of Hispanic and Latino heritage. Many of the relationships that would shape the anti-racism dialogue in the late 1980s and the early 1990s that led to the 1992 General Assembly resolution on racial and cultural diversity were also informed by the unfinished business that shaped these events. For this reason, efforts to address issues of race carried into their basic blueprints the unhealed injuries, the unresolved conflicts, and the unsolved dilemmas around the right approach and relationship for a predominantly white, liberal denomination in trying to eradicate racism. In this same era, the Association began efforts to create "intentionally racially and ethnically diverse congregations," which, while not given the "anti-racism" label per se, shaped key relationships with ministers of African-American, Latina/o and Hispanic descent. The miscommunications and negative feelings from these efforts shaped the relationships that would be carried into the early 1990s.

Dr. Norma Poinsett, an African-American leader and activist since the Empowerment Controversies days, saw one challenge of relationship this way: "We are an association of people who you don't tell what to do. You don't require them, you don't say you must do it."

Those concerned with ministering in urban areas became involved in race relations as well because, as Rev. Robert Eller-Isaacs, minister of First Unitarian Church in Oakland, California, from 1982 to 2000, said, "It was very clear that part of having a presence in the urban areas was learning to be in conversation with people of color." The urban concerns work inherited the unfinished business of the Empowerment Controversies, Eller-Isaacs said, because "many of the people on that committee were carrying that agenda as ministers and as human beings." The intentionally racially and culturally diverse congregations also offered a glimpse at what was to come, he said, observing, "This problem exemplified how hard it would be to become an anti-racist institution. . . . The inherent institutional racism is so difficult to root out and the stories are not being told."

Part of the heritage was also a link between the struggle for racial justice and a struggle for youth empowerment which would emerge again as important as the twenty-first century dawned. Rev. Wayne Arnason, who became a youth leader in the years immediately after the Empowerment Controversies, noted that an unusual number of youth attended the fateful 1969 General Assembly and thus became part of that narrative. "The huge effort to get youth to attend the UUA GA and the birth of the whole concept of a youth caucus was associated with the 1969 GA when that issue was again before the Assembly. There was not only a youth advocacy role for the agenda of the Black Affairs Council, but where there was an understanding on the part of youth leaders that the same anti-oppression understanding that they had learned in engaging with the issues around the Black Affairs Council was one that had a resonance with their own situation as a group that had a certain degree of oppression," he observed. "I realize this is hard to compare, but a to certain degree, they experienced oppression by virtue of their age and were experiencing the inability that they had to control some of their own resources and destiny as an organization as having parallels, or at least things they could learn from the understandings they achieved from the Black Affairs Council."

At its deepest level, faith was at issue, in the sense of faith that theologian Henry Nelson Wieman summons when he describes it:

> Faith is not essentially belief at all, although faith generally has a belief. Religious faith was basically an act—the act of giving one's self into the keeping of what commands faith, to be transformed by it, and to serve it above all. More specifically, it was the act of deciding to live in the way required by the source of human good, to maintain association with a fellowship practicing that commitment, to follow the rituals designed to renew and deepen this commitment, to search one's self for hidden disloyalties to this devotion, to confess and repudiate these disloyalties. All habits, interests and structures of personality were thus condemned when they hinder the living of the life demanded. This complex act was faith: the beliefs are merely incidental to it.

A number of the people interviewed for this project noted that in the 1960s, Unitarian Universalists viewed racial issues through a justice rather than theological lens and that our lack of theological clarity contributed to the difficulties we have discussing our views on racial justice. Rev. Dr. Victor Carpenter observed that "justice was the presenting issue, as they say in the shrink's office. . . . The theology had not been worked out."

Sinkford said,

> The language of justice was the language I was most familiar with back then. And that can be theological language,

but I think you have to remember that humanism was very much the order of the day in most of our congregations and religious language was very little used. There were some exceptions, but for the most part it was very little used, so it's not surprising that our folks didn't go to theological depth because they didn't have the language tools available to them to do it. They basically, we basically—it's hard for me to know when to say "we" and "they"—sort of appropriated King's language of the beloved community, but we never actually sat down and said what does that look like? What does that mean? . . . That was in some sense what the . . . Empowerment Controversies were all about. It became very clear that there were radically different images of not only what that beloved community looked like, but how you got there.

Hindsight, the old adage says, is 20/20. History viewed from an idealistic perspective exposes some unsavory and painful truths as well as many noble and courageous acts. Held together, these form a sort of inheritance that framed the conversation about race and power that took place in our Association starting in 1992 with the adoption of the General Assembly Resolution on Racial and Cultural Diversity in Calgary. For many of the individuals involved, this was merely one step in a long trajectory of planning, organizing, and acting.

CLOSING WORDS

Affirmation of Hope
By Loretta F. Williams

We, bearers of the dream, affirm that a new vision of hope is emerging.
    We pledge to work for that community in which justice will be
    actively present.
We affirm that there is struggle yet ahead.
    Yet we know that in the struggle is the hope for the future.

We affirm that we are co-creators of the future, not passive pawns.
    And we stand united in affirmation of our hope and vision of a
    just and inclusive society.
We affirm the unity of all persons:
    We affirm brotherhood and sisterhood that allows us to touch upon
    each other's humanity.
We affirm a unity that opens our eyes, ears, and hearts to see the
different but common forms of oppression, suffering, and pain.
    Yet we are one in the image of God, and we celebrate our hopes for
    human unity. Within ourselves and within the gathered commu-
    nity, we will discover the strength not to hide in indifference.
Affirming that hope, publicly expressed, energizes and enables us to
move forward. Together we pledge action to transcend barriers—
be they racial, political, economic, social, or religious.
    We pledge to make our tomorrows become our todays.

PART 2

Reclaiming an Identity

*When you begin to look at oppression and how it operates, one of the
things you understand is that there is always a gross imbalance of
power. . . . So a vaccine for oppression . . . has to reduce that gross
imbalance of power. . . . DDT—diagnosis determines therapy. The
treatment is characterized by the diagnosis. . . . When you go back
and analyze your policies and programs, past and present, you're going
to find that an overwhelming number of them are based on a false
modality. . . . Why do we have this continued problem with racism?
Why is it that we have attacked more substantially issues of gender
and sexual orientation? [Because] this neo-racism is invisible. . . .
[N]eo-racists look at the good they are doing. Oppression is legitimated
as good and moral. A breakthrough is to begin to look at oppression in
the good that we do. . . . Whoever has the power to label has the power
to control.*

—Rev. Dr. William Jones, UUA Board member

1989

UUA president William Schulz creates the
Office of Racial Inclusiveness to provide a
specific focus on groups historically under-
represented in Unitarian Universalism.

The Unitarian Universalist Association
publishes Rev. Dr. Mark D. Morrison-
Reed's adult multimedia curriculum, *How
Open the Door?: Afro-Americans' Experience
in Unitarian Universalism.*

The new *Welcoming Congregation* program
to affirm bisexual, gay, and lesbian people
is unveiled at the UU Ministers Association Professional Days.

1990

The Board of Trustees directs the
UUA administration to develop
a feasibility plan for racial and
cultural diversity.

1991

The Board of Trustees presents
a basic list of changes needed to
achieve diversity within ten years.

51

THE EFFORTS OF PREVIOUS YEARS were beginning to bear fruit. Unitarian Universalist Association president William Schulz and the advocate he had hired, Rev. Melvin Hoover, along with the Racial and Cultural Diversity Task Force, formed a coalition of people once again concerned about bringing the issue of race and Unitarian Universalism into the open.

At the same time, a few members of the Association staff were assessing the lessons of an experiment in congregational development—the intentional initiation of congregations designed to attract more multiracial membership. With limited resources, unclear expectations and slower growth than predominantly European-American congregations, most were to fade from the scene during the 1990s, yet not without bringing in a number of people who would be future leaders of anti-racism advocacy within the Association.

1992

The Unitarian Universalist Network on Indigenous Affairs (UUNIA) is created as an advocacy group championing Native American issues.

The UUA Board issues the report Long-Term Initiative for Racial and Cultural Diversity.

A group of UUA affiliate organizations presents a resolution on Racial and Cultural Diversity in Unitarian Universalism. Delegates to the General Assembly in Calgary pass it by a large margin.

The UUA Board of Trustees appoints a Racial and Cultural Diversity Task Force to develop a plan and process for achieving diversity.

1993

The UUA staff hires Crossroads Ministry to lead an anti-racism team training in Newton, Massachusetts.

The first of four annual Racial Justice Days at General Assembly is held, titled, Racial Justice: For Such a Time as This. Other programs are offered in 1994, 1995, and 1996.

The Thomas Jefferson Ball is held at General Assembly in Charlotte, North Carolina. Hope Johnson, representing the African American Unitarian Universalist Ministry, asks at a plenary, "Should blacks wear rags, or a ball and chain?"

James Brown becomes the first black UUA district executive, of the Southwest Conference.

1994

The Black Concerns Working Group creates and offers the first "Creating a Jubilee World" workshops at the congregational level.

The General Assembly of Congregations became the stage for many of the efforts to raise awareness about anti-racism efforts. In 1992, a resolution calling on the Association to explore ways to become more racially and culturally diverse passed at the General Assembly in Calgary. In the following years, General Assemblies became the place to showcase nationally known experts on race relations and to present training models.

On a much lesser scale, a number of delegates took the ideas from General Assembly home and tried to put them into practice in the congregational arena. Research conducted by Rev. Olivia Holmes in 1996 found that a wide variety of initiatives were being tried in congregations, though many members of those congregations were fearful that explorations of racial and cultural differences could mean conflict. Though a number of training approaches, including the Building a Jubilee World workshop of the Black

1995

The Latina/o UU Networking Association (LUUNA) is created with the help of the UU Urban Coalition and the Unitarian Universalist Association Religious Education Department.

The Young Adults of Color Caucus (YACC) is formed at General Assembly in Spokane, Washington.

1996

The UUA publishes *Weaving the Fabric of Diversity*, a curriculum for adults.

The Racial and Cultural Diversity Task Force presented its initial findings to the General Assembly in Indianapolis, titled *Journey Toward Wholeness, The Next Step*: From Racial and Cultural Diversity to Anti-Oppression and Anti-Racist Multiculturalism.

General Assembly delegates pass a resolution that all congregations, districts, organizations, and professional and lay leaders participate in a year-long reflection-action process using the Task Force's materials.

LUUNA critiques the Task Force's recommendations as a "dichotomous program taking into account only blacks and whites."

The UUA staff chooses sixteen "pilot project" congregations to undertake anti-racism trainings because of their existing commitment to racial justice.

Starr King School for the Ministry diversifies its faculty by adding people of color.

Members of the UUA staff create the Diversity of Ministry Team, to which two representatives of DRUUMM (Diverse and Revolutionary Unitarian Universalist Multicultural Ministries) are added in 2000.

Concerns Working Group, remained popular in this period, the model developed in partnership with Crossroads Ministry was being used more and more often for training the national leadership of the Association. The analysis of racism used in this model would become the basis of a new national effort launched in 1997.

Perhaps more important than the training models used was the fact that by reopening hard conversations, advocates were seeking to reclaim an identity as people who cared about racial justice.

CHAPTER 5

Building an Infrastructure for Interracial Dialogue

A multi-faceted pattern of events, conversations, and relationships leading up to passage of the 1992 resolution on racial and ethnic diversity at the General Assembly in Calgary revealed a growing intricacy in relationships and choices about what sort of identity Unitarian Universalists would have around issues of race.

For some, the identity was a source of pride—to try to reconnect to the ways white Unitarian Universalists took leadership in the Civil Rights era. For some, the identity needed to be repentant:

> There was a clear request from one congregation to the UUA for a "formal apology to African American ministers to whom the UUA may have done harm intentionally or unintentionally." The sentiment was shared by others present. . . . Drawing attention to our nascent multi-ethnic theology of right relationships may be one of the most important consequences of the consultations.

For others, the focus was on building the capacity for the Unitarian Universalist Association to understand itself as a majority Euro-American community with learned assumptions that were a factor in the continued failure to achieve racial and cultural diversity in congregational life. This would be the seed that led to the idea of an anti-racist identity.

Office of Racial Inclusiveness

In 1989, Rev. William Schulz, Association president, created the Office of Racial Inclusiveness and appointed Rev. Melvin Hoover to head it. By establishing this portfolio for a staff member, Schulz wished to signal that he thought the issue of race relations was a priority. Hoover's job title was changed from director of urban and international programs/extension (his title since 1987) to advocate for racial inclusiveness and director of international congregations. Under the new structure, Hoover reported directly to Kay Montgomery, the executive vice president. At the same time, Jacqui James became the Association's affirmative action officer, responding to one of the recommendations of the Institutional Racial Audit, which the Unitarian Universalist Association's Board of Trustees had adopted in 1980.

To have a part of the Association structure carrying an explicit agenda around race was significant and other events seemed to coalesce around this. Also in 1989, Rev. Dr. Mark D. Morrison-Reed published his adult multimedia curriculum, *How Open the Door? Afro-Americans' Experience in Unitarian Universalism*, which provided a way for congregations to engage in a direct conversation about the Unitarian and Universalist history with race.

And the Black Concerns Working Group released a new report, titled "We Have No Problem . . . Again." It contained an introduction by Horace Seldon of Community Change Inc. in Boston that seemed to capture the frustrations of some who had been laboring long to bring about greater attention and awareness of racial issues in the Unitarian Universalist Association:

> The "no problem" response to racism is usually heard from white people, and usually in institutional settings where there are few people of color. Since I have not yet found an institution where there is no problem, my assumption always is that we have simply to uncover it. . . . It doesn't take long for most people of color to say there is a problem. . . . People of color can tell you where the problem is, and what its affects are. . . . Don't fear it; discover it; uncover it; even stir it up if necessary. Then we can begin to deal with it. If we

don't do that, then we'll soon be right back at the same old place. . . . "we have no problem" . . . again!

Feasibility Plan for Racial and Cultural Diversity

In 1990, the Board of Trustees directed the UUA administration to develop a feasibility plan for racial and cultural diversity. In 1991, a basic list of changes needed to achieve diversity within a ten-year period was presented to the Board of Trustees.

This effort was part of a longer-term organizing effort. Hoover recalled, "We built networks that had not always worked together. We built across the isms and themselves, but we built in a strategic way and we also built institutional strength with committees, and structures, not just individuals." A number of people working to shape the Association's race relations efforts attended a 1990 conference in Chicago featuring black activist and author Angela Davis, whose analysis became a shaping influence.

A number of forces came together including the leadership of President Schulz and moderator Natalie Gulbrandsen, both of whom had been involved in civil rights and other equity issues such as women's rights. "When they came into office, I think in that sense, that was always part of what they carried in terms of their personal visions and beginning to look for ways to move, and histories, and moving it into various structures," Hoover said. "We had some key board members at that time and several board members of color during that era who were pushing, again, for revisiting and reconnecting to racial justice work. They weren't calling it anti-racism, but racial justice activities and racial diversity concerns."

Schulz said that in the fall of 1990, members of the Committee on Urban Concerns in Ministry met in Boston and the decision was made to appoint a committee to make recommendations on "what at that time we very foolishly thought was a ten-year plan for racial and cultural diversity." Schulz said that the Board of Trustees was supportive and that Gulbrandsen was very supportive.

Crossroads Ministry Pilot Training

In an era when methods and models for approaching conversations about racial divides were springing up from many sources, the

EXCERPT

"We Have No Problem . . . Again"

The following was written by Horace Seldon of Community Change Inc., a Boston-based social change organization that was hired by the UUA Board of Trustees to conduct an institutional racism audit in 1980.

About twenty years ago whenever the issue of racism was mentioned in the presence of my white suburban friends there was always someone to assure us that "we don't have that problem here." Pursuing that statement usually led to another one that went something like this: "Well, there aren't many black people here" . . . so the logic seemed to say . . . of course . . . "no problem."

I knew then that my friends were wrong for a number of reasons. First, they assumed that the problem of racism existed only when people of color were present. The assumption "located" the problem among black people and other people of color; it failed to see that racism is rooted in white people and in white institutions whether or not there are black people present. Second, I knew that the absence of many black people was itself part of the problem; attitudes and practices by the majority white population limited the choice of blacks who may have wanted to live in the suburbs. Third, the "no problem" argument was an attempt to avoid responsible action; if there is "no problem," or if the problem is somewhere else then [we are] absolved from doing anything. Fourth, I knew that a lot of people in the suburbs were there precisely because they wanted to avoid "urban problems," and that many of my friends equated "urban problems" with the presence of racial minority groups. To assert that "we have no problem here" was to distance themselves from the city.

That was some time ago, and while the "no problem" attitude still persists it is argued in slightly different forms now.

One of the "new" statements of the "no problem" syndrome proceeds from an assumption that there is no problem of racism unless there is some overt incident which expresses hatred and bigotry. Recently a high school principal assured me, within minutes of our introduction, that "we have no race problem here." That meant there had been no stabbing, no violence, no racially motivated incident in the school. Before seeing the principal I had already talked with a number of students, both black and white, and a couple of teachers; they had all told me of the presence of racism in a variety of forms in classrooms, corridors, and school activities. But the principal made it his priority to assure me that there was "no problem."

In the "no problem" view, the word "problem" is used almost exclusively to refer to an incident of bigotry; someone calls a name, a racial slur appears in graffiti, an openly discriminatory act occurs. When something like that occurs people on the site and in the community are quick to respond, ready to condemn it, and hopefully, equipped to administer a just solution. In many instances after that initial response, everyone goes back to "business as usual" as quickly as possible. A collective sigh of relief goes up as everyone says, again, "we have no problem." It is the underlying, ever-present problem that is seldom addressed. Most white people don't believe it is there, they don't want to have it pointed out, are eager to leave it alone. So the acculturated, institutionalized base of the problem goes untreated. It remains the festering bed of the next incident.

writings of Rev. Joseph Barndt, a Lutheran minister, had caught the attention of several key leaders.

Rev. Marjorie Bowens-Wheatley was working for the Veatch Program of the Unitarian Universalist Congregation at Shelter Rock, in Manhasset, New York, long a source of funding for the Association's racial justice efforts. She recalled making the case for an early grant for Barndt's approach, which focused on the importance of whites acknowledging their complicity in a system that oppresses people of color. "Joe Barndt introduced this idea and I thought it was a worthy idea, but at that time it was strictly interfaith work," she said. "It wasn't specifically with the UUA, and it was based out of New York. And I thought it was a worthy project as an interfaith project. It wasn't well developed, but I thought it was worthy of development. And the next thing I know, all other sorts of things had taken place."

Hoover had asked the Black Concerns Working Group to read Barndt's book, *Dismantling Racism*. Because of Hoover's conviction that Barndt's was the approach that could address the particular, persistent problems of a predominantly white Unitarian Universalism around race matters, he began to try to make connections with the organization Barndt headed, Crossroads Ministry. The organization was still young and seeking its own identity. Barndt recalled that Hoover and the Association and Crossroads came together at a particular point in all of their development that was like "a confluence of rivers."

"We started Crossroads in 1986, but we did not really begin to center in on anti-racism work as the exclusive work of Crossroads, and institutional organizing as the central piece of our anti-racism work, until 1990," Barndt recalled. "Among the many other great influences was the Unitarian Universalist influence that made us shift early in the Crossroads years from being a Christian organization to being an interfaith organization." Hoover and a colleague from the Lutheran Church were instrumental in helping to shape the identity of the emerging organization, Barndt said.

Hoover recalled that the earliest interactions with Crossroads went well and generated support. "The early ones were quite successful," he said, "and everybody said, because we were looking at

60

VOICE

Rev. Marjorie Bowens-Wheatley

This article was published in the Community Church of New York newsletter on April 21, 1996. Bowens-Wheatley was a long-time advocate for racial justice.

For several years, we have been dreaming (through the strategic planning process) about who we wish to become. As important as it may be, our goal of Growth Through Diversity will not be achieved by simply wishing it or dreaming it, or by passive action. It's been nearly 100 years since DuBois said the problem of the 20th century would be "the color line." Derrick Bell argues that racism is a permanent condition in this country, part of our cultural landscape—unless and until people of European heritage organize to eliminate it. I cannot envision growing through diversity without also addressing racism. Here's why:

1. Many of us have not moved from the 1960s' assumption that integration is *the* goal: that people of color are willing to assimilate and accept European American perspectives, while the reverse is not true.
2. There is a perception that racism expresses itself as personal prejudice and, to a lesser extent, as unjust laws. Since many Unitarian Universalists believe that they harbor little personal prejudice and since the Civil Rights Movement accomplished much, there is a failure to understand how they participate in sustaining racism.
3. Most of our efforts have focused on solving the problems of the oppressed rather than on deconstructing systems of institutional and cultural oppression.
4. We say that all people and cultures are created equal, but we do little to challenge assumptions that say they are not. European culture, history, and philosophy are still presumed to be normative and superior. However, the philosophical assumptions and values of many European Americans are fundamentally different from many people of color. This complicates communication in critical ways.
5. Racism is often unconscious. It is supported by denial, defensiveness, quietude and inaction.
6. If we do little or nothing to dismantle racist institutional policies and Euro-centric cultural norms, assumptions and practices that uphold one culture as supreme over all others, we participate in sustaining racism.
7. We often assume that if we simply "get the right mix" of people that we will have solved the problem. Though we would like to see more racial diversity, when people of color become a critical mass (between 15 and 30 percent), European Americans tend to feel threatened and find it is difficult to genuinely share power and authority. The risks associated with fundamental change seem to be too high for many to remain at the table.
8. Many approach racism in a linear, quantitative manner—as a task to be solved within a finite time—rather than as a process of learning and unlearning.
9. Multicultural programming, as it has been formulated in recent years, helps us to gain a deeper appreciation for those unlike ourselves and to value diversity. But multiculturalism does not address systemic oppression. It is often presented as a disguise, as a way of avoiding the issue of racism.
10. European Americans often don't recognize or acknowledge racism until there is a crisis. Further, they often expect (or wait for) people of color to teach them about racism.

what do we do next, . . . 'Oh yeah, this is a direction to go.' That's part of what we're doing in that era, looking for models. . . . We knew we needed to have an umbrella structure or comprehensive structure that works together."

At the time when the UUA was entering into relationship with Crossroads Ministry, its approach was in its infancy. "We were cutting our eyeteeth on this institutional organizing model and the UUA was one of the major ones," Barndt said. "The Unitarian Universalists, the Presbyterians, the Lutherans, and the Mennonites were the principal denominations in the early years that really shaped a whole lot of what we were doing."

Black Concerns Working Group

In 1991, the Black Concerns Working Group planned programming for General Assembly including a sing-along featuring Rev. Alma Crawford, with a focus on songs that have been sung by both African Americans and whites; a workshop on the Canadian connection in the Underground Railroad; and a workshop called "Watch Your Mouth: Everyday Racist Language" as well as workshops to introduce the Jubilee trainings.

These events brought new interest from people such as Dr. Norma Poinsett, an active black layperson who had remained in the UUA when other African Americans left after the Empowerment Controversies. By 1992, she saw a new commitment emerging that added import to the work of the Black Concerns Working Group, of which she was a part. "I think what we had done from 1985 to 1992 was to start getting a few people aroused to the fact that, yes, this is something either I've been thinking about or I believe in, and I will do something to help our church to move a bit," she said. "But one of the problems I always had with that is, even if we did a second workshop in a church, we only affected a few people and quite often we were singing to at least half of the choir, the ones who were at least halfway convinced. People who were there were some way convinced already, and then we had to get some of the others on board, and then there were some who would argue, you know—you don't know where you left them. I think that our biggest, one of the biggest things is not having the continuity. . . . If you're going to work on these oppressions and ending racism, anti-racism, the emphasis has to be . . . very obvious, total, working at it all the time." She said a comprehensive structure working with the Association's districts was needed and was not available.

Other approaches to generating race relations dialogue were also being tried. Rosemary Bray McNatt, an African-American layperson who later became a minister, worked with Ann Reeb, the daughter of James Reeb, the white minister killed in Selma answering Dr. Martin Luther King Jr.'s call for support in 1965, to stage a performance piece about Reeb's death at the 1990 General Assembly in Milwaukee. Unable to get it in the official program, they did it on their own. "We booked a room at GA at the conference center in Milwaukee," McNatt recalled, "and paid for it ourselves, and did flyers, and did the stuff. People came, and we got a standing ovation. . . . For me, that was an example of the kinds of things I wanted to do," she recalled. "I wanted to do anti-oppression work across racial lines and talk about some of those things that were sticking points in the history of our movement. Because I was a writer at that point, the creative process was a way to do that, and because institutions are institutions, that's not necessarily how institutions see their role, so I just kind of ignored them."

Momentum Gathers
In April 1992, the Board accepted a ten-year plan from the Black Concerns Working Group, which was beginning to feel resource constraints and was looking for ways to get congregational funds to support its workshops. In debriefing the Board's reaction to the plan, which included one comment that growth in the Association might be slowed by a focus on multiculturalism, the Working Group noted that "people of color come in, look around to see how the church feels, and leave if there is a bunch of 'crap' to put up with." Dr. Norma Poinsett noted that because of this "Unitarians are also becoming homeless." The Group also talked about the fact that the discussion was moving toward discussing the needs beyond "black and white."

A month later, Hoover and consultant Bob Snow proposed that the Association undertake research into the methods that congre-

VOICE
Rev. Dr. Anita Farber-Robertson

Farber-Robertson was co-chair of the Racial and Cultural Diversity Task Force when she wrote this in 1996.

We have an American culture in which European culture is the norm and standard and from which anything else is perceived as deviant or not "right." It was within this context that Unitarian Universalism was created and flourished. Therefore, it is reasonable to turn a sharp and critical lens on our history and practice and presuppositions, to reveal in what ways Unitarian Universalism, as a creation of the white European culture, was designed to perpetuate white power and privilege.

What becomes obvious is the way in which our expression of our faith, European religious language, music, form, color, texture and story have been *the* culture, normative, definitive. By focusing on removing the understanding of European culture as "right" and normal for our faith, we create the context in which people of color can shape a Unitarian Universalist faith which is compelling for them, and in doing so, create a Unitarian Universalism which can more authentically and congruently lives its principles. Similarly, we need to study our history with new questions and heightened awareness, so that we might better tell an authentic story of who we have been. That must include the ways in which Unitarian Universalism supported the oppressive structures, behaved in ways which were oppressive ourselves, protected white interests, and resisted changes.

gations have successfully used to increase racial and cultural diversity. Those who engaged in this project later became advocates or critics of the Association's anti-racism initiatives; some of the searing experiences of people of color in this time became part of the untold stories that became an almost unbridgeable divide.

A report from the time noted,

> The first group were the historically integrated urban churches (e.g., All Souls Church Unitarian in Washington, D.C.; Community Church of New York; First Unitarian Church of Chicago; Unitarian Universalist Church of the Restoration in Philadelphia). The second were the African-American new starts with African-American leadership (e.g., Church of the Restoration Unitarian Universalist in Tulsa, Oklahoma; Sojourner Truth in Washington; The Thurman-Hamer-Ellington Unitarian Universalist Church in Atlanta . . .). The third were the intentionally multicultural new starts currently headed by whites (e.g., [UU Congregation of the Palisades,] Englewood, N.J.; [First Unitarian Society of Westchester], Hastings-on-Hudson, N.Y.; North River in Chicago). And the last were the suburban and/or predominantly White churches that have forged links with inner city congregations of color (e.g., the Unitarian Church of All Souls, New York); other congregations of color (e.g., Eno River [UU Fellowship, Durham, N.C.]; [Unitarian Universalist Church of] Reston, VA); non-church organizations that serve people of color (e.g., the Benevolent Fraternity [in Boston], which was the group that had held the urban agenda).

This search for new congregational approaches took place in an era of extreme tension in the country, Schulz, the Association's president, observed, adding,

> I find it hard to believe, given the growing black middle class, given the huge numbers of Hispanics immigrating to the United States, given the high educational levels of many

Asian Americans . . . that there are no more than 3,000 minority people in the entire continent who would find Unitarian Universalism a compatible religious home. . . .

The verdict of the jury in the Rodney King case [involving the 1991 beating death of an African American man by police in Los Angeles] has sparked an explosion of anger in our country. If we believe that the rage being expressed in so many of our cities is merely about this one incident, we are deluding ourselves once more, and tragically so. Wrong as it is, this rebellion is about something far greater. It is the anguished cry of an ever-larger group of people who are dispossessed from the core of this society, lacking access to equal education, housing, employment, and adequate health care. We can blame no one but ourselves. Our own society, from the Executive Branch down, has worked to create a system that is unequal, discriminatory, and fed by suspicion and fear.

We can afford to behave in this way no longer, for we do so at the peril of our country's survival. We must act, now, to begin a national dialogue that will result in tangible equity and instill mutual respect in the hearts and lives of all people. When Unitarian Thomas Jefferson called for "equal and exact justice," he spoke of a vision that is yet to be fulfilled. For the sake of all our dreams of tomorrow's promise, we must work together, now, to achieve that justice.

CHAPTER 6

A Resolution at Calgary

In 1992, delegates to the General Assembly held in Calgary, in Alberta, Canada, adopted a resolution that was designed to recast the Association in a leadership role in dealing with racial identity. This bold step both reconnected us with our history as the Association of Congregations that sent many leaders to Selma in 1965—and that required us to temper our pride with a new humility and understanding of the complex web of relationships that support the dysfunctional racial divide within our nation and our communities.

The Resolution called for the formation of a task force and the Association's Board of Trustees appointed the Task Force on Racial and Cultural Diversity to determine which of the recommendations from the 1980 Institutional Racism Audit had been implemented. Rev. Susan Suchocki, then a member of the Board and of the Task Force, recalled that the task force went through the list and determined that most of them had been addressed in some way. More than a decade later, however, the awareness of what was needed was greater. Suchocki remembers that the Audit had called for a seat on the Board of Trustees to be reserved for a person of color and that by 1992, the Task Force knew that one seat was inadequate.

The new Task Force embraced a prophetic identity, noting in a 1993 report to the Veatch Program of the Unitarian Universalist Church at Shelter Rock, in Manhasset, New York, a major funder of its initiatives,

> This is a watershed moment in time, as it was when our Association responded to the Call to Selma from Dr. Martin Luther King. Our Board of Trustees gave leadership to

Precursors to the 1992 Resolution

Rev. Dr. Mark Morrison-Reed, the African-American historian and author of Black Pioneers in a White Denomination, *offered his reflections on some of the events that led up to the resolution at Calgary.*

President Rev. Dr. Eugene Pickett's Leadership: Morrison-Reed wrote in an email in March 2009, "Gene immediately made efforts to address the vacuum left after the Empowerment era. . . ." When Eugene Pickett became president in 1979 he hired Dr. Loretta Williams, an African American and UUA Board member, as director of the Section on Social Responsibility. He brought all the African-American ministers to Boston for a meeting; that included Revs. Jeff Campbell, Thom Payne, John Frazier, Grayland Hagler, Ron White, Morrison-Reed, and others. Pickett and Rev. William Schulz, the executive vice president of the Unitarian Universalist Association, met with Vernon Jordan, then the executive director of the Urban League, to explore ways the League and UUA might work together. Other significant policy developments ensued. "Under the Pickett administration the Committee on Urban Concerns and Ministry, which was chaired by Jack Mendelsohn, put forward the idea of dual fellowship," Morrison-Reed noted. "The Committee went to the MFC and said, 'We are having trouble settling African Americans and despite that when a transfer comes to us we say drop your accreditation in your current denomination and then we'll see if we can settle you. That is wrong.' After the MFC agreed the Committee went to the UUMA. They were reluctant but the logic was compelling. It was debated at the 1981 General Assembly in Philadelphia. It was this which opened up the possibility for Mel Hoover and Dan Aldridge and others to enter the UUA ministry."

Publication of Key Resources: *Black Pioneers in a White Denomination* was published by Skinner House Books and later the UUA Identity Curriculum team worked with Morrison-Reed on developing *How Open the Door?*, a curriculum dealing with race in the Association. Morrison-Reed wrote, "This team made sure that African-American content was part of all the other curricula it developed: Peg Gooding's *Growing Up Times*, published in 1988; and *The Stepping Stone Year* (1989), which included a lesson on Lewis Latimer; Jan Evans-Tiller's *Around the Church, Around the Year* (1990); Elizabeth Strong's *Messages in Music* (1993) encouraged youth to bring all forms of music including soul, blues, and jazz; and Lois Eklund's *Travel in Time* included a story about Errold Collymore, the first black AUA Board member. In addition, the *In Our Hands* social justice curricula released during the same years touched on the theme of diversity."

Development of Worship Resources: Morrison-Reed also highlighted the critical work of the Hymnal Commission, which had an African-American member and was staffed by Jacqui James. He recalled that the group discussed at length the use of white/black, light/dark imagery. The Hymnal Commission had readings from African-American UUs to choose from because in 1991 Skinner House published *Been in the Storm So Long*, edited by Jacqui James and Morrison-Reed. He notes, "It was and is one of the few UU liturgical resources that addresses the African-American experience." These efforts were important precursors to the efforts by the Unitarian Universalist Musicians Network to broaden and diversify the music used in our congregations.

Morrison-Reed points out that much reflection, change, and anti-racism thinking had gone on prior to the 1992 Calgary GA resolution. "These actions are what actually set the scene for what followed," he said, adding that progress on addressing issues around race continued throughout the 1970s and early 1980s.

the Association by adjourning their meeting and reconvening in Selma in order to participate in the march. They issued a call to our Unitarian Universalist ministers and members to join them in their witness with . . . civil rights activists. Our participation as a predominantly white religious organization publicly exhibiting new attitudes, behaviors, and response was instrumental in the involvement of large numbers of European Americans in the civil rights movement. It was one of the most vital times in our Association's history. What the Racial and Cultural Diversity Task Force has learned from our experiences of the past two years is that racism has mutated, as Dr. William Jones says, and that we need a new diagnosis for a new day and new resources for creating a new anti-racist antidote.

Coalition for a Resolution

In 1989 General Assembly delegates voted to establish the Welcoming Congregation certification process for congregations wishing to learn more about gay and lesbian issues, and the Association staff had responded. The process has raised awareness of the kinds of resources needed to make social change of any kind and the checklist from the Institutional Racism Audit seemed inadequate. "We were just ticking them off," recalled Suchocki, "We had just come through the Welcoming Congregation process and thousands of dollars had been spent. And I said, I am not going to play this game anymore. . . . We need to bring this to the General Assembly."

Suchocki recruited Denise (Denny) Davidoff to strategize about an approach. Davidoff, who had been active in the Unitarian Universalist Women's Federation and was known to be skilled with parliamentary procedures, had made it known that she would be running for election as the Association's moderator. A draft resolution was floated among a broad coalition of leaders, including the African American Unitarian Universalist Ministers.

The initial idea had been to present the resolution to the 1993 Assembly. Yet events overtook this schedule and the decision was made to have President Schulz address race in his remarks to the

VOICE
Rev. Susan Suchocki

The following remarks are excerpted from a sermon delivered on October 24, 1993, entitled "Unity and Diversity." Suchocki is the former chair of the Journey Toward Wholeness Transformation Committee.

A question that we must begin to explore—especially if we are going to be a viable religion into the future, is how can we applaud, appreciate, celebrate, honor, and nurture the diversity of each person, yet at the same time come together as a unified community that has a common core with which to unify us in our diversity. Does the coming together in community mean that individuals' uniqueness and preciousness must be left at the door? (Will a sign be posted that reads, "Leave your individual selfhood at the door please"?) Or is there a way to combine and use all the diversity that we each have. I fear that if we forced the submission of the individual character or did not encourage individuality we would become a very bland and boring religious group, yet I have also seen that diversity has caused considerable problems.

These problems are not just specific to our church community or our Unitarian Universalist Association either but show up in our secular lives. America—the home of the free, the new frontier, the place to come to and explore and expand your individuality—has led us into times of turmoil and upheaval. We have long been the nation that hailed the individual as the keeper and harbinger of the good, of the best; the rugged individualism of persons is front-page news. But this creates two problems, one is that not only do we tout individualism as an ideal but we end up having a vision that the only persons who can benefit from our country are those who think, look, and act like us. The second problem is that though our words speak of the importance of individuality, and our words speak of the freedom of the

individual, more and more of us are feeling that we are only an insignificant being in the mass of society, that we are only an infinitesimal part of a group that is at the whim of the lowest common denominator and we end up feeling very non-individualistic, very controlled, very limited, very much a small part of a whole, that we do not have any control over nor even understand. We are lonely in a group and it becomes harder and harder to find a place to exercise both the desire for our individuality and the pull to be part of a meaningful group.

As a solution, I would like to suggest that a religious community, and our religious community to be specific, is the place where we can meet to explore these competing needs and these confusing thoughts.

James Luther Adams, the Unitarian theologian, provided me with new understandings about diversity and unity. He gave me new thoughts to ponder, and new ideas to pursue. One of the ways that he accomplished this was the novel way that he translated the story about the Tower of Babel. You may remember this ancient biblical story about the people building a tower that would reach high into the heavens. The common group joined together for the singular purpose of building a high tower that was higher than anything in existence. They did this to prove their value and worth and their strength as one unified group. Supposedly, when God observed this tower, God became angry and decided that they should be divided by language and culture and that they should become a diverse group not unified in culture, language, or ethnicity. They were scattered. I read this Biblical story suspecting it had great significance but never quite grasped it until James Luther Adams' interpretation helped to clarify it. He stated the reason that the people were scattered was not as punishment but rather as a reminder that we all are dependent on the many and that we are all connected under a higher order. The scattering of the peoples and the confusing of language can then be seen as a blessing not a curse.

1992 Assembly so that a "responsive resolution," which the UUA bylaws allow delegates to make from the floor in response to official business could be introduced. "I tried every year in my president's address to address either urban concerns or race or both," Schulz recalled. Moderator Natalie Gulbrandsen spoke to it in her report as well. Also at this Assembly, the Board of Trustees issued the report *Long-Term Initiative for Racial and Cultural Diversity.*

The General Assembly at Calgary was unusual in several ways, recalled Rev. Dr. John Buehrens, who was then running for election as the Association's president. That it was held in Canada meant that attendance was smaller than at many other Assemblies. Also, because a new president and moderator would be elected the following year, a great deal of energy was focused on politicking.

Behind the scenes, "we ran around tremendously in Calgary building the coalition" to support a resolution, recalled Davidoff, who noted that groups in support included the youth caucus. At the right moment in the Assembly's business meeting, the coalition led by Davidoff, representing the Unitarian Universalist Women's Federation, presented a responsive resolution, *Racial and Cultural Diversity in Unitarian Universalism*, which read:

WHEREAS President Schulz and Moderator Gulbrandsen have called on Unitarian Universalists to support a vision of a Unitarian Universalist faith which reflects the reality of a racially diverse and multicultural global village; and

WHEREAS the candidates for President and Moderator of this faith community stand in solidarity with this vision; and

WHEREAS the Board of Trustees and staff of the Unitarian Universalist Association have worked to bring this vision to life; and

WHEREAS the individuals in our congregations who bring our visions to life need a process to articulate their concerns and ideas on how we can make this vision a substantive reality; and

WHEREAS our first principle calls on us to affirm and promote the inherent worth and dignity of every human being; and

WHEREAS this resolution was prepared by a coalition including the African American Unitarian Universalist Ministry, the Black Concerns Working Group, the Coalition of African American Unitarian Universalist Organizations, the Continental Women and Religion Committee, the Covenant of Unitarian Universalist Pagans, the Ministerial Sisterhood of Unitarian Universalists, the Network of Black Unitarian Universalists, the Society for the Larger Ministry, the Unitarian Universalist District Presidents' Association, Unitarian Universalists for Lesbian and Gay Concerns, Unitarian Universalists for a Just Economic Community, the Unitarian Universalist Service Committee, the Urban Church Coalition, the Unitarian Universalist Women's Caucus, the Unitarian Universalist Women's Federation, Young Religious Unitarian Universalists, the Youth Caucus, and others;

THEREFORE BE IT RESOLVED that we, the delegates of the 1992 General Assembly of the Unitarian Universalist Association, affirm and support this vision of a racially diverse and multicultural Unitarian Universalism;

BE IT FURTHER RESOLVED that the 1992 General Assembly urges the Board of Trustees of the Unitarian Universalist Association to develop and implement a process involving a broad representation of congregations, organizations, and staff to realize this vision of a racially and culturally diverse Unitarian Universalist Association; and

BE IT FINALLY RESOLVED that the 1992 General Assembly of the Unitarian Universalist Association call on the Board of Trustees to present to the 1993 General Assembly a report of progress in research and planning to realize this vision of our faith community.

The informal coalition had decided that Rev. Dr. Victor Carpenter would be the best to speak in support of the resolution, and Davidoff pulled him out of a session where he was presiding as chair of the Unitarian Universalist Service Committee so he could address the delegates. "We have been provided with that rarest of human opportunities," Carpenter told them, "a second chance. Twenty-five years ago we had the opportunity to lead this country's religious community in the direction of racial justice. We rose up and fell back. The vision was too blurred, the rhetoric too harsh, the pain too deep. Now we are again given a chance to lead this nation in generous response to the social crisis symbolized by the Los Angeles civil disturbances. We are called to do justly, to love mercy, and to work humbly for the empowerment of our brothers and sisters. Let's not blow it!"

Dr. Norma Poinsett, chair of the Black Concerns Working Group, seconded the motion and highlighted the multi-faceted coalition that had co-sponsored it. The resolution passed overwhelmingly.

Poinsett said Davidoff's leadership was key: "Denny has . . . that kind of respect for what she was doing and that kind of involvement," she said. "I thought she did a lot of pushing and a lot of convincing people around several things—a lot of things within the Association that had to do with people of color, not only people of color but the movement, you know. . . . To begin to have blacks recognized as human beings who were giving something to the association. Because once upon a time, I can remember when there were few women! It was just all men, as if other people didn't exist, other than white men."

The resolution was not specific about the work it called on Unitarian Universalists to do. "It was the first time I think that as a national movement, UUism had been able to come close to touching the topic of race in a long time, which I think explains the vagueness," said Rev. William Sinkford, who was elected as the Association's first African-American president in 2001. "It was clearly diversity-oriented. You know, Rodney King said, 'Why can't we just get along,' and I think that was some of the emotional tone of it, although it clearly was prophetic. It said we have work to do, but it was not analytical. At the same time, very hopeful. My faith community had finally re-engaged at some level. So my spirits were buoyed."

Responses to the Resolution

In the main official response to the resolution, the Board of Trustees appointed a Racial and Cultural Diversity Task Force to develop a plan and process for realizing its vision.

On a personal level, many who witnessed passage of the resolution were deeply affected. Phyllis Daniel, a member of the Unitarian Universalist Church of Long Beach, California, who would later be instrumental in addressing anti-racism through the Ministerial Fellowship Committee, the accrediting body for clergy, recalled,

> I happened to go to General Assembly in 1992 in Calgary because friends were going—I hadn't been to GA for awhile. At that GA the resolution was introduced for the first time. . . . I was just very affected by that. I don't recall right now what the presentations were, but in any event, I felt like this was very, very important work, it was something I was very happy the denomination was engaging, and I wanted to be part of it. And I made the decision that I might run for district trustee. . . . So that's what happened. I ran for district trustee, and I know that I talked about this as part of my campaign.

Rev. Dr. Tracey Robinson-Harris, who had been active in racial justice advocacy as a white person since the 1980s, reflected, "For me it was significant that the elected delegates said what they said. That was huge," she said. "I think it was the only way to get it in front of us."

Others had more mixed reactions. Dr. Rev. Fredric Muir, a white minister serving the Unitarian Universalist Church of Annapolis, Maryland, had been working on race relations issues for more than a decade when the resolution was brought before the Assembly. His reaction reflected the complex dynamics and emotions that surrounded these issues. "One response was 'Well, it's about time,'" he said. "In my ministry up to that point I don't feel like there'd ever been an institutional attempt to address issues of racism since all the way back to the empowerment controversy, and it just had felt as though the UUA had abdicated any responsibility, any interest, to congregations as well as the larger society around us. There didn't seem to be any program available for any direction. There was nothing going on at all, so at least this was a glimmer of hope. At the same time, I realized quite frankly my response was, 'Here we go again.' What's going to happen? This is just going to be another opportunity for failure, and everybody's going to be able to say, 'See, we told you this was going to happen.' I anticipated a lot of resistance, resistance that might even be seeded with anger, and so it was mixed feelings. I was really, really pleased that something was appearing, that something was going to happen, that the elephant in the room had been named, and at the same time, it was like, 'Boy, where are we going to go with this?' Are we really ready, and what does it even mean to be ready?"

Some advocates for a more inclusive Unitarian Universalism were pained by the resolution. Looking back, Rev. José Ballester, who would become one of the founders of the Latina/o Unitarian Universalist Networking Association in 1995, expressed what he felt should have been different. "When the Task Force on Racial and Cultural Diversity was formed I would make sure there were a variety of voices and not a binary [black-white] conversation," he said. "Personally it would not have been necessary for me to continually remind the UUA that our voices and insights were being ignored. It would have been obvious that Crossroads Ministry's programs were limiting." Moving programming out of the Black Concerns Working Group was an opportunity to include other racial and ethnic groups, he said, pointing out that the Black Concerns Working Group initially designed key programs such as the Jubilee workshops. "You can't correct Jubilee I and Jubilee II simply by adding the names of the other marginalized groups and not delving into their oppressions," Ballester said. "I and others would have been spared the denigration we endured for having a differing opinion."

Rev. Dr. Rebecca Parker recalled,

I've never been a voting delegate to GA, but I was there and listened to the debate and in 1992 where the rhetoric was at and the arguments that were made for why we should pass the resolution . . . I personally was so uncomfortable with the rhetoric at that point that I walked out of the room in the middle of that vote. And my heart was not rejoicing at that vote, and at that moment of where the UUA was at . . . I remember the extent to which the vote reflected a ground-swell of a sense of white failure and white desire to make things right and have a second chance and be committed to anti-racism work, and it felt like it was coming from the wrong place. . . . It felt like it was an expression of issues in white identity. . . . I had a sense of desire or longing for a different center, a different grounding for why anti-racism and counter-oppressive work was important for Unitarian Universalists to be doing.

Another concern was the location. "For everything you can say about Calgary," said Gini Courter, who became the Association's moderator in 2003, "anti-racism was not a grassroots movement. It was a political movement. . . . Why would we do this in a General Assembly in Canada? That was one of the two years I know I couldn't afford to go." She noted that passage of a resolution does not indicate commitment. "The goal is not to pass something. The goal is to get something to affect congregational life," she said, noting that the resolution did have some impacts. "It did inspire some folks and the vote in Calgary committed the Board."

The resolution set the precedent that General Assembly would be a focus for educating about racial justice issues. Rev. Wayne Arnason observed that this was the natural outcome of the training and education efforts of the late 1980s. "What we started to see was GA programming that was being built out of the experiences that leadership was having with anti-racism training, with having themselves open up to the ethical commitment and the power of the education that we were involved in, and wanting to have that be part of General

Assembly," he said. "What we were up against, we realized, was that because of our polity and because of the role that ministers play in leading churches and being sensitive to church culture and being able to change church culture, the only place that UUA leaders had direct access to members of congregations who possibly could be converts, or who could go through some kind of born-again educational experience of seeing anti-racism work as something that was intrinsic to their own well-being, health, to the health of their congregation, to the future of the Association—the only place we had that access was at GA, because we could not make people come to these conferences beyond the leadership level. There was a limited kind of authority that the Association could invoke, so we had to do education at the GA level, and also do resolution work. I think that's why the resolution in Calgary becomes important."

The sense of many was not that this was a new dialogue, rather it was a continuation of an unfinished conversation that had long been part of the challenges facing Unitarian Universalism. "In the Journey struggle, not really beginning in Calgary but resumed there, the UUA as an institution and many Unitarian Universalists as caring leaders took on the hard work of understanding the deep systemic issues still sickening our society and our own immersion in those dynamics," said Rev. Linda Olson Peebles, minister of religious education at the Unitarian Universalist Church of Arlington, Virginia, and later a trustee on the Association's Board who identifies as "a straight white female of Scandanavian heritage":

> We had to take a step back from our extreme individualism, and begin to revision ourselves as part of a covenantal community. Personal salvation cannot be separated from community-wide and institutional transformation. We had to begin to mature away from our self-focused narcissism, and towards a relational-focused stewardship, to truly minister to the hurts and needs of a broken world.

Yet the sense of alienation was growing in other quarters, especially for those who identify as Latina/o and Hispanic, for the focus remained on black/white relations. Ballester recalled,

Now we have this program, that's going to change that, because we've learned the lessons from the past, but we still have the same people in place, with the same initial training, with the same views. . . . Shall we define madness again? How often do we have to do this? How awful that, from Calgary, we put together a racial and cultural diversity task force that included [only] blacks and whites.

The Racial and Cultural Diversity Initiative

The new Task Force on Racial and Cultural Diversity was chaired by Dr. Leon Spencer of the Black Concerns Working Group and Rev. Dr. Anita Farber-Robertson, minister of the Unitarian Universalist Church of Greater Lynn, in Swampscott, Massachusetts. The task force was made up of representatives from the Unitarian Universalist Ministers Association, the Youth Caucus, District Presidents, Black Concerns Working Group, Urban Concerns and Ministry Committee, Women's Federation, and the Board of Trustees and staff, representing the coalition of groups that had supported the 1992 resolution. In another response to the resolution, the Association's administration changed the Office for Racial Inclusiveness into the Office for Racial and Cultural Diversity and staffed it with a full-time director and a full-time administrator.

"The most important decision we made, we actually made the first day we met," said Farber-Robertson, whose ethnic identity includes Jewish and Lutheran roots. "We decided . . . that it is easy to infer from the color of Unitarian Universalism that there is racism existing in the institution—otherwise it would not be so white. If that was the case, it didn't make sense to do outreach to communities of color. . . . The first order of business was to put our house in order and deal with the institutional and personal racism. That was the scary thing we did—if we had done the thing everyone expected us to do, which was to reach out to communities of color and recruit, everyone in the UUA would have been happy. . . . I am really proud we made it about us and not about converting people of color."

The task force appointed a research group to design a multiphase research effort, the overall purpose of which was to build a foundation of understanding of what the racial and cultural diversity initiative means to Unitarian Universalists within our congregations. One goal was to gather insight on how to become more racially and culturally diverse, and to identify barriers to doing so. People were asked about their perceptions of the advantages and concerns regarding an initiative to promote racial and cultural diversity and to help identify models within for implementing such an initiative. The Task Force was looking for ideas. Spencer recalled, "There was not any model or a ten-year plan that had already been mapped out for us. . . . There was a realization that we had to address some piece institutionally and structurally."

A report drafted in June 1992 described the Research Group's work:

> A total of 18 focus group discussions were conducted within congregations in Boston, MA; New York, NY; Montclair, NJ; Decatur, GA; Tulsa, OK; Dallas, TX; Denver, CO; San Francisco, CA; and Chicago, IL. Two discussion groups were held in each congregation. Congregations were selected by the Research Group for inclusion based on the presence of a large enough number of African Americans or other diverse population so that between eight and twelve non-Caucasian people could be invited to participate in a discussion. District Executives in each District being considered were contacted for their counsel on congregations that might be appropriate for inclusion in this initial phase of research.

> The Research Team actually conducting the discussions consisted of four Unitarian Universalists—three women and one man, two African Americans and two Caucasian Americans. All members of the Team are professional facilitators, two with professional backgrounds in market research, two with professional backgrounds in diversity (one professor at Occidental University, one consultant to industry). Each facilitator was assigned three congregations based on regional accessibility. . . .

Some churches felt their members would be more comfortable discussing diversity in racially diverse discussion groups. Others felt their members would speak more openly if they were interviewed separately, Caucasian Americans in one group and African Americans in another group. Ultimately the research design included every combination possible.

The black-and-white nature of the research design was striking. Spencer said that this was not an oversight, that how inclusive or exclusive to be was an explicit part of the conversation. "We had an agenda to close," he recalled. "The fear was that people would skip that and move on to the next."

The Task Force's research found much fermenting and fomenting around unaddressed issues of race for Unitarian Universalists. In their research, which led to a series of findings, they also interviewed and surveyed people to generate lists of comments that revealed how broad the spectrum of opinions was:

"Are we trying to make UUs out of multicultural people, or are we trying to make UUs multicultural?"

"There is an intellectual barrier. Minorities are not comfortable in an intellectual environment."

"We would finally be willing to dialogue with each other about racism, not just be a bunch of intellectuals preaching about good works, but really getting into each others' hearts. We would be a connected rainbow, we would understand each other."

"I integrate my workplace and my neighborhood. My daughter integrated her school. I was not going to have my family integrate our church, too."

"I do believe it is a moral imperative. If we can't live together in our churches then how in the world will we impact the larger community to live together?"

FINDINGS
From the Racial and Cultural Diversity Initiative

A. Diversity is most often understood to mean acceptance of and affirmation of the complete spectrum of human differences, not simply as racial or cultural diversity. It is critically understood as an attitude embracing co-equality of all people.

B. Benefits of diversity frequently mentioned include personal growth and enrichment, a need to reflect demographic trends, living the Unitarian Universalist principles we preach, and sharing this potentially healing religion with the larger world.

C. The concerns most often raised seemed to concentrate in these areas: fear of change and of sharing power among Caucasian Americans, perceptions of programming which is not relevant to the concerns of African Americans or other diverse groups, and considerable difficulty in learning how to confront racism, in learning how to deal with racial differences and racial conflict in an affirming way within our congregations.

D. African Americans report coming to Unitarian Universalist churches primarily because the minister and/or congregation are actively engaged in social justice causes relevant to

African Americans; and because they're looking for a church where their own commitment to diversity, where their possibly racially mixed family, or where their non-Eurocentric theology will be accepted. They stay because they feel accepted, like the programming, or are committed to learning how to live in a diverse world.

E. Signs and symbols that indicate an openness to diversity to a newcomer in the congregations interviewed are primarily limited to including materials from the African-American (or other) tradition in Sunday worship services. Art from diverse traditions, an actual increase of African Americans (or other diverse groups) attending worship, and an increase in social programs relevant to African Americans (or others) were all suggested as appropriate signs for the future.

F. There is a strong indication that individual Unitarian Universalists are not comfortable with the concept of an initiative to diversify "legislated" from the Unitarian Universalist Association. Rather, people expressed interest in and support for the Unitarian Universalist Association to provide vehicles to meet congregations where they stand on the appropriateness of such an initiative on an individual basis, adaptable to the particular types of diversity relevant within their communities.

"Selfishness, complacency. . . . I don't want to change or make the effort to change. We don't perceive of it as selfishness, but that's really what it is."

"You can't change another person. If there are whites in the congregation who don't want to examine their own racism, what does that mean for those who want to move in another direction? We argue about this . . . all the time."

Of particular note were the comments of African Americans and people in other historically marginalized groups:

"In the black churches hymns are about the struggle, surviving, salvation. Our hymnal is about nature and flowers."

"They don't want us to have chicken dinners. You can raise a lot of money that way, but they look down on it; it's not a traditional thing to do here. We had volunteers, but they never asked. We get asked to volunteer for white activities."

"As African-Americans we're bi-cultural or we don't survive. We have to be able to slip in and out of both of those worlds. Maybe we're hoping one day the Eurocentric people will be able to slip into our world a little bit."

"As a black person new in this church going into coffee hour I am very aware that there are some people in this congregation who are very uncomfortable with blacks, as they may be with gays or with aggressive women. Two things bother me. As an African American I don't see myself as a minority in this society. Minority is a weapon in this culture used against African Americans and Latinos to reinforce what racism does, which is inculcate a sense of negative self-worth. Our language is pregnant with white racism."

"I had a miserable experience there [at a suburban UU church]. I went to a concert. Afterwards they had cheese and crackers and wine. Someone gave my host and hostess [white UUs] a glass of wine. By the time they got to me there were no more glasses. And it happened again. This is childish, and awful. So I never drank any wine and asked to leave soon after."

"One of the problems with unconscious racism that's denied is that they aren't in touch with themselves. We're not safe because racism's hurtful and can come up any time."

"UUs lack space for Jesus and the Bible. We do OK with Buddha. Until we can resolve our own issues with Christianity we will have trouble including a lot of people, not just people of color."

"White people are cold."

"Each church should involve itself in what makes sense for the individual congregation. There should not be a blanket diversity formula. The UUA should provide some models that are successful and funds to do it."

"Each congregation should go about doing the stuff the way they want to. We shouldn't legislate how to do it."

"Look at our RE resources . . . they're all written by white people. We need to offer our children who are not white resources in RE from their own traditions."

RECOMMENDATIONS
From the Institutional Racism Audit

While the 1992 task force that reviewed the findings of the 1980 Institutional Racism Audit found no villains or heroes, it found apathy, wariness, and middle-of-the-road skepticism pervasive among UUA staffers. It had become apparent by early 1983 that some of the recommendations had been implemented, but that insufficient resources prevented substantive adherence to the actions mandated.

1. *Increase the number of people of color on the UUA Board of Trustees.* Mechanisms suggested: Increasing the number of at-large Trustees or reserving two of the current at-large seats for people of color.

2. *To adopt an official statement of UUA intention to be involved in work against racism as an ongoing imperative.*

3. *Adopt and implement a long-range plan for the renewal of the UUA role in and through city churches, to include at least seven emphases.*

4. *Instruct the Office of the President to give major emphasis to identifying the things which have been learned about how to create more authentic black-white relationships within the structures of the UUA.*

5. *Instruct the Office of the President and other appropriately designated instrumentalities to plan a way to bring symbolic closure on the feelings left over from the Black Empowerment Controversy.*

6. *Establish and staff six new churches*: two in predominantly Hispanic areas, two in predominantly black areas, two in areas of multiracial populations, in different parts of the continental jurisdiction, by the year 1990.

7. *Fully implement the guidelines and policy recommendations of Project Equality, and urge societies and fellowships also to become active members of Project Equality.*

8. *Adopt an Affirmative Action Policy and Program for employment of people of color—with plans for recruitment, goals, and timetables.*

9. *Designate a staff person to assume total responsibility for the portfolio of Affirmative Action Officer with necessary support services to implement and monitor an Affirmative Action Plan.*

10. *Adopt an Affirmative Action Plan for volunteer leadership recruitment, with goals and timetable.*

11. *Review all standards of fellowshipping ministers of color, with particular attention being given to ways of accepting non-Unitarian Universalist performance and experience in lieu of academic criteria.*

12. *Develop an intern program for ministerial students in already existing Unitarian Universalist churches which are bi/multiracial in composition.*

13. *Vigorously pursue a program to recruit ministerial students of color and provide necessary support services for them during training.*

14. *Establish an Office of Racial Justice charged with developing and implementing programs to eliminate racism.*

15. *Provide racism awareness training for all employed staff.*

16. *Cooperate with programmatic efforts of other religious groups to eliminate racism.*

17. *Establish and maintain meaningful liaisons between UUA official structures and the National Urban League, as well as with similar groups of Hispanic, Native American, and Asian peoples.*

18. *Continue regular reporting of ways in which investment decisions have been based on guidelines for maximum social responsibility impact and report the same in the UU World.*

19. *Develop and train teams of persons prepared to go into districts, churches, and fellowships to facilitate anti-racism actions, networks, and strategies.*

continues on page 82

20. *Distribute a summary of this Audit Report to all Unitarian Universalist churches, districts, fellowships, and interested individuals.*

21. *Develop racism audit processes for use in member societies and districts.*

22. *Establish a committee and empower it to conduct a study of current multiracial churches, to determine the potentials and guidelines for the development of multiracial Unitarian Universalist churches.*

23. *Enter into negotiations with the author of* Black America/White America *to determine the possibilities for timely publication.*

24. *Conduct an immediate review of existing printed and audio-visual materials by a team of persons representing different racial backgrounds, prior to purchase or production.*

25. *Adopt criteria for the elimination of racism for use in evaluating all printed and audio-visual materials purchased or produced.*

26. *To request the administration to develop study materials for use among Unitarian Universalists which will facilitate exploration of stereotypes and ways in which they might be behaviorally countered.*

27. *Develop materials from a multicultural perspective, including bilingual works to interpret liberal religion among French and Hispanic people.*

28. *Produce video cassettes, role-plays, and other experiential learning instruments for use in societies and district meetings.*

29. *Develop materials designed to communicate liberal religious views especially among people of color.*

30. *Develop Spanish-language materials for use in interpreting liberal religion among Hispanic peoples.*

31. *Require the President to report on the implementation of audit recommendations to each General Assembly.*

CHAPTER 7

Congregations, a Congress, a Curriculum Lost

As Unitarian Universalists struggled to reclaim an identity as people who address racial justice as a religious imperative, the congregations started in the 1980s to be racially and culturally diverse were faltering, due in part to resource constraints. The adult curriculum for congregations called *The Language of Race* never made it to press. And the Continental Congress of African American Unitarian Universalists, which drew more than a hundred people to Philadelphia in September 1992, was never convened again.

As the racial/ethnic new start congregations failed to meet the goals set for them, as funding decreased, and as a number of the congregations dissolved in the late 1980s and early 1990s, discussions about them were limited. The lessons learned through them—about how to target historically underrepresented racial and ethnic groups, for example—were not disseminated broadly to inform other congregations that might have benefited. They lived on only in the hearts of those who had experienced them, in a few reports at Unitarian Universalist Association, and for the ministers of color who had led them, in a legacy of deepening distrust in the Association.

Relationship and faith were both tested for those who sacrificed and led in the efforts to achieve racial and ethnic diversity at the congregational level, both through the new start congregations and through the pilot projects to address racism in predominantly white congregations. The stories of these sacrifices and the division they incurred are too extensive to do justice to in this book; suffice it to say that they added to a climate of distrust and broken relationships.

In addition to the perception that they were under-funded and under-supported, often the leaders—people of color and those of Latina/o and Hispanic origin—felt they took the blame for the failure of these efforts. These feelings have not left those who were placed in these positions. The fact that the learning that could have been gleaned from these efforts was not openly aired to benefit and inform greater Unitarian Universalist circles recalled the avoidant behavior around the history of the Empowerment Controversies. In a similar way, unpublished works such as the *Language of Race* curriculum remain as unclaimed parts of our heritage, creating a new subterranean network of hidden shames.

Congregations Under Stress

In 1991, planning was under way to assist congregations that could demonstrate diverse membership in order to help them increase that diversity. This built on the work of the Racial and Ethnic New Start Congregations, many of which were still struggling.

Financial limitations plagued the new start congregations. The Black Concerns Working Group noted in 1992, "These congregations continue to suffer from lack of financial resources." Two additional congregations were started, informed by the lessons of those that came before them, but they were not able to escape falling victim to some of the same challenges, especially around resources and support from predominantly white sponsoring congregations.

The new start congregations were very focused in their identity as multicultural churches and had a set of core values not found in the predominantly white churches that surrounded them. Through extensive community involvement, many of them carried the Unitarian Universalist name into places and groups and neighborhoods where it had never been heard before.

The struggles of these congregations were many, some specific to a congregation, others common among them. Their leadership, both professional and volunteer, carried heavy burdens because of their small size and slow growth. Some of the congregations also established issues that would continue into other aspects of anti-racism advocacy.

How these experimental congregations would be evaluated was not clear and the expectations for their performance were set by those who had conceived and funded them. Congregational leaders "asked for assistance in developing evaluation procedures," a 1991 report said. "Since many are new to Unitarian Universalism and to working in a partnership with a minister," it added, "they requested guidelines and good process for communication and decision-making." The demographics of the Association created awkwardness as well. "The need for European-American staff members to evaluate African American New Congregations has had the apparent effect of leaving everyone cautious while trust is built," the report noted.

Enthusiasm for these congregations was often reliant on the abilities and talents of a single minister or leader, according to a 1994 evaluation:

> The Thurman-Hamer-Ellington Congregation in Atlanta, GA, was led by the Rev. Daniel Aldridge as organizing minister; the Rev. Michelle Bentley organized the North River Unitarian Universalist Church (NRUUC) and the South Loop Unitarian Universalist Church in Chicago in 1987 and 1988, respectively, with support in planning and funding of a sub-committee (all European American) of the Central Midwest District Extension Committee. The Korean seed church was organized by the Rev. Hyun Hwan Kim first in Anaheim, CA, and then moved to the First Unitarian Church in Los Angeles. The El Salvadorean Oscar Romero Congregation, a nested model within a larger, majority white, congregation, was organized in 1985 under the lay leadership of Ricardo Zelada, a Salvadoran refugee who received sanctuary in the First Unitarian Church of Los Angeles. The Oscar Romero Congregation in Anaheim, CA, had two Salvadorean organizers, Dagaberto Zavala and Juan Castillo, who trained at the UUA's New Congregation Training.

Financial issues were rife, especially around compensation of their professional ministers.

CONGREGATIONAL STORY
Church of the Restoration, Philadelphia

Warren Ross wrote this story for a 1993 issue of the World.

The congregation moved from downtown Philadelphia [to the Mt. Airy neighborhood] in 1937. The first black family joined in 1961, when Mt. Airy was still overwhelmingly white. Three years later, the Rev. Rudolf Gelsey was called to the Restoration pulpit. It was the decade of civil rights and Vietnam protests, and Gelsey was controversial even among Unitarian Universalists. . . . Gelsey's concern for social justice took him to the Alabama protests, where James Reeb, a fellow Unitarian Universalist minister, was killed, and then into the thick of racial battles back home. Gelsey noticed that the demographics of Mt. Airy were changing. Suspecting blockbusting by real estate agents, he organized a neighborhood association—with his own parishioners at the core—to halt panic selling by whites. His initiative more than helped stabilize the neighborhood: as Pat DeBrady, a long-time African American member recalled, "He made the church a place where we could feel some level of comfort. . . ." When [Rev. Robert] Throne took over the ministry in 1987, Restoration's membership, by then about one-third black, had plateaued at about 100. Today, membership stands at over 150, and attendance at Sunday services has doubled. "There is certainly twice as much going on," says Throne, "with new faces and new music and new social ways."

Also, a basic shift has taken place in what it means to be a multi-racial church. In the 1950s and 1960s, black Unitarian Universalists were willing to settle for a church where they could be accepted "as if they were white." Today many insist on being accepted as people of a particular culture, with their own proud traditions and with a special contribution to make to the religious life of the congregation. In response, says Throne, the church not only celebrates Kwanzaa as well as Christmas, Hanukkah and the solstice, but it is talking more deeply about race and culture. . . .

By the time Marion Napper joined in 1980, the church was sufficiently biracial that she felt immediately at home. Seven years ago, she became the church's second—and first female—African American moderator. "This was my first exposure to Unitarian Universalism. I had a Pentecostal background, but here I felt at home. Have I ever felt any racial tension at Restoration? Oh yes, but it's very subtle, and I don't think it's intentional. It's a reflection of the larger society. I'll tell you something: when I first joined, I made a point of not working in the kitchen," she laughs. "That's what blacks are expected to do. After I became moderator, sure I worked in the kitchen. By that time I felt fully accepted. And I felt willing to speak up when someone is insensitive and say, 'You shouldn't do or say that. That hurts our feelings.'"

A high point of her Restoration membership, she says, came when following the Los Angeles riots, black members remained silent. "I do not want whites to feel our pain," she explains. "But I do want them to understand it."

In the fall of 1990, Restoration Church conducted a racial audit to check on its attitudes and practices. "It was reassuring to see that our commitment was deeply rooted among us," Throne recalled. "We were and are widening our worship and social style—to speak more authentically to the African American experience and to other cultural resources. And it is good for us to share our story, to help others take steps we have found not only morally right but also richly nourishing. But we also discovered how hard it is to talk frankly about racial matters at a personal level," the minister continues. "We have to keep digging deeper to understand—and overcome—the remaining barriers. We who are white need to educate ourselves about the black experience, need to risk being hurt a little ourselves. We may not solve all the problems of the world, but we can learn to love one another a bit more deeply, more authentically."

The presence of religious leaders who mirrored their racial identity helped African Americans feel more at home in Unitarian Universalism. Carol Carter Walker and Carmelita Carter, African-American sisters active in the Sojourner Truth Congregation of Unitarian Universalists in Washington, D.C., noted that the presence of Rev. Dr. Yvonne Seon, the first African-American woman to be fellowshipped as a Unitarian Universalist parish minister, was a draw for her. Vivian Pollard recalled that the planned arrival of Rev. Daniel Aldridge, an African American, at the Thurman-Hamer-Ellington Unitarian Universalist Church in 1991 encouraged her to become a charter member.

These congregations offered the Association a chance to learn more about the religious appeal of Unitarian Universalism to different communities such as the Latino/Latina/Hispanic populations. Real experience offering Unitarian Universalism in these contexts led to insights about the challenge of intentional outreach based on racial and ethnic factors. "The Latino community is no more homogenous than the Anglo community," a September 1991 report noted. "It is diverse in national background, dialects and colloquialisms of language, life experience, class-interests, religious and political affiliation and length of residence in North America."

These real-time encounters showed the cracks in the veneer of Unitarian Universalist understanding about these diverse cultures. "It is important for Unitarian Universalists to learn about Latino life in North America, not just about the solidarity and sanctuary movements," the same report observed. "For example, it is important to know that government oppression of Latinos exists in the U.S. as well as in Latin America, including labor legislation which has worked different standards for migrants compared to all other workers; life in recent political refugee communities versus Latino communities that have been stable for several generations versus migrant communities which move throughout the year; rural versus center city settings; educational opportunities and disadvantages for Latino children, including whether Spanish, as well as English, is spoken in schools serving Latino children; economic realities for Latino communities and individuals in North America, and how those realities benefit or harm the economies of Mexico, the United

States and Canada. For example, do farm workers make less than a living wage so that U.S. consumers can pay less and agribusiness interests can make more profit on their backs?" Knowing the different issues was important when establishing the outreach strategies of these congregational efforts. For example, the Los Angeles Oscar Romero Congregation started in 1984–85 to bring Unitarian Universalist Purposes and Principles to the Hispanic community as part of solidarity with the Salvadoran movement.

These congregational efforts yielded important information about the resources needed and issues faced with doing outreach into a more diverse spectrum of racial and cultural groups, as the 1991 report stated:

> [T]he issues faced by the Anaheim Oscar Romero Congregation illustrate the struggles of these congregations which were charting new ground with very limited resources as this cryptic account of the history reveals: "[In] 1985 began efforts with encouragement from LA Oscar Romero. The congregation was not geographically close to the Latino community. Had to compete for time and space with Anaheim congregation and encountered overlap in program needs. Noise and confusion problems reported as well as carpool and transportation issues since people could not get there. In 1987, representatives of the congregation visited UUA headquarters to ask for help. District gave $2,000 in credit but no cash. The focus became providing community services—legal and referral and this attracted people (around 3,000 from 1987–89) with some support from District funding. [A participant noted that] growth became threatening—Latinos began to use church building more than Anglos . . . parties brought in people, but not seen as positive by the Unitarian Universalist congregation. Some of the Latino leadership became involved in the regular congregation and played a key leadership role there as well as providing human services. . . . It took a while to figure out the Unitarian Universalist way of doing things."

The congregations also modeled a way of being that was ahead of their times. Rev. Rosemary Bray McNatt noted of the Sojourner Truth effort,

> Yvonne Seon's congregation was the most interesting, fascinating congregation I've ever set foot in my whole life. I went to her congregation in Washington. I thought they were the neatest group of people in the world. And what she was trying to do is the norm for a lot of our congregations now. When you went to her congregation, there were gay people and straight people and interracial couples, and when you go to urban congregations now in UUism, it's so ordinary and boring now to see that. It was like being on another planet in UUism, when you went into her congregation. She was ahead of her time.

Organizers of these congregations often left disillusioned and burnt out. The attempt to form intentionally multiracial congregations was a microcosm of the relational tensions that arose between the lofty goals and the practical needs of a religious institution. With the focus on demographics and cultural change, and on documenting results, anti-racism efforts could become exhausting and stray from their original intent. "Dropping the spiritual was certainly not my intention," said Seon. "It was a byproduct of some other things. I think it was a byproduct of diversity becoming the focus (within the UUA). . . . I think if you drop the focus on diversity and focus on the spiritual . . . and social justice, we'll have the diversity. By focusing on the diversity, the different subgroups become politicized and the spiritual becomes lost in the process of politicization."

And these experiments began to document target groups within the Latino population who might be attracted to Unitarian Universalism:

> People with a strong social conscience and/or those involved in similar concerns/activities as Unitarian Universalists; for

example, individuals who work with refugees, provide sanctuary, are involved in political work to end U.S. involvement in Central America, religious work to increase church assistance to people in Central America, bilingual literacy. . . . People with similar values; education, professional concerns, child-care, multicultural awareness, community development, the arts. . . . Recent immigrants searching for community survival skills/entry points, such as sanctuary residents. . . . College students. . . . People who discover the UUA Principles and Purposes, which are largely unknown in the Latino community. . . . People who are looking for alternative theology, liturgy, practice or lifestyle to that of religions they have known and left.

The very theological diversity that attracts many Unitarian Universalists made these racial and ethnic new starts a challenge. An unidentified member of the Unitarian Universalist Church of the Restoration in Philadelphia put it this way:

We're into this spiritual potpourri and let's not let one thing dominate. I don't mind the fluidity, but for me, there is a lack of sincerity if you can't commit to something. That's what keeps getting tossed back to us. This is Unitarian Universalism (and) you can't commit to any one thing. You have to honor diversity. I don't see a lot of growth that way. In terms of religious education, Black people come primarily out of a Jesus [background]. There was a lot of discomfort about the lack of commitment to God among Black members. To be a Unitarian Universalist meant you couldn't be committed to God and couldn't acknowledge Jesus. Part of Unitarian Universalism is to maintain doubt. What I get from Unitarian Universalism is doubt, debate and ridicule as a path to faith.

Rev. Marjorie Bowens-Wheatley analyzed other constraints in her evaluative report as well:

The fact that Unitarian Universalists base their system of governance on congregational polity represented another area of cultural difference. In many Black churches, not only is there some degree of deference to the minister, but it is often assumed that the minister will have the last word about any major decision (for example, holding a board meeting without the minister).

Heterosexism was a very real issue; at the same time (in one congregation) a politically savvy (gay member) exploited an opportunity to act without congregational support which may have exacerbated existing sentiments around the issue of sexual orientation.

According to the lingo of the UUA Department of Extension, congregations included in [the 1993–94] survey adopted the "planter" model of growing a new church. It should be made clear that this model was used for two reasons: African American Unitarian Universalist ministers (a) were not getting settled through the established channel—the UUA Settlement process; and (b) some wanted to start congregations that were diverse in racial/ethnic/cultural terms), Afrocentric or rooted in the African American experience. Though the affirmative action/full employment approach was well-intentioned, the UUA had little experience or programmatic support in terms of how to build or sustain these congregations which face unique challenges.

This survey seems to confirm what some African American Unitarian Universalists have suspected for decades: that there are people in historically Black churches who are unhappy with dogmatic theology and authoritative structures and in search of a place where spiritual or theological diversity is encouraged. There is a great potential for attracting such people to Unitarian Universalism if—and only if—two conditions are met:

[First] there is a greater tolerance for theistic perspectives and honoring the fact that the experience of Jesus has been a great source of inspiration in the African American community and [second] there is an educational process on issues of polity—one that values the positive contribution of the Black church.

In addition, it should be recognized that the lack of acknowledgment of a collective decision-making process within congregations is disruptive and unhealthy for congregational growth.

The efforts to establish racial and ethnic diversity in congregational models also fueled the awareness that attitudes about race were a barrier to advancing Unitarian Universalism. Bowens-Wheatley noted, "Because racism is ill-understood within the congregations surveyed resulting in an unfair burden for African Americans and other people of color in a multicultural setting, anti-racism training or racial reeducation is needed from the onset."

These well-intentioned and much-hailed new congregations faltered and with the faltering came distrust and alienation, particularly by clergy from traditionally marginalized groups. The frustration and anger of those who had led these efforts came forward in "An Open Letter to Unitarian Universalist Leaders":

We, the leaders of the racial/ethnic new start congregations while meeting in Atlanta in November 1992, recognize that our relationship with the Unitarian Universalist Association must be changed. There are problematic dynamics which need to end so that we can move into new and more effective structures. Though each of our congregations has a distinct character and profile, we have identified some common aspects of who we are and the directions in which we are moving. We differ from the typical "growth model" of Unitarian Universalist congregations.

We share common beginnings: all of our churches were "planter models" dependent upon African American ministers, have been in existence for two to six years, began with a strong liberation/social justice emphasis, and are rooted in urban communities.

BYLAWS
All Souls Church Unitarian Universalist, Durham, North Carolina

The new start congregations continued to experiment with practices and procedures from which predominantly white congregations could have learned. For example, All Souls Church Unitarian Universalist in Durham, North Carolina, under the leadership of Rev. William (Chester) McCall, put months of effort into the development of anti-racist bylaws which, while perhaps not useable in their original form for all congregations, offered an important model as to how to honor the minority voice, as these provisions on caucusing illustrate.

ARTICLE IX: CAUCUS—OR AFFINITY GROUPS
All Souls shall institutionalize Caucus- or Affinity Groups into the decision-making process as another way to create an inclusive environment where the best possible nonoppressive decision may be reached. As with the Standing Committees of the Committee of the Whole [COW] Caucus- or Affinity Groups shall be created at the discretion of the COW and each group shall be an official body of the congregation, afforded the same rights, privileges, and responsibilities as other Standing Committees. The People of Color Caucus shall be a Standing Caucus with a representative on the board. Other groups may also form caucuses.

Caucuses shall exist to evaluate the potentially oppressive impact specific institutional and/or organizational decisions and/or decisions regarding policy may have on members of the congregation who identify themselves as members of a group that has been historically marginalized and disenfranchised in larger society.

Membership in any caucus and/or affinity group shall be open to any person who publicly lives and/or self-identifies as being a member of the specific target group for which the affinity group or caucus has been formed.

Though there have been difficulties, we pause to celebrate our achievements:

- Establishing a new, racial/ethnic Unitarian Universalist presence and mission in urban communities of Atlanta, Georgia; San Francisco, California; Tulsa, Oklahoma; and Washington, D.C.;
- Attracting to the movement people who would never have considered Unitarian Universalism as a religious option—both in our congregations and seminaries;
- Broadening and enriching Unitarian Universalist worship in form, style, and content;
- Providing opportunities for individuals, congregations and districts to receive our gifts and support our efforts;
- Discovering unique theological and cultural experiences; and
- Helping the Unitarian Universalist Association better define what has been a previously ill-defined endeavor.

The racial/ethnic new start congregation program emerged from a Unitarian Universalist public need to appear racially inclusive, a private need for many Unitarian Universalists to have a multi-racial, multi-cultural religious experience, and the need of some African-American Unitarian Universalist ministers to be settled in congregations with a significant African-American identity. Our collective efforts have been particularly frustrated by the failure of the Unitarian Universalist Association to deal with race, class and other prejudices in its own operations. For example, outside of this program, there is not one African-American, settled, full-time, senior minister in the entire United States.

An ambiguous institutional commitment and noteworthy staff turnover in the Extension Department have hindered our efforts. We have had to deal with a lack of institutional memory and changing expectations. We must have a clear, reliable, consistent commitment to our mission and presence with adequate funding and support. At minimum this includes:

- Leadership which doesn't capitulate to ministers, staff or local churches which subvert efforts to confront racism;
- Leadership which will not capitulate to resistance to our very existence;
- Recognition of our experiences as vital resources for the Association in its programs and decision-making;
- Being directly consulted in matters which affect our existence and the Association's efforts to be culturally, ethnically and racially inclusive;
- Resources and materials which reflect our communities and other non-European cultures;
- Technical assistance for our leaders and congregations;
- Flexibility and creativity in the ways we relate to traditional Unitarian Universalist practices; and
- A new process for developing milestones for evaluations and celebrating accomplishments.

Our vision for our churches has changed from its initial conception and has grown out of our varied experiences. It includes our new awareness of our accountability to one another as leaders of the racial/ethnic new congregations. It should inspire a new kind of learning for the institution; one of renewed support based upon commitment to continuing Unitarian Universalist presence and mission in our urban communities.

[Signed]
Raquel Sneed, Sojourner Truth Congregation,
    Washington D.C.
Donald C. Bliss, Sojourner Truth Congregation,
    Washington D.C.
[Rev.] Charles Johnson, Church of the Restoration,
    Tulsa, Oklahoma
[Rev.] Daniel W. Aldridge Jr., Thurman-Hamer-Ellington
    Church, Atlanta, Georgia

> Keith Chapman, Thurman-Hamer-Ellington Church,
>   Atlanta, Georgia
> Dorothy DeWitty, Church of the Restoration,
>   Tulsa, Oklahoma
> [Rev.] Toni Vincent, New Community Congregation,
>   San Francisco, California

In the final analysis, the Extension Department was not able to state with definitive proof that the new starts added greater diversity to the ranks of Unitarian Universalism because membership statistics based on race were not tracked until after the initiative had begun. An evaluative report prepared for the Veatch Program conjectured,

> Although our statistics are based on somewhat limited information, it can be shown congregations under the sponsorship of the Extension Department do contribute significantly to the racial and ethnic diversity of Unitarian Universalist membership. Our statistics report such a minimal number of people of color that any modest effort to increase persons of color membership would be a positive and necessary step.

The lessons learned from these new starts were many. Rev. William Sinkford, elected the Association's first African-American president in 2001, was once asked, "What kind of response could an uncredentialed black minister trailing an impoverished congregation expect from the UUA today?" He paused for several seconds and then said,

> I wish that I could tell you it would be a completely enthusiastic one. Since the 1980s, we have tried to support—have in fact supported—congregations built around particular ministers of color. None of them have proved to be self-sustaining over time. If I were talking to a [black minister] today, and what he or she said was that we need support but we're going to make this work ourselves, I would say

absolutely, welcome in. The problems we've had have been creating dependent relationships with ministers of color and congregations that were formed around them. And that's a dangerous place for this largely white institution to travel. Things aren't quite as simple as we would like.

In his first job at the UUA, Sinkford was charged with overseeing the new starts. "One of the hardest things that I had to do in those years was oversee the shrinkage and the closure of almost all of them," he recalled.

The efforts of the "extension" work were controversial, resented by existing congregations, which saw scarce resources going into the gambles of new congregations. Rev. Dr. John Buehrens, Association president from 1993 to 2001, observed,

> It became very apparent that we didn't know how to do new starts anyway. And then when we started doing it with heavy subsidies for populations of color, it was just a mess. That needs to be really owned up to as a failure. We continue to delude ourselves about what it takes to start new congregations and think we can imitate the evangelicals.

He noted that the track record was poor—with only one of the original six congregations surviving. "This track record compares poorly with other denominations doing similar outreach," he said.

These experimentations did bring in some individuals who were drawn to their particular spirit and style and way of being and when several of the new starts floundered, those individuals were cast adrift. Bill Norris, who now describes himself as "inactive" as a Unitarian Universalist, described his journey:

> I began my anti-racism work with the Pilot Program which was begun in Atlanta and continued with the Journey Toward Wholeness program and I was a member of the Mass Bay District's Anti-Racism Transformation Team. My work on the Team continued even after I ceased active church membership. The outcome of this work seems to me

VOICE
Jacqui James

This reading was published in the UUA meditation manual Been in the Storm So Long *in 1991. James is the former anti-oppression programs and resources director in the Religious Education Department of the UUA.*

Blackmail, blacklist, black mark. Black Monday, black mood, black-hearted. Black plague, black mass, black market.

Good guys wear white, bad guys wear black. We fear black cats, and the Dark Continent. But it's okay to tell a white lie, lily-white hands are coveted, it's great to be pure as the driven snow. Angels and brides wear white. Devil's food cake is chocolate; angel's food cake is white!

We shape language and we are shaped by it. In our culture, white is esteemed. It is heavenly, sunlike, clean, pure, immaculate, innocent, and beautiful. At the same time, black is evil, wicked, gloomy, depressing, angry, sullen. Ascribing negative and positive values to black and white enhances the institutionalization of this culture's racism.

Let us acknowledge the negative connotations of whiteness. White things can be soft, vulnerable, pallid, and ashen. Light can be blinding, bleaching, enervating. Conversely, we must acknowledge that darkness has a redemptive character, that in darkness there is power and beauty. The dark nurtured and protected us before our birth.

Welcome darkness. Don't be afraid of it or deny it. Darkness brings relief from the blinding sun, from scorching heat, from exhausting labor. Night signals permission to rest, to be with our loved ones, to conceive new life, to search our hearts, to remember our dreams. The dark of winter is a time of hibernation. Seeds grow in the dark, fertile earth.

The words black and dark don't need to be destroyed or ignored, only balanced and reclaimed in their wholeness. The words white and light don't need to be destroyed or ignored, only balanced and reclaimed in their wholeness. Imagine a world that had only light—or dark. We need both. Dark and light. Light and dark.

"business goes on as usual." The work has not reached far enough into the pews. The one thing I have noticed that is different is a few Unitarian Universalist congregations have congregants less reluctant to discuss the issue of racism as long as they aren't made to feel uncomfortable.

That these lessons were not spread more widely in the movement remains a testimony to the tendency to choose covert conflict over overt.

The Language of Race

Just as the lessons of the new starts were closely held, Jacqui James, then one of the few African-American members of the UUA staff, was producing an adult curriculum intended for congregations that would focus on privilege and oppression within a broad frame including heterosexism, disabilities, classism, and racism. The result, entitled *The Language of Race*, was never published. This huge piece of work, which drew from the *Beyond Categorical Thinking* program for churches in search for a new minister, was symbolic of many efforts started and never completed in this era.

First Continental Congress of Unitarian Universalists

The first Continental Congress of African American Unitarian Universalists, a group of 120, gathered in Philadelphia in September of 1992, journeying from seventeen U.S. states and one Canadian province. One participant, Sherry Weston of Boulder, Colorado, said the event created "a roomful of commonality." The Congress was organized by Rev. Daniel Aldridge, who was then minister of the Thurman-Hamer-Ellington Congregation of Decatur, Georgia, which was 60 percent African-American. The gathering inspired attendees, with Rev. Dr. Mark Morrison-Reed predicting, "My hunch is that we will double the number of black ministers to thirty in seven years . . . [and] we'll be developing a liberal black liturgy, and increasingly trying to articulate a uniquely African American perspective on liberal religion." The event also included a service of commemoration for the life and work of African-American Unitarian Francis Ellen Watkins Harper.

EXCERPT
Definitions

This is excerpted from The Language of Race, *an anti-racism curriculum that was written for the UUA in the late 1990s by Robette Dias, Rev. Keith Kron, and Vivian Carlo and edited by Rev. Marjorie Bowens-Wheatley but never published.*

Racism. The systematic subordination of members of targeted racial groups who have little social power in the United States (African Americans, Latino/as, Native Americans, and Asians) by the members of the agent racial group who have relatively more social power (Whites). This subordination is supported by the actions of individuals, cultural norms and values, and the institutional structures and practices of society.

Racial prejudice coupled with the structural power to impose values and policies on others and to restrict their freedoms; misuse of power + [racial] prejudice = racism.

A set of beliefs, ideologies, and social processes that discriminate against others on the basis of their supposed membership in a so-called racial group. The term has been used in a variety of ways to describe both systems of thought and doctrines that justify the supposed biological superiority of one social group over another.

Modern Racism. A subtle form of prejudice that incorporates negative feelings about [non-dominant] groups but not the traditional stereotypes. Modern racism assumes that discrimination no longer exists; that [non-dominant] groups are responsible for their own disadvantages; and [that] special programs addressing ethnic and racial inequality are unjustified and unnecessary. (Victor Rodriguez, sociologist, Concordia University)

Individual Racism. The beliefs, attitudes, and actions of individuals that support or perpetuate racism. Individual racism can occur at both an unconscious and conscious level, and can be both overt and covert. Examples include telling a racist joke, using a racist epithet, or believing in the inherent superiority of Whites.

Overt Racism. Actions which have as their stated or explicit goal the maintenance of the system of racism and the oppression of those in the targeted racial groups. People who participate in active racism advocate the continued subjugation of members of the targeted groups and protection of "the rights" of members of the dominant group. These goals are often supported by a belief in the inferiority of People of Color and the superiority of White people, culture, and values.

Covert Racism. Beliefs, attitudes, and actions that contribute to the maintenance of racism, without openly advocating violence or oppression. The conscious and unconscious maintenance of attitudes, beliefs, and behaviors that support the system of racism, racial prejudice, and racial dominance.

Institutional Racism. The network of institutional structures, policies, and practices that create advantages and benefits for Whites, and discrimination, oppression, and disadvantages for people of color. The advantages created for Whites are often invisible to them, or are considered "rights" available to everyone as opposed to "privileges" awarded to only some individuals and groups.

Cultural Racism. Those aspects of society that overtly and covertly attribute value and normality to white people and Whiteness, and devalue, stereotype, and label People of Color as "other," different, less than, or render them invisible. Examples of these norms include defining white skin tones as nude or flesh colored, emphasizing individualism as opposed to a more collective ideology, defining one form of English as standard, and identifying only Whites as great writers or composers. Supports and sustains institutional racism.

Power. The ability to define, control, manipulate, or enforce; the ability to reward and penalize individuals and groups based on the way in which social goods and services are distributed.

Racialism. The unequal treatment of a population group purely because of its possession of physical or other characteristics socially defined as denoting a particular race.

Some tensions did surface around this event when white Unitarian Universalists, including an editor from the Association's *World* magazine, participated. "My joy at the weekend was marred by the unexpected shift in the congress," Adrienne Morrison, assistant moderator of the Unitarian Universalist Church of the Restoration in Philadelphia, reported to her congregation, which had helped host the event. "Would the congress as originally called mean that we are fostering separatism? What attracted me and keeps me working so hard is our community. But having lived in this society for too many years, I am sick and tired of being sick and tired—of refighting for every inch of progress."

"I thought it was an enormously successful event," said Sinkford, who attended. "It was successful because it brought people together. It was an opportunity for people to tell their stories, and there was a lot of storytelling involved. And then honoring Frances Ellen Watkins Harper and putting a new gravestone on her grave was just a wonderful experience. Sadly, it was a one-time event."

Unitarios Universalistas de Habla Hispana
Another experiment in racial and ethnic diversity took place at the congregational level. The Unitarian Universalist Church of San Jose, California, under the leadership of Rev. Lindi Ramsden, a white minister, and member, Ervin Barrios, of Latino heritage, formed Unitarios Universalistas de Habla Hispana (Spanish-Speaking Unitarian Universalists). At the first meeting in December 1993, thirty-five people showed up, drawn by word-of-mouth and materials distributed by PROLATINA, a group advocating for Latino gay and lesbians. An article in the *World* described their services as:

> Like any Unitarian Universalist worship service, UUHH services reflect . . . theological diversity, but they also have a distinctly Latino feel. At a service earlier this year, a piano played a hymn with a march-like rhythm, but then a bongo drum entered and the music was transformed into something more playful and less ponderous. Much of the music at UUHH comes from the Latin American "new song"

RESURRECTION
Frances Ellen Watkins Harper

David Reich wrote this article for the World *in 1993.*

On September 26–27, 1992, African American Unitarian Universalists joined Unitarian Universalists from nine Philadelphia area congregations, members of the city's Mother Bethel A.M.E. Church, and representatives of the mayor and the governor, to commemorate the life and work of African American Unitarian Francis Ellen Watkins Harper.

Born in 1825, Harper, an activist, orator and author who wrote *Iola Leroy*, recently reprinted by Beacon Press and traditionally considered the first published novel by an African American woman. She also taught college, published poems and essays, and helped the Underground Railroad shelter freed slaves. Her public speaking on abolition and women's suffrage was so powerful that some in her audience, succumbing to the period's extreme stereotypes, refused to believe she was African American, claiming she was actually a man or a white woman in disguise.

Harper and her work had been largely forgotten from her death in 1911 until recent years when scholars and ministers like the Rev. Daniel Webster Aldridge, chair of the Coalition of African American Unitarian Universalist organizations, turned their focus on her. Aldridge places Harper among the many "progressive and prophetic African American Unitarian Universalists who did not receive appropriate recognition." He first learned of Harper and her work in the 1960s, when he was studying 19th century African American women writers, many of whom, he says, "are far less known than some men whose work is of inferior quality."

More recently, Aldridge learned that Harper was a Unitarian who belonged to the city's First Unitarian Church, a "tremendously exciting" discovery, he says, for someone "in a predominantly white denomination that has ignored African American contributions." And then he heard that Harper lay buried in an unmarked grave. Determined she not be "insulted" in this way, he says, he brought the matter up at a meeting of the coalition. As coalition member the Rev. Melvin Hoover, UUA Director of Racial and Cultural Diversity, recalled, "a number of us pulled out our checkbooks." Several meetings were held to plan the dedication of the new headstone and other commemoration activities, which came to include a Continental Congress of the Coalition, a Saturday night service at Harper's home church, and sermons preached by Coalition members at nine predominantly white Philadelphia city and suburban congregations.

The Saturday night service involved the full participation of the Mother Bethel A.M.E. Church, where Harper also worshipped. "Theologically, she saw herself as Unitarian," explained Lola Peters, associate director of the UUA Department for Social Justice, "but she needed the sociological and cultural connection to the A.M.E. [African Methodist Episcopal] Church." Like today's African American Unitarian Universalists, she had to "live in two worlds, bridge two cultures," Hoover added. . . .

The weekend culminated with Sunday's headstone dedication. According to Throne, over 150 people stood in the city's Eden Cemetery on the cold, rainy day and heard "moving words" from Hoover, Aldridge, and Sister Falaka Fattah, Harper's grand-niece. . . . The headstone dedication offered participants a dramatic surprise. As the cemetery workers were preparing the ground for the new headstone, they had unearthed an old headstone for Harper that no one had known about. "It was striking to see" the headstones side by side at the dedication, said coalition administrator Nikki Whittingham—the old ornate headstone with three levels representing the trinity, and the simple and dignified new headstone, made of African marble and designed by Olivine McCoy, the only African American headstone designer in the country, according to Aldridge. But more to the point, says Whittingham, finding the buried old marker "was symbolic of resurrecting Harper's work."

movement which emphasizes spiritual and social conscious-ness in its lyrics.

Readings for that Sunday's sermon included a story about Mexico's Zapatista rebels and how the Zapatista women were forcing changes in women's social roles, to the general discomfort of the men. The sermon itself—written in English by Ramsden, then translated bilingually by UUHH members and delivered by Ramsden in Spanish—dealt with changes in our lives and ways of accommodating them.

This congregation-within-a-congregation also influenced its parent congregation, which conducted its 1995 Easter service bi-lingually. The lack of culturally appropriate materials reflecting Unitarian Universalism and a shortage of funding for the ministry, which had a high number of people with limited economic means, were challenges for the congregation.

VOICE

Layla J. Rivera

Rivera was a junior at Smith College when this was published in Ferment, *a publication of the Association's Young Adult and Campus Ministry office.*

When I sat down to write this article about Unitarian Universalism I realized that I have never felt further away from it. I have not been affiliated with a church in about three years. I am about thirty days away from being a senior at Smith College and I have had many questions on my mind including: what do I do after this, where do I call home, and where is my spirit most at ease? My connection with UUism has been primarily on a social work level. The UUA is a place where I have learned to be a leader and how to question structure and policy. I have met some of the most wonderful people through my involvement with the Jubilee World Working Group for Anti-Racism. Even though I am at a point in my life where I have isolated myself into a community of color, being involved with the UUA reminded me that there were still good white people out there. My active participation with the Young Adults of Color Network made me realize I was not alone and that there are people of color within Unitarian Universalism looking for their place and demanding that their voices be acknowledged. At Smith I have learned about my history and the history of people of color. I have learned of the injustices that social and biological sciences have committed against people of color. I found a new language, the language of race, and I learned to be angry. I have become very involved with my community and now realize that I am going to follow my dream of going to medical school. I will follow this dream no matter how many times my advisor tells me I need to be more realistic. No matter how many times he tells me that there are no longer preferences so people like me might not get into medical schools as readily anymore. No matter how many times I am told that I don't fit the profile because I have not abandoned my identity as a Black Latina woman. So when I say that I feel disconnected from UUism I feel like I can do the work, but the religion is just not feeding me right now. I need a place where I can go and cry my sorrows away, I need a place where I can scream from anger when the world seems so cold, and I need a place to rejoice in my spirit. I need a church. The UU churches have been lonely places of nice white people with strained smiles. These visits are pleasant, but almost painful. When I enter these spaces my soul feels on edge and so alone. I know that Unitarians are good-hearted people but I need my space to worship in my way. The hardest transition from YRUU to the young adult world was leaving experimental worships behind, even though I think I have outgrown the whole hippie, touchy-feely vibe. I find myself, from time to time, attending my boyfriend's church in Boston. It is a Baptist church made up of many West Indians and African Americans. I love the ritual; the music, the shouting, call and response, the moving of the spirit, the liveliness, the joy and the tears. Yet, my soul just can't seem to harmonize with all the teachings. I have learned to take from the sermons what I feel can be applied to my everyday life. I realize that I have taken my UUism into another space. I will always be a UU at heart. I have made my own religion, found that my spirit's home is right here at my side and that I never really left UUism.

CHAPTER 8

Contradictions and Complications at General Assembly

After the Racial and Cultural Diversity resolution was adopted in Calgary in 1992, General Assemblies became gatherings where anti-racism initiatives were showcased—and where the difficulties of assuming an anti-racism identity surfaced.

General Assemblies also became the place where opposition to these efforts coalesced, with voices emerging such as Rev. Dr. Thandeka, then a professor of theology at Meadville Lombard Theological School, whose thinking became important to those uncomfortable with the Associational approach and the Crossroads Ministry approach.

Because so much of the discussion occurred at General Assemblies, an odd disconnect developed between what went on at the Associational level around race and what happened in the congregations. During the 1990s, a commitment to addressing racism began to be built at the highest levels of Associational leadership. Rev. Wayne Arnason, a member of the Board of Trustees at the time, recalled,

> I came on just when there was an internal struggle and a lot of resistance in the Board among four or five members who were very resistant to the desire to have an internal monitoring process on our own anti-racist policies and work as the UUA Board. [The consultant] U.T. Sanders [an African American] was invited to facilitate a process. . . . One night, which proved to be very powerful, we had some breakthrough around that resistance. We realized that our Board,

by and large except for a few voices, were really willing to engage with anti-racism work and more training, as an ongoing part of who we were. This was not going to be a passing fad; it was part of every meeting, every day that we met. We began to address better how we functioned as the board of a racist institution, and how we could be more conscious of addressing that.

Arnason chaired an internal group on the board that monitored how the board was doing in the area of anti-racism processes.

Two Faces of General Assembly

At the 1993 General Assembly in Charlotte, North Carolina, the first of a series of planned Racial Justice Days was held. It was the result of months of planning and strategizing by the Racial and Cultural Diversity Task Force. The official account related:

Meeting in plenary session style, approximately 1,800 Unitarian Universalists gathered to hear a moving presentation by the Rev. Mark Morrison-Reed, Co-Minister of First Unitarian in Toronto, and UU Women's Federation President Kay Aler-Maida on the history of our movement and racial justice and a keynote speech by [Rev.] Dr. William Jones, UUA Trustee and Director of Florida State University Black Studies Program. Delegates at GA learned about our racist Unitarian Universalist history and how our Unitarian Universalist culture of racism has hurt each one of us. In his presentation, the Rev. Mark Morrison-Reed asked delegates to seek answers to the question, "When and how did I become aware of racial difference?" In asking that question Mark said we will discover where the pain began—the seed of our disillusionment. For all of us to explore the mistrust and rage, misinformation and fear, and shame and guilt that we harbor will take time. This was the beginning of a process of reflection that needs to be broadened to all Unitarian Universalist congregations and members and explored in even greater depth.

As Mark said in his talk, "Our history in regard to racial justice is brave enough to make you proud, tragic enough to make you cry, and inept enough to make you laugh once the anger passes. We also have a future. Today's task is to learn from what was and move on. To move on will mean creating a vision for the future. May concern for our faith and love for one another guide our efforts."

This presentation led up to the keynote speech by Dr. William Jones based on his work "Toward a New Paradigm for Uncovering Neo-Racism and Oppression in Unitarian Universalism." Dr. Jones teaches that if you have a disease and it is a virus that can be treated but you do not properly diagnose it then you can never develop an effective vaccine to cure it. Racism is a disease! If racism still exists then we have to look at our diagnosis to see what has gone wrong. Jones challenged people to "get rid of misconceptions about oppression. . . . Since the 1960s racism has become more subtle and thus harder to attack." The vaccines to combat the racism of the 60s and 70s are no longer effective for combating the racism virus of the 90s. Dr. Jones provided the delegates with a framework to understand today's racism in order to begin new processes to effectively change our attitudes, behaviors, policies, practices, and structures to those of an anti-racist institution. He will have an opportunity to implement his concepts as a newly elected trustee-at-large of the UUA.

After the morning's speeches 100 facilitators met with participants in small groups to discuss Dr. Jones' ideas and how they applied to their own experiences and to Unitarian Universalism.

This event was significant in that it put forward some premises that would shape the future of efforts to address race issues. Morrison-Reed and Jones both spoke of the issue not as a matter of personal prejudice but as a larger systemic issue. Both called attention to the intractable nature of issues of race in our Association, versus other areas of oppression where more progress was evident. Morrison-Reed spoke of the need to be "whole."

Rev. Dr. Anita Farber-Robertson and Dr. Leon Spencer, co-chairs of the Black Concerns Working Group, chronicled the response to Racial Justice Day:

The Office for Racial and Cultural Diversity recently received the 1993 General Assembly participant evaluations. The comments from the Racial Justice Day section are very positive and include the following:

"Superior programs. Great opportunity to speak out. Revelation to me about systemic injustice." "Made me proud." "William Jones was excellent and forced us to re-examine painful beliefs!" "I wanted to attend more workshops!" "Very thought provoking and valuable." "The keynote was good, explained new ways to identify racism. Small discussion groups were good and enabled people to learn how to relate to other ethnic groups." As well as: "Repetition of numerous workshops in the past. Everyone knows where they stand. These workshops should be done in other religious denominations." And: "Well done. Good first step. Please let's remember that there are a number of racial/ethnic groups not at our table." "An emotionally and physically exhausting day. Hard but valuable." "I am from a city that has been working on this issue for years. The people in my group were not at a place where years of thought and effort was a part of their history." "It was moving, as was Mark Morrison-Reed on Monday." "This was very good and needed. I had no idea that many congregations are almost as bad as ours in race relations and diversity."

Racial Justice Day was indeed a success, not only because people actively engaged the issues on that day, but because the requests to continue this work have been pouring in since GA. The Task Force and the Office for Racial and Cultural Diversity received dozens of letters praising the experience and numerous phone calls requesting assistance and resources for holding workshops and starting Racial Justice/Diversity committees. Many people have requested copies of Dr. Jones' keynote speech on oppression and the

EXCERPT

Racial Justice for Times Like These

These comments are from Rev. Dr. Mark Morrison-Reed's introduction to the video, Racial Justice for Times Like These.

There are today seventeen African American Unitarian Universalist ministers, but I have also identified at least that many who considered it and wanted to become ministers. . . . The UUA writes and talks a lot about racial and cultural justice . . . and so it is and so it goes. From blanket discrimination to the subtle—and we can be very subtle—today's attitudes are less overt, but no less pervasive. . . . [This is] the underbelly of our heritage. . . . Our culture of racism has hurt each of us. It has hurt each of us. . . . Part of our hard struggle will be not to walk away from the pain, concerns. . . . Part of our hard struggle is going to be listening to things we don't want to hear.

No one is born a racist—racism is not a genetically transmitted disease. It is a systemically transmitted disease. . . . Our move towards racial justice is a move towards health, towards wholeness.

In his presentation for the video, Rev. Dr. William Jones included these words. [There are] myths about oppression . . . such as oppression is evil. If you operate from that understanding of oppression you will never see it. The oppressed is always "other." We do not see the oppressor in ourselves. . . . The only way I have found to get out of the dilemma of being the oppressor is to understand that to survive, you have to feed on something else. . . . Whoever has the power to label has the power to control.

Rev. Mark Morrison-Reed and Kay Aler-Maida's history piece "Setting the Context." Requests for Black Concerns Working Group "Creating a Jubilee World" workshops have increased. The districts have been sending in their pledges of individual commitments to action. These actions, proposed strategies, and requests for assistance are as diverse as our movement is in its anti-racism and racial justice history and efforts. Among the commitments are efforts to build coalitions, hold workshops and trainings, study Dr. Jones' oppression model, develop partnerships with urban churches, start reading groups around Dr. Cornel West's book *Race Matters*, diversify church music and religious education programs, make linkages with community organizations, participate in the "How Open the Door?" curriculum, work on environmental racism . . . and the list goes on. A complete report will be compiled by the Office for Racial and Cultural Diversity once all the district reports are sent in.

The Task Force on Racial and Cultural Diversity proclaimed after the 1993 General Assembly, "Once again we are on the cutting edge in terms of racism, race relations, and religion as evidenced by the publication by Beacon Press of award winning books: *The Measure of Our Success* by Marian Wright Edelman and *Race Matters* by Dr. Cornel West." At the 1993 Assembly, 1,500 people heard West speak about race relations and racial justice efforts. His address provided an analysis that characterized the problems of blacks as part of a systemic discrimination that linked race with economics. "There can be no black freedom struggle, no radical democratic tradition without some universalism," said West, a philosopher on the faculty of Princeton University. "It will not be a universalism from above that dictates and then tries to force assimilation in the cheap sense—'fit in, adjust to our mainstream and things will be nice.' But it must be a universalism from below in which we all differ within our own histories and heritages and yet reach that common affirmation of who we are. . . . It has much to do not just with empathy and sympathy. It has much to do with love . . . the kind that asks your neighbor, 'What are you going through?' 'Can I be of service?'"

With this explicit focus on race as part of the planned activities for this General Assembly, protest erupted a few days later around a planned "birthday party" commemorating Thomas Jefferson. "Saturday night there was to be a dance—the Thomas Jefferson Birthday Ball," recalled Rev. Keith Kron, who was a member of the General Assembly Planning Committee. "People were supposed to come in period costume."

The September/October 1993 *World* has this to say about the protest:

> [T]he struggle for racial justice and inclusiveness was kept on the front burner . . . especially by the controversy over Saturday night's so-called Thomas Jefferson Birthday Ball, which occasioned a protest demonstration led by the African-American Unitarian Universalist Ministries (AAUUM).
>
> In response, the African-American Unitarian Universalist Ministry organized a protest that drew hundreds of delegates outside the ballroom. In a leaflet distributed at the demonstration, AAUUM members cited Jefferson's record as an "unrepentant slave-owner" and declared themselves "outraged" by the event, which delegates and others had originally been urged to attend in period dress. "Should African-Americans attend [the ball] in chains?" the leaflet asked. An estimated 300–400 people attended the demonstration, which took place near the foot of an escalator leading up to the Omni Hotel ballroom. To the Rev. William Jones, director of black studies at Florida State University and a newly elected UUA trustee, it was "symbolic that the administration of the denomination was up [in the ballroom] and I and other African-Americans and whites who had a clearer idea of the problem were at the bottom of the escalator. Which side was the authentic mainstream of Unitarian Universalism?" Jones asks.

It was a spur-of-the-moment protest. A number of concerned observers had raised questions weeks before General Assembly. Rev. Hope Johnson said that members of the delegation of Community Church of New York noticed the implications of the Thomas Jefferson Ball and raised concerns during a pre-General Assembly planning meeting. Janice Marie Johnson, also a member of the delegation, asked her congregation what she should wear as a person of African descent attending a ball to honor Jefferson in period costume. Rev. Joseph Santos-Lyons described this event in his 2006 seminary thesis, noting it as a galvanizing event for people of color: "In 1993, a year after the Racial and Cultural Diversity resolution established the Racial and Cultural Diversity Task Force, General Assembly was held in the Thomas Jefferson District in Charlotte, North Carolina. As part of the program, the GA Planning Committee sponsored a 'Thomas Jefferson Ball' with instructions to come in period dress circa 1776. In the months leading up to GA, protests were issued by Unitarian Universalists, including African descent Unitarian Universalists, deeply concerned that this would mean People of Color having to attend in chains, as slaves, as those were their circumstances during that era. Due to the miscommunication and misplaced intentions, the Thomas Jefferson Ball was still held despite concerns and communications raised in advance of GA.

During the first Plenary Session in Charlotte, Hope Johnson read the following statement of protest, which she adapted from the original AAUUM statement by Hope Johnson, Janice Marie Johnson, and David Barus:

> We, members of the African American Unitarian Universalist Ministers (AAUUM), and our many friends of differing racial and cultural backgrounds are outraged by, and strenuously protest the inclusion of events described as "The Most Famous Unitarian in the World" and the "Thomas Jefferson Birthday Ball" in this UUA General Assembly Program. We refuse to participate in these activities which reflect a profound lack of sensitivity and judgment, particularly in view of the UUA's stated thrust this year toward

racial and ethnic diversity. We urge all Unitarian Universalists to look at the total picture before lending your presence to the planned events. Please consider these elements:

"The Most Famous Unitarian in the world" as described for one of the GA events was an unrepentant slave holder; advocated the extermination of indigenous peoples in America; had an enslaved consort, Sally Hemings, who bore his children; refused to set free his slaves, many of whom were his own children.

This example of the selective creation of heroes and heroines within the UUA perpetuates continuing racial oppression and promotes neo-racism in our Association, and in this nation. Thomas Jefferson's role in the racial history of the United States is not one which African Americans, native Americans, or others victimized by the "founding fathers" wish to honor. Is his life style one that Unitarian Universalists should really celebrate? Must African Americans attend such events in rags and chains?

To turn briefly to another source of our deep concern at this GA, we find that too few Unitarian Universalists know, or care, that Africans were recruited into Universalism in America as equal children of one God.

There were African-American Universalists in the 18th century. There were also Black Universalist ministers, including Gloster Dalton [a signer of the 1785 charter for the initial Universalist congregation, in Gloucester, Massachusetts]. Why were they not included in the history of Universalism presented at our opening GA event?

The racial message of these incidents is insulting to people of color and all those who sincerely believe in racial justice. Do not support this message through indifference, or acceptance of this narrow view of history.

The ball was held, although more than four hundred people chose not to attend it. The same day, Rev. Dr. John Buehrens was elected as the Association's president and Denise (Denny) Davidoff as its moderator. Davidoff joined the peaceful protest though it meant skipping some of the official celebrations of her victories. "To me it was, and always will be, a perfect example of how asleep we good people can be," she said of the ball.

Kron, the General Assembly Planning Committee member, recalled,

> No one on the committee, of which there were two wonderful African-American people, talked about what period costumes would mean for African-Americans. When this was brought to the attention of the GA Planning Committee, the white folks wondered why the people of color said nothing. If nothing else, the white folks, myself included, were pretty unconscious about race issues. But then this is how oppression works well in our society—people remain unconscious.
>
> The Planning Committee discussed this as a group, tried to blame Gladys McNatt and Arthur Morrison for not bringing this to our attention, and then worked on a statement. The chair, [Rev. Dr. Daniel] Higgins, read a statement to the Planning Committee to be read to the General Assembly to address the issue. It was a nice statement. We authorized him to read it. He then went and changed it, moving away from acknowledging the problem was ours.
>
> That Saturday night, the day Dr. John Buehrens was elected president, the day before the entire General Assembly was to have a general session on anti-racism, a protest ensued. People of color and allies rallied against the dance. The police came not realizing these were our people, assuming these were folks from the far right protesting our previous night's candlelight vigil to support the end of sodomy laws. The Omni Hotel was witness to an internal protest, the likes of which the UUA had not seen before in a long time, possibly ever—or at least since the last time we tried to do anti-racism work in the late 60's. It was a dramatic evening.
>
> I am not sure what the white people learned from it. Many blamed others. Few took responsibility. Some stood

with the people of color. Some hid. Some were disgusted. But I still don't know what people learned, or what the white people learned. If anything, white folks learned to double their efforts to not make mistakes, how to walk on eggshells. I am not sure we learned however how to make amends. Though I may be too hard on us. Perhaps learning this just takes a long time.

The origins of the ball represent how differently Unitarian Universalists of different races could view context. "I'm in Charlottesville at that time and I'm involved with the governance process," recalled Arnason, who was then minister at the Thomas Jefferson Memorial Church Unitarian Universalist in Charlottesville, Virginia, a church whose main building was built in part by money raised by Unitarians nationally as a tribute to Jefferson. He went on:

[It] is the 250th anniversary of Thomas Jefferson's birth, and Charlottesville is at the center of that celebration. We're in the Thomas Jefferson District, and [my colleague, director of religious education] Leia Durland-Jones is on the Planning Committee. So Leia and I are talking about, in the winter of '93, about how GA is coming along and unfolding, and I'm saying to Leia, well there should be something that honors the Jefferson birthday anniversary. "Good heavens, we've got to have something," I argue. So Leia takes this back to the Planning Committee, and that's where this idea of a birthday ball gets birthed. . . . Not only does the idea of the ball get birthed, but the Planning Committee comes back to me and says, "Will you do a workshop on Thomas Jefferson?" So I created a workshop that is entitled "The Most Famous Unitarian in the World," and that's the workshop title. . . . The Planning Committee ultimately has to deal with the consequences of planning the Thomas Jefferson Ball as a costume party event. . . . But I had to deal with rewriting and rethinking what I had to do with the workshop. Of course it was a huge oversight to miss the racism inherent in the Jefferson heritage, and indicative of the racism blindness that I suffered from in suggesting this kind of event.

Rev. Dr. Tracey Robinson-Harris recalled how tense the situation was: "I had folks stop me in the hall and tell me they were afraid we were going to split the denomination—they remembered the black empowerment controversy." She felt good about the response: "We did it collaboratively with people of color taking leadership. It was for me a microcosm of how we address particular moments when racism is not subtle, when it can be brought to awareness."

The story of the Thomas Jefferson Birthday Ball, as with so many other events in this period, cannot be concluded in one neat way. Interpretations remain dynamic. "We think of racism as being an overt thing," Kron reflected. "As someone who had lived in the South and had seen, as a 5th grader, my elementary school become integrated, I knew what racism was. And I was right. Or half-right. There are a lot of people who consciously want people of color to be second-class citizens. What I and the rest of the Planning Committee didn't know at the time was that much of racism is not conscious—just part of the system, and you have to be awake to see it."

This collection of intense good and bad experiences would continue to mark subsequent General Assemblies.

Racial Justice Day II
Building understanding and momentum for addressing issues of race was part of the strategy for the 1994 General Assembly. One of the most remembered parts of the Assembly program was a presentation by Barbara Major, who was working with two groups devoted to anti-racism, Crossroads Ministry and the People's Institute for Survival and Beyond. She presented an exercise that linked issues of poverty and class with the issues of race. The questions she asked included: "How many of you work or have relationships with poor people?" "Why are they poor?" "If you're in the grocery store and overhear two people talking about poor people, what would they say about why people are poor?" She concluded: "No one has a right to

work with poor people unless they have a real analysis of why people are poor."

General Assembly had become a key part of anti-oppression organizing and that strategy would continue after the more formal Journey Toward Wholeness program was developed. "I think we did enough at GAs," recalled Dr. Norma Poinsett. "We used to have a lot of mini-workshops. I mean, we drew people to them. We would put on programs and we'd have our worship services that enriched delegates' convention experience. I think if we could really have all Unitarian Universalists attend one, two, or three General Assemblies, we would have had much more conversion of souls."

The continued programming at the 1994 General Assembly also had resource implications. As the Task Force on Racial and Cultural Diversity noted,

> Many of the people and resources that are most needed in the UUA efforts to become more racially and culturally diverse are not Unitarian Universalists. Their costs and expenses are not accounted for in existing budgets because it is a UUA policy not to pay Unitarian Universalist speakers and workshop leaders. Last year would not have been the culture-changing experience that it was without the participation and contributions of Dr. Cornel West; the Rev. Joseph Barndt, author of *Dismantling Racism*; the Rev. Marvin Chandler, a Howard Thurman Scholar and lecturer; Dr. Elias Farajaje-Jones, Howard University professor; Dr. Charles Foster, professor at Emory University, and others.

Report and a Resolution at the 1996 Assembly
The Racial and Cultural Diversity Task Force planned to present a report to General Assembly, in Indianapolis, proposing a survey for congregations to assess where they are in a continuum of anti-racism. In their deliberations, they discussed the fact that there is "still a problem with stereotyping black people wanting gospel music and emotional services" as well as the fact that "many evaluations say that the participants want some concrete suggestions about what works and what doesn't." They were also revisiting charges and

goals in light of the fact that "other interest groups (Asian, Hispanic, Native American) have emerged and have become a part of our work."

The report, entitled *Journey Toward Wholeness: The Next Step— From Racial and Cultural Diversity to Anti-Oppression and Anti-Racist Multiculturalism*, contained recommendations, resources for congregations, and the summary of a research report on where Unitarian Universalists stood on issues of racial and cultural diversity. Then moderator Davidoff said the report was extraordinary because it was unusual to have research to support an advocacy effort. "By March of 1996," she recalled, "we could report that the Team had completed three separate research studies. In 1993 focus group discussions were conducted with members of nineteen congregations having experienced intentional efforts to become diverse. In 1994 over five hundred Unitarian Universalists, including one hundred persons of color, were interviewed by telephone to gain an understanding of the attitudes and activities that move us forward toward or hold us back from becoming more diverse within our congregations. That second study indicated that the attitude and support of the minister are critical to the attitude of a congregation in making—or not making—such an effort. So, in 1995, just over two hundred Unitarian Universalist ministers were interviewed by telephone to gain insight into ministers' perceptions of their own roles and responsibilities regarding congregational efforts to become more diverse. At the 1996 GA in Indianapolis, the research team report was made by the Reverend Olivia Holmes . . . former partner in a well-known and widely respected market research organization, Trost Associates."

For Davidoff, that research was very significant. "It predicted all the obstacles," she recalled. A major finding was that without the support of the ministers, efforts at attitudinal change such as the anti-racism push faced a long uphill road. The report noted:

> The research suggests, in a variety of ways, that for real change to occur, the congregation and the minister, together, need to put diversity onto the church's agenda. When they do, the results are consistent and positive. Ministers are clear

STATISTICS

Programs Tried by Congregations

This information was gathered through the research of Rev. Olivia Homes, "Racial and Cultural Diversity: Where Unitarian Universalists Stand," conducted in March 1996.

	Reported by		
	Total	White UUs	UUs of color
Acknowledging Diversity:			
Sunday service programming	87%	86%	95%
Religious education curricula	80	79	83
Diverse art displayed in congregation's space	59	58	62
Congregation space rental to diverse groups	49	45	68
Supporting a Diverse Community:			
Raised money to help racially diverse groups	72	70	80
Joined community coalitions	70	68	81
Created racial justice outreach program	46	45	59
Organized to Address Our Own Prejudices (Racism):			
Congregational committee to promote racial diversity	27	24	39
Participation in a district anti-racism workshop	25	19	52
Congregational committee to reduce racism	18	14	33
Examining Our Own Prejudices:			
Welcoming Congregation (homophobia)	58	54	70
How Open the Door (racism)	16	13	29
Beyond Categorical Thinking (racism in selecting a minister)	11	9	19
Jubilee World Workshop (racism)	5	3	12

that they cannot lead such an effort well without congregational support. Lay Unitarian Universalists are clear that more can be done when they have the support of the minister.

Congregations evaluated by their ministers as having an extremely long commitment to becoming diverse reflect higher levels of actual diversity, and, as a result, have far fewer concerns and fears of conflict than less diverse congregations worry about. It is important to realize that only 15 percent of the ministers evaluate their congregations as being extremely committed to an effort to become more diverse. The overwhelming majority of ministers find their congregations either somewhat committed (38%) or not very committed (41%).

At the time of this research, ministers were also asked about the language of anti-racism. Holmes found that most seemed to "understand the idea of moving toward 'anti-racism' as facing both personal and institutional or systemic racism, and doing something about them. However, some express concern that 'anti-racism' is negative language. Those ministers hope that over time our language might evolve to a more positive choice of words."

For some, it felt as if the direction was more important than the details. Rev. Gordon D. Gibson, minister of the Unitarian Universalist Fellowship of Elkhart, Indiana, became involved when he noticed some mistakes in the timeline. His efforts to get them corrected convinced him that factual accuracy was not being given enough focus by those leading efforts on behalf of the Association.

When the Journey Toward Wholeness report was presented at the 1996 General Assembly in Indianapolis, I found myself in the odd position of rushing to a "con" microphone. It wasn't that I was going to vote against receiving the report, but I urgently felt the need to say, "There are some serious errors in the timeline on pages 25–31." I was assured that corrections and updates would be made as needed. Later, in conversation with a friend who had served on the Racial and

Cultural Diversity Task Force, which had created the report, I got a response that amounted to, "What's the big fuss?" For me, the big fuss is that if we are serious about this work we need to get our facts right. . . . Had such blatantly wrong information appeared in [the sexuality education curriculum] "Our Whole Lives" (say an incorrect failure rate for condoms), I have every confidence that each purchaser of the curriculum would have been notified. There would have been some sort of mailing or prominent on-line posting to alert anyone who had missed the notification. Trainers using the curriculum would have been alerted to the mistake and asked to have people write the correction into their copies to be sure it was there. . . . I am, at long last, pleased to report that in 2002 the UUA did devote staff time to putting together a much fuller and more accurate timeline. But I continue to be disturbed that we spent six years circulating information that was just blatantly, obtusely, unnecessarily wrong. It hinted to me that some of our "anti-racism" efforts were given a low priority, or that feelings were perceived as vastly more important than factual accuracy.

The report included a curriculum, the "Congregational Reflection and Action Process Guide," created by Rev. Nannene Gowdy, religious educator Jacqui James, and Rev. William Sinkford.

In response to the report, the General Assembly delegates "resolved that all congregations, districts, organizations, and professional and lay leaders participate in a reflection-action process throughout the 1996–97 church year using the Congregational Reflection and Action Process Guide and the Anti-Racism Assessment." This resolution would set up one authorizing a major new push for anti-racism at the 1997 General Assembly.

The emphasis on action at General Assemblies had a cost. Sinkford, who became president of the Association in 2001, said,

Some of our colleagues would argue that the General Assembly does not represent the congregations very well. And in point of fact, we continue to work on that to try to improve. That meant that's the authorizing structure. In my judgment, the leadership that was shown was prophetic leadership and this is religion. You have to make a place for prophetic leadership or give up what it means to be religious, it seems. So I believe that [former UUA president Rev. Dr. William] Schulz was correct to name this as a priority. I think he was right to make sure that both Dr. John Buehrens and Carolyn Owen-Towle [the candidates to be elected president at the 1993 Assembly] supported it. I think he was right to staff it. I think, you know Dr. John Buehrens [who succeeded Schulz as president] was right to support it as well. With 20-20 hindsight, I think we all might wish that it had been done somewhat differently. But I think the Association national leadership has an absolute right and responsibility to lead. That's an opinion that would not be shared by all of my colleagues, of course.

Said Arnason,

The observation that some would make is that we ended up creating initially a continental leadership that went deeper and deeper into the work, but it was a bifurcated leadership. You had your continental culture, which was struggling with, but moving toward, this model at some level, and then a congregational culture which was unaffected by it except in the cases where either there were some pilot programs that brought Crossroads Ministry Trainings to the congregational level or there was a minister who wanted to move forward.

CHAPTER 9

Organizing for an
Anti-Racist Future

Even before the General Assembly Resolution in Calgary, Association staff leaders such as Rev. Melvin Hoover and members of the Black Concerns Working Group, the African American Ministers Association, and the Unitarian Universalist Women's Federation, were thinking about ways to spread a broader understanding about the racial divide in the UUA. One strategy involved training, bringing people together to be exposed to a particular analysis of the problems and the needed solutions. The Black Concerns Working Group took this approach in its Building a Jubilee World anti-racism workshops; it also brought the Association into relationship with Crossroads Ministry. The key here was to focus on critical relationships with people in a position to make change at the Associational and the congregational levels.

The other source of momentum was efforts already under way in congregations working with models developed by Rev. Dr. William A. Jones, a long-time Unitarian Universalist activist, and others.

Bringing about a widespread change in mindset in an Association of Congregations where the power to change was diffused and held at the individual congregational level was very difficult. And unlike the changes that had occurred a generation earlier through the women's movement, in most congregations those who would have the most stake—those from racially and culturally diverse backgrounds—were not present in any numbers in the majority of congregations. Though some congregations pursued racial justice as a program or special initiatives, many more did not. "It's the whole question that the Association is always struggling with, whether it's with anti-racism work or any other congregational cultural change, and that question is how does the Association have an impact on changing congregational culture?" observed Rev. Wayne Arnason, who had been active in Associational initiatives since he was part of the youth movement.

Crossroads to the Forefront

Though most of the training being delivered at this time was through the Jubilee workshops and other models of the Black Concerns Working Group, supporters of the Crossroads Ministry approach were gathering momentum, especially with some key Association staff members and institutional leaders.

Denise (Denny) Davidoff, elected the Association's moderator at General Assembly in 1993, was involved in some of the Crossroads pilot efforts. "For me, it was transformative," she recalled. "It was an amazing experience. I can still remember whole pieces of it." Some saw the theological grounding of the Crossroads model as too Lutheran—Crossroads director, Rev. Joseph Barndt, was a Lutheran minister—but for Davidoff it was not a problem. She appreciated the way Barndt laid out the role of white privilege. As one who had been a supporter of the Black Affairs Caucus in the Empowerment Controversies, she said she was already on board. "I wasn't looking for ways to push back. I wanted to go forward."

Yet others thought it important that a number of training options remain available. The Racial and Cultural Diversity Task Force concluded in September 1993,

> [W]e need to look at different models and scenarios as to how this can happen. Let's create different approaches and give people choice. . . . Cultural change is very hard and very slow. At the UUA we do not have a uniform culture. We have Unitarian and Universalist, we have North and South, urban and suburban. Models that have the maximum flexibility as their point of entrance are going to be the best for us. We want to create something that can be used at all these entry points. What we're trying to do is

122

VOICE

Rev. Kurt Kuhwald

Kuhwald was a member of the Jubilee Working Group and serving as minister of the Unitarian Universalist Church of Boulder, Colorado, when he wrote this piece. He identifies as an elder, European-American, temporarily able-bodied, heterosexual male.

Our understanding about racism has come slowly. Through years of struggle within Unitarian Universalist communities and anti-racist working groups, many of us have begun to develop an intellectual comprehension of racism that ever more deeply is informed by the heart.

It has always been clear for many that we are all prejudiced. Many, too, claim to have always had some awareness of our own race prejudice. We have seen how it grew within us, even without our being conscious of it. As we looked around at our white friends, friends of color, and fellow UUs, it seemed clear to us that we were not alone. Many of us who are white have carried guilt about our racism, and still do. Many of us who are persons of color have carried our own self-hate, and still do.

What we have been coming to learn, however, in a rudimentary way, is how to transform those debilitating emotions, and our own ignorance, into a proactive commitment to be openhearted and honest, and to take on the work necessary to reduce the power of our own racist attitudes, and our own internalized racism, to as low a level as possible.

What has helped the growth of many UUs has come from two commitments: the first commitment has been to do the work, to seek out the opportunities to deal with the issues, to be honest with ourselves, to be compassionate with ourselves, and to stay at the table—that is to keep trying no matter how discouraged we have become, no matter how scared, no matter how defensive, no matter how blind we have found ourselves to be. To stay at the table of social dialogue with an anti-racist, multicultural commitment.

Many of us have drawn strength to do that from the fact that we understand this work to be at the heart of the spiritual journey. . . .

The second commitment has been to truly try to understand what racism in America really is. The analysis developed by the Jubilee Working Group for Anti-Racism of the UUA, Rev. Bill Jones (UU minister and professor at Florida State University), and other anti-racist groups, has given us the definitional tools we needed to understand our own racist psychology, our own internalized racism, as well as the sociology of institutional racism.

The definition of racism advocated by the Jubilee Working Group is: Race Prejudice plus Power equals Racism.

The simplicity of this definition belies its sophistication, accuracy, power, and utility. It is its utility that is most important for our UU congregations. Simply put, this definition keeps our focus on the one issue that is key to understanding racism's imperviousness to change. This definition allows us to see that racism's power comes from the fact that white individuals are positioned, both psychologically and institutionally, within an orbit of authority that thoroughly dominates the whole of society. Being within the circle of power for whites means that they and they alone have direct access to the controls that govern society. Being within the circle of power means that whites unconsciously profit from patterns of oppression even when they are not aware of them. Being within the circle of power means that whites carry its imprint within their own psychology, even though this is largely unconscious to them.

Being outside that circle of power means that persons of color struggle continually with internalizing the fact of their exclusion, their lack of access, their being targets for hate and rejection. Being outside that circle of power insures that persons of color must live out of a dual consciousness that is continually fueled by mistrust, which often results in mistrust of self, as well as of others. Being outside the circle of power means people of color carry its imprint within their own psychology, even though this is largely unconscious to them.

The uncomplicated definition of racism offered by the Jubilee Working Group never lets us lose the critical awareness of the centrality of power in creating and maintaining racism. We are thereby able to gain a serious foothold into a clarified vision about our own complicity, both personally and institutionally. A gift of power, indeed.

actually embody the value we're promoting—there is an incongruity in trying to promote diversity through uniformity—we have to respect diversity within our structure and have a model with diverse entry points and methods. The entry point should allow the hurts people have experienced to be heard.

In the 1994–95 program year, one major emphasis was training, with a goal of training more than two hundred people by mid-1995. A variety of vehicles existed, including the Crossroads anti-racism workshop, William Jones's oppression workshop, and the Jubilee workshops of the Black Concerns Working Group. After the 1994 General Assembly, twenty-seven Building the Jubilee World workshops were scheduled. Most were organized on a district or regional level and some drew nearly one hundred people.

The first groups to be trained by Crossroads Ministry were the Board of Trustees, the Association's executive staff and some of its program staff, the district executives, some members of African American Unitarian Universalist Ministry, and the executive committees of the Unitarian Universalist Ministers Association, Interweave (Unitarian Universalists for Lesbian, Gay, Bisexual and Transgender Concerns), and the Women's Federation.

Members of the Board of Trustees, the executive staff, AAUUM, and the executive committees of the Ministerial Association, the Liberal Religious Educators Association, and Interweave took part in a Crossroads training held September 29–October 2, 1994, in a Boston suburb. In a 1995 memorandum to the Association staff, Hoover, the director for racial and cultural diversity, wrote that "the Racial and Cultural Diversity Task Force and the UUA Executive Staff have determined that an essential step in becoming an anti-racist multicultural association is to train the major institutional groups of the UUA and to create a leading corps of anti-racists. This training will provide a common language and a common understanding that is necessary to build the leadership corps which is essential for transformation."

Yet, as noted before, these trainings were not without difficulties. Rev. Dr. Tracey Robinson-Harris, one of the initial white ally trainers, observed that the initial trainings caused tensions. "Early on there were both theological and process assumptions in the trainings that were abrasive to some folks. Whether that gave some the excuse not to engage and whether there were folks that just couldn't engage can't be known." She described what she called "predictable negative aspects," especially the "misfit between some of the very earliest efforts that involved Crossroads which created some resistance. . . . Controversy over the early trainings diverted some effort and was frustrating and made it hard to stay in relationship." Another strategic issue was how to lead "when anti-racism work is not negotiable." She also noted a tension between leadership and vision. Finally, she said that, in the end, anti-racist transformation has to be grassroots and at the congregational level.

Sinkford recalled the early strategizing around the Crossroads approach:

> It was the fall of 1994, just after I had joined the UUA staff as Director of District Services. I attended one of the first anti-racism trainings organized by the UUA. The participants included members of the UUA Board, the UUA's Executive Staff (what we now call the Leadership Council), the Unitarian Universalist Ministers Association Executive Committee [UUMA Exec] and other continental leaders, including members of the African American Unitarian Universalist Ministry group. The strategy then in place was to start by "converting" the continental leaders rather than beginning at the congregational level. Few of the white leaders were there by choice. They had been instructed to attend.
>
> I use the term "convert" intentionally. The training was conducted by Crossroads Ministry and the language and theology were heavily Christian. There was considerable pushback about the theology in open session and even greater pushback expressed in private. Or put more optimistically, the persons present felt that they were being pushed away from work they wanted to do by the theological frame. Denial perhaps, or a wish to preserve a belief in innocence. But the tone was one of resistance.

Every leader in the room was well intended. Everyone, if asked, would say they wanted to end racism in our faith community. The training, however, was not going well. Finally, after testimonials from the persons of color present, after fighting about "the analysis," after reactivity to the theology, some version of grace happened. The UUMA Exec, led by Rev. Wayne Arnason, "got it." Or put more accurately, began to "get it." They accepted the fact that they had some responsibility for maintaining our ministry as a white institution. They acknowledged that their white skin did give them privilege. And, as the training closed, in the segment where the various constituencies were asked to report out their action plans, the UUMA leaders promised to add a person of color to the Exec. It was a beginning.

At the Board of Trustees level, the iterative nature of training was becoming apparent. Phyllis Daniel recalled,

Soon after I had come on the Board, I attended one of the first trainings that was done by the Crossroads Ministry for people who were on major leadership groups, and there were several of us from the Board of Trustees, there were some UUMA people there, and other groups. Those were the two I remember. Joe Barndt conducted that training at the Newton Center. I thought it was great. It spoke to the kinds of issues I needed to clarify for myself and there was a lot of learning for me, and I just kind of drank it all in. I was very much enthusiastic about that training, more so than some of the other Board members, but people were fairly accepting. This was a new thing, and so forth. Then, in 1995, a new group of trustees were elected and they went off to training, and it did not go over well with them. They came to the next Board meeting really not wanting to continue to support the work in the form it was then being presented. I wasn't part of that group; I tried very hard to understand what their experience had been. It didn't seem like it had been very much like my experience. But I don't really know

FLYER

Creating a Jubilee World

"Creating A Jubilee World" Weekend

Sponsored by the Jubilee Working Group for Anti-Racism

The Friday evening through Sunday morning "Creating A Jubilee World" Workshop has been developed by the Jubilee Working Group for Anti-Racism, formerly known as the Black Concerns Working Group. This workshop is designed to help Unitarian Universalist congregations dismantle racism by allowing participants to examine both personal and institutional racism, and by empowering them to develop a realistic plan that can move their congregations forward in working for racial justice.

Objectives of the workshop are to:

- *Increase awareness of racism within the church and the larger community.*
- *Recognize the power/privilege of racism from personal and institutional perspectives.*
- *Identify activities and responses that promote the elimination of racism.*
- *Identify the challenges and barriers to working toward eliminating racism.*
- *Examine our denominational values, principles, and purposes in relation to the vision of a Jubilee World.*

- *Begin the process of building an anti-racism transformation team*

The Jubilee Working Group recommends that before a congregation participate in a "Creating A Jubilee World" Workshop they:

- *Have completed the Action/Reflection Process found in the 1996 Racial and Cultural Diversity Task Force's Report Journey Toward Wholeness*
- *Have held a Journey Toward Wholeness Sunday*
- *Have sponsored a racial justice curriculum or program, such as the Jubilee Working Group Video Series, Weaving the Fabric of Diversity, How Open the Door, Study Circles, Healing Racism, or the equivalent.*
- *Have done a social justice project that has worked on racism in their community*

The "Creating A Jubilee World" Workshop Format

The Friday Night Event

The Friday evening program begins with a social gathering or reception for all of the workshop participants. Afterward, a 25–45 minute video (supplied by the Jubilee facilitators) is shown. This is followed by a discussion.

The Saturday Workshop

All of Saturday is dedicated to the anti-racism activities led by the Jubilee facilitators. Lunch and snacks for all the conference participants should be planned by the hosting committee.

The Sunday Morning Worship

The "Creating A Jubilee World" Sunday Service is designed by the hosting congregation and the Jubilee facilitators to reflect the workshop themes of racial justice, multiculturalism, and anti-racism. The Jubilee facilitators are often available to share in the Sunday morning worship service. It is important to inform your congregation's minister and worship committee in advance of the planned Sunday Service, thus securing this time for the workshop date requested.

what their experience was because I didn't have it. We talked about it a lot. This was not immediately after they joined the Board. They had been on the Board for a while before this training was scheduled for them to attend. Again, I don't know if it was a year, or what. There was a real emotional discussion at the Board level, at the Board table, about continuing to support the work in the form it was then being done as exemplified by that training. And as a result of that discussion, we did not abandon our commitment to anti-racism work, and I recall looking across the table at Gini Courter who was really (and she remembers this well), really one of those who was voicing concerns about the kind of training that was being done. And I said, "It will break my heart if we turn our back on this initiative." And she looked at me and said, "It will break my heart, too."

In 1994, Hoover wrote in a memo that he and his staff were still exploring a variety of workshop options, saying it was important to have a variety of options for congregations. Yet William Jones noted that a full pilot program to test several models was never attempted. "I would have done a more competitive set of pilot studies which would have identified some of the problems in each of the different models and helped us to avoid some of the dead ends," he observed.

A year later Hoover wrote to the Unitarian Universalist Association staff,

In order to increase the probability of success in our efforts to become more racially and culturally diverse, a number of education and training approaches for Unitarian Universalist leadership and congregations have been examined. As a result of this exploration, the Racial and Cultural Diversity Task Force, Research Group, Staff Team, and the Black Concerns Working Group are participating in the Interfaith Multicultural Education and Training (InterMET) Anti-Racism Transformation Team Training Program led by Crossroads Ministry to dismantle racism and create anti-racist institutions. The training provides the opportunity to do in-depth analysis of our UUA institutions, policies, practices, and procedures and trains people to assist others in looking at their structures in order to develop multicultural education training programs and processes.

Hoover also delineated how the training strategy was developing, with a warning about the need for additional funding, stating,

> The Crossroads Ministry Anti-Racism Transformation Team training on May 7–10, 1995 . . . is fully enrolled with sixty people registered. Approximately thirty-five staff members will be participating. These include all program staff who have not yet taken the training and support staff in program areas. The entire LREDA Board, including designates will be participating, along with three UUA Board members, two new District Executives, six District Presidents, four more AAUUM members and members of the Urban Concerns and Ministry Committee and the MFC. Board designates have also been invited. We have had many more requests than we are presently able to accommodate for this training. We are being encouraged to request that we sponsor another training event as soon as possible. This would mean finding the funds if we are to honor this request.

Because of the concern that the Crossroads Ministry model had a Lutheran orientation, members of the UUA staff began translating materials into a Unitarian Universalist context. "There was a sense that there was a fence around the training—we didn't do as good a job as was needed with what to take home to the congregation and how to do so," Robinson-Harris recalled. "Participants needed to responsibly address these issues with their leadership and their congregations. It is difficult to bring the work back home. And one person is not sufficient to change congregational culture. There needs to be a critical mass of people. We needed to do better in developing and supporting leaders to lead this change in our congregations."

District Transformation Teams

In his report to the Board of Trustees in January of 1993, Hoover reported on efforts "for assisting the UUA Headquarters in becoming a racially and culturally diverse workplace":

> That goal has been successfully achieved and currently approximately 20 percent of the UUA staff are people of color. An Affirmative Action Officer oversees these efforts in conjunction with the Human Resources Administrator and Executive Vice President. The UUA is a member of Project Equality, a national organization that promotes equal opportunity in employment, use of vendors and purchasing. The UUA utilizes their guidelines in its hiring practices, purchasing decisions, and site selection for General Assembly. The Treasurer incorporates principles of ethical investing, sensitive to racial and cultural diversity, in the use of UUA funds.

Looking ahead, he also reported on a plan to help the Thomas Jefferson District Racial Justice Task Force develop a "transformation team," a cadre of anti-racism trainers to work on racial and cultural diversity and justice issues both within their congregations and local communities.

By the end of 1993, the Thomas Jefferson idea had become a national strategy and the Northeast, Southwest, Pacific Southwest, Prairie Star, Central Massachusetts, Massachusetts Bay, St. Lawrence, Michigan, Metropolitan New York, and Pacific Southwest Districts had made a pledge to follow suit. An expansion of this model was envisioned through the development of other transformation teams, some of which would focus on oppressions other than racism.

The Thomas Jefferson workshop provided training in anti-racist strategies, application skills, training techniques, and facilitation skills. About forty participants were involved in the training, including Black Concerns Working Group members and ten three-member teams. Four were from existing congregational racial justice task forces that were a result of previous collaborative efforts of the

Black Concerns Working Group and the District Racial Justice Task Force.

The Thomas Jefferson District, in the Southeastern United States, had begun an annual anti-racism conference that continued as an annual event into the twenty-first century. Participant Margaret Link provided this report of an early conference:

> The Thomas Jefferson District Board launched a major effort to identify and combat racism when they sponsored the first Anti-Racism Conference in Columbia, SC in 1990. Led by the Black Concerns Working Group and local resource people, participants explored issues of racism in the community, workplace and church and began to plan ways to promote racial inclusiveness within local churches, the District and the larger community.
>
> From this modest beginning has sprung a growing network of conferences, trained workshop leaders, local church workshops, local anti-racism task forces and a measurable increase in racial diversity in those congregations which have participated.
>
> The District Anti-Racism Conference has become an annual three-day event featuring prominent activists . . . as well as UUA staff and lay leaders. The four conferences have been held in Durham-Chapel Hill, NC, Norfolk, VA, Savannah, GA and Knoxville, TN. Attendance has averaged 100 people per conference.
>
> In an effort to bring the conference experiences to more people at the local level, six congregations have held one-day workshops led by members of the Black Concerns Working Group. For the first of these, the BCWG developed a model titled "Creating a Jubilee World" which leads participants through exercises that help them identify racism around them and then invites them to design concrete, practical projects for the congregation which can be completed in a reasonable time period.
>
> This second level of training has resulted in the establishment of local anti-racism task forces and a number of interesting projects. Columbia, SC has a gospel choir made

up of members from a Black church and the Unitarian Universalist Fellowship; Eno River, NC sponsors an ongoing lecture series in cooperation with a Black Lutheran church.

At its February 1993 Anti-Racism Conference the District inaugurated the third level of training. Sixty individuals were invited to attend a pre-conference training session conducted by the Rev. Joseph Barndt, author of *Dismantling Racism*, and members of the BCWG. Aided by a grant from the Unitarian Universalist Funding Program, the Working Group encouraged churches in the District and elsewhere in the Southeast to send up to three people for this training. The grant funds covered hotel expenses, meals and conference registration fee. The goal of this phase of District efforts is to develop teams of lay leaders who will conduct District level workshops and possibly join Working Group members for workshops in other parts of the continent.

At the 1994 Knoxville conference, members of the UUA Racial and Cultural Diversity Task Force were included in the second level of creating anti-racism transformation teams. Participants in this conference were also introduced to the Black Concerns Working Group's "Jubilee World II" workshop model which looks at developing a strategic plan for individual congregations to become anti-racist in all committees and functions.

Hoover recalled that initial efforts in the districts were mixed:

We picked the Thomas Jefferson District because there was a lot of activity to try and move to showing how a district could do it, and make it strong, as a model. We also had a lot of resistance during that era. The [Joseph Priestley District] was absolutely opposed to what we were doing, and we had a couple of others on the other coast who were quite honestly not working to make it real. And we had worked with Metro New York, thinking again that was a logical place. Again, that was very interesting there because it was still a lot of racial justice consciousness, had difficulty moving into anti-racist consciousness. . . . We were doing some things in

Massachusetts, but again the district didn't really get behind it in the early stages. . . . They appointed a committee that was going to coordinate all the kind of, what was it, I forgot now, justice work or something, and they'd appointed a transformation team before and then they spent a year or two fighting about who had the authority to do what.

Use of a training-heavy strategy for promoting an anti-racist ethic had resource implications. Additional funds were needed to support the work of those trained as part of the Thomas Jefferson District conference, for a newly formed Anti-Racism Trainers Collective, to provide staff support for these efforts, and to develop the resource materials to expand the effort. "This training event which integrates so many important components of Unitarian Universalist life cannot occur without additional funding," the Task Force warned.

Ambitious Undertaking

In 1995, the Office of Racial and Ethnic Progress, which was primarily responsible for implementing the 1992 General Assembly Resolution on Racial and Cultural Diversity in Unitarian Universalism, revealed ambitious plans in pursuit of its mission "to transform Unitarian Universalism into an anti-racist multicultural faith that promotes and creates racial justice in the world."

The office, headed by Hoover, was charged with designing and implementing a long-term strategy for anti-racist multicultural diversity by working with the Racial and Cultural Diversity Task Force, Research Group, the Staff Team, the executive staff, the Black Concerns Working Group, the districts, congregations, and Unitarian Universalist organizations on various levels with the aim of dismantling racism and increasing racial and cultural diversity. It was also to work on education and training, programming, models for change, research, assessment procedures, and resources for creating anti-racist institutions, policies, and practices as well as a long list of other tasks including working with the Departments of Ministry and Extension in recruitment and settlement of potential ministers of color.

PLAN
For Congregational Action

These work plans for Eno River Unitarian Universalist Fellowship in Durham, North Carolina, were developed at a 1993 Black Concerns Working Group workshop in Savannah, Georgia.

1) Mission statement concerning anti-racist multicultural/racial diversity
   a) Get Board support
   b) Opportunity to cultivate new leadership.
2) Ask Minister for sermon on diversity.
3) Send members to be trained by National Council for Churches in Durham or other Thomas Jefferson District training.
4) Long range goal—common understanding and definition of racism.
5) Offer specific training for groups within larger Fellowship on anti-racist diversity. As many groups as we can get done within Task Force framework.
6) Highlight to the congregation that multiculturalism is a denominational priority.
7) Contacting relocated Unitarian Universalist African Americans who are not part of ERUUF for feedback.
8) Continue networking with other community and Unitarian Universalist groups.

General Assembly showcasing promoted anti-racism training, at least for congregations that already had resources in place. Rev. Dr. Laurel Hallman, minister of the First Unitarian Church of Dallas, remembered, "Some of our people went to 'Dismantling Institutional Racism,' led by Joseph Barndt, and were very favorably impressed by him." The group brought their learnings back to the church and in 1996 a group called Kaleidoscope formed to offer "intercultural" movies, events, dinners, and other opportunities for exchange. The congregation had a history of speaking out on racial justice issues, with ministers who had addressed issues from the pulpit since the 1950s. Hallman said that when she began her ministry in the 1980s, there was a "generalized feeling that we were out there on the front edge with a lot of individual and small group work going on, but institutionally not so much inside the congregation." This began to change in the mid-1990s, when an intern minister, Suzelle Lynch, worked with an African-American parishioner to offer the adult religious education curriculum designed by Mark Morrison-Reed, *How Open the Door?* This led to receptivity to the ideas presented at the 1995 General Assembly.

Youth and Young Adults Provide Leadership
Also by 1995, organizing was happening. The Young Adults of Color Caucus (YACC) formed at General Assembly that year in Spokane, Washington, with Kristen Harper, Alyce Gowdy Wright, and Danielle Gladd as key leaders. Rev. Donna DiSciullo from the Association staff provided institutional support.

Rev. Joseph Santos-Lyons, then a young adult, has this recollection of what was for him a transforming moment:

At the General Assembly of Unitarian Universalist congregations in 1995 held in Spokane, Washington, I was approached by a stranger, someone who had obviously done a quick visual imaging scan before introducing themselves to me. I was asked, after a brief introduction of names, if I would be interested in attending a meeting of Young Adults of Color sponsored by the UUA (Unitarian Universalist Association of Congregations) Office of Young Adult Ministry.

My reaction was one of euphoria, in part because I had not anticipated any opportunity to meet in religious community with other Unitarian Universalist People of Color, and in part because this belief had been gnawing at my soul as I debated my future in the church. I had loved my Unitarian Universalist experience as a child and youth, and I had embraced my experience of understanding my identity and responsibility as a Person of Color. The spiritual experience was in the miraculous nature of these two loves, that I had once thought paradoxical, meeting together with harmony. The sense of connection was overwhelming with the dozen or so young adults who gathered, and the simple process of checking in provided a satisfying spiritual strength that has become a wellspring for my continued activism around People of Color ministry in Unitarian Universalism today.

Santos-Lyons identifies as "hapa," a Hawaiian term that means "half" and refers to a biracial heritage.

In this same period of time, the infrastructure to support multiracial dialogue was growing with the formation of a number of organizations, including the Unitarian Universalist Religious Professionals of Color and the Latina/o Unitarian Universalist Networking Association.

Black Concerns Working Group

The Black Concerns Working Group met in October 1995 and reviewed progress, which seemed encouraging. The financial picture generated concerns, and yet a review of the Association's anti-racism initiative included General Assembly events by the Working Group and by the Racial and Cultural Diversity Task Force, including a worship service featuring Rev. Alma Crawford, minister at the Church of the Open Door in Chicago. "The racial justice morning program was different from previous ones and touched many people," minutes from the Working Group concluded.

The Association's executive staff had a retreat to look at how they would work together to carry out their anti-racism mandate and established eight categories by which they would measure the effectiveness of their work. One was anti-racism: "Staff anti-racism training is being funded even when other things are having to be cut," according to minutes of a Black Concerns Working Group meeting. The Anti-Racism Staff Team, made up of program staff people with anti-racism as part of their portfolio as well as some support staff, was up and running. Departmental annual plans now were to include anti-racism efforts. "Departments are trying to work in teams across departments, which causes some confusion," the minutes said. "There is commitment to change." Another level of Crossroads training was introduced and the executive staff, task force, and the Anti-Racism Staff Team all participated, and the plan was for all new board members and staff to have this training.

The Black Concerns Working Group also continued offering its Jubilee World workshop and its successor model, the Jubilee II training, which was designed to offer more of a look at the systemic nature of racism. The early trainings were important points of entry for some. Jean Shepard, a white member of the Thomas Jefferson Memorial Church—Unitarian Universalist in Charlottesville, Virginia, recalled,

> The weekend in January 1995 that [Dr.] Leon Spencer [co-chair of the Working Group] and Mel Hoover came to TJMC to lead our first Jubilee Workshop was life-changing for me. I was fairly new to Unitarian Universalism then and delighted that the denomination was sponsoring the anti-racism movement. . . . That day I knew that there were others who were willing to talk realistically about racism and who were willing to help congregations move to better understand and combat it. That day I knew that I would put anti-racism work on my list of life's top priorities. I have carried that cause into employment situations, church leadership, district participation, my extended family, community work, and deep into my soul.

The Working Group saw a clear need to continue its workshops alongside the Crossroads trainings, despite increased calls for approaches that embraced more than a black and white paradigm.

Member Sherry Weston composed a statement on behalf of the group that read,

> In our Association, we have moved to a stage that makes anti-racism work more dynamic. With the diversifying of our congregations through increased membership by many different ethnic and racial groups, comes a time to add a dimension to our charge. We, the members of the Black Concerns Working group, affirm and support the unique perspectives of our other sisters and brothers of color. It is our intention to continue to provide anti-racism training to the churches and fellowships of the UUA. We will continue to hold up the issues specific to the African American experience in the UUA, but will advocate for inclusiveness in the discussion of the issue related to other ethnicities. Coalition-building between us and entities which represent other ethnic and racial groups has begun and we look forward to more dialogue about how to continue this path together.

A special focus session at General Assembly 1995 called "Racial Justice: A Community Celebration!" was held on Saturday, June 17, 1995, with Working Group participation.

Congregational Initiatives—Pilot Project

In 1996, sixteen "pilot project" congregations with existing commitments to racial justice were chosen to test anti-racism at the congregational level. They were the Unitarian Universalist Congregation of Atlanta, Georgia; First Unitarian Congregational Society of Brooklyn, New York; First Unitarian Universalist Society of Burlington, Vermont; Thomas Jefferson Memorial Church—Unitarian Universalist, Charlottesville, Vermont; the Unitarian Universalist Church of Greater Lynn, in Swampscott, Massachusetts; Arlington Street Church in Boston; the Community Church of New York; the Unitarian Universalist Society of the Palisades, in Englewood, New Jersey; the Unitarian Church of Montclair, New Jersey; First Unitarian Society of Plainfield, New Jersey; the Unitarian Universalist Church of Evanston, Illinois; Tennessee Valley

Unitarian Universalist Church, Knoxville, Tennessee; First Unitarian Church of Detroit; First Unitarian Church of Chicago; Second Unitarian Church of Chicago; and First Unitarian Church of Denver, Colorado. The congregations participated in two anti-racism training weekends, followed by an anti-racism self-appraisal.

Rev. Marjorie Bowens-Wheatley, who staffed the effort, recalled that the pilot project grew out of an experience at a training held in the early 1990s that contained Crossroads elements yet it was not limited to or by that approach. "We were talking about how we could be effective in this work at the congregational level," she recalled. "Then it was a training that was mostly affiliates and associates, and Kay [Montgomery, the executive vice president of the Unitarian Universalist Association] said, 'You know what we really need is to try out this work with a group of congregations. . . .' It was a two-year project, so basically we had about eight trainings together and I didn't use the Crossroads model. I used a variety of different resources from different organizations and some things I developed myself and I would say that that work had a huge effect on the congregations involved. I believe that all the congregations that participated . . . are still involved in the work and not only that, but those in the New York area developed a district project, which has had an annual conference every year. . . . So that work has been sustained over the years, and it's always been very flexible."

Yet training was not the only approach. Many other churches sought to build relationships through partnerships with other community groups. The Neighborhood Church in Pasadena, California, took a different tack, opening its doors and becoming more of a public institution, hosting a variety of community groups. "For instance, when the Urban League would meet at the church, and the Urban League in Pasadena was primarily, if not exclusively, an African American group," recalled Rev. Dr. Lee Barker, minister during these years, "we would make sure that there were opportunities before the meeting (or after), where there was social interaction with other groups that were meeting in the church that evening. We would put in place those kinds of opportunities."

One result, Barker said, was that Latinos and Latinas found their way to the church in larger numbers. "And what I found myself doing was getting to know kind of who each of those persons was and what their experience was and what it was about our church that they found to be most nourishing and nurturing and comforting," he recalled. "And here's the generalization—probably not true in any one case—but the general pattern that I could see emerging was that they were people who were usually at least second generation Americans. They were college educated people, mostly. They had children that they wanted to give a religious education to, so they tended to be younger and they tended to be families, and then the last, most interesting generalization (in my book at least), was that they had been raised in either Roman Catholic homes or fundamentalist homes. So they were reacting from the religion of their upbringing and coming to church because they wanted a liberal religious education for their children and for themselves.

"What I also was able to say is that that was the same generalization that I could make about virtually everyone who came to that church: college-educated, not recent immigrants, and either raised in fundamentalist or Roman Catholic homes, or no church at all, and they were looking for something for their kids. . . . They came from nearly the exact same demographic as all Unitarian Universalists. And that tells you something else: one way to have more diverse communities is to reach out to those who have the commonalities with who we are, exclusive of race and culture, and to see if there's enough there to build a bridge."

Starr King School for the Ministry

One of the two Unitarian Universalist theological schools had became actively involved in anti-oppression work in 1992. The Starr King School for the Ministry Board of Trustees, led by its long-range educational planning committee, undertook a process of theological reflection. During that project, students, faculty, trustees, graduates, invited guests, and consultants considered the mission and vision of the school. By 1996, that work became more tangible when Rev. Dr. Rebecca Parker, Starr King's president, wrote "Educating to Counter Oppressions," a summary of the work done by the Board. In the fall of 1998, the faculty formally voted to establish the "Educating to Counter Oppressions Committee" with Parker's document as "the working document to which we hold ourselves accountable." The major themes of the document were integrated into the faculty handbook.

Parker noted in a 2006 interview that Starr King was wary of the direction set by the official Unitarian Universalist Association Journey Toward Wholeness efforts because they were perceived as being too driven by white guilt. Starr King during this time was seeking to develop its own models, with a focus on being "counter-oppressive."

The Black Concerns Working Group met with Parker and asked what the school was doing to train or retrain African-American ministers. Efforts she outlined included "having had conversations with African-American graduates and former teachers to determine what needs to be done in seminaries; developing a liberation theology intended to foster change; providing a course geared to racial justice led by the Revs. Bill Gardiner and Mel Hoover [of the UUA staff] once a year; racism/sexism course and another 'Search for Common Ground' based on the theology of Howard Thurman as well as drawing on a broad range of resources and human experiences in their materials overall." Parker observed that the associated faculty gave them a chance to achieve diversity, but the core faculty was still white and that she had concerns about the bridges to the African-American community being one-way.

Starr King School for the Ministry continued a quiet trailblazing in their "educating to counter oppression" focus. The resistance they encountered was at a real cost to the institution and to the individuals leading the effort. A 2005–2006 report remembered,

> Since beginning this work over ten years ago, the school has been challenged by people within and beyond the school who question its importance and actively oppose the high priority we give to it. Some of the resistance has been ugly. Much of it has shown us that we need greater insight into how white privilege, in particular, "performs itself" in Uni-

tarian Universalism, sometimes in the guise of arguments for greater attention to "Unitarian Universalist identity."

In 1996, when we diversified our faculty to include people of color and a queer activist, a number of donors, including the school's largest contributor, withdrew their financial support protesting that we had succumbed to "political correctness." We received hate mail directed against faculty members. For her support of the school's new faculty, the president of our school was attacked as "unbalanced" and "immoral" in a letter sent to 50 major contributors and the UUA board of trustees, prompting the head of the department of ministry to follow-up on the letter-writer's accusations.

The school responded to this challenge by endeavoring to speak personally to as many of the naysayers as possible. At one point, the chair of the board drove four hours to talk with one writer of an especially angry letter. She listened to his concerns and defended the school's actions.

Faith in Action Department

In 1996, discussion began about creating a new department to carry out the racial justice initiatives. The Black Concerns Working Group discussed in April 1996 that a new department was to be created by combining the social justice, racial and cultural diversity, and diversity resources offices. The mission of the new department went through several refinements and ended up as:

> The mission of the Faith in Action Department is to assist Unitarian Universalist religious leaders, congregations, districts, and affiliate groups in their efforts to create inclusive multicultural religious communities committed to justice-making in the world. The department collaborates with Unitarian Universalists in congregations, districts, seminaries, and associate and affiliate groups to work for the transformation of Unitarian Universalism into an anti-oppression, multicultural religious community. The department works with other appropriate interfaith and secular organizations for social transformation.

CONGREGATIONAL STORY

First Unitarian Church of San Jose, California

The following is from the congregation's web site.

In 1986, the church declared itself a sanctuary for refugees fleeing the wars in Central America, and it has been active in supporting the legal rights, housing, and job needs of refugees. With the leadership of the Rev. Lindi Ramsden, this effort was eventually expanded into an interfaith community organization called CERCA (Comite Ellacuria para Refugiados de Centroamerica).

In 1993, we began an intentional ministry to serve Spanish-speaking people who were seeking a liberal religious home. While the growth of the ministry was interrupted by the fire, in 1998, Rev. Lilia Cuervo, the first Latin American immigrant woman to study for the Unitarian Universalist ministry, was called to serve as our Extension Minister for Spanish Speaking Ministries, offering a weekly Sunday service in Spanish, as well as pastoral counseling and other support services.

For over 100 years, the church building had served, not only as our spiritual home, but as a de facto community center. [Even after suffering a damaging fire] the church kept the needs of the larger community in mind. In 1998 the church founded the Third Street Community Center, a separate non-profit housed in the lower level of the building which has expanded and improved the non-sectarian community use of the building. The Third Street Community Center houses the Don Edwards Computer Learning Academy, an afterschool program, and ESL classes serving low-income and immigrant neighbors.

Hoover and Rev. William Gardiner were appointed as co-directors and Susan Leslie as program coordinator. The Anti-Racism Staff Team was also to be reconfigured so that someone from each department would be a member of the team; anti-racism forums were planned for twice a year.

By the October meeting of the Working Group, more details were available. "The Faith in Action office is talking about using the anti-oppression concept as an 'umbrella' for all of its work," the minutes read. "They are developing a new mission statement that will reflect this. We can consider that racism cuts across all other oppressions." That meant the Working Group needed to rethink its functions based on the new department's existence. The Working Group saw itself as providing technical assistance, training, education, monitoring, resource development, motivation, leadership development, and agitation—"will have to do this," the minutes noted.

Faith in Action's work with the congregations remained very significant for some. "I thank the UUA Faith in Action programs for bringing anti-racism challenges out from behind the cloud," wrote Jean Shepard of Charlottesville, Virginia. "I appreciate that hundreds of people in our denomination now have a slightly better understanding of the impact of racism. We are beginning to have a common vocabulary about and understanding of racism as well as a better understanding of the work that needs to be done. The sharing of language, tools, and strategies aids our abilities to make a difference."

Yet from the beginning Faith In Action had its concerned observers. Rev. Clyde Grubbs saw concentrating efforts in the department as "not bringing many other Unitarian Universalists into the conversation."

Faith in Action also worked in collaboration with Crossroads Ministry. In September, at a Crossroads training for trainers in Chicago, a number of the concepts that would later become controversial were presented:

Leadership development and accountability go hand in hand.

Need to make space for new people to keep from getting stuck (The Frozen Chosen).

GETTING STARTED

A Congregational Action Plan

This excerpt is from a report of the Racial and Cultural Diversity Task Force and Faith in Action: A UUA Department for Diversity and Justice. It was presented to the delegates at the 1996 General Assembly.

Congregational Consciousness Raising. For many of our congregations, simply increasing member awareness of racism is a meaningful and important starting point. A short list of possible actions steps follows. Use your imagination and your knowledge of your congregation to define ways in which to increase your congregation's understanding of their own needs and the needs of your community.

- Avoid describing or picturing African-Americans, Latinos, Asian-Americans, and American or Canadian Indians in essentially subservient roles.
- Guard against loaded words like civilized, uncivilized, primitive, savage, emerging nation, third world, minority, etc. that imply that European Americans are the norm.
- Be aware of the privileges that you benefit from if you are European American. Read Peggy McIntosh's paper on white privilege available from the Center for Research on Women, Wellesley College, Wellesley, MA 02181 or *Convictions About Racism in the United States of America*, a collection of essays by Horace Seldon which can be ordered from Community Change, Inc., 14 Beacon Street, Room 602, Boston, MA 02108.
- Present a video and workshop on the UUA's history of racism and resistance. Suggested videos include Rev. Dr. William Jones's *Grid of Oppression* model and *Black Pioneers in a White Denomination* by Rev. Mark Morrison-Reed, both available from the UUA Video Loan Library.
- Organize a discussion group using the *Eyes on the Prize* video series or other relevant videos.

- Learn about the concept of "whiteness." Toni Morrison's book *Playing in the Dark* might serve as a starting point.
- Establish a forum for elected officials to address their antiracism efforts and achievements.

Worship and Religious Education. The following suggestions are made for the consideration of your congregation's Worship and Religious Education Committees.

- Introduce a multicultural calendar into the church's worship context bringing congregational awareness to holidays such as Kwanzaa, Yom Kippur, and Islamic high holy days—not in such a fashion as to co-opt these traditions, but rather, to increase awareness regarding other races and traditions.
- Review the congregation's religious education program to ensure that the program eliminates racism and incorporates the numerous multicultural and antiracist curricula available through the UUA's Office for Religious Education.
- Review the music and services offered for racial and religious inclusiveness. The UUA's multicultural hymnal *Singing the Living Tradition* is a valuable resource. The UUA's Department of Worship and Diversity Resources can also assist your congregation in its efforts.
- Include in a prominent place in your building pictures of people of color who have led struggles for social justice and antiracism such as local congregation members, local leaders, Martin Luther King, Malcolm X, Gandhi, and Caesar Chavez.
- Establish children's programs to recognize and combat racism.
- Undertake a series of pulpit exchanges including Unitarian Universalist ministers of congregations active in multicultural and antiracism efforts, ministers of local congregations dedicated to creating antiracist religious structures, and ministers of churches

of color to discuss critical issues such as power-sharing, agenda setting, and possibilities of alliance building.

- Regularly champion the theological basis for anti-racism activism through adult education and religious education programs.

Congregational Actions. Viable antiracist activities that the congregation could begin with the following:

- Provide free or low-cost use of church facilities to people of color and groups dedicated to eliminating racism.
- Establish a pro bono legal service for people of color, to provide services that *they* require, through the church utilizing the legal expertise of the numerous church members who are local attorneys.
- Provide antiracism training for interested congregation members.
- Form discussion groups that examine issues of white power and privilege.
- Sponsor symposia on political issues critical to people of color that often do not receive fair reporting such as welfare reform, the criminal justice system, affirmative action, toxic waste, international racism, racism in the media, etc. to which the congregation and the community at large are invited and encouraged to attend.

What are the accountability relationships of:
- team members to one another?
- the team to the internal bureaucracy?
- the team to the external UU community?
- the team to the external world?

If we agree that our accountability should always be to communities of color . . .
- All people of color are not anti-racist.
- How do we decide which people of color are anti-racist?
- Are they chosen by and accountable to a community of color?

A Step Ahead—For Ministers

Also during this time, an effort was made to do special training for ministers to allow them to be in a position to help guide their congregations. Bowens-Wheatley recalled that she and Gardiner were trainers. Workshops were held in the Ballou-Channing District, in the Joseph Priestley District, and with a cluster in the Southwest District. A few years later, she expanded the model to include a conversation about theology. "Theology wasn't in the model at all," Bowens-Wheatley said. "I kept saying this is a spiritual issue, we have to bring in theology, especially with ministers. So I created a portion of the model that elicited from the ministers how they felt our Unitarian Universalist theological foundations formed our anti-racism work. They were extremely appreciative of that. That's what led to *Soul Work* [a book she co-authored]. It really came out of working with ministers around theology. Yes, there was some resistance, but . . . it was a very different approach than the Crossroads model because we tried to localize it, get them to tell us about the areas they were working in, what were the geographic and sociological characteristics of the area, the congregations, etc. I still have the model filed somewhere. I would say "A Step Ahead" was a far more successful program than other models we worked with in congregations in general. We didn't get everybody, but it was much more conversational, much more dialogic, much more input from them, and much better received, frankly."

PART 2

LEARNINGS

As the 1990s began, Unitarian Universalists were beginning to envision themselves once more as people who could talk about issues of race. The long period of silence and coded language that had been in place since the early 1970s was passing away, though the unhealed wounds remained like subterranean caves, revealing abysses and fissures that could make for dangerous travels. Yet as the country wrestled with harsh, new forms of racism seen in events such as the 1991 Rodney King beating in Los Angeles, it became hard to ignore that changed laws did not mean changed attitudes.

The pivotal event for the Unitarian Universalist reengagement with racial issues was passage of the 1992 resolution on racial and cultural diversity at the General Assembly in Calgary—a public statement that said out loud that the Association would be talking openly about its racial divide once more. And yet, even with this statement, passed largely by delegates who had little knowledge of the divisions remaining from the 1960s and 1970s—and with new language and many new players, the developments that led to the declaration at Calgary were tempered by unresolved histories and hurts.

Rev. Dr. William Schulz, president of the Association from 1985 to 1993, noted the large role that staff played in starting the race initiative: "Probably if I were doing it today," he said, "I would engage people well beyond the staff. . . . In retrospect, it was probably not the best decision." Despite this, Schulz said concerns about racial issues had deep roots. "This was not just an edict from the Association: We truly wanted to provide resources to congregations. These issues had emerged in good measure out of the Urban Concerns Committee, that this was a grassroots committee that had itself emerged out of the Urban Church Coalition, that there were congregations that were not urban that cared about race and anti-racism."

Rev. Dr. Anita Farber-Robertson of the Racial and Cultural Diversity Task Force agreed: "I think the key mistake we made was that we didn't work enough with our ministers and we could have known better." Farber-Robertson also noted that the support for ministers who did engage in anti-racism advocacy was not adequate and that more skills in conflict management were needed. "You just don't do 'top-down' with ministers and then ask them to risk their jobs." Those who carried memories of the Empowerment Controversies brought their own mixed reactions to the new developments. The resolution passed in a very different climate than those passed during the late 1960s and was more about aspiration than allocation. Rev. Dr. Victor Carpenter, author of a book on the Empowerment Controversies, was chosen by those organizing the resolution effort to speak in favor of it, in part because he was from a large church. He recalled, "My thinking was okay, here we go again. Maybe this time it'll work. Resolutions at GA don't usually go very far, just because denominational gatherings are not places where initiatives really get off the ground. . . . It is not what those gatherings are for."

General Assembly, the setting for the Empowerment Controversies of the Civil Rights era, also became the setting for the renewed discussions about race, although changes in the process for making monetary commitments had made it nearly impossible for an Assembly to make large financial pledges, such as those made to the Black Unitarian Universalist Caucus in the late 1960s. This was another outgrowth of the Empowerment Controversies and made seasoned observers, such as Carpenter, more wary.

This reclaiming of a prophetic, if tentative, voice and an advocate's posture on racial issues became critical to the identity of many Unitarian Universalists, and this time the focus was on the majority white identity and its views on race. A focus began to emerge that saw racism within the Association itself as an avenue to solving the perennial challenge of why more racial diversity was not seen within our pews. From the beginning this approach was controversial and represented a major shift in direction. Rev. Clyde Grubbs had this observation about the context of the 1992 resolution at Calgary: "The theory before Calgary was that the reason we did not represent the diversity of the U.S. was because of internalized racism; therefore, overcome internalized racism and we would become more inclusive." He observed that this, in some ways, flew in the face of our history because Unitarian Universalist civil rights work in the community was what brought in African Americans in the 1960s. Yet Grubbs's personal experience as a Native American growing up within the movement affirmed this difficult choice:

> We had to tackle what we had neglected (our own racism as experienced by people of color within the UU movement). I grew up UU in a racialized family. I knew about the racism in the movement. . . . Up to Calgary the UUs did work on racism out there . . . external to the UU community . . . and this work gave us a reputation and some growth . . . but again I was there in 1970 when the internal racism undermined our work.

For others, especially newcomers, the time had come to move ahead. "Speaking with very limited knowledge, I wonder at what took us so long!" mused Rev. Dr. Jerome Stone, an adjunct professor at Meadville Lombard who visited his first Unitarian Universalist congregation in 2000. "For decades after the 'Black Empowerment controversy' we seem to have crawled back into our shell."

In this period, new organizations emerged that fostered the identity of particular groups; some survived and some disappeared, such as the African American Unitarian Universalist Congress whose historic 1992 gathering brought together an unprecedented number of African-American Unitarian Universalists but proved to be its only one. The African American Unitarian Universalist Ministers Association continued to grow in influence while new players such as the Latino Unitarian Universalist Networking Association emerged. Other more informal gatherings were held, bringing Unitarian Universalists who shared a racial or cultural identity together for the first time in what could be very moving events.

Paradoxical tensions in Unitarian Universalist identity became more apparent in this era. "The difficulty with the Unitarian Universalists was twofold," observed Rev. Joseph Barndt of Crossroads Ministry, the nonprofit organization that worked with the Unitarian Universalist Association to develop the training program and later was paid by the UUA to deliver it. "One, their history with the black empowerment, which essentially shut down the Unitarian Universalists' ability to work for racial justice for a number of years . . . and the other difficulty was the issue around theology, of not having a theology that could support an analysis of racism. . . . [Anita Farber-Robertson noted that] the UUA cannot progress very far in the anti-racism work without coming to grips with their need for a theology of evil, that there's a strain of the UUA that says don't talk to me about guilt, don't talk to me about sin, or anything but the goodness of the human being, the goodness of man. . . . So that strain responded to the Crossroads stuff and to me with, 'Damn you, stop trying to make Lutherans out of us! Take your guilt someplace else!' . . . But how does the Unitarian Universalist understand brokenness? . . . If you didn't have a Lutheran answer, then what would the Unitarian Universalist answer be?"

Differences in analysis of how to improve racial diversity damaged relationships. In this era, a series of trainings was offered to help people gain a greater understanding of the complexity of modern race relations and the power dynamics associated with them. Controversial, theologically challenged, and underfunded though they were, the early trainings offered hope to people of color who had struggled in the Association to find a way to negotiate relationships with the white majority or who sought others who shared their vision.

Ministers who chose to engage in anti-racism work did so at some risk. "I was one of those ministers who took those risks and was out on the front lines and I suffered the consequences of it," Farber-Robertson said. "We asked [ministers] to do something that was outrageous. . . . There was not support from the UUMA or anywhere once stuff started coming down." She noted that congregations also had little support. "There was no support for me or for them. . . . I tried to see it through to the next level and I really didn't know how to do it. There was nobody who was going to say to the congregation, 'This is scary work.'" For Farber-Robertson, the tensions caused her to decide to leave the congregation. Even in this difficult time, she was proud that the congregation funded a large needs-based scholarship in her honor.

Fear over the loss of relationship played in as well. The landmark research conducted by Rev. Olivia Holmes found that "fear holds us back." After conducting three phases of her research, Holmes wrote, "Fear is the critical factor that keeps coming up as holding us back from making a strong commitment to become more diverse. Fear of conflict, perhaps in ourselves, as well as in our congregations, seems to be the key issue." In her research, Holmes found that 31 percent of the lay members surveyed agreed with the statement that "people will be uncomfortable with the possibility of conflict" while 26 percent agreed that "we will lose our sense of being a safe and healing community if there is racial or cultural conflict."

The debate was also about faith and theology. The need for a deeper examination of the theological questions about issues of race was also identified as part of a consultation around race held in 1991:

> We recommend that the UUA Administration and the Extension Department articulate the theology . . . behind the Association's work in this area. While this was done previously in the Extension Department through the articulation of a mission statement and in a series of assumptions underlying the department's work, it is a new era. . . . We recommend, as a part of this theological articulation, that the Administration and Extension and District Services staff members consider ongoing public confession of our limitations and shortcomings. As long as predominantly European American and socially privileged people administer the programs for the gathering of congregations of color and mixed economic class, there is a need for confession. Many European Americans, recipients of the land and products of the poorly compensated labor of Native Americans, African Americans and other ethnic immigrants, or oppressions of third world countries through our endowments of our institutions are in part garnered from surplus labor accumulated on the backs of slaves and poor wage earners. As members of an educationally and economically privileged religious community, we have also inherited the responsibility to make amends. This is a critical point we have only just begun to address. It is one, however, for which our movement is historically well-suited to provide leadership. We have a recurring history or caring about right relations among all peoples. We name ourselves Unitarian Universalist.

CLOSING WORDS

A Call To Worship
By Rev. Melvin Hoover (adapted)

We'll build a land where we bind up the broken.

We can't control the future but we can shape it and enhance the possibilities for our children and grandchildren. More than 6,000 of our Unitarian Universalist children are multiracial.

We'll build a land where we bring good tidings to all.

We can't discern in the present the fullness of our actions and their impact but we can be seekers in our time exploring fully the crevices and cracks where knowledge and new insight might be found.

We'll build a land building up ancient cities.

We can explore our spectrum of relationships and confront our complacency and certainty about the way things are. Within our congregations we can begin to review our mission and vision statements and how we might fulfill the promise of our heritage and our future.

We'll build a promised land that can be.

We can dare to face ourselves in our entirety.
To feel the tears.
Of the individuals and groups who feel marginalized.
Of the individuals and groups who risk and make mistakes.

We'll build a land where peace is born.

To listen to our frustrations and confusion.
From ministers in congregations who are seeking direction.
From struggling racial justice committee members.

We'll build a land of people so bold.

To discover new capacities and capabilities that will empower and transform us.

Come build the land my people we seek.

Revelation and Resistance

I teach my children the game of chess. Why chess? Because it is an excellent game for the mind. It teaches that you must never think that your back is up against the wall with no way out. In the game of chess, as in life, your mind must always be working—thinking about options for yourself. If people tell you, you're not smart enough to do this, or you can't do that, and for all the wrong reasons, you must find another way to survive, to stay alive, and not just to survive, but to stay healthy and achieve your goals. You must always remember that you are somebody—equal to all others—a child of the universe—strong and proud. Stay alert and plan how to go around, over, through obstacles that are placed in your way, obstacles that tell you, because of the color of your skin, "you do not matter, you are unimportant." Make another move for your health and for your success, remembering always to stay on a path with a heart of goodness.

—Rev. Dr. Michelle Bentley, minister,
Third Unitarian Church, Chicago

1996–97

The first District Anti-Racism Teams form in the Massachusetts Bay District and in the Thomas Jefferson District.

The administration of President Dr. John Buehrens creates the Faith in Action Department as part of the Unitarian Universalist Association staff to coordinate anti-oppression efforts.

1997

The Liberal Religious Educators Association Board conducts an anti-racist self-assessment in February, and creates an anti-racist transformation team in October.

The Anti-Racism Core Organizing Team convenes itself, in June, to coordinate efforts and resources that congregations could follow to become anti-racist.

At the General Assembly in Phoenix, delegates pass the business resolution *Toward an Anti-Racist Unitarian Universalist Association*, which calls for a program for anti-racism.

The Unitarian Universalist Association Board creates the Journey Toward Wholeness Committee, and it holds its first meeting in October.

The Black Concerns Working Group changes its name to Jubilee Working Group (for Anti-Racism), to reflect its expanded focus.

The African American Unitarian Universalist Ministry becomes Unitarian Universalist Religious Professionals of Color.

From 1997 to 1999, the Unitarian Universalist Association was building an infrastructure to support anti-racism programming. While the Association staff built formal structures such as the Faith in Action Department, more informal structures came together. These included the Core Team, a self-appointed coalition of staff and consultants who advised on program development.

As awareness grew about how much change an anti-racist strategy would require, the Board of Trustees began to assert its leadership, proposing a resolution to begin an anti-racist "Journey Toward Wholeness" and shepherding it through the General Assembly. This initiative vested more power in the Board, which appointed a committee to coordinate anti-racism initiatives.

A debate intensified over whether anti-racism dialogue and trainings should focus on the black-white issues that remained since the days of the Empowerment Controversies or whether such efforts should broaden to reflect the increased racial and ethnic diversity of

1998

The Meadville Lombard Theological School hosts, and the Starr King School for the Ministry co-sponsors, a consultation on race and theology entitled "Theology, Faith and Action," in January.

Unitarian Universalist Religious Professionals of Color changes its name to DRUUMM (Diverse and Revolutionary Unitarian Universalist Multicultural Ministries).

DRUUMM sponsors Multiracial and Families of Color Camps in the Pacific Southwest, Pacific Central, and Northwest Districts.

Latina/o Unitarian Universalist Networking Association (LUUNA) publishes a critique of the Association's anti-racism efforts, *The Baltimore Papers*.

The UUA Board invites congregations to participate in the first Journey Toward Wholeness Sunday in December.

Unitarian Universalism. In particular, Latina/o leaders such as Revs. Patricia Jimenez and José Ballester repeatedly raised questions about how their experiences could be embraced if the primary focus was on black-white relations.

This was a time of revelations about how critical it was to speak of these issues—and of resistance to the pain, cost in relationships, and simple awkwardness that these efforts caused. As the decade went on, more and more groups and voices came into the discussion and debate over anti-racism goals and training. As new groups formed, relationships grew more complex. The stakeholders coming to the table included youth and young adults, who were growing their ability to be advocates for anti-racism, anti-oppression, and multicultural goals.

Language and affiliation defined relationships. Labels began to be applied. For some, a label "anti-racism" might mean one thing and for others it meant something else. "Journey Toward Wholeness" became synonymous with "anti-racism" and all of that became

1999

The Journey Toward Wholeness Transformation Committee brings thirty people to Boston in January for an assessment and planning meeting.

The Transformation Committee convenes the Next Steps on the Journey Toward Wholeness stakeholders meeting, which brings about eighty-five people to Kansas City. To protest a lack of cultural diversity and sensitivity, Latina/o and other participants walk out.

The Anti-Racism Core Organizing Team disbands "with the understanding that there will be ongoing conversations about the best structure with which to support this work."

Rev. Dr. Thandeka presents "Why Anti-Racism Will Fail" at General Assembly, critiquing the Crossroads/Journey Toward Wholeness approach and publishes her remarks later that year in *The Journal of Liberal Religion*.

LUUNA publishes *Bringing Gifts*—alternative analyses and methods to raise awareness of racial issues.

The UU Ministers Association considers and rejects a resolution to guarantee DRUUMM positions on its Executive Board, and one on its Continuing Education Network for Training, Enrichment and Renewal (CENTER) Committee, pending action by its Executive Board.

linked with the particular approach of Crossroads Ministry. In reality, many people were experimenting with different strategies. Even the most-aired controversy, which pitted Rev. Dr. Thandeka against the Journey Toward Wholeness Transformation Team and the Faith in Action Department, was more about method than ends. Scarcity of resources and a scarcity of attention, except in the hothouse environment of General Assembly, seemed to add to this. People were wondering what it meant to be a Unitarian Universalist and how that related to the dialogue about anti-racism.

1999

The Continental UU Young Adult Network (C*UUYAN) presents its first anti-racism workshop, before its conference, OPUS, in July.

DRUUMM welcomes laypeople into its membership.

The UUA Board of Trustees agrees to take anti-racism training.

The Liberal Religious Educators Association (LREDA) Board undertakes anti-racism training.

C*UUYAN Steering Committee sends members to UUA-sponsored anti-racism trainings in November.

CHAPTER 10

Toward an Anti-Racist Unitarian Universalist Association

The Racial and Cultural Diversity Task Force's work in the early 1990s had reopened a discussion with a direct focus on race. Those who had been eager for such a discussion to reopen began to build the infrastructure necessary to sustain it and to sustain relationships within the Unitarian Universalist Association that could help keep the discussion going. The passage of a second resolution at the 1997 General Assembly in Phoenix, Arizona, provided a much clearer and more distinct focus for the conversation—the resolution named it as "anti-racism," an identity that would generate resistance as time went on.

Many congregations would ignore the resolution; some would use the materials produced by the Black Concerns Working Group and members of the Association's staff. Rev. Dr. Laurel Hallman of the First Unitarian Universalist Church of Dallas recalled introducing anti-racism efforts to her congregation in the fall of 1997 this way: "We [can] use tools from the recent very intelligent and constructive work in the area of anti-racism that would make us less helpless, less overwhelmed and more able to constructively confront the problem of racism so deeply embedded in our culture. . . . The board and I agree that this is not just a good intention on our part. We have recognized the cost of racism in our own lives. That the path to wholeness is our path to take together. We hope you will join us in the journey."

The new resolution helped shift the focus from individuals to systems, with an open analysis of the damage oppressive systems could do. Rev. Keith Kron, who became director of the Association's Office of Bisexual, Gay, and Lesbian Concerns in 1996, recalled,

> The most amazing thing for me about our anti-racism work is a sense of awe of the people who began this work in the early '90s—who risked a conversation I thought would never happen. As a gay man, I sort of assumed that the best I could hope for was that people would not discriminate overtly against me, that often I would be given a chance to "show folks what I got." When I first went to an anti-racism training and they began to talk about systematic oppression I was dumbfounded. "You mean we get to talk about this?" I asked. I had never thought we would talk about these things in my lifetime. I just figured I had to live with them.
>
> So to be a part of the conversation where we looked at systematic oppression as well as individual oppression was a gift to mc. It gave me great hope that we might in fact get somewhere one day.
>
> This took me to anti-racism trainings, where despite the utter lack of the pastoral element to them, where I began to see many similarities between the oppressions. I began to notice that all our good work on sexism was in some ways a detriment. Many of our folks thought we had "done" sexism and could move on to other oppressions. Similarly, I saw the danger of our Welcoming Congregation work [to help congregations welcome gay, lesbian, bisexual, and transgender people]. The congregation had a certificate and had therefore "done" the work. Why do more? This changed the way I did my work and the way I said things when I visited congregations. I spoke continually about processes more so than final outcomes—of getting to a place in the work which would lead to a next place. It also led me to learn how to lead anti-racism training.

For me, the greatest outcome was realizing the trust and hope that were involved from the people of color who risked opening the conversation about oppression on a systemic level. It made me want to earn it and have great respect for those who tried.

Phyllis Daniel, who served eight years on the Board of Trustees during this period, put it this way: "The systemic analysis is really important. I don't know how to get to that except in a didactic way, so somehow or other that's got to be. . . . This is just stuff that people still need to be grappling with."

Money issues strained relationships in this era. For many, money had been the breaking point for relationships during the Empowerment Controversies, so distrust built as the dollars were less forthcoming than rhetorical support for addressing racial inequities. Rev. Melvin Hoover recalled,

A major effort was made to have all the congregations buy into the anti-racism, anti-oppression, multicultural vision. The next logical step for effective transformation was to revision a new UUA rooted in and guided by the principles and understandings of the anti-racist, anti-oppressive, multicultural vision that was adopted. Unfortunately, that isn't what happened at all. It was a new level of the old UUA approach of appointing a committee to monitor racism and then not funding it. The vision that the UUA Board and leadership teams had developed in terms of the thirty-year plan for truly becoming an anti-racist, anti-oppressive, multicultural institution called for a refocusing of institutional resources, people, and dollars. There was great momentum in many congregations to move and the need was to make available consultants and develop resources on a large scale that would help many of our UU congregations still operating from a racial relations or transitional understanding of institutional change to grow into a transformational vision and capacity. That didn't happen.

Faith in Action Department

Wishing to give more visibility to race relations work, Association president Dr. John Buehrens reorganized the social justice segment of the Association staff to create the Faith in Action Department. Buehrens recalled that he allowed the new group, with Hoover and Rev. William Gardiner as co-directors, to name itself. "One of the things I had done was to recognize that a lot of the decisions were made by the executive staff and I had expanded the executive staff," Buehrens recalled. By extending membership to all department heads, once Faith in Action was launched the executive staff included two African Americans, Hoover and Rev. William Sinkford, then director of the Department of Congregational, District and Extension Services.

For Hoover, creation of Faith in Action was significant because it represented an important hallmark of the approach to anti-racism he championed: that change could be made inside of an institution, not only by external forces "knocking down" the structure.

Core Team Expands

To support the development of training initiatives, Association staff had put together an informal "Core Team," whose mission was "to promote the adoption and implementation of the Racial and Cultural Diversity Task Force's proposed vision and resolutions for becoming an anti-racist, multicultural religious organization." Association executive vice president Kathleen Montgomery said the team began operating in the mid-1990s as an ad hoc group. The Core Team was made up of UUA staff members with particular responsibilities seen as critical to advancing an anti-racist agenda as well as lay members with an interest in racial issues who enhanced the diversity of the team. By October 1997, members of the Core Team were Hoover and Gardiner, the Faith in Action co-directors, and Rev. José Ballester, Rev. Marjorie Bowens-Wheatley, Vivian DeCarlo, Robette Dias, Judith Frediani, Alyce Gowdy-Wright, Jacqui James, Susan Leslie, Joseph Lyons, Rev. Dr. Tracey Robinson-Harris, Sinkford, and Rev. Cheng-Imm Tan.

The Core Team diversified the conversation outside of the Association staff, expanded it beyond black and white voices, and added lay voices to those of ministers. The team operated in a quasi-staff way because of the need to hear the perspectives of people of color and to the shortage of those perspectives on the Association staff. Dr. Leon Spencer, who had co-chaired the Racial and Cultural Diversity Task Force, noted that "if you were a lay person and a person of color, you became quasi-staff." Hoover said the informal Core Team grew to become a more formal and expanded entity. It took on the name Anti-Racism Core Organizing Team.

"The whole concept of the Core Team," Buehrens said, "was a manifestation of the staff attempting to implement the Calgary resolution prior to the broad leadership of the Association getting training or taking significant ownership of the initiative. . . . Before my first term was up, I was very aware that what we had developed was a coterie of people who thought they owned anti-racism."

The team's influence was seen when the fledgling Journey Toward Wholeness Committee, which the Board of Trustees appointed in response to the 1997 resolution, met with the Core Team to try to figure out how to work cooperatively. The minutes of this meeting sum up both the clarity and the ambiguity:

> The Core Team is involved in justice work, resource development, training for congregations, districts, affiliate and associate organizations, and religious professionals.
>
> JTWC is responsible for oversight, monitoring, political role, and funding.
>
> Areas of overlap include: Coordination, communication, marketing, vision, strategic planning, goal setting, evaluating. . . .
>
> Mel [Hoover] reminded us that "The challenge is to learn to live with ambiguity with intentionality and consciousness." It was also noted that "much of the front-line advocacy, promotion, and marketing of the initiative is being done by the Core Team, at a level and on a scale that JTWC does not have the resources to do. JTWC should use whatever clout it has to advance the agenda in a variety of ways, including identifying places where work is being stymied because of lack of resources, funding, people, etc.

Over time, some raised concerns about the fact that the Core Team was a staff-driven initiative. Robette Dias, who worked as a volunteer and then later joined the staff, noted that the issue of being staff-driven "only gets raised in terms of doing anti-racism work. . . . In reality, the UUA is incredibly staff-driven." Bowens-Wheatley recalled,

I was a part of the Core Team from the beginning even though I wasn't UUA staff, so I had a lot of input from the beginning, and we split up the Core Team into three, maybe four, different subgroups, and one group was research. . . . This research team ultimately persuaded the Core Team that you could not do this work effectively without bringing in history and class. We developed a critique of the Crossroads model and Christine [Murphy of the Faith in Action staff] and Robette [Dias] actually expanded the model to include colonialism as a historical piece that had to be brought in, and some elements of class. I wasn't involved in that critique, they did it, but I responded to the critique. Ultimately that led to a broadening of the model . . . in 1997 or 1998.

Dias noted that the Core Team also provided leadership development for people of color. "It was the only place in the UUA," she said, "that was doing any intentional people of color leadership training." She also said that it was the broader inclusiveness of this group that would later allow the Black Concerns Working Group to broaden its focus as the Jubilee Working Group and that would later produce an organization for lay and professional people of color known as Diverse and Revolutionary Unitarian Universalist Multicultural Ministries [DRUUMM]. "There was no structural way for people of color to have a voice," Dias said. "The Core Team was a way to have coordinated power." Spencer noted that "the Core Team really helped make the shift from black to people of color."

In 1997, the Core Team became involved in discussions about a sculpture called "That Which Might Have Been," which was white artist John Henry Waddell's interpretation of what the four young

VOICE
Rev. Marjorie Bowens-Wheatley

These remarks are from an address delivered by Rev. Marjorie Bowens-Wheatley at a 2002 Convocation of the Unitarian Universalist Ministers Association.

What continues to challenge my personal faith is wondering whether I will ever see the day when our religious movement moves beyond its Eurocentric norms. We would probably all agree that a life of faith cannot be nurtured in the face of endemic evil. But it's more difficult to see that it is also impossible for many people from non-European heritage to be nurtured by an upper middle-class Eurocentric norm blessed by self-satisfaction.

Someday, I'm going to update W.E.B. DuBois' book, *The Ways of White Folks*, that will focus on the cost of Eurocentrism and of cultural indifference in a multicultural society.

In our movement, there seems to be a canon of language that "educated" people are supposed to be familiar with and love. There is a canon of literature that is presumed to have been read. There is a canon of music that too often does not allow the spirit to emerge freely.

In most of our congregations that I have been a part of or worked with, structures that create and sustain whiteness are normative. There is presumption from some clergy and some laity that these canons of music, and literature, and art, and language, and social discourse, rooted in the European experience, are normative. Eurocentrism is seen as logical and rational, and those who express a need for a spirited form of worship or those who use a different language set are somehow made to feel less educated, less than worthy. These presumptions make it extremely difficult for culturally oppressed groups to find a place in our congregations. Speaking personally, while I enjoy and appreciate a wide variety of cultural traditions, when I cannot find myself in a worshipping community, it drains the life of the spirit out of me, and I must go elsewhere to nurture my soul.

If I and other colleagues who are rooted in cultures outside Europe are to be nurtured in our movement, then I must keep the faith that things can be different. Being open to and supporting new possibilities in ministry, different cultural forms in worship, new ways of seeing—these too are important to keeping the faith, to nurturing the spirit. If you will stand with me in solidarity in an expanding circle of culture so that it includes *all of us*, you too will be keeping the faith.

girls killed in 1963 church bombings in Birmingham, Alabama, would have looked like had they lived. The Unitarian Universalist Congregation of Phoenix, which had commissioned the sculpture, had proposed displaying it at the 1997 General Assembly in their city. Women of color on the staff raised concerns that the depiction of the African-American women was very sexualized. Hoover recalled that Bowens-Wheatley and staff members Lola Peters and Jacqui James asked the team to become involved. Spencer was among those asked to enter into a dialogue with the sculptor and members of the Phoenix congregation. "I remember for myself, as the father of a black daughter, it raised concerns," he said. After the conversation, the sculpture was not displayed at General Assembly.

Another focus the Core Team brought was a concern about children of color, including transracial adoption and multiracial children, in the congregations. "Those of us who had kids were aware of the need for a place to raise Unitarian Universalist kids of color," Dias said, recalling that Lola Peters provided leadership on this issue, conducting workshops and trainings on transracially adopted and biracial children. The Journey Toward Wholeness Committee was also concerned about the children. "First of all, we need to share this new awareness that our 'downstairs' is more diverse than our upstairs," note the minutes of the committee's May 1998 meeting. "Our survey indicates that we have somewhere around 10 percent multiracial."

Thomas Jefferson District Name Debate

In the Thomas Jefferson District, a process established to consider changing the district name because of Jefferson's legacy as a slave-owner who never freed his slaves had been under way for several years. This effort emerged, in part, because of the protest against the request for "period costume" at the Thomas Jefferson Ball at the Charlotte General Assembly in 1993. The *TJ Connection* newsletter recalls the history this way:

> Following the Charlotte General Assembly, the President of the TJ District, Barbro Hansson, was convinced that the Thomas Jefferson District must allow dialogue to take place

concerning our district name. "We," she said, "must, as sensitive Unitarian Universalists, listen to and talk with each other regarding the meaning of a name, specifically the name Thomas Jefferson." The discussion continued with workshops, "What's In A Name," held at the 1994 TJ District Anti-Racism Conference, '94 TJ District Annual Meeting, and the 1994 Fall Leadership Conference. The TJ District Board, at its Fall 1994 Board Meeting, decided that the issue should be addressed formally. They had been made aware that the name of Thomas Jefferson did not represent some district Unitarian Universalists, including . . . African American, Native Americans and other non-European peoples, Universalists, and feminists who have difficulty with his relationships with women.

A committee was appointed with the charge to develop a process to formally consider changing the district name. Committee members were Mike Harbour, chair; William (Footsie) Edmundson, Lewis Walker, Rev. Audrey Vincent, A.L. (Sandy) Peaslee, and Leon Spencer.

Ultimately, the proposed change was defeated by a small margin. The District web site reported,

At the Annual Meeting of the Thomas Jefferson District held on Saturday, April 26 [1997], at the Unitarian Universalist Church of Charlotte, North Carolina, some 175 UUs, including 121 delegates from 40 of the District's 54 congregations in the Carolinas, Virginia, Tennessee and southeastern Georgia, voted to retain the name of Thomas Jefferson in the District's name. The motion to change the district name to "Southeastern," a by-laws change, required a 2/3 vote (84) for passage; the vote was 75 in favor of the change and 51 opposed.

The vote on the emotionally-charged issue attracted both local and national press attention, especially in a year in which much media attention has been paid to the enigma of Thomas Jefferson. At issue was the concern of many in the District that calling it by the name of a slave owner is offensive to African-American members. Some delegates, however, were offended by the implication that their championing of the name of Jefferson, whose doctrine of the separation of church and state and freedom of religious belief is central to Unitarian Universalist belief, implied that they were racist.

After the vote, there was further discussion about what should be done. A motion, which passed, charged an Anti-Racism Task Force with continuing to study the issue of the name as well as how Unitarian Universalists in the District can best work to combat racism both within the denomination and in the larger community.

Spencer later wrote, "The meeting was a tense, painful experience which resulted in the formation of the District Anti-Racism Transformation Team (DARTT). It became apparent that our district name only touched the surface of the deeper issues we face around justice, race, and institutional oppression." Reflecting on the vote outcome years later, Spencer noted that it remained a source of irritation and hurt. "It wasn't just about TJ, it was about our vision for the future and who we attract. . . . It was an opportunity for reconciliation and isn't a faith community a place for reconciliation?" he asked.

"Toward an Anti-Racist Unitarian Universalism Association"
Denise (Denny) Davidoff, who had been instrumental in the passage of the 1992 resolution on racial and cultural diversity and who had been a member of the task force it created, said that by 1997 a stronger statement was needed, one with a focus on the congregations. "By that time, we had five years of pushback," said Davidoff, who by then was the Association's moderator. "The whole purpose of the Journey Toward Wholeness was to involve the congregations and get out of the preliminary part." She remembered Hoover's efforts to get the resolution passed as "brilliantly aggressive."

Buehrens noted that the resolution came about because the Board was taking more ownership of the anti-racism work and was no longer comfortable with the leadership for it coming from the Association staff. Rev. Susan Suchocki, a member of the Racial and Cultural Diversity Task Force, said that the task force was aware by this point that institutional change was needed. "We weren't going to be an authentic transformed institution; we would just be about prejudice reduction," she said. "We needed to have a new resolution." The Task Force's 1996 report was titled "Journey Toward Wholeness."

This planning, strategizing, and organizing led to a reaffirmation of the 1992 resolution on racial and cultural diversity. At its April 1997 meeting, the Board of Trustees voted to place a resolution on the General Assembly agenda. The one adopted in 1997 was more specific in its directives about who was to participate: The 1997 General Assembly Resolution was titled, "Toward an Anti-Racist Unitarian Universalist Association" and read:

> WHEREAS the 1996 General Assembly resolved that all congregations, districts, organizations, and professional and lay leaders participate in a reflection-action process throughout the 1996–97 church year using the Congregational Reflection and Action Process Guide and the Anti-Racism Assessment; and
>
> WHEREAS our Unitarian Universalist principles call us to affirm and promote "justice, equity, and compassion in human relations" and "the goal of world community"; and
>
> WHEREAS our history as Unitarian Universalists includes evidence of both great commitment and individual achievement in the struggle for racial justice as well as the failure of our Unitarian Universalist institutions to respond fully to the call for justice; and
>
> WHEREAS racism and its effects, including economic injustice, are embedded in all social institutions as well as in ourselves and will not be eradicated without deliberate engagement in analysis and action; and

WHEREAS because of the impact of racism on all people, and the interconnection among oppressions, we realize we need to make an institutional commitment to end racism; and

WHEREAS the social, economic, and ecological health of our planet is imperiled by the deepening divisions in our world caused by inequitable and unjust distribution of power and resources; and

WHEREAS we are called yet again by our commitment to faith in action to pursue this anti-racist, multi-cultural initiative in the spirit of justice, compassion, and community;

THEREFORE BE IT RESOLVED that the 1997 General Assembly urges Unitarian Universalists to examine carefully their own conscious and unconscious racism as participants in a racist society, and the effect that racism has on all our lives, regardless of color.

BE IT FURTHER RESOLVED that the General Assembly urges the Unitarian Universalist Association, its congregations, and community organizations to develop an ongoing process for the comprehensive institutionalization of anti-racism and multi-culturalism, understanding that whether or not a group becomes multi-racial, there is always the opportunity to become anti-racist. Early steps toward anti-racism might include using curricula such as Journey Toward Wholeness for all age groups, forming racial justice committees, and conducting anti-racism workshops.

BE IT FURTHER RESOLVED that the General Assembly urges all Unitarian Universalist leaders, including ministers, religious educators, leaders of associate and affiliate organizations, governing boards, Unitarian Universalist Association staff, theological schools, and future General Assemblies to engage in ongoing anti-racism training, to examine basic assumptions, structures, and functions, and, in response to what is learned, to develop action plans.

BE IT FURTHER RESOLVED that Unitarian Universalists are encouraged to enter into relationships of sustained engagement with all people of color with a goal of opening up authentic dialogue that may include, but is not limited to, race and racism. Such dialogue should also include how to appropriately honor and affirm the cultural traditions of all people of color.

BE IT FURTHER RESOLVED that the General Assembly requests that the UUA Board of Trustees establish a committee to monitor and assess our transformation as an anti-racist, multi-cultural institution, and that the Board of Trustees shall report annually to the General Assembly specifically on the programs and resources dedicated to assisting our congregations in carrying out the objectives of this resolution.

BE IT FURTHER RESOLVED that in order to transform the racist institutions of our world, the General Assembly urges the Unitarian Universalist Association and all its parts to establish relationships with other international and interfaith organizations that are working to dismantle racism.

At the same time this resolution was introduced at the General Assembly, a packet of materials for congregations prepared by the Racial and Cultural Diversity Task Force the previous year and titled "Journey Toward Wholeness, the Next Step: From Racial and Cultural Diversity to Anti-Oppression and Anti-Racist Multiculturalism" was distributed. For a handful of congregations, this was an opportunity to move ahead.

The tools developed as part of the Journey Toward Wholeness effort were designed to chart a course for congregations. Rev. Dr. Fredric Muir of the Unitarian Universalist Church of Annapolis, Maryland, was receptive and took them back to his congregation after General Assembly. "I said to myself we're going to do this and take it and see where it goes. Here's exactly what the congregation has been asking for," he recalled. "I had a feeling this is what every congregation in the UUA has been asking for, and that is a direction. There was a three- or five-session curriculum, and we did that. We

VOICE
Tomas Firle

Tomas Firle is a member of the First UU Church of San Diego, California.

In the mid-80s I had gotten a wake-up call about "male privilege" through participation in UU men's groups. I got a wake-up call in March 1998 at an anti-racism weekend training in New Orleans. Here I was, a whit e immigrant [who had] experienced racial discrimination—I did not recognize that I now had white privilege in American society. And I was not conscious of it. And I still have white privilege.

My partner Joan Cudhea and I got turned on by an AR [anti-racism] weekend training in 1998. We asked Revs. Tom and Carolyn Owen-Towle to reactivate AR work via the JTW Program. . . . We were encouraged and trusted to move forward responsibly. First off, we insisted on a formal Board action designating that anti-racism be a major policy focus. The Board, as elected Trustees, must "own" this commitment. We then formed a JTW Transformation Team [not the UUA version] to bring [to] the entire congregation awareness of oppressive inequalities, including those in our own institution.

We insisted on participation by a Board member, active, not just as liaison. Tom [Owen-Towle] attended most of our monthly meetings. We have benefited greatly from the wise guidance from Robette Dias and Rev. William (Chester) McCall during his interim ministry with us. We deliberately delegated AR action issues to a separate task group, "Organizing for Justice."

Our church is allied in coalition with more than 20 other churches, with mostly people of color membership, for community organizing and civic actions. We had to learn to be "allies," letting affected groups identify their own needs and decide how and what they wanted to do. We continue to participate as an accepted equal partner.

We have formed a covenanted "white allies" caucus and people of color meet on their own and with us. We have DRUUMM people and a Board member on our JTW team. Both of our search committees had people of color and LGBT members on it and so has our Board of Trustees.

Yet there has been denial and resistance from individual church members with harassment of people of color. White members involved in this work have also been harassed with telephone calls. Weekly refreshed clippings of bias incidents, local as well as national, on our bulletin board have been repeatedly removed and others defaced. Despite these acts by individuals, our congregation has been supportive of AR work and training. Our Jubilee I and II's and other events are well attended by an increasingly wider range of members.

[We] continue in this work, focused on building individual awareness of our members, and focus on our own institutional racism. This work has been and continues to be our ministry. We have made mistakes and failed. We were and are blessed to be actively supported by our ministers and Board and many church leaders. I say blessed because apparently many UU ministers had not been supportive of the UUA's JTW program, even resistant, fearful of the reaction of their congregation.

did the curriculum and I led it. I came back, and kind of the way I often do things when I want to get people's attention, is I'll preach a sermon about it and I'll have people get really excited and sign up. I had seventy people sign up for the class. . . . At the beginning I said what I really want to come out of this eventually is an ongoing JTW team that will pick up some of these themes, set an agenda for addressing the initiative, and become a part of the church structure. That's what happened. I ran the five classes and then eventually had about twenty people want to keep going and they became, for approximately three to four years, the church's voice of anti-racism in the church and interfacing with the community."

Other efforts were more home-grown. At First Unitarian Church of Dallas, Hallman recalled,

> In 1997, we started a group called CDARE—Cultural Diversity and Antiracism Empowerment group. And in 1997–98 they planned events and again, it was trying to bring people in and have informative discussions and have a variety of programs. It wasn't a sort of driving, ongoing program; it was an adult religious education program, a social program of the church. Then in 1998, we signed on for the Jubilee World workshop from the UUA Faith in Action, a day-and-a-half event, and we had seventy congregants.

The Dallas church had found that the general program from the UUA, based on the Crossroads Ministry approach, was aimed at smaller congregations than theirs and so sought their own resources to accomplish the larger goal put forward by the 1997 General Assembly resolution.

Fulfilling the Promise Effort

Passage of the 1997 resolution seemed less of an event, perhaps because a number of other initiatives were introduced during that General Assembly. Concurrent to the work of the Journey Toward Wholeness, the Board of Trustees appointed a strategic planning team to consider how the Association might think about and plan for the years ahead. The committee met for the first time in January of 1997 and proposed renaming itself the "Fulfilling the Promise Committee." The Board approved the name change as well a statement of purpose: "to call the UUA member congregations into a participatory process of ongoing renewal so that needs and aspirations will be made explicit, [and] a covenant of shared goals, resource commitments, and supportive structures will be realized, and Unitarian Universalism will fulfill its promise in the world."

The committee undertook a survey and received about ten thousand responses. Some of the questions addressed the new Journey Toward Wholeness initiative. In presenting the survey results, Rev. Clark Olsen, Fulfilling the Promise Committee member, noted,

The challenge is to better understand, for our time and the future, what we shall do together, in our congregations and in our association of congregations. That may seem abstract, but beneath the words lies a deep sense that we have not yet understood our potential, not yet put our purposes and principles adequately to work, not yet discovered the full promise of our faith and of our association.

. . . As the Unitarian Universalist Association—our bylaws say we are member congregations in covenant with each other. *How do we define that covenant? What does it mean to be "We, the member congregations"? Given who we are, what shall we do together?*

About that last question—both as individual congregations and as an association of congregations, "What shall we do together?"—if we answer only in terms of committees, structures and programs, we shall have failed to accept the depth of the challenge. If we answer in terms of fundamental understanding of our covenant, we shall find we have said something deeply important to ourselves and the world.

Journey Toward Wholeness Committee

The 1997 resolution called for the establishment of a Journey Toward Wholeness Oversight Committee and the UUA Board of Trustees appointed the initial members at its June 24 meeting. The first com-

FINDINGS
Fulfilling the Promise Survey

The Fulfilling the Promise Committee designed a survey in 1997 to "stimulate deep thought and as profound conversation as possible throughout our association." These are questions that pertain to anti-racism and anti-oppression.

Question #4: *What is missing for you in your UU experience?*
Virtually tied for first: "Greater intensity of celebration, joy and spirituality" and "More racial and cultural diversity and diversity of perspectives."

Question #7: *How do you respond to the call for greater racial/cultural diversity in our membership?*
41%—"It's about time. This is central to my faith and theology."
6%— "This whole thing is just about political correctness."

Question #9: *What are the deepest yearnings of your heart?*
The answers were fairly well balanced across all six choices:
• To make a difference, help build a more just world
• To become whole/find meaning
• Happiness, nurturance and love for my children/family
• Peace and harmony
• To be known and loved
• To feel I am part of a wondrous creation

Question #13: *To what extent should your congregation contribute to spreading the UU faith?*
66%—"Be outspoken in our community, a voice for justice based on our principles."

mittee meeting was held on October 21, 1997. The members present were Ruth Alatorre, Rachael Brown, Ivan Cottman, Robette Dias, Rev. Galen Guengerich, Hoover, Jacqui James, and the chair, Rev. Susan Suchocki. Member Dr. Leon Spencer was absent. The committee discussed its mission statement, provided by the UUA Board:

> The mission of the Journey Toward Wholeness Committee is to strategically plan, guide, facilitate, coordinate, and monitor the transformation of the UUA into an Anti-oppressive, Anti-racist, Multicultural faith community.

The identity of the committee was ambiguous even before it was established. Particularly unclear was the committee's role in setting the direction of anti-racism training. At the Black Concerns Working Group meeting before General Assembly, Spencer expressed "frustration that there is a conception that JTW Oversight Committee was supposed to implement JTW. This is not right. The committee is just gathering and presenting information. Accountability is now on the institutional system to move forward."

The committee's discussion began by dealing with the ambiguity of the group's charge, something that would be revisited over and over in the coming years:

> We discussed the name and role(s) of the committee. Some concern was expressed about the word "oversight" and the possibly loaded aspects of it for some people. The resolution makes it clear that this group is to monitor and assess, but does not use the phrase "oversight." Susan said the language in the resolution outlines responsibilities and scope of the committee's work. She reminded us that this is a Board committee and one of its responsibilities is to annually give a report to the General Assembly. Galen would like to see this as a coordinating committee but would remove the element of monitoring and assessing. He doesn't particularly like the use of "oversight," but did feel it might give it added clout. Ivan likes the monitoring and assessing and is won-

dering about the coordinating aspect. To him, coordinating means a great deal more than monitoring and assessing function. We need more discussion about this because it defines the role of the committee.

The meaning of the phrase in the resolution, "toward an anti-racist UUA" was also raised. Ruth feels there needs to be clarity about our language and the scope of our charge (institution versus association; bureaucracy versus rank and file, etc.). We agreed that "institution" encompasses all UUA organizations and affiliates as well as headquarters.

Decision was reached that our name should be the Journey Toward Wholeness Committee (JTWC). This allows for flexibility and gets away from the term "oversight."

The new committee's role in measuring progress was also discussed. The minutes reported: "Effective justice work that results in change, requires different staging at different levels. We need to create a measurement tool so we can know how this work is progressing. It's not possible for us to know exactly what outcome the GA delegates had in mind when they voted for this resolution but we need to determine how we will know when we have fulfilled the mandates of the resolution."

How much authority the new committee could have was also discussed with this summarized conclusion:

One of the realities of the resources we create to help dismantle racism is that once created, we have no control over how they are used. They assume a life of their own; some people/congregations use them effectively, others don't. The best we can do is to try to create resources to meet the needs as we perceive them. We are not in a position to police how they are used. We need to evaluate the effectiveness of resources created, but evaluating and policing are not the same.

VISION
Rev. Susan Suchocki

Suchocki was the first chair of the Journey Toward Wholeness Committee. Later she reflected in a sermon the significance of this experience, which she considered an honor.

The Journey Toward Wholeness Transformation Committee has been involved in strategically planning, coordinating, monitoring, guiding and assessing the transformation of the UUA into an antiracist, anti-oppressive, multicultural faith community. As spiritual leader in a congregation, I work for that same vision. Most often it will probably be the minister to be the first one to step ahead. In fact, according to a survey from 1996, congregations look toward their ministers to be the leaders on the journey toward wholeness. "Unitarian Universalists who believe their minister's attitudes are extremely important in forming the attitudes of the congregation consistently report higher levels of diversity, higher levels of diverse programming in the church, higher levels of outreach into the community on issues of social justice and higher levels of activity in the congregation to reduce racism." But to be successful the congregation and the minister must together decide to put diversity and anti-oppression on the church's agenda.

The process I engage in to build a genuine beloved community has been to walk and work with all groups and persons to build relationships of covenant and commitment so that we can together help to transform our religion into an antiracist multicultural faith.

Do you wonder what an antiracist, multicultural faith institution would be like? [I say that] at its core it would have a genuine love for all and it would have an institutional understanding of oppressions. The operating and guiding principles, the Bylaws and the use of all resources fiscal, personnel and property would reflect an understanding of linked oppressions: heterosexism, ableism, classism, sexism, ageism, classism, racism; for when any person or group is not fully involved in the life of the institution the entire institution suffers.

If we as spiritual persons are successful we will pave the way for others within our UU world and the larger world to be in relationships of accountability, of spiritual nurture and sustenance, of advocacy and of organization. If we as spiritual persons are successful we will pave the way for communities to engage in authentic relationships committed to rejoice, mourn, learn and explore together ways of making a difference in the world.

The General Assembly in Rochester

At the 1998 General Assembly, the Journey Toward Wholeness Committee received fifteen minutes to address the plenary session and Davidoff addressed its work in her moderator's report.

Before the Rochester Assembly, the Unitarian Universalist Native and Indigenous Americans initiated conversations about bringing up that the site of the General Assembly was on Seneca land. Ill feelings arose when UUNIA leaders went through the process of trying to get a session to discuss these and other issues and were denied. The new Journey Toward Wholeness Committee, established as part of the 1997 resolution, discussed what sort of outreach they could make to the General Assembly Planning Committee to point out a pattern of acts seen as disrespectful to people of color that had occurred at Charlotte and Phoenix.

Suchocki, the Journey Toward Wholeness Committee chair, said that at that General Assembly, the committee "presented its report to the delegates and we handed out buttons. [Rev.] Kurt Kuhwald and I, with input from the committee, had written a responsive reading that spoke of failing-succeeding, trying-rethinking, commitment and willingness to get involved. It was hard to see the faces of the delegates but I do know that I saw many persons around me in tears, and throughout that GA I heard comments made that the report had affected a shift in the focus from the negative to a willingness to engage. . . . As a member of my congregation who had been in the audience to assist remarked, that presentation showed them that the delegates wanted to engage even if the UUA didn't."

Also at the General Assembly, sociologist Robert Bellah, author of *Habits of the Heart*, presented some stark statistics about race and the UUA, revealing the demographics to be 97.6 percent European-American or white; 2.5 percent Native American/Indigenous, 1.3 percent African-American or of African descent, 1.1 percent Latina/o/Hispanic, and .8 percent Asian American (with participants able to mark more than one racial category).

An incident at the Rochester General Assembly became a marker for youth and young adult anti-racism advocates. Rev. Joseph Santos-Lyons described it in his 2006 seminary thesis:

At the 1998 GA in Rochester, New York, a young adult of color was informed upon reaching the front desk to check into her room, that she had no reservation. After a period of discussion, intensified by frustration and the crushing presence of other GA delegates seeking to check-in, the young woman was dismissed with condescension. She had to seek out the UUA Director of Young Adult Ministry, a White minister with whom she had a working relationship, and together they approached the manager. In this follow-up, the room was secured. A complaint was made with the hotel and with the regional office based on the discourteous and patronizing behavior of the front desk staff and management. The loosely organized network of Young Adults of Color also came to the young woman's aid, and similar stories were shared. In conclusion, the manager of the hotel came to a gathering of the Young Adults of Color meeting to apologize and ordered a buffet of foods for the final group meeting of GA.

As part of the youth movement, Elandria Williams, a youth member of the newly formed Thomas Jefferson District Anti-Racism Team, a district-based vehicle for generating discussions about anti-racism ideas, recalled moments of great connection—and moments of great disconnection: "All these white guys were talking slang. . . . We all walked around as a collective. I thought, 'This is beautiful.' And people looked at us like we were crazy. We spent a lot of time talking about gangs and violence because that was what we were dealing with. It was deep." And yet she felt resistance from others who didn't want to room with a "black girl." At a coffeehouse held one evening, degrading comments were made about the sexual prowess of different ethnic and racial groups and Williams said she left in tears: "I didn't go back until Long Beach GA" in 2004. Because of her experience in Rochester, she chose not to get involved at the continental level and worked instead at her high school where her town was embroiled in a debate about displaying the Confederate flag.

Article Highlights Controversy

An article in the July/August 1998 issue of *World* magazine featured a cover story on race and class. The lead article was a group interview with Hoover, co-director of the Faith in Action Department; Rev. Dr. Thandeka, a Unitarian Universalist theologian, and Tom Turnipseed, a lay leader, discussing race. The opening of the story described the atmosphere as contentious. One slice of the dialogue exposes some of the tensions:

WORLD: Can you talk more concretely about how UUs might heal themselves?

THANDEKA: I start by asking Euro-American UUs to recollect their earliest memories of the formation of their white identities. What comes forth is feelings of exile and abandonment because they did something wrong—usually by showing what their parents saw as undue interest in a nonwhite person or people—and when they go back to these feelings, more often than not they begin to cry because they pull up into consciousness extreme feelings of risk they had as a child, feelings that somehow they weren't loved enough, so that there was something wrong with them.

My approach gives them a vocabulary to look without guilt at the way they've been injured. As a result, they're interested in developing rituals for their Sunday morning services that help them deal with the way congregation members have been injured and in developing healing practices that will transform them into people who can stay the course when they do social justice work.

HOOVER: This is what, 1998? And I started asking whites that question about early racial memories, along with the UUA Black Concerns Working Group, in 1986. We probably asked 10,000 to 20,000 UU's in that time. And you're right—a lot of folks have trouble finding language for their experience. But even if they get in touch with the personal dynamics, what we discovered about five or six years into asking the question Thandeka's now asking is that whites say to us, "My getting myself healed doesn't change the culture, either for whites or people of color. There's another, systemic level of this that we have to look at changing." Otherwise, it's like pulling the bodies out of the river instead of going upriver and finding out why bodies are ending up in the water.

THANDEKA: Oh, I agree with that . . . .

TURNIPSEED: We're all saying the same thing. Beyond the rituals and beyond examining our belly buttons and our shame and guilt, for liberal faith people the ultimate healing is in the doing—in interaction and doing social justice.

HOOVER: I'd like to add that obviously class is very tough for us to talk about. Folks with money don't talk about money publicly. We think of ourselves as good people, justice-seeking good folks, and we know there's an awful lot of wrong in the world, and we don't want to see ourselves in that wrong. But we have to really wrestle with that and begin to own that because, if we want to talk about seeking truth, we have to admit that we can distribute our assets differently. We can make choices about what we benefit from and what the culture gives us and how we apply it. To really own that as part of the faith would change some behaviors. I mean we wouldn't be begging for money for justice issues if our folks truly believed in making justice in the world.

We have got to start saying, "We're not a middle-class culture; we're an *upper*-middle-class culture. We're the shapers of this damn world. We're the gatekeepers sitting in key places all around the country that impact people's lives in policies and programs." Because we're not using our faith as much as we could in those places and spaces, and we clearly don't have a collective vision that we're putting out for the culture to challenge what's out there currently. If we really want to talk about speaking truth to power, we have to speak it first to ourselves because we *are* power.

Growth Versus Diversity at GA

At the Nashville General Assembly in 1999, the Journey Toward Wholeness and Fulfilling the Promise shared the focus. "I thought the coherency of vision was missing," recalled Paula Cole Jones, a member of All Souls Church in Washington, D.C., who is of African descent.

Hoover recalled,

"Fulfilling the Promise" was launched and managed as a separate major effort requiring attention and resources. In fact it became, no matter what its intent, a separate and more equal agenda. Instead of working from the strength of a comprehensive plan integrated with the anti-racist, anti-oppression, multicultural initiative, it was often experienced by many as a competing vision. . . . There was always a tension in our faith between growth and diversity. The Journey Toward Wholeness leadership was saying if we are going to become a diverse institution, we might have to grow more slowly. We might have to lose some people in the short term even in order to lay the right groundwork to both assist and allow people to truly grow into the vision of being an anti-racist, anti-oppression, multicultural faith and learning how to live that faith in all we think and do.

The Board and Anti-Racism

Rev. Dr. William Jones, long an active voice on issues of race within Unitarian Universalism and member of the Board of Trustees, felt the attention paid to racism in this period of time was important, noting,

It provided a particular model for addressing the problem which can then become, or which then became, the basis for criticism and renegotiation, correction, and so forth. To me, getting started down this path was something that was very positive. . . . People started discussing it and people began . . . to look at their faith communities in light of, and making a judgment about, the essential character of their faith community in light of how it was responding to this issue of oppression. And that, to me, is all to the good.

Jones eventually resigned his Board position. He reflected later that he found himself in a position of "frustration and problematics of trying to solve this problem from a position on the Board. My model [of how to address race as an issue] indicated at the very beginning that this was not going to work, but that was based on my model, so I'm in the context of the Board, where a different model is being presented, and I'm called upon to make evaluative judgments about that and that, to me, creates a conflict of interest situation, which I finally resolved by resigning from the Board, which would give me the space and freedom to challenge the model in what I thought was a more appropriate venue."

Jones was not supportive of the approach the Journey Toward Wholeness efforts took, reflecting in 2006,

> The failure, the problem, to me, has to do with the choice of a faulty methodology at the outset. If you're trying to correct a situation, trying to reduce oppression, to me, you have to adopt what we call a virus-vaccine model. When a hostile virus enters our life's circle, we try to develop resources and strategies to protect ourselves from it, and one of those strategies, following the virus of oppression metaphor, is we develop vaccines or antitoxins. But an effective vaccine production does not start off focusing on the vaccine. You first must focus, give dedicated attention to the virus and map its life cycle, what it's vulnerable to, what nurtures it, and know its maintenance needs. Only after you have developed that kind of specific profile, do you start to focus on vaccine production, because the vaccine has to identify the vulnerabilities of the virus and attack those.
>
> The UU analysis of oppression had several problems or errors with it. One, it did not recognize that racism, oppression, has mutated. Racism has mutated. . . . A mutant virus—there's no universal vaccine. The vaccine is always virus-specific. We may have developed an effective vaccine for the premutant form, but when we apply that to the mutation, it's not going to work.

That, to me, was the problem. We did not have an accurate understanding of the racism or oppression that we were attempting to correct. We made some errors in thinking that increasing diversity effectively reduces oppression, and to me, it does not. But the faulty understanding of the nature and operation of oppression and the consequences of that, to me, was a major problem.

Another Board issue with anti-racism was maintaining a continuity of opinion in an organization run by volunteers who work on limited terms. The turnover meant that a group might reach consensus on anti-racism and then see its membership change; with the new members could come a new understanding—or lack of understanding—of the commitment. This was true at all levels, including the Board of Trustees. In 1999, six new Board members entered and took part in a training with a consultant. The minutes describe its outcomes thus:

> The Board meeting started with a very intense retreat with six new Trustees, with the theme of "What Does It Mean To Be a UUA Trustee?" led by U.T. Saunders [a Boston-based consultant]. At the end of the retreat we confirmed a Covenant with one another. Here they are in a preliminary, slightly edited form:
> We will stay in relationship even in disagreement or conflict; we will respect our communal meeting time, using it to advance the designated agenda; we will focus on policy issues, not management; we will work to find balance between good, inclusive process and closure on substantial matters; we will presume good faith; we will not re-do the work of the working groups and committees, and we will own that work; we will be honest and direct with each other; we will speak out when something is of serious concern, asking questions rather than making attributions, working on an issue directly with the person(s) concerned, supporting and encouraging others to do the same; we will practice

confession and forgiveness; we will attend to and manage
the energy level and spiritual tenor of the meeting; we will
treat each other with respect, not interrupting nor speaking
when we have not been recognized, listening to and respecting the recognized speaker, minimizing side comments.

Other Developments

New name. A lack of cohesiveness on the Journey Toward Wholeness Committee itself was an issue its membership discussed when
they met again in October 1999. As the group struggled to identify
their mission, they renamed themselves the Journey Toward Wholeness Transformation Committee. Tensions with the Core Team
also led to a recommendation from that group that they disband
and reform as a working group with members of the JTWTC. Once
again, the focus was on the need for communications and outreach,
as this excerpt from the minutes illustrated: "There is a lack of
knowledge among our people and ministers are key to getting out
the message. We need to develop sound bites for ministers and REs
[religious educators]."

Culture shift. The GA Planning Committee opened a dialogue
around anti-racism and anti-oppression. Suchocki recalled,

> [T]he GA Planning Committee shifted its culture and ways
> of doing business. From 1998–2003, they maintained a close
> relationship with the Journey Toward Wholeness Transfor-
> mation Committee, asking questions, engaging in difficult
> dialogue, demonstrating a transparency and vulnerability
> while trying new ways of structuring GA, assessing policies
> and practices that were perceived as being oppressive and
> then changing many of these. Plus they changed not just
> about "racism" but were willing to engage in and look at all
> areas of oppression.

UUSC's focus. Valora Washington, an African American, became
director of the Unitarian Universalist Service Committee in 1999
and began to take the organization in directions that certainly could

be seen as sympathetic to the work of anti-racism. In an interview with *UU World* in 2000, she described the priorities of her administration as the empowerment of women; protecting the rights of indigenous people and oppressed racial and ethnic groups, particularly around their civil and political rights; environmental justice; protecting children, and responding strategically to wars and natural disasters. As part of the planning process, she noted,

> Of course, when we come to this vision about what we want to become and the areas in which we're going to focus, we do that very mindful of our history. For example, the Service Committee has played a courageous role in combating racism and injustice related to race and ethnicity. The Service Committee was taking stands in the 1940s and 1950s—ahead of the curve—for desegregation and to protect the rights of oppressed minority groups. Today, when we set out on new projects in communities of color, we can build on our former strategies and ideas, and our history helps us build credibility and trust. People respect that we've been doing this kind of work for more than 50 years.

Though Washington's tenure was to be less than four years, for a brief period of time Unitarian Universalists could point to African-American leadership in two of the major Unitarian Universalist institutions.

CHAPTER 11

Strategies for Training

With the passage of the 1997 General Assembly resolution and the formation of groups interested in promoting an anti-racist position, more emphasis was put on training people to become more effective at seeing race through an anti-racist lens. The approach developed by the partnership between Crossroads Ministry and the Association's Core Team, made up of Faith in Action Department staff and key volunteers, was the focus of discussion while the Jubilee I workshops of the Black Concerns Working Group continued to reach more congregations.

Trainings based on the approach of Crossroads Ministry, a Chicago-based nonprofit founded by Rev. Joseph Barndt, a Lutheran minister and social activist, were developed in this period. For many who attended these trainings, a real change in perspective took place, which later would be linked by some observers to institutional changes. Rev. Danielle DiBona, an Association staff member from 2000 to 2003, observed,

> As an association, the UUA began "training" people to be anti-racist. They began with groups like the Board of Trustees and the staff. At the same time people were being trained to go out into the congregations to do anti-racism work. Although there were many fits and starts at the Association level, I think it became apparent to all that the UUA was going to move forward no matter what. . . .
>
> I think the Association did hear the demand for better, more real, more transformative anti-racist change . . . then go with the model that was at hand in an effort to get moving on the process. It is very clear to me that there has been

significant movement. The Board of Trustees, for example, continues to make an effort to view their work through an anti-racist lens. That works in fits and starts because of the regular turnover and, I sense, the back-sliding around training up new members. However, because of the anti-racism work in the 90s, there are enough white folks out there to continue to raise the anti-racist questions. For example, the [Association's Ministerial Fellowship Committee, which credentials clergy] finally, finally heard from DRUUMM [the Diverse and Revolutionary Unitarian Universalist Ministries] and POC [people of color] that they needed to do more to prepare seminarians to begin to have an anti-racist lens.

POC are being heard at the national level. I sincerely do not believe that that could have happened without the anti-racist work/Jubilee work/Transformation Committee/and Crossroads. Some examples: As the VP of DRUUMM, I was invited to meet with the MFC to share with them some of the needs of POC; when all hell broke loose at Meadville Lombard, there was an attempt to address the issues at a systemic level rather than at an individual level; when the leadership of the UUA began to meet to discuss the futures and presence of ministers and seminarians of color, POC were able to get a voice at the table.

Before the UUA began its anti-racist work, these examples would have been either ignored or identified as issues between/amongst individuals. There would never have been a concept of white power and privilege and how it played out in all of these situations.

Advocates who experienced the trainings found them illuminating. Rev. Dr. Anita Farber-Robinson recalled that the Racial and Cultural Diversity Task Force experienced one of the first trainings. "We got so much out of that meeting," she recalled. The Task Force decided to expand the training to other stakeholders.

The trainings offered a different framework than had been offered before and had pluses and minuses. "Crossroads brought two important assets to the UUA's anti-racism work, the power

PRINCIPLES OF
Organizing to Dismantle Institutional Racism

Crossroads Ministry detailed these principles of organizing to dismantle institutional racism in a 1996 handout.

1. The task is organizing for systemic change.

Racism is a systemic issue, more than personal or attitudinal; it is manifested individually, institutionally, and culturally.

Institutions need to be equipped to implement new expectations of racial justice.

An institution needs to develop an analysis of its own systemic racism.

2. The organizing task is to develop an anti-racist institutional identity.

Multicultural diversity is either racist or anti-racist.

There needs to be a marriage of anti-racism and multicultural diversity.

Anti-racism is not negative, but a positive identity and action.

3. The organizing task is an "inside job."

Past institutional changes have been mostly responses to outside forces.

The 1990s bring a new opportunity to initiate institutional change from within.

Internal change requires institutional endorsement, mandate and acceptance.

4. A specific model for change is needed for each specific situation.

There are no generic models.

Each model for change must reflect the language/structure of the institution.

For religious institutions, a faith-based model is required, reflecting the language, beliefs and structure of the religious institution.

5. Trained, equipped leadership teams are needed.

Each team must be affirmed, endorsed, called and sent by the institution.

Each team must develop a common team and analysis.

Each team must develop organizing and teaching/training skills.

6. Anti-racism transformation is long-range, even generational.

A 20- to 30-year plan is necessary.

The eventual goal is the institutionalization of anti-racism.

7. Institutional change is a component of community change.

The task is not only transformation within the institution, but also for the institution to participate in societal change.

In dismantling racism, the institution is accountable to the communities of color that racism oppresses.

analysis and the internal institutional organizing model," recalled Robette Dias, a lay leader at this time. She added,

> The power analysis Crossroads introduced to the UUA began to develop some shared language and conceptual understanding of race issues that was very helpful to begin to build a critical mass of UU's who were moved to deal with institutional racism in the UUA. On the downside, Crossroads' power analysis was narrowly focused on a Black/White analysis of race; this frustrated a number of People of Color, especially those of us who were not African American. This was one of the first things addressed by the Jubilee II trainers when they started doing the UUA's version of the analysis training and it was a significant and important contribution to the whole Crossroads network. The power analysis, with its focus on white supremacy and white identity as the problem of racism was resisted by a significant number of UUs because of its discomforting impact. Crossroads' internal institutional organizing model of building an internal "transformation team" to strategically guide the anti-racism initiative was also a powerful contribution to the UUA's work. Although the UUA did not fully adopt the model as designed and recommended by Crossroads, the Journey Toward Wholeness Transformation Committee made significant contributions to the work. The part of the model the UUA left off is also significant in that it left JTWTC vulnerable around its accountability, because of this JTWTC was not able to leverage the power of the anti-racist constituency when the JTWTC priorities diverged from the administration's, thus weakening JTWTC and the overall initiative.

Elandria Williams, a founding member of the Thomas Jefferson District Transformation Team, recalled,

> Crossroads, like the few other organizations that were doing cutting edge transformational work around race, were made

up of people who had been involved in the work for some time, many since or before the Civil Rights Movement. It is important for organizations to work with people and organizations that are trusted and ones in which relationships have been built. That has and still does create a challenge for younger leaders and organizers that due to their age will not have these relationships. They however stuck with me through those challenging times and because of the many lessons that I learned from them as an organization as well as the People's Institute for Survival and Beyond I am able to still continue with the work. The funny thing is that I now go to gatherings or events and since I started so young— at 29, I have known people 10–12 years, which makes me an "old head"!

The trainings strained relationships from the beginning. Rev. William Sinkford, who would become the first African-American president of the Association and who had witnessed the effects of the trainings as a staff member, recalled,

The trainings continued and the pushback became enormous, particularly from ministers, and I'm talking particularly about older white ministers who found the theological language of basically Lutheran-informed language and theological concepts more than they could tolerate. They didn't want to engage with the issue because many of them had been burned in the earlier period, so the pushback became enormous. It was difficult to get congregations to engage with the trainings beyond what we now call the Jubilee I, which everybody was happy to do—it was kind of a 101 which leaves people feeling good.

The basic premises of the approach were challenged by many. Dr. Jon Rice, an adjunct faculty member at Meadville Lombard Theological School, gave voice to one type of opinion:

There is a good sentiment here. The anti-racism initiative wants to create a world free from racism. The people who run it are willing to embrace those who admit their "race" and are in pain, and are willing to share that pain. That is noble, but lacks critical analysis and thereby it fails at understanding. When you fail to challenge what you may come to know are a person's misperceptions, based often times on the damaging experiences they have had, you are not helping that person. I think that ending racism begins with acknowledging the illogic of race, and then acting as if race did not exist. For those of us who are openly black to take up the responsibility that goes with our power and to help those who regard themselves as white to work past the illusion that they are a part of, and thereby responsible for, the ruling institutions on this planet. Most so-called white people are as victimized as everyone else, and as hurt, and without the cultural apparatus for healing themselves, which is why white people often borrow black cultural coping apparatus— in order to survive.

Rev. Clyde Grubbs, a Native American, noted that references to "Crossroads" became a code that expressed dissatisfaction with a wide range of anti-racism issues. For some it captured their dislike of focusing on racist attitudes within the Association rather than in the outside world; for others, it captured their dislike of the training methods used by the organization and Barndt, its founder; for others, resistance to the strong leadership of Rev. Melvin Hoover; for others, discomfort with the increased organization of those historically marginalized into groups such as DRUUMM and LUUNA (the Latina/o Unitarian Universalist Networking Association).

Working Group Changes
The Black Concerns Working Group marked its tenth anniversary in 1995 and noted in a report it published that year that the number of Jubilee I workshops it delivered in congregational and other settings had quadrupled over the decade. Those events continued to be received positively by many who participated. "I will take home awareness that I have racist attitudes and practices simply by the fact that I was born a white American. I can't change the past but I can change today," one Jubilee participant wrote. Wrote another,

"In the first couple of hours, I was distressed by the misunderstanding of racism many people seemed to express. Later I felt honored that many people shared genuine feelings and experiences. I leave feeling hopeful that little by little we might make a change."

With new groups emerging, the Working Group's agenda became less clear, especially since some of its members were also participating in the training model developed with Crossroads Ministry. For example, after the Journey Toward Wholeness Committee was established, identities and roles were uncertain, and when the Faith in Action Department was formed and began developing its own training strategies, the Working Group faced more competition for resources and for those seeking training. In the fall of 1997 the Working Group wrestled with what its role should be:

> We agreed that the name of the group is no longer reflective of the actual work we do. In the discussion, the following issues were considered: In the past, broadening the emphasis to all oppressed groups was a tactic used to dilute the effort to eliminate racism against blacks; Other people of color who are not black feel that what we do is not about them; Our work is already about anti-racism and multiculturalism and our name should reflect that; It might be presumptuous of us to change when we don't have other people of color involved in the discussion; and the change is really about what we do, not who we are, changing now would help us recruit people for the committee.

Only two years later, the Working group was changing its name because "Black Concerns" was no longer a broad enough agenda; two years after that, the group was defunct.

By 1997, the Working Group was also raising questions about the relationship with Crossroads Ministry. "We discussed the relationship of the Crossroads training to our training," the minutes reported. "The 3½ day Crossroads training makes you a UUA Core Trainer but not a 'Crossroads trainer.' The UUA is a member of Crossroads. The hope is to have a UU model which uses UU theological language." At a previous meeting, the Committee had reviewed the Crossroads video and determined that it was too "bor-

MEMBERS

Jubilee Working Group 1997–1998

Rev. Nannene Gowdy
Susan Gershwin
Larry Hutchison
Betty Holcomb
Rev. Kurt Kuhwald
Margaret Link
Rev. Melanie Morel Sullivan
Layla Rivera
Harvey Thomas
Sherry Weston

Staff: Hyh'nes Bakri, Rev. Melvin Hoover, Susan Leslie, Christine Murphy

ing" and too focused on the 1960s to be used in entirety as part of the Jubilee trainings. Later, it sent a letter to Hoover expressing the opinion "that the model should be a uniquely UU one, and not one based on any other religious tradition or tied to any particular leader."

The goals of the Jubilee Working Group were loosely defined as "raising awareness of racism and promoting anti-racism; support for people of color including involving them in the process and identifying potential leaders; training which includes developing a cadre of new Jubilee trainers; and record-keeping, assessment and analysis."

Group members also concluded that they had expertise to offer:

> After a long and very difficult discussion, we decided we would be the best group to design the next phase of the Journey Toward Wholeness. . . . [Our representatives] will write a letter to Bill Gardiner [of the Faith in Action Department] telling him we wish to undertake this task and that we would like to be the team that will work with him in January to begin developing this process. It will mean that along with an entirely new role, we will still be responsible for overseeing the Jubilee World workshops and continuing to foster the training of new Jubilee trainers.

The letter stated their position: "Creating a Jubilee World is the longest running anti-racism program of the UUA, with over 200 workshops conducted in every District over the course of 13 years. Over $0.5 million and 1300 person hours of UUA sponsored training experience have already been invested in developing this program to this point." The letter also noted that forty-five Jubilee trainers were in the network. It concluded, "We feel it is vitally important to bring other groups (Latino/Latina, Native American, Asian, disabled, gay, lesbian, bisexual, transgender) to the table so that all members of the UUA family can move towards wholeness. We have created a network that enables us to identify talented people and to nurture them in leadership positions." Later, the "Creating a Jubilee World" workshop would become known as Jubilee I and a workshop based on the Crossroads Ministry model would be known as Jubilee II.

The Working Group did not get clear responses to their proposals to become the primary training delivery system for the Association's anti-racism work. The lack of responsiveness by the Journey Toward Wholeness Transformation Team appears to have led to apathy and a feeling that it no longer made sense to meet. No other formal minutes exist from the group, which stopped meeting formally after this point. The impact of this group is perhaps best illustrated by considering the congregations they touched in 1988, their last year of formal operations. The Jubilee workshops continued under the Faith in Action umbrella. The original Jubilee workshop became "Jubilee I" while a "Jubilee II" contained more of the materials developed in conjunction with Crossroads Ministry.

The Working Group's dissolution was hard. "People had so much of their identity wrapped up in that," said Dr. Leon Spencer, a member, remembering that the disbanding was particularly hard on those who were white allies. "They had no place to go," he said.

"These people are still lost today," added Dias, who was on the UUA staff at that time.

District Teams Form

The Faith in Action staff facilitated the formation of anti-racism teams at the district level. In 1996, Massachusetts Bay became the first district to experiment with the model. Thomas Jefferson District joined the efforts in 1997 and the Joseph Priestley District came aboard in 1999. "I love working with these teams," Gardiner reflected in 2005. "These teams are actually living in multicultural reality. It's really powerful. It feeds my soul."

Yet work through the districts would prove a challenge. Barndt, the Crossroads Ministry founder, observed in 2006,

> One question Crossroads is still about the business of trying to answer is that of an association of congregations. If you can only change an institution from the inside, how do you relate to the association of congregations with the congregation? But the other piece of that in Unitarian Universalism is the weakness of the districts. . . . And one of the presuppositions in Crossroads' model is that there can be a district, or a diocesan power, to help congregations get into this work

EXAMPLE

A Year of Jubilee: Workshops Planned by the Jubilee Working Group for 1998

Birmington Unitarian Church, Bloomfield Hills, MI
Community UU Church, Daytona Beach, FL
Connecticut Valley District, CT
UU Church, Fargo, ND
First Parish in Concord, MA
First Unitarian Church of Orlando, FL
First Unitarian Church of Dallas, TX
First Unitarian Universalist Church, Detroit, MI
First UU Church of Stockton, CA
First Unitarian Universalist Church of Nashville, TN
First Universalist Church, Denver, CO
James Reeb UU Congregation, Madison, WI
Kitsap UU Fellowship, Bremerton, WA
Metro Detroit Churches, MI
Monte Vista UU Congregation, Montclair, CA
Olympia UU Congregation, WA
Second Unitarian Church of Chicago, IL
St. Cloud UU Fellowship, MN
Third Unitarian Church of Chicago, IL

Unitarian Church of Montpelier, VT
Unitarian Church of Norfolk, VA
Unitarian Church of Baton Rouge, LA
UU Church of Annapolis, MD
UU Church of Chattanooga, TN
UU Congregation of Greensboro, NC
UU Church of Palo Alto, CA
UU Church of Berks County,
    Reading, PA
UU Church of San Mateo, CA
UU Church of Savannah, GA
UU Church of Tallahassee, FL
UU Congregation at Shelter Rock,
    Manhasset, NY
UU Fellowship of Gainesville, FL
UU Fellowship of Huntington, NY
UU Fellowship of Raleigh, NC
UU Fellowship of Waco, TX
UU Society of Oneota, NY
The Unitarian Society of
    Ridgewood, NJ
West Hills UU Fellowship,
    Portland OR
Southeastern UU Winter Institute
Meadville Lombard Conference,
    "Engaging in Racial Justice"
President's Council Training in
    New Orleans, LA
Thomas Jefferson District Anti-Racism
    Conference
Urban Church Conference in
    Baltimore, MD

without having to force themselves on congregations. But groups like the Thomas Jefferson District have been struggling with that. And who in the UUA attributes any power to the district? . . .

Crossroads doesn't have any good answers to that either because it has a lot to do with authority. An archdiocese of Chicago of the Roman Catholic Church can have a cardinal who says, "We're gonna have three anti-racism teams, and they're gonna change the way congregations function." And, you know, at least it doesn't stop there. You know, there's nobody who stands up and says, "You can't do that." But there's still a bunch of pastors of the congregations, according to the cardinal, who say, "We don't care what the cardinal says, this is what we're gonna do." So at every level that question is . . . how do you take this to the depths of an institution? For five hundred years of white privilege and white power, you've got to be thinking in long-term. How do you make this enter into a UU congregation? So you all have been trying it, sometimes with a congregation, sometimes with a district.

Crossroads Influence Grows

The Association's Faith in Action Department, which was in a position to choose the Association's training models, promoted the Crossroads Ministry approach to anti-racism training. Hoover, who became a Crossroads board member in this period, said the Crossroads approach was particularly helpful because it addressed the black-white power question lingering since the Empowerment Controversies and because it put responsibility on white people for developing understanding of systemic dynamics around race.

"One positive outcome of the UUA's efforts is that I personally had a vocabulary to use when addressing these issues around race and racism in this country," Rev. Michael Carter, who experienced some of the earlier trainings and later became a trainer, noted. "That is to say that I could articulate my views without being easily written off as just another angry male person of color. I also was impressed by the fact that when we offered our workshops that there were interracial teams so as the dominant culture could listen to one of their own talking about the history and privileges that are shared just because one is 'white.' This always reminded me that there are some European Americans who are willing to speak truth to power around this issue because I used to work side by side with some of them."

In this new role of institutional transformation, not all went smoothly. "We did a series of national trainings in Boston," Barndt noted. "I don't remember how many . . . it must have been some- where between five and ten in the early years. And two of the most influential trainings were trainings that didn't work; we called them 'Trainings from Hell.' . . . Like adversity shapes character, it was some of the resistance and particularly those two trainings that shaped the commitment, the direction, of the UU folk about mov- ing forward. And so they stand out not only because they were such traumatic events, but because they became such an influence."

"The first groups always go through an intensive learning process—the first trainers, the first in congregations, the first anti- racism teams," observed Gardiner, of the Faith in Action Depart- ment and an anti-racism trainer. "The change processes that Crossroads developed were used in large denominational structures. We tried to adapt their models to congregational and district set- tings. It takes two to three years to create a team in a congregation. Then the team takes on a life of its own. Some of the teams are suc- cessful and some of them aren't."

Rev. Kurt Kuhwald, who also became a trainer working with white people exploring anti-racism work, said his most memorable moment as a participant in a discussion on race occurred "at the Crossroads Training when Thandeka, who would go on to become a Unitarian Universalist theologian, screamed 'bullshit!' at the trainer. . . . We need to be able to yell 'bullshit!' at each other." He noted that this moment revealed to him "the intensity of the oppo- sition to following a program focused on the systemic structure of racism, and that exposed white privilege and white complicity."

Others recall these trainings with more reservation. "I still hear negative feedback, to the point of resembling abuse victims, of white folks talking about going to early Crossroads anti-racism trainings," said Rev. Keith Kron, director of the UUA's Office of Bisexual, Gay, Lesbian and Transgender Concerns. "I wonder if those people will ever recover." Still, he sympathized with the need to find a model capable of reducing prejudicial thinking. "I lead Beyond Categorical Thinking trainings, workshops to help congregations think about calling a minister who is not white, straight and/or able-bodied. I hear the same things from our folks after nine years of doing it: Will a minister of color be intellectual enough? Will the worship service be too emotional? Will she or he understand me? Will he or she only preach about racism? Will they have an agenda?"

Rev. Abhi Janamanchi, who was born in India and came to Unitarian Universalism from a liberal Hindu tradition, participated in an early training when he was a seminarian. "It was too focused on pain," he said, "and did not leave enough room for healing and wholeness that it claimed in its title. That became evident as we started the journey with about forty people and had to shift gears after the second or third session to incorporate things that weren't in the suggested curriculum plan to make it more meaningful for people and not just feel as if they had spilled their guts and had nothing to clean it up. . . ."

Grubbs had a more mixed assessment of the Crossroads model, distinguishing between its training methodology and its analysis of the systemic nature of racism. "Their trainings of our people and our people's implementation of their programs created problems from at least 1995 on, good people turned off because of 'get with the program attitude,'" he said, adding that it exemplified a non-collaborative style that often created divisions.

The analysis Crossroads presented identified racism as a product of prejudicial systems designed to benefit the majority white culture and reinforced by the disproportionate share of the decision-making and resource-allocating power of that culture. This contrasted with the more prominent view that racism was only vested in particular persons, not systems. Grubbs said this aspect of the Crossroads approach was very valuable. "The notion that racism is simply a prejudice held by bad people continues to be held by UUs," he said, "and the work that was done helped UUs become clear."

Gini Courter, who joined the UUA Board in 1995 and became Moderator in 2003, said the model generated hostility. "That model could not have been better designed to turn me off. . . . The whole process started with how racist you are. . . . I also know that model worked incredibly well for many people but they have had a different experience growing up than I have." She said that the model, targeted at the demographic majority of those in the Association, assumed that all UUs were white and middle-class and that people who were not found no place in it. She felt it was designed to work best for southern whites and people whose racial context was primarily black and white.

The persistence of the training began to permeate key institutions in the Association. Rev. Wayne Arnason recalled his experience as a part of the Unitarian Universalist Ministers Association in the mid-1990s. "We had our own personal epiphanies in the Crossroads training," he said. "I became a Crossroads fan in the sense that I felt comfortable with the level of confrontation that Joe Barndt and his trainers would do. . . . The agitation, the shaking you up, and the extreme challenge that is represented by the position that all white people are racist, if we accept this group of definitions, was a kind of born-again experience in terms of my understanding. . . . I just never saw things the same way after that. It put my previous experience in LRY [Liberal Religious Youth, an organization for Unitarian Universalist Youth later supplanted by another organization] into a different perspective. I guess that's how I would summarize what the experience meant to me. We tried to institutionalize this in the Unitarian Universalist Ministers Association."

Transformation Committee Agenda

The JTW Committee was working on implementing its huge charge, which included overseeing training. Some of their priorities from this era included:

- Reaching out to support ministers and to help educate them, especially in face of the fact that it was acknowledged that engaging in or promoting anti-racism training might endanger their jobs because it was controversial.
- Talking with the Department of Ministry about the need for seminarians to be exposed to anti-racism training.
- Beginning to look at training in terms of religious education and the specific needs of multiracial youth.

CHAPTER 11: STRATEGIES FOR TRAINING

- Developing a strategy for working with groups affiliated with the UUA.
- Trying to develop financial support from within the UUA for continued training.
- Coordinating with the "Fulfilling the Promise" initiative which had been charged with implementing a "re-covenanting" process.
- Field-testing a conflict resolution model.
- Responding to an article in the *UU World* perceived as critical of the consultation.
- Addressing concerns raised by the UUA Board about the lack of an assessment tool for evaluating its work.

Funding and Resources

As mentioned earlier, also during this period came the need to begin to develop an alternative source of funding for the Journey Toward Wholeness. The Transformation Committee held a sobering conversation with Hillary Smith of the Unitarian Universalist Funding Panel that raised the perennial spectral question of how to continue paying for the work. The notes concluded,

> The UU Funding Panel sees itself as done with funding anti-racism training. They see this work as something that is institutionalized, the responsibility of the UUA and the folks who want to do the training. Taking on this responsibility shows a readiness to do the work. The panel tries to be a couple of steps ahead of the institutionalization of work; funding organizations in their adolescence so that they may move to adulthood. We need to start encouraging congregations to use the money that they have raised from the JTW Sunday for training. Also the UUA Board of Trustees needs to take ownership on this issue, so that anti-racism work is funded to be effective; this is beginning to happen.

In a letter sent to large congregation presidents in May 1998, Unitarian Universalist Association president Dr. John Buehrens described one strategy, a "Journey Toward Wholeness Sunday" to raise money for local congregations to do anti-racism work as well as Association funds.

The Whitney Young Sunday program, a racial justice funding approach, became the Journey Toward Wholeness Anti-Racism Sunday. The goal was to raise $150,000, which would be used 2/3 for training and 1/3 toward urban ministry. At the Jubilee Working Group meeting in April, it was reported that the Board saw all of this going to pay for Journey Toward Wholeness training and that the motion that they would pass at the next meeting should be specific about what percentage was to go for urban church programs. It was also reported that the Core team was working on an anti-racism training model for youth.

The October 1998 minutes note that the Jubilee Working Group was operating under resource constraints that did not allow them to meet the demand for the "Jubilee" workshops.

Hoover said resource restraints were linked to the lack of progress, especially on the congregational level. In 1995–96, congregations were invited by the Faith in Action department to give input and a study of ministerial attitudes was conducted. By 1997, energy had been diverted to other efforts. "The other thing is that people were hot to trot in terms of getting what became [the comprehensive sexuality curricula] *Our Whole Lives* because we were working with the [United Church of Christ] and got the grant and stuff," Hoover said. "So the energy of RE, our education department, resources department, which I had anticipated was going to be available for anti-racism and anti-oppression stuff, really wasn't. . . . And so we didn't have the internal staff developing the resources at that level for congregation-based stuff. . . . And we actually had a training program; we actually had a program for a bunch of consultants which we did that year to equip about fifty folks to be able to work with congregations. And we didn't have any travel money. And we didn't have a chance, we didn't get out to congregations to catalyze them to say, "Who wants to do this?" . . . The next level was to go back and try and find people where they were and give them materials to help them move into that, which we saw as another three, four, five years of work just to get some key congregations doing that. But we didn't have the resources to do that."

Critical Voices Heard

Those uncomfortable with an explicit emphasis on anti-racism began to give voice to their concerns during this time. One of the key tensions articulated around the relationship with Crossroads Ministry was around the perception that underlying assumptions were not in sympathy with Unitarian Universalist beliefs, and yet the range of beliefs was large. Barndt noted, "Everybody was really right in saying to me, sometimes in great anger, 'Damn you, stop trying to make Lutherans out of us!' But that accusation was, at least in part, a deflection of, 'How do we as Unitarian Universalists understand evil?'"

Anti-racism efforts had attempted to adopt the agenda abandoned after the Empowerment Controversies. This meant a focus on the black-white relations that had been at the center of those conversations. More than two decades later, the racial and cultural landscape was more complicated. Another criticism of anti-racism efforts such as the Jubilee and Crossroads trainings was that they looked at race through a black-white paradigm. "Coming at it from a person of color perspective, from a different culture, both [my co-trainer] and I felt that it was too focused on racism as a black and white issue, and him being Japanese-American, and my being Indian," recalled Rev. Abhi Janamanchi. "We had to reorganize some of that because we found ourselves being asked questions which didn't fit with the overall scheme of things within the JTW program as well as one of the things I remember doing is to spend probably a couple of sessions on focusing on Mark Morrison-Reed's book, *Black Pioneers in a White Denomination*, which again, I felt was an important piece of our history which somehow did not get as much attention as it ought to have."

Other concerns arose as well, including those of people who identified as Hispanic or Latina/o. Rev. Peter Morales, a founder of LUUNA, remembers attending an early version of the weekend. "I actually went, trying to not be my cynical self," he recalled. "It was held at First Unitarian, Denver. Once again, it was frustrating. The two people, who were well-prepared, one was an Anglo woman and one was an African-American man. Every single—without exception, over a day and a half—every example given was a black-white example. This is in Denver, where there are four Latinos for every

African American. . . . It was like, what was being presented had no relationship to us in the front ranks, to our lived experience. And I can imagine what it must have been like in Tucson."

Gini Courter, who joined the UUA Board in 1995, recalled that she was in the second wave of those exposed to anti-racism training. In that year, six new board members entered and the culture that had begun to be developed had to be reimagined. "Before I was ever at a board meeting, I was sent to training," she said. The training that she went to was one that did not go well. Several key members of the training team were sick and that combined with the fact that this training attempted to work with a larger number of trainees combined for a negative experience. "It just really irritated us," Courter recalled. "Staff people were saying they didn't feel safe. . . . I called Denny [Denise Davidoff who, as moderator of the Association, chairs the Board] and told her we were going to make a statement and she said she would never stop Board members from saying something they felt they needed to say." Later Courter saw the struggles of maintaining momentum. "Being on the Board, I didn't realize that new folks come in and you have to reimagine the community every time you have significant transition. What you thought was your culture just walks away. . . . It took me six years to get enough history to realize that they had just worked so hard to get the agreement to be an anti-racist Board—and then here comes these new folks."

Writing in 2005, Rice, a Meadville Lombard teacher, illustrated another common concern. "Over the past two decades," he wrote, "I have usually found myself at odds with the philosophy of the UUA's initiative, while endorsing the sentiments behind it. I find myself ardently opposed to solutions to social problems that paint the problem with broad strokes, assuming one group of people to be powerless and without responsibility, and the other, dominant group to be guilty and inordinately powerful and thereby responsible. . . . There is no going back. What is done is done. . . . You cannot do ANYTHING about the trail of tears, nor the Atlantic slave trade. It is done! Let it go. We survived it. Celebrate that! We are the survivors! Our ancestors protested it. They did all that they could. Praise John Brown, and Henry Thoreau, Harriet Beecher Stowe, Robert

Shaw, Frederick Douglass, Martin Luther King Jr., all of our ancestors who fought for good causes. They are OUR heritage."

Others charged that the model did not leave room for claiming the sacrifices of the past that many had made. Rev. Marjorie Bowens-Wheatley observed,

> One of the biggest responses that I heard as a trainer was that the model left no space for affirming people who had been doing any form of racial justice work for ten, twenty, thirty, forty years. I'm not just talking about Selma, I'm talking about people who were actively involved around organizing racial justice in their communities. There was no place in the model to affirm that.

Courter looked at the choice of models as primarily a business decision, one without proper choices:

> We got to choose one vendor. Crossroads was looking for a partner to acquire and keep a client. Leon [Spencer] would say, "JTW is not Crossroads Ministry." The JTW was an initiative of the General Assembly and the UUA Board, but it got taken over by Faith in Action. . . . I don't think we ever chose a method, we chose a vendor.

She was a consistent voice calling on the financial relationship with Crossroads Ministry to be more closely examined and in her tenure as chair of the Board's finance committee, she did a "back of the envelope" analysis of the resources that had flowed to Crossroads, pointing out that the amount was "significant." (Her recollection was that about 12 percent of program funds was being spent on anti-racism training. Looking back in 2008, Association executive vice president Kathleen Montgomery said it was difficult to separate expenditures on anti-racism from expenditures on social justice.)

The lack of transparency was one of the issues Courter returned to in her analysis of the problems with the JTW efforts. She said the lack of transparency was a systemic problem for the UUA, which

MAP
Journey Toward Wholeness

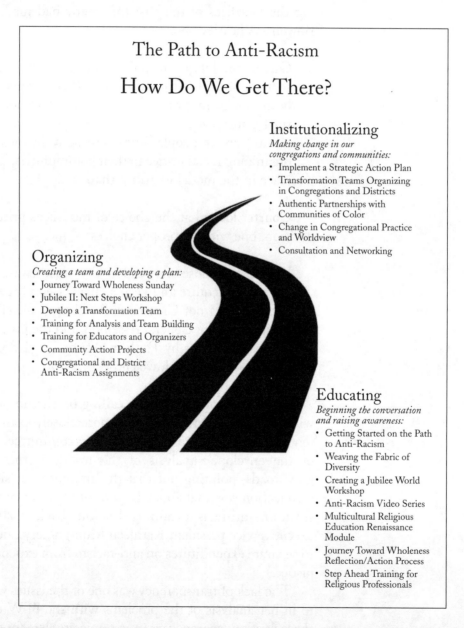

addressed it at the General Assembly in Long Beach in 2004 when it set in place new rules requiring meeting documentation and other open meeting procedures. And yet the functioning of some of the leadership of anti-racism efforts, especially Faith in Action, seemed particularly difficult to Courter.

Rev. Dr. William Jones noted that he thought using Crossroads was a critical decision. "If I would make any suggestions for a future kind of problem, it would be to handle the initial modeling differently," he said. "What I had recommended was to identify the different sort of the spectrum of models and positions on the issue in the denomination, and then select three or four representative positions or persons and have them develop a model for addressing the problem and do some kind of initial pilot study where you would select a church or denomination or religious education, or something, and test out each of these models initially and then do a sort of a resumé or synopsis or summary of the case studies to see what common features, if any, you could find and take that summary or have another way to do it. Take one or two, three, or four models, and put them into competition with each other in terms of how they would approach a different issue and so forth, and gather that data and at that point attempt to come up with a preliminary model that you would then again do different pilot studies on and work out in more detail. What they did was to select one model based primarily on the necessity to have a common language or something to work with. That, to me, was really a fatal error. Fatal in the sense that it did not provide a context, and there has never been a context within which the different models were translated into a concrete competitive strategy for dealing with some aspects of racism, genderism, whatever . . . but there was no effort to critically assess the different models from their respective differences. Until you do that, you don't have any kind of evidence about the value, the merit of it."

Though the focus was on the Crossroads and Jubilee models, other independent efforts were under way as well. Funding from the Whitney Young Fund provided a number of interesting models, including Unitarios Universalistas de Habla Hispania, sponsored by the First Unitarian Church of San Jose, California; Community

Language School of Open Door Community Ministry, sponsored by the Church of the Open Door in Chicago; and "Art and Soul, Teens Beyond Racism," sponsored by the First Unitarian Church of San Diego, California.

Journey Toward Wholeness Transformation Committee

Relationships were the focus of the October 1998 meeting of the Transformation Committee: relationships with the UUMA and its Center Committee (in charge of continuing education for ministers), relationships with the Fulfilling the Promise campaign and with the Salt Lake City Task Force of the General Assembly Planning Committee. How to get these bodies to see themselves as accountable to the Journey Toward Wholeness structure and as candidates for its educational efforts was laced through these discussions. The Transformation Committee discussed the need to be in dialogue with a number of key voices, including Rev. Dr. Thandeka of the Meadville Lombard Theological School; Julio Noboa, who had been part of the Racial and Cultural Diversity Task Force; and Rev. Dr. Michelle Bentley, who had founded two intentionally racially diverse congregations in the Chicago area, the minutes stating, "We need to write to everyone who participated, thanking them for their exchange and input, letting them know that they have been heard, and asking that they feel free to continue to bring their ideas to the table."

Funding for anti-racism training was a concern as well, both looking for new sources of funding and shoring up relationships with established funders. A shortage of funding overall meant that congregations were going to the same funding sources as were funding the continental work, such as the UU Funding Program and the Veatch Program of the Unitarian Universalist Church at Shelter Rock in Manhasset, New York.

The Committee's minutes include this summary of a conversation with President Dr. John Buehrens and Moderator Davidoff:

Questions have come up as to why are we behind in our training process. UUMA did [a conversation around the movie] "Color of Fear" three years ago. The ministers were given the impression that there would be follow up from this. Where is it? There is a perception that it is two years late. Ministers don't understand what the expectations of the denomination are on this issue.

We need to be able to answer these questions. What we need is a solid report explaining where we are, what has happened, etc. We need a high profile action plan with accomplishments followed by a marketing plan and policy.

We need to exhaust every communication vehicle open to us. A major learning has become that you need to communicate what you are doing while you are doing it. People have a tremendous need to know. And communication does not have to be perfect. You have to 'fess up to all of the struggles, frustrations, etc., as well as successes. The other piece is that you have to communicate to several different groups simultaneously. Another thing has to link JTW with Fulfilling the Promise. All of this is, however, tempered by the history of anti-racism work with the Racial and Cultural Diversity Task Force and the Communications Department.

Veatch has signaled that they are going to cut funding on our anti-racism work. We have a window of opening there to do anti-racism training in that they have requested a Jubilee World Workshop for April 9–11, 1999. The Veatch Board of Governors should be asked to treat themselves as gatekeepers and do an Analysis and Team Building Training. . . .

We need help identifying 100 key leaders.

We have asked [Rev.] John [Buehrens, then the Association president] to identify the most important ministers of the 40 largest congregations.

The need for priorities and more communication with key players or "stakeholders" gave rise to the idea of having a summit to set a strategic direction for the JTW work. In 1999, the Committee also met with Barndt around the relationship with Crossroads Ministry, seeking a "discussion of a non-defensive statement or definition of our relationship, both present and historical, with Crossroads." The notes from that meeting reveal the flavor of the conversation was both cordial and confrontational, summarizing:

Veatch introduced the UUA to Crossroads, when Joe [Barndt] was seeking funding from them and the Racial and Cultural Diversity Task Force approved the Crossroads model and directed Mel to make relations with them.

The negative perceptions come from two trainings which went awry.

What needs to be said/brought up:

Issues around theology, sexism or male approach, and the concept of the interlocking oppressions being present (or not present) in the model

People who have personal problems with Joe Barndt

Discounting the model because it has Saul Alinsky principles of organizing

Being able to name the underlying organizing principles of the model

Class is "not addressed"

Focus is on training not organizing/action . . .

In a discussion of theology, "three pieces that are present within Unitarian Universalism and are barriers" were noted:

Anti-Christian tenet

A lack of theology of evil and repentance

Individualism

We need to deal with these in order to create a strong spiritual resistance to racism.

We need to find out how to capture the identity of our social consciousness.

Demographics show that social consciousness has "gone underground" and we need to tap into it.

These conversations were part of the ongoing identity issues for the group that centered on accountability and the scope of their authority due to congregational polity. The amount of training that could be offered was determined by relationships. An example is their discussion of the GA Planning Committee:

The GA Planning Committee coordinates the annual gathering of UUs. The GA Planning Committee works with the GA office, and also divides itself into several working committees. There is also an informal network of people that the GA committee relies on for sub-committee work. Planning Committee members are elected at GA, and nominated by the Nominating Committee. The Planning Committee reports to UUA Board of Trustees. . . . What do we want from them:

- Do a GA anti-racism assessment
- An ongoing relationship with Transformation Committee
- Integrate anti-racism into every part of the General Assembly
- Go through anti-racism training as a team, geared specifically to equip them with the skills to integrate the analysis into their charter, and they should pay for it.

The Committee also discussed frustrations with its ongoing communications with the Core Team, which was responsible for coordinating training strategies and the need to address "[q]uestions around review of product and accountability relationships between the Transformation Committee and the Core Team. The Transformation Committee really wants to view the curricula, without micro-managing by evaluating it. The committee really just wants to be knowledgeable of it, to speak on it at GA."

Another Curriculum Unpublished
The Language of Race curriculum—written in the late 1990s by Robette Dias, Rev. Keith Kron, and Vivian Carlo and edited by Rev. Marjorie Bowens-Wheatley, but never published—captured much of the content knowledge and group dynamic knowledge of the anti-racism training community. Its introduction discusses its purpose, which was to bring antiracism to the congregational level:

So often the topic of racism is intimidating, raising fears of confrontation, guilt, and frustration. *The Language of Race* is intended to build religious community and inspire action for justice. Participants will have the opportunity to share their own experiences, beliefs, feelings, and hopes for themselves, their congregations, and society. This ten-session introductory anti-racism curriculum for adults and senior high youth explores basic concepts in understanding race, racism, and anti-racism. In this highly interactive program participants will address issues such as identity, colonialism, multiculturalism, power, and the linkages between oppressions. Themes explored in the ten sessions are:

Identity

Oppression

Race

Racism 1—definition and power

Racism 2—institutional and cultural

White Skin Benefits and Middle Class Privilege

Colonialism and Neo-colonialism

Multiculturalism and Pluralism

Claiming an Anti-Racist Identity

Action/Celebration

The Language of Race is intended to be introductory, not comprehensive; a beginning, not an ending.

Bowens-Wheatley said,

There were chapters in it on different things, and one chapter was on oppression, one chapter was on history, one on class. In any case, Robette Dias and I were two of the authors, and Robette simultaneously brought in the colonialism history piece for Crossroads and wrote some of that for this curriculum that had several names: it was *The Language of Race*, it was *Under the Baobab Tree*, it was several things.

That the curriculum was never published followed a pattern from the 1980s, as Rev. Joseph Santos-Lyons documented in his seminary thesis. He noted that three efforts to publish materials on race designed for congregational use were made over the last twenty-five years. *Black America/White America: Understanding the Discord*, was envisioned in the 1970s and planned for completion in the early 1980s. Later in the 1980s, Rev. Dr. Mark Morrison-Reed sketched out an approach for a curriculum building on his book *Black Pioneers in a White Denomination*, which he called *How Open the Door?*, yet as Santos-Lyons notes, "attention and focus of the UUA lagged to the point that he gave up pushing for the finished product." It was eventually published in 1989.

The 1980 Institutional Racism Audit had this to say about the first attempt:

> In the late 1970s, the UUA entered into negotiations for the design and publication of *Black America/White America*. A long history of writing, testing, revision, and correspondence surrounds the controversy that developed over the curriculum. In September of 1980, a letter from the major author of the curriculum suggested twice that some resolution about whether or not to proceed with publication be made by January of 1981. In early December, Community Change team members (responsible for the Institutional Racism audit) found that no decision had then been made or at that time was envisioned for January 1981; again in early January no decision had been reached.
>
> Somehow, persons responsible never got around to making a decision, or even getting the matter onto the formal agenda. Like a dead albatross, the unresolved matter of the curriculum drifts along behind the ship, whose wake periodically forces it to turn over, rise again to the surface, then silently slide once more toward oblivion.

Core Team Disbands

By the June 1999 meeting of the Journey Toward Wholeness Transformation Committee, evidence of conflict within the Core Team had emerged. The minutes reflected, "Several members decided that they could not work until these conflicts were resolved. . . . Some of the conflicts on the Core Team generate from the work around oppression, and others deal with interpersonal issues."

Lack of clarity about the role of the Core Team was becoming more problematic. Again, the minutes reflect this:

Questions need to be posed to the Core Team around accountability, and thus about the possibility of restructuring itself so that it can do its work. Also we need to ask what does the Core Team need from the Transformation Committee, the UUA "Structure," and who in addition does it need to do its work. How is it a team? Should it be a team (vs. a coalition)? Finally, we need to ask the question about how does the spiritual/reflective personal dimension fit into the work. These questions need to be posed to the Transformation Committee and the JWG [Jubilee Working Group] as well. . . . Does the Transformation Committee even have the expertise to evaluate and make recommendations to the Core Team? These are the questions of accountability and authority. Questions about trust and power. . . .

The Committee did an analysis of the Core Team at this meeting, concluding that the Core Team was made up of seventeen people, a majority of whom were on the Unitarian Universalist Association staff: "In this mix is all kinds of lateral and hierarchical relationships," they concluded. The staff-driven nature of the Core Team was a continuing source of conflict. "It was important to consider the volunteer context of our congregations," said Paula Cole Jones, an active member of All Souls Church Unitarian in Washington, D.C. "You can mandate changes for staff, volunteers choose whether or not they'll participate. They can walk away from it anytime they want to."

UUA President Buehrens noted that creation of the Journey Toward Wholeness Transformation Committee transferred decision-making from a staff-controlled function (the Core Team) to a Board-controlled body (the JTW Committee). Eventually the team stopped meeting and disbanded.

EXCERPT
Colonialism Defined

This is excerpted from The Language of Race, *an anti-racism curriculum that was written for the UUA in the late 1990s but never published.*

To those who followed Columbus and Cortez, the New World truly seemed incredible because of the natural endowments. The land often announced itself with a heavy scent miles out into the ocean. Giovanni de Verrazano in 1524 smelled the cedars of the East Coast a hundred leagues out. The men of Henry Hudson's Half Moon were temporarily disarmed by the fragrance of the New Jersey shore, while ships running further up the coast occasionally swam through large beds of floating flowers. Wherever they came inland they found a rich riot of color and sound, of game and luxuriant vegetation. Had they been other than they were, they might have written a new mythology here. As it was, they took inventory.
—Frederick Jackson Turner, historian, 1861–1932

Operational Definitions

Colonialism:
Colonialism is comprised of a complex set of relationships stemming from the underlying condition of subjugation in which one power has control over another people's education, language(s), customs, lands, and economic means of sustenance. (Dobles & Segarra, 1998)

A system in which one nation exercises military, economic, and political control over another. The era of colonialism was begun in the sixteenth century by European nations, later followed by the United States. (American Friends Service Committee, Resistance in Paradise, 1998)

Colonization:
The process by which a nation occupies and settles in territory belonging to another people (or unoccupied territory).

Decolonization:
Freeing a colony from dependent status.

Deculturalization:
Stripping away a people's culture and replacing it with a new culture.

Congregational Initiatives

In other congregations, the paths varied as a glance at the activities of three congregations showed.

In 1999, Connie and Guy Loftman formed the "What Color Is Community?" Racial Justice Task Force at the Unitarian Universalist Church of Bloomington, Indiana. They offered this account in 2005:

> We have carried on annual Journey Toward Wholeness Sundays, and a one-time weekend Journey Toward Wholeness training/workshop. We have had a variety of movie and book discussions, and organized and led racial justice workshops for our members. We have reached out to Muslims since 9/11, and had a Ramadan fast-breaking in our church the last two years. We have organized regular visits to the Bloomington Juvenile Correctional Facility, a state detention facility for juvenile delinquents. Our choir has organized annual Martin Luther King Day ceremonies for three groups of medium and maximum security inmates at a state prison 60 miles away for six years with African American choirs.

Another initiative concerned reparations. Repairing the Breach: The Monroe County Race and Justice Project was formed from interested community members. We have made a documentary named "Living with Jim Crow in Monroe County." It is gaining wide viewership. We organized the application for a state historic marker which will be erected this February 13 at the site of the original segregated "Colored School." This is one of the very few historical markers in the state that deals with African-American history, and only the second historical marker on any topic in Monroe County. More dealings with African-American history are now planned by various groups in the community.

One of our goals was to partner with African-American groups. We built on pre-existing relationships with the local NAACP branch. That led to a study of race and criminal justice in Monroe County published in 2000 showing

CONGREGATIONAL STORY
First Unitarian Church of Dallas, Texas

Some large congregations reported finding anti-racism efforts particularly challenging. In 1997, First Unitarian Church of Dallas started the CDARE (Cultural Diversity and Anti-racism Empowerment) group. And in 1997–98 the church offered a variety of programs; seventy congregants took part in a UUA-conducted Jubilee workshop. In a newsletter column written in June 1998, senior minister Rev. Dr. Laurel Hallman wrote:

As you may have noticed in the last *Dallas Unitarian*, our board of trustees has unanimously endorsed the continuation of our Journey Toward Wholeness project begun in the enlightening and stirring Jubilee weekend held at the church in March. It was then that many of our board members, staff and leadership recognized, along with the other attendees—70 people attended—that there were resources available and understandings to be gained. . . . We could use tools from the recent very intelligent and constructive work in the area of antiracism that would make us less helpless, less overwhelmed and more able to constructively confront the problem of racism so deeply embedded in our culture. With the board's wholehearted support, I have had conversations with people at the UUA about what is possible. While I am at our UU [General Assembly] in Rochester, NY, I plan to talk with UU students and ministers of color, or as one advisor has said, "Don't talk much. Listen, to get their recommendations." By fall we should have a plan in place. The board and I agree that this is not just a good intention on our part. We have recognized the cost of racism in our own lives. That the path to wholeness is our path to take together. We hope you will join us in the journey.

Yet making a plan proved difficult. "We had some very practical problems," Hallman recalled, "including finding programs and resources to help us. We had very real questions about organizing the trainings and shaping a long-range plan which could start where we were and move us forward. Who would run a follow-up program to sustain the effort? How would we fund the program?"

The congregation, Hallman said, found that "there weren't any next steps available to us as a large church. We just thought that was an anomaly of the group that arrived, but it turned out to be a big issue all along the way, every time. This frankly is a problem often with programs that have been designed for small or midsize churches and then are brought into our church. They are very difficult to implement because the leaders who come aren't prepared to deal with the large groups that we have taking part in the program. So it makes it less effective."

The church set aside $30,000 to be matched by $15,000 from the UUA to provide training through Crossroads Ministry. That relationship broke down and the church eventually contracted with Visions, a Boston-based multicultural training company. This work seemed more suited to the congregation, perhaps in part because it looked at multiple oppressions and the Dallas congregation had done a lot of work to fight oppression of gay and lesbian people.

Over time, Hallman's sense was that the congregation got tired of bringing in programmatic trainings and turned the work to interfaith organizing, which connected them to people of many cultures and races in Dallas, while accomplishing real change in the city. It too was challenging, because the priorities weren't always the congregation's priorities, and the decision-making process was shared. "Something would be decided by the interfaith leadership and the Unitarian Universalists would ask, 'When did we talk about that?'" she said.

numerous racial disparities between blacks and whites in our criminal justice system. While the report was highly controversial, it led to the formation of the Monroe County Racial Justice Task Force, including the local prosecutor, sheriff, chief of police, judges, city officials, Indiana University faculty and UU and NAACP members. We undertook a new study which was accepted for consultation by The Sentencing Project, an outstanding national organization on these issues. Dedicated work by IU graduate students was vital. Our published study was recognized by the American Bar Association as a national model for communities across the nation. Our congregation was expressly identified in that report. We are deeply involved at this time in challenging but exciting efforts to see more of our recommendations implemented. Some already have been.

The Unitarian Universalist Church of Arlington, Virginia, which was active in the Civil Rights movement of the 1960s, formed a Task Force on Racial Diversity in 1993, which followed UUA courses on anti-racism, had book groups, speakers, potlucks, and tried without much success to increase the racial diversity of the church. Their account recalled,

> After our Jubilee II workshop in 2001 those in attendance went to the Board who agreed to charter the Anti-racism Transformation Team. Although we have had ideas, it has taken a couple of years(!) to get organized enough to start implementing much.
>
> Having a continuing (if low-level) presence over time has kept issues alive in our congregation. This is the fourth year since our church has joined two other local congregations to share a service honoring Martin Luthur King, Jr. This is the first year that our three congregations are trying to do more together than just the annual service. We have started three joint activities: voter registration, Christmas in April, and tutoring.

The Jubilee workshops have been significant influences. We have used documents from them—the Continuum, the Congregational Assessment tool, etc. It has been very helpful to have ministers engaged in anti-racism work. [Rev.] Linda Olson Peebles [minister of religious education] helped us plan a "stakeholders gathering" or leadership summit, which was a half day workshop which she and Paula Cole Jones led as a way to introduce this kind of work to those outside our group. Summer religious education intern Manish Mishra was another valuable resource. *Soul Work* has been the basis of a book group and a sermon by Michael McGee [the congregation's minister].

We have learned how slow this work can go—sometimes it feels like the blind leading the blind. We have learned that it can be meaningful and rewarding. Keeping at it over time seems to build something not there before. There have been definite shifts since the JTW started. For example, when we met with the Search Committee for our new settled minister, a member of the search committee said, "Let me see if I understand—you used to be focused on getting more people of color into our church, but now your goals are to work on the issues, the structural pieces that we can do something about." Our goals are getting clearer. Now we're trying to get more structured and efficient about implementation, since we floundered so much in the last few years, despite having lots of good ideas.

The Unitarian Universalist Church of Annapolis, Maryland, has been increasingly engaged in racism issues over many years. In 1995 the Ku Klux Klan held a rally in Annapolis. Members and friends of the congregation joined with other churches, social action groups, and citizens in a march in opposition to the Klan's presence in the city. Shortly after this occasion an interested group of members and friends of the congregation began meeting as a small discussion group. The discussion led to the formation of the church's Journey Toward Wholeness Committee in 1998. Here is an account of the Committee's activities from 1999 to 2003:

Supporting a community Unity Day Rally.

Sponsoring a Fieste de Halloween party for children of Hispanic origin.

Organizing and presenting an annual Kwanzaa service at the church.

Organizing and presenting an annual Journey Towards Wholeness Sunday at the church.

Sponsoring a trilogy of videos on various racial themes.

Partnering with Banneker Douglas Museum to provide a two-part lecture series featuring local historians specializing in African-American history in Annapolis.

Providing tutoring and mentoring for elementary- and middle-school children at an Annapolis housing complex.

The results of the racial justice or anti-racism work are increased awareness within the congregation regarding racial justice issues, recognition in the community-at-large as a church interested in being involved in diversity efforts, and the participation in a tutoring/mentoring program at a neighborhood after-school program.

In addition, Committee members are encouraged to work in the community-at-large on various social action projects. Some of these activities include:

- The Martin Luther King Breakfast Committee
- The Martin Luther King Dinner Committee
- NAACP/NAACP Freedom Banquet
- Kunte Kinte Festival
- Leadership Anne Arundel—Neighborhood Leadership Academy

Working in cooperation with diverse groups in the community has revealed sameness and differences, and resulted in forming strong bonds and ultimately enriching the spiritual and social lives of all concerned.

V O I C E
Robette Dias

This is excerpted from an address at the Urban Church Conference in 2001. Dias is a former staff memer of the UUA's Faith in Action Department.

I want to take us back to the beginning. To the beginning of when all these "problems" we have been talking about first came to this land. When did classism, racism, sexism, homophobia, ableism, and all the rest become such a problem? When did they get woven into the fabric of society?

As an Indian person, as a Karuk person, my elders have taught me that these things did not exist before the White invasion of the Europeans; that all these oppressions, these "isms" came with the White folks. Concepts of race, class, heterosexuality, ability are all culture-bound concepts, and they are not *indigenous* cultural concepts.

I am not trying to idealize Native peoples; back in the old days they also had the concept of "the other" and there were often competitions for resources and territory. But Indian conflicts before the Europeans came were highly ritualized and were never, ever attempts to dehumanize the enemy, nor to obliterate them from the face of the earth. All that changed with the coming of the European invaders. And Indians have been suffering ever since. . . .

When I come to events like this, I always listen very carefully to the discussions; I listen especially carefully to the suggestions for fixing the problems because I wonder how the fixes are going to impact Indian people. . . .

Indian people still are tribal, but everyone was at one time. And this is important because as tribal people, all of our ancestors had a very different sensibility, a different perceptual reality than we have today. The difference is that they knew who they were. They knew they were sacred beings, they knew because they knew the land on which they lived . . . knew it like a mother, because it was. Gradually, however, tribal people in Europe began to change and evolve in very dangerous and destructive ways, and they forgot who they were, where their lands were, and who and where their mother was. At one time all our cultures were based on the peoples' harmonious relationship with the earth and all creation; culture told the people who they were as members of tribal groups, and what their responsibilities in life were. But at some point in Europe, that started to change and the cultures became cultures of forgetting. The people forgot who they were, forgot their relationship to the earth, their mother, and forgot their responsibilities. And they brought this forgetting, and all its problems, with them when they came to the so-called New World.

Now culture is a collective enterprise. Individuals don't have culture. I can talk about "my" Karuk culture, or "my" Indian culture, but I am talking about me as one person within a larger collective of an identifiable group of people. And I am a bicultural person because I also exist within the larger United States society, which also has a distinct, well-defined culture. When I say culture, I mean the language, life ways, and most importantly, the world view of a people.

When I talk about a people forgetting who they are, I am talking about all three of those things: people forgetting their language, their way of life, but most importantly I am talking about people forgetting a world view that puts them in harmony with creation rather than at odds with creation.

What we have in this country is a dominant world view that is a *dominating* world view. We have a culture that is based on domination, a culture based on oppression. We have a culture of violence, violence toward the earth, violence toward the plants and animals of the earth, violence toward all the peoples of the earth. . . . Violence is everywhere around us, between us, within us. We cannot escape it; it is in the air we breathe. It is the culture in which we live. That is why we *have* to forget; who wants to remember that?

So what does this mean for us as Unitarian Universalists? Are we above or outside this culture of violence? No, we are fully within its mix, right smack in the middle of it. It controls and dominates our lives. And it defines who we are. *But!* It does not define who we *could* be. We *are* intelligent, emotional, sacred beings. We could begin to remember who we are; we could begin to take responsibility for our lives, our actions, our families, our faith, our religious community, our country, and our world. Take responsibility for creating a just world.

I believe we want to do that, that we, as a religious community, want to accept our responsibility to create justice. Some of us *have* done it. We have set ourselves, our lives, on a course of justice making. I think of José Ballester and his dedication to the UU Service Committee. Of Mel Hoover, the director of the Faith in Action Department and the Faith in Action staff. Of Dr. Norma Poinsett in the many leadership roles she plays in our institution. Individuals are taking responsibility and leading us, prodding us to take responsibility too—not as individuals but as a *collective*. As a religious *movement* for justice.

This requires a new cultural consciousness. This requires us to think of the *collective*, of the *group* as the unit of action—not the *individual*. Individuals accomplish very little—it is the power of the collective that makes real and lasting changes. In this new cultural consciousness it is a question of what can we do? What must *we* do? Where are we going as a religious collective? . . .

Where are we headed? I see a very clear justice-making vision [in individuals]. . . . But do we have a collective justice-making vision? Are we *sharing* the vision? I wonder if we do.

If we had a collective vision, does that mean we would all have to work for justice in the same way? No, as long as we are working toward transforming this culture of violence, we can work in many ways. We must work in many ways.

I personally have chosen anti-racism, because that is the place I found in Unitarian Universalism to work on issues that are important to Indian people. The place I can dig in and be most effective. It's the place from which I can talk about colonialism, culture and cultural racism, and this culture of violence in which we live. And the Journey Toward Wholeness allows me to strategize processes to change our Unitarian Universalist culture toward justice. Toward a culture of taking responsibility and relationship. A culture which supports and nurtures people for remembering, for actively opposing the forces in our dominant society that make us forget who we are as sacred, powerful beings.

CHAPTER 12

Stakeholders and Identity Groups

In this period, the number of people considering themselves "stakeholders" in the conversation about race and anti-racism increased. Part of this was the formation of identity-based groups that provided a forum to address concerns individuals had long harbored. The Latina/o Unitarian Universalist Networking Association (LUUNA) emerged, joining the Unitarian Universalist Native and Indigeneous Americans group.

Also notable during this time was the emergence of a youth voice committed to anti-racism ideals.

Rev. José Ballester, a Unitarian Universalist minister since 1987 and a member of the Core Team, recalled the need for a forum for Latina/o and Hispanic people:

> When we complained, they said, "Oh, we're sorry. We'll include you." Then in 1997, when they rolled this out at GA, and everybody is out there saying, "This is wonderful; we have the Journey Toward Wholeness." We were forgotten. Again. There was black/white. Excuse me—we've been here all along! And so the promise is made: we will change, we will include you. Bring in somebody to serve with us—and it has to be a white woman, it has to be a lay person. The leadership was not included, at that time. And as time went on, everything, all our contributions, were ignored. Everything we said was ignored. We were publishing stuff; we're trying to educate; we're trying to be a part of this system, and it was like spitting into a hole in the ground. Nothing.

Rev. Peter Morales observed,

> The worst experiences I've had in the Association are around anti-racism. The nastiest, most hateful kinds of experiences, and the way I characterize it is, I kind of felt like, as a Latino in this thing, like Poland between Germany and Russia. They just run over you back and forth. They're not interested in Poland, they just fight each other, but Poland gets caught in the middle of every war through history. I get feeling invisible, or the other impression is there's this family that's had this bitter feud for a long time and I walk into the middle of it and I'm having trouble figuring out who's on which side and why they're so mad at each other.

LUUNA

The original members of the group first met at the 1995 General Assembly in Spokane and the Latina/o Unitarian Universalist Networking Association (LUUNA) got its official status as a Unitarian Universalist affiliate group at the Phoenix General Assembly a year later. In its early years, the committee met at General Assembly and two other times each year. LUUNA was open to everyone. Its purpose and goals were described by founding members this way:

> LUUNA is a continental association of Unitarian Universalists dedicated to spreading the liberating message of our faith to Latinas and Latinos and enriching our denomination with their involvement, leadership and spirituality.
>
> Goals of LUUNA: We recognize that the realization of these and other efforts depends as much on our involvement and commitment as anything else. LUUNA is open to all UUs interested in contributing towards the achievement of our common goals:
>
> 1. To develop and activate a strategic plan for attracting more Latinos/as to our faith and for enhancing their participation within it.
> 2. To educate UUs about Latino history, culture and diversity, and facilitate UU involvement in current issues that affect Latinos.

3. To share aspects of Latino spiritual heritage and personal journeys with all UUs and thus enrich the worship, theology and spirituality of our chosen faith.
4. Through our fellowship and involvement, bear witness to UU principles and practices in Latino communities and in the wider society.

To illustrate LUUNA's perspective and approach, it published "Bringing Gifts," a statement on their perceptions about race and ethnic differences, which read,

> The LUUNA (Latino/a Unitarian Universalist Networking Association) steering committee would like to offer a Latino perspective on the work before us in our Journey Toward Wholeness. LUUNA is deeply committed to this labor. We applaud and honor the work that has begun and we dedicate ourselves to take an active part in extending it. We share a vision of a rich, multicultural, multiracial movement that values each human being.
>
> As part of our effort to extend the work of creating a multicultural and diverse UUA, we in LUUNA are committed to bring the insights from our own experience. We believe the experience of Latino peoples has much to teach us. To be a Latino, particularly a Latino in North America, is to be multicultural and multiracial. We are a mixture of European, indigenous and African cultures. We are a mixture; we are mestizos and mulattos. A gathering of Latinos is a gathering of racial and cultural diversity. Some of us are light skinned; some of us are dark. We bring a history of oppression—we are both the oppressed and the oppressor. Yet, regardless of our differences, we share a need to form and sustain communities which in turn support the family members of that community.
>
> We do not pretend to have all the answers. However, we would like to offer some observations and ideas.
>
> Candidly, we Latinos are troubled by much of the language and categories used in the UUA's attempts to achieve a more multiracial and multicultural religious movement.

We are not comfortable with thinking that focuses on white and black, on racism, on oppression. We feel left out, marginalized, when our experiences, oppressions and insights are not counted. We feel belittled when a recounting of Civil Rights struggles does not include our struggles, setbacks and accomplishments; nor are our leaders, writers and activists mentioned.

This is not a matter of mere vocabulary, of changing a few terms to make our language more inclusive. The problem is much deeper and much more serious. Ultimately, it not only propels us to unwittingly alienate portions of our UU community but it threatens the very fiber of that community by turning one against the other.

Categories tied too closely to the history of the racism experienced by African Americans at the hands of white Americans are too limiting. Latinos and Latinas do not fit easily into the present scheme. Neither do Asians. Neither do Native Americans. Perhaps most importantly, neither do the growing number of children in our congregations who are part Latino, part African American, part White, part Asian, part Indigenous.

Furthermore, we believe that what ultimately binds us together is a vision of a common future. Each of us—black, white, brown, gay, straight—longs for a community of faith that values us for who we are. We bring a deep need to be in a faith community where we are loved and known, where we can bring our gifts and our pain. We in LUUNA believe that we are better served by organizing around our common vision for the future rather than on our injuries in the past. That does not mean we deny the past, that we do not take hard instruction from it. We believe that an overemphasis on past injuries makes oppression something that gives us legitimacy; it devalues those who do not have "enough" oppression. There is nothing which can adequately compensate us for past oppressions, and ultimately, little is to be gained from dwelling on past failings. The end result of such a process will be an overwhelming and paralyzing sense of guilt in some and resistance and denial in others. Most significantly, to dwell on oppression divides and distracts us from our true tasks. Our true tasks are to create a common vision and make that vision a reality. In sum, we feel we need to concentrate more on what will unite us despite our differences and despite the injustices we have suffered. Our process for ending racism must create loving community.

Lastly, we criollos, mestizos and mulattos in LUUNA believe that our varied pasts are precious gifts that we want to share. Part of spiritual growth is learning to appreciate the gifts and wisdom of different traditions. We also grow spiritually when we come to know another deeply and intimately, to understand his or her experience, to take it in and make it part of us. We would like to see our work in multiculturalism focus more on the gifts we each bring to our communities of faith rather than on our injuries. Or, better put, we need to reframe our injuries and make them into gifts. Someone who has experienced pain is more sensitive to pain in others; this sensitivity is an enormous gift. Our varied backgrounds give us so much to offer each other. Our variety can be a source of wisdom that helps revitalize worship, religious education and community life in our congregations.

In summary, we in LUUNA feel we need to take time to rethink and reframe our discussion. We want to be part of a religious movement with a common vision—a vision founded on sharing the wonderful gifts we are. We in LUUNA are eager to work with joy and love to help make our shared vision a living reality.

[signed] LUUNA Executive Committee
The Rev. Patricia Jimenez, Chair
The Rev. Lilia Cuerva, Vice Chair
The Rev. José Ballester, Treasurer
The Rev. Peter Morales, Communications
Louis Schwebius, Outreach & Education
Ruth Alatorre, Finance
Ervin Barrios, GA & Events Coordination
Julio Noboa, Publications

At a meeting after the paper was released, the Journey Toward Wholeness Committee had "more discussion on the genesis of 'Bringing Gifts' and its relationship to the JTW, including these points: that 'it is not understood as a critique of JTW by LUUNA, but rather a statement of opinion.'" They also expressed concern that "LUUNA does not see itself as an organization with the goal to dismantle racism." They also had a "discussion about participation of LUUNA in the JTW vs. Latinos who want to do anti-racism in the JTW" and a "discussion of racist multiculturalism, Latino/a identity."

Rev. Joseph Barndt, the director of Crossroads Ministry, acknowledged that some of the criticism of the black-and-white focus was valid and yet said that a dilemma existed for him and other members of the Crossroads organization:

> It was always present in the Crossroads model, but never in the kind of depth it needed to be, and one of the things that is happening in Crossroads right now, and needs to be happening any place, is not just Latino/Latina but Asian-American, and Arab-American, and Native American components to be really clear about the analysis and how the understanding of racism is different in its effects on each one of those groups. It's not a one-size-fits-all. . . . But the danger behind all of that is of losing the centrality of the black experience while you're going deep into the other stuff. So it's a combination of needing to go equally deep into all of the groups, but not losing what to me is the centrality of the black experience. And not losing sight of the real question—it's not the black experience, or the other people's of color experience, but the real question we're trying to address is the white experience. . . . Racism exists for the empowerment of white people. And the disempowerment of people of color—all of those groups—is a product of that, but the primary goal of racism is the empowerment of white people.

Through "Bringing Gifts" and other outreach, LUUNA helped deepen the dialogue in the religious education community. Ballester recalled,

ASSESSMENT

Identity-Based Organizations

This excerpt is from Belonging: The Meaning of Membership, *a 2001 report by the Commission on Appraisal.*

Although the UUA is and has been firmly committed to civil rights for persons of color and those of differing ethnic backgrounds, there have often been strong disagreements about what this means within the Association and how best to achieve and practice an openness to non-European Americans. Since the early to mid-1990s, the Association has taken on the goal of becoming an anti-racist organization that strives to be open to people of various racial and ethnic diversities. However, as the journey has not always been easy, members of various racial and ethnic minorities have created Affiliate organizations to provide support and counsel in the process of the UUA's transformation. The most recent of these organizations are UU Network on Indigenous Affairs (UUNIA), Diverse Revolutionary UU Multicultural Ministries (DRUUMM), and Latino/a UU Networking Association (LUUNA). African American UU Ministers (AAUUM) helped found DRUUMM, and it no longer exists as a separate organization. . . . Members of the focus group [assembled by the Commission] explained their involvement in these organizations this way:

- "AAUUM provided a place for African Americans to meet, share concerns that only applied to them. It also was a safe place where I could say things that might not be understood elsewhere. That helped me stay with the UUA. It filled gaps that the congregation did not meet."
- "On a personal level, the congregation has been important to me . . . the sense of community. At the level of LUUNA, it supplements the involvement at the congregational level. It's a way of working on important projects; it is fun and comradeship. There's probably not a UU church that has a half-dozen Latinos in the country."
- "As an Indian person whose ancestors have been oppressed and exploited by organized religion, joining a church was probably the last thing I wanted to do. A professor said the UUA is 'not that bad,' not really much of a church at all, good people, inclusive, it'll work. . . . I found UUNIA at General Assembly, 'thank God.' It's

very much a reason why I have stayed through thick and thin. It's hard for me to sit in our congregations. I feel so completely invisible, calling myself a member is problematic. . . . There is a home for me with these groups [UUNIA], but not in a congregation. I cannot be fully who I am in a congregation."

For most, their involvement in UUNIA, AAUUM, DRUUMM, and LUUNA are important parts of their involvement in Unitarian Universalism, and for many these organizations are their primary loyalty and community of nurture and support. For some, their participation in Affiliate organizations is the only thing that keeps them in Unitarian Universalism, for through these groups they link up with others who share their identity and are committed to ensuring that the UUA becomes (and then remains) an anti-racist organization.

These groups have served almost as political action groups within the UUA to push for equality of all, regardless of racial or ethnic definition. AAUUM began both to offer support to African American ministers, as well as to lobby with the Department of Ministry for those ministers who experienced difficulty getting into Fellowship and into congregations once in Fellowship. DRUUMM has worked within the UU Ministers' Association to make sure that issues of concern to ministers from various minorities are raised and dealt with and to help further the UUMA in its goal of becoming anti-racist. LUUNA has worked to ensure that material is available in Spanish for individuals who may be interested in Unitarian Universalism.

The majority of the members of these organizations are also involved in local congregational life, though the degree of individual involvement varies greatly (as it does for individuals who are not members of extra-congregational associations). However, many still feel marginal or invisible in their congregations. Frequently, these individuals are also expected to bear the burden of explaining themselves and justifying their existence within the congregation to other congregational members.

The tensions felt in congregational life for members of these groups are similar to tensions arising from differing theological orientations, primarily the questions of who gets to define the culture of the congregation and the amount of diversity in style of worship and other programmatic areas of congregational life.

In 1985, the Religious Education Department of the UUA heard my objections about exclusion and brought a variety of voices to their curriculum efforts. The RE Department did extensive research into the various institutions and resources and selected a methodology that was inclusive, respectful of differences and grounded in our UU values.

In 1994 they worked with the Urban Concerns Ministry to help us found the Latina/o Unitarian Universalist Networking Association (LUUNA). In this movement the Religious Educators have long championed our cause and lived closest to our UU values. If it had not been for the continuing support and efforts of the religious educators I would have long ago left the ministry in this movement. When we members of LUUNA felt embattled, belittled or ignored we knew the religious educators sympathized from their own experiences.

LUUNA also continued to advocate its views to the Journey Toward Wholeness Tranformation Committee. Ballester recalled,

At the January 1999 meeting, the Transformation Committee held a discussion to reflect. The Rev. Patricia Jimenez, president of LUUNA, participated and gave background on LUUNA, including their goals to educate, bring Latinos to congregations, enhance worship, and ties to the Latino community. A committee member began by asking about Latino concerns about the JTW program. . . . The point was made that "LUUNA had moved from wanting to be heard to wanting a seat at the table to wanting to take part and shape the work."

Rev. Joseph Santos-Lyons noted that "Bringing Gifts" was important to his deepening understanding of anti-racism, writing on his blog: "I find this type of analysis and commentary very helpful for us to understand each other and deepen the conversation around race."

VOICE
Rev. José Ballester

These comments were made in March 2001 at the Theology, Class and Race Dialogue at the UUA Urban Church Conference in Chicago.

I was born in New York City. My family came from Puerto Rico. I identify myself as a Puerto Rican, and a Nuyorican, with different influences. . . . But there are a lot of assumptions that are made about my life.

What does it mean to be a Latino? What does it mean in this particular setting, in working with my fellow UUs? . . . There are major differences between us, not all of them good, not all of them bad. It is the differences in class that concern me. An assumption is always made when you hear the word "Latinos." Do we understand UUism and how important a higher education is to understanding UUism? I have heard people say about reaching out into the Latino community, "We have to wait to have literature in Spanish." [But] I am quatri-lingual. Many of my fellow UUs are at least bilingual. . . .

I speak before you as an ordained UU minister, and I speak in a way so that you would not know that my first language is Spanish. You don't hear what my normal speaking voice is, how I grew up in NYC. If you did, you would again make an assumption about who I am, how intelligent I am, and [you might not know] that this person has a 161 IQ. It is a learned behavior, so that I can take part in this world.

[W]e have tried to oversimplify who we are, what we are. I do not object to you trying to learn more about me, the objection is to making assumptions about who I am and what I am. I did not grow up poor, I did not grow up uneducated, or working-class. I hate those titles. I did grow up not really feeling the effects of poverty. . . .

I now make a salary that, with my spouse, puts us comfortably in the middle class, but because I can connect with the people I work with . . . people who have been destroyed by the economic system in which we live, I hope that we [here at this conference] can suspend any presumptions we make about what the lower class, poor class are doing. . . .

Until you have groveled for food, you don't understand poverty. If you do not understand poverty, you do not understand the solutions. We as a group understand that we are called forth to make a difference in the lives of other people. Yes, we are. But we have to leave the confines of our world and enter into another world. . . . We have to be proud of who we are and be proud of who they are. We can not simply hold up Thoreau, Emerson, and the other greats who wrote about theology. We need to be with UU itinerant ministers, going up and down the dusty roads, spreading a faith, living a faith as completely as we can. There is hope; there is always hope.

Recently, I attended a chapter meeting of the Latino Professionals Network. Here was a room of about 100 to 125 people—professionals, CEOs, COOs, IT professionals, lawyers, doctors—and young people coming in. And I looked around that group, and they were all Latinos. . . .

I went up to the first person and introduced myself. She explained what she did, and I said what I did. I said, "I'm a UU." She told me she was too. And told me what church she attended. I was excited. I met another man. He said, "Well I'm a UU, in a suburban UU congregation." A third person, from New York City, we talked about 125th street, the barrio, and then got into the "what do you do for a living" talk: I'm a UU." . . . [In their congregations], these three UUs, prominent people in their industry, . . . did not share their background. . . . If they did, people would stop looking at them as powerful movers and shakers in industry, and look at them as those people who need, as those people who have English as a second language.

I hope you have the courage to address this openly. I invite you to go through this process, and remember that injustice anywhere is a threat to justice everywhere.

DRUUMM

In 1997, African American UU Ministers (AAUM) invited individuals of color to a meeting to talk about "providing personal and professional support, advocacy and reflection for its members; and promoting racial justice and harmony in our UU institutions for all professionals of color. Calling themselves UU Religious Professionals of Color (UURPOC), they created a steering committee of Robette Dias, Jacqui James, Gordon Bailey, Rev. Timothy Malone, Bea de Muinck Keizer, Rev. Patricia Jimenez, and Rev. Abbi Janamanchi and advertised their first annual meeting at the 1998 General Assembly. Rev. William (Chester) McCall, then minister in Durham, North Carolina, noted, "AAUUM had a plan for anti-racism; we have a similar plan, the exact same, seven years later."

By 1999, some had become aware of the need for an organization that served more people of color than those who were religious professionals. Diverse and Revolutionary Unitarian Universalist Multicultural Ministries was formed to meet that need. DRUUMM was seen as the heir of previous organizations, such as the African American Unitarian Universalist Ministers. What for some was divisive and difficult was for others what kept them active participants as Unitarian Universalists. "UUism has allowed me to continue doing the anti-racism work I'd started before," observed McCall. "This work has given me a community—professional and lay, friends and people who support me."

Malone, a founding member of DRUUMM who served as its first president, said creation of the organization was the most significant aspect of the anti-racism work for him. Paula Cole Jones, a later DRUUMM president, recalled, "DRUUMM was where I was part of a community where different racial groups could share a common identity." She noted that she experienced a great deal of personal and professional growth through listening to the stories of others and working together to make change. "A PhD could never have given me that," she said. "I am forever thankful."

As with many, she experienced a time in her journey through anti-racism "feeling discouraged" and being a part of DRUUMM was her path back. "You need community, you need a place where people are building confidence and operating with integrity. Then

"People of Color"

This controversial term was unpacked by Rev. Joseph Santos-Lyons as part of his Harvard Divinity School thesis. His research included a survey.

"People of Color" is a term that has come into widespread use over the last decade. With no apparent roots with respect to the common parlance of today, it has been used historically to identify multiracial persons, particularly of African descent. In French New Orleans, Louisiana as early as the 18th century there were groups, including a battalion in the War of 1812, which organized as "Free People of Color," for example. The idea of identity based on color can be directly connected to the racism and identity of European-Whites, predominately in North America, who have a long record of passionate fixation over color and people. Over time the meaning of the term has changed significantly, and nowadays the term is generally used to identify those persons who have been racially, culturally, ethnically, and economically oppressed. For all intents and purposes, this has meant broadly persons of Latino/a, Native American/Indigenous, African, Asian/Pacific Islander, and Arab/Middle Eastern descent, in part or wholly.

The UUA continues to struggle however with People of Color and has made a significant modification internally by adding "Latino/a." People of Color/Latino/a has now become the standard phrase articulated by the UUA administration. . . .

A group of Latino/a ministers, the Rev. Patricia Jimenez, the Rev. Lilia Cuervo, the Rev. José Ballester and the Rev. Peter Morales, advocated for the change in language to the UUA administration after the election of the Rev. William Sinkford, an African-American and one of the founding members of DRUUMM. Misunderstanding and confusion as to the purpose of these changes, coupled with the continued presence of Latino/as within DRUUMM who identify as People of Color, continued to be a source of tension in the UUA.

From the survey:

"People of Color is a political term to me, used to identify many different racial and ethnic groups bound by similar political circumstances." —Asian/Pacific Islander descent

"People of Color is a term of racialized resistance. It's a term adopted by racially oppressed peoples to bind us together in order to resist the divide and conquer paradigm that characterizes our lives and our collective relationship to White, as the dominant racial group in the U.S." —Native descent

"It is an umbrella term intended to both identify the common experiences of brown-skinned people in a white world and, also, it is a way to build a sense of solidarity around those experiences across ethnic lines. —African descent

"When I speak of 'People of Color' in the anti-racism community, I mean people who are descended from any of the indigenous people of Asia, America, Africa, Australia, Pacific Islands, and people from the Middle East. I include people who are multiracial as "People of Color." I understand, however, that most of these people have never heard of the designation." —Latino/a descent

"It is both a personal and political identity. It brings a name to my personal experience, without having to walk around 'bleeding for folks,' and it is a comment on my political analysis of the system of oppression. I think it also implies a personal and political commitment to an engaged resistance around issues of oppression rooted in my experience of racism." —Arab/Middle Eastern descent

. . . A few respondents [6.59%] showed a personal disapproval of the term. Responses did not make claims as to the use of the term more broadly in community as those who identified it in a political or movement-building sense sought to convey. Instead, these respondents commented that they personally would not employ the term to describe themselves because it had a neutral to negative meaning. An example includes:

"Honestly I would have to say Person of Color is extremely rude when referring to anyone. Yes there may be differences in the way different cultures raise their families, but to make a statement regarding People of Color just sounds politically incorrect. I would be offended if say a Teenager on up to an adult would say this, but maybe a smaller child would probably not upset me as much." —Latino/a descent

we can hold ourselves accountable for improving things rather than leaving because of disappointments."

By 2000, DRUUMM was working with the Association's Faith in Action Department to deliver anti-racism training and with the UUA Staff Team on Diversity and Ministry, which was created to recruit and support people of color in ministry. DRUUMM had been asked to intervene with this committee by people of color who felt that they were being assessed rather than supported.

Stakeholders Meeting Walkout

In part because of the need to be more inclusive, two stakeholders meetings were organized by the Journey Toward Wholeness Transformation Committee. In a 1999 report, the JTWTC discussed this:

> [W]e wanted to share what we were all learning among the stakeholders and provide them with a way to know each other. We hosted two stakeholder gatherings in 1999 to reflect on what people were learning and what was working in confronting racism. This was also an opportunity for stakeholders to let us know what assistance and resources they needed.
>
> The first gathering, Journey Toward Wholeness Assessment and Planning Meeting, was held in January 1999 in Boston with thirty leaders, including the JTWTC, the Board, the president and moderator of the UUA, UUA executive staff, Fulfilling the Promise (FTP) leaders, UUMA [Unitarian Universalist Ministers Association] Executive Committee members, the Latina/o Unitarian Universalist Network Association (LUUNA), DRUUMM, and others. Its purpose was to assess the progress of the initiative and to plan for a larger stakeholder gathering in June. At that meeting, a huge map on the wall showed all the district profiles from anti-racism transformation teams to Journey Toward Wholeness committees to accessibility committees to Welcoming, Jubilee, and JTW Sunday congregations. Participants added stories and information about congregational

and district efforts. We also compiled data on anti-oppression curricula and materials sold and distributed. Together, we analyzed the progress of the initiative and obstacles to going forward. One of our major conclusions was that while it was very encouraging and exciting to see a visual representation of the progress in each district, it was still clear that we needed to broaden the initiative.

Three major areas of focus that the gathering identified were getting the word out about the changes in the training, involving more ministers in the initiative, and surveying congregations about how they were relating to the Journey Toward Wholeness initiative. Other constituencies identified as needing particular support were religious educators, youth, young adults, activists, and social and racial justice committees. Materials from that meeting, which identified accomplishments, concerns, needs, and hopes for outcomes of the June stakeholders gathering were compiled and mailed to all participants.

"The Kansas City meeting was designed as a conscious shift in strategy," said Rev. William Gardiner of the Faith in Action Department. "At the stakeholder meeting we invited a wide variety of groups from throughout the Unitarian Universalist Association to participate in the meeting. It was a way of getting more of these groups involved in the process and creating broader ownership of the anti-racism movement." The meeting would prove contentious, but the plan produced from there is worth noting because it was comprehensive and gave a sense of the extent of the changes needed to make the "Journey."

Taquiena Boston, then a Faith in Action consultant, recalled that the people of color and/or Latina/o and Hispanic people gathered in caucuses to develop agendas for advancing anti-racism. "From the People of Color Caucus," she recalled, "agenda items that emerged were the following: developing anti-racism trainings that spoke specifically to the identities and experiences of people of color; incorporating more of the histories and experiences of diverse people of color groups into the anti-racism power analysis used in the JTW

Path to Anti-Racism; bringing more identity work into the anti-racism power analysis; developing programming that addressed the specific needs and concerns of multiracial families and families of color; and incorporating the intersections of oppressions, i.e., the links between racism and other forms of oppression such as sexism and heterosexism, homophobia, and classism and economic oppression."

Yet the meeting was difficult, as the JTW Transformation Committee reported:

> We hosted a larger gathering of eighty-five people in Kansas City called Next Steps on the Journey Toward Wholeness. . . . Many of the tensions involved in our anti-racist transformation, including dynamics of exclusion and control, our partnership with Crossroads Ministry and use of their training model, and the perception that the analysis operates from a black/white paradigm of racism, were present at this meeting and difficult to manage. In fact, the keynote speaker for the event, Dr. Janet Helms, spoke to the emotional dynamics associated with anti-racism efforts. We knew we had to address these very tensions as part of bringing the stakeholders together and broadening the initiative to the congregations. We knew that it was not enough to have an anti-racist analysis; it was also necessary to understand the dynamics of institutional change and how they affect individuals and groups.

The Kansas City stakeholders meeting illustrated the many agendas that were in the room. Confusion erupted over the role that Barndt, of Crossroads Ministry, was to play in the meeting. When presenter Janet Helms was conducting a session on identity, he interrupted and created more conflict in a tense situation. Dias, who would later join Crossroads Ministry as co-director, noted that the organization had "dysfunction" at that time and that "the JTWTC as a group was not strong enough to balance some of the stuff that Crossroads brought in as a group and we got hit full steam ahead at Kansas City." Dias noted that some of the expectations participants brought to the Kansas City meeting were not realistic. "They wanted to have the perfect curriculum where no one got upset," she said. "Unitarian Universalists want to stand on a bully pulpit."

Another rift widened at the Kansas City gathering. Rev. José Ballester recalled,

> This conference was, for some of us, the starting point of our disenfranchisement from the UUA's efforts. As Latinos and Latinas, we had long experienced being forgotten, overlooked or ignored. Much of the efforts had been dichotomous with a black-white focus. In 1985 when some of us protested that the creation of a Black Concerns Working Group without some concerns for other "minority groups" was unfair, we were ignored.
>
> Despite its name we were largely left out of the 1992 Racial and Cultural Diversity Resolution. Our voices were not on the Racial and Cultural Diversity Task Force, with the result that the creation of the Journey Toward Wholeness (JTW) Resolution of 1996 did not include us. When we protested and refused to endorse the resolution we were promised a place on the new committee. When selection time came we were restricted to naming one Latina layperson. This disqualified much of our leadership who were ministers, male or non-Latina/os.
>
> From that point on we were invited to "participate" in gatherings, conferences and/or committees but our contributions were ignored, opposed or dismissed. The Kansas City stakeholders gathering promised to change all that. In January 1998 there was a pre-conference gathering at UUA Headquarters. Despite all our protests about being marginalized the conference room had quotations from only African American writers and the participants in the open worship service were either white or black. Gratefully, Leon Spencer noticed our exclusion and asked one of us to take his place in the worship service. We finally had a ray of hope that things would be different. We prepared a statement for the conference that showed our commitment to the effort

and our insights. It was called "Bringing Gifts." We heartily awaited Kansas City.

The first night was promising, with the leaders, including Leon Spencer, acknowledging the wider agenda we needed to address. However, the next morning, it was evident that the gathering would be business as usual. By mid-morning, it was clear that the gathering was to sell us on the current JTW effort, that there would be little change, and that we had been left out, yet again. The Latino Latina contingency walked out of the conference.

From that time until fairly recently, those who have differed with the official UUA/JTW have found ourselves being openly attacked, deliberately excluded and marginalized by the UUA staffers, committees or supporters. . . . Regardless of the criticism, and experiences that the UUA's efforts were not working, we stuck to this one single ideal and viewed any other suggestions as hostile. We have learned very little.

Jimenez recalled,

I found myself just getting more and more and more upset, and finally I got up . . . and I was standing out there, talking to Susan Suchocki [a minister and chair of the Journey Toward Wholeness Committee], who had put this thing together, and I was saying, "I am furious," and the next thing I see is José coming out, and after him was . . . practically half the room. And we were promised that this would be addressed. I asked [Leon Spencer], "Are we going to address this?"and he said, "Yes," and we did not.

A huge gulf opened up, fueled in part by the perception that the loss was not noted or mourned by those participating. "We tell the story of the African Americans and their supporters walking out in Boston GA [in 1969 as part of the Empowerment Controversies], and it's a whole part of our history," Ballester observed. "Here you have your Latino contingency walk out and the only thing that resulted was then we were branded as rabble-rousers and enemies and from that point on, it seems like we were being targeted."

The Emergence of Caucusing

At the same time that differences were causing divisions, they were also a reason for coalescing. Caucusing or grouping by identity categories was emerging as a powerful force to provide support for members of historically marginalized groups. Caucusing itself would become a lightning rod for criticism, attracting charges of separatism. Rev. Manish Mishra, then a seminarian, reflected in 2006 from his position as president of DRUUMM about these reactions:

> Caucasian Americans, the majority culture, caucus together all the time, and that's nothing new or surprising unless you haven't looked at it that way. When you actually stop to consider it that way, that white folk get together all the time—what in our particular demographic tends to be suburban, white folk—they share the common experiences of being suburban, white folk who also tend to be highly educated and middle- to upper middle-class. So in a way, the whole culture supports that type of networking. And what that leaves, then, is the question of how people who don't necessarily identify with those majority demographic aspects of UUism find the space and the ability to talk about our somewhat different experiences and issues?
>
> What I hear most frequently with regard to the criticism against caucusing is the phrase, "Well, I don't know why you all have to do that. I don't see color. I don't treat people differently. Everybody is the same. I'm color-blind. So why do you all need to make it a big deal, and why do you all need to do this identity caucusing and therefore promote segregation and promote difference, when I'm trying to be a good person and not focus on difference?" . . . Cory Edwards helped me in her book, *Against All Odds*. What she talked about in there, with her other co-authors, is how this idea of color-blindness really shifts the entire responsibility of the nonwhite experience onto people of color, and it does so by

saying, "Because I'm not going to recognize color, because I'm color-blind, if you are recognizing color, you are the problem. I'm not the problem." So it becomes a way of shifting the responsibility to do something about societal and cultural racial discrimination off the shoulders of somebody who is probably good at heart and well-meaning, but it shifts that burden directly and exclusively onto the shoulders of people of color, which is not anybody's idea of a valid outcome, if you were to sit around and dissect it and analyze it in that way. I think most UUs would not want people of color to feel like they're carrying the water all by themselves, carrying the burden of diversity all by themselves, and yet this language of not seeing color, of being blind to it, does exactly that. It absolves the person who is from the majority culture of any sense of responsibility to hold the pain and troubles of people of color and to do anything to try and be supportive of the fact that those struggles and that pain exist.

Yet identity groups were coalescing at a time when tensions existed between them. At 1999 General Assembly, the Transformation Committee and LUUNA met to follow up on what had happened in Kansas City. The JTWTC version of the meeting indicated that little was resolved. A number of other efforts were made to bridge differences and yet distrust was now sown. In the many debriefings that followed, several themes emerged:

- Lack of communication that led to a number of people feeling disenfranchised and "dissed." These feelings were not just from LUUNA members they came also from some of the Core Team.
- Unresolved issues between the Association staff and people of color surfaced in the exchanges at Kansas City.
- An accidental meeting of LUUNA and AAUUM furthered the distance between key individuals.
- The situation among people of color was exacerbated by the expectations of white people that all people of color/Latina/

Latino/Hispanic people should share one perspective when in fact they do not.

- Caucus time was needed for people of color/Latino/Latina/Hispanic and whites. We learned that we need to always design events with caucuses. The POC caucus was the largest at that time that had ever officially been convened by the UUA.

LUUNA responded in part with a collection of essays known as the *Baltimore Papers*.

Youth and Young Adults

From the beginning, some youth and young adults seemed predisposed to addressing issues of race. The Continental Unitarian Universalist Young Adult Network (C*UUYAN) held its first anti-racism workshop in 1999. And the first youth and young adults of color conference took place in Atlanta the same year.

Among more difficult issues facing the Journey Toward Wholeness Committee as 1999 began, a bright spot was the work of the Youth Council, the governing body of YRUU. The Youth Council's efforts, included development of an Anti-Racism Task Force by a resolution sponsored by the YRUU Steering Committee, a General Assembly workshop, and "Coming Out of Denial," a day-long training at Youth Council.

Gardiner, of the Faith in Action Department, recalled that it became apparent that youth needed their own approach to anti-racism work. "We invited the youth to multigenerational anti-racism trainings but we finally stopped doing these programs," he recalled. "Our training models didn't match with the learning styles that most youth feel comfortable with. In addition, many youth of color are working on core racial identity issues. Our trainings were not designed to work with those issues. Now the youth and young adults are developing their own anti-racism training models. We are supporting them in that work."

Yet for others, particularly those who came from historically marginalized groups, the beginning work was essential to keeping them in relationship with the Association. Rev. Joseph Santos-Lyons recalled his experience as a young adult:

EXCERPT
Baltimore Papers

Ruth J. Alatorre wrote the following piece, "Urban issues & Latinos," for the Baltimore Papers, *a critique of the UUA's anti-racism efforts published by LUUNA.*

Whatever you think of when you think of "Latinos" is almost certainly wrong. The Latino community in the United States today is so diverse that any attempt to have a single approach to Latino ministry is almost surely doomed to fail. When we speak of "Latinos" we are simultaneously speaking about recent immigrants and people whose families were here long before George Washington was inaugurated. Among the recent immigrants, we are talking about families from Mexico, Guatemala, El Salvador, Nicaragua, Colombia and Peru. When we speak of "Latinos" we are talking about people who cannot speak English and also about people who speak little or no Spanish. Those who speak Spanish as their mother tongue may have trouble understanding each other. A Mexican-American family in Los Angeles is likely to think of a Puerto Rican family from New York as more "foreign" and different than the Anglo family next door. Lastly there are Latinos who are seemingly invisible, middle class and living in suburbs, sometimes married to non-Latinos. . . .

One possible reason for the invisibility of middle-class Latinos is that our lifestyles are completely integrated with mainstream America. We often live in Anglo middle-class communities, we often marry non-Latinos, we sometimes do not speak Spanish, and we often do not fit Anglo's perceptions of what a Latino should look like. We need to learn more about the successful middle-class Latinos and stop lumping all of us together for the purpose of demographic analyses.

How should our congregations respond to this overwhelming diversity among the Latino populations? How do we establish a ministry that simultaneously meets the needs of the poor, uneducated family who just immigrated from El Salvador and the family of Mexican-American professionals who live in a prosperous suburb? The answer is that we respond with different ministries, ministries based on knowing real people and their real needs. Recent immigrants are more likely to benefit from English-as-a-second-language classes, citizenship assistance and a place to congregate than to adult religious education on Transcendentalism. Unchurched Latino families in the suburbs are likely to need a ministry much like the one we provide already at worship, religious education, a liberal religious home where they can grow spiritually free of rigid dogma and where they can unite with others on their religious journeys.

There is no way a set program developed by LUUNA or the UUA can possibly respond to the nuances of each congregation's actual situation. Our ministries must be unique and grow out of a deep knowing. We begin with open doors and open hearts. We listen to people's stories and tell our own; we hear their needs. When we know people in depth, we know how to respond.

I had become very committed to the idea of building a multiracial community, and was slowly learning the theories of racial justice, anti-racism, the linkage of oppressions, confronting racism, institutional, cultural and systemic racism. When I was invited in 1996 to take on the responsibility of moderator for the Continental Youth organization (Young Religious Unitarian Universalists or YRUU) for their annual business meeting, I was honored but skeptical of feeling at home in the community that had once been so meaningful for me. With my worldview newly informed by my college education and experiences, I had already begun a careful and detailed interrogation of my birth-faith of Unitarian Universalism. I had become wary of the extreme Whiteness within the church, and the institutional and cultural racism therein. My experience at the University of Oregon introduced my maturing self to racism of the White liberal through my activism with Students of Color. Reflecting on my childhood in the church, I concluded that I gained little knowledge or insight about race relations. Given where I was personally, Unitarian Universalism's White guilt, tokenizing and color-blind behaviors fueled my growing disenchantment towards the church. Even so, attending the 1996 Continental Youth Council at Reed College was an honor and gave me a long moment to reflect on my own religious and spiritual identity. I concluded this event with a renewed interest in our liberal religious faith. I experienced serious questioning about racism within Unitarian Universalism that inspired me, paralleling the questions I was asking as a Person of Color within the church. At Youth Council I learned much about myself and came to look upon the virtue of Unitarian Universalism with fresh eyes in part through the mandatory and daily Anti-Racism workshops.

ANALYSIS

Identity as a Spiritual Process

Dr. Leon Spencer wrote this piece in the 1990s for use in identity workshops and in trainings for identity trainers.

Wherever we are, we deal with identity. We are often tempted to try to find one category that describes all of who we are and yet, ultimately, we find that all such attempts end in frustration. In truth, we have multiple dimensions to our identities, which are products of what we value, what we believe, what our institutional affiliations are, and cultural and racial scripts that affect us individually and collectively. Identity has a spiritual aspect. When we ask "Who am I?" or "Who are we?", we are asking a deeply theological question. And identities will shift over time and will continue to evolve over our whole lives.

Identity Statuses: William Cross in his work has found that several "statuses" exist as far as identity is concerned. These are not so much a progression as labels for a point in time because people can often shift between these statuses. The statuses are:

1. Pre-Encounter—Here a person has never encountered a person from a different identity group. While in this stage, people will put a high value on reinforcing the dominant culture. They will have an almost naïve belief that "all is well." They will have a preference for members of different groups to do everything together and will be threatened by attempts to differentiate among groups. (Example: Many white UUs living in our predominantly white UU culture.)
2. Encounter—An encounter occurs when an event, which can be either positive or negative, takes place which makes the person realize that differences do exist among groups. This can be a time of self-assessment and even a time of dissonance. In almost all cases, the individual has a compelling desire for more knowledge after the encounter and there is a certain chaotic ele-

ment in identity as new information is received. (Example: A transracially adopted child who has a negative experience around race in the congregation or a multiracial couple who discovers another multiracial couple and feels an immediate affirmation and bond.)
3. Immersion/Emersion—Because of the strong need for additional information after the encounter experience, individuals may choose to immerse themselves in experiences that reinforce their own identity. They may want only to be with people who share their identity as they look for a stronger sense of that identity and seek to verify their own experience. After this experience, they emerge with their new identity into a world which may or may not embrace their stronger identity. (Examples: Men joining men's groups or women joining women's groups; a multiracial family or families of color gathering.)
4. Integration/Commitment—When the individual embraces their identity as something they value and are prepared to act on. (Example: The use of identity caucusing as a way to provide a safe space for members of one racial group to support one another while affirming the value of multiracial gatherings in other activities.)

Identity Enactments (based on the work of William Cross): Because of the many identities we hold, we have learned ways to deal with the reactions we may get by being part of a particular identity group that is not part of the dominant culture. William Cross has identified five kinds of behaviors that he believes occur when people "enact" their identities.

1. Buffering—Sometimes being part of a marginalized group, people have strong negative experiences such as those around race in our culture. To minimize these, people have learned to "buffer" or protect themselves or others. (An example might be a husband of African descent who chooses not to engage with his white in-laws, or parents of multiracial children who seek to

shield their children from negative attitudes toward racial difference.)

2. Code Switching—Another method for dealing with identity-related issues is to "code switch," which is to become multilingual in a real sense. Those who are adept at this may speak one language (literally or figuratively) with members of their identity group and another with the society at large. (An example would be someone who uses certain terms, phrases, and mannerisms when with her family than she does when at her predominantly white UU congregation.)

3. Bridging—People may see themselves as bridgers between members of one of their identity groups and the society at large. In this way, they keep a sense of their identity both within the specific group and as a member of the larger culture.

4. Bonding—For some, spaces where all share one important aspect of identity may be most important and they seek opportunities to deepen their sense of identity through these groups. (An example would be caucusing by race as part of an anti-racism training event.)

5. Individualization—Others may have had little experience with others who share an important aspect of their identity and thus may see themselves solely as individuals with very little need or ability to share a group or collective identity. (An example might be someone who defies all labels and groupings.)

These enactments are neither positive nor negative. If they are done to the exclusion of other behaviors, they may limit the experiences a person has with members of their identity group or with the larger culture.

CHAPTER 13

Ministry Steps

Coming into focus in this period was the difficulty ministers faced in adding anti-racism into their complex stew of relationships. Rev. Kurt Kuhwald, a parish minister who became an anti-racism trainer, noted that in Unitarian Universalism ministers serve at the will of the congregation, so raising controversial issues can be risky. "I wanted to be a Methodist sometimes," Kuhwald said, "because I would then know I am going to be [a congregation's minister] for four years no matter what." He said parish ministers need to look at how raising difficult topics can restrict their ability to do other important work: "How can I talk about that when I also have to do the food drive next week?" Yet, he said, being willing to take on conflict could make Unitarian Universalism more relevant in the twenty-first century.

Rev. Danielle DiBona, then on the Association's Faith in Action staff, noted tension with pastoral care—if a parish minister raises painful issues such as racism, some people might be loathe to look to them for support. She also noted the paradoxical truth that not naming the difficult things also undermined ability to minister. "If you serve a church long enough, something is going to hit the fan," she said. "Because we are non-creedal, we have to identify our ministerial authority very differently than the Methodists or the Baptists. Until we claim our authority, they don't respect us as a pastor."

The efforts of President Dr. John Buehrens' administration met resistance from many ministers. "This is hard work and the work of many generations and most ministers don't want to go near it," said Rev. Rob Eller-Isaacs, a long-time proponent of urban ministry efforts. "Most of our churches have relegated anti-racism work to the social action corner of the church."

DiBona observed, "There was little or no preparation or pre-work [about anti-racism] for the folks in the pews or the clergy. This permitted many [ministers] to accuse the process as being flawed and then to pass on the anti-racist work, with an arrogant understanding that they were protecting church polity."

Eller-Isaacs agreed. "Some of the ministers of the large churches," he said, "are more comfortable articulating disdain for the Association."

Structure Changes

In this era, the Unitarian Universalist Ministers Association was trying to honor the commitments it had made to support anti-racism dialogue. Attending anti-racism training became one of those commitments. Rev. Gary Smith, who became UUMA president in 1998 and who identified as white from Scots-Danish-Irish descent, recalled that parts of the anti-racism training seemed designed to produce guilt and turned him off, yet overall it "was really transformational for me. . . . I have to say, it got in there and changed me in terms of an understanding of systemic racism, which I had not understood before."

The insights gained caused change in the UUMA, Smith said. "Rev. John Gilmore was appointed (or elected, memory fails) to the [the UUMA Executive Committee] and not only kept issues of racism before the group, he also delivered able service, handling the UUMA's difficult publications portfolio," Smith said. "But there was no institutional change to ensure that a person of color would continue to serve on that body. At the end of John's term, the UUMA Exec became all white once again. A new group of UUMA leaders, several years later, would have to 'get it' again."

Smith also observed, "It took us a long while to get away from the notion that there were people out in front [anti-racism advocates] who were kind of disappointed with us, that we didn't see the light, that they did and we didn't. And I think I would have to say, and now I can only speak for myself, that was my feeling, that and I really want to give a lot of credit to Sue Suchocki [chair of the Journey Toward Wholeness Transformation Committee], because she really helped me understand that it was more a partnering, and they were walking with us. They were trying not to walk out front and be arrogant. That was extremely helpful to me to just reframe it, because I felt so frustrated . . . that I wasn't quite where some of the leaders were in the anti-racism work."

Theology, Faith and Action Conference

To develop a Unitarian Universalist race and oppression vocabulary was clearly a challenge. In 1998 the two Unitarian Universalist seminaries, Meadville Lombard Theological School and the Starr King School for the Ministry, co-sponsored an event titled "Theology, Faith and Action," held January 16 to 18 at Meadville Lombard's Chicago campus. The design called for seven or eight presenters to look at anti-racism efforts from different viewpoints and different theologies. It featured Unitarian Universalist seminary faculty as well as prominent people of color including Rev. Dr. Michelle Bentley, Dr. Elias Farajajé-Jones, Rev. Melvin Hoover, Yielbonzie Charles Johnson, and Rev. Dr. Thandeka, as well as Unitarian Universalist academics from other institutions, Rev. Dr. William Jones, Dr. Sharon Welch, and Rev. Dr. Ian Evison of the Alban Institute. Rev. Dr. Rebecca Parker, the Starr King president, and Bentley, of Meadville Lombard, served as facilitators.

For Starr King, this had been a difficult time. Parker noted that in 1996 and 1997, the school had diversified its faculty, hiring two men of color who were also gay. She remembered,

> When we called two men of color to our faculty [Farajajé-Jones and Johnson] and we got a whole lot of backlash for that, and couldn't always tell if it was backlash because they were men of African descent, or if it was because they were queer, or in the case of Ibrahim Farajajé, because he was UU-friendly but didn't identify as a UU, or some of the backlash to Yielbonzie was he hadn't had enough parish experience. At any rate, there was backlash for having hired them as somehow inadequate.
>
> That backlash also was where I got accused of having lost my senses and being sexually immoral. That was a moment in which we appealed to the UUA Board for support and help. I don't know if we appealed to the JTW Com-

VOICE
Rev. William (Chester) McCall

For ministers of color, the struggle persisted, as this account from a Preliminary Fellowship Renewal request reveals.

Being an African-American bi-sexual male in a long-term same-sex relationship thus perceived as a gay male, made the selection of a mentor difficult. During my mentoring relationships in Tulsa I began to realize that I was having professional experiences and challenges of my ministry that my Euro-American (White) colleagues did not and could not understand. While I found that there was empathy for the issues that were arising as a result of these two factors of being black and seen as gay, there existed as a result of no fault of their own, an inability to engage in depth in a conversation about these issues and their impact upon my ministry. . . . There existed a very basic fundamental difference in what I perceived as an experience of racism and homophobia and what my Euro-American colleagues believed what I was experiencing. In most cases, before I could have what I believed to be an in-depth meaningful conversation, I had to first convince my colleague that I was in fact experiencing racism and homophobia. If the mentoring relationship for ministers of color is to be more than a superficial one that exists only for the purpose of meeting an MFC requirement, then there will be times when there may not be available an appropriate mentor for a minister of color, a minister who is homosexual and/or a minister that is a person of color and bi-sexual. In these situations, there needs to be an institutional alternative.

mittee, or whatever form it would have been, at that point. And the silence in response to our appeal was pretty loud. In fact the [UUA's] Department of Ministry felt they had to investigate the charges that I was sexually unethical. In other words, there wasn't an analysis that said, "Oh this is backlash. . . ."

When we got slapped, the UUA could have said, "There's all this anti-racism work going on; this is a priority of the UUA," so what kept the UUA at that point from stepping out boldly in support of the directions in which its theological school was moving? The [UUA's] Panel on Theological Education could say, "Bravo for you guys and since you've lost funding for this, we're going to make sure we boost your funding." [Missing was] even a letter from the UUA Board that said, "Hey, we appreciate what you're doing, and we understand you're getting flak, but we're with you." Even that kind of moral support. We weren't at a place in '96 or '97 where that was where the UUA Board and leaders went.

We soldiered on at Starr King anyway, but we didn't feel like we were working in the context of commitment. And I remember Yielbonzie saying at one point, "This is a sign that the UUA's approach to AR [anti-racism] work is not working." . . . Our counter-oppressive and AR commitments have only skimmed the surface of the kind of cultural transformation that's needed in a historically white liberal context for various kinds of peoples of colors to be able to flourish and function wholeheartedly and fully. So Yielbonzie's comment that when Starr King got a lot of flak and then didn't get a lot of support that . . . it made it look like the UUA's anti-racism work and commitment was all surface. And maybe it was, how to translate some consciousness-raising into solidarity kinds of action, especially when resources become an issue.

Buehrens, who described his identity as "the product of a multi-ethnic, Euro-American Midwestern family in which my father did not have the benefit of a college education," considered this meeting a great disappointment because little cross-fertilization occurred, in his opinion. "It ended up being eight different presentations, all crammed into too small a compass," he said. "They were sequential presentations that were designed to be sort of rah-rah rallying things rather than people wrestling with one another." He also noted that no record emerged from the conversation, as many of the presentations were not written.

This illustrated some of the challenges the theological schools faced. Rev. Rosemary Bray McNatt was on the Starr King board from 1993 to 2001. She recalled,

> We were very interested in trying to figure out how do you educate people to deal with issues of oppression when you have a faculty that's all white, and hasn't even coped with that. It being all white in and of itself wasn't a problem. The problem was, if this is an important issue for you, how do you model a multiracial culture in the school? What do you do to make that happen? . . .
>
> I think the most important thing was to get people to talk about it. That was the most important thing. We couldn't get anybody to talk about it before that. And the most important thing was once the Board was able to talk about it, was that the Board was willing to take action on behalf of what we talked about, and to withstand the enormous pushback from the movement and from donors about it. Because people stopped giving money.

At Meadville Lombard, the Jubilee Working Group said that "the race and theology program . . . presented a wide perspective on the subject [though] there were pieces missing since the group was white or African American." This awareness led the Working Group to design a General Assembly meeting, with representatives from LUUNA and UUNIA invited, to talk about trying to include multiple perspectives of oppression in anti-racism workshops.

Ministers Association Steps

The Unitarian Universalist Ministers Association had taken the step of appointing a member of its Executive Committee, which is known among ministers as "the Exec," to hold an anti-racism, anti-oppression, and multicultural portfolio. Gilmore held a temporary position. The first member to hold the permanent position was Rev. Peter Morales. The difficulties posed by these sorts of advances are illustrated by Morales's appointment. Attending a meeting of the Diverse and Revolutionary Unitarian Universalist Multicultural Ministries (DRUUMM) when he was fresh out of seminary, he was asked to serve as a representative "person of color" on the Exec. He recalled:

> Three people turned it down, said they couldn't do it. Michelle Bentley was one who turned it down, and a couple of others I can't remember. So then someone turns to me and says, "Would you do it?" And honest-to-God, my response was—I'm just getting out of seminary—"What's the Exec? I don't know anything about the Exec or what's involved." "Well, it's the executive committee of the UUMA." "Well, what do they do?" "Well, they meet a few times a year," and I said, "Why me?" It wasn't anything I was anxious to do or even had enough knowledge to know what I was being asked to do. So I ended up getting on it because it seemed like nobody else was going to. . . . I had just graduated and was about to go into my first settlement. . . . I know how these things work: "We got one at Starr King!" You know. And it's been kind of funny that way to be offered all these things and invited into this and that. I've joked at times it was odd to be the first this and the first that. It's not something I had the experience of before, and it says something about our movement.

The background as to how the position was established was complex. A key question was how the individual holding the portfolio should be accountable to larger communities, such as DRUUMM. At the UUMA's annual meeting on June 24, 1999, three resolutions were introduced that addressed structural responses to anti-racism work. First, at the January 1999 meeting, a petition signed by Revs. Sarah Clark, Laurie J. Auffant, Dr. Mykel Johnson, and Sherri Puchalsky asked the UUMA to "guarantee that DRUUMM (Diverse and Revolutionary Unitarian Universalist Multicultural Ministers) be represented with one position on the UUMA Executive Committee and one position on the CENTER Committee, the continuing education arm of the UUMA. These two people to be appointed by DRUUMM to monitor and address the needs and concerns of UU ministers and ministerial candidates of color." Though this was eventually ruled as exceeding the authority of the UUMA Executive Committee, it did start a discussion of having a designated position which was the focus of the second resolution. The third resolution addressed the need to have an educational event for ministers as well as "encourage creation of a full-time staff member at the UUA for the sole purpose of addressing issues surrounding professionals and people of color in general within the UUA." This last resolution caused debate about whether the work was needed most at the Association or the congregational level and then it passed. The UUMA approved a single appointed position and having an educational event.

Morales, minister at Jefferson Unitarian Church in Golden, Colorado, did not support the idea of DRUUMM appointing the Exec position he held. Based on his experience, he said, he saw this as neither necessary nor appropriate. "I said, 'Y'know, these folks are not resisting having this portfolio on the Exec,'" he recalled. "I think it's going to be a tough sell for any professional organization to give another group the right to appoint somebody to the Executive Committee. And I was actually saying they have a nominating process. One, not all DRUUMM members are ministers. It's not even a ministerial organization. And to have a non-ministerial organization appointing someone to the Executive Committee of a professional organization seems kind of goofy."

A number of people of color such as Rosemary Bray McNatt, then a seminarian, saw theological diversity and racial diversity in the ministry as linked issues:

For me, it's been an ongoing issue that if we want to expand the number and kinds of people of color in the UUA, we have to expand theologically and stop having an allergic reaction to more traditional forms of Christianity. That was something that was very important. I made a conscious choice to be able and willing to talk about those things and to back up my conversations about those things with service in the UUA so that I was known to people in the movement as someone who would work on behalf of the movement on things in addition to race and class and gender.

244

VOICE
Rev. Fredric Muir

An excerpt from the sermon "White and Anti-Racist," which Rev. Fredric Muir preached February 27, 2000, at First Unitarian Universalist Church of Annapolis, Maryland.

When I was a child growing up in Oak Park, Illinois, on many Christmases my family would take the food our church had collected to the Jane Hull House in downtown Chicago. These were in the days before the Eisenhower Expressway was complete, the massive interstate that connects Chicago and the western suburbs. Our only alternatives were the three or four streets that ran through my village and ended at Lake Michigan—Division Street is the way we usually went.

I remember the first time we made the Hull House trip. About 20 minutes into Chicago, the neighborhoods began to change. The people on the streets and in their cars didn't look like the people in Oak Park—Puerto Ricans and African Americans mostly. We were all very quiet—my brother, mother, father and I, we just stared out the windows. Then my dad broke the silence "Did everyone remember to lock their doors?" He didn't need to say any more. He never named names, he said nothing derogatory, he made no generalizations—and we didn't ask for clarification because his tone of voice said it all. And the message was quite clear—I just had to look out the window to understand, or least understand as best as an eight-year-old might understand. Of course he wanted us to be safe. I'm sure he had our best interests in mind. And it was just one of the first of many racist messages I grew up with, stepping stones affirming prejudice and privilege.

It was the 1960s. Oak Park was a white enclave surrounded by communities where redlining, panic-peddling and civil rights disturbances had already erupted and shaken the status quo. Oak Parkers lived in a delirious and unfounded fear of race riots—something so far from reality that even then I had a hard time making sense of it. What

my family didn't want to talk about on car trips or around the dinner table was read in the paper, seen on the television, talked about at school. It was all happening right before us—in the hometown of Frank Lloyd Wright, the birthplace of Ernest Hemingway, who had described it as a village of "wide lawns and narrow minds"—I can now see that the times were a'changing though not without a hard fight from those who felt their power and privilege being threatened.

Twenty-five years later, I was driving my family to Howard University, where they were going to drop me off at a meeting so they could use our one car. As I turned off Route 50 onto Florida and then over to Georgia Avenue, I hit the power locks button. "Who did that?" my daughter asked me. I did, I told her. "Why did you lock the doors? Is something going to happen?" she wanted to know. I was just concerned for their safety, I told myself. And what was the message I was sending to them? I quickly changed the subject not really sure what to say. Evidently the silent and demonstrated lessons of my childhood weren't easily forgotten, but burned deep into my psyche and emerging without much thought. My racism will only be exorcized with a lot of struggle.

Don't misunderstand what I'm saying: there are still many neighborhoods where I lock my car doors. As I said, my father had our best interests at heart, I had my family's safety in mind. But it was the silence that was damaging. Children hear the words, look around, and draw their own conclusions, conclusions that can last a lifetime.

One of the revelations I [gained attending anti-racism training] was something I'd read before but never fully understood. Race is an arbitrary and false social construct and distinction. Freely we talk about "the races"—we read about it, we hear others speak about it. But there is only one race—the human race. Within the human race there are people of different color, different genders and sexual orientations, people from different nations, but it's all the human race. The very idea of there being races was invented during the time of European expansion, colonization and domination—I mean, how much easier to oppress a people when it's believed that they are of a different race, that they are not the same as you.

Racism, then, is the result of this deceptive and error-filled means of categorization. Racism is color prejudice and the misuse of institutional power. Let me unpack this. We all have prejudice, we all prejudge, it's a part of living. . . . Some do their prejudging of people based on the color of skin, facial characteristics, and accent. In and of itself, this may not be all that bad. But racism is more than color prejudice, it's prejudice enforced by power, by institutional power, as in the institutions which make the rules that determine who's in charge.

This racism is expressed at three levels. First, individually, and perhaps it's individual racism that is the least effective in a wide-ranging way, individual racism often has very little impact on society as a whole. As I've said, my own color or ethnic prejudices don't carry much weight all by themselves. But, when coupled with the second level, institutional racism, then it's felt much more. Racism at this level is power over, it's when the rules and privileges are set in our institutions and closed to people of color, which is to say that institutional racism makes a big difference. But not the difference that cultural racism can make: cultural racism is when people's lives are shaped by color prejudice, the very way they think about themselves has been determined by distortions, discountings, and discredits as seen in our language and expressions, images and stories, history and heroes.

When I first heard this definition of racism and all of the pieces and levels, I've got to admit that I could agree that I have lots of prejudices, I prejudge all the time and often I prejudge by the use of skin color. But power? Me having power, authority and control? Yeah, right! I don't have any power, I've told myself. So I have to admit to you that I now understand that I have quite a bit of power and a great deal of it is simply in the fact that I am white: our society has been created by white people for white people and whether I want it or not I am a beneficiary of all those years of white control and power. This is a privilege I don't even think about—it just is.

CHAPTER 14

"Why Anti-Racism Will Fail"

Resistance among ministers was persistent. Rev. William Sinkford, who was elected president of the Unitarian Universalist Association in 2001, recalled that the push-back continued despite the fact that anti-racism trainings and approaches were modified to address concerns. "Over time, far too long a time, these trainings were modified, making them more UU friendly," he recalled. "But the 'buzz' among the ministers, that the trainings were theologically inappropriate and almost creedal, became widespread. For me as a black man, and the highest ranking person of color on the UUA staff [as Congregational, District and Extension Director before being elected], this early work was a source of both comfort and frustration. Comfort because the institution to which I had committed my ministry was taking seriously the issue of race. Frustration because the pace was halting and agonizingly slow, especially outside the continental leadership groups."

Rev. Dr. Thandeka's 1999 address at a 1999 General Assembly workshop, "Why Anti-Racism Will Fail" (published later that year in the *Journal of Liberal Religion*) was a lightning rod for all the discomfort. Those who had reopened painful work around race felt that the address had attacked them in an unjust and agenda-laden manner. Those who did not support efforts to look at racial biases within the Unitarian Universalist Association saw the address as a vindication. Relationships polarized around the perception of two divergent positions, though hindsight would reveal that the positions were not that far apart in critical ways. Both positions articulated a need to create a dialogue across differences in race and ethnicity; both saw the barriers to such as systemic.

Rev. Melvin Hoover, then directing the Association's Faith in Action Department, said Thandeka's opposition was harmful because she was a strong communicator and had access to a number of channels for communication. He said her arguments were used by more "conservative" elements in Unitarian Universalism that were fighting the Journey Toward Wholeness effort because it came out of UUA lay and professional groups. He recalled that she was not the only one resisting: "[Rev.] Bill Jones [professor and anti-racism educator] was always saying, 'Well, I'm not sure, this is not going to work because of this and this and that.' He said, 'They're going to come up to the point of real change and not do it.' . . . He might have been right."

Rev. Robert Eller-Isaacs, then minister in Oakland, California, said, "The Crossroads model became a flashpoint that reflected concerns about anti-racism."

Rev. Dr. Thandeka's GA Presentation

A presentation by Thandeka, a professor of theology at Meadville Lombard Theological School whose thoughts had also been featured in a 1994 *World* article, garnered attention from those with concerns about the focus on anti-racism. Her statement included:

I must begin my remarks with a critique of the anti-racist programs described by the *Journey Toward Wholeness Path to Anti-Racism*, the information packet developed by the UUA's Faith in Action Department for Diversity and Justice. The packet itemizes the steps we need to take to develop an anti-racist UU identity, none of which, we're told, can be skipped if one wishes to become an anti-racist. The first step is to take an anti-racism training workshop led by an authorized trainer.

I took one of these workshops and read the accompanying material. As a result of these experiences, I learned three things: One. All whites in America are racists. Two. No blacks in America are racist. They're prejudiced just like everybody else, but they lack the power of institutional resources to force other racial groups to submit to their will. Thus they can't be racist because racism in this conceptual scheme is defined as prejudice + power. Three. Whites must be shown that they are racists and confess their racism.

Based on my experiences of the training and on my work with some of the anti-racism advocates at the UUA on a racial and cultural diversity task force, I concluded that the anti-racist strategies have three basic problems: First. They violate the first principle of our UU covenant together to actively affirm and promote the inherent worth and dignity of every person; Second. They make an erroneous assumption about the nature and structure of power in America; and Third, they misinterpret actions resulting from feelings of shame and powerlessness as evidence of white racism.

Now in more detail:

Problem #1: The UUA's anti-racist programs tend to violate the first principle of our covenant together. Evidence. Anti-racists assume that congregations and their leadership mirror—and I use the anti-racist language here—the larger society's racism by excluding people of color as well as other socially oppressed groups such as gays and lesbians, people with disabilities, Third World citizens, etc., through the congregations' often unexamined policies, practices, teachings, and decisions. What these anti-racists fail to notice is that most of our thousand or so churches are closed to virtually everyone regardless of race, color, class, or creed. Half our congregations have fewer than 250 members. A great many of them function as clubs. A case in point. One white friend told me that the former white minister of his UU church left after the congregation met to decide whether he should be ordered to shave off his new beard.

Rather than recognize that our congregants often find all difference threatening, anti-racists conclude that these congregations stay small and virtually all white because of the members' racism. With this caricature in place that UU congregants are, like all whites, racists, the anti-racists then, through careful and protracted training, call upon these congregants to confess their racism. Thus the anti-racists have created what they describe: whites who have learned to think of themselves as racists.

The theological principle behind all this is expressed in Joseph Barndt's book, *Dismantling Racism: The Continuing Challenge to White America*, which was sent to me compliments of the UUA anti-racism program to reinforce the lessons of the anti-racism workshop. Barndt, a white Lutheran minister, conducts anti-racism trainings for the UUA.

Barndt's belief that all whites are racists is based explicitly on the Christian doctrine of original sin, which claims that through Adam's sin in the Garden of Eden human nature was corrupted—a doctrine linked to the Trinitarian claim that only through the death of Jesus and with the assistance of the cleansing work of the Holy Spirit can human nature be saved. In every age, Christian theologians have found new language to explain this doctrine. The anti-racist doctrine is just such a recent example.

As Unitarian Universalists we reject this doctrine in its pure form, but we have inadvertently brought it into our midst by using anti-racist rhetoric informed by Barndt's Christian dogma. Barndt, for example, tells us we're "Enslaved by sin and freed by grace,"—classic Christian Trinitarian language. In other words, only a savior can free us from sin and human imperfection because we humans lack agency to help ourselves. Following this Christian doctrine to its logical conclusion, Barndt thus urges whites to seek forgiveness for their racism and, to quote him verbatim, face the fact that "our [meaning whites'] unwitting and unwilling imprisonment in racism . . . continues even after we have repented, confessed, and been forgiven." In short, Barndt insists that whites will always remain sinners because their nature is corrupted. They are thus slaves to what Barndt calls—and again I use his language—the original sin of racism.

Lacking all agency, they thus can't effect their own salvation. In short, they need a savior. And in the Barndt theology, this savior isn't Jesus but, in a brash leap, "people of color." Listen to what he says:

"Leadership and direction can only come from [people of color because they] understand racism far better than we do, and they know what needs to be done to eliminate it. Thus, the first step toward breaking the chains of this prison [for white people] is to recognize that we cannot be in charge of the changing."

When it comes to specifics, though, Barndt and his colleagues call for no other action on the part of the white sinner except confession. Surely the moral passivity advocated by such a theology is one reason why anti-racism programs can claim so few concrete results.

Further, the doctrine of human helplessness goes against the entire sweep of our religious traditions. As Unitarian Universalists, we affirm human moral agency and reject the orthodox, Protestant Trinitarian dogma that makes the cruxificion of Jesus the justification for our salvation in the eyes of God. The first principle of our covenant together is a pointed rejection of this Christian doctrine of original sin. Rather than affirming that human nature is corrupt, we celebrate it as inherently worthwhile and filled with dignity. This affirmation sets aside the need for a Messiah to sacrifice himself to redeem a corrupted nature.

William Ellery Channing declared as much in his 1819 sermon "Unitarian Christianity," which Unitarian Church Historian Conrad Wright calls, "our party platform." Listen to what Channing said in this sermon which marked Unitarianism as a distinct religion from its orthodox Trinitarian kin. Channing, of course, uses the non-inclusive language of his era:

"All virtue has its foundation in the moral nature of man, that is, in conscience, or his sense of duty, and in the power of forming his temper and life according to conscience. . . . [N]o act is praiseworthy, any farther than it springs from [human] exertion. We believe that no dispositions infused into us without our own moral activity, are of the nature of virtue, and therefore, we reject the doctrine of irresistible divine influence on the human mind, molding it into goodness, as marble is hewn into a statue."

In our tradition, we are always active agents in our own salvation. This is core to our teaching as Unitarian Universalists. So why have we accepted a doctrine of race that indicts 95 percent of our congregants as helpless, passive sinners?

To answer this question, we have to turn to the second problem I have found in UU anti-racist strategies: the errant assumption that white America works for white Americans.

Anyone who cares to look will quickly discover that it doesn't—at least, not for the vast majority of them. The privilege that, according to the anti-racists, comes with membership in white America, actually belongs to a tiny elite. Let me illustrate this point.

Imagine that business and government leaders decreed that all left-handed people must have their left hand amputated. Special police forces and armies are established to find such persons and oversee the procedure. University professors and theologians begin to write tracts to justify this new policy. Soon right-handed persons begin to think of themselves as having right-hand privilege. The actual content of this privilege, of course, is negative: it's the privilege of not having one's left hand cut off. The privilege, in short, is the avoidance of being tortured by the ruling elite. To speak of such a privilege—if we must call it that—is not to speak of power but rather of powerlessness in the midst of a pervasive system of abuse—and to admit that the best we can do in the face of injustice is duck and thus avoid being a target.

My point is this. Talk of white skin privilege is talk about the way in which some of the citizens of this country are able to avoid being mutilated—or less metaphorically, to avoid having their basic human rights violated. So much for the analogy. Here are the facts about so-called white skin privilege.

First, 80 percent of the wealth in this country is owned by 20 percent of the population. The top 1 percent owns 47 percent of this wealth. These facts describe an American oligarchy that rules not as a right of race but as a right of class. One historical counterpart to this contemporary story of extreme economic imbalance is found in the fact that at the beginning of the Civil War, seven percent of the total white population in the South owned almost three quarters (three million) of all the slaves in this country. In other words, in 1860, an oligarchy of 8,000 persons actually ruled the South. This small planter class ruled over the slaves and controlled the five million whites too poor to own slaves.

To make sense of this class fact, we must remember that the core motivation for slavery was not race but economics, which is why at its inception, both blacks and whites were enslaved.

Second, let us not forget the lessons of the 1980s. As former Republican strategist Kevin Phillips reminds us in his book *The Politics of Rich and Poor: Wealth and the American Electorate in the Reagan Aftermath*, "For all workers, white-collar as well as blue-collar, their real average weekly wage—calculated in constant 1977 dollars—fell."

Third, let us also not forget that today, numerous companies are opting to lower standards for job qualifications for their work force rather than raise wages and thus cut into profits. Jobs paying $50,000 a year or more have twice the share of the job-loss rate than that they did in the 1980s.

The result of these contemporary economic trends is the most acute job insecurity since the Great Depression. As economist Paul Krugman has pointedly argued in the November 3, 1997, edition of the *New Republic*, the modern success story of America's booming economy rests on the bent backs of the American wage earners. The economy is booming because wages, the main component of business costs, are not going up. And wages are not going up because the American worker is presently too fearful to stand up and make demands. Downsizing has shaken worker confidence. Unemployment insurance lasts only a few months, and the global labor market has undermined the American worker's bargaining power. These basic economic facts, Krugman argues, have created one basic psychological fact for the typical American worker: anxiety.

A strong economy no longer means job security for most white middle-class Americans—and they know it. This awareness, however, has not produced a rebellion against the rich but, rather, frenzied attempts by downwardly mobile middle-class whites trying to keep up the appearance of being well-off. Such appearances, however, include a penalty: debt. As Harvard social theorist Juliet B. Schor reminds us in *The Overspent American: Upscaling, Downshifting, and the New Consumer*: "Between a quarter and 30 percent of all American households live paycheck to paycheck; and in 1995, one-third of families whose heads were college-educated did no saving."

I do not call this economic condition in white America white skin privilege. I call it white middle-class poverty. Talk of white skin privilege is a distraction from this pervasive problem in white America. Talk of white privilege, to paraphrase a statement of Martin Luther King Jr., can feed the egos of poorer whites but not their stomachs.

So why have white UUs accepted a doctrine of race theory that is economically naïve, sociologically counterfactual, and racially damning? The answer is that by and large we haven't. In so far as we have, it's because the talk of privilege inflates some egos.

As we know, Unitarian Universalists are, collectively, the second wealthiest religious group in this country. Our members are also the most highly educated. This means that 49.9 percent of us are college graduates and that our median annual household income is $34,800. In other words, members of our association tend to have a big brain and a small purse. UUs also tend to be politically active, environmentally conscious, nature-oriented, and live in the suburbs. This is not the profile of the power elite. It's the profile of civil servants, school teachers, small business persons, and middle managers. In effect, middle America—

the group of professionals who keep America running by training its children, maintaining government, and paying taxes.

Two hundred years ago, the Unitarian part of our tradition had a very different profile, as Conrad Wright notes in his essay "Ministers, Churches, and the Boston Elite." Between 1791 and 1820, Unitarianism was called "the faith of the well-to-do, urban New Englanders." Harriet Beecher Stowe noted in the 1820s [that], "All the literary men of Massachusetts were Unitarians. All the trustees and professors of Harvard College were Unitarians. All the elite of wealth and fashion crowded Unitarian churches." Calvinist Jedidiah Morse described his liberal opponents as "a formidable host . . . combining wealth, talents and influence." But that was then and this is now. Today, most Unitarian Universalists are not affluent.

Yet we seem fond of describing ourselves in this manner. We find this hinted at even in the Commission on Appraisal's 1997 report on congregational polity, *Interdependence*, which presents one of church historian Tex Sample's generalizations about the cultural left: "They are mostly affluent." The members of the Commission go on to tell us that Sample's description is in general quite consistent with the demographic and psychographic profiles of the members of our association. I am increasingly persuaded that most of us do indeed imagine we're well off. I'm also persuaded that some of us impoverish ourselves trying to live out this myth of our lives.

The truth is that to be white in America and not affluent is for many persons—embarrassing. No contemporary writer has chronicled the story of this middle-class shame better than Juliet B. Schor in her book *The Overspent American*. Schor notes that if debts are subtracted from assets, the typical middle-class American household's net worth is less than $10,000. Does this mean that even though almost three-quarters of UU's own their own homes, their net worth might still rank a great many of them as members of America's middle-class poor? I suspect so.

The simple truth is that most middle-class white persons, including UU's, are not part of the economic ruling elite in this country. They have not amassed structural power and control. Our UU anti-racist rhetoric, however, claims that they have. Such a claim seems to produce three kinds or categories of ego responses in white UU's.

First category. For some, it is an ego boost. Bereft of real power and prestige in the eyes of America's ruling elite, what a tweak of the ego to have a so-called person of color tell you that you are all-powerful. Who could resist? Loads.

Thus the second category. Some egos are deflated. The egos of whites who are not racists, but have sometimes acted in racist ways in order to retain membership in their own social groups. . . .

The third group affected by anti-racist rhetoric I will call the silent majority. These Unitarian Universalists know that the anti-racist rhetoric that pervades our religious association runs counter to the economic realities of this country and their own lives. I believe that these persons simply dismiss the rhetoric as insulting to their intelligence and walk away. This doesn't help us build a strong, vibrant religious community. Quite the contrary. This is the way in which our community is broken. One withdrawal at a time.

Enough. This anti-racist rhetoric and its fallout must be stopped.

Thandeka's presentation became a magnet for those who had been made uncomfortable by the Journey Toward Wholeness/Crossroads approach and a lightning rod for the proponents of that approach. "Thandeka's point of view, unfortunately, became one of the most serious challenges to the UU work," observed Rev. Joseph Barndt of Crossroads Ministry. "And the reason I say unfortunately is because I think that when I read Thandeka's work, we're not that far apart. . . . I don't know, I think it may have to do with the difficulty in the UUA of bringing together individuals into a collective struggle. . . . That's made it difficult to have Thandeka's point of view considered in the context of an anti-racism analysis rather than as a resistance to anti-racism analysis."

An official response was received a year later when the Journey Towards Wholeness Transformation Team issued its own statement, challenging key points in Thandeka's narrative. The statement, in part, read,

> The printed form of Rev. Thandeka's workshop contained numerous points and several threads of argument. Our letter is intended to address some of those we consider to be the most egregious. There are several major points regarding the content of her workshop that we want to address. There are also a number of issues regarding the manner and the venue in which she chose to express her critique that deserve response. She asserted that there are three "basic problems" in the UUA's anti-racist strategies. We will address them one at a time.
>
> (1) "They violate the first principle of our UU covenant together to actively affirm and promote the inherent worth and dignity of every person." Her analysis leading to this conclusion is based on two basic points. First, she argues that those of us who support the initiative have blamed the exclusiveness of our congregations on the fact that they are racist, rather than on their clubbish exclusion of just about everyone. She cites a white friend of hers who reported about a minister's leaving his congregation when its members met to consider whether he should be ordered to shave off his new beard. That the clubbishness of many of our congregations has been known to lead to such prejudicial action is certainly true. We agree that the exclusiveness of clubbish congregations results in the lack of admission to a range of identifiable social categories (e.g. class). In response to this critique, however, we would ask two simple questions: "Who does make up the racial majority of our congregations?" and "What races are most consistently excluded from our congregations?" Analyzing who remains and who is, in fact, excluded along racial lines gives us an important window into UU exclusiveness. The percentage of people of color versus whites in our Association is nowhere near the percentages in society at large. If our congregations were

excluding almost everyone as Rev. Thandeka asserts (who would remain is an interesting question), why would the demographics demonstrate a bias against persons of color so out of line with the configuration of society? As a linked oppression, class is certainly interwoven into the institutionalization of exclusiveness, but to deny that race plays a critical and significant part seems, at best, like tunnel vision.

A further error concerning demographics and congregational size is her assertion that the UUA's Journey Toward Wholeness actually teaches that our congregations are small due to their racial exclusiveness. This is simply false. Our focus is not on size, but rather on constituency and the quality of their members' experience. Our analysis does concern itself with why people of color are not in congregations, and how they are kept from participating—but that is not our only focus. How we can participate in dismantling racism, both in our congregations and in society, is equally important. An additional and compounding difficulty with Rev. Thandeka's critique is the blurring of just who she is critiquing in her workshop. When she says "What these anti-racists fail to notice is. . . ." We ask, who are the "anti-racists"? To which programs is she directing her remarks? Does she know what UUA anti-racism programs actually exist? In this response we will demonstrate that her confusion about the UUA's anti-racism programs is so great her analysis cannot help but be seriously flawed.

The lack of substance and the uninformed nature of her critique leads us to question why she chose to assault an initiative which she seems to so thoroughly misunderstand. Why has she distorted the fundamental facts about the Journey Toward Wholeness Initiative?

Secondly, she states that as a result of believing that all whites are racist and "through careful and protracted training, [JTW's strategy is to call] upon . . . congregants to confess their racism." She then spends considerable time critiquing some dimensions of the theology expressed in Rev. Joseph Barndt's book, *Dismantling Racism*. She assumes that her interpretation of those aspects of his theology is what the JTW advocates and teaches, and upon which it bases its strategies for transformation. Her assumption is wrong and her conclusions are far off the mark. Three points are relevant here: (a) Selecting out portions of Rev. Barndt's theology for critique and criticism and assuming that they are what JTW bases its analysis of racism on is guilt by association, rather than by actual observation. Had she observed any of the actual workshops led by UU trainers, she would be unable to find any such doctrine serving as the underpinnings of our understanding of racism. (b) She has distorted Rev. Barndt's analysis of a relationship of accountability that whites must develop with people of color in order to come into right relationship into an argument for a "savior." Setting up a straw dog of a savior as being necessary for "salvation" from racism is an achingly unfair and mistaken interpretation of our theology and practice. (c) Her erroneous assertion that our programs cause UUs to depend upon some outside salvation from their racism leads her to state that our workshops indict 95 percent of us as helpless and passive sinners. This is a distortion that can only be due to a thorough unfamiliarity with UU facilitated workshops. One of the major sessions of each Jubilee weekend workshop is the creation of action planning groups. Participants consistently leave these sessions empowered, enthusiastic and more deeply committed to transformative action than ever before.

We have statistics and anecdotal evaluations of several hundred Jubilee workshops written by thousands of UUs. The data has been accumulating for over twelve years and was freely available to her had she chosen to use it.

(2) The second critique Rev. Thandeka makes is accusing the JTW of being in error about the nature and structure of power in America. She claims that the privilege that exists in white America only belongs to a "tiny elite." We wonder which privileges she is talking about. Surely she cannot mean the ability to purchase property with virtually no restriction, as long as the funds are available. Surely she was not referring to the freedom to drive an automobile

without the fear of being stopped by the police because of one's color. Nor could she have been referencing the privilege of consistently seeing one's race reflected throughout the media, represented in government, and holding the vast majority of the upper levels of management and ownership of U.S. companies of all sizes. We know she must not have not meant the safety of escaping incarceration in percentages radically lower than those for people of color, especially with sentences of death. Nor could she have meant the freedom from tragically high rates of alcoholism among the indigenous peoples of our land, nor from the major crises in indigenous health care whose proportions and oppressive neglect are unknown in white communities. But then she could also not have been suggesting the privilege of white Americans whose (on average) net worth is 50 percent higher than Latino Americans no matter what their socio-economic level. We would assume that she did not mean the privilege of consistently learning a version of history from textbooks sanctioned by state education programs that make the white race appear to be THE most creative, productive, moral, and important people on earth. If she was not referring to all of these privileges, securely held by the white middle-class, just which privileges was she referring to?

The list is one that could go on, and we are surprised that she avoided trying to factor it into her analysis. Further, her denial of white middle-class privilege disregards its role as gatekeeper for the elites. Rev. Thandeka has rightly cited the use of the lower classes to create a buffer for the elites. What she has failed to understand is the similar role held by the white middle-class, which is an even more powerful tool in keeping the races divided, and people of color oppressed. We applaud any discussion that shows links between oppressions such as racism and classism, but to excuse the profit that whites of all classes derive from the oppression of people of color, misses the complexity and, more importantly, the tragedy in the day to day degradation experienced by persons of color. That degradation is intensified in today's unstable financial reality because people of color at the bottom of the economic scale must vie for lower and lower level jobs as those above them push them out of their already substandard employment.

Rev. Thandeka's analysis of the present financial instability we are experiencing that causes so much anxiety and economic vulnerability for whites is accurate, but what she fails to include is the deeper trauma that this causes persons of color, which is experienced in a reality that is much more brutal and murderous. Leaving the trauma and oppression of people of color out of her arguments creates an aura of eerie disconnection that has caused many UUs of color to ask, "Where are we in her analysis?" Labeling the vulnerability of whites as "middle-class poverty" can be helpful to see the fallacy of living by appearances—but it does not eliminate nor account for the privilege of being able to avoid living at or very near the bottom, economically, politically, and socially that is the lot of the majority of persons of color in our nation. Nor does it account for the better housing, employment, education, police protection, nutrition, geographic mobility, cultural support/affirmation, media representation, etc., etc., etc., that middle-class whites enjoy.

(3) Third Rev. Thandeka states that we misinterpret actions resulting from feelings of shame and powerlessness as evidence of white racism. She is making a critical distinction here that misses the complexity, subtlety and systemic nature of racism in our times. She seems to be arguing, as some whites do, that racists are those people who act out of a conscious conviction of race prejudice, e.g. members of the Klan. She places high priority on exposing the shame that some (and we emphasize the word "some") whites carry about their conditioning about persons of color, and their "capitulation" to authority in order to belong. We believe that her emphasis is out of balance and disregards the holistic and devastating nature of learning racism which few, if any, white persons can escape in our society. She seems not to have been listening when Shirley Chisholm, esteemed African American legislator, said, "Racism is so universal in this country, so widespread and deep-seated, that it is

invisible because it is so normal." Her emphasis upon shame is helpful, but limited. It does not take into account how other powerful formative emotions which contribute to the individualization and internalization of racial prejudice do not just contribute to shame, but are powerfully debilitating in their own right. Such emotions as the lust for power, fear, helplessness, and rage—as well as the processes of denial— all serve to betray an individual's sense of relatedness to others and are powerfully present in constructing white identity.

But more importantly, the shame some whites experience can not discount their behavior. Although Dan [a person used in Thandeka's address as an example] was ashamed of himself, he did in fact act in ways that were oppressive. Her denial that his behavior was racist, because he was not acting out of an overt, personal desire to oppress blacks is far too superficial an analysis of how oppression operates. Her argument suffers from a lack of understanding of the difference between intention and impact, which are hallmark dynamics used in most diversity trainings—and were especially developed in relation to the gender oppression of women. Dan needs understanding regarding his intentions, AND he needs to be accountable for the impact of his behavior. Early childhood education has shown us the deep complexity of learning that goes into the building of values and behaviors. It is clear that something as complex as racism is built out of a thick web of interactive forces that certainly include shame, but also include many other factors in the shaping of the child's malleable mind and heart, not the least of which are overt and covert racist actions witnessed and/or carried out by the growing child. It is also clear that unlearning negative personal attitudes and behaviors (such as racism) requires consciously directed corrective action.

Finally, her emphasis upon shame as the central construction of racial separation in whites, and her denial that racism exists except in those consciously convicted of their prejudice, misses the reality of the systemic nature of racism in today's world. The Journey Toward Wholeness programs do not hold that any of us are racist at birth, we "have to be carefully taught." That teaching comes from and results in the construction of ideologies, language, life ways—in short, culture. This sets up patterns of oppression within institutions and the systems to which they belong. No individual alone can dismantle them and all individuals suffer from them whether or not they are conscious of it. That teaching sets up target populations and non-target populations which serve the underlying dynamic and structure of oppression. In our society today we believe it is eminently clear that nonwhites are the target of oppression no matter what their class; it is also clear that whites of all classes profit from that targeting on many levels and in many ways. To disregard or minimize this reality is to live in an illusion that is both costly and dangerous.

There is another problem in Rev. Thandeka's analysis that is troubling: Casting the racial dynamic on this continent in Black/White terms. There are several points we want to make in this regard. First, although there was an oligarchy in the south who owned the majority of slaves, their rule would have been impossible without the direct involvement of the other classes in enforcing the institution of slavery: night riders and patrols, overseers, and the very consciousness of gaining status as whites which served as a wedge between the elites and the imported Africans that she also cites, created a wide spread commitment of whites of all classes throughout the south against blacks; the undermining of reconstruction was also a widely systemically coordinated assault on "Negro" freedom by all classes of southern whites.

Further, what her arguments concerning slavery leave out, and the omission is glaring, is the struggle between the colonizing white population and the indigenous peoples they oppressed. Certainly there were class issues intermixed with the overt practices of conquest, removal and extermination, just as there are today with the strategies employed by modern corporations; the problem is that it is impossible to remove race from the equation; it is impossible to declare that the only reason populations of color were so widely targeted was solely due to economics. To do so is offensive to persons of color throughout the history of this continent who have suffered no matter what their class membership. To do so represents academic thinking in its most arcane and narrow form.

A further error Rev. Thandeka made in delineating the origins of racism is that of arguing that etiology determines maturity. That is, although a cancer might start because of the exposure to carcinogenic material, once the cancer takes hold in the body, it does not matter how it started. Its infection spreads. Its destruction dominates. Its life-threatening potential has a life of its own. The same is true of racism. Once the institutionalization of racism has fully taken root, its effects extend well beyond class issues alone, if they were ever solely limited to them, which we dispute. Once white individuals have been "infected" with the internalization of race prejudice, the oppressive use of power, the life numbing forces of denial, and the continual seduction into taking advantage of the florid expression of that prejudice as it exists in its systemic institutionalization, to argue that it can't be racism because it originated in economic causes, is simplistic and misses seeing the reality of the on-going tragedy. Beyond responding to the specific content issues of her workshop, we want to address some dynamics of process and history that we find unacceptable and misguided.

A first point is the failure on Rev. Thandeka's part to collaborate with her UU colleagues (especially those of color) and with lay folk who are responsible for promoting the Association-wide Anti-Racism Initiative. We believe that personal anti-bias and healing work are a necessary part of any authentic effort to dismantle oppression. Her lack of intentional and collaborative dialogue, however, leads us to believe her interpretation of the social justice mission of our religious movement is thoroughly privatized and suffers a disconnection both from the facts and the spirit of the Anti-Racism Initiative. Her lack of collegial conversation clearly underlies many of the serious errors in her thinking and in her perception of what she believes are the facts. Her workshop was filled with errors in judgment, scholarship, perception and reasoning.

Rev. Thandeka distorted the learnings and the underlying intention of the Crossroads training she attended and disrupted the workshop itself by shouting expletives at the trainer. She distorted the interfaith collaborative effort of our work by unfairly and inaccurately characterizing our interfaith partners as being locked into a belief in a debilitating conception of original sin. Her gross critique of Christianity is a parody that would offend the faiths with whom we have so successfully collaborated at the cutting edge of anti-racism work.

We are saddened by the above list of misperceptions and distortions; we believe their negative impact is even more serious due to Rev. Thandeka's status as a responsible teaching professional and clergy person. Rather than the GA Initiative, and the institutionalization of it through the Journey Toward Wholeness Anti-Racism programs, violating our First Principle, we believe Rev. Thandeka's workshop did a serious disservice to the UU women and men who have worked for so many years to collaboratively forge a dynamic and multifaceted process for addressing one of the most debilitating oppressions in human history.

Our sadness, however, does not prevent us, and will not prevent us, from moving ahead inclusively and collaboratively with a healing vision of freedom, equity and justice based on clear analysis and articulated through practical, concrete and powerful anti-racism programs that are consistent with and in the spirit of the General Assembly vote in Phoenix, June 1997.

[Signed] In the Faith,
The Journey Toward Wholeness Transformation Committee
The Rev. Susan Suchocki, *chair*; Ruth Alatorre, Dr. Ivan Louis Cotman, Ken Carpenter, the Rev. Linda Olson Peebles, and Dr. Leon Spencer; the Rev. Kurt A. Kuhwald, *liaison from the Jubilee Working Group*; the Rev. Melvin Hoover, Robette Dias, Susan Leslie, *staff.*

Thandeka's remarks also became the catalyst for other responses, some of which critiqued both her work and that of the Journey Toward Wholeness efforts. James Brown, who, in 1993, became the first African-American UUA district executive, also crafted his own response to Thandeka's ideas:

It seems to me that there are two serious flaws in Thandeka's position. First, she considers the term "racist" only as a pejorative appellation, an accusatory smear, a condemnation of some "sin." Although the term is most often used in this manner, it is also simply an appellation, the name applied to people identified with a pervasive phenomenon that almost everyone (except Thandeka) acknowledges as existent in the USA. What makes the issue difficult and complex is the definition of the phenomenon—racism.

The UUA's definition of racism: "racial prejudice plus power and privilege" unnecessarily complicates our understanding of U.S. racism. Simply put, racism is the unquestioned, deeply held group belief that one "race"—in the U.S. it is the White race-is superior to all other races, and (this is vitally important) all the People of Color "races" are inferior. The second part is vital to our understanding, because the belief in White superiority is more than egocentric chauvinism (we are the best), it is inextricably coupled with the deeply held belief that people of color, as a group (not necessarily as individuals), are inferior (they are not up to acceptable standards). This (superiority/inferiority beliefs) definition of racism is used by most social scientists currently involved in these discussions. These beliefs are inculcated in the psyches and souls of Americans from the day they are born, and for immigrant Americans, from their first exposure to American culture and media of all types.

I have only found two reactions to the above definition from American Whites. The first group fully agrees with the definition—the great majority. The second agrees that it is true "for some white people" but they, themselves, "don't see skin color"—everybody is equal. The evidence of denial on the part of those holding the second position is easily discernable. Their neighborhood, their friends, their doctor/ lawyer, their spouse or partner, their church, their heroes or role models, their favorite performers, etc. etc. are all white. Since all White people more or less agree, in words or deeds, that they, as a group, share the superior/inferior belief, and that belief according to most social scientists, defines racism, then it is not untrue or unfair to say all Whites are racist. (I will accept 99.9% if you simply cannot accept absolutes.) . . .

The second flaw in Thandeka's position is: "That the real problem is economic classism, not racism." I submit that both are oppressive. POC's suffer from racism, and from economic classism along with many Whites in our market-based capitalist society. A disabled POC suffers from racism and ableism. A homeless POC suffers from racism and economic classism. Whites may suffer from ableism and economic classism, but not racism. Inequities and oppression continue to exist. Our own James Luther Adams and great historical minds such as Engels, Marx and many others crafted various approaches to resolve this problem, but it persists. This global, complex problem only obfuscates the issue of American racism. It is an important, but different issue.

Hoover, the Faith in Action director, recalled the escalating effect of resistance during this period:

Once it got out, then people started interpreting it. . . . Thandeka was clear she didn't believe in the strategy and the direction of the end product and she could throw out stuff that we couldn't really counter. . . . And a lot of other folks who didn't want to change, and quite honestly another factor in all this is that a number of our key ministers. . . . When we were able to work with leadership groups, and work the small groups, we were able to work the concepts and the intellectual understandings, underpinnings of the analysis, in a way that people could wrestle with those and they would have to know that in fact whether they liked some things or not, they were true. And that or some things were true and whether you like the approach or not, that if things were going to be different they had to be addressed. But when it got out into the congregational arena, that was where we felt huge loss in not having the consultants and people, in the grassroots curriculum that we had hoped for, that that kind of work wasn't done at the grassroots level. And therefore people weren't prepared enough.

The controversy was felt in those congregations that were aware enough to understand. For opponents of anti-racism efforts, Rev. Thandeka provided a reason to reject the ideas it professed. For others, her work motivated response. Rev. Dr. Fredric Muir, senior minister at the Unitarian Universalist Church of Annapolis, Maryland, recalled,

[Thandeka's presentation] made me so angry, I just came back and said, "We're going to make this work." That was a pivotal moment for me, actually. So it was shortly after that that we began this work. I think a lot of people came into the room hearing that this Crossroads training was really, really Christian-oriented, that there were problems with language, that it wasn't a very good UU model. . . . A lot of people came to the meeting [where Thandeka presented] wondering what this was all about. By that time the UUA had done a pretty good job of adapting it to UUs, and it was very, very powerful. For many of the folks it was the first time they had ever, ever experienced something like that. It was especially that way for some of the people who had been born and raised in the mid-Atlantic area. I remember people in my congregation who went to that [version of the training] and were just blown away. The stories they told—they had never participated in an event like that. It was very powerful and very well received. Quite a few of the people who were there are still involved in doing this work.

PART 3

LEARNINGS

If reopening a dialogue about race was part of the agenda of the late 1980s and early 1990s, by the end of the 1990s, the focus was more on the vocabulary used when Unitarian Universalists talked about race.

Part of the identity question was whether it was important for Euro-American Unitarian Universalists to claim either the identity of "oppressor" or identify themselves as "anti-racist." Some saw that as a critical first step. "Did we need to start there? Yes," said Rev. Kurt Kuhwald, a proponent of white people such as himself claiming their "whiteness."

At the Unitarian Universalist Church of Annapolis, Rev. Dr. Fredric Muir saw it this way:

> Largely people who were very, very social justice-conscious in their jobs, or African Americans, and/or both, who would come into the [congregation's] JTW Committee, stick around for a month or two, and then leave. I finally started to talk to some of those folks. What was going on? . . . They kind of felt like the Committee wanted to go out and fix everybody else's problems. They didn't want to look at themselves, and they didn't want to look at the church. I think this is an ongoing issue in a lot of our congregations. Probably it's just human nature in our institutions. . . . Where do you start doing this work? I think in UUism, my sense is part of our heritage is we're these really bright people and we've got a lot of interesting, creative answers, let's go share that with everybody else. Rarely do we ever hold the mirror up and look at ourselves.

A key question was whether those who did not wish to label themselves as "anti-racist" were thus "racist" by default. A thorny question was whether those who saw a need to address racial issues and yet did not endorse the Crossroads Ministry approach to anti-racism training were "racist." Rev. Peter Morales, who served on the Unitarian Universalist Ministers Association Executive Committee, observed that he saw divisiveness, especially coming from the leadership of Diverse and Revolutionary Unitarian Universalist Multicultural Ministries (DRUUMM) and from staff members in the Association's Faith in Action department. "This is not the Ku Klux Klan," Morales said.

> These are ministers who in their own way are committed to anti-racism, multiculturalism, so this is picking a fight we don't need. Just as an overall thing, one of the things that would trouble me with the whole anti-racism effort as I saw it was it ended up picking fights with people who should be strong allies. When your tactic is doing that, it should tell you something is wrong. When people who share your values and are your natural allies are being put off, I said, this is just crazy.

Rev. Clyde Grubbs, a founding member of Unitarian Universalist Native and Indigenous Americans and minister in North Hatley, Quebec, and Austin, Texas, in this period, stressed that the attempt to find one way to generate dialogue and change attitudes about race that worked for all was against the Unitarian Universalist culture, which stresses individual paths to truth.

"What I saw was railroading. I didn't see the open discussion," said Dr. Finley Campbell, a member at First Unitarian Universalist Church of Chicago. "The whole system was an artificial system." He said his preference would have been an approach that stressed multicultural unity. He also noted the challenges of finding one approach that could bring Unitarian Universalists together. "It's like herding panthers," he said. He said over time, he has come to see that what was most missing was a systematic way to offer critique of the approaches taken. "There has to be a place for multiracial unity," he said. "Some of us now want to peacefully coexist. Can't there be a Journey Toward Wholeness that incorporates that?"

If trying to find a single approach that met all needs was impossible, it raised the question of whether group interest had any place among Unitarian Universalists. "It's not ingrained in UU culture to do things collectively," Rev. Melvin Hoover, director of the Association's Faith in Action Department in these years, said in a 1998 interview in *World* magazine,

> We have an individualistic culture, and the skills of being a collective have to be learned. One place that can happen is in our congregations, in our organizations. Right now, one of our gifts is being an upper-class powered white denomination. But our people don't own that. They need to understand that they have power and that the issue is how will they use that power, and for what ends?

Another identity question was whether the goal for Unitarian Universalism's culture should be to incorporate a few other voices or to be changed by the presence of other experiences and ways of being. Rev. Susan Suchocki, a white minister who would become the first chair of the Journey Toward Wholeness Committee, preached this from her pulpit in Leominster, Massachusetts, in 1992:

> In my opinion, one of the problems is that we Unitarian Universalists have been working with an assimilation model as the exclusive way to be welcoming. In other words, if you think like us and have a theology compatible to us—we are for you. If we continue with this as the primary model of welcoming, I think we end up sacrificing a lot. Instead, I prefer a model of diversity. A model of diversity recognizes differences in skin color, in sexual preference, in physical capacities, in age, in gender, and those differences are applauded, enjoyed, and celebrated though sometimes struggles and disagreements may emerge.

Anti-racism engaged many people of color, often setting them into antagonistic relationships with others. The most aired controversy involved Rev. Dr. Thandeka's public denunciation of anti-racism efforts in 1999. Other conversations were also polarizing. "Some people of color got marginalized in the UUA, because the only thing they could talk about was anti-oppression issues," observed Rev. Rosemary Bray McNatt, an African-American seminarian during this period. "It was the only thing they knew to talk about. It was their only level of service in the UUA. It was the only ministry they had, and it seemed as though it was their only interest."

The conversation about anti-racism, which began as a way of resuming a conversation about black and white relations that had been silenced in the 1970s, was now much more complex, due to the growing influence of a number of other identity-based groups, including Unitarian Universalist Native and Indigenous Americans and the Latina/o Unitarian Universalist Networking Association (LUUNA).

This added richness to the dialogue—and a focus was lost for some long-time advocates. Long-time black activist Dr. Norma Poinsett said,

> I don't like the term people of color because it erases me. I like the word black. If they somehow could just go ahead and use everybody's name, everybody's race, it would be good . . . but the one thing I know is that in this world no matter what's going on, other than the Indians, the blacks are always going to have the hardest time.

Relationships grew heated during this time when the focus was on intra-group relations. With many of the efforts growing out of or tapping into unresolved emotions from the Empowerment Controversies, the tendency to focus on issues through a black and white lens was prevalent. The concerns raised, especially by Latina/Latino/Hispanic Unitarian Universalists became more pronounced as the training model became better known.

About this time, some observers began to notice a distinct pattern of conflict aversion within Unitarian Universalist circles. Because conversations about race were by their nature conflicted, bias against these conversations grew.

As for faith, this period saw a growing disconnection among people who did not see the specific Unitarian Universalist religious context for the trainings that came to be identified with the Journey Toward Wholeness umbrella. McNatt characterized the JTW efforts at this time as "political" because they were about managing power dynamics rather than motivating people through their beliefs and passions. "Nobody had any interest in it because we were acting out of a political model," she said. "Everybody forgot this was a religious movement. . . . By the time I had made the transition from an active lay person to a seminarian, I had made the decision that I wouldn't touch this stuff with a ten-foot pole because I didn't want to have a conversation around this in political terms. . . ."

"The models were not broad enough," Rev. Danielle DiBona, then serving in Cleveland, Ohio, observed, stating that the starting point was dictated by the Associational governance structure. "As an association of congregations, we are theologically immature. And the immaturity is that our theology has no place for sin, so we don't have a place for redemption." And no place existed for elders as well in a faith that often prized the new over the traditional. "There has been exploratory work around the role of our elders," said Grubbs, adding that the idea of establishing a "council of elders" has been discussed extensively. DiBona agreed. "So many of our elders have skipped town," she noted. "Get burned out and go away."

In terms of relationships, while conflicts over the Journey Toward Wholeness work divided some into "pro" and "con" camps, individual perceptions were much more complex.

Tomas Firle, a member of the San Diego congregation, recalls that while he felt the anti-racism efforts were essential, he was troubled by many aspects. "On-going anti-racist consciousness and congregational awareness-building was left to local lay leaders with no guidance or mentoring from UUA," he said. "It appeared that throughout the country there was little anti-racism commitment by ministers. We were blessed with the exception. . . . In my opinion, the JTW 'training' approach was structured on an academic, multi-year, sequential event-oriented curriculum—via weekend workshops—built on the Crossroad Ministries model. It was finally tweaked by UUA trainers, but is disconnected by its lack of emphasis on UU values."

Monetary resources were a real factor in this period. The strategy devised by Faith in Action and others required training and travel expenses to spread its ideas. Outside trainers were often required because a given congregation was likely not to have non-white participants to share their perspectives. Initially, several groups were funded, though none at the levels they requested. "When the money crunch came, the effort was to try to consolidate the groups and bring them into alliance under a single strategy," recalled Robette Dias of the Faith in Action staff, noting that the disbanding of the Jubilee Working Group, which developed the Jubilee anti-racism trainings in the late 1980s, allowed for more trainings to be held since the funding from that group became available.

Rev. Dr. John Buehrens, president of the Unitarian Universalist Association during this period, said the Association's financial situation was such that new initiatives had to be funded from grant or special money. He said anti-racism efforts, and the extension work to grow new, intentionally diverse congregations, was funded largely by grants from the the Unitarian Universalist Congregation at Shelter Rock in Manhasset, New York. Speaking of this time, he wrote in an email, "The bulk of the UUA budget derived from congregational and individual contributions is typically allocated, by constituent pressure through the Board of Trustees, to semi-permanent services and staff positions serving the existing congregations and professional groups. Most income from endowment is for purposes restricted by the donors in the past. So new initiatives, both before and during my administration, were indeed heavily dependent either upon grants from what became the UU Congregation at Shelter Rock, Long Island (earlier called the Northshore UU Congregation, Plandome, New York)."

Buehrens and Denise (Denny) Davidoff, the Association's moderator in these years, agreed that Rev. Melvin Hoover, director of the Faith in Action Department of the UUA, was key to the events of 1996 to 1999. "None of this would have happened without Mel," said Davidoff. "He worked tirelessly and he absorbed punches and they got harder and harder. He became the lightning rod."

Said Buehrens, "The work never would have gotten off the ground without Mel being on staff. Mel maintained an ability to talk to everyone, even during the least enlightening ideological fights. He was a pretty sound theologian about it, but humble. He didn't have the need to be the mouthpiece; he was willing to be a catalytic presence who didn't have to get the credit. And that is worth its weight in gold."

Rev. Dr. Laurel Hallman, senior minister of the First Unitarian Church of Dallas, looked back on these years and observed, "I think we're going to have to figure out what, for want of a better word, is a kind of institutional maturity . . . which allows us to say we'll do this, not that. We have had a hard time making choices because we wanted to be open. I think that's one of the things that made the anti-racism work difficult. We wanted to be so radically open that we often got done very little."

CLOSING WORDS

JAMES LUTHER ADAMS

Rev. Adams was a parish minister, social activist, scholar, and professor who died in 1994.

We of the middle class are tempted, indeed, almost fated to adopt the religion of the successful. This religion of the successful amounts to a systemic concealment of and separation from reality—a hiding of the plight of those who in one sense or another live across the tracks. In the end this concealment comes from a failure to identify correctly and to enter into combat with what St. Paul called "the principalities and powers of evil." The religion of the successful turns out then to be a sham spirituality, a cultivated blindness, for it tends to reduce itself to personal kindliness and philanthropy costing little. Thus it betrays the world with a kiss.

Time of Paradox

Resistance is a natural part of any change process. It is also an indicator that people are involved in that process in significant ways. We therefore expected that we would encounter resistance when we confront racism because of the deep change this confrontation demands. (Fears are common about change: not knowing what the future will bring, losses of all sorts, shifts in identity, and fear about institutional change are all examples.) The bottom line is that people must engage in a process that is meaningful and transformative in order to keep moving forward. As Journey Toward Wholeness leaders, we have become more mindful of reflecting, through our own behaviors and language, a need for a common understanding and commitment; this has led some to perceive the Journey Toward Wholeness as being overly rigid and dogmatic rather than the open, inviting, dynamic process of change we are striving to co-create. This perception came in part from the inevitable process of resistance to change and from our emphasis on the power analysis approach; however, we have learned to listen to critiques offered in good faith and to be flexible in making needed adaptations.

—"Continuing the Journey" Report to the 2001
General Assembly From the Journey Toward
Wholeness Transformation Committee

2000

LINC (Linked Identities Networking in Coalition) forms and holds the coalition's first event, a forum at General Assembly for the three candidates to be president of the UUA.

C*UUYAN (Continental UU Young Adult Network) mandates that anti-oppression education happen at all C*UUYAN-sponsored conferences.

The Liberal Religious Educators Association (LREDA) undergoes an institutional assessment by consultant and anti-racism trainer Taquiena Boston.

Four UU leaders meet at the White House as part of President Bill Clinton's "Initiative on Race: One America in the 21st Century."

The Diversity of Ministry Team, a staff committee formed in 1996, adds two representatives of DRUUMM (Diverse and Revolutionary Unitarian Universalist Multicultural Ministries).

Members of the UUA President's Council, the UUA Staff, and the UUA Board, C*UUYAN leaders and other youth and young adults attend UUA anti-racism training.

As THE NEW MILLENNIUM DAWNED, anti-racism was filtering into the organizational structures of key Unitarian Universalist groups. The leadership of Rev. Gary Smith, the Unitarian Universalist Ministers Association president, was significant and helped create ongoing anti-oppression channels within the UUMA. The creation of two positions on the UUMA Exec, as its Executive Committee is known among ministers, focused on racial diversity and a new committee focused on anti-racism, anti-oppression, multicultural issues was notable, as was the lack of consensus among members of historically marginalized racial and ethnic groups about who the representatives should be.

Other groups stepping up included the Liberal Religious Educators and Directors Association and the Ministerial Fellowship Committee, the credentialing body for new ministers. General Assemblies became meeting grounds for ideas and people, with more groups coalescing around particular identities and for discussions of anti-racism theologies.

2000

C*UUYAN holds its first intentional caucusing of people of color and white identity groups.

Young Adult and Campus Ministries holds its first annual strategy and review meeting with UUA anti-racism consultants.

DRUUMM struggles with identity and accountability; no founding LUUNA (Latina/o UU Networking Association) members remain in DRUUMM.

The UU Ministers Association (UUMA) holds a facilitated conversation about race and ministry and asks for another DRUUMM appointee, who is Rev. José Ballester, who is then working for the Unitarian Universalist Service Committee.

DRUUMM YaYA—Youth and Young Adults of Color, a DRUUMM sub-group, holds its first conference, in Atlanta

2001

UUA president Rev. Dr. John Buehrens convenes the "Consultation on UU Theologies and the Struggle Against Racism" in Boston in January to further develop a theology of anti-racism for Unitarian Universalists.

LREDA changes its bylaws to reflect an anti-racist, anti-oppressive, multicultural stance.

Karen Eng, Young Kim, and Mark Watanabe hold the first "meeting" of Asian or Pacific Islander UUs, near the message boards at the General Assembly in Cleveland.

For some, the fact that Unitarian Universalists were trying to be cutting edge in anti-racism matters was worth celebrating. Four UU leaders met at the White House as part of President Clinton's "Initiative on Race: One America in the 21st Century." On March 9, 2000 (almost thirty-five years to the day after Rev. James Reeb was martyred in Selma answering Rev. Martin Luther King's call), Rev. Melvin Hoover, director of the UUA's Department of Faith in Action; Rev. Laurel Hallman, senior minister of the First Unitarian Church of Dallas, Texas; UUA Mid-South District Executive Eunice Benton; and UUA consultant Robette Dias were among 150 religious participants. The April 2000 minutes of the Journey Toward Wholeness Transformation Committee contain this comment: "It is impressive to our constituents that we went to the White House. The Journey Toward Wholeness is cutting edge."

The election of the Association's first African-American president, Rev. William Sinkford, was another pivotal event in 2001.

General Assembly delegates protest against the name and mascot of the local professional baseball team, the "Indians," and its mascot, "Chief Wahoo."

On June 25, the delegates elect Rev. William Sinkford as the first African-American president of the Unitarian Universalist Association at the Cleveland General Assembly.

LUUNA (Latina/o UU Networking Association) lacks a quorum at its annual meeting, reorganizes, and appoints a Steering Committee.

The UU Ministers Association creates an anti-racist, anti-oppressive, multicultural portfolio as an elected position on its Executive Committee, plus another position on the Exec, appointed by Diverse and Revolutionary UU Multicultural Ministries.

The Ministers Association creates a Committee on Ministry to deal with issues around anti-racism, anti-oppression, and multiculturalism.

C*UUYAN offers its first self-sponsored anti-racism training, in Madison, Wisconsin, led by young adults Revs. Dr. Kristen Harper and Joshua Pawelek.

C*UUYAN caucuses at General Assembly in June and engages in anti-racism trainings at Opus, the Network's annual spiritual retreat, and ConCentric, its annual business meeting in August. The Network agrees to create an Accountability Committee for anti-oppression work.

Unitarian Universalist Service Committee Executive Director Dr. Valora Washington speaks at the United Nations World Conference against Racism, Racial Discrimination, Xenophobia and Related Intolerance.

CHAPTER 15

Leadership at the Unitarian Universalist Ministers Association

Resistance from ministers grew as anti-racism encountered congregational cultures, though efforts were made to reach out to ministers. "We met with ministers," recalled Rev. Melvin Hoover, then director of the UUA's Faith in Action Department. "We thought the ministers were key. We tried in several ways and we actually had strategies ready to go. There were some critical leaders of that time, in our larger churches particularly and others, who basically had come together and said they weren't going to do it. . . . Some of those say it now, 'It's not what we want to do—we want to grow the numbers, and this isn't going to get us there.'"

If individual ministers continued to be outspoken critics, leadership of the Unitarian Universalist Ministers Association was working to be intentional about its approach to race and ethnicity concerns, making a number of changes to make its structures more responsive.

Another issue was the particular trials of ministers from racial and ethnic groups historically under-represented in Unitarian Universalist ministry. As stories spread, especially within communities of color/Latina/o/Hispanic circles, people grew discouraged about their opportunities within the professional leadership. This was also discouraging for lay leaders who wished to see a ministry that wore their face, as exemplified in these observations of long-time black Unitarian Universalist advocate Dr. Norma Poinsett:

> One of the things that is so terrible about this Association is our black ministers just cannot make it. . . . Not as parish

ministers. I mean people are mean; people are nasty to them. I think sometimes they forget. If I were a minister, there's not any way in the world I'd ever forget I'm black. And I'd never forget white folks are white. And some of my best friends are white folks.

But I don't forget that, and I know that they will just sometimes, no matter how good people are, they will forget and say, "Well, I don't want you to marry me. No, I don't want my daughter to be married by a black minister," or "I think his sermons are not intellectual enough." You know, it's always something. Or "Oh, they broke a verb." Or "It's a little too Jesus-y." . . . I think the Unitarian Universalist Ministers Association and the Ministry Department could help change the minds of our congregations to accept all our ministers.

Unitarian Universalist Ministers Association

As the anti-racism discussion entered into the new millennium, tensions that had been vague rumblings became louder, especially from the professional ministry. The UUMA held a "conversation about white allies in anti-racism" before the 2000 General Assembly in Nashville. Rev. Linda Olson Peebles, serving in Alexandria, Virginia, and a former UUA trustee, recalled,

At the Nashville GA my naiveté was brought to an end. Following the many years of General Assembly "on-stage" inspirational signs of support for the ideal of doing this work, and the education of Jubilee trainings which I thought had been pretty widespread; following the valuable learnings about the complexities of being aware and accountable gained from the 1993 "TJ Ball" issue, and the 1997 Phoenix sculpture issue; and following the challenging discussions in response to the 1999 Kansas City Crossroads-facilitated "stakeholders" gathering and the 1999 GA confrontation with Rev. Dr. Thandeka's analysis; I had come to the 2000 Ministers gathering before GA in Nashville with the assumption that UU ordained leaders were aware of the need, the complexity, and the mutuality of the "Journey." Instead, I found an astonishing and shocking "stone-walling" from many of my UU colleagues, separating themselves from some "other" who was imposing this on them. There were UU ministers who denied the need for the work; who diminished the skills and intent of those engaged in the work as being marginal to the "real" UU ministry; and who ignorantly maligned the analysis, process, and openness of the work. I felt assaulted by my colleagues, by those very people for whom I had had the greatest regard, respect, and even affection; by those very people to whom we entrust the leadership and ministry of our congregations. And in that painful series of encounters during Professional Days meant to inspire ministers in their work, I realized—in my bones and deep in my soul—that the transformation that is needed is vast and deep. And I realized that my allies and colleagues were not one and the same.

Progress was still perceived in 2000. At the Journey Toward Wholeness Transformation Committee fall meeting, it was noted, "Mel Hoover, Director for Faith in Action, reported that the UUMA is taking significant steps forward with the leadership of Rev. Gary Smith, UUMA President."

Likewise in its fall meeting the UUMA Executive Committee (known as the Exec) noted that "[f]eedback for the June 2000 conversation [as part of the continuing education events before General Assembly known as CENTER] was very affirming. There is strong support for our doing it again in 2001. The Exec support for this is to be transferred to the anti-racism portfolio. Conversation needs to be broadened to include other minorities than African American." The decision was made to continue the conversation during the professional development time, CENTER Day, at the 2001 General Assembly in Cleveland.

Others had less optimistic assessments. Rev. José Ballester summed up the Nashville events:

The UUMA Conversation on Racism and Oppression falls far short of expectations. Rev. Patricia Jiminez, who was serving as a community minister in San Jose, CA, rises in objection that she and other members of the Latino, Asian and Native communities are being ignored and their concerns are being marginalized. After a moment of silence, the presentation continues totally ignoring what has been said. Rev. Kay Jorgensen, [co-founder and president of Faithful Fools street ministry in San Franscisco, CA] stops the proceedings and forces participants to acknowledge the marginalization that has just occurred and to concentrate on the issues of oppression.

The UUMA had invited selected members to the Nashville conversation in a letter signed by Revs. Karen Matteson, Kate Walker, Chris Buice, Melanie Morel Sullivan, Cynthia Cain, Roy Reynolds, and Peter Morales, on behalf of the UUMA's Executive Committee, which read in part,

> We recognize the UUA has been conducting anti-racist, anti-oppression and multicultural training and workshops for many years. We wish to assess what we are doing in our ministries, and facilitate communication amongst ourselves. This conversation is an opportunity to share your story and hear the stories of your colleagues. We wish to focus on the successes, while acknowledging the challenges.

The minutes note,

> This will be a celebration, lifting up some of our colleagues who have been dedicated and effective and will mentor the rest of us to do some learning . . . it will inspire us and give us models for continuing this work . . . and [will be] focused on the ministers' role in bringing this work to their congregations.

Anti-Racism Portfolio for UUMA

In January 2000, the Unitarian Universalist Ministers Association changed the bylaws to add a new member at large for anti-racism, anti-oppression, and multiculturalism to the Exec. At the same meeting, the Committee met with Robette Dias and Rev. Melvin

Hoover of the UUA staff, and the Rev. Susan Suchocki of the Journey Toward Wholeness Transformation Committee, to have a conversation about how to lead the racial justice issues involving the UUMA and UUA. At issue was a disagreement between DRUUMM leadership and others, particularly leaders involved with LUUNA, which had arisen months earlier when the UUMA had agreed to create a special position for someone holding the anti-racist, anti-oppressive agenda.

How to fill the position was to prove controversial. The person in the position would hold an "Anti-Racism, Anti-Oppression and Multiculturalism 'portfolio.'" The Exec would commit to adding another member to the Committee and Morales, who had volunteered to serve in an ad hoc position created in 1999, asked for a few weeks to determine if he would stay for the rest of the year. A proposal was developed that DRUUMM would make a recommendation for a year-long appointment to this portfolio at the June 2000 Annual Meeting; the Exec would appoint this person. Rev. Danielle DiBona, a founding member of DRUUMM, said, "They came to DRUUMM because they saw it as an accountable organization by white people. . . . Gary [Smith] wanted to be in an accountable relationship with an accountable organization."

Under the proposal, the Exec would propose a bylaws change at the June 2001 Annual Meeting to make the position hold an elected, three-year term, with the initial term being 2001–2004. DRUUMM would make recommendations to the Nominating Committee to fill this position in 2001.

This proposal did not resolve issues about who should or could represent the voices of those racial and ethnic groups historically under-represented in Unitarian Universalist circles. At issue in this complex set of events was a provision that had been enacted by DRUUMM that the nominee "self-identify and live as a Person of Color." Rev. Patricia Jimenez had already raised the issue that this did not relate to the realities of the Latina/o/Hispanic experience. Ministers raised questions about whether the candidate needed to be endorsed by DRUUMM, how such an endorsement would take place, and whether someone not endorsed by DRUUMM should be allowed to hold the portfolio.

Unwilling to ensure DRUUMM seats on the Executive and CENTER (Continuing Education Network for Training, Enrichment and Renewal) Committees, the UUMA asked for another DRUUMM appointee. DiBona recalled that she spoke to Smith about the need to separate the portfolio holder from the representative person-of-color/Latina/o/Hispanic seat. Ballester volunteered to serve on the Exec while Rev. Marjorie Bowens-Wheatley agreed to serve on the CENTER Committee. JTWTC minutes note,

> The Rev. José Ballester has been appointed to the anti-racism seat that has been created on the UUMA Executive Committee. This seat has been created for one year and there is discussion to make it a permanent member of the Exec. One of the issues under discussion is to make sure that this position does not carry the entire anti-racism portfolio but that it be a recommended person by DRUUMM and that the whole committee carry anti-racism.

While in this role, Ballester wrote,

> We need to put together a team of people to help with transformation. Some people from Exec, plus others doing diversity work. [They need to] look at what has been done, bring a number of models to the larger group. We also need to look at what other UU affiliated organizations are doing. We know what the goal is, we know where we want to go; we just don't know how to get there.

Ballester surveyed ministers of color to ask them who they wished to represent them in the permanent position. He reported that the top candidates, Rev. Dr. Mark Morrison-Reed and Rev. Dr. Michelle Bentley, declined to serve. Jimenez was the third choice. As Ballester recalled, later Rev. William (Chester) McCall submitted his name and, still later, Rev. John Gilmore's name was submitted. Ultimately, Gilmore was elected; Jimenez was appointed. "It was a complete breakdown of trust and process," Ballester said. DiBona recalled that the ministers who were members of

PERSPECTIVE

A Latino View of the Journey Toward Wholeness

This article was written by Revs. Peter Morales, Patricia Jimenez, and José Ballester, all members of LUUNA.

As our movement travels on our Journey Toward Wholeness, in what way are the issues we face different for Latinos? The three of us, all Latino members of the UUMA but of widely different backgrounds, would like to offer a Latino perspective. Our comments are based on an analysis of our situation and upon a theological sensibility that centers on the sanctity of community and relationships.

We are troubled by much of the language and categories used in the UUA's attempts to achieve a more multiracial and multicultural religious movement. We are not comfortable with what scholars call the "black/white binary paradigm." Many Latinos feel left out of a discussion that is based on categories that grow out of the experience of African Americans.

It is not that we believe racism and skin color are not important in North American life. Clearly, they are. However, for Latinos the critical dimensions are culture and language, not race. . . . Categories tied too closely to the history of the racism experienced by African Americans at the hands of white Americans miss the essence of Latino experience. We Latinos do not fit easily into the present scheme.

Neither do Asians. Neither do Native Americans. Perhaps most importantly, neither do the growing number of children in our congregations who are part Latino, part African American, part White, part Asian, part Indigenous.

If our movement is to attract the growing Latino population into our congregations and into our pulpits, we need to broaden our language and expand our paradigm. The language we Latinos use among ourselves is telling and points the way. Latinos rarely talk of Euro-Americans as "whites." Rather, the term is "anglo." *Anglo* captures a sense of cultural difference, not racial difference. The oppression that poor recent immigrants from Nicaragua share with upper middle class Latino professionals is a cultural oppression, a sense of being robbed of their language and traditions. As we move to heal the relationships in our movement and in our larger society, we need to talk about race and also about culture and class. A focus on any one is too narrow and dismisses the experience of too many people.

As we travel on this path toward wholeness, we believe we need more emphasis on what binds us together. We need to come together as a people who share a common vision and a common destiny. Each of us—black, white, brown, gay, straight—longs for a community of faith that values us for who we are. We bring a deep need to be in a faith community where we are loved and known, where we can bring our gifts and our pain. We believe that we are better served by organizing around our common vision for the future rather than on our injuries in the past.

That does not mean we deny the past, that we do not take hard instruction from it. However, to dwell on oppression divides and distracts us from our true tasks. Our true tasks are to create a common vision and make that vision a reality. In sum, we feel we need to concentrate more on what will unite us despite our differences. Our process for ending racism must create loving community.

Lastly, we blancos, indios, negros, morenos, mestizos, and mulattos who make up the Latino population believe that our varied pasts are precious gifts that we want to share. Part of spiritual growth is learning to appreciate the gifts and wisdom of different traditions. Our varied backgrounds give us so much to offer each other. Our variety can be a source of wisdom that helps to revitalize worship, religious education, and community life in our congregations. One example of this revitalization is the way the ancient Día de los Muertos traditions are being adopted in UU churches as a way to grieve and celebrate those who have died.

We need to take time to expand and reframe our discussion. We want to be part of a religious movement with a common vision—a vision founded on sharing the wonderful gifts we are. We are eager to work with joy and love to help make our shared vision a living reality.

DRUUMM had put Gilmore's name forward, which was how it came to be considered.

About the same time, the decision was made to create a Committee on Anti-Racism, Anti-Oppression and Multiculturalism within the UUMA. A report from Gilmore and Jimenez recalled the next development:

> Beginning in June of last year, the UUMA Executive Committee began its recruitment of members for a newly formed Committee on Ministry for Anti-Racism, Anti-Oppression and Multiculturalism. The committee consists of [Revs.] Clyde Grubbs, Rudolph Gelsey, and Suzelle Lynch and Executive Committee members John Gilmore and Patricia Jimenez. The Committee will support John [Gilmore] and Patricia [Jimenez] to carry out their portfolio of anti-racism, anti-oppression, multiculturalism on the UUMA Executive Committee. The Committee on Ministry also has the task of identifying areas where the UUMA can make changes to its institutional structure and practices to become anti-racist and anti-oppressive, and bringing recommendations to the UUMA Executive Committee for consideration and implementation.
>
> At its April meeting, the UUMA Executive Committee asked this Committee on Ministry to bring back recommendations for eliminating the classist assumptions that deny many UUMA members full accessibility to, and limit participation in, UUMA programs such as Ministry Days.

DiBona said the new Committee on Ministry had the delicate job of handling incidences of alleged racist behavior against ministers of color by their white colleagues. She said both the appointed positions and the new committee were part of a change that some saw as essential to changing the racial dynamics within the UUMA. "Overall, one of the things that was lacking in the UUMA was any kind of understanding of how racism affected their members of color in the churches. Without codifying a relationship in the community, there was no way to recognize the problem that people of color were having in the congregations."

Meadville Lombard Theological School

At its April 2000 meeting, the Transformation Committee discussed the lack of responsiveness of the General Assembly Planning Committee and of Meadville Lombard Theological School's perceived unwillingness to be actively engaged with the institutional anti-racism analysis developed by Crossroads Ministry, which had been conducting trainings of the UUA leadership. Several Transformation Committee members including Suchocki, Robette Dias, Rev. William Gardiner, and Dr. Leon Spencer visited Meadville Lombard to try to have a conversation with faculty and students, which turned into a confrontational debate. The Committee's summation revealed deep concerns:

> Had to keep reminding them that they were not there for an intellectual debate, but rather to build a relationship and have conversation. Issue not clear that ML is a stakeholder in the anti-oppression initiative. After the meeting, there were several people who felt that they did have a place at the table. Leon and Susan went to meet with students; Robette and Bill met with faculty. Bill and Robette spelled out what JTW is. Dr. Thandeka argued against the anti-racism initiative. Bill and Robette stressed using power effectively as anti-oppressive voices. . . . Susan and Leon had a very difficult time with students. They would not listen to find out what JTW was about. Students of color—some came in the morning, but left in afternoon. Leon got angry and finally spoke out about how he felt as a person of color. Student body president defended Leon's speaking out, and things began to shift. Others who wanted to hear about Transformation Committee began to speak up, and Susan and Leon were able to present. . . .

Transformation Committee

The Transformation Committee also discussed courses of action with ministers not supportive of their work, noting,

> What should be done when Transformation Committee hears about ministers and others misrepresenting the JTW?

Try to use the existing structures to raise the issue with them. Transformation Committee can raise this issue with the UUMA and MFC: how to hold ministers to a standard of professionalism and accountability. Write a letter to UUMA: we notice that some of our ministers are behaving in a racist way and attacking the JTW, not expressing differences of opinion, but telling lies, etc. The Transformation Committee needs to contact the seminaries too, and to do a stakeholder analysis for them. Monitoring and assessment are extraordinarily powerful tools—the Transformation Committee is at a place where it can own its power and hold stakeholders accountable. Language to UU Ministers Association and Board of Trustees should be something like: "Transformation Committee is charged to assess and monitor UU systems. If ministers tell lies about the JTW initiative or advise congregants to resist the initiative how will you respond? This is a new question and Transformation Committee needs your advice on how Transformation Committee should respond." It is part of the monitoring function to call attention to resistance.

The Transformation Committee devoted a great deal of time on issues related to ministry in non-parish settings. Community ministry had been raised as a key issue for ministers of color. The Committee's minutes included this summation of a part of that discussion:

Discussion began with examining the lack of support for community ministry by the UUA. In the discussion, it was noted that the core constituency of the Unitarian Universalist Association were the congregations and that community ministry, which was not necessarily congregationally based, had no place at the table. This was important because a high percentage of ministers of color choose community ministry and community ministry work was often involved with work against racism and oppression. Community ministers were seen as a resource in helping congregations with their transformation into anti-racist institutions. Of the 44 ministers of color—10 were doing community ministry and 18 were parish ministers or working at the UUA.

The Committee also discussed ministers' discomfort with the Journey Toward Wholeness. Tensions had arisen with the UUMA Executive Committee when the Transformation Committee had not supported the UUMA's proposal to use the National Coalition Building Institute's race relations training approach. The UUMA had sought funding from the Association's Panel on Theological Education to spread the NCBI approach. Department of Ministry staff reported that they were hearing negative comments about this, that "the Association has a party line," and that the "UUMA folks felt that they were being told that they should only use Crossroads." The Committee also raised concerns about the lack of support for ministers of color, noting that "[a] special start-up process is needed for new ministers of color who are settled in a parish that has never had a minister of color. This should be ongoing past start-up."

Diversity of Ministry Team

Ministers of color and Latina/o/Hispanic ministers became aware that a special Diversity of Ministry Team consisting of UUA staff members had held meetings to discuss ministers of color. Association president Dr. John Buehrens recalled that he established the group around 1996 and chaired it himself out of a concern for the historic difficulties around ministers in historically marginalized racial and cultural groups. The Committee operated for three years before its existence generated concern with some seminarians and ministers of color. The fact that the team had been meeting without the consent of those discussed raised ire. Gilmore's and Jimenez's summary of the discussion highlighted key tensions:

> UUMA: Is there a minister of color on the task force? *Bill Sinkford and Mel Hoover.* Is a candidate or minister being discussed on a personal level? *Yes.* How is confidentiality kept? *We assume it doesn't go outside the room.* Does the minister know s/he is being talked about? Are you sharing "illegal to hiring" information? *This is an advocacy organization. We*

gauge our success on getting more ministers of color into our ministry. We are trying to stay in dialogue with people who have concerns without injuring the work we do.

"Conduct Unbecoming"

In January 2001 the UUMA Executive Committee held a discussion about anti-racism and professional ethics:

The Exec discussed the question: At what point do our professional guidelines hold someone accountable for racism and make this "conduct unbecoming [of a minister under the Guidelines for the Unitarian Universalist Ministry]"? We are not talking about changing our codes, but about whether we live up to them.

[Rev.] Diane [Miller, director of the UUA Department of Ministry]: *Do you act without a complaint? Do you notify the MFC?*

[Rev.] Gretchen [Woods]: *We are back to asking people who have been hurt to talk about their hurts again.*

[Rev.] José [Ballester]: *They are willing to talk if some action is to be taken. . . .*

José asks the Exec to think about what the long-term issues might be regarding racism among colleagues. [Rev.] Gary [Smith] asked José to put together a one-page paper about the issues. Betsy [Rev. Elizabeth Stevens] would be willing to meet with Gary and José to continue this work. Discussion:

[Rev.] Craig [Roshaven]: *Is the language in our guidelines adequate and we simply haven't thought to apply them this way?*

[Rev.] Kendyl [Gibbons]: *I don't want us to find ourselves in a place where our thoughts are illegal. We need to define this in terms of behavior. That public statements are effective in letting people know what is expected of them.*

Gretchen [Woods]: *Case studies and education before implementation will be important. It will help get chapters to take this step toward education.*

VOICE
Rev. Patricia Jimenez

This address, entitled "Facing the Challenge, Dreaming the Possible," was delivered at the Unitarian Universalist Association's 1998 Urban Church Conference in Baltimore. Jimenez is a founding member of LUUNA.

When I joined the Unitarian Universalist church in Tucson I was one of two Latinos in the congregation, and I believed, quite mistakenly I was to learn much later, that we were the only ones in the whole denomination. I have to say that it was a very lonely feeling. Since then I have met many more Latino and Latina Unitarian Universalists. We come from many parts of the world—Puerto Rico, Mexico, Spain, Colombia, Chile, El Salvador, to name just a few of the countries of origin—and we all have our own unique stories of how we came to Unitarian Universalism.

And, despite the fact that we know that there are many more of us in the denomination, and in our various congregations, some of the isolation remains. Most of us would like to see more Latinos and Latinas in our congregations. But what does this mean to our denomination? What does this mean within our individual congregations? And what does this mean to each of you as individuals? . . . In order to do this, however, it means that we will have to broaden our perspectives on race and culture, and we will have to come to terms with our issues around class.

It means that when we talk about diversity we have to move beyond skin color as a way to describe what we'd like to see. It means that we probably will have to find a new language.

For example, many Latinos and Latinas are uncomfortable with the use of the phrase "people of color." Not because you cannot use color to describe us, but because it does not go far enough! It leaves out culture and language, and any expression of individual ties to a particular country that are such an important part of individual identity. . . .

Today, I would like to invite you to use your imaginations. Can you imagine what it might be that connects you to that Latina or Latino who just might happen to come to your church some Sunday and then stay? Think about it. I am making an assumption, of course: that many of you would like to have Latinos and Latinas in your congregations, or if you already have some, that you would like to see more of us; taking part in the worship services, serving on committees, and maybe, just maybe, becoming your friends.

But just so your imaginations don't run too far amok, let me give you some ideas of how this might affect a congregation. It has taken me a long time to both realize, and appreciate, what it is from my own culture that informs my ideas of an ideal religious community. For me these include: a respect for elders; a profound sense of the importance of family and community; the inclusion of children in all activities; and of the need for celebration which includes the joys of both culture and language.

Now, how might this play out in the congregation? For example: there might be more events that are multigenerational; in fact, I could also see a ministry involving the elders in the congregations, but one that encourages an open exchange of learning and wisdom; someone just might question why we send our the children out of a worship service; and on a lighter, but no less important note, parties might be more fun, certainly probably noisier.

I wish I could tell you some magic formula for attracting new members, particularly Latinos and Latinas. There isn't one. I hope you will realize, however, after learning more about us that there are some things you need to find out about the Latinos and Latinas you want to attract. Things such as where do these potential new members come from? What historical, social, or political circumstances have caused them to be where they are now? And, finally, but not least, what social class do they represent?

Classism is a factor in any discussion about Latinos and Latinas and our Unitarian Universalist congregations, and I do not want to underestimate its importance in this discussion. Classism is real, and we as UUs struggle with it. For all of our talk, and yes, for all our very real, and sincere, and exceptional efforts on behalf of those less fortunate, we have not come to terms with it, particularly when it comes to representation within our individual congregations. . . . So, just who might these Latinos and Latinas be? The ones who will come and stay? Perhaps we can take a look at the Latinos and Latinas who are already in our congregations. Take for example, the three of us [speaking on the panel]. All three of us come from other faith traditions; we all three have graduate degrees; and we are all professionals. We fit the profile of a lot of UUs. In addition, we all speak English. What I do suggest is that here among the educated, professional, and bilingual Latinas and Latinos is a good place to start. For very practical reasons:

First questions: How many UU congregations have members in the congregation who speak Spanish? Fluently. Enough to make a person feel welcome and at ease, and not awkward because he or she can't converse with you? Not all Latinos and Latinas speak Spanish, but I would suppose that among those whom you've already attracted—from that pool that I was describing above—will be some who are bilingual, and who would make it a point to welcome Spanish-speaking newcomers, or those who don't feel very comfortable speaking English.

At a workshop at GA, someone pointed out that many businesses have signs in their windows, "se habla Espanol," and suggested that congregations put a little note on the name tags of members who speak Spanish.

Second question: How many UU congregations are now prepared to offer services in Spanish? Very few, let me tell you. There are several factors that come into this: again, the lack of Spanish-speaking members plays a role. You have to have a fairly large pool of volunteers to prepare services in Spanish over a number of years.

Still another factor that hinders this happening is the lack of resources in Spanish. Only recently has the book, *Our Chosen Faith*, been translated into Spanish. It was translated by Ervin Barrios, a member of the San José Unitarian Church, and a LUUNA board member. There are no other widely available resources in Spanish.

Nor can you look to the Latina and Latino ministers within the denomination to meet this challenge. At the present time there are barely a dozen Latino and Latina Unitarian Universalist ministers and/or ministry students. There are just not enough of us.

I know I have just said that most of us believe that we need to start by attracting Latinos and Latinas who are at least bilingual, and I have said that there is no magic formula for attracting any Latinos and Latinas at all, but I want to tell you about [a congregation] . . . my own church in San José. The minister, Lindi Ramsden, has devoted a great deal of her time to learning Spanish, and there are a number of bilingual persons in the congregations. For a while we had separate services in Spanish, and then we changed to bilingual joint services. Today, five years later, we still struggle with a worship format that meets the needs of the congregation. Members who speak only Spanish are few, and we struggle with financial resources, as well as leadership resources. During this time, however, the group has developed their own worship resources. They have many insights that they could share with us.

The other congregation that I want to tell you about is the Oscar Romero Congregation which meets in the building of the First Unitarian Church of Los Angeles. It was born out of the sanctuary movement and has been in existence for several years.

Its membership, including its lay leaders, come from the community that surrounds the church, and are primarily from Central America. Its focus has been around social justice issues.

Now they are struggling with a waning membership, lack of financial resources, and how to become a worshipping community. However, there is a new effort supported by several of the ministers and churches in the Los Angeles area to help this congregation.

There is one thought that I would like to leave you with, and it comes from my experience as a chaplain. In my work, every single time I encounter another person there is something I seek to do: to make God manifest in that relationship. What that means to me is that we stand together, together in a holy place. May we, in all our encounters with each other, and with those who seem to be different, find a way to manifest the divine or holy. May we stand together.

CHAPTER 16

Transforming the Transformation Committee

Under the Crossroads Ministry approach to anti-racism favored by the UUA as the century turned, institutions were expected to develop a Transformation Committee to facilitate the change toward being an anti-racist institution. While the goal was clear the process was not, and whether the Journey Toward Wholeness Transformation Committee could or should take the role was an ongoing point of discussion.

During this era, the annual General Assembly became the event that raised both awareness of and controversy around the work of those advocating a UUA anti-racist agenda. Discussion of anti-racism permeated the 2000 General Assembly in Nashville, ranging across theology, tensions with the UUA's Fulfilling the Promise initiative, and the need to include economic class as an oppression within the Unitarian Universalist movement.

In 2001, at the General Assembly in Cleveland, the Journey Toward Wholeness Transformation Committee issued a report, *Continuing the Journey*, that assessed progress and provided a suggested guide to resources. The multipurpose nature of the report indicated the Committee's continuing multiple roles.

The leadership of Rev. Melvin Hoover, then director of the UUA's Department for Faith in Action, was wide ranging. Rev. Joseph Barndt of Crossroads Ministry recalled,

> Mel, with all his ability to work on six tracks at once, was also very influential, not just as a Unitarian Universalist person but as a Crossroads person. He wasn't just simply there

as a representative of the UU anti-racism program but . . . he could use Crossroads and say "we." . . . Mel was a partner, was just an enormously powerful influence [who] provided the opportunity for the UUA to get back into racial justice.

Shifts on the Transformation Committee
Membership on the Transformation Committee began to change. Member Ken Carpenter resigned because of other commitments and Rev. Frank Rivas resigned because of differences over the Committee's work. The minutes noted,

> Frank Rivas was present Saturday so that he and the committee could discuss his resignation from the Transformation Committee. The discussion sought to address several questions: How does the committee deal with a member taking a stance different than the rest of the committee? How can Frank help the committee to understand its own functioning better? . . . On what terms was Frank leaving? There was a general feeling that issues had been discussed thoroughly and with mutual respect.

The Committee also engaged in a lengthy conversation with Denise (Denny) Davidoff, who as the UUA's elected moderator chairs its Board of Trustees, about whether the Committee should serve as a "Transformation Committee," as Crossroads Ministry, the interfaith anti-racism consulting group, advised the UUA. From the beginning, the Committee had resisted the idea that it was an "Oversight Committee."

"None of that oversight stuff," Rev. Susan Suchocki Brown, the Transformation Committee's first chair, remembers saying. "That right there smacks of what we are talking about needing to change!" This discussion revealed continued confusion about key Journey Toward Wholeness issues, including confusion between what the Transformation Committee was doing and what the UUA's Faith in Action Department was doing; the role of the Transformation Committee versus the role of the Board; the need for a strategy to extend the reach of anti-racism trainings beyond the Association's leadership level; and the need to understand whether the role of a Transformation Committee was to help facilitate change or evaluate it. Suchocki Brown observed that the Transformation Committee idea came from the Crossroads Ministry trainings and yet "one of Joe Barndt's great failings was that he could not define what a transformation committee should do."

Another question was whether the Journey Toward Wholeness Transformation Committee could be a leader for change when its membership did not include many decision-makers. On this last point, a memo written by the Core Team, an informal group of anti-racism trainers, some of whom were UUA staff people, was considered: "The memorandum imagined a team with a larger number of board members. Denny [Davidoff] took it to [the Board's] Committee on Committees, and they felt that they had already created a committee, which is the Transformation Committee. . . . Denny and the Board are waiting for the transformation committee to tell them what the model is."

Tensions with UUA Committees

The Transformation Committee initially found the General Assembly Planning Committee lacking in anti-racism responsiveness. Suchocki Brown recalled that this gradually changed and the Planning Committee became receptive to an anti-racist awareness as part of General Assembly. "At first they were resistant: 'We're the Planning Committee, we plan GA,'" Suchocki Brown recalled. Yet the planners increasingly saw the Transformation Committee as a resource as it continued to raise issues, such as the desire of Unitarian Universalists of Indian and Native American heritage to have elders from the area bless the land where General Assemblies were held.

The Transformation Committee also experienced tension with "Fulfilling the Promise," the strategic planning and resource-raising initiative launched by the Association's Board of Trustees. The April 2000 Transformation Committee meeting minutes reported that Ruth Alatorre, the member involved with Fulfilling the Promise planning, had said the Fulfilling the Promise leadership was "not receptive" to the concerns she had raised about their plans for

General Assembly workshops. She concluded that "the workshop process is not welcoming to marginalized people."

Rev. Melvin Hoover, of the Faith in Action Department, said the Department and the Core Team initially supported Fulfilling the Promise as necessary to raising the funds needed to move anti-racism forward. "It supposedly was going to incorporate the anti-racism stuff right at the heart of it," Hoover said. "But Fulfilling the Promise moved from justice-making to fundraising. . . . And a number of key leaders who had been leading the anti-racism piece did not, in fact, carry the next steps of what were needed to institution-alize anti-racism/anti-oppression/multiculturalism into the actual incorporation of Fulfilling the Promise. It didn't systemically move anti-racism ahead. . . . It actually in many ways undermined it."

Rev. Dr. John Buehrens, the Association president who launched the Promise campaign, disagreed. He said Fulfilling the Promise was the strategic planning process to lay the groundwork for an ambitious capital campaign. A seven-person Steering Committee guided the effort, including Buehrens, Davidoff, and as staff coor-dinator, Rev. William Sinkford, then head of the Association's Congregational, District and Extension Department. Rev. Clark Olsen, an organizational development consultant as well as a min-ister, "had long observed that the UUA needed to ground new intitivies in a strategy planning process," Buehrens said. "Some persons associated with the Journey Toward Wholeness evidently thought that no other planning than their own was necessary, but the very controversies surrounding the various ideologies and approaches to anti-racism undercut any effort to turn all planning over to that team." Buehrens also observed, "The UUA, like many of our congregations, prefers to operate by lurch and veto," Bueh-rens observed. "Just the fact that there was another initiative aimed at strategic planning, aimed at getting the resources that could actu-ally do transformation work, meant some of the people in the Jour-ney Toward Wholeness saw it as a competition."

Buehrens said the multiple approaches were intentional. "In effect, the UUA in my era needed to have a multi-layered approach to strategic change—involving not only 'grass roots' opinion, includ-ing that of marginalized and underrepresented groups, but also such key constituencies and power brokers as the Board of Trustees, the staff, the ministers of the large congregations, the UUA's major donors including [the Unitarian Universalist Congregation at] Shelter Rock [in Manhasset, New York], and its partner organizations, from UUSC to the seminaries to camps and conference centers."

UUA Staff Efforts

The Faith in Action Department was heartened by progress at the district level, as they noted in a report to the grant-making Veatch Program of the Unitarian Universalist Church at Shelter Rock, New York. The Joseph Priestley District Transformation Team had completed high-level anti-racism educating and organizing training in March 2000. "The team now has a well thought through organizing strategy for the next five years," the report noted, adding that in fall 2001, "Building a Jubilee World-Two" workshops, focused on developing an analysis of the ways oppression translates into institutional power, were scheduled for representatives from three congregations in and around Washington, D.C., and five in the Philadelphia area. The report continued,

> Thomas Jefferson District has a 30-person transformation team. The team is sponsoring a district anti-racism conference in February, piloting the delivery of Jubilee workshops, and obtaining a grant for interfaith work. We are working with the district team to train district people in the Jubilee model.
>
> Two congregations in the Clara Barton District, the Unitarian Society of New Haven, [Connecticut,] and the Unitarian Universalist Society of Greater Springfield, [Massachusetts,] completed the phase three educating and organizing training in October 2000. In addition three congregations in the Hartford area (the Unitarian Society of Hartford, the Universalist Church of West Hartford, and the Unitarian Universalist Society: East Manchester) have formed Greater Hartford UUs Against Racism. We are supporting them in their anti-racism work and in the development of congregational anti-racism teams.

The Mass Bay District has a fifteen-person transformation team. We will be doing a Jubilee Two [power analysis of racism training] program for their board and leaders on February 9–11 of 2001.

Leaders from [Colorado congregations in] Denver . . . Boulder . . . Fort Collins, Cheyenne, and Colorado Springs participated in a Jubilee Two . . . training last November. These congregations make up the Front Range Cluster in the Mountain Desert District. We are in dialogue with these congregations about the formation of anti-racist transformation teams for the cluster and their congregations.

We are also working with several congregations in the Metro New York District, including Brooklyn and Community Church of New York. On April 20–22, 2001 we will hold a Jubilee Two in Ridgewood, New Jersey, that will include leaders from Paramus and Palisades.

We are working with the district anti-racism committee in the Pacific Southwest District. In November of 2000, we held an Introduction to Building a Transformation Team training for several congregations in the district. Jubilee Two . . . workshops will be held [in California] with San Diego (March 16–18, 2001) and Long Beach, Rancho Palos Verdes, and Orange Coast (March 23–25, 2001).

Mid South District board members and leaders will be doing an introductory Jubilee workshop in February of 2001.

Florida District leaders have just completed a survey of the racial justice work being done in their congregations. The district is going to form a district anti-racism committee. We will be providing support for the next steps that they take.

Leaders in the Central Midwest District are going to survey the racial justice work being done in their congregations. We are in conversation with them about how to form working relationships with their district leaders and congregations.

In the program year 2001–2002, we hope to offer approximately 25 Jubilee World workshops to churches

EXCERPT
Explaining Anti-Racism

This article by Tom Stites, the editor of the UUA's World *magazine, appeared in the March/April 2000 issue of* World. *Stites identifies as a white American with roots in the Great Plains.*

Antiracism, as used in the UUA's Journey toward Wholeness initiative, means a commitment to dismantling the structures of the status quo that build racism into our culture.

Thus, antiracism goes beyond tolerance, which is the passive acceptance of people who are different, beyond the wish for diversity, beyond proactive efforts at inclusion, beyond a nonracist stance that is neutral and thus does not challenge the status quo. Antiracism requires taking on the daunting challenge of reshaping society's structures so that justice is built into our culture in place of the racial oppression that has been part of it since Europeans began colonizing North America five centuries ago.

By focusing on antiracism as more than a personal matter, the definition used by the Journey toward Wholeness is more sweeping—and more abstract—than definitions, often used in workplace diversity trainings, that focus on personal attitudes and practices. Several other religious denominations are among the groups committed to structural antiracism.

Amending the U.S. Constitution to outlaw slavery was structural change of the first order. So was the Supreme Court decision that outlawed official school segregation and the civil rights movement's successful fight for laws that ended official housing segregation and required equal opportunity in employment. Other examples include Congress's 1924 law that ended the ironic classification of Native Americans as "resident aliens" in favor of "people eligible for citizenship." But these changes did not end racism. In the words of the Rev. William R. Jones, an African American UU theologian, "racism mutates." Now that segregation is no longer sanctioned by the Constitution and in law, racism remains in less explicit forms that include substandard education for people of color, discriminatory lending by financial institutions, racial profiling by police, and discriminatory hiring and promotion in the workplace.

According to the Rev. Melvin Hoover, director of the UUA's Department for Faith in Action, racism is part of the core of all U.S. institutions and expresses itself almost invisibly in status quo assumptions such as choices of language and symbolism. He says this is why the Unitarian Universalist Association has created and leads workshops whose goal is for participants to make a commitment to dismantling racism.

The UUA's trainings are based on the idea that people all have culturally assigned roles according to the groups they are born into, that the roles are held in place by racist social structures, and that the culture thus resists change. The trainings make the point that because of racist social structures, as white children grow up, they are socialized into a role that places them at the center of power relative to people from other racial groups; in the language of racism theorists, this is called unearned white privilege. Conversely, the culture assigns marginal roles to people of color.

"We insist on examining privilege," UUA President the Rev. Dr. John Buehrens says of the UUA's view. "Most of the other training models don't."

Hoover says the UUA's workshop for congregations—called Creating a Jubilee World after the biblical jubilee years when liberty was restored to the enslaved, debts were forgiven, and property was returned to its original owners—use this definition of racism: Race prejudice plus the misuse of systemic power equals racism. Thus, given white people's dominant role in the culture, racism cannot exist without whites' complicity, witting or unwitting. And it follows that racism cannot be removed from the culture without the active commitment of whites to use their power to this end.

In the UUA publication *Creating a Jubilee World: Antiracism Resources*, the Rev. Kurt Kuhwald, a member of the Association's Jubilee Working Group, writes that its definition of racism "never lets us lose the critical awareness of the centrality of power in creating and maintaining racism."

The Journey toward Wholeness initiative addresses racism as only one of many forms of oppression. Others it strives to end are based on people's gender, class, sexual preference, and ability.

and districts. We will continue to identify and train new lead and co-trainers and apprentices across the continent. Additionally, the Anti-Racism Program Coordinator will spend time in the churches and districts familiarizing Unitarian Universalists with the Faith in Action Phase I programs. Not all congregations will be appropriate candidates for a transformation team, however we believe that we will identify and provide programming for at least five more.

Several anti-racism trainers came to realize that efforts in a predominantly white context such as the UUA put a heavy burden on people of color, Latina/o, and Hispanic people and did not serve to address their developmental needs around race issues. In response the Faith in Action Department conceived a new training, Anti-Racism for People of Color.

"These are the people who are called up for leadership in every place they are. They are carrying the weight of responsibility and leadership and trying to live life too," said Taquiena Boston, who was a consultant to the UUA at that time. The training was piloted before the 2000 General Assembly. Boston recalls,

> This workshop explores people of color identity, the diverse experiences of racism among distinct people of color groups (including the impact of colonialism), the internalization of racist oppression, and agenda setting for continued community building and leadership development among Unitarian Universalists of color. Another important aspect of this workshop is that it incorporates visual expression, dialogue, story-telling, worship, and ritual—multiple modes of communication and learning. . . . In addition to Unitarian Universalists youth, young adults and adults of color and multiracial people, the workshop included members of the Crossroads interfaith anti-racism collective from other religious communities such as Disciples of Christ.

Also, the UUA staff worked with DRUUMM (Diverse and Revolutionary Unitarian Universalist Multicultural Ministries) developed camps for multiracial families and families of color. The retreat-format camps were held in the West and became the prototype for other multiracial and families of color activities. James Coomes, Robette Dias, Young Kim, Joseph Lyons, and Rev. Suzelle Lynch provided leadership.

UUA Leadership and Anti-Racism

In February 2001, the Transformation Committee was concerned about creating forums for the candidates for UUA president and moderator to make their anti-racism positions clear and explicit. Transformation Committee members met with the Association's Executive Staff Council, which was composed of the president, executive vice president, and heads of all UUA departments, to reflect on how their work with anti-racism was going. The Council, the committee noted at its next meeting, "has a very difficult time figuring out how we're going to manage the work of anti-racism in our departments. Also tends to be too much focus on staff rather than congregations." The Committee mourned the death of Committee member Ruth Alatorre, who died in December of 2000.

The Transformation Committee Chair asked the Exec Staff "What has been the most fun, challenging change in the departmental mission and work?" The Department Directors responded:

- *Religious Education*: Having people of color in the department has made a huge difference. We have anti-racism/anti-oppression on every agenda. The staff has companioned the director on this issue. A new life span curriculum is being developed that incorporates an anti-oppression lens throughout. This is a big change from having selected modules on this issue. The youth work on anti-oppression has been tremendous.
- *Finance*: Meeting needs of people of color and anti-oppression activists who are living on a shoestring. Finance committees have taken training and are applying an anti-oppression lens to investment and other major financial decisions and strategies. Finding multicultural investment managers.

VOICE
Joseph Santos-Lyons

This was broadcast on KBOO 90.7 in Portland, Oregon, on July 19, 2006, and was titled "Parents Shouldn't Take Their Children's Race Personally." Santos-Lyons was a founding member of DRUUMM and a young adult leader.

Coming of age I found myself thinking and living through a different racial lens than my childhood. I moved beyond an abstract, intellectual understanding of being a mixed-race person, Chinese and White, and found myself identifying as, being seen as, and living as a multiracial person.

I am adopted, by White parents, who intentionally and unintentionally ignored any discussion about my racial identity. Upon reflection, they've shared that they had hoped that I would see myself as white, and were deeply perplexed by my wish to live as a mixed-race person.

Why be proud of my racial and cultural heritage? Why give care and attention to the ancestors who have come before me? Why be concerned about my racial identity in such a deeply racialized society? These questions were important to me, and my attitudes and beliefs changed as a result.

My parents took this personally, in the sense that they had a personal expectation about how I would believe and live racially and culturally, and that my choice to live as I wanted to live offended them personally. They were unhappy with me, impatient with my explanations, frustrated with my developing sense of racial identity. It was a difficult time for all of us.

Parents shouldn't take their children's racial identity personally. We have a right to our racial and cultural identity, we have a right to interpret and define our existence. Racial identity is fluid and dynamic, race today defies the definitions of the 1960's.

My wish is for our parents, and our religious and social institutions, to support people who search for the truth and meaning of their racial identity in our racialized society. We seek this knowledge not only for our own dignity and self-respect, but for our health and safety.

- *Development*: Presidents Council work has been fantastic—they took the training at their own expense, they are boosters of the JTW initiative, they have increased their diversity. The two most successful Friends letters have been anti-oppression—responding to hate crimes and the White House recognition of the UUA anti-racism effort as one of the best practices in America.
- *Beacon Press*: People of Color internship program: Very difficult to raise funding for this program. 16 interns every year. We are helping to transform the industry. The books, the books! Not just race, really looking at class. Best book on class in this decade—Michael McDonald's *All Souls*. The Bluestreak series of books—women of color, lesbians' voices. Annual collection of Beacon's best. Democracy Forum—proportional representation. Lots of people of color on staff—and only 1 is at the entry level—others have been promoted to or hired at upper levels. Helen and a staff member sit on the PEN (Poets, Playwrights, Essayists, Editors, and Novelists) diversity committee.
- *Ministry*: Role of the iconic figure in a transformational time. There is an enormous pressure on those in minority oppressed groups to lead the transformation, be the voice for the oppressed. This puts extra burdens on a small number of people.
- *Congregational District & Extension Services*: Still struggling with extension ministries and diversity.
- *Communications*: Lots of struggle around this issue. Focus has been on the *UU World*. One of the results of this has been an entirely new staff who have a much greater understanding of anti-oppression work. The magazine expresses a new culture. The new editors are committed to having an editorial advisory group.
- *President*: Board is putting together a committee on socially responsible investing. John has been doing a lot of interfaith work with the Progressive National Network. . . . UU clergy are well-situated to know who are the other progressive clergy in their areas.

The Transformation Committee's notes from the discussion also reveal both the large sense of mission Committee members felt and the day-to-day frustrations:

> There are limits to moral exhortation. It is work of grace. Our job is to set the conditions for grace to happen. . . . We're all broken and we're all in this together. That means changing the work of this committee from institutional superego to healthy ego work of transformation. So, we need to be strategic collectively to help make grace happen. We really need to work with the ministers and religious educators—companioning is needed for religious professionals and others to be prophetic and pastoral. It's not just in your face—it's companioning. The question is how to make anti-racism, anti-oppression, and justice reside at the heart of congregational life.

Continuing the Journey Report

The Transformation Committee's *Continuing the Journey*, which was to be introduced at the 2001 General Assembly, was a subject of discussion at the Committee's April meeting. The report included the rationale for taking on the hard work of talking about race:

> In every generation, Unitarian Universalists have responded to the prophetic call to create beloved community. We have sought ways to fight oppression in all its forms, to build a more just and anti-racist society, to bring much needed social and economic change to our communities. Today we celebrate the many successes in our racial justice efforts. We also feel compelled to understand our many failures. Success and failure intertwine, leaving us with one sure truth: UUs have historically put themselves in the struggle for racial justice, and participation in this struggle is one of our hard-won traditions. Consistent with this tradition, the Journey Toward Wholeness Path to Anti-Racism is Unitarian Universalism's new and growing response to the prophetic call to create anti-racist, multi-cultural beloved community.

The Journey Toward Wholeness Path to Anti-Racism was born out of the premise that racism and its effects, including economic injustice, are embedded in all social institutions as well as in ourselves and will not be eradicated without deliberate engagement in analysis and action. The path begins internally. We take a fresh look at ourselves and learn to identify our personal and institutional relationship to oppressive systems. We then learn the skills we need to dismantle racism in our own institutions and restructure ourselves into anti-racist institutions. Finally, we move from this new focus on internal change into authentic multiracial, multi-ethnic, and interfaith coalitions for effective, spiritually-driven action for justice.

The Journey Toward Wholeness Path to Anti-Racism achieves its goals using the "transformation team" model. Congregational and organizational transformation teams participate in a series of anti-racism workshops, trainings, consultations, curricula, and assessments—each designed to teach team-members how to analyze institutional racism in UU congregations and organizations, and how to "coach" their own institutions along the path to anti-racist transformation. By learning to apply this powerful anti-racism/anti-oppression lens to our theology, our worship, our structures, our justice work, and our relationships with other institutions, UU anti-racism transformation team-members become empowered to develop strategies, actions, and relationships that will make Unitarian Universalist congregations not only visionaries for, but participants in the anti-racist, multicultural beloved communities we long for. In short, transformation team members learn a new, anti-racist way of being in the world, and they learn how to spread the good news! This is deeply spiritual work that calls us into a new awareness of how racism has impacted all of us. It calls us into new ways of relating to the communities in which we live and to whom we are accountable. It requires a commitment of the heart as well as analysis and skill. It renews our faith. It fulfills our promise. It is, truly, a journey toward wholeness.

The report also laid out what it saw as "The Path to Anti-Racism" as a series of steps that might take a congregation two to three years to complete. The steps included:

- Anti-racism educational resources and curricula
- Creating a Jubilee World introductory anti-racism weekend workshop
- Introduction to Building an Anti-racism Transformation Team workshop (1 ½ days)
- Creating a Jubilee World II advanced anti-racism weekend workshop
- Planning and Design of Anti-Racism Initiatives Consultation (1 day)
- Anti-racism Analysis and Transformation Team Building training (3 ½ days)
- Anti-Racism Educating and Organizing training for anti-racism transformations teams (4 ½ days)
- Resources, consultation, and networking for anti-racism transformation teams

The Association's Board of Trustees also reviewed *Continuing the Journey* before General Assembly, which laid out a new "Council" structure that would formalize input from various "stakeholders" groups, and, according to the Committee's minutes, raised the following points:

- What the Board is concerned about is whether the Journey Toward Wholeness Council will be effective. The Finance Committee asked about what funding would be required. They indicated that this should be figured out by the Executive Staff at the August budget meeting. Obviously, the new president will have a significant role in these decisions. Depending on who is elected, the Transformation Committee may need to rely more on the Board. . . .
- The Board expressed concern about moving the anti-oppression, anti-racism, multicultural work into the congregations. They want to know how this would be done and how the proposed steering committee and council would promote and facilitate this?

Rev. Joshua M. Pawelek

Joshua M. Pawelek was minister of the UU Church of Norwich, Connecticut, and a program associate in the UUA's Faith in Action Department when he wrote these words for the March/April 2000 issue of the UUA's World *magazine. He identified his racial/ethnic identity as white with Polish, German, and Scandinavian heritages.*

The Racism Embedded in Our System

I started volunteering as an antiracism organizer in UU congregations in August 1997, after attending a three-and-a-half day antiracism analysis and team-building workshop led by Crossroads Ministry of Chicago, the primary consultant to the UUA's national antiracism initiative, the Journey toward Wholeness. Crossroads, an interfaith antiracist collective, helps religious denominations (beginning usually and sensibly with denominational leaders) transform themselves into antiracist, multicultural institutions.

Before the workshop I knew very little about antiracism transformation teams and certainly had no plans to join one. I'd been invited to the workshop not as a prospective team member but as a UUA staff member. But by the end of the workshop, I couldn't imagine not joining the team. The workshop had transformed me.

How was I transformed? First, I began to understand some of the institutional obstacles that keep liberal religious people like me from becoming effective agents of justice in the post-civil-rights era. Second, I learned to see the world with an antiracist vision that helped me think strategically about how to overcome these obstacles. All in all, I felt empowered. I left the workshop believing I could and should work for antiracist change in my own institutions.

People who know me well inform me that I'm politically naive. I sure felt naive a few months into my volunteering with the Mass Bay District's Antiracism Transformation Team when I began to hear that the Crossroads workshops were coming under heavy criticism from a variety of UU sources. At the joint Meadville Lombard-Starr King Consultation on Race and Theology in January 1998, I heard white ministers claiming that Crossroads was dogmatic, that its approach to fighting racism was essentially creeping Calvinism. Back in Boston I heard people say that Crossroads' focus on white privilege—how racism benefits white people—was too heavy-handed, that it made people feel bad about themselves and therefore wasn't a good workshop for UUs. I also heard questions about why we need to always focus on race: "Isn't class the root of the problem?" Well, I hadn't thought any of these questions through. Had I just unthinkingly accepted a dogma?

I went back to the notes I had taken during my Crossroads workshop. The workshop consists of a variety of exercises in which participants grapple—intellectually and emotionally—with a set of propositions. One proposition states that all white people in the United States participate in and benefit from systemic white racism, whether or not we recognize it. Another states that all people of color internalize racist oppression, whether or not they recognize it.

These propositions did sound potentially dogmatic, not to mention alienating. After all, in the UU congregation where I was raised, I'd learned I couldn't be a racist, that racism was something the KKK did, not something I was connected to. In fact, being nonracist was a major part of the way I saw myself—until the Crossroads workshop showed me a different perspective. In the workshop context, the two propositions I mentioned above don't pretend to imply that all white people secretly harbor racist intentions or that all people of color are helpless victims. Rather, they refer to the racism embedded in the system we live in, a system that, on the whole, offers social, economic, and cultural advantages to white people and disadvantages to people of color. You might say we find ourselves in a racist social situation. For example, my wife and I recently needed to move on short notice. A potential landlord told us he only rented to "good" people. We took his apartment without giving this declaration much thought. It was the only

continues on page 306

apartment we could find that was convenient to both our jobs. Only later, after seeing that everyone in our complex was white, did we realize that his term "good" was code for "white." All we had done was rent an apartment, and yet we'd helped perpetuate racism.

From this perspective, I don't mind exploring the term "racist" in relation to myself. In fact, I find it helpful. It keeps me focused on what I as a white person must strive to change. Claiming my racism doesn't mean that I've come to believe I'm inherently bad. Recognizing my unintentional complicity in a racist system has nothing to do with my inherent worth and dignity as a white person. There's no creeping Calvinism here. This is not about who I am; it's about how I've been shaped—how we've all been shaped—by a system we didn't create. It is also about what I choose to do. That is, now that I understand how I benefit from racism, I don't wallow in white guilt and self-loathing, but instead I choose to struggle against racism, first by changing the institutions where I have the power to bring change. One such institution is my church. Therefore I will work for antiracist change in my church and my beloved UUA.

I commend Crossroads for challenging Unitarian Universalists to look at the depths of racism in our congregations.

Examples include the ongoing difficulties we as a movement have in finding secure settlements for some ministers of color; our unexamined European American cultural norms; the way we often try to hide those cultural norms by appropriating the traditions of people of color; the way we tell our own history, often leaving out our forebears' relationship to the extermination of Native Americans in New England or to the slave trade; and the way we often expect the few people of color among us to speak on behalf of "their people."

When we can accept the overwhelming, crushing power racism has over all of our lives, when we can grasp just how deep our inability to form relationships across lines of race results from the racism in our midst, then and only then can we begin to know our personal and communal responsibility in relation to the problem, and then and only then can we begin to act, not with long-distance, Band-Aid responses but with transgressive, transformative solutions.

Let's stop resisting the change that must happen. If you reject my analysis because it's calling you to change in ways that don't feel good, I implore you please to stay with it. Racism doesn't feel good, either. So don't panic. Don't run away. Take a breath. Check your step. And notice that you're on the journey.

CHAPTER 17

Laboratories for Change

As the new millennium opened, Unitarian Universalist advocates for an anti-racist identity began looking at particular ways to retool key parts of the Unitarian Universalist Association. The Journey Toward Wholeness Transformation Committee helped spur these changes, serving sometimes as a broker of resources and sometimes as a monitor.

Three places where struggle and change were seen were in *World*, the magazine of the Association; in the work of the Department of Religious Education; and in the work of the Ministerial Fellowship Committee, the credentialing body for ministers. In addition, at the General Assembly of Congregations each year, anti-racism initiatives were showcased—in 2001, it was in an act of public witness and protest against the mascot of the Cleveland Indians baseball team.

Rev. Danielle DiBona, who joined the Faith in Action staff in 2000 and who was prominent in raising issues of concern to Native Americans, noted that this was a time when a significant shift was being made, from understanding issues around race as the "personal problems" of individuals to understanding them as systemic problems of the Association:

> Calgary began a process of looking at race from an institutional perspective rather than a personal one. Those in Calgary and, later, in Phoenix, who voted for the UUA to become an "anti-racist, anti-oppressive organization" were, in fact, voting as individuals and, I believe, imagining individual change throughout our churches and the UUA. In

retrospect, it appears that there was not a concept in the larger UU world of institutional racism. I think this had far-reaching ramifications—as follows:

As an Association, the UUA began "training" people to be anti-racist. They began with groups like the Board of Trustees and the staff. At the same time people were being trained to go out into the congregations to do anti-racism work. Although there were many fits and starts at the Association level, I think it became apparent to all that the UUA was going to move forward no matter what. Consequently, individuals may have "gone along to get along" although many did not even do that.

Although the process and programming was, indeed, flawed and there was resistance at all levels, there was also a public understanding that the UUA was talking about institutional change and transformation. Consequently, the whole conversation about race was raised to a higher level and took on an urgency and public place within all work of the UUA. Imperfect though it was!

When I became a UU in the mid-80s there was no discussion around race and almost no discussion around diversity. The "front burner" placement of anti-racism changed that in ways that changed the face (if you'll pardon the pun) of UUism, what it meant to be a UU and how UUs interacted.

This coincided with a significant increase in people of color at the national level. People of Color began to show up at General Assembly. This was not my experience in the late 80s.

I think, for traditional UUs (read white), these years have been hard because most believe that they have done good work and have good thoughts, so they are OK. The change from individual anti-racist experience to collective continues to be a hard learn for most UUs.

Ultimately, for the UUA to look at anti-racism, anti-oppression issues from an institutional perspective allowed and continues to allow People of Color to find a place (albeit, often an uncomfortable place) in the larger UU world.

World Magazine and Anti-Racism

The Transformation Committee had an ongoing conversation about *World*, the magazine published by the Unitarian Universalist Association. Tensions had existed since 1998 when the magazine had published excerpts from an interview with Rev. Melvin Hoover, director of the UUA's Faith in Action Department; Rev. Dr. Thandeka, a professor at Meadville Lombard Theological School; and Unitarian Universalist activist Tom Turnipseed. Tom Stites, then the UUA's director of communications as well as the editor of *World* magazine, recalled, "Bigger tension arose from *World*'s coverage of the conversation on race at Meadville Lombard, particularly because it reported about the tensions among participants and especially because of the black and white photographs the magazine ran, which several advocates thought the editors had selected to make black people look dangerous." At the 1998 General Assembly, an "open hearing" hosted by the Journey Toward Wholeness Committee had leveled criticism of the magazine's staff.

After Thandeka's "Why Anti-Racism Will Fail" speech at the 1999 General Assembly, *World* not only included coverage of her speech but also published an unrelated article by her in its next issue. At its fall 1999 meeting, the Transformation Committee had this to say about the periodical:

> There is disagreement (in the UUA) over the role of *World* Magazine. The mission of the *World* is to be informative, useful, provocative. They are a part of the UUA and need to be accountable to General Assembly. Are they a mediator or house organ? Tom Stites has two roles. As Editor in Chief he has editorial freedom; as head of Communications he is responsible to get the word out for JTW. There needs to be clarification on the mission of the *World*. Executive Staff Council is an advisory body to the *World*, and it is stepping up to that role. In contrast, Beacon Press has made a con-

VOICE
Tom Stites

Tom Stites, the editor of World *magazine, delivered this sermon at UUA Chapel on November 21, 2000.*

One year ago, at a meeting in this very room, I was confronted along with the other editors of *World* magazine. The meeting was set up in response to strong feelings by UUA antiracism advocates, many of them people I know and admire. The advocates were troubled by articles and photographs we had published. This, in the words of one, showed us to be "opponents of antiracism." No one said outright that we were racists, but it wasn't hard to infer.

This room was electric with tension that day. Antiracism advocates had flown in from all over the country. When the meeting ended it could hardly be said that everybody in the room saw eye to eye, but there was a lot less tension and more clarity than when it began.

I can tell you from both my heart and my intellect that I have a much deeper understanding now of the privilege that comes with being white, and the further privilege that comes with being middle class. This leads to a deeper understanding of the racism that is woven into our culture and institutions, and of my inevitable part in it as a white person and as a gatekeeper in a powerful institution.

Despite my taking part in an antiracism training led by [Rev.] Joe Barndt of Crossroads Ministry I have never found the theory behind the idea that all whites are racist either valid or useful. Indeed, I'm pleased that UUA-led trainings now address the role of whites in our racist culture in terms that I think will prove far more effective in helping whites come to grips with their privilege. From the day I finished the Barndt-led training I lived with the fear that by resisting the all-whites-are-racists concept some of my colleagues would categorize me as a white in denial of his racism. I was still carrying this fear a couple of years later when the tensions began to rise.

As things escalated, I was so reactive that it felt like the advocates were picking on me and my staff. I said to myself, rather indignantly, What about the right to conscience here, *my* right to conscience? What about the inherent worth and dignity of every person, especially *my* dignity? What about *MEEEEE?!* I sought friendly counsel from whites and people of color. No one was much help until the last friend I told my story to. When I was done he said, "I hear you, but I don't hear you mentioning empathy. You won't get out of this unless you work on your empathy."

"Empathy?" I said incredulously. "Empathy for whom? For the people who are accusing me unfairly?"

"Exactly," my friend said, and walked away.

Alone in my office, my head spun for a moment, and suddenly I realized that he was right. I immediately let go of the notion that all this was about *MEEEEE.* It's not like I made a conscious decision to let go, it's more like this realization hit me in a way that shook my grip loose. At the same time, I let go of thinking that all this was about *them.* Suddenly, I understood that we were all in it together, the antiracism advocates and I, that we are part of the same system, that this was bigger than any of us. Suddenly, I understood that we all had roles in a real-life drama about broken relations between groups of people that, tragically, has been running for several centuries. Thanks to my friend's perfectly aimed blow to my reactivity, I did not have to struggle to summon empathy. It just came.

Now the last impression I want to leave is that I feel smug and self-congratulatory about this. What I feel is more like amazement, even awe, because something amazing happened to me and I had so little to do with it.

Going into the meeting, the point was no longer to win the argument about whose truth is the better truth, it was to show up for the meeting understanding that my truth is no more complete than anyone else's. Our meeting was going to be just one more scene in the act of this drama that happens to be playing here now, part of the messy but holy process by which people grapple for better truth. This holy tension leads us closer to harmony with the divine.

certed effort to publish marginalized voices, and it has a policy that it will publish things that meet the UU principles. There has been active opposition to JTW among *World* staff. This is not freedom of the press.

Controversy over this coverage prevailed until a meeting was convened to bring anti-racism advocates to meet with the staff. Stites recalled that the "fishbowl" conversation, facilitated by consultant U.T. Sanders, raised issues and tensions and resulted in the departure of a key staff person.

The Transformation Committee also discussed the coverage of anti-racism in the *UU World* and the frustrations of being misinterpreted and misunderstood. Though the coverage was perceived as much more positive than the 1999 coverage and Stites was noted as an ally by those promoting anti-racism, concerns were voiced about the amount of dissension in the pieces and in the letters that followed though it was perceived that such discussion "opens the door for deeper communication." Also, *World*'s decision to publish one article in Spanish generated a great deal of discussion, with concerns being raised that the publication of bilingual articles without further context: "Confusion about bilingual articles (what was the rationale?) There has been reaction from Diverse Revolutionary Unitarian Universalist Multi-Cultural Ministries (DRUUMM) and some Latina/os. Assumption that it was a 'good' thing, without a critical lens."

For the March/April 2000 issue, the magazine ran a special issue on anti-racism, based largely on the Faith in Action work. It engendered conflicts on all sides. Rev. Susan Suchocki Brown remembers as ultimately positive the "the incredibly moving, painful, challenging and ultimately positive interactions I and the committee have had with Tom Stites, the editor of the *UU World*, and the changes the magazine and publications underwent."

Liberal Religious Educators Association
In 1997, the Board of the Liberal Religious Educators Association (LREDA) conducted an anti-racist self-assessment in February and created an anti-racist Transformation Team in October, including

From Exclusive to Inclusive: Signposts and Stages

CONTINUUM ON BECOMING AN ANTI-RACIST MULTICULTURAL INSTITUTION

Racial and Cultural Differences Seen As Deficits→ →→Tolerant of Racial and Cultural Differences→ →→Racial and Cultural Differences Seen as Assets

STAGE ONE: *EXCLUSIVE*	STAGE TWO: *PASSIVE*	STAGE THREE: *SYMBOLIC CHANGE*	STAGE FOUR: *ANALYTIC CHANGE*	STAGE FIVE: *STRUCTURAL CHANGE*	STAGE SIX: *INCLUSIVE*
Policies and Practices	Policies and Practices	Policies and Practices	Policies and Practices	Policies and Practices	Policies and Practices
A De Facto Segregated Institution	A "Club" Institution, Taking No Action	An Open Institution, Recognizes and Takes Action	Awakening Institution, Educating Self And Others	A Redefining Institution, Initiating, Preventing	A Transformed Institution
Actions	Actions	Actions	Actions	Actions	Actions
Denying/Ignoring	Recognizing, No Action	Recognizing, Taking Action, Educating Self	Educating Others	Supporting, Encouraging	Initiating, Preventing
Social Justice	Social Justice	Social Justice	Social Justice	Social Justice	Social Justice
Nil	Noblesse oblige	Service-oriented	Reassessing	Collaborative	Accountable, Engaged
Moving Forward	Moving Forward	Moving Forward	Moving Forward	Moving Forward	Moving Forward
Raising Awareness	Understanding The Nature of Oppression	Symbolic Change	Awakening	Redefining	Antiracist and Multicultural

Jacqui James
Anti-Oppression Programs and Resources Director
UUA Religious Education Dept.

religious educators Rev. Dr. Tracey Robinson-Harris, Lucy Klaus-Li, Chris Parker, Rev. Linda Olson Peebles, Judith Frediani, and Lynn Bacon.

By 2000, LREDA leaders arranged for an anti-racism assessment by consultant Taquiena Boston. Her report showed both work done and areas yet to be explored, and it reflected the tensions other organizations faced when approaching anti-racism. In the section titled, "How has LREDA institutionalized anti-racism in its identity and practice to date?" Boston referred to the five structure levels of the Crossroads Ministry anti-racism model and assessed LREDA's current place on this continuum, warning that "the Continuum is an impressionistic tool." She then laid out her assessment of where LREDA was on a number of key indicators using the model's six stages, with Stage 1 being the least anti-racist and Stage 6 being the most:

Personnel: Continuum Stage 2: Passive or "Club" Institution

As an organization with few staff, LREDA depends on volunteers to carry out many programs and functions. At present, few religious educators of color serve on volunteer committees. Fall Conference attendance and comments of those who attended indicate that LREDA membership is predominantly white. Current staff is also predominantly white. The small number of people of color who are LREDA members and who serve on volunteer committees means that people of color will have less access to various leadership and professional opportunities for which LREDA membership and volunteer opportunities provide entry. This includes higher-level staff positions in the UUA's Religious Education Department and other volunteer leadership opportunities in LREDA and the larger UU community.

Efforts to bring more people of color into UU religious education is limited by the fact that LREDA currently does not recruit people into the profession, though this may change soon. In addition, the tendency to focus on religious educators as a marginalized group, which they are, hinders the ability to recognize how LREDA may marginalize peoples of color in its structures and practices.

Programs, Policies, Procedures: Continuum Stage 3:
Symbolic Change or Multicultural Institution

This is the area in which LREDA best demonstrates a commitment to anti-racism and where leadership has been most active in incorporating multicultural diversity. Efforts include the Anti-Racism Lending Library, a resource for religious educators; a policy that requires congregations to indicate commitments to anti-racism and anti-homophobia/anti-heterosexism when applying for the grants program; continuing education modules that include anti-racism and anti-oppression curricula; participation of persons of color in the Fahs lecture; regular reporting on the activities of the Anti-Racism Task Force; and inclusion of anti-racism and anti-oppression credentialing units among the proposed Professional Standards. In addition, the Fall Conference included worship resources from diverse religious and cultural traditions. . . . Absent is a strategy for helping the larger membership understand and implement anti-racism in their congregations. While members who spoke to me indicated an awareness of the importance of multicultural diversity, few were actively involved in programming or in relationship with communities that address the needs and interests of the children and youth of color and multiracial families in their congregations. It is also unclear what role anti-racism plays in the Good Officers recruitment, hiring and training. [Good Officers provide support to religious professionals in times of conflict.]

Constituency: Continuum Stage 2.5:
Moving from Passive/Club to Symbolic/Multicultural

LREDA's current membership is predominantly white. If the emphasis is on serving the needs of existing membership then logically LREDA reflects the interests, culture, and norms of its predominantly white constituency. Based on this reality, the challenge is how to incorporate the interests, values, and norms of peoples of color, that is to develop practices and structures that are accountable to peoples of color.

Also, LREDA does not have a formal accountability relationship with an organization that represents the interest of peoples of color. This is significant because LREDA makes decisions that influence all religious educators in the UUA. Without the voice and involvement of peoples of color who will feel the impact of LREDA's decisions, there is the risk that policies, programs, and structures may foster exclusivity rather than inclusiveness for religious educators of color.

Establishing "accountability relationships" with peoples of color is a way of involving those "under-represented voices." . . . By establishing "accountability relationships" with communities of color, predominantly white institutions begin to develop structures and practices that open access to their institutions, and engage with peoples of color in creating institutional change. It is also important that the persons representing the under-represented voices (in this case, peoples of color) are recognized and designated by community/ies of color to perform this role. In other words, the representative needs to have an accountability to for whom s/he speaks.

Organizational Structure: Continuum Stage 2:
Passive/Club Institution

LREDA's leadership (Executive Committee, At-large Board, Nominating Committee) currently reflect the predominantly white membership. Few people of color are involved in committees that shape organizational direction with regard to priorities, programming, and policies. In addition, it does not appear that anti-racism is part of the "portfolio" of all board members and committees in shaping policy and strategic priorities. Nor is there a procedure for ensuring that new leadership receives the JTW [Journey Toward Wholeness anti-racism] analysis training.

Mission/Purpose/Values: Continuum Stage 3.5: Moving from Symbolic/Multicultural Institution to Identity Change (Analytic)/Anti-Racist Institution

LREDA has been a predominantly white organization for much of its history, though religious educators of color were involved in the organization from its earliest history. In addition, LREDA is a leader among UU affiliate organizations because it is the first to make a public commitment to becoming anti-racist and welcoming [to bisexual, gay, lesbian, and transgender individuals]. This public position is prominent in LREDA's membership brochure, newsletter, conference literature, and anti-racism task force brochure. However, there is no statement of LREDA's commitment to anti-racism in the by-laws, one of the primary "identity documents" of an organization.

Ministerial Fellowship Committee
The Ministerial Fellowship Committee created a new policy to permit a waiver request of "Rule 17," which holds that ministers who provide professional services in a congregation in search for new leadership are barred from serving in that congregation. This was seen as important to opening opportunities to ministers of color because they could now visit congregations in search to do anti-racism, anti-oppression, multicultural training. Previously some ministers of color had visited a number of congregations and thus reduced the number of congregations where they might be settled. As Rev. Joseph Santos-Lyons noted in his senior thesis at Harvard Divinity School, this rule was an important acknowledgment that extra efforts were needed to ensure ministry placements for those historically marginalized because of race and ethnicity.

DiBona saw this as an example of where the institutional focus made a difference. "I think the Association did hear the demand for better, more real, more transformative anti-racist change," she said, "then went with the model that was at hand in an effort to get moving on the process. It is very clear to me that there has been significant movement. The Board of Trustees, for example, continues to make an effort to view their work through an anti-racist lens. That works in fits and starts because of the regular turnover and, I sense, the back-sliding around training up new members. However, because of the anti-racism work in the '90s, there are enough white folks out there to continue to raise the anti-racist questions. For example, the MFC finally, finally heard from DRUUMM and people of color that they needed to do more to prepare seminarians to begin to have an anti-racist lens. People of color are being heard at the national level. I sincerely do not believe that that could have happened without the anti-racist work/Jubilee work/Transformation Committee/and Crossroads. Before the UUA began its anti-racist work, these examples would have been either ignored or identified as issues between/amongst individuals. There would never have been a concept of white power and privilege and how it played out in all of these situations."

The 2000 General Assembly in Nashville

At the Nashville General Assembly, anti-racism efforts were very visible. As the meetings convened, Moderator Denise (Denny) Davidoff reported about a new role for the Transformation Committee, anti-racism process monitoring. The debate widened to include issues of class. David Reich, covering the event for *UU World* magazine, called his piece "To Nashville, with Class" and noted,

> Moderator Denise Davidoff invited comments from the floor about the UUA's Journey toward Wholeness anti-racism initiative. Attendees who accepted the invitation gave the initiative mixed reviews. Speaking favorably, the Rev. Barbro Hansson, extension minister of the Plattsburgh, New York, fellowship, said, "The work of anti-racism and the Journey toward Wholeness is the most important work I have been involved in as a lay leader and minister," while delegate Gladys McNatt of Greensboro, North Carolina, said, "It's a hard program, and I don't see the end, but we need to be there working on these issues. We have to stick

with it." More critically, [Rev. John] Corrado who hails from Grosse Pointe, Michigan, expressed relief that the anti-racism program had "been modified to eliminate name-calling, harassment, and disrespect" of trainees, and Finley C. Campbell of Chicago disputed what he called the program's "white skin privilege theory of racism," explaining, "I can't see that any white brother or sister on welfare has privilege." Finally, a delegate from Massachusetts asked the Journey Toward Wholeness leadership on behalf of her congregation "to address the elephant in the middle of the living room, and that is the issue of class. We never talk about it."

It was as if the Massachusetts delegate had turned on a spigot, for after her remarks "the issue of class" was talked about repeatedly during this GA, briefly and at length, in forums ranging from a reading by the author of a hot new book to [UUA President the Rev. John] Buehrens's report to the delegates—the second-to-last of his second four-year term. Buehrens, suggesting that the GA might do well to hold over this year's statement of conscience, titled Economic Injustice, Poverty, and Racism, for another year, said that his travels among UU congregations "do not give me much evidence that we UUs have found . . . even the words to talk about class."

Nashville was also the site for continued dialogue around theology and race, with a session featuring the theologian Rev. Dr. James Cone. While his remarks made a huge impact on the large audience that attended his session, the responses by those in the Unitarian Universalist fold best showed where we were as a movement:

Saying "There is no justice without memory," Cone suggested that silence is racism's best friend. "Most whites don't like to talk about racism because it makes them feel guilty, a truly uncomfortable feeling." But how uncomfortable does racism make its victims? When oppressive history is hidden, the victims are made the oppressors, and the oppressors, victims.

"No one can be neutral or silent in the face of this great evil. We are either for it or against it." . . . Cone challenged the UUs in the packed hall to develop an enduring race critique, embedded in our faith, and to make the analysis so explicit that no one can avoid talking about it.

Expanding on this theme, Rev. Dr. John Buehrens, UUA President, noted that the UUA's Journey Toward Wholeness program requires that all UUs become theologians. "For some of us," he said, "engaging with the painful history of oppression makes theology possible again." . . . Buehrens closed his remarks with a warning against the temptations of a false universalism, projecting outward middle class economic success and scientific attainments that are not available to all people.

The Rev. José Ballester spoke, too, of his own experience from the 1960s (in his case, it was in New York as an anti-war activist and member of the Young Republicans) and his realization of the importance of not just reading and talking about acts, but doing action. . . .

"Justice is what we need to establish," not a theory of justice, Ballester said. "We need to do justice, not talk about it." But he also cautioned that justice can never be achieved at the expense of others, and closed with a strong message to remember that nothing is more important than the community and the family. Only if we have right relationships can we work effectively in the community.

The Rev. Dr. Rebecca Parker, president of Starr King School for the Ministry, spoke of how black theology has made more space for other critical theology, including feminist theology, with a shared focus on personal experience as the basis for analysis. . . .

Using [Rev. Dr.] William R. Jones' concept of "whiteianity"—the idea that Christianity may be inherently about white racism—she noted that Christian theology defines ignorance and innocence as being in right relationship with God. To be in the Garden of Eden, the ideal state, is to be without the knowledge of good and evil. Acquiring the fruit of knowledge forces an alienation from God. The sacrifice of a human being restores right relationship with God, so Christianity blesses redemptive sacrifice and helps us not to recognize that the sacrifice of human life is a crime. "Christianity cannot tell the truth about a fundamental act of violence," she summarized.

Parker noted that theology can bless our ignorance, disconnect us from seeing reality and stand in the way of our doing justice. But, she also noted, theology can open our eyes. She drew from William Ellery Channing's theology of the wonderful array of human power as a reflection of our creation in God's image. Our whole being is divine, and unfolding our powers is our reason for being. Channing came to realize the social implications of that theology: anything that gets in the way of that unfolding is a way of killing God. Slavery, Channing came to see, was an evil because it kept slaves from coming into the fullness of divine living.

As UUs, Parker noted, we value those who stand against their culture with open eyes, people who see more clearly and who dare to say what they see. But she also noted that Channing's congregation had rejected his analysis of slavery, and she asked the institutional question: what would have transformed Channing's congregation? What the collective community knows and recognizes is also important, because people learn from and are supported in community. . . .

Knowledge, Parker closed by saying, allows us to disrupt injustice. To know is to love.

Youth and Young Adults Step Up

In 2000 a Task Force of Young Religious Unitarian Universalist Advisors issued a report on the state of Young Religious Unitarian Universalists (YRUU) that included a pitch for anti-racism training, stating,

While the denomination has made great strides to instill its leadership and adult membership with anti-racist values, the message of anti-racism, anti-oppression work has not reached the youth advisor community adequately. It is paramount to reach youth advisors and youth in anti-racism and other anti-oppression trainings as these groups have not been adequately targeted for participation in these resources.

Later the same year, the YRUU's governing body, the Youth Council, adopted a new way of doing business:

Steering Committee decided to use formal consensus process instead of Roberts Rules because (a) they were inviting a people of color caucus and they wanted them to be participants in the work, (b) consensus is much less oppressive. Consensus is inclusive of everyone at the table, and intentionally anti-oppressive, anti-racist, and feminist. Consensus is based on the idea that a group can make decisions that no one person can. They can make decisions that are the best for the group while feeling like everyone is heard, everyone is accountable to the decision; instead of people feeling like they were against it, but were in the minority.

Also in 2000 a new coalition group, Linked Identities Networking in Coalition (LINC), was conceptualized by Continental UU Young Adult Network (C*UUYAN) members Rob Cavenaugh, Barb Greve, Joseph Santos-Lyons, Kent Matthies, Kevin McCulloch, Alison Miller, Christine Murphy, and Justice Waidner as well as Rev. Donna Disciullo, staff support to the group, as a coalition with DRUUMM (Diverse & Revolutionary UU Multicultural Ministries), YRUU (Young Religious UUs), Interweave, and the UU Women's Federation in May. Initially, it sought to ensure anti-racism concerns were addressed by the candidates for UUA president and moderator in the 2001 elections. As the leaders within LINC began working together significant energy and enthusiasm emerged for continuing to work together as a coalition. LINC brought together the following five Unitarian Universalist affiliate organizations:

- Continental Unitarian Universalist Young Adult Network (C*UUYAN)

Melanie Griffin

This article, "Start Becoming an Actively Anti-Racist Youth Group!" was written in August 2000.

This September I'm beginning college. As I leave the familiar surroundings of the D.C. area, there are some things that I am worried about. For example, will my roommate be racist? Will it be uncomfortable for me as a black female to be around her? Will the institution I am enrolled in have built in advantages for some and disadvantages for others? These are subjects I think about every day when I meet new people, even YRUUers. Being the open, accepting and comfortable group we are, YRUU as a whole is looking to become an anti-racist organization so that YRUUers, especially YRUUers of color, can feel more at home in this community.

Racism and Anti-Racism

As one central Floridian YRUUer said, "It's all tricky stuff." That it is and a whole lot more. It is very complex, painful, and awkward, but I am confident that YRUU can take steps to address these issues. To begin this process we have to have a common understanding of what we are looking at. So let's get to some definitions! These definitions are those in the *Creating a Jubilee World* anti-racism resource book. *Creating a Jubilee World* is a wonderful UU program created to fight racism.

Definitions

Institutional Racism

The systematic use of power by a dominant racial group at the expense of non-dominant groups. "Institutions have great power to reward and penalize. They reward by providing career opportunities for some people and foreclosing on them for others. They reward as well by the way social goods are distributed by deciding who receives training skills, medical care, formal education, political influence, moral support and self respect, productive employment, fair treatment by the law, decent housing, self-confidence, and the promise of a secure future for self and children." (*Institutional Racism in America*, Knowles and Prewift, Prentice-Hall, 1969)

Cultural Racism

The assumption that the values, standards, and cultural habits of one racial, ethnic, or cultural group (e.g., in the U.S., Northern European white culture) are normative; a dimension of the collective identity of the dominant racial group.

Anti-racism

A conscious, intentional effort to eradicate racism in all its forms—individual, cultural, and institutional. With this common understanding we can move on as an organization, both on the continental level and on the local level, to become anti-racist. There are many steps that we can take, as we take them we must remember that this is a life long process, that racism is not going to go away over night, so we have to have patience and faith. Activities that a youth group can do to begin work towards anti-racism: There are all kinds of anti-racism organizations, many of these organizations will come and do workshops for your congregation or your youth group. Look into finding local groups who do anti-racism work and have them come talk to your youth group. Many churches have had the UU anti-racist groups, like Journey Towards Wholeness or Jubilee World, do workshops for the congregation. Make sure that your youth group participates in this! If you would just like to begin discussing these issues with your youth group there are different activities you can do to begin a dialogue. For example, there are movies about racism and race that you could watch with your youth group to begin a dialogue, such as *The Color of Fear*, which your church might have or that you can order from the UUA. Another good way to begin looking at this issue within your youth group is to do an activity that will make you aware of all the perspectives and backgrounds that are present. Have a facilitator arrange for people to go to certain sides of the room depending on their answers to questions about themselves. . . . This activity can lead into a discussion about each others' similarities and differences; the group can learn about where each other is coming from. This is a fitting manner to begin talking about issues of race. There are countless other things your youth group can do to begin its path towards anti-racism.

Brainstorm! Plan! Talk! Act! Just get going!

- Diverse and Revolutionary Unitarian Universalist Multicultural Ministries (DRUUMM) and DRUUMM Youth and Young Adult Caucus (DRUUMM YaYA)
- Interweave Continental—for Bisexual, Gay, Lesbian and Transgender Unitarian Universalists
- Unitarian Universalist Women's Federation (UUWF)
- Young Religious Unitarian Universalists (YRUU)

The 2001 General Assembly in Cleveland

In preparation for General Assembly, plans were laid for a major protest against the Cleveland Indians baseball team and their "Chief Wahoo" logo as an example of derogatory cultural appropriation. Committee minutes reveal some tensions: "Some local UU ministers are worried about this protest because they have congregants that wear the logo, like it, etc. They want to know if they will be supported when GA leaves town? A problem is that leaving it at a vigil does not place a demand on the Cleveland Indians."

The protests went forward. At the same General Assembly, 4,500 copies of *Continuing the Journey* were distributed. A report was given on anti-racism trainings for youth, which were said to be well received within youth culture, despite problems getting youth of color to participate.

Santos-Lyons noted one incident that was discussed extensively among the young adult community:

A group of African descent youth attended GA 2001 from the Neighborhood [Unitarian Universalist] Church of Pasadena, California. Through the Youth and Young Adults of Color caucus that had started meeting collaboratively at GA 2000 in Nashville, Tennessee, they shared experiences of being questioned by other GA delegates despite wearing their nametags. They articulated pain at being unwelcome in their own faith.

As part of one workshop, Moderator Davidoff also addressed how the intentions of ministers and congregations affect work on issues of race:

Over 70 percent of Unitarian Universalists interviewed think it is possible for their congregation to become more culturally diverse, more racially diverse, or both. This is true of white Unitarian Universalists and Unitarian Universalists of color, Unitarian Universalists in urban and suburban locations, Unitarian Universalists in congregations of all sizes, Unitarian Universalists who are men and those who are women, Unitarian Universalists who think their congregation reflects the diversity in the community and those who think it does not.

What Unitarian Universalists think is required for our congregations to become more diverse is intentionality. An attitude that diverse people will come simply because the doors of a Unitarian Universalist congregation are open to all is not sufficient to create a diverse congregation. The research suggests, in a variety of different ways, that for real change to occur, the congregation and the minister, together, need to put diversity onto the church's agenda. When they do, the results are consistent and positive. Ministers are clear that they cannot lead such an effort well without congregational support. Lay Unitarian Universalists are clear that more can be done when they have the support of the minister.

Congregations evaluated by their ministers as having an extremely strong commitment to becoming diverse reflect higher levels of actual diversity, and as a result, have far fewer concerns and fears of conflict that less diverse congregations worry about. It is important to realize that only 15 percent of the ministers evaluate their congregations as being extremely committed to an effort to become more diverse. The overwhelming majority of ministers find their congregations either somewhat committed (38 percent) or not very committed (41 percent).

Ministers who believe their own attitudes are extremely important in forming the attitudes of their congregations, and those who see an effort to become more diverse as extremely appropriate to their congregation, are consistently more likely to evaluate their congregation's commitment as extremely strong.

Unitarian Universalists who believe their minister's attitudes are extremely important in forming the attitudes of the congregation consistently report higher levels of diversity, higher levels of diverse programming in the church, higher levels of outreach into the community on issues of social justice, and higher levels of activity in the congregation to reduce racism and promote diversity. Unitarian Universalists who believe their minister is extremely supportive of congregational efforts report similar results. This is why it is so critical for ministers and congregations to be intentional about doing this work together. It works. It's a two-way street on which the minister and the congregation walk together.

326

VOICE

From *World* Magazine's Racism Issue

For the March/April 2000 issue of World *magazine, the editors sent out a call via the* World *web site and email lists read by UU ministers, activists, and others, soliciting essays on race and related topics. Among the responses published was this by Rev. Richard Trudeau, who, at the time of publication, was minister of the UU Church of Weymouth, Massachusetts.*

I'm white. In 1950, as I was about to enter kindergarten, my mother said, "There may be Negro children at school. Other children may call them 'niggers.' Don't ever say that. It hurts people's feelings!"

I was puzzled. Why would some children want to hurt other children's feelings?

"Because," my mother explained, "some people don't think Negroes are as good as other people."

Thus I learned about racism. The lesson continued through the 1950s and 1960s, as the civil rights movement unfolded on TV. I saw the firehoses and the dogs. And I felt: Racists are slimeballs. Even when I learned about more subtle forms of racism, that feeling never left me.

I therefore find it hard to keep listening to some in the UUA leadership when they solemnly assure me that, as a white, I can't help but be some kind of racist. The term "racist," no matter how prefixed with modifiers (like "institutional"), still feels like an insult. It's as if they're telling me, "Richard, we have a more advanced understanding of what it means to be a slimeball, and we've concluded that, in this more advanced sense, you, Richard, are a slimeball."

But there was more to that conversation with my parents back in 1950. If there might be Negroes in school, I asked, where did they live? Why had I never seen any? My father said, "They stick with their own kind." That meant, of course, that we whites were also a kind, and that we stuck with our kind, too—though that was never said. (One of the rules of being white is that you never talk about it, except by indirection.) My father was teaching me about racial boundaries, and that it was important to respect them. I was being racialized.

My racialization has handicapped me all my life. Fifty years later, it still affects me. Whenever I'm getting to know a person of another race, for instance, I notice an extra awkwardness. I feel a conflict within me—between what I learned at age four (racial categories are important) and what I believe now (racial categories are meaningless).

If the UUA leadership would like to help me, they can stop calling me a rarefied racist and advise me instead on how to deal with my racialization. (How can I minimize its effects? How can I avoid transmitting it to younger people?) That, it seems to me, would also promote the UUA's announced goal of "dismantling racism."

Racialization is the more fundamental evil, in that it makes racism possible. Eliminate racialization, and racism, in all its forms, will evaporate.

This response to the World *editors' call for essays came from Rev. Frank Rivas, at the time minister of First Universalist Church in Minneapolis.*

As a child, I heard the story of Moses' ascent to the holy mountain, the place where he stood in the presence of God. I was surprised to learn that meanwhile his people were so impatient that they began to worship golden calves. Golden calves! What kind of people worship golden calves? This story did not increase my esteem for grown-ups.

Now an adult, I begin to understand. I, too, have grown impatient. Too often I've been willing to cast idols in metal.

I'm heartened that our denomination confronts the reality of racism at a time when many are fatigued by an issue that just doesn't seem to go away. I'm also grateful that our tradition doesn't make an idol of any one particular way of thinking about this problem but remains ever open to new understandings. One of the strengths of liberal religion is our willingness to challenge our own priorities and programs. I interpreted in this spirit Rev. Dr. Thandeka's 1999 General Assembly workshop titled Why Anti-Racism Will Fail, which critiqued the current UUA anti-racism program.

Moses wanted to share what he had encountered in his 40 days and nights on Mt. Sinai, but his words just weren't adequate. The best he could come up with was two tablets on which he described a life of gratitude and justice. That summary, largely negative in tone, didn't really get at what he had experienced. Later prophets who sat on other mountaintops offered words that broadened and deepened Moses' description, but those words, too, fell short. What matters most in life resists being clearly framed in anyone's words, anyone's model, anyone's institution.

Race is still an issue decades after civil rights legislation. No, the playing field has not been leveled. An ethical issue that was once painfully clear has become more nuanced, more complex, touching on a broader spectrum of ethnic identities, confused with class and economic issues, reaching beyond equality under the law. Addressing race requires the free and unfettered speech of all who care about justice—and the critical dialogue that will push each of us beyond our own narrow vision. Unless we understand the depth and breadth of the problem, our fixes will be partial, and the fix—action—is what it's all about. Like Moses . . . we must act and reflect, act and reflect: acting from partial understanding, reflecting on our action, adjusting our action to our broader understanding, then reflecting again. To act without ongoing reflection or to reflect and diagnose without committing ourselves to the work of justice is not living in good faith.

Like Moses, Martin Luther King Jr. stood at the mountaintop. Like Moses, he knew he might not get to the Promised Land with us but that we as a people will get there. We will not get there as a people who seek guidance for every step in the revelations of the past but as a people open to ongoing revelation.

The affirmation of ongoing revelation, revelation to which each voice contributes, is why I signed on to liberal religion. And working for an end to racism, classism, economic injustice is far too important to leave to any single understanding. It requires everyone's wisdom, everyone's commitment, everyone's love.

If we do it right, we may yet redeem the reputation of grown-ups.

This response to the World *editors' call for essays came from Ervin Barrios, a Spanish–English translator who, when this was written, was events coordinator for the Latina/o Unitarian Universalist Networking Association (LUUNA) and a member of the General Assembly Planning Committee and of First Unitarian Church of San Jose, California.*

When the Zapatista rebels first struck in Chiapas, on January 1, 1994, I was not surprised at all, for I had witnessed how badly the Indians there were treated by the mestizos and whites. I was a 9-year-old boy when my father was called to be the Presbyterian minister in Villa de las Margaritas, in the northern region of Chiapas. In that little village, people greeted all passersby politely, even strangers—that is, if the passersby were white or mestizo. I saw many of those friendly people crossing to the other side of the street in order to avoid greeting an Indian. The region's Indians, mostly Tojolabal, came to town once or twice a year on colorful religious pilgrimages, dancing and playing flutes and drums. They also came to town to sell their agricultural products or to buy at the stores. Each time, they were treated with disdain by almost everyone whose path they crossed.

I had first learned about the Indians just before coming to Chiapas. As a seminarian, my father wrote his dissertation on the impact of the Christian gospel on the indigenous peoples of Chiapas. This took him to the mountains of the state, home of the Tzeltal and Chol Indians. When he got home, he brought back many pictures and cherished memories of the time he had spent there. He taught me that the Indians were intelligent, clean, hard-working, and above all loving people who deserved respect. But everything I saw around me in Chiapas contradicted that concept of having respect for the Indians. More generally, in Mexico to this day, the word indio is used as an insult among mestizos and whites. Institutionalized racism is blatant and permeates all social and economic strata, as well as institutions like politics, religion, and the media. To see this, all you need to do is watch a Mexican soap opera on TV. Though 95 percent

continues on page 328

of Mexicans are mestizos with Indian blood, the actors on these shows look so European that a Canadian friend of mine says they remind him of TV in Scandinavia. As a light-skinned mestizo, I was among the winners, enjoying many social privileges that I took for granted and believed I deserved. I used them whenever I could, and just like many others I made fun of Indians.

Then I came to live in the United States. My world of privilege collapsed. Here, I am the Mexican immigrant who speaks with a foreign accent and belongs to a sub-world where people make comments about my "wetback" brothers and sisters as if I am not there. A sub-world where other Latin American immigrants get offended when asked if they're Mexican. I no longer feel I'm automatically welcome; in fact, I represent the persona non grata. I have to struggle to prove that I don't fit the stereotype of the Mexican: lazy, ignorant, and drunk, sitting under a cactus, wearing a hat that covers his face—and his shame.

This is not because of the accent per se, because my French and Austrian friends have it a lot easier socially in spite of their heavy accents. It is the Indian blood in me, of which I now am proud.

When I first arrived in the United States, I couldn't understand why so many Mexican Americans preferred not to speak Spanish, or why they had forgotten how to speak it, even though their parents and grandparents speak only Spanish at home. Now I have figured it out: the dominant culture has stripped them of their ethnic cultural pride.

Race, Theology and Reconciliation

As the conversation about anti-racism progressed, it was framed more and more often in terms of the beliefs underlying it. One response was criticism that the Journey Toward Wholeness effort was primarily based on ideas about anti-racism developed by Crossroads Ministry, a Lutheran-oriented organization hired to advise the UUA, and was, therefore, theologically incompatible with Unitarian Universalism.

Another response was the search for a distinctly Unitarian Universalist theological perspective. Two important events were a 2001 General Assembly presentation on evil by the theologian Rev. Dr. Paul Rasor and a gathering to talk about race and theology that would eventually yield the book, *Soul Work: Anti-racist Theologies in Dialogue* (Boston: Skinner House, 2003). This dialogue was an opportunity for people to discuss openly whether they thought Unitarian Universalism had an appeal beyond middle-class white people. Rev. Rosemary Bray McNatt, minister of the Fourth Universalist Society in New York City, said, "I believe that our historical Universalist message has enormous potential to reach African Americans and people who have been—and are—oppressed." Yet she also asked, speaking of people of color, "Are we here to provide interior decoration for our congregations, here to do spiritual domestic work on behalf of those wounded by God, by racism, by white privilege, or by the circumstances of their own lives?"

And as the discourse grew richer, some Unitarian Universalist congregations took action to address racism and classism directly.

Race and Theology

As part of the Unitarian Universalist Association's effort to deepen theological reflection on racism, the UUA hosted an invitational consultation on Theology and Racism on January 28 to 30, 2001, at its headquarters in Boston. A small group of scholars, ministers, and activists from within and outside Unitarian Universalism participated. The opening presentation was given by Rev. Dr. James Cone of Union Theological Seminary, a leading black theologian. Rev. Dr. John Buehrens, the UUA president, responded to Dr. Cone's presentation. Essays were presented by McNatt, Rasor, Rev. Dr. William R. Jones, Rev. Patricia Jimenez, Rev. Gary Smith, Rev. Dr. Thandeka, all Unitarian Universalists, and Rev. Dr. George Tinker, a professor at Iliff School of Theology in Colorado. Responses were offered by Revs. Marjorie Bowens-Wheatley, Tom Schade, Dianne Arakawa, Dr. Tracey Robinson-Harris, José Ballester, Jo-Ellen Willis, Peter Morales, Ken Olliff, Elizabeth Ellis, Dr. Fredric Muir, George Kimmich Beach, Dr. Anita Farber-Robertson, and Danielle DiBona, as well as Dr. Leon Spencer. Others presenting and responding were Rev. Dr. Rebecca Parker, president of Starr King School for the Ministry, and Rev. Susan Suchocki Brown of the Journey Toward Wholeness Transformation Committee and Rev. Melvin Hoover of the UUA's Faith in Action Department. Buehrens facilitated the event and Bowens-Wheatley was its convener.

Buehrens said he advocated for the meeting, seeking an interactive dialogue on race. In his introduction to the *Soul Work* book, Buehrens writes,

> During my own tenure as UUA president (1993–2001) several further steps were taken on what became known as the Unitarian Universalist "Journey Toward Wholeness." . . . The journey came to be seen as not just an institutional or political process, but as one of spiritual transformation. . . . It became clearer that deep theological reflection would be essential to continued progress on the journey.

For many, the opportunity to talk about anti-racism in theological terms was crucial, though differences of opinions surfaced once more and the discussions became heated. Attendee Morales recalled the consultation as a divisive and difficult experience with relationships very strained and "nasty."

Buehrens said the consultation was a critical juncture. "That tracing of at least the rough outlines of a theological consensus, a social psychology that would work for us, was way overdue," he said.

Third Annual Urban Church Conference

Urban concerns, which for many years had served as the de facto conversation about race within Unitarian Universalism, now became a venue for talking about race and faith. Bowens-Wheatley, then on the staff of the Religious Education Department of the Unitarian Universalist Association, set the stage at the start of the third annual Urban Church Conference held in Chicago in March 2001:

> When Tracey [Robinson-Harris] asked me to reflect on the broad topic of this conference, my first inclination was to decline, because of the impossibility of saying what needs to be said in the short time I was designated. But when I began to think about the relationship between race, class, and theology, I realized that for me, it boiled down to three points—three "simple" points. As I thought about it, I had to acknowledge that theology is never simple. Nevertheless, here they are:
>
> 1. The world was created for all of us to live together and share its resources. At the heart of the universe is love— love for all creation. Or to proclaim the language of a theist, God created the world in love, and with concern for the well-being of all of us.
> 2. Not everybody agreed with God. Some people thought they deserved more than their fair share, and began to systematically exploit and dominate others at will. In this country, it was manifested not only as personal superiority, but as colonialism, slavery, neo-colonialism, and imperialism—which in these modern times, gets translated as "globalism."

3. These systems of exploitation are supported by racism and classism. These and the other "-isms" are rooted in the practice of "other-ing"; that is, holding up some people as superior, and putting others down as inferior. To make someone "the other" is a form of domination, power-over (rather than power with . . .). Most institutions in this country, including religious institutions, have been part of a system of *structural* domination, which is a form of violence. Structural violence is evil, and thus it is a theological problem that calls religious people to respond. The Rev. Barbara Hebner suggests that the antidote to domination is "the one and only commandment": thou shalt not *other*, which she says, covers absolutely everything, and how to treat everybody (and here I would add no matter their class, racial or ethnic background).

We have forgotten who we are—that we are brothers and sisters in covenantal relationship with each other and with the creative forces of the universe. We have bought into the dominant narrative: that individual effort will lift people out of class or racial oppression; that individual interests are more important than the interest of the whole community; that capitalism is the best—indeed the only—system that "works," and we could go on and on. But where is justice?

I believe that what we need is a new narrative—a theology that empowers people to remember what Dr. [Martin Luther] King said: that none of us is free until all of us are free; and to understand that we can unite across all the artificial boundaries that divide us from each other and from God.

The new narrative cannot ignore the fact that we live in a capitalist society, and to a great extent, are controlled by it. Latter day capitalism has, in effect, become a false God, which the power brokers hold up as the answer to all our troubles. . . .

Let me mention briefly some of the factors I think prevent us from remembering who we are and why we are here, that we are sisters and brothers—even across class, race, ethnicity, gender, or other differences. And here I'm going to cite two of the nearly 30 theologians, ministers, scholars, and activists who participated in a consultation on Antiracism and Theology sponsored by the UUA this past January, which I had the privilege of convening. . . .

The intersections of class and race, it seems, are among the most difficult conversations we will engage in, partly because they are theological problems. Several of the participants at the consultation said that what inhibits us from addressing race (and by extension, class) is fear. The opposite of love is not hate, but fear. Fear of sustained engagement with others, said participant Paul Rasor, is one of "the barriers we erect around ourselves in the name of individual autonomy." It is what keeps us from loving those we label "the other."

. . . The gap between rich and poor, between people of different class, ethnic, racial, and cultural backgrounds continues to carve walls of division between us. The way out, I believe, begins with remembering who we really are and why we are here; that we are *spiritual* beings, connected to something larger and more trust-worthy than ourselves or the differences that divide us. If we want to see a world in which we are not divided by race and class, then we must also work to create a social and an economic system rooted in justice. But to work for this change, we must do more than sing "Where is our holy church, where race and class unite." We must answer the question with conviction, with a prophetic voice, and with actions that lead to justice.

Race and Evil

The theological discussions around anti-racism continued, this time with a session led by Rasor, a theologian who had been examining liberal religion's relationship with evil. He posed this challenge in a workshop at the 2001 General Assembly:

VOICE

Rev. Cheng Imm Tan

This excerpt is from a sermon by Rev. Cheng Imm Tan, an associate minister at the UU Urban Ministry in Boston and director of Renewal House, a ministry with women in crisis and their children. She preached at the UUA's third annual Urban Church Conference.

I remember when I first came to the U.S. some 23 years ago. I saw the U.S. as a land of opportunity, of freedom, equality. Where I came from, color racism did not exist. I had learned a lot of history of racism. I knew that it existed. But I did not know how it would affect me as an Asian woman. I knew nothing of experiences of the Chinese or Japanese in the U.S., of the treatment of railroad workers in the U.S.

I did not understand why I could not "get in." I did not understand why people seemed not to hear me when I spoke. I did not know why people treated me as if I did not exist—as if I was wallpaper. I did not know why people told me to go home. I did not know what to make of these experiences. I knew something was wrong, and I thought it was me. I began to blame myself, thinking that there was something wrong with me, and that I needed to change.

As an Asian and immigrant woman, I learned, finally, how to fit in. Assimilation. Leaving the parts that are different behind. You learn to speak at the right time, speak about the right thing, and an Asian woman shouldn't be too outspoken or pushy, should eat the right foods. And don't bring up anything that is different. Don't make waves. Agree a lot. . . .

When racism is this divisive, everyone loses. There is no chance to learn from the wisdom of various communities, or experience the richness or wealth of various cultures.

We need to learn from the mistakes of the past, to build effective relationships. For many immigrants, the experience of discrimination is based not only on color, but on language, relationships, many things. People have low paying jobs, little accessibility to health care, no choice in schools.

Taking the bus or subway can be very challenging. Many of us have been penalized because we did not understand the mainstream culture. A young immigrant man was arrested and jailed because he answered "yes" to everything the police officer was asking him. Another person lost his job because his religion called for him to pray several times a day.

As director of Renewal House, I saw Asian women forced to face their batterers over and over again because no interpreters were available. I saw Asian women killed because they could not access support services. Anti-immigrant sentiment is born out of oppression.

Anti-immigrant sentiments are aroused by people's fear of differences; they are ignited when immigrants are viewed as competitors in a world where there are too few resources. Immigrants are seen as commodities to be used at will. Even in the current economic times, the debate shows the white portrayal of immigrants as separate, competitive, the "other."

This separation, this "other"-ness, this dehumanization of groups, can not survive . . . yet I am always struck by how much good will people have; the willingness to help one another. . . . [I]n the final analysis, we are more alike than different. The differences that have divided us are superficial differences. We are all alike in wanting happiness, and not wanting pain. As human beings, we are essentially the same, part of the complex web of life. If this is true, we cannot turn away when part of the universe is at our knees. We don't have a choice about whether to be in relationship—we already are. . . .

We need self-love and acceptance . . . opening our heart to those things we do not like, to the shortcomings, where I do not meet my expectations, and [can embrace] the spirit of generosity and love. This is spiritual work, to embrace those things with a loving heart. Only there, is there transformation. Our inner selves can not be destroyed. . . . [S]ome people think spirituality is not justice oriented, but we know that is not true . . . spirituality calls us to care more deeply, to let our hearts be open and caring, and to see pain around us and within us. . . .

My claim is that the tensions I have identified will continue to weaken our prophetic voice and interfere with our anti-racism work unless we recognize that racism is an evil that poisons not only our institutions, but also our hearts. We must, in other words, attend to its spiritual dimensions. And, in order to do this, we must begin to see racism not only as a matter of institutional structures and social power disparities, but a profound evil.

This is a difficult message for liberals to hear, so let me be as clear as possible. I am not simply making a moral judgment that racism is wrong, nor am I making an anthropological claim that human beings have the capacity to do horrible things and create oppressive institutions. These statements are of course true; in fact, they represent the way religious liberals usually think about systemic evils. Instead, I am making a theological claim. Racism is an evil, a profound structural evil embedded deeply within our culture and within ourselves. It is a "power" in the biblical sense.

It is hard for liberals to talk in these terms because we have no real theology of evil, and therefore no language or conceptual reference points adequate to the task. Indeed, this language has been difficult for me. But as I have thought about white racism in the context of our ongoing denominational struggle, I have come to believe that any other approach is inadequate. Treating racism as an evil, a power that has us in its grasp, may help us realize more clearly what we are up against. This does not mean that we need to think of it as a disembodied supernatural demon or the like. White racism is of course a cultural construct, the invention of human beings in specific historical settings and social contexts. But to approach it as a human construct, and nothing more, misses its profound power over us. We are tempted to think it can be dismantled with the right motivation, proper analysis, and good programs. It will take all of these and more, but these, by themselves, are not enough.

Instead, racism, once unleashed onto the world and embedded within human structures and institutions, takes on a life of its own. Like all cultural and institutional structures, it eventually becomes self-perpetuating and, to some, self-justifying. Despite our best and most persistent efforts to dismantle it, it keeps coming back in newer and more subtle forms. As [United Methodist minister] Bill Wylie-Kellermann says, "no force in U.S. history has proven more relentless or devastatingly resilient than white racism. It is empirically a demon that again and again rises up transmogrified in ever more predatory and beguiling forms, truly tempting our despair."

When we begin to see it from this perspective, we can more easily recognize that the evil of racism poisons our spirits as much as our institutions. It gets inside us despite our best efforts to block it out, eating away at our hearts, eroding our capacity for expanded community. . . .

In other words, the evil of racism is not only structural and institutional, it is also spiritual. This means that all of our analysis, no matter how sophisticated, and all of our programs, no matter how well designed, will never be sufficient by themselves to make us anti-racist. We must also be "willing to do the difficult soul work necessary for spiritual transformation."

. . . This . . . is not the place to work out a full-blown theology of evil for liberals, or even to suggest specific spiritual practices or techniques for addressing the particular evil of white racism. As a necessary first step, however, we must at least recognize these dimensions of the struggle we are engaged in. We have been shaped by the very powers and structures we now want to dismantle. The social transformation we seek requires spiritual transformation as well. Without this, our anti-racism work, like other prophetic practice for social change, becomes difficult to sustain or retreats into the safety of disengaged analysis or internal debate.

Reconciliation in Cincinnati

As the theological conversation advanced, some congregations took direct action to address racism. The following excerpt from a *UU*

VOICE
Qiyamah Rahman

This is taken from a 2000 issue of TJD Connections, a publication of the Thomas Jefferson District of the UUA. Qiyamah Rahman was serving as district executive at the time of publication.

I am aware that a number of UU's of European descent in the TJ district are very upset about the use of the term "racist." I cannot know what it feels like to be called a "racist," but I do know what it feels like to struggle to name parts of myself that were almost too hideous for me and others to identify, name and embrace.

I grew up in an abusive family. My mother was a battered woman and my siblings and I were battered by my parents. When I first became a parent I beat my children when they misbehaved. I deliberately do not use the word "spank" here, although that is how it was referred to by everyone including those from whom I sought help to change. The language allowed me and others to justify this behavior and normalized the behavior. We have learned to sterilize our acts of violence through such neutral language. The act of naming the behavior for what it was was part of my self education and my decision to step outside the conspiracy of silence. In seeking to change I had to remove myself beyond the reach of those who would seek to aid and abet my behavior.

My name is Qiyamah A. Rahman and I am a child abuser. Those words allowed me to move toward healing and to non-violent parenting. To call myself a child abuser seemed extreme to some but in the face of a society that sought to accommodate my behavior I needed to rename my use of corporal punishment as violence. It was painful to name myself a child abuser. But one cannot begin to heal until one speaks the truth, as painful as it may seem.

World article by David Whitford, entitled "A Step Toward Racial Reconciliation," describes efforts by Unitarian Universalists in Cincinnati to apologize for the treatment of a Depression era African-American Unitarian minister:

Leslie Edwards believes it was a "miracle," that's the word he uses. A miracle that he was even in the sanctuary to hear the sermon that day. "A lot of times I didn't come to church," he says now, nearly four years later. "In fact, during that time I was bouncing in and out of church. Maybe I may miss church for two months. And how it happened I came that time in *May*, you know." He just smiles and shakes his head.

The Rev. Sharon Dittmar's year as interim minister at the Northern Hills Fellowship in Cincinnati, Ohio, was almost over. In the fall she'd be moving downtown to the pulpit at the historic First Unitarian Church, some of whose members founded Northern Hills in the early 1960s. The sermon was on her list of things to do before she left. The idea for it arose from a class she had taught on Unitarian Universalist history—specifically the section on the African-American experience in Unitarian Universalism. "The members of the class were surprised, concerned, and fascinated by what they learned," Dittmar explained by way of introduction. "One member said, 'You have to share this with the congregation. They need to know.'"

Drawing from the Rev. Dr. Mark Morrison-Reed's *Black Pioneers in a White Denomination*, Dittmar traced what she described as Unitarian Universalism's long "history of dis-ease" on matters of race—a history all the more troubling, she argued, for there being so many genuine Unitarian Universalist heroes, from famous abolitionists like the Rev. Theodore Parker to civil rights martyrs the Rev. James Reeb and Viola Liuzzo. She pointed out that in 1998 African Americans filled a mere 1 percent of UU pulpits, and roughly the same percentage of UU pews. . . .

Flipping through her copy of *Black Pioneers* while preparing for the sermon, Dittmar continued, "I came upon a section I had never noticed before, a paragraph about an African-American Unitarian church that formed in Cincinnati in 1918, probably the only one of its kind in America at the time. The church was called the Church of the Unitarian Brotherhood." Other Unitarians in Cincinnati knew about the church and its founder, the Rev. W.H.G. Carter, but turned their backs. They made no effort to forge personal connections, and offered no material support to the struggling congregation beyond a box or two of old hymnals. For two decades no one even bothered to inform the American Unitarian Association (AUA) in Boston of its existence. When the AUA finally did find out, in 1938, it sent the Rev. Lon Ray Call to investigate. Call's official report captured perfectly the tone and substance of mainstream Unitarian attitudes at the time toward blacks. It described Carter as "a kindly man, quite intelligent." It noted, however, that the neighborhood surrounding his storefront church was "poor and characterized by rowdiness" and that two local Unitarian ministers (one from First Church) who had spoken there agreed that the response they received was "not very intelligent." Call's conclusion: "I do not recommend Unitarian fellowship for Mr. Carter, or subsidy for his movement." Shortly afterwards the Church of the Unitarian Brotherhood closed down and its sixty or so members dispersed. Race and class trumped a genuine spiritual bond.

Many who heard Dittmar's sermon were powerfully affected, but none more than Edwards, seventy-six, a retired meat inspector and now a member of the Northern Hills board. Edwards says that before joining Northern Hills, in 1993, he spent two decades searching for a spiritual home, a place where "if I needed to express myself in any way about how I truly felt, I would not have any problem whatsoever." But until that Sunday in May 1998, he had no inkling that the roots of his quest were buried deep in family history.

"That's my grandfather you were talking about," Edwards said to a hushed congregation during the discussion period after the sermon. "I never thought I'd hear his name mentioned in a Unitarian church."

It was "a moment of grace and awe," says Dittmar. . . .

Part of the answer lay in closely reexamining First Church's past. That summer, after learning about the National Underground Railroad Freedom Center (set to open in Cincinnati in 2004) some parishioners began researching how members of First Church had responded to the moral challenge of slavery in the nineteenth century. As expected, they found many outspoken abolitionists, as well as evidence of involvement by some church members in the Underground Railroad. But it soon became clear that many of First Church's most respected members at the time had profited, at least indirectly, from the slave economy. A mixed legacy, in other words, exemplified by the parishioner who made his fortune selling salt pork to the Southern plantations, even while his wife was venturing out at night on horseback, presumably to aid runaway slaves. But nothing galvanized First Church like the story of W.H.G. Carter. "My feeling was, 'My God, where have I been?'" says Walter Herz, who has been a Unitarian since 1958. "Here I am the church historian and have published work on the church's history, and I knew nothing about this."

You don't have to be a member of First Church to feel shame at the way Carter was rebuffed by Cincinnati church officials and the AUA. Even Call, more than half a century after filing his report with the AUA, expressed his remorse to Morrison-Reed in a letter written shortly before he died. "Sorry if I kept a good man from fulfilling his mission," Call wrote . . . .

. . . [An] ad hoc Carter committee at First Church [discussed] starting a memorial fund, . . . writing an article for *UU World* or making a presentation at General Assembly, or posthumously welcoming the Unitarian Brotherhood Church into the UUA. But the keystone, they decided, should be an apology to the Carter family, some kind of formal admission, as Herz put it in a letter to Dittmar, of the "stain on the Unitarian Movement and on our local Unitarian Churches occasioned by our rejection of Carter's Brotherhood Church sixty years ago."

January 13–14, 2001. Racial reconciliation weekend at First Church. Two days of sermon and song, food and fellowship, hugs and tears, among and between the parishioners of First Church and the more than one hundred descendents of Beulah and W.H.G. Carter and their families (including a one-year-old great-great-great-grandson, Santi Sander) who crowded into First Church on that cold, bright mid-winter Sunday, having flown in from all over the country. Among the other visitors were members from Northern Hills and Morrison-Reed, down from his home church in Toronto, who delivered the main sermon on Sunday morning, entitled "The Burden of Guilt."

"Remembering the past with regret can strengthen the resolve to do the only thing we can do together to shape a more just tomorrow," was the point Morrison-Reed landed on. "For in that moment when the one person feels hurt and the other feels sympathy, a bond is established. That connection can be built upon. And as the relationship grows, we can move beyond avoidance, guilt, and self-hatred, and let go of the anger and recrimination to embrace the only things that can sustain us over the long haul—the love of God, which we find in one another, and our shared vision of tomorrow. For alone our vision is too narrow to see all that must be seen, and our strength too limited to do all that must be done, but together our vision widens and our strength is renewed, and that is cause, as it is today, to celebrate and recommit with our souls."

But the most memorable speaker that day wasn't even listed in the order of service—a deliberate omission, says Dittmar, who thought it presumptuous to assume the Carter family would accept her apology before they'd had a chance to hear it. But when Dittmar stepped down from the pulpit,

CONGREGATIONAL STORY
The Jericho Road Project

In 2001, members of the Social Action Council of the First Parish in Concord, Massachusetts, were considering how to effect social change; they were interested in contributing time as well as money. The conversations grew out of a series of gatherings initiated by Rev. Gary Smith, the senior minister.

"We began to identify people who would be influencers in the field of anti-racism and anti-oppression and multi-culturalism," Smith said, "and I can remember several weeks in a row just having them come early in the morning just to chat with us about if we were to begin all this new, what would we do. The name Jericho Road came from a sermon that Martin Luther King preached on the parable of the good Samaritan and he said that really the focal point of that parable should not be on any of the people. It should be on the road itself, and why isn't the road to Jericho safe for everybody? The road to Jericho should be safe for everybody."

For the Jericho Road Project, congregation members chose to work with the nearby old textile mill city of Lowell, where needs are great, many, and various. The project obtained nonprofit status separate from the church's in 2002. Volunteers—including lawyers, architects, accountants, engineers, and designers—assisted institutions in Lowell with board development, strategic planning, and business essentials. Budding entrepreneurs can get guidance and coaching, while organizations are shown how to be sustainable. By 2005, the project had contributed 107 volunteers to 178 collaborations with 48 different charities in Lowell—over 4,000 service hours and many thousands of dollars' equivalent in services. The model was also replicated in a number of other nearby cities.

While the project helps Lowell, it also helps the volunteers from First Parish. Said Smith: "We try to keep the transformational piece for our own people so that it's a reflective piece for people to say, how am I changed by this work I am doing. When we light our chalice, very often it's someone who's speaking about the work they're doing in Jericho Road and how their life has changed as a result. It's been a real powerful piece for our congregation."

Starita Smith of Denton, Texas—mother of two grown children, graduate student in writing, practicing Baja'i, and great-granddaughter of W.H.G. Carter—took her place.

Smith admitted she was skeptical of "the recent wave of apologies to black people for everything from slavery to neglect of Africa. . . . We read the headlines and we say, 'So what changes now?'" She expected more from Unitarian Universalists. "You are supposed to be the most liberal of the mainstream denominations," she said. "It is very meaningful to me that you took the initiative to acknowledge a history that must be embarrassing for you, and to attempt to make amends in the present for what was wrong in the past. . . . But we must also acknowledge that racial reconciliation, true racial reconciliation, requires commitment. . . . I hope you will reflect on this weekend often and let it galvanize you. I hope that it will cause you to go beyond the comfortable friendships you have with your black Unitarian friends to attempt to bring honesty, light, and compassion into the thorny arena of race relations beyond the boundaries of your church. We Carters encourage you to continue to look into your hearts, ask difficult and complex questions, and take action. We accept your apology."

The silence in the sanctuary was broken by a sudden burst of applause. Smith found herself in Dittmar's arms. The minister's black robe enveloped them both. "When the hug seemed to go on a beat or two too long," Smith later wrote, "it dawned on me that she was crying and leaning on me for support."

. . . [When Cincinnati faced a series of race-related riots], Dittmar joined publicly with other concerned clergy, black and white, in calling for a deeper understanding of the roots of racial violence. She opened the doors of First Church to a series of citywide teach-ins, and participated in a pulpit exchange program with a nearby black church, West Cincinnati Presbyterian, which has led to an ongoing relationship. In October, members of First Church and West

342 of Part 4: Time of Paradox

Cincinnati Presbyterian, marching side by side, were among the several thousand Cincinnatians who participated in a six-mile walk to raise money for the National Conference for Community and Justice and the National Underground Railroad Freedom Center.

All of which Starita Smith praised when she returned to Cincinnati this past January [2002] for the one-year anniversary of the Carter weekend. "So many people jump to condemn black people for rioting before they understand what drives them to express their rage in the streets," she said in her sermon. "Destruction of property isn't right, but then neither is destruction of human beings through neglect and oppression. The important thing to me about your work is that it continues, and you remain committed to a mission that sometimes has no big, dramatic victories in sight. I think that my great-grandparents would be pleased that you are willing to try to continue their ministry."

VOICE
Rev. Dr. Kristen Harper

Youth and young adults began being much more visible as advocates of anti-racism work at the General Assembly gatherings. Youth of color raised as Unitarian Universalists offered a particularly powerful perspective. Here is an excerpt from a 2000 General Assembly worship service where Harper, serving in Ormond Beach, Florida, shared her own analysis of where Unitarian Universalists were with race and racism.

Bridges go both ways. So often when we speak about racism or race relations it is as if only one person, only one group is hurt, one group responsible, only one way to solve it. I begin my doctoral dissertation "Being Black in America is not easy . . . ," and yet I know that being White in America is not all joy and light. The amalgamation of cultures and traditions in this country is often negated by the lumping of everyone into the White box. As a college student I watched in sympathy as my classmates, young White men and women, fought to find a piece of culture for themselves. They would buy African, Asian, Native and Latino/Latina clothes, books and music and show them off to proclaim their okay-ness, their coolness. And, we Unitarian Universalists of color call this cultural appropriation, or Lost Soul Syndrome. They called it a search to find a place to belong, a space of individuality.

White Americans are responsible for purchasing 75 percent of Black music. As much as past centuries honored milky white skin untouched by the sun, many in my generation and others before have spent hours in the sun trying to burn the color they were not born with in order to be more beautiful. And although the Black Power movement in the 70's chastised Black women for processing their hair, claiming we were trying to be White, I have seen many White young people dred, cornrow and perm their hair; perhaps they're trying to be Black.

I have seen many of our teenagers talk and walk and imitate Black rappers and musicians, basketball players and other athletes. They seem not to want to be who they are, who they feel they have to be—White. They have lost their Scottish, English, Irish, Ukrainian cultures in order to fit in, to become American. These young people know that it isn't only the Black people living in the projects. They know that it isn't only the Latinos who suffer from poverty and poor education. They know that Native Americans aren't the only ones who feel displaced. What does being identified as White do for their soul, for their dreams of happiness and friendship? Bridges of Pain go both ways. . . .

One day after church this winter I was driving west on Granada Blvd. in Ormond Beach, Florida, to visit Wanda Cassidy, a member of the congregation I serve. A truck with a confederate flag and four young men was driving eastbound. As the light turned green the truck, that appeared to be turning in front of me, changed directions and headed towards me. The driver honked and when I looked up he gave me the finger and the group of them yelled expletives and an ethnic slur at me. I sat for a long time at that light and for the first time in my life I was terrified. When I got to Wanda's home I sat for a little while still feeling that terror and when it was apparent to me I could not be present I told her what had happened. We talked, I don't really remember what was said, she just listened mostly and after a while the terror left and we were able to move on to why I was really there. The bridge of fear goes both ways. As does the bridge of healing.

Although I have been a UU all my life, I have only been involved on a national level for about seven years. I watched as we as an association have struggled with how to define and redefine the race issue. It seems as if every year we push ourselves harder and harder to understand the ultimate causes of racism and to discover solutions to those causes. In spite of my own experiences, many very painful, with the racism in this Association and in our churches I wonder about the spiritual damage this push has caused.

It is not that I am not angry. I am angry that I am called a Nigger when I am taking a walk down the street or driving in my car. I am more angry that I care. I am angry that

continues on page 344

people of color are used and abused by the media, by political parties, by some in the White community. And I am angry that some White people seem not to believe or notice or care enough to try to change that. I am also afraid. Afraid of White people's anger towards me and what some have done and tried to do. I am afraid that by being honest I might change how people in my congregation see me. I am afraid of losing my ability to minister with them.

But I have listened to White people in the congregations I have served, in those with which I have worshipped. I have listened in ministers' groups, and in seminary. You too are angry. Angry that we are still dealing with the race question, angry that you feel forced to address an issue over and over again that seems never ending; angry that you are blamed for a system you did not create and oppression you did not participate in; and angry that you are told that something in your childhood made you white. And you too are afraid: afraid to say the wrong thing, afraid to be called a racist, afraid to be honest and perhaps lose the community of faith you hold dear. Bridges always go both ways.

. . . [W]e can still build bridges and I believe that we must build the bridge of relationships first. The bridge that must go both ways is one of friendship and trust. You must know that I am going to stick around even if you say something I think is racist. You must know that I will be there when you're sick or hurting or confused even if we talk about race. You must know that even if we fall short of our promise, I will not walk out. And I must know that, even if I am angry. Even if I am hurt. Even if you don't understand or we don't agree, that you will still trust me to be there and that you will still listen to my guidance and respect me as a minister, as a fellow journeyer in faith. There must be people who are willing to remain at the table, share their stories, but more importantly share their friendship.

During a recent Black and White Dialogue held in our church, we were asked to talk about racial incidents that happened, what did we do, and whether we thought we should confront them or back off. I said that for me, I had been taught to confront head-on injustice. But over the years I have realized that saying something to the person who calls me an ethnic slur, or who follows me around in a store because they think I might steal, who makes assumptions about who I am or how I feel because of my color, or who rolls up their window because they are afraid I will carjack them—saying something to these people is often futile. Although silence is a form of collusion, sometimes walking away, staring, turning your back can be a form of protest or at least protection. I do not believe that there can be a bridge built between strangers.

CHAPTER 19

New President, New Direction

At the 2001 General Assembly in Cleveland, the Unitarian Universalist Association of Congregations elected its first African-American president, Rev. William Sinkford. For Dr. Norma Poinsett, a long-time African-American UU activist, Sinkford's election was a watershed, for it opened the door for recognition of others who had been historically marginalized. "The most positive step for the Association was finally being able to elect a black president," she said. "It's important for an Association that claims it wants to become an anti-racist, anti-oppressive, multicultural association to have some of everybody at the table."

The worship service after the election results were announced was led by Revs. Wayne Arnason and Kathleen Rolenz, serving as co-ministers in Cleveland, Ohio. "We held that service at the same ballroom at the same hotel that the 1968 GA vote on funding the Black Affairs Council was taken," noted Arnason, referring to the decision to provide funds for organizations in the black empowerment movement.

Others saw the election of the first African-American president as a challenge. Rev. Joseph Barndt of Crossroads Ministry said electing Sinkford released a sense of duty:

> Part of the unconscious identity is: we've got a president who's black, therefore we've made it. Or at least, we've fulfilled the obligation. . . . In the end, a black president ends up being at least partially incapacitated from carrying out an emphasis on racial justice, in order to be a bishop of, and a pastor to, those who are against a program of racial justice. At least it feels to me like that happens in a number of our

CENSUS

People of Color on UUA Headquarters and District Staff

	UUA Leadership Council	Staff Managers
2005	14.29%	7.58%
2004	17.53%	8.82%
2003	16.59%	n/a
2002	n/a	n/a
2001	20.95%	n/a
2000	20.77%	n/a

345

[Crossroads] settings, and probably that's also happened to one degree or another with Bill.

"One of the things that hurt anti-racism the most was electing Bill Sinkford because people assumed we were done," said Rev. Danielle DiBona, a member of the Faith in Action staff at the time of the election.

"Beyond my many gifts and skills, an awful lot of UUs liked the fact that they could vote for an African American for the presidency. I need to acknowledge that," Sinkford recalled in an interview. "It was just a reality. I can't tell you how many conversations I had with UUs in the course of the campaign where the conversation would be, 'Well, you know that I've adopted a Mexican-American daughter, and I'm so glad because of that we'll stand in solidarity shoulder to shoulder.' It was very common."

For many, especially people of color who understand the costs and the difficulties of being a "first," Sinkford continued to be an icon of leadership. "Bill Sinkford is my hero," said Kok-Heong McNaughton, one of the founding members of the Asian Pacific Islander Caucus.

Sinkford's election would result in a change of direction in the UUA's approaches to anti-racism with new programs and a new approach to staffing. Sinkford's position regarding race was illustrated in a sermon he preached in January 1996 at the First Unitarian Church of Dallas:

What draws a person of color into this very white religious community? Let me share with you a little of my personal history.

I walked into my first UU church in 1960, in Cincinnati, Ohio. I was 14, just starting the 9th grade. And even at that young age, I knew I didn't fit in traditional Christian churches . . . at least as I had experienced Christianity in the Black Baptist church in small town North Carolina and the Black Episcopal Church in Detroit. Damnation and hell-fire were too much a part of the Baptist experience, despite the wonderful sense of community. The high Episcopal church in Detroit was light on hell-fire but filled with liturgical mysteries (transubstantiation? and the strange notion of the triune God?) which didn't make sense to me. And beyond that, the upper middle-class Black folks in that church seemed to care far more about what kind of car your family drove and what labels were in your clothes, than they did in what you thought, or how you saw your spiritual path.

Cincinnati in 1960 was a very Black and White world. There was no visible Asian, Latino, or Native American presence that I remember. And Cincinnati is just across the river from Kentucky, the "South" where legal segregation . . . American Apartheid . . . was still the law of the land.

In that UU church, as I moved about during coffee hour, as I went to a church school class and the youth group meeting that night, I experienced something truly remarkable. Although the congregation was largely European American and the minister was white, there were a number of dark faces, enough in fact that the presence of people of two "races" together seemed incredibly . . . ordinary and accepted.

It was no big deal.

I didn't take any polls, or conduct any formal surveys, so I don't know if African Americans represented 10%, or 15%, or 20% of the congregation. What I do know is that the presence was sufficient. It was enough to let me know that this was a place where it was OK to be Black and where it was OK to be Black in the company of Whites.

Most of the persons of color in the pews had been drawn to that church because of the prominent and public role the minister and members of the congregation had played, and were playing, in the civil rights struggle in Cincinnati. Their presence grew out of the living out of that church's mission in that world.

And beyond the mere numbers of persons of color, the Director of Religious Education, Pauline Warfield Lewis, was an African American. So my first UU experience showed me a person of color in a position of power in the congregation . . . charged with the religious education of the children of the community.

And beyond the racial justice issues, what was preached from the pulpit was the radical right of the individual to find her or his own meaning. Mostly his meaning in those days. There was no hell-fire. No Trinitarian mystery, requiring the suspension of disbelief.

I spent my adolescence in that church, then left that and all UU churches for 15 years. But I rejoined that church 12 years ago. Married then, and with a young family, I felt the need for a church home again. Does any of this sound familiar to you?

Why do I begin with this story about another church in another city? Well, in part it is to introduce myself to you, to give you some idea of who is speaking this morning. It is certainly not to judge this congregation against another. Congregations are highly individual and exist in unique environments with unique histories. But we . . . each of us carries around a picture, deep in our person, of what a UU congregation looks like. And it is only fair for me to tell you that my picture is of a congregation where folks of different racial and cultural groups worship and live together, and where persons of color are in positions of power. To me, that's what UUism is supposed to look like.

In the conversation about race and our churches, I have heard European Americans speak as if people of color had never darkened the doors of UU churches. I have heard people say that UU churches will have to make dramatic changes in order to attract people of color. Some say that people of color are not interested in a faith like ours, a faith not reducible to simple creeds. I hear people say that they don't know how to attract people of color to the church, don't know how to make people of color welcome when they do come, and frankly, don't think it's appropriate to make the effort. People of color just don't find a spiritual nourishment at the UU table. People of color need a simpler salvation.

Well, I'm here to tell you that African Americans have been part of UUism not for decades, but for centuries. From Gloster Dalton, one of the signatories of the Gloucester

Universalist Society Charter of Compact in 1785, through Frances Ellen Watkins Harper, poet and activist who maintained membership in both the First Unitarian Church of Philadelphia and Mother Bethel AME, through the Universalist and Unitarian ministers who tried to call and serve congregations in the 19th and early 20th centuries, through William Carter whose Unitarian Brotherhood Church, founded in 1927, in my own beloved Cincinnati, could get no recognition from the local Unitarian clergy, let alone the denomination. . . . And I can testify that I find our faith to be a sustaining and empowering one for people of whatever "race." And I'm also here to say that the discussion about race in UU circles, just as in the larger society, still reflects a view which cannot be supported scientifically, which blurs our vision, distorts our understanding and deadens our spirit.

As people of color come to worship with you, welcome them. Do not expect them to be a credit to their race, any more than you are a credit to yours. And do not apologize for your church. People who come in this sanctuary, come to be nurtured, just as you do. They do not come to hear an apology.

In the Black church tradition, preachers are instructed to always close with the Good News, to find some ground of hope on which the congregation can stand. Well, I have some very good news to leave you with. The good news is that our faith knows how to embrace and affirm people who have been oppressed and marginalized. Witness our leadership in ordaining women ministers. We know how to do this work. Witness the number of gay, lesbian, bi-sexual, and transgender persons who find affirmation and support in our communities. We know how to do this work. Witness the number of persons who come to us after disappointment and even pain in other faiths. We know how to do this work.

We have been almost paralyzed around issues of race for too long. We need to inspect who we are and how our values inform our lives. UUs are very good at analysis.

EXCERPT

Congregational Efforts

This excerpt is from "Creating Partnerships for Anti-racist Actions" by Susan Leslie in the book Soul Work.

In March of 2001, the Journey Toward Wholeness Transformation Committee (appointed by the Unitarian Universalist Association Board to monitor and guide our anti-oppression, anti-racist multicultural initiative) wrote to all UU congregations asking them to report on its activities to provide information on anti-racism/anti-oppression resources, as well as about their needs. Responses from over fifty congregations revealed a broad range of activities. The efforts that involve active engagement with the surrounding community and that are undertaken in partnerships involved the greatest degree of transformation. Some highlights follow.

The Anti-Racism Working Group of First Unitarian Society of Wilmington, Delaware, was designated as an official committee of the church, with line budget support to do strategic planning for participation in the Unitarian Universalist Association Journey Toward Wholeness initiative. Four anti-racism forums were held that reflected on what the church could do to address racism. The culminating event was a major forum with all seven African American state judges gathering (for the first time!) to discuss racism in the criminal justice system. The sanctuary was overflowing; the event received wide press coverage, and sparked much interest and debate. All the judges called for a statewide review. The church is at the center of these efforts in partnership with Stand Up for What's Right and Just, a community group fighting crime, racial profiling, and mandatory minimum prison sentences.

Mountain Light Unitarian Universalist Church in Ellijay, Georgia, was welcomed into the Unitarian Universalist Association of Congregations in June of 2000. By August, this new congregation had held its first Journey Toward Wholeness Sunday, and began using the curriculum *Weaving the Fabric of Diversity* as a resource for interactive, inter-generational, lay-led worship services. Two public meetings were held featuring Native American elders who spoke on the theme "Healing the Family Circle." These events brought church members and Native American residents together, leading to both collaboration and accountability. Together, they have begun to actively support a local food pantry, sponsor a PFLAG [Parents, Families and Friends of Lesbians and Gays] group, establish special parking for the differently-abled, and add pictures of people of color to the walls of their religious education space.

The Journey Toward Wholeness Committee of the UU Church of Cheyenne, Wyoming, partnered with Love and Charity, an African American women's service organization, and the school department to offer anti-racism programming during Black History Month to fifty classes of twelve hundred students. Programs included videos and discussions on prejudice and racism, re-enactments of Martin Luther King's "I Have a Dream" speech, visits with Buffalo soldiers, African American art tours, talks on African American and Cheyenne history, and an opportunity to hear folktales and view African art. Teachers were given a packet with follow-up discussion suggestions, interactive ideas, and bibliographies. The week of classes culminated in a community-wide gospel extravaganza on Friday night and an all-day Saturday celebration featuring African dance, art, history, food, and music. The trust and relationship that were developed between church members, Love and Charity, the teachers, the children, and the parents had a transforming power in the work to dismantle racism. . . . "Miracle in Cheyenne" will be a General Assembly 2002 workshop. . . .

The Social Action Committee of the Boise [Idaho] Unitarian Universalist Fellowship is working with a large coalition to gain the minimum wage for farm workers—the majority of whom are Mexican Americans. In the course of this work, church members have struggled to learn about "the food on our tables," to fast in solidarity with the farm workers, and "to learn more about different people and the needs in our community."

Why would anyone doubt that our faith, our radical belief in the inherent worth and dignity of every person, our trust in the spark of divinity which each of us carries . . . how could anyone doubt the appeal of such a faith and the need for such a faith in this very broken world. We HAVE good news to share. We have an abundance of good news . . . that sometimes we can't even recognize.

PART 4

LEARNINGS

In the first years of the new millennium, many Unitarian Universalists were aware of anti-racism, especially those involved at the Association level. In this time period, groups worked hard to establish an anti-racist identity for themselves and Unitarian Universalism—and to embed anti-oppression awareness in the culture of several key UUA structures.

"A major outcome is that antiracist, anti-oppressive, multicultural work is on the radar screen of all our staff groups, elected leadership groups and professional groups on the Associational level," observed the Rev. Linda Olson Peebles, then a member of the UUA Board. "Association-wide elected and appointed leaders are expected to receive education in anti-racism, anti-oppressive, multicultural work. The Board has an institutionalized and internalized process of assessing its work and the work of committees and administration with this lens."

The Ministerial Fellowship Committee, the accrediting body for ministers, was another group that began to experiment with weaving an anti-oppressive orientation into its activities, recalled Phyllis Daniel, former chair.

Rev. Danielle DiBona, observed,

The 1992 General Assembly in Calgary began a process of looking at race from an institutional perspective rather than a personal one. Those in Calgary and, later, [at the 1997 General Assembly] in Phoenix, who voted for the UUA to become an 'anti racist anti oppressive organization' were, in fact, voting as individuals and, I believe, imagining individual change throughout our churches and the UUA. In retrospect, it appears that there was not a concept in the larger UU world, of institutional racism. I think this had far-reaching ramifications.

The level of conflict in many relationships grew. Among the conflicted relationships were those among ministers. Dr. Norma Poinsett, a long-time black activist and trainer with the pre-Journey Toward Wholeness anti-racism education program, "Building A Jubilee World," observed that ministers often were not involved in their congregations' anti-racism dialogues. "Jubilee was when they had a Sunday off," she said. Rev. William Sinkford, the UUA's first African-American president, observed,

> The reality is if you don't have the support of the ministers, you're not going to get to the congregations. It's just a reality of life. That was a piece that was not done well. It just wasn't. I think there are many, many reasons that can be cited. We operate so much on buzz, and the early negative buzz to the initiative, I think was just deadening for it. I don't think we've really recovered from that. I still have unproductive conversations with people who are complaining about the early [anti-racism] trainings.

Rev. Dr. Fredric Muir, senior minister of the Unitarian Universalist Church of Annapolis, noted that many of the larger churches balked. "There's an awful lot of the larger churches or soon-to-be larger churches that don't want to do this work," he observed. "It's too bad, because a lot of our smaller, program-sized churches look to the larger churches to see what they're doing. They have a real leadership role, and I think again part of the either reluctance or unwillingness for the larger congregations and larger ministers to do this work is, I think that there's a distrust of the UUA, that they want to do it their way. I also think that many of the larger churches are focused on growth and they don't see how doing anti-racism work is going to foster growth in numbers."

Michael Sallwasser, a founding member of the Anti-Racism Transformation Team at the Unitarian Universalist Church of Long Beach, California, recalls one such incident for him:

> I organized a conversation among a group of Unitarian Universalists to reflect on essays/sermons that confronted

racism, particularly focusing on white privilege. All of the participants were white. The conversation did not unfold as I hoped. The near universal reaction was to dismiss the writings, characterizing them as misplaced finger wagging. White privilege was a phantom to evoke unproductive guilt, not a malady to be confronted.

Someone I had considered an ally seemed to provide cover for those who wanted to avoid the issues. A few months later I mustered the courage to express my disappointment and feelings of betrayal. To my delight, I understood my friend's discomfort with providing others cover, but that he had no tenable means of effectively addressing the issues being raised with the format and personalities involved. I learned that I did indeed have an ally and I also learned the importance of maintaining right relationships with those involved in the struggle and how deeply personal the issue is to me.

On the faith front, much of the support for and much of the rejection of the idea of bringing an anti-racist lens to the work of Unitarian Universalism was cast in theological terms. The importance of doing so was underscored when Rev. Dr. John Buehrens, then UUA president, convened a consultation on race and theology in January of 2001 with invited guests from within and beyond the Association. Years later, and after many difficult confrontations, the conversation at that consultation would become the book *Soul Work*, edited by Rev. Marjorie Bowens-Wheatley.

On every front—identity, relationship, and faith—what was clear was that this issue of race, an unspeakable topic for years, was fair game for conversation again. Rev. Gary Smith, an officer of the Unitarian Universalist Ministers Association during this time, said, "I think what was accomplished was making much more normal this conversation. . . . This is something we own. It's not a constituent group that's going to solve this. It's got to be part of our whole language."

During the elections for moderator and president of the Association in 2001, anti-racism was a hot issue. "Hindsight is, of course,

20/20," observed Sinkford. "The decision to focus on continental leadership (large system change) left the vast majority of our congregations uninvolved. Those that did try to engage, far too many of them, felt unsupported. I wonder what our position might look like today if more emphasis, resources and flexible support had been offered to congregations. Though the issues of homophobia and racism have different dynamics and different demographics in our congregations, the success of the bisexual, gay, lesbian, and transgender-focused Welcoming Congregation program, which works one congregation at a time, should make us all ponder."

The election of the Association's first African-American president was a mixed victory. For many, this was a sign of how far the Association had come. For others, it was a stop. "The personal achievements of one individual, however impressive," said DiBona, "were a distraction from the systemic issues around race and culture."

CLOSING WORDS

WORD WARRIOR
By Christopher Donshale Sims

Christopher Donshale Sims, a spoken word artist, was active in work with youth and young adults of color in the Association.

I am a word warrior
Sorcerer of sonic sounds
who's infinitely bound to
the beauty of the Universe
which I bring to life through verse!

I am a word warrior

I use words as weapons
to combat ignorance, injustice,
negativity, and self-destruction

Each word is encoded. . . .

PART 5

Building the New House

Saying we are accountable to each other, we make a statement about our whole lives as human beings. We acknowledge that the community of Unitarian Universalists, in one sense, represents the whole human race, past, present, and future, to which we are accountable—the ancestors, the people who aren't UUs, the people yet to be born, the seventh generation.

—Rev. Wayne Arnason, UUA Board member

2002

Youth and Young Adults of Color, the Continental UU Young Adult Network (C*UUYAN), and Young Religious UUs (YRUU) set anti-racism priorities in a joint meeting in Tampa, Florida.

The UUA Board of Trustees "recommends that all members of committees elected by the General Assembly engage in anti-racism and anti-oppression training/consultation."

Youth and Young Adults of Color (YaYA) holds second annual conference in Chicago.

The first annual "White Allies" conference, for people of Euro-American heritage who support anti-racism work, is held separate from but near the YaYA conference in Chicago.

C*UUYAN holds its second young adult anti-racism conference.

The UUA Youth Office holds its first training of trainers/organizers for youth.

Introducing its study, *Belonging: the Meaning of Membership*, the Commission on Appraisal presents a skit at General Assembly in Quebec City in which a character played by a white man shoves aside a character played by a woman of color. Concerns are raised.

After Young Kim has worked throughout the year to invite other Asians and Pacific Islanders, twelve attend a meeting at General Assembly, the first step in organizing an Asian/Pacific Islander group.

UNDER THE NEW ADMINISTRATION of Association president Rev. William Sinkford, UUA anti-racism efforts were under review. Sinkford had received feedback while campaigning for office that convinced him that the educational and outreach strategies efforts known as the "Journey Toward Wholeness" needed refocusing.

Sinkford initiated a process to comprehensively reorganize the UUA staff and over the course of 2002–03 a new structure emerged, with the creation of a new "Identity-Based Ministries" staff group reporting to the president and led by Taquiena Boston. The Faith in Action Department was disbanded and every staff group was made responsible for anti-racism efforts that had been its focus. A number of the key Faith in Action staff members left the UUA and other mainstay groups such as Crossroads Ministry, which had advised the UUA on anti-racism since the early 1990s, and the Jubilee Working Group took a lesser role.

2002

The UUA is restructured on July 1—the Faith in Action Department is disbanded, with staff dispersed into the Identity-Based Ministries and the Advocacy and Witness staff groups. Key staff members begin to depart.

Jubilee Working Group disbands and its work is "interspersed through our community."

The Journey Toward Wholeness Transformation Committee hosts Common Ground meetings in Washington, D.C., and San Francisco to talk about UUA anti-racism efforts.

Two youth and two young adults, from the Youth and Young Adults of Color (YaYA), pilot a youth weekend workshop in New England.

DRUUMM (Diverse and Revolutionary UU Multicultural Ministries) forms a Youth Council for accountability in C*UUYAN and YRUU.

DRUUMM YaYA (Diverse & Revolutionary UU Multicultural Ministries' Youth and Young Adults) Committee meets for the first time.

The UUA youth staff makes funding for youth and young adult anti-racism training a budget priority for the next fiscal year.

President Sinkford holds a "seminarian consultancy" in September to determine how better to support seminarians of historically marginalized racial and ethnic groups.

C*UUYAN passes new anti-racism policy to set standards and raise awareness at all C*UUYAN-sponsored events.

At the same time volunteers struggled to build the infrastructures to maintain an anti-racist identity. A number of groups, including the groups supporting youth and young adults, worked to strengthen the anti-racism infrastructure at the Associational level. And a number of new identity-based groups organized during this period, including the Youth and Young Adults of Color and what would become the Asian-Pacific Islander Caucus of DRUUMM (Diverse and Revolutionary Unitarian Universalist Multicultural Ministries).

Ministerial leadership continued to be a focus. The Unitarian Universalist Ministers Association continued its efforts to respond to calls that it become more accountable to the needs of historically marginalized groups.

The theological conversation deepened around anti-racism efforts at this time.

Of note also was the publication of the book *Soul Work: Anti-Racist Theologies in Dialogue*, an effort to expand the conversation

2003

Faculty, students, and staff invite UUA leadership to their Catalyst for Change: Undoing Racism at Meadville Lombard conference.

Asian/Pacific Islander UU Caucus holds its first annual meeting in Berkeley, California.

Journey Toward Wholeness Transformation Committee hosts Common Ground meetings in Chicago and Dallas.

YaYA holds its third annual conference and Youth and Young Adult White Allies holds its second annual conference, both in March.

Youth and young adult trainers identify the need for a Transformation Team focused on youth and young adults in May; C*UUYAN and YRUU formally endorse this request in August.

The UUA Ministerial Fellowship Committee (MFC) makes anti-racism part of its core mission.

The first Leadership Development Conference for Youth of Color is held, sponsored by a coalition including DRUUMM, the UUA's Youth Office, and the Young Adult and Campus Ministry Office.

The UUA's Youth Council devotes the majority of its business meeting time to anti-racism training.

The Unitarian Universalist Service Committee offers the "What's Your Profile" program for teens to explore and dismantle racism.

The UUA's Skinner House Books publishes *Soul Work*, the proceedings of the discussion on race and theology held in 2001.

about the theological grounding for the difficult work of anti-racism. Dialogue at Meadville Lombard Theological School, continued efforts at changing institutional culture at Starr King School for the Ministry, and support by the Ministerial Fellowship Committee raised these issues for seminarians.

The intentionality with which the youth and young adults active at the Associational level took on anti-racism work in this era is worth note. "The positive possible outcomes will be with our youth," said religious educator and UUA staff member Jacqui James.

CHAPTER 20

The Search for Common Ground

In January 2002, the transitional staff of new Association president, Rev. William Sinkford, convened two Finding Common Ground meetings to get feedback on the Association's anti-racism efforts. Sinkford requested these meetings because of concerns he heard as he campaigned for the presidency and as part of an effort to shift the Journey Toward Wholeness work away from the controversial focus on the oppression of race and toward the more accepted idea of working against a range of oppressions. A new administration inevitably meant new approaches, some of which were met with resistance, as change often is.

Many of those who had been the front-and-center leaders and advocates of anti-racism as an approach left as part of the transition. With all the changes came a larger question—of accountability and who should be controlling the anti-racism agenda.

Changes in Focus for Anti-Racism

In October, a few months after his election, Sinkford met with the Journey Toward Wholeness Transformation Committee and gave a candid assessment of anti-racism efforts. The Committee's minutes noted,

> Bill found on the campaign trail that JTW was the most controversial thing that the Association is doing. Much of this revolved around the feeling that JTW is top down; that it does not recognize the good work many congregations are doing in interfaith, relationship, partnership work; that the

Crossroads [Ministry consulting group's] approach [which had served as one basis for early UUA anti-racism efforts] does not resonate with UU theology. He would like to reach the people who are shutting down and/or resisting JTW. A lot of this is about more effective communications and knowing that there is a lot to be learned where there is resistance.

One example he gave was a church that has been involved in a community organizing effort and has a long-term partnership with an African-American church. He asked, "Why not approach that kind of church and explore together what's working, what isn't, etc.?"

. . . Bill's concern is that a polarized, unhealthy climate is developing of who is for and against the Journey Toward Wholeness. . . . Bill believes there is a real opportunity to shift things dramatically in the next year. "You have to be smart about it. You need to touch a few opinion leaders. Reconciliation can happen."

It was agreed that there is a unique opportunity with Bill's election to shift the mood and enable more to join the journey. Transformation Committee needs to figure out who it's important to talk to and who on Transformation Committee needs to do it.

By early February 2002, the Transformation Committee was in flux. The Committee had proposed a JTW Council, which had not become reality, and a new proposal was developed for restructuring the Transformation Committee itself. Executive Vice President Kathleen Montgomery, meeting with the Transformation Committee at their winter meeting, advised them to scale down this proposal as well.

In his first year Sinkford engaged his senior staff and others in a process that led to reorganization of the Association's staff departments and relationships with some other groups. By April, as the reorganization plan was taking shape, the Transformation Committee expressed concern about the new administration's commitment to anti-racism. "It was agreed that the restructuring offers both opportunities and threats for forwarding JTW work and that Transformation Committee's work will be crucial in this next period," report the minutes from the April 2002 meeting.

The Committee and the new president agreed to meet regularly. They discussed with him ministers' resistance to anti-racism and what could be done, agreeing that "no 'magic' way to get ministers on board existed. This is very relational work and the Transformation Committee needs to reach out and initiate conversations with ministers and ask them to get involved, find out and talk through their resistances, find out what they are doing, etc."

The reorganization took effect July 1, 2002. The Faith in Action Department, which had coordinated anti-racism efforts under the leadership of Rev. Melvin Hoover, was disbanded and its members and responsibilities were reassigned to the Congregational Services Department and two new departments called Identity-Based Ministries and Advocacy and Witness. Where Faith in Action had been responsible for the UUA's anti-racism efforts, Sinkford held all departments responsible for advancing anti-racism. And under the reorganization Sinkford became the staff liaison to the Transformation Committee.

In September, Sinkford hosted a Seminarian Consultation in Boston, which he called to explore how the UUA staff can support seminarians and ministers from racially and culturally marginalized groups. A major focus was the Diversity of Ministry Team, UUA staff that monitored the progress of students from these groups. The consultation suggested some principles that team members could use to guide their work, which had been previously unknown to the seminarians and candidates involved. Sinkford emphasized the commitment of the Settlement Office and Ministerial Education Office to supporting ministers of color and Latina/Latino ministers.

A teleconference between Transformation Committee members and Sinkford as part of its fall meeting revealed the Committee's key issues of concern: resources for anti-racism trainings and other anti-oppressive work, what Sinkford was hearing about the Journey Toward Wholeness in interactions with UUs around the country, especially ministers, and how to get feedback from UUA staff. Of particular concern was Sinkford's decision to stop trainings for a year and to hold gatherings to hear opinions on anti-racism work. Sinkford gave his vision, reported thus in the minutes:

> [Sinkford] stated his hope that the Transformation Committee would serve as an accountability construct for UU congregations, and that it would focus on information gathering from congregations. He affirmed the need for the Transformation Committee "construct," and asked the Transformation Committee to prepare a statement that assessed the JTW's progress to date and its future for reflection at General Assembly.
>
> Further, Bill described optimistic signs that anti-oppression and anti-racism work will be embedded throughout UUA staff work, noting that [the new] Ministry and Professional Leadership Staff group is taking more ownership around the work with ministers of color and Latina/o and Hispanic ministers. He also emphasized the need to make the work more concrete, and to draw on the experiences of congregations across the broad UU community and to share it, which is an opportunity that "Finding Common Ground" gatherings present.
>
> Bill noted the negative energy generated by the "Crossroads-derived training," and the need to find ways to make people who had shut down and felt shut out engage in anti-racism work. The decision to "take a year to imagine different ways to move forward" had been interpreted as a retreat from the anti-racism agenda. His intention was to "find some better ways to make more people available to the work." Bill asked the Transformation Committee to bring him a vision [for continuing anti-racism initiatives], including the budgetary commitment to take to the UUA Board of Trustees (BOT), so they could talk about it as a priority. He affirmed that he is deeply committed to the work, that staff had never brought anti-oppression work forward so the board could make decisions. He stated his willingness to be a partner in getting support through the Board of Trustees for Anti-Oppression.

Another topic of the meeting was the state of resources and programming, with former Faith in Action staff members Revs. Josh Pawelek and William Gardiner presenting a grim assessment, including:

- Fewer staff to fulfill requests for anti-racism training and consultation (from eight program staff in Faith in Action to two straight white men in Congregational Services),
- The absence of staff who are people of color as a way to ensure accountability in the shaping of anti-racism programming,
- Need to develop consultant capacity—part of the "new plan" of approach to delivering anti-racism/anti-oppression services to congregations,
- Figuring out how to do anti-racism training for UUA staff using non-staff facilitators. Note: there's no UUA sponsored anti-racism training for staff this year. However there is contracting with [a multicultural training] group called VISIONS to train UUA staff,
- Concern that Transformation Committee's recommendation re: taking a "consultation approach" to anti-racism [focusing conversation on the specific needs of a particular group] was overemphasized and taken out of context. "If you can't get people into an analysis training, what's the point of a consulting process?"
- Concern that focus on "consultation" removes focus from anti-racism organizing (to make systemic change), and
- There are not enough resources for Jubilee 1 and Jubilee 2 trainings. Training for board leaders and staff is on hold for a year.

A perception grew among other concerned observers that the reorganization reduced the emphasis on an Association-wide conversation around race and ethnicity. Dr. Norma Poinsett, whose involvement in training and education around this issue long predated the Journey Toward Wholeness era, said,

The emphasis is not on workshops anymore. I have the feeling that we should keep having anti-racism workshops as long as there is an Association because nothing is going to change that much that fast, and if anything, if the emphasis is off, we regress. If it's too quiet about what's going on, we regress. I think that's been one of the biggest disappointments for me. That we really, we are just kind of thinking that people are going to go off and start their own JTW committees and they're going to carry this work on in their districts and in their various churches, and just because they read about how you can set it up, they're going to do it. But they're not.

Poinsett also wondered who was leading the charge. She recalled the Black Concerns Working Group, which predated the Journey Toward Wholeness: "It was not a group of people to think out something, we actually did the work. It would have to be some kind of group like that who would actually help develop regional . . . groups that would try to transform the Association."

"We've changed how resistance was dealt with," Rev. William (Chester) McCall of Church of the Restoration in Philadelphia, said. "With institutional change, you have to expect resistance: validate it, acknowledge it, talk about it within a context of change, instead of allowing it to undermine the work." While McCall was speaking of the resistance anti-racism advocates encountered, it would also apply to the resistance the new president encountered, resistance to the reorganization and to his appeal for a broader discussion of religious language in the Association.

Others found the new approach useful and responsive. Phyllis Daniel, chair of the Ministerial Fellowship Committee, recalled,

The MFC was one of the first organizations to ask for training from the Congregational Services. . . . And so we again were kind of trying something out to see how it worked. And Josh Pawelek and Paula Cole Jones were asked to work with us. And that was a really wonderful experience for me because I had phone conversations with Paula and Josh, and email conversations—they did a wonderful job of trying to understand what the needs of the MFC were.

Crossroads Ministry

The Association's relationship with Crossroads Ministry was also evolving, with tensions developing between Crossroads and the Transformation Committee, whose membership had evolved as well. The Committee minutes include this reference: "[Rev.] Joe Barndt [founder] of Crossroads asked Taquiena Boston [head of the Identity-Based Ministries staff group] to convey to Transformation Committee that Crossroads would still like to get in right relationship and have Transformation Committee at the strategy table. Susan Suchocki Brown [of the Journey Toward Wholeness Transformation Committee] reported that she sent a letter to Joe to which she never received a reply. As for joining the Crossroads Strategy Table, it was agreed that this is something that should be examined in terms of an overall discussion of what groups Transformation Committee might partner with."

One continuing perception was that the Crossroads approach was impenetrable and unchangeable, a criticism its defenders were quick to challenge. "Those who resisted hadn't been to training," observed Rev. William (Chester) McCall. "Those at trainings who raised issues—those issues were addressed. The program changed over time, responding to critique."

Barndt saw this as evidence of resistance and noted,

There's a pattern we at Crossroads, or at least I and others—I'm not sure how inclusive that "we" is—have been noticing. . . . There appears to be a point in every institution's life that we work with, a point at which institutions regress from collective decisions they have made or from progress they have made. . . . The institution's systemic unconsciousness recognizes that these folks are serious about changing the identity of this institution, and there's a hand that goes up that says, "Talk to the hand." And the real resistance goes up. . . . You've fought tooth and nail to climb half way up a mountain, and there's a landslide. And you have to gather yourself back from the landslide before you continue the rest of your climb. . . . It appears to be at some point where the institution's leadership, or the institution's whatever the systemic unconsciousness is, feels really threatened by the historic identity change behind that.

Those who supported the established anti-racism approach found their commitments tested and in some cases deepened by encounters with those who did not share their opinions.

Common Ground Gatherings

The first two of four regional Finding Common Ground gatherings were held in early 2002 with the aim of giving congregational leaders, religious educators, social justice activists, and others a chance to express their concerns about the Association's anti-racism efforts and their hopes for the future.

A gathering in the Washington area attracted seventy-seven people and one in the San Francisco area attracted ninety. Transformation Committee members attended as listeners, and the convenors encouraged open dialogue. What emerged was the fact that people were appreciative for the chance to give feedback, that they felt it should have come sooner, and that the "story" of the Journey Toward Wholeness was not clear or consistent.

Paula Cole Jones, a consultant to the Association around issues of race, said she was not surprised that the initial efforts generated "push-back." In anti-racism work, Cole Jones said,

The first phase attracts the diehard people who are most ready for change. Resistance to change by others is a normal response. The first phase of anti-racism in the UUA identified and equipped leaders. We needed to build a movement and to create a new environment where anti-racism was a normal way of operating. That meant we needed to find ways to bring the average UU to the table. Compare our efforts with the scuba industry, where the first divers were serious athletes. They had to have brawn, strength and courage. When the industry wanted to grow, it had to find ways to include the everyday person. Industry leaders changed the rules, used technology to improve the equipment, expanded outreach and marketing, and then scuba diving became a sport that the average person could do.

Congregational representatives who spoke at the Common Ground gatherings made it clear that ministerial support was critical to their engagement with anti-racism. They also said they needed simple approaches and guidance along the way. That huge misperceptions and miscommunications had occurred in the first decade of anti-racism work was also clear.

In January 2003, another Common Ground gathering was held in Dallas. Based on the written record, some participants came hoping for an anti-racism training and expressed disappointment to discover that the meeting was an "information-gathering event." When asked what puzzles or questions they had for the Committee, participants generated a list that included:

- Are we more concerned with acting correctly "anti-racist" or actually working to dismantle oppression?
- When is UUA JTW going to draw from Crossroads training and others they may have had to establish guidelines for congregational JTWs? Many congregations want to start, but don't know how, others need directions.
- What resources are there?
- How can I invite people (friends), colleagues, and acquaintances from marginalized groups to my church without being an evangelist or seeming to be valuing them only as tokens, etc.? Any suggestions? Perhaps I should not be so self-conscious.
- How can small congregations effectively conduct JTW?
- How can we move from intellectual assessment to spirit-infused action?
- How do we do justice work with joy and vigor? And in ways that attract others.
- Why can the UUA not develop a JTW prototype from which congregations could take our cues?

- [How can we] find a way to evaluate "hostility towards Christianity" in UU fellowships. I appreciate the concern over how to be cool with pagans.
- Does it ever get any easier?

Leadership from the UUA Board

Tamara Payne-Alex, a member of the Association's Board of Trustees from 2000 to 2009, recalled that this was a volatile time for the Board, which was being asked to take a large leadership role in anti-racism work. "[Denise Davidoff, who as UUA moderator served as Board chair] had taken a real leadership role and decided the Board should step up to the plate," she said. Payne-Alex, who had worked as a professional diversity consultant, arrived when concerns about the Crossroads model were circulating. Payne-Alex saw the model as "one of the best" available and yet felt it was in some ways a "cultural mismatch" with some aspects of Unitarian Universalist culture, especially the expectations that each congregation should be able to choose its own methods as well as the unwillingness of an activist- and justice-minded laity to follow strong leadership. "We have some really bright, competent, passionate individuals," she said.

Payne-Alex's approach to anti-oppression work differed from some others on the Board due first to her corporate perspective as one who had worked as both a business systems consultant and a diversity consultant, and second, to being younger than many of the other players. This was a difference she had observed in her work life as well. "I saw a real generational difference between the folks who were senior consultants and those of us who were younger," she said. "I experienced them as angry, needing to reallocate some of the power structure. I cared less about having people share power than to get them to use the power they had to make change." Her approach proved a useful fresh perspective on a Board divided about issues such as the effectiveness of the Crossroads Ministry approach. She continued, "I said, 'If you are not a racist, prove it—what are you going to do to change the system you are in, because you've been elected to leadership.'"

For Payne-Alex, the timeline was longer. "I thought it would take another five generations to get people's attitudes to change in real ways," she said. "Change had to come from sustained inter-action."

Reorganization in UUA Staff

Sinkford announced the new organizational structure for the Unitarian Universalist Association staff at General Assembly in 2002, and later recalled,

> During the campaign, I used the language of the beloved community and talked a good deal about both racial justice and the need for transformation. It was not the top of my list, however. I was very concerned and, really, through the first term of my presidency, concerned that I would be seen as a one-issue president, and made the conscious decision not to make in a public way the work of anti-racist transformation seen as the top of my agenda. It was a judgment call. I think it was the right one, but it certainly was a judgment call.
>
> At the same time, I started immediately working to unblock the congregational system in terms of access to the work, and to reshape the staff support for the work. Neither of those was easy. I invested, actually, quite a lot of time and energy in working with the large-church ministers' group to get them to say, "Okay, we'll go one more round on this." The staff changes were even more complicated to effect. . . . It was clear to me that with the then-existing leadership the work was not going to move ahead. The reactivity was just too great. That was hard.

Shortly after Sinkford was elected the economy softened, reducing income from the Association's endowment. Thus restructuring also had to mean fewer people. News of the change was shared with the trainers who conducted the weekend-long Jubilee II anti-racism analysis trainings, to an unenthusiastic reception:

From the perspective of the trainers, it is difficult to see the vision and values at the heart of the restructuring. Questions were raised: What is the vision driving the restructuring? What values are driving the restructuring? How is the commitment to anti-racism and anti-oppression reflected in the restructuring? . . . Some trainers expressed skepticism. On paper, the restructuring does not appear to be grounded in anti-oppression. The UUA's commitment to anti-racism and anti-oppression appears marginalized. It feels like the main factors determining the shape of the restructuring are 1) increasing the effectiveness of status quo services to congregations and 2) financial constraints the UUA is currently facing.

Sinkford's widespread staff reorganization took effect in the weeks after the General Assembly. The largest department—Congregational, District and Extension Services—was divided into two, Congregational Services and District Services; two new departments, Identity-Based Ministries and Advocacy and Witness, were also formed. The departments of Religious Education and of Ministry received expanded portfolios and were renamed Lifespan Faith Development and Ministry and Professional Leadership, respectively. Most troubling to anti-racism advocates, the Faith in Action Department was disbanded and anti-racism responsibilities were distributed among other staff groups.

Hoover, the director for Faith in Action, told the Jubilee II trainers that "political realities" made it necessary to eliminate Faith in Action. Staff members were shifted into Identity-Based Ministries and Advocacy and Witness, with some of its functions dispersed into the Congregational Services and Lifespan Faith Development departments. In the months after the changes, it was announced that Robette Dias and Rev. William Gardiner of the Faith in Action staff would leave the UUA; Hoover left the next year.

The decision was made to spread the staff across other staff teams to ensure a wider dissemination of the work. This decision was not well received by the Jubilee II trainers:

We are concerned that in breaking up Faith in Action, anti-racism and anti-oppression programming will not have the same level of resource commitment from the UUA as it has had in the past. For example, members of the proposed Identity-Based Ministries staff-team who formerly engaged in anti-racism and anti-oppression programming are hearing from the administration that in their new capacities they are not expected to be anti-racism and anti-oppression trainers. The entire anti-racism training and consulting program (Path to Anti-Racism), which formerly existed in the portfolios of at least six program staff and three support staff, now exists in the portfolios of two program staff and one support staff in the Congregational Services staff-team. We wonder how the same or similar levels of programming are possible given this massive redistribution of work.

The trainers feared a lowered commitment to the Journey Toward Wholeness and raised concerns about the absence of any people of color on the staff assigned to work directly with anti-racism. Another concern arose from the perception that these changes had come about because of the resistance of particularly powerful ministers in the Association. Pawelek continued,

[W]e are concerned about an apparent power differential between some large church ministers and others who have used their access to the UUA administration to dissent against the Journey Toward Wholeness, over and above the voices of those who've been doing the work of anti-racist and anti-oppressive transformation mandated by the 1997 Anti-Racism business resolution. Often, those volunteers who've been doing the work of anti-racism and anti-oppression in congregations do not have the same kind of access to the UUA administration as those who've historically opposed the work.

[Rev. Dr.] Tracey Robinson-Harris assured the Jubilee II trainers that she did not understand her mandate as the Director of Congregational Services to be the silent dismantling of the UUA's anti-racism and anti-oppression programming. Regarding anti-racism specifically, she stated that her commitment is to 1) review the current structure of the anti-racism program; 2) discern ways to make it more effective and more efficient; 3) help develop networks among congregations; 4) obtain the necessary resources to run an effective and efficient anti-racism program. She also talked about developing an anti-racist and anti-oppressive approach to the work of Congregational Services.

Announcements from the new Office of Community Justice-Making indicated that the Journey Toward Wholeness Sunday program, which raise money in congregations for anti-racism efforts, was being continued and not expanded; that fewer Jubilee I basic introductory workshops were expected in 2003; and that smaller consulting teams were to be used for a revised Jubilee II organizational analysis training. Training for new transformation teams and further education modules was planned, including a module on action reflection processes and community partnerships.

Supporting a Historic Presidency
Important in the context of these times was the need for Journey Toward Wholeness proponents to be supportive of the administration of Sinkford as the UUA's first African American president. As the notes from the Jubilee II trainers' meeting indicate, they were conscious of this need, noting,

> The Jubilee II trainers are very supportive of Bill Sinkford. . . . We are very clear that Bill Sinkford is our leader. We are also clear that our specialty as anti-racism trainers and the resources that have been invested in our development as trainers obligates us to lead in areas related to our expertise.

Pawelek offered his personal assessment of the changes in February 2003:

The UUA restructured as of July 1st, 2002. This included the break-up of the Faith in Action Department (FIA). FIA had as many as eight full and part-time staff working on anti-racism. Some FIA staff were sent into the new UUA Department for Advocacy and Witness, directed by [Rev.] Meg Riley. Some were sent into the new Department for Identity Based Ministries, directed by Taquiena Boston. And some were sent into the new Office of Congregational Justice Making (OCJM), which is part of the new Department of Congregational Services, directed by Tracey Robinson-Harris. The underlying goal of the break-up of Faith in Action was to begin spreading the reach and influence of anti-racism staff throughout the UUA. (I must admit I was skeptical at first. But having worked in the new structure for half a year, I am now beginning to see signs that anti-racism is moving deeper into the UUA. A good example of this is the introduction of more in-depth anti-oppression questions on yearly staff evaluations.)

One of the current dilemmas we face is the reality that FIA had as many as eight program staff dedicated to anti-racism, and yet we now have two program staff dedicated to anti-racism. . . . Thus, there has been a large cut in staff hours dedicated to anti-racism program development and implementation. Despite the staff changes, we are positive that the traditional UUA anti-racism programming will continue. There is a solid pool of Jubilee I and Jubilee II volunteer trainers. We also are beginning to envision the creation of a consultancy program which should alleviate some of the dilemma posed by the reduction in anti-racism staff (see below).

Feelings of Concern and Loss
"I really wish that Faith in Action was not put out of business," Gardiner said in 2005. "Members of the Faith in Action staff were building relationships with leaders in districts and congregations. Josh Pawelek was working on the East Coast and Robette Dias was

working on the West Coast. After Faith in Action was dismantled, we lost that organizing capacity."

Pawelek offered this further analysis:

I think it is true that the UUA's Department for Faith in Action, which had the majority of the responsibility for creating anti-racism programs, as well as the UUA administration and Board of Trustees, which had the majority of the responsibility for overseeing the anti-racist transformation of the UUA based on the 1997 General Assembly resolution, made numerous mistakes, some big, some small. However, none of these mistakes were fatal mistakes. None of these mistakes were any different than the kinds of mistakes a UUA department or the administration or the Board of Trustees would make whenever a new and somewhat controversial direction or program is introduced. The work of changing an institution's identity is bound to include mistakes. Whatever the mistakes were, they don't really bother me.

If I could go back and change one thing about the UUA's efforts, I would not have radically altered them upon the election of Bill Sinkford to the UUA presidency. I would like to have seen them hold steady and continue with the same message about anti-racist accountability. I would like to have seen the Department for Faith in Action continue. I would like to have seen 30 Jubilee I and 20 Jubilee II workshops continue to take place every year in UU congregations and districts, as opposed to the current six or eight workshops that take place now. I would like to have seen the UUA proudly continue its relationship with Crossroads Ministry. I would like to have seen Rev. Sinkford tell the large church ministers something of the importance of accountability to people of color, instead of agreeing to alter the UUA's anti-racism programs because the large church ministers didn't like them, which is exactly what Bill Sinkford told the Faith in Action staff a month after his election. The UUA's original anti-racism efforts were intended to support a long-term process of anti-racist institutional transformation. In my analysis, we did not give them a long enough time to work. We changed the approach before we could even adequately measure the success of our original approach. Frankly, I wouldn't have changed a thing.

In the congregations that had been most engaged with anti-racism, the change created unease and even anger. "I am very disappointed that the UUA has dissolved the Faith in Action section of our denomination," said Jean Shepard, a member of the Undoing Racism Committee in the Thomas Jefferson Memorial Church in Charlottesville, Virginia. "Although everyone in every department within the UUA is supposed to be working in non-biased ways, I think that we have lost a very important 'message center.' Our denomination should be leading the anti-racism movement among predominantly white churches. But instead, I think that we have lost a nationally recognized voice in that community. Having a Boston-based educational department also sends the message to all congregations that this work is truly valued by the UUA. I believe that we have lost our momentum in this work since everyone now needs to find their own way in this struggle. We need more leaders/messengers, not fewer!"

For some who had been committed to the efforts as Faith in Action had shaped them, the sense of loss was huge and the departure of leaders such as Hoover, Gardiner, and Dias was a betrayal. Rev. Kurt Kuhwald said,

> [A] flow of activities [was] crystallized in several particular actions: the dismantling of the Jubilee Working Group, the later removal of the Rev. Mel Hoover from leadership of the Social Justice efforts of the UUA, and the ultimate marginalization of racism in the UU national agenda.
>
> The lack of a clear conversation, Association-wide, about the [Sinkford] administration's choices for abandoning the UUA's focus on Anti-Racism, that involved the Working Group's termination and Mel's dismissal, represents a clear bureaucratic avoidance of the real issues facing our Association and our nation in the matter of race.

The fact that the new administration no longer lifts up dealing with racism as central to the vision of modern UUism is shocking . . . and expected. Anti-racism is one of the hardest spiritual tasks/paths a person, a group or an institution can take on. The UUA has fundamentally failed to live out its goal-specific, public commitment to address racism. In this failure it has demonstrated not how "uncommon" it is, but how similar it is to other religions which its members so often criticize for being too doctrinaire, rigid and oppressive. . . .

The frequently proffered argument across the board in the current administration that anti-racism has been so integrated into our institution that it is being dealt with on all levels and in all areas of our Association is simply untrue. Our congregations continue to be bastions of white, liberal privilege. Our public witness continues to avoid the difficult work of consistently and coherently addressing matters of racial justice/anti-racism. Those who argue that change has been made, and that much anti-racism work goes on, speak the truth. The question that begs an answer, however, is: "What, now, is our public agenda and commitment regarding racism?"

What stands out for me about the UUA's effort toward anti-racism is how thoroughly it has been eliminated from public discourse, how quickly the effort has been subsumed beneath other goals. What stands out for me is how we have essentially submitted to the current national forces that refuse to deal with race and, which in fact, encourage and strengthen racism. Certainly our efforts to support a few other justice issues (one wonderful example: Marriage Equality For All) have been strong and visible, but why, too, could we not have equally strong efforts to address the virulent inequities of race that continue to grow and deepen across our land, particularly when so much of the essential anti-racism groundwork has already been laid?

I am finally left with a few simple questions: Why have we backed off? What are we protecting? What are we afraid of? What pay-off are we truly gaining? If there are clear and strategic reasons for decreasing our anti-racism work, what are they? What, now, is our dream?

For those who had taken up the anti-racism mantle and endured stressful interactions championing it, feelings of abandonment were real. McCall observed,

> Sinkford . . . found a way to bring people into the conversation who were opposed . . . but dismantled the existing program. . . . [The Identity-Based Ministries staff group] was created without the responsibility to continue the existing anti-racism programs. The anti-racist community that had been created was now dispersed . . . devalued . . . disrespected.

For others who had become increasingly uneasy with the Crossroads Ministry approach to anti-racism, relief came with the change in direction. "Now there is an understanding that racism isn't just an issue for African Americans," said Jacqui James, a religious educator and long-time UUA staff member. "That was a problem with the Crossroads model. . . . You're guilty, you're racist. . . . The whole approach of guilt. We didn't spend much time helping people think about their identity and that's important. Racism affects all people of color but our histories are different and it took us a while to understand that. My experience as a light-skinned African American is different than that of a darker-skinned African American. That doesn't mean I don't experience racism." James said the Crossroads approach had not allowed exploration of colorism, the impact of region, or other factors which affect identity.

In October 2003, President Sinkford, perhaps to counter the many unofficial interpretations circulating, released a memo articulating where he stood on anti-racism work:

> As I promised at the pre-GA Board meeting, I've now assembled the charges/mission/status of the many institutional groups within the Association which are engaged

with this work. It gladdened my heart. Anti-racism work has "seated" itself both deeply and broadly in the life of the Association. From YRUU to the UUA Board, committees/transformation teams/task forces are at work. We couldn't stop this work now, even if we wanted to.

The extent of congregational buy-in and engagement is another matter. A couple of our districts have formal structures in place and some congregations are in relationship with the Association around this issue. But at the congregational level, the engagement is neither broad nor deep.

That is why I asked the Journey Toward Wholeness Transformation Committee to begin serving as our accountability link to the congregations. (The Common Ground gatherings, which were enormously helpful, were the result.) Now the JTWTC is returning to its original broad charge.

Perhaps that is best, but I see a terrain very different from 1995 when the JTWTC was created and charged. Then the Association was "selling" and the task was to obtain broad buy-in from leadership groups. The charge of the committee was appropriately broad: "plan, guide, facilitate, coordinate and monitor" our transformation. As all of us involved at the time knew, we didn't have a clue what the work might actually look like.

Given the broad buy-in at the institutional/leadership level today, and the still uncertain engagement of most of our congregations, I continue to feel that my impulse to shift the focus of the work of the JTWTC was sound. But beyond that, in light of the widespread commitment to this transformation, I believe it is time for the Board to revisit the charge of this committee.

Let me say clearly that I believe we need some broad Associational structure, but I wonder if the center of the charge does not need to be congregationally focused, or if not that, more directly focused on sharing information/best practices among the array of committees/teams/task forces which are hard at work.

Identity-Based Ministries

Taquiena Boston, who had entered Unitarian Universalism through the multiracial All Souls congregation in Washington, D.C., had developed a history as a volunteer, consultant, and staff member working on anti-racism training and assessments since the late 1990s. She was the one asked to head up the new Identity-Based Ministries staff group after Boston conceived the idea with Faith in Action members Robette Dias and Revs. Danielle DiBona and Keith Kron.

"We asked what it would look like to have a group that would focus exclusively on the Unitarian Universalist communities which experience marginalization and exclusion within the UUA," Boston said, noting that the idea was to include a range of oppressions. This fit what was happening in the Association, where identity-based caucuses such as LUUNA (Latina/o Unitarian Universalist Networking Association) and DRUUMM (Diverse and Revolutionary Unitarian Universalist Multicultural Ministries) were emerging. "I think the value is in having an internal staff group that can advocate for people when it is not possible for them to advocate for themselves," Boston said. The Department operates under this mission statement:

> Identity-Based Ministries seeks to make Unitarian Universalism a welcoming, inclusive, empowering, and just faith for Unitarian Universalists who identify as bisexual, gay, lesbian, and/or transgender; economically oppressed; Latina/ Latino and Hispanic; multiracial families; people of color; and people with disabilities. Ministries of this staff group focus on advocacy, education, and support related to policies, practices, and programs that support leadership development, community building, and organizing among constituents identified above. In addition, Identity-Based Ministries works collaboratively with Unitarian Universalist Association staff groups, and consults with continental committees, affiliates, and constituents to develop resources that educate congregations about how to dismantle institutional and cultural ableism, classism, heterosexism/homophobia, and racism.

The idea was to infuse anti-oppression in all the work of the Association staff, rather than making it an "add-on." Still, a new structure did not guarantee an easy path. "You can make pronouncements, but then you have to provide the resources and the trainings," Boston said.

Language of Reverence

Another conversation was shaping up, tangential to anti-racism efforts in some ways and related in others, that fed into the mix. Sinkford began to discuss what he called "the language of reverence," which he connected to a move toward greater wholeness as a religious association. These excerpts from a January 2003 sermon capture some of his message, which caused a strong reaction, particularly at Meadville Lombard Theological School and in humanist congregations and groups. He preached,

> I believe that Unitarian Universalism is growing up. Growing out of a cranky and contentious adolescence into a more confident maturity. A maturity in which we can not only claim our Good News, the value we have found in this free faith, but also begin to offer that Good News to the world outside these beautiful sanctuary walls. There is a new willingness on our part to come in from the margins. . . .
>
> Our Purposes and Principles date to the merger of the Unitarian and Universalist movements in 1961, when the effort to find wording acceptable to all—Unitarian and Universalist, Humanist and Theist—nearly derailed the whole process.
>
> The current revision of our Purposes and Principles dates back to 1984. It deals with the thorny question of whether or not to mention God or the Judeo-Christian tradition by leaving them out of the Principles entirely but including them in the section on the *Sources* from which our living tradition draws. It was here that we placed reference to "Jewish and Christian teachings which call us to respond to God's love by loving our neighbors as ourselves," as well as "Humanist teachings which counsel us to heed the guid-

ance of reason and the results of science, and warn against idolatries of the mind and spirit." And even that compromise went too far for those in our movement who feared "creeping creedalism," and not far enough for those who would have preferred more explicitly religious language.

Given the differences of opinion that needed to be bridged in one document, it's really not surprising that the wording adopted completely avoided anything that smacked of traditional religious language. And the Purposes and Principles have become an integral part of our denominational life. Many of our congregations print them on their orders of service. They open our hymnal. They hang in our vestibules. Many of us carry them in our wallets.

They serve us well as a covenant, holding out a vision of a more just world to which we all aspire despite our differences, and articulating our promise to walk together toward making that vision a reality, whatever our theology. They frame a broad ethic, but not a theology. They contain no hint of the holy.

Now while Unitarian Universalists reject any hint of a creed, we do affirm the importance of the individual credo: we are all charged, individually, to pursue our own free and responsible search for truth and meaning. And I wonder whether the language of our Purposes and Principles is sufficient for that purpose. UU Minister Walter Royal Jones, who headed the committee largely responsible for their current wording, wondered aloud how likely it is that many of us would, on our death bed, ask to have the Purposes and Principles read to us for solace and support. I fear, in words borrowed from former UUA president Gene Pickett, that "they describe a process for approaching the religious depths but they testify to no intimate acquaintance with the depths themselves."

. . . Our resistance to religious language gets reflected, I think, in the struggle that so many of us have in trying to find ways to say who we are, to define Unitarian Universalism. I always encourage people to work on their "elevator speech"—for when you're on the sixth floor and you're going to the lobby and somebody asks you, "What's a Unitarian Universalist?" What do you say? You've got about forty-five seconds. Here's my current answer: "The Unitarian side of our family tree tells us that there is only one God, one Spirit of Life, one Power of Love. The Universalist side tells us that God is a loving God, condemning none of us, and valuing the spark of divinity that is in every human being. So, Unitarian Universalism stands for: one God, no one left behind."

. . . Religious language places us in a larger context, whispering of a larger meaning, and carrying with it implications for how we should live., these too are names for the unnameable, which I am now content to call my God." . . . My growing belief is that, as a religious community and as individuals, we may be secure enough, mature enough, to find a language of reverence, a language that can acknowledge the presence of the holy in our lives. Perhaps we are ready. Perhaps, this faith we love is ready to stop calling itself a movement, and call itself a religion. Religion: to bind up that which has been sundered. To make connections in a world which would isolate us. To engage in the real journey toward wholeness.

Who knows? Perhaps we're ready.

As noted earlier, the lack of consensus around religious language was seen as an impediment to building a sense of urgency for addressing race as a religious imperative. The "language of reverence" discussion pitted many of the same people against one another who had found themselves with opposing views on anti-racism.

Crossroads at a Crossroads
One of the results of this time was a change in the relationship between the Unitarian Universalist Association and Crossroads Ministry, though it was a gradual, rather than abrupt, shift and key Associational leaders continued to attend Crossroads trainings.

"I was constantly asking the question, 'When are we going to get together to talk about the next step?'" said Barndt, the Crossroads director. "There were very formal steps that did take place that said 'the UUA has its own trainers, the UUA can use Crossroads material, the UUA can do the two-and-a-half-day training, the UUA is now independent of Crossroads, in charge of its own process of anti-racism training,' but always assuming that when that was said that we were still partners in anti-racism work. And so we still had that relationship. . . . I'm not even sure it's possible to describe when and where or how or *if* the end of that ever came."

For some, anti-racism and Crossroads Ministry were linked and the gradual end to the relationship with Crossroads was seen as an end to anti-racism efforts. "I would have acted to implement and support a component of the work that directly addressed the feeling and very personal levels of racism, where it lives in the human heart—along with a clear analysis of classism and its endemic presence throughout the UU world and its institutions," Kuhwald said when asked what the lens of hindsight revealed to him. He said the elimination of Faith in Action interrupted work against oppression and kept it from going to the next level. "Combining heart and class work with the power of the systemic anti-racism work that had already been developed could have resulted in a wider awakening about the actual realities of racism and oppression, and about their immediate and terrible corruption of authentic spirituality and heart-centered ethics. Had this change been undertaken, though my guess is that in the end the Association would still have abandoned anti-racism work because its demands are so high, I would have felt like we had given it our best shot."

At its November 2003 meeting, the Transformation Committee asked questions about vendors and contracting, and specifically about Crossroads Ministry. "The Committee was informed that the UUA/Crossroads Ministry relationship is a partnership, not just a contractor or vendor relationship," the minutes for the meeting relate. "The UUA has worked with Crossroads in adapting the anti-racism power analysis to the UU context, organizing congregational and district anti-racism transformation teams, and developing anti-racism leadership and trainers/organizers. In addition, the Crossroads relationship involves other denominational partners that have shaped the anti-racism power analysis used by the UUA."

Accountability
Over the years since the 1992 Calgary resolution, many questions about accountability were raised. At issue was how a white majority could be accountable to those who had historically been marginalized in its midst.

One tricky dynamic was that, at times, more people from racial and cultural groups historically marginalized by Unitarian Universalism were on the Association's staff than in its volunteer leadership. As Rev. Susan Suchocki Brown, the first chair of the Journey Toward Wholeness Committee, noted, this led to questions as to whether the staff should be accountable to the Board or the Board to the staff on matters of anti-racism.

The existence of identity-based groups such as LUUNA and DRUUMM provided an alternative to asking one representative of a group to speak for the whole racial or ethnic group. For Boston, director of the UUA's new Identity-Based Ministries staff group, providing arenas where people from historically marginalized groups could come together was a way of ensuring that people of color/Latina/o and Hispanic people could be accountable to one another.

VOICE
Rev. Joshua Pawelek

Pawelek, minister of the Unitarian Universalist Church of Norwich, Connecticut, worked as an anti-racism program associate at the UUA from 1999 to 2003, three years in the Department for Faith in Action under the leadership of Rev. Melvin Hoover and one in the Congregational Services Department under the leadership of Rev. Tracey Robinson-Harris. In offering the following sermon excerpt, Pawelek said, "In my view, the most important concept we tried to teach UU congregations through the Journey Toward Wholeness anti-racism programs was that of white accountability to people of color. How do historically white institutions make themselves accountable to people of color within the institution and within the community in which the institution is located?

Amazing progress has occurred in the struggle for racial justice over these past few hundred years, and we must celebrate that. But I always ask this question: if we can recognize racism's embeddedness in the very foundations of our country, can we also take an honest look at our history and identify when those foundations were intentionally transformed and gutted of their racism? Racism did not end with the end of slavery, nor the end of Indian wars, nor the end of legal segregation, nor with the economic success of the Pacific Rim—nor did it end in the wake of the 9/11 terrorist attacks despite claims of "one nation under God." When was our nation's racist legacy transformed once and for all? Can we answer that question definitively? And if not, how on earth can we expect to just get along? We cannot. Certainly *individuals* can cross racial lines and get along, even fall in love. But as a collective—as a society—it is naïve to believe we can get along. . . . Martin Luther King [said]: "America owes a debt of justice which it has only begun to pay." That debt will be fully paid—and we shall truly be able to get along as a multi-racial society—when the racist legacy at the heart of our institutions and systems has been dismantled and transformed.

I have discovered only one promising and reliable way to do this. White people must learn to make themselves and their institutions accountable to people of color—and not just to individual people of color, but to organized communities of people of color. Communities of color must learn how to function in situations where white communities are trying to be accountable. That's a nice, abstract concept. Clears things right up! Let me explain what I mean by telling you a story from my ministry in Norwich. It's the story of the Elks Lodge. If you've heard me tell it before, it won't hurt you to hear it again.

News broke in December 2000 that a qualified African-American man named Mannie Cooper had been denied membership in the Norwich Elks Lodge. Mannie had a number of business ventures in Norwich, and because networking and deal-making were part of the Elks' culture, Mannie felt it would be good for him to join the lodge. Of the 700 members of the Norwich Elks four were women, none was a person of color. You need a 2/3 favorable vote to be accepted. Every time a vote came up, Mannie missed by only a few votes. Elks leaders who had sponsored Mannie's candidacy for membership hoping to integrate the lodge alleged that the only reason anyone was voting against Mannie was the color of his skin. No one denied this allegation.

A few activists, including myself, had recently founded a multi-racial organization called the Norwich Area Anti-Racism Collective or NAARC. When we heard the news, another white member of NAARC and I hatched the idea of organizing a demonstration. Our initial plan included engaging in civil disobedience, blocking the lodge entrance on one of their meeting nights. I was excited, wondering if this might be a moment to get arrested. Almost sounds like the 1960s!

As a white anti-racist, there is one critical question I must ask before I proceed with such an action. How is this action accountable to people of color in our collective and in the local community? Just because I have good intentions, just because my heart is in the right place, just because I'm

continues on page 388

willing to get arrested, does not mean my actions are accountable; nor does it mean the institutions I represent are accountable.

NAARC was beginning to develop what we called an anti-racist accountability structure. With this structure as part of the organization, white activists would not act independently. We would bring our ideas to the people of color who were part of this structure. We did this, and although they liked our intentions and our passion, they felt the action had problems. They said the event should be planned in conjunction with the NAACP. Since the NAACP often engaged in public events, our organization should not steal the limelight from them. If the NAACP wanted to participate, their approach should take priority. When we contacted the president of the NAACP, she agreed that a public response was a good idea. However, she felt uncomfortable with civil disobedience. It seemed unnecessary. Then she requested that we do something we hadn't thought of: contact Mannie Cooper and see what would make the most sense from his perspective. We did this, and Mannie was adamantly opposed to the idea of civil disobedience. He felt it would destroy his chances of ever getting into the Elks. He liked the idea of an organized public response to the situation, but not a demonstration. Instead, he asked that we organize a rally in support of the Elks who had voted for him. This would be a much more positive action, and would not alienate the majority of Elks.

Now we had a plan that was accountable to the people of color involved. Notice how if this action had happened based on my initial plan, it would have worked against Mannie. Notice that even without racist intent, a failure of white accountability to people of color in this situation would have led to a racist outcome. That happens a lot, sometimes in obvious ways, sometimes in very subtle ways. President Bush was criticized this week for going to Atlanta and conducting a program at Martin Luther King's grave on the 15th without connecting with local activists who'd been planning events for a year. Once again, a white person tells people of color what he intends to do on their behalf. How different would it have been, if the White House had contacted the King family and the various activists in the Atlanta community months ago to ask: "What are you planning? How would you like the president to participate?" It doesn't sound difficult, but the foundations run deep.

On December 21, 2000, 75 people marched for forty-five minutes in front of the Norwich Elks Lodge. Speakers praised the Elks who voted for Mannie's membership. Signs proclaimed "Thanks to those who voted yes!" The marchers cheered and sang. The event was covered in the local papers, on local radio, and on two local TV news. Even the *New York Times* ran an article. A photo of the rally appeared in the Jan 7th *Times* showing members of NAARC and the NAACP.

Most white people cannot answer the question: who are the people of color to whom I am accountable? Who are the people of color to whom my institution—for example, my church—is accountable? And most people of color have some trouble answering the question, who are the white people who are accountable to me, who will respect my power, who will take my suggestions seriously, who can take direction from me? What are the historically white institutions that are accountable to people of color? These are very difficult questions to answer. I suppose it's no wonder people in my trainings get frustrated and say "why do we need this, why can't we all just get along?" The foundations are still in place. Their legacy is the absence of white accountability to people of color, which can lead even the most well-intentioned white people to perpetuate racism. That is why we don't get along. And that is what we must change.

CHAPTER 21

Ministerial Involvement

During 2002 and 2003, ministers and other professional leaders faced serious challenges in their anti-racism engagement. A conversation at Meadville Lombard Theological School focused on long-standing allegations that the school was not welcoming to people of color. The Ministerial Fellowship Committee began requiring an exposure to anti-racism work for the candidates for ministry. And the Unitarian Universalist Ministers Association [UUMA] worked to create structures to reinforce anti-oppression by providing forums for training.

As Rev. Gary Smith, UUMA president, said, "I think it helped the leadership of the UUMA and to some extent as it carried down into some of our district and chapter leaders, just recognizing some of the complexity of this journey was not such a simple one at all." Smith noted that the focus on anti-racism was in the context of other changes, such as a new dialogue about valuing religious educators, and part of a complex conversation. The big switch came when the white ministers took responsibility. Smith recalled that the Committee came to realize that they had to take ownership and not rely on representatives from racially and culturally marginalized groups to educate them.

Rev. Clyde Grubbs, a member of the Unitarian Universalist Ministers Association's Executive Committee at the time, said it was during this period that the Ministers Association took several important steps, including anti-racism training for the Executive Committee, working closely with Center Days to assure anti-racist content in programming, and creating the Committee on Ministry for Anti-Racism, Anti-Oppression and Multiculturalism. He also saw a new level of understanding within the new Ministerial and Professional Leadership Staff Group. He observed,

> The UUA has become more focused and much more concrete around anti-racism work in its programming. I meet with the new Ministerial and Professional Leadership Staff Group around anti-racism concerns once a year. The last few years the Ministry and Professional Leadership staff group has become very concrete and we have dealt with cases that pointed to institutionalized racism and taken steps to deconstruct those policies and practices.

He noted that the group still had issues understanding the cultural context of ministers and other professionals from historically marginalized groups, stating, "We continue to have concerns relative to cultural competency."

Other Approaches

In this time, some experimented with approaches to conversations around race. For example, Revs. Rosemary Bray McNatt and Charlie Ortman led a program about race entitled "Whose Job Is It Anyway?" as part of the 2002 pre-General Assembly professional development gathering known as Center Days. This kept the focus on anti-racism and established a continuity of the theme, if not the approach, from previous years.

McNatt and Ortman refined anti-oppression training to create their own approach. "We had lots of opinions about the work people were doing and why we didn't like it," McNatt recalled, "and both of us had this thing about when people sit around and whine about what they don't like, and don't want to do anything about it. So we said, well okay, instead of sitting around whining, why don't we do something about it and see if it works on the ground. So we did this at the Mountain Desert district's annual meeting, and people really liked it." Because of its success they then presented it at a number of other venues including Center Days, the annual meeting of the UUA's Metro New York District, and the Unitarian Universalist Congregation at Shelter Rock in Manhasset, New York. McNatt described their approach:

We're asking people to understand themselves and to decide for themselves where they're going to sign up in this struggle. We're assuming . . . that they want to sign up for the struggle against oppression, but they don't know what they want to do. Our goal is to give them some insight and some tools and to help them figure out what their role is in the struggle, because they're the only ones who know. We can't tell them what their role is; we can't tell them what their work is. But we assume everybody has work to do, work that only they can do. Our job is to help them discover it. And to give them at least a beginning set of tools to go do it.

Part of our approach includes having people report out at the end, saying, "Now that we've done all this, what do you know that you didn't know when you came in? What's your work?" Sometimes their work is personal, because we take people to those levels. The first conversation we think people should be having is with themselves. We think people start talking to each other and to other people and they haven't talked to themselves yet. They don't know what they don't know, and what they feel, that they haven't admitted to themselves, and that they don't remember, and that they're ashamed of because they can't admit it. And that's all grist for the mill.

We already begin with a whole set of stuff, we get all kinds of stuff out of the way. Like, okay, the culture is racist, sexist, homophobic, classbound—everything you can imagine—we already know this, and you should know it if you don't already know it. That's good news and it's bad news. It's bad news because it's harming all of us. It's good news because it means that there's something that we can do about that if we know it and understand it. We tell people that's where we are coming from. . . .

If you're white, particularly if you're white . . . you will particularly be penalized and singled out. Because you're not supposed to resist. You're supposed to go along with the program. . . . And when they bust out of being white, bad things happen to 'em. Very, very bad things. So we talk about that. We talk about acknowledging that. We talk about our approach to talking about this, which is amnesty and honesty. And we don't call people racist. We don't do name-calling, just like we wouldn't do name-calling in church, do you know what I mean? We're a church. We're a church! We don't call people names in church! So we're not going to call 'em names in here. We don't let 'em call each other names.

I mean, to me, it's just all basic stuff. We try to get people to tell each other the truth, and to assume well-being and well-meaning on the part of people, and that we're starting at this place, but we're not going to stay at this place, and the idea is to help people grow. Because this is all part of a spiritual experience, so you have to give people room to make mistakes. We're basically trying to act like we're in church. On some level, it's what pastors are doing every day, just it has moved to this particular arena. It's not rocket science. . . .

We talk about the fact that there's a through-line in UU history and values that is an anti-oppressive line. It's not like there aren't racist, oppressive UUs. There always have been and there always will be, but there's also a long stream of justice making in UUism that goes back to its founding, and there are very specific people and events and circumstances that bend toward justice: Theodore Parker, Clarence Russell Skinner, Dorothea Dix. These are people and events and history and circumstances that have always been part of who we are. We can rely on them, look at them, study them, depend on them. The 1917 Declaration of Social Principles that Clarence Russell Skinner wrote talked about equality among races. And in 1917, at the height of the Ku Klux Klan, that was not a small thing. But we don't talk about those things. We think that our history of justice making kind of ended at the Civil War, started up again in the Civil Rights movement, and in between is this big void. We actually have a whole lot of history around this stuff. We have Joseph Fletcher Jordan, we have all these other kinds of things, but what we don't do is put them together.

First, we work in small groups. We don't make them do it in a big room. And we talk about our own experiences first. Part of it involves our own vulnerability. See, we don't care about telling on ourselves. One of the things we [McNatt and Ortman] do is talk about all the stupid things we did to each other and said to each other, and all the mistakes we've made, and mostly people are reassured. . . . What most people wind up saying is, "If you guys can survive making the kinds of stumbles that you have made with each other, then we can survive it, too." . . . And then we ask them to go into groups and talk about the same stuff, so they know that we've done dumb stuff, and we're friends. And they figure, "Well, they won't make fun of us because they've done dumb stuff too." It's safe to say dumb stuff. God knows, they've done dumb stuff. It kind of takes the pressure off of them, and that, I think, is one of the big reasons that people will talk about some of the things that they might not otherwise talk about. We don't necessarily need them to report to us. What we try to do is get people together in groups of no bigger than six. Usually it's four or five, and we get them to repeat the same kinds of stuff and we walk around and kind of listen. We tell people you can report out or not. And we ask people to stay together in those groups the whole day, or over the couple of days. We've done it as long as a week and as short as seven hours, and somewhere in the middle, but we like people to have time to be together. It's very experiential. People cry, because they remember things they hadn't remembered in a long time. We tell people that everybody makes mistakes about—for example, one of the stories I tell is being five years old and talking about the grocery store in Chicago where I'd been watching these old war movies and there's a Filipino woman who runs the store near us, and she'd always been really nice to us, but I'd been watching these old war movies, and I go in with my Mom and I said, "Look at that Jap," because I think it's an okay thing to say because it's in the movies. And I always remember how everybody looked at me, and how that lady who had been so nice to me looked so hurt. And Charlie remembers being on a tennis court playing with his brother, and he got really mad at his brother because his brother was beating him and he called him a nigger, and what his mother did.

When you tell those stories in front of people, they get to know that just because I'm black doesn't mean that I don't have experience with having said something or done something that is reflective of the culture in which I live. African Americans are not the only peoples who are victims of racism in the culture. So you have to get up and be willing to say to people, see, I've done this too. And after that, it's okay.

Meadville Lombard Catalyst for Change Conference

In an effort to come to grips with anti-racism, Meadville Lombard Theological School held a consultation in January 2003 with its faculty, students, and board. Rev. Dr. William Murry, who served as president and dean from 1997 to 2003, recalled the events leading up to the conference:

I went to Meadville Lombard because I felt very strongly that the preparation of students for our ministry would pretty largely determine the nature of our movement in the years, for a generation or two to come. I think the perspective of theological students is very important, and it's important to begin to change some of their attitudes, or try to enable them to change some of their attitudes toward race, if it could be done, and then that will be transmitted to and communicated to their congregations for ten, twenty, or thirty years. I think [attitudes about race] go back to the 1967 controversy with the Black and White Alternative and Black Affairs Council and so forth, with all of that, and that I think was simply symptomatic of us good liberal UUs. We don't see ourselves as having a problem with race. We were all in favor of the things Martin Luther King stood for. We opposed segregation and so on, and we're sort of in that category where we are blind to some of the things that are actually happening in our culture with people of color.

Some things that happened before . . . at Meadville Lombard would not happen today. I know of one situation . . . in which a Meadville Lombard student who was a person of color, a woman, was locked out of her room by another student and locked out of her building, Fleck House, where both students lived, and was called a nigger bitch by one of the students. I don't think that would happen today. I'm sure there were other incidents of discrimination against people of color as students of color at Meadville Lombard, that I don't know the particulars about, but I know that Meadville had a very bad reputation towards students of color to the point where some of the young ministers of color were saying, "Don't go to Meadville, if you're going to study for the ministry," to young students of color. That's pretty damning.

The consultation on race, under Murry's leadership, grew out of some students' concerns. Rev. Archene Turner, a Meadville student of African and Caribbean heritage who was one of the students, along with Kate Lore and Leslie Takahashi Morris, whose concerns prompted the consultation, was among those who attended the consultation. She recalled that her first General Assembly was 1999 when Rev. Dr. Thandeka, a Meadville Lombard professor, made her presentation entitled "Why Anti-Racism will Fail." As a lay person who had been advocating anti-racism efforts within her congregation, Turner felt conflicted. "I had already been accepted to Meadville Lombard," she said, "and as a person of color was trying to figure out what my place would be."

The school-wide consultation, known formally as the Catalyst for Change Conference and facilitated by Boston-based consultant U.T. Sanders, consisted of a series of open "fishbowl" conversations. Many participants complained that the consultation left them with feelings of incompleteness and pain. Some challenged the method in which it was conducted, others challenged the fact that it was held at all. Dr. Jon Rice, then an adjunct faculty and staff member at Meadville Lombard, reflected on his experience in the consultation:

One of the most startling encounters I have had with the anti-racism initiative occurred here at Meadville. . . . It seems that a professor here at the school was being accused of racism by a student. As there had previously been a case of a school administrator being charged with discrimination against a prospective teacher—the charge of discrimination was based on the teacher's sexual orientation—I assumed that this case would be handled in a similar way. In that case, an outsider was called in to investigate the charge, people were interviewed, and it was determined that the charge itself was unwarranted.

However, concerning this racism charge no such procedure was followed, in fact the anti-racism committee, as far as I could ascertain, did not follow a just procedure. Here is why I say this. Rather early on in the meeting over the racism charge, I asked the committee how they defined racism. I was told, by several committee members, "You cannot define racism because everyone sees it differently." Which seems peculiar to me. We all experience the sun somewhat differently, yet we can define it. Upon reflection, is there ANYTHING we do not experience differently? Nonetheless, my response was, "How can you charge someone with something you cannot define? Perhaps we can re-define the charge," I suggested, "so that we could get to the bottom of the matter. Maybe it is a case of racial discrimination, or prejudice, or simply something we CAN define."

One person on the committee agreed with me, the rest clearly did not. The chair said, "No, we will not do that!" I asked if the accused person had been notified that she was being charged with racism. I was told she had not been. I mentioned that the accused has the right to face her accuser. I was told that IF we demanded that the accusation be verified we "are, in fact, challenging the veracity of the claim—which is insulting to the accuser." The committee, for the most part, seemed satisfied with this answer. The sentimental ruled over the logical, and over the just. . . .

Kate Lore, social justice director at First Unitarian Church in Portland, Oregon, was one of the seminarians most involved with the consultation. "A minister came to me right after the conference and told me she was seriously considering filing an ethics claim against me," she said. "Not only did I get a clear view of the personal risks to do this work but it also told me something about the solidarity around white people. . . . You may not publicly question these white people." Lore, a white student who was enrolled in the Modified Residency Program, in which students were on campus only in January, spent most of her residential month that year trying to have follow-up conversations one-on-one. Lore also noted the attendance of many prominent Unitarian Universalists whose participation was made less effective because of the "fishbowl" format. "We had such an amazing array of experts in the mix, but they weren't willing to sit in a fishbowl," she said.

Turner, who was a member of the All Souls Church in Washington, D.C., said the consultation and the years that followed it demonstrated "how hard it was to turn this ship around." She felt that a community worship in 2001 was perhaps more effective at reaching hearts of her fellow seminarians. She said the support of more seasoned colleagues such as Revs. Michelle Bentley and Danielle DiBona, and of UUA staff members Taquiena Boston and Robette Dias, were important to her. "I don't think I would have gotten through," she noted, adding that personal contact from Rev. Dr. Mark Morrison-Reed also kept her going in the harder moments. "He helped me understand community for ministers of color in this denomination." Turner was also personally inspired by Bentley's example, which Turner felt illustrated the position of many people of color. "She who has endured incredible amounts of personal sacrifice and energy has stayed at the table out of her love for Unitarian Universalism even though it has come at such a high price."

Turner said the consultation raised issues for her about the nature of seminary education within Unitarian Universalism and how it addressed controversial issues such as race. She said regular spaces for deeper engagement and spiritually grounded conversations were needed. Lore said her goal would be to get all seminarians to do fieldwork in a setting that allowed them to have face-to-face contact with those affected by these issues. "You cannot understand how this liberates us into a new oneness until you experience this," she said.

After the consultation, the Meadville Lombard Board of Trustees met and discussed its role in undoing racism at Meadville Lombard. Murry included this reference in his report to the Board in February 2003:

> As you know, Meadville Lombard has had a poor record in the matter of race. In order to address this problem, the January Modified Residency Conference this year centered on racism at Meadville Lombard; classes were dismissed and the entire community was urged to attend. Over 130 people participated—residential and MRP students, faculty, staff, MRP field advisors, five Board members, and a dozen or so guests, several from the UUA staff and several former students of color. [UUA president] Bill Sinkford attended and the UUA gave us $10,000 to pay for the expenses of those who came from outside the Meadville Lombard community. Facilitated by U.T. Saunders and his colleague, Bruce Albert, we had an opportunity to hear about some of the racist treatment of students of color in the past, to confront the things that have happened in recent years and to discuss what we can do now to make ML a safer and more supportive environment for all students.

President Murry's report set the context, noting,

> We have a lot of work to do but the conference gave us a chance to start that work by providing an opportunity for healing and for learning what has been wrong and what now needs to be addressed. The conference concluded with lists of work that needs to be done to continue the progress made by the conference. The two Undoing Racism committees will meet at the Board meeting and assign various tasks to working groups. The conference has given us the opportu-

nity to change the culture of Meadville Lombard on the matter of race. Now the work begins.

At the Board meeting, the discussion led to the following resolution:

> VOTED: Consistent with the Board of Trustees resolution of March 9, 2002, regarding undoing racism, The Board of Trustees directs the President to establish procedures to continue the work of the January 2003 Catalyst for Change Conference and to insure that such procedures include a process of accountability.

A report by Rev. Marjorie Bowens-Wheatley provided background to the Board, which decided not to distribute the report due to the confidential nature of the stories shared by current and past students—though a summary was made available.

The March, 2003, JTWTC meeting heard a report on the consultation from Rev. James Hobart and Dr. Leon Spencer, who attended. They noted that "one of the goals is that the work of anti-oppression does not become the work of the Board committee but of the entire Board and the whole institution."

The consultation left strong divisions. Rev. Patricia Jimenez, who was present at the consultation along with others who played an observer role, described the event as "pathetic." In a memo to the UUMA Exec in April 2003, she wrote, "Since the meeting at Meadville Lombard, I have had a chance to reflect on that meeting. . . . One of the conclusions I have reached is that we should not confuse catharsis for change. I remain very skeptical about these meetings."

Reflecting four years later, Murry saw the conference as part of a larger process:

> It seems to me the most important outcome has been a growth, at least as I see it, in the students that I work with, a growth in racial sensitivity. A sort of a consciousness-raising, as it were. I know that Meadville Lombard had a

EXCERPT
A Seminary's Challenges

In a report entitled "Challenges to Doing Anti-racism/ Anti-oppression/Multicultural Work at Meadville Lombard Theological School," Lee Sanchez, who was a Meadville Lombard student, wrote the following.

In reflecting upon those challenges that have surfaced during the past three years of doing anti-racism/anti-oppression/multicultural work at Meadville Lombard School of Theology, six categories quickly come to mind:

1) **Influx**—There has been a tremendous amount of influx in terms of Meadville Lombard staff, faculty and students during the past three years. We have a new school president, many of our faculty and staff are no longer with us, and the student population has changed drastically—both in terms of new students coming in and former students graduating. This has had a dramatic effect on the institutional memory regarding the anti-racism/anti-oppression/multicultural efforts at Meadville Lombard.

2) **Accountability**—Although several attempts have been made to create systems of accountability, there is still a great deal of confusion over who is accountable to whom in this work. Examples include:
   • Is Meadville Lombard accountable to DRUUMM, LUUNA [Latino/a Unitarian Universalist Networking Association]. . . .
   • Are white students accountable to historically marginalized students?
   • Is the [Meadville Lombard] Undoing Racism Committee accountable to the [Meadville Lombard] Catalyst for Change Steering Committee?
   • Are the faculty and staff accountable to the Meadville Lombard Board of Trustees?

3) **Fear of Conflict**—Conflict is inherent in anti-racism/ anti-oppression/multicultural work; it comes with the territory. Yet according to the professional assessment of our Catalyst for Change consultants, the people involved in the community of Meadville Lombard are generally conflict-avoidant. This is particularly troublesome because it hampers effective communication. When issues arise, people often respond with awkward silences. People also tend to take things personally, instead of looking at the "big picture."

4) **Diversity of Opinion of Best Approaches**—People have strong opinions about which anti-racism/anti-oppression/multicultural approaches are most effective and align most closely with the shared spiritual values of our Unitarian Universalist heritage. Thus, energy that could be used in addressing anti-racism/anti-oppression/ multiculturalism has been diverted by arguments about "method."

5) **Lack of Regular Training Opportunities**—Although a few anti-racism/anti-oppression/multicultural training workshops have been offered, it has not been a regular course offering. Neither has attendance at these workshops been mandatory.

6) **Lack of Social Analysis**—Many students who have struggled to understand the anti-racism/anti-oppression/ multicultural efforts at Meadville Lombard have had very little exposure to any sort of social analysis. Their knowledge of sociology and systemic oppression has often been lacking and this, in turn, effects their grasp of anti-racism/anti-oppression/multicultural fundamentals (i.e., systems of accountability to historically marginalized persons have been interpreted as "reverse racism").

very bad reputation with respect to race. Of course, we did some things . . . to try to change that. But I think the main thing at this point is that people are a little more sensitive to racial issues, racial sensitivity. There is definitely more conversation going on. There's greater awareness of racial issues and racism and its demonic nature. The fact that there has been a workshop of some kind for five years in a row has had some impact. It is not the answer to everything, but I think it helped to raise people's sensitivity.

On the other hand, I want to point out that I think what we're working with here is a change of the UU culture and when you're talking about culture change, you're talking about something that takes a long time. My guess is that the real outcomes of the anti-racism work, the Journey Toward Wholeness, will not be apparent to us for another generation.

Rev. Dr. Lee Barker, a member of the Meadville Lombard Board, was appointed President of Meadville Lombard shortly after the consultation and continued to hold anti-racism events at least annually. He noted that the institution faced a long road to a fuller multicultural capacity and that the early years of the millennium had seen a changing awareness around race. "The Catalyst for Change conferences we've been doing—sometimes they've been successful and sometimes they haven't—but each and every one of them is a chance to say, 'What we're talking about here today is ministry,'" he said. "Here's the subset, but what we're really talking about is ministry. What does this have to do with your ministries? That's what we're going to try to get at today. It really is a way of helping students form the multicultural competencies that we've talked about, but to do so by asking them, and not just them, all of us, to continually reflect on what this has to do with ministry is amazing. What had changed, to some extent, was the willingness to see engagement with issues of oppression as part of the collective faith life of Unitarian Universalism."

Meadville Lombard's consultation tapped into decades of frustration about the commitment of the professional ministry to race and class issues. Dr. Norma Poinsett, long-time member of the Black Concerns Working Group, observed,

> I really think both of the theological schools should have institutionalized antiracism training. Institutionalize it, so that every teacher and every student would have to have some training, you know. I think what worked well was the total immersion of all the board members and staff at Headquarters.

The Ministerial Fellowship Committee

Meanwhile, the Ministerial Fellowship Committee, in charge of credentialing new ministers, was proceeding with plans to include anti-oppression as a part of the credentialing process. The MFC's work caused a backlash, as Phyllis Daniel, who was chair at the time, recalled,

> I read a number of email lists . . . and somebody would say something about the MFC's party line about anti-racism—you better know it or you're in trouble. And that would make me smile, because it was clear the word was getting out that you were going to be asked about anti-racism. And that was our goal. We wanted people to get it that they'd better be able to talk about their understanding of anti-racism work, and anti-oppression work because the MFC was going to ask questions about it. One of the things that's evolved is trying to figure out what kinds of questions to ask. We've talked about that some, and I know they'll continue to talk about that.

The MFC asked the Transformation Committee to conduct an audit of the forms and practices it used with seminarians seeking credentialing and also began to ask seminarians direct questions about anti-racism exposure as part of the credentialing process. Some found value in actions they were asked to take as a result. "One of the concerns expressed by the MFC when I was granted Preliminary Fellowship in 2004 was that I become accountable

---

VOICE

Rev. David Bumbaugh

This piece entitled "From the Stairwell Wall," was initially published in The Stairwell Wall, *the in-house newsletter of Meadville Lombard Theological School. Bumbaugh is a professor at Meadville Lombard.*

In the ongoing conversation concerning the antiracism initiatives of Meadville Lombard and the Unitarian Universalist Association, my voice has been largely silent. A recent experience, however, has provoked me to enter the fray.

I was sitting as a panel member in a mock MFC [Ministerial Fellowship Commission] interview [with a ministerial candidate], when we engaged the question of antiracism. I remember saying to the candidate that it would be well to pay attention to this area, since it involves a clear party line and an acceptable response must reflect that party line. My colleagues on the panel were quick to demur—insisting that there is no party line, that the MFC simply wants to know that the candidate has engaged the question and that the question is on a par with insisting the candidate have a theological position.

I have been thinking about that in the intervening weeks and find I must respectfully disagree. To begin with, I have never sat through a mock MFC where a student was asked specifically about his or her theology. But more than that, I find the importance attached to this question revealing.

No candidate is asked to present a paper outlining his or her position on war and peace. Indeed, we boast of the Unitarian Universalists who have served as Secretary of Defense and the Unitarian Universalist Association, at all levels, has gone out of its way in recent months to assure those who engage in and support the military adventures of this nation that they are fully welcome in our congregations. No candidate is required to define his or her relation to an economic system that deliberately and consistently transfers wealth from the poor to the rich—a system from which most of our people benefit. Indeed, the UUA at all levels has gone out of its way to assure capitalists, large and small, that they are welcomed in our churches. No candidate is required to submit a position paper regarding the ongoing global ecological catastrophe occasioned by our life style, even though it is clear that this moral issue trumps all the others. But every candidate must present a paper on antiracism.

That, in my mind, defines a party line. Let me be clear. Questions of race and racism have dominated my personal life and my public ministry. I do not question the importance of this concern for individuals or institutions. I am, however, troubled by a kind of group-think which inhibits our ability to place this issue in a larger context. And above all, I am affronted by a mindset that uses the real challenges of racism to allow us to feel better about ourselves rather than to address the larger world. When I see this kind of problem institutionalized in such a way that we are discouraged from asking fundamental questions, my teeth begin to itch.

to Native American scholars in my teaching of Native American religions," recalled Rev. Dr. Jerome Stone. "This has been a very positive experience. The retiring president of the American Indian Philosophical Association has agreed to mentor me. She has provided me with a marvelous reading list by Indian authors which has been very helpful."

Ministers and Accountability

In seeking to replace Rev. John Gilmore as a member of its Committee on Ministry for Anti-Racism, Anti-Oppression and Multiculturalism, the UU Ministers' Association had discovered that a number of the ministers of color/Latina/o/Hispanic were not UUMA members. The Executive Committee decided to reach out to these ministers and to seminarians from these groups, including a special effort to identify Latina/o students. The October Transformation Committee minutes stated,

> [Rev.] Patricia Jimenez is requesting that the UUMA Executive Committee gather information about the experiences of ministers and seminarians of color and Latina/Latino and Hispanic minister and seminarians. Danielle DiBona is organizing ministers of color on behalf of DRUUMM [Diverse and Revolutionary Unitarian Universalist Ministries]. Marta Valentin, Interim Latina/Latino and Hispanic Concerns Program Associate for Identity-Based Ministries, is summarizing information she gathered on behalf of DRUUMM in summer 2000.

The Ministry and Professional Leadership staff group also asked the Transformation Committee to audit its policies. Sinkford remarked at a Transformation Committee meeting that this decision indicated that "the terrain is radically different now than it was when the JTWTC was started." He also found it meaningful that the Senior Ministers of Large UU Congregations organization had agreed to include anti-racism and anti-oppression as part of its annual meeting. This was seen as "a big shift."

VOICE
Rev. Peter Morales

Morales was senior minister of Jefferson Unitarian Church in Golden, Colorado, when this was published in Quest *in 2002, the newsletter of the Church of the Larger Fellowship, the congregation for Unitarian Universalists who are isolated from bricks-and-mortar congregations.*

It has become something of a cliché to call Sunday morning worship the most segregated hour in American life. Though the work is unfinished, we have done much to integrate our schools, our military, our government bureaucracies, even much of our workplace. Yet on Sunday morning, all across America, many of us seek the comfort of people who look and speak as we do.

So, here we are, Unitarian Universalists, overwhelmingly white and Anglo. Why is a group that is so genuinely dedicated to anti-racism, anti-oppression, and multi-culturalism (a mouthful I have dubbed "Anti-Anti-M") so homogeneous? Why do so many of our people react with indifference to anti-racism workshops in our churches?

And what, if anything, does all this Anti-Anti-M stuff have to do with religion? What, if any, is the spiritual significance? And, if Latinos and African Americans and Koreans want to worship with people who look like them, isn't that fine? What more are we to do? I mean, if an African American or Latino or Asian American comes to church, we welcome them. Indeed, at many of our churches, we fall all over ourselves to show how welcome they are.

This is, as you can imagine, a deeply personal issue for me. Let me tell you a little of my experience. Shortly after entering seminary, I was invited to a gathering of ministers and seminarians of color from all across the country. Then, I was invited to attend the extension ministry training, a training designed for established ministers. Soon after, the Department of Ministry offered to help pay my expenses to General Assembly.

I was invited to participate in a panel at GA while a first year seminarian and have been a presenter every year since.

I was asked to serve on the Latino UU Networking Association steering committee. Last summer I was asked to serve on the executive committee of the UU Ministers Association. And I have just begun a term as our district's trustee on the UUA Board. And I haven't even reached final fellowship. Now, as much as I would like to think that I am being asked to serve because everyone thinks I am wonderful and capable and witty and charming, I know that the real reason is that I am named Morales.

The reason I am being offered all these denominational opportunities is that we are caught in an awkward bind. On the one hand, we want our boards and committees to look the way we hope our association will come to look some day. We want diversity. But when it comes to having members who are "minorities" or "people of color" (neither term is perfect), we have so few that we have to ask the same people to serve over and over. The sad truth, which we must face honestly, is that our efforts in Anti-Anti-M have been tragically disappointing. We have about as many "minority" ministers now as we did a generation ago. During that same period, women have gone from a small fraction of our ministry to occupying more than half our pulpits. In the last 20 years, gay and lesbian people have made enormous strides in our ministry. Why is this? Why are we stymied? Why can we make radical changes in our openness to leaders who are women or gay or lesbian or transgendered, and yet we get almost nowhere with racial and ethnic minorities? What are we doing wrong? What do we need to change?

First, I believe we are coming face to face with the reality that racism is deep, pervasive, and toxic in our culture; it traps us all. To be white is to be in a position of power and privilege, whether white people seek that or not. This inequality poisons relationships. Racism, especially as directed against African Americans, is a fundamental injustice we need to confront wherever we see it.

And yet I have come to believe that to focus on skin-color racism is too limiting. As terrible as it is, the real problem is even more difficult. The problem includes issues of social class and culture that may be more difficult to face than issues of race.

For example, let's think about the amazing strides we have made in including women and gender minorities in our ministry. Why was that so much easier? I believe it is because these people were already part of our culture and our social class. They are our partners, children, coworkers, friends. We have been able to transcend race and ethnicity only when the minister is comfortable in white, middle-class, educated, professional culture.

Part of our journey is to broaden our vision beyond race relations between whites and blacks. As important as that issue is, it is too limiting. We need to look at issues of class and culture as well. For example, the language of race utterly fails to capture the experience of Latinos. Our issues have more to do with culture and language than with race. When I grew up in San Antonio, Latinos did not call Euro-Americans "whites." We called them "Anglos." For us, the differences were cultural and economic, not racial. Similarly, I believe we need to think of Anti-Anti-M as much more than an issue of justice. Again, I do not mean to diminish the horrible injustices that are all around us. As a religious community, as religious people, we must combat injustice.

And yet, we must have a vision that is more than "anti." We have to stand together for something. We need to go beyond justice to create a community where we view our differences as gifts, as opportunities for personal and spiritual growth. There is a critical spiritual issue at stake here. Our differences are ways of exploring what it means to be human. Diversity—whether theological, ethnic, cultural, or racial—is an opportunity to learn and grow.

The tragedy—and it really is a tragedy—is that there are tens of thousands of Latinos, African-Americans, Asians, and, increasingly, people who come from mixed ethnic and racial backgrounds, who are UUs but do not yet know it. They are isolated, religiously homeless people. These are people who are living in two cultures, often feeling as if they belong to neither. They need the kind of community we provide; and we need them. They are the natural cultural and religious bridges to our more diverse future. But we do not reach these people. Why don't we? Because we don't get to know them. Because, like me, they become invisible. And, especially, we never invite them to church. I am a recent UU, but I would have been a UU 20 or 25 years ago if someone had invited me and welcomed my family.

My dream for Unitarian Universalism is that we confess that we do not have all the answers. We need to admit that this is hard work, that Anti-Anti-M is as rigorous a spiritual discipline as we will encounter. I dream that we will begin a conversation, a deep spiritual dialogue, about how we can learn to be open to each other and, especially, to work together to create a community and a culture that celebrates all that it means to be human.

We not only have gifts to give each other, we are gifts to each other. We must not forget that.

Our journey toward wholeness has just begun. We are not sure of the way. We have often lost our way in the past, believing our destination was in sight and easily reached. We were a bit arrogant and a bit naive. We are wiser now. We know we will not get there soon. And we know we need to walk together and walk humbly.

Come. Let's us make that journey together. One step at a time; paso por paso. Hand in hand; mano en mano. Come. Leave no one behind. Together, we can make this journey. Come.

CHAPTER 22

Transformation Committee Responds

The Journey Toward Wholeness Transformation Committee, charged with holding the Association's anti-racism vision, faced many changes as the Sinkford administration began to define its approach.

At its spring 2002 meeting, the Committee adopted a new structure designed to make its membership racially diverse; encompass bisexual, gay, lesbian, and transgender people; and have class diversity as well as familiarity with accessibility issues. It also set out to give voice to the people in the congregations and to encourage regional gatherings. Under the leadership of Rev. James Hobart, the Transformation Committee also explored these major topics:

- Linking anti-racism efforts with the work of groups such as the UUA Accessibilities Committee and the Office of Bisexual, Gay, Lesbian and Transgender Concerns.
- The idea of a congregational certification process similar to that used to address BGLT concerns through the "Welcoming Congregation" program.
- To whom it was responsible and accountable.
- Ways the Committee could be more accountable to ministers of color and Latina/o/Hispanic ministers by focusing more on what happens during their preparation for the ministry, early years of ministry, and the special challenges they encounter as settled ministers.
- Concerns about the status of the fundamental Journey Toward Wholeness anti-racism trainings, Jubilee I and Jubilee II,

and resources available to support anti-racism training and innovations.
- The process for ensuring anti-oppression training for the Association's new Board and key Committee members.

The spring meeting minutes also noted, "DRUUMM [Diverse and Revolutionary Unitarian Universalist Ministries] and Youth and Young Adults are so far ahead of the rest of us, there's a lag."

By fall, concerns that had been bubbling now began to boil as the Transformation Committee became more uneasy about the new administration's direction. The minutes state,

[Rev. William Sinkford, the Association's president] described optimistic signs that anti-oppressive and anti-racism work will be embedded throughout UUA staff work, noting that Ministry and Professional Leadership is taking more ownership around the work with ministers of color and Latina/o and Hispanic ministers. He also emphasized the need to make the work more concrete, and to draw on the experiences of congregations across the broad UU community and to share it, which is an opportunity that "Finding Common Ground" gatherings present.

Bill noted the negative energy generated by the "Crossroads-derived training," and the need to find ways to make people who had shut down and felt shut out engage in anti-racism work. The decision to "take a year to imagine different ways to move forward" had been interpreted as a retreat from the anti-racism agenda. His intention was to "find some better ways to make more people available to the work. . . ."

On New Congregation Growth Strategies, Bill said that the wish for UU congregations to grow in diversity was included in the growth effort, but there is a question about whether "we're healthy enough to take this on as an objective." He acknowledged Unitarian Universalism's failure to be inviting to people "not like us," and said that our congregations need to prove that they can replicate themselves

CONGREGATIONAL STORY

Unitarian Society of Ridgewood, New Jersey

A number of congregations struggled to define their approach to anti-racism work. The following represents one congregation's approach.

Our Anti-Racism Statement

Whereas, The Unitarian Society of Ridgewood's Statement of Purpose asserts that we are a caring, religious community, welcoming and respecting diversity and working for social justice at home and in the world; and

Whereas, our membership is open without regard to creed, faith, national origin, race, color, gender, sexual orientation, physical challenge or other similar test; therefore be it:

Resolved, that we, the members of The Unitarian Society of Ridgewood explicitly and publicly affirm our identity as an anti-racist religious community; and

Whereas, we, the members of The Unitarian Society of Ridgewood, are guided by the Unitarian Universalist principles which affirm and promote the inherent worth and dignity of every person, with justice, equity and compassion in human relations; therefore we

Resolve that our anti-racism commitment be reflected in the life and culture of the congregation through our policies, programs and practices as we continue to learn about racism. We Further Resolve to develop and work to implement strategies that dismantle racism through our adult religious education, children's religious education, Sunday services, and community outreach and action.

Adopted May 5, 2002

DISTRICT STORY
Metro New York Efforts

The Anti-Racism and Diversity Committee of the Unitarian Universalist District of Metropolitan New York serves fifty-one congregations in southeastern New York, northern New Jersey, eastern Pennsylvania, and southwestern Connecticut. This is a statement of the Committee's approach as of February 2007.

Recognizing that each congregation is on its own unique "journey toward wholeness," the Anti-Racism and Diversity Committee (ARDC) of the Metro District works to nurture and support the broad range of diversity and anti-racism work being done within our district.

Through networking and bringing together the multitude of ideas, talents and resources that we offer each other, the ARDC works to assist our congregations in whatever ways they find most useful and empowering.

The District Board of Trustees makes the work of the ARDC possible both with its funding and encouragement.

We are a proactive programming resource—ARDC arranges guest lecturers, film series, programs for youth, Sunday speakers, discussion leaders, and other services to assist your congregation in its anti-racism work. Volunteers are available to share their expertise in evaluation, training, and program planning. No matter your point of entry to this work, no matter the question, it will be treated with the utmost concern and respect!

Examples of ARDC Programming
Anti-Racism Training Workshops—ARDC's highly-experienced workshop leaders can assist you with planning and implementing anti-racism training programs for small groups on up to large-size congregations. We can either work with you on a consulting basis or come in and run the whole program for you.

Program for Teens—"Race Realities/Youth Power!" an ARDC curriculum for middle school and high school: How are race and racism "real" for you—in your school, your neighborhood, your camp? How can you use your youth power to stand up to racism wherever you find it? Through games, talk, song, dance, drama, and a film or two, we'll take on these issues in your world! Facilitators can tailor this to your needs.

Film Forums: Project in a Box!—". . . Designed to entertain, inspire, explore and inform, [ARDC offers] film and videos that address the question of race, their collective impact profoundly anti-racist."

The Middle Passage Program—. . . "The Middle Passage" was the journey of African slaves from the coast of Africa to the Americas. It was a part of a triangle of trade and a horrific part of American history. The program consists of readings, songs and a dance, and depicts the history of the African enslavement from the villages in Africa to the slave plantations in America. "We look at this moment in history as a reality that we must acknowledge if we are to move on in our understanding and accepting of one another. This program is one step towards healing the wounds of the past in reconciliation so that we can move ahead to a meaningful future."

The leaders and designers of this program are from a group based at the Unitarian Universalist Fellowship of Huntington, NY. They have studied the subject in depth and have given numerous workshops and lectures. This program has been presented at the following UU churches: at Bellport, Water Mill, Shelter Rock, Muttontown, Freeport, and Huntington on Long Island; and at Morristown, Plainfield, and Englewood in New Jersey. The program has also been given in a number of public libraries.

CONGREGATIONAL STORY

First UU Church of Nashville, Tennessee

InterConnections *published the following article in March 2002:*

First UU Church of Nashville, TN (383 members), is part of a community group, Tying Nashville Together, which explores racial discrimination and holds rallies to lobby elected officials.

The congregation also sponsors an annual human rights lecture and holds a joint service with an African-American Baptist congregation. Director of Religious Education Emily Green organized Camp Neighborhood last summer, bringing together for five days children from the congregation and from a racially diverse elementary school.

The congregation is also involved in "Diversity in Dialogue" groups—small racially diverse groups that discuss racism. "Our members feel good about the anti-racism work we do," says Carleen Dowell, board chair. "Many haven't had sustained interactions with people of color before."

before they take on becoming more diverse. He admitted his conflict about this but also said that JTW is not absent from the UUA's plans for growth.

In the face of all this change, the Transformation Committee found itself again discussing what its role should be. Underlining the magnitude of change was heavy criticism of some of the language of Journey Toward Wholeness anti-racism trainings as well as in need to align Transformation Committee work with Sinkford's advocacy and witness priorities of racial justice, gender justice, and economic privilege. The committee questioned, "What does this work have to do with congregations?"

Rev. Susan Suchocki Brown, a founding member of the Committee, said the lack of consensus about what it should be led to the repeated reevaluation of its role. "One of my biggest frustrations was that the Journey Toward Wholeness got merged into being an educational effort," she said, adding that this prevented a more activist role. "It is a function of our Unitarian Universalism that we can educate ourselves away on anything."

Transformation Committee's Five-Year Plan

In 2003, the Transformation Committee began implementing a new five-year plan for anti-racism efforts across the Association. The members began by assessing the Association's anti-racism work, finding far more signs they perceived as negative than positive ones, including:

- Lack of diversity on the UUA staff;
- Dearth of people of color, people with disabilities, bisexual-gay-lesbian-transgender people on emerging staff;
- The integration of anti-oppression/anti-racism work into a number of staff groups rather than in a separate department;
- A lack of financial resources to support anti-racism efforts;
- A shortage of training for UUA volunteer leadership;
- The failure to reflect back and learn from mistakes;
- That people of color were overtaxed;
- A general gap in communication.

As for signs of progress, they saw only a few: use of anti-oppression criteria in the Association's staff performance evaluations, the emergence of the Asian/Pacific Islander Caucus of DRUUMM, and the Lifespan Faith Development staff group's incorporation of anti-oppression concepts into religious education curricula.

Three broad strategies for the plan emerged, including creating a covenantal statement of relationships with stakeholders (those who had an interest or "stake" in the areas where change was sought), recognizing congregations as stakeholders, and training the Transformation Committee in internal organizing, noting, "The community we are organizing is not an oppressed community, and it does not see itself as a collective, so we have to create an identity." The Committee focused heavily on congregations as stakeholders, in that it had no clear channel to communicate with them. The spring meeting minutes observed, "The JTWTC is supposed to be in relation to the delegates from the congregations at GA, but there is a tension there that needs to be worked with, as well as a resource. JTWTC needs to look at how districts can take responsibility for stakeholder analysis of congregations. Transformation Teams provide this function."

Other Committee Concerns

The Committee discussed new momentum growing in key groups such as the UUA Board of Trustees in January 2003, based on an institutional racism audit the Committee conducted. The Board was talking a great deal through the "anti-racism lens" and had participated in a conversation on who matters and who is marginalized with Paula Cole Jones, president elect of Diverse and Revolutionary UU Multicultural Ministries (DRUUMM).

At its spring meeting, the Transformation Committee had a frank discussion of some of the issues current members felt had hampered anti-racism progress. These included unclear boundaries in that some UUA staff members also served as members of the Committee and in sometimes competitive roles with the staff Core Team.

The Committee also returned to the discussion of its role, both at the March and November meetings, concluding that the "JTWTC

CONGREGATIONAL STORY

UU Church of Cheyenne, Wyoming

Interconnections, *the UUA newsletter for congregational leaders, published the following article in March 2002.*

When the UU Church of Cheyenne, WY (127 members), teamed with an African-American women's group to develop an anti-racism education program and offered it to public school teachers for Black History Month a year ago, it expected a modest response.

Instead, requests flooded in. The same thing happened this February. Each year about 1,200 third- through sixth-graders were bused to the church for two hours of black history, music, and art. The project is one example of anti-racism projects undertaken by UU congregations as part of the Journey Toward Wholeness program through the UUA Department of Faith in Action.

The Cheyenne congregation's anti-racism interest developed in 1999 after

First Unitarian Church of Denver sponsored a free anti-racism workshop for UU congregations and Cheyenne's new anti-racism team attended. Fired up by the workshop, the team joined with the black women's group Love and Charity and organized a community celebration and the school program. The program includes videos about prejudice and the Civil Rights era, Martin Luther King Jr.'s "I Have a Dream" speech, Buffalo Soldier reenactors, African-American inventors, African folk tales, spirituals as freedom songs, and quilts as "freedom maps."

Accompanying the week-long educational program has been a Friday night gospel extravaganza and a Saturday music and history celebration, plus a soul food taster. The program cost, excluding volunteer hours, has been $1,000 to $2,000, mostly for copying resources for teachers and students, feeding volunteers, food for the taster, and hiring an African dance group. About half the money has come from the Wyoming Arts Council.

charge is to monitor, assess, report, and reflect to the General Assembly—not to train, give talks, lead workshops, etc. It is not the committee's role to be the manipulators of the system." Members also noted that a "distinction should be made between what exactly is being monitored and assessed: the UUA or congregations?" The observation was made that the work had to reach the congregational level.

At the November meeting, Taquiena Boston, director of the UUA's Identity-Based Ministries staff group and former Faith in Action Department associate, reported a new UUA initiative called the Anti-Racist Multicultural Welcoming Congregation that had emerged from the recommendations of congregational representatives at the Finding Common Ground gatherings. The idea was to have a race and ethnicity curriculum similar to Welcoming Congregation, the program for congregations to prepare themselves to make bisexual/gay/lesbian and transgender people feel at home.

A Transformation Committee youth presence was also discussed. Jazmin Sandoz said, "Youth feel it's very important to have a youth representative on the JTWTC and want to bring themselves to different tables to be listened to. . . . This generation is really cool. They're going to change a lot. . . . Let us come to the table."

Rev. Charles Ortman, a Committee member, asked Sinkford about his larger frustrations. Sinkford listed the difficulty in finding settlements for male African-American ministers, the lack of information about what congregations are doing, and the challenges of being the first African-American president and trying to stay in touch with the communities of color.

Sinkford also said that, in his opinion, the Transformation Committee's two primary tasks were to be in relationship with congregations as they engaged in anti-racism and anti-oppression work, and to create a community of learning for the various continental committees.

In a parallel development, the Canadian Unitarian Council, which was emerging as a body independent of the UUA, passed its own statement on racism in May 2003.

CONGREGATIONAL STORY
First UU Church of San Diego, California

This account is offered by Tony Brumfield, a lay leader at First Unitarian Universalist Church of San Diego and head of its DRUUMM group, the only such congregational-level organization.

I will never forget when at the beginning of a Jubilee I workshop, Rev. Kurt Kuhwald asked us why the problem of race and racism won't go away. He said it's because racism is about power. This has certainly been true at First Unitarian Universalist Church of San Diego. Our ministers for 24 years, Rev. Drs. Carolyn and Tom Owen-Towle, started the most recent movement at our church but the power transformation didn't begin until their retirement three years ago. It was in the power vacuum following their retirement that the local Journey Toward Wholeness and DRUUMM [Diverse and Revolutionary Unitarian Universalist Ministries] group at our church flexed its muscle in insisting that 1) a person of color be on the search committee, 2) that the search committee participate in an anti-racism training, and 3) that we develop together interview questions to help us discern where ministerial candidates were regarding oppression issues and their commitment to developing an accountable relationship with the anti-racism community at our church and within Unitarian Universalism.

A congregation transforming into an anti-racist institution requires the support and commitment of its ministers. First Church of San Diego has had that in Revs. Carolyn and Tom Owen Towle, and now in its new lead minister, Rev. Dr. Arvid Straube, and assistant minister, Rev. Julie Kain. . . .

The search survey . . . has been very revealing. Many members desire a congregation that is more diverse and at the same time don't believe that identity, such as race, should be a factor in selecting a minister. They see a person's age, sex, and race as being neutral factors, like being left handed, that have nothing to do with one's life experience, world view, or qualifications as a minister.

Like many Unitarian Universalist People of Color, I am from a multiracial family and have spent much of my life living in mostly-White neighborhoods. My father's family is a White family from the Deep South, and my mother's family is a Mexican family from Los Angeles. I was working as an electrical engineer at General Dynamics when I encountered Unitarian Universalism. Working at General Dynamics was difficult for me. Most of the people there revered President Reagan and I despised him. To address my social isolation, I sought the assistance of a counselor who recommended that I seek a peer group that felt as passionate as I did about social and environmental issues. She suggested that I check out the First Unitarian Universalist Church of San Diego. . . .

[Church members] Tomas Firle and Joan Cudhea started a Journey Toward Wholeness group at our church, which I joined. Joan, Tomas, Jan Gallo, and I have been the core members of this group for the last six years. At a district "skills" conference, I was approached by Ruth Alatorre who asked if I'd be interested in sitting with her and other People of Color for lunch. She and Robette Dias invited me to a DRUUMM conference in Santa Cruz. I drove up to Santa Cruz that spring in 2000 where I met Joseph Lyons, a UU young adult and Person of Color organizer from Portland. They convinced me to organize a regional DRUUMM conference in Southern California which I did. Forty UU People of Color from all over California attended. The following year, I organized, with Jan Carpenter Tucker, a DRUUMM group at our church in San Diego.

Annie Abernethy, one of the youth from my church who was involved in YRUU at the national level, invited me to serve as an adult advisor at Youth Council, the annual gathering of youth delegates from every district in the United States and Canada. For our youth, anti-racism workshops are not a side attraction. Anti-racism work is central to everything that they do. They are much further along than the adult UU community and have much to teach us. They taught me much about institutionalizing anti-racism, lessons which I have taken back to my congregation.

This last year, we have developed White Ally support groups so that White members of this church who are working with DRUUMM and JTW to transform this church can, in a safe environment, struggle with what it means to be White, learn the history of racism in this country, and learn how they personally have benefited and been hurt by racism.

First Church of San Diego is part of a coalition of urban churches in San Diego called the San Diego Organizing Project (SDOP). SDOP is part of a larger organization, Pacific Institute for Community Organizing (PICO). Through PICO and SDOP, our church is acting with other churches, mostly churches of color, to address the high cost of housing in San Diego and the high cost of health insurance. With our Peace and Democracy Task Force, we are a powerful presence in the anti-war movement and other justice causes in San Diego. We are part of a coalition that provides temporary housing and food for homeless people in San Diego. Recently, our Clean Elections Campaign is organizing to reform election law in San Diego and California.

My congregation in San Diego hosted the first DRUUMM leadership development conference for UU young adults of color. It is this collaborative spirit that binds together and benefits our People of Color community, our youth and young adult communities, and our congregations.

CHAPTER 23

General Assemblies

Events at the General Assemblies in 2002 and 2003 kept the idea of being intentionally anti-racist on the table. One plenary session incident also raised the need for clearer expectations of groups that would be presenting priorities before the assembled representatives of Unitarian Universalist congregations.

Janice Marie Johnson, then president of DRUUMM (Diverse and Revolutionary Unitarian Universalist Ministries), noted that people of color and those of European descent had different experiences of the incidents. "People of color are a part of the public General Assembly, and then we have our own private GA," she said. "It's pretty difficult reconciling the two. Most people of color steel themselves prior to going to any major UU gathering. In addition to all of the work that everyone has on their own respective plates, persons of color have the added pressure of issues around race that in some fashion invariably show up. When do the realities within the people of color communities become real, or shall I say 'believable,' 'acceptable,' and 'undeniable' for the white community?"

The incidents focused attention on the idea that people needed to be accountable to those who have been historically marginalized. The increased opportunities for people to come together in identity groups was an important part of this discussion because group positions carry more weight than the position of one individual person from an historically oppressed group.

During this period the purposes of General Assembly became a topic of discussion. At a meeting of the General Assembly Planning Committee, UUA president William Sinkford noted,

General Assembly is seen as a free-standing event. There have been few attempts at coordinating the work of the UUA with that of the GA. This gets reflected in how we budget for GA (a set aside, self-paying operation). The budget is never reviewed by the Association. There's a lot of parallel play—play, but parallel. . . . We've never had a conversation about where GA stands in relation to the other programmatic areas of the Association.

2002 General Assembly in Quebec City

An incident during presentation of a report in skit form by members of the Commission on Appraisal attracted a lot of heat. The Commission is elected by the General Assembly delegates and charged with reviewing "any function or activity of the Association which in its judgment will benefit from an independent review and report its conclusions to a regular General Assembly." Here is the incident as described in the *UU World*:

> Delegates packed a Friday-afternoon workshop to respond to the Commission's provocative topic, "Where is the unity in our diversity?"
>
> But as the commissioners were introducing their new topic in a brief skit at Friday's plenary session, they inadvertently dramatized an old conflict that quickly moved to the top of the Commission's agenda. Here is what the delegates saw: The chair of the Commission, Dr. Janis Sabin Elliot of Portland, Oregon, introduced the Commission and described its mandate. She then turned the podium over to Janice Marie Johnson, director of religious education at the Community Church of New York City. Johnson, who is a young black Caribbean woman, spoke about the Commission's last report. The large video screens to the left and right of the stage were showing a close-up of her face—she had just started to say, "And members of the Commission are available for autographs"—when Mark Hamilton, a tall young white man from Toronto, broke in. "Moving on to

our next topic," he said, and nudged Johnson away from the microphone.

The next day, Moderator [Diane] Olson opened the plenary session by telling delegates that a number of people of color had been alarmed by the sight of a white man pushing a black woman. She invited people with concerns to meet with the members of the Commission on Sunday evening. At least thirty people attended. Several said that the incident was one in an ongoing series of offenses that diminish the experience of people of color in the Association. Robette Dias of Sonoma, California, told the Commission: "What I experienced was a woman of color being pushed aside."

Janice Johnson responded that she had raised a concern about the skit's original script, in which the Rev. Earl Holt, minister of King's Chapel in Boston, would have been the interrupted speaker. "My comment to Janis [Eliot] was, 'Are you aware that a commissioner of color is not speaking?'" Eliot asked Johnson to take the role; Johnson agreed, but said she was uncomfortable because it depended on hamming up a punch line. "What I saw on paper was an interruption, but what I experienced was a push," she said. "Mark [Hamilton] is one of my closest friends. But I felt it, and I was taken aback."

Many, including the Youth Caucus, voiced concern. Though acknowledging the good intentions of the Commission participants, Rev. Hope Johnson said, "They didn't just brush it aside. The youth stepped up and said what they saw. . . . The world saw what it saw and we had to affirm that it was not okay." Responding to a request for a point of personal privilege from the floor of the plenary session on Monday, the Assembly's last day, the moderator recognized Rev. Susan Suchocki Brown, of the Journey Toward Wholeness Transformation Committee, and Paula Cole Jones, president-elect of DRUUMM. The women presented this statement:

[Rev.] Susan Suchocki Brown: The purpose of the Journey Toward Wholeness Transformation Committee is to monitor, access, coordinate, and guide the Association in its anti-oppression, anti-racism, multicultural work and DRUUMM is the community of color in the UUA to which we hold ourselves accountable. We come together to model a true relationship of accountability.

A significant number of persons present are concerned and feel the issue of the Commission on Appraisal (COA) is still unresolved and not a good way to end the General Assembly (GA). So we have been asked to come to you opening up the deeper and unresolved issues not presently being offered to the GA attendees. We find it regrettable that the COA was not able or willing to make a joint statement, but that a member of the COA had to speak as an individual.

Paula Cole Jones: My name is Paula Cole Jones and I am the president-elect of DRUUMM. DRUUMM is organized to support People of Color in our movement and to help the Association understand what it means to be in right relationship with People of Color. As Dr. Leon Spencer said yesterday in the meeting with the Commission on Appraisal, "For People of Color, just being present is no longer enough."

The situation that brings us here is not a private or a personal issue; it is a community issue. Usually we do not hear the community response when a situation leaves someone feeling slighted or devalued. This time we did. In order to establish right relationship, we have to be able to trust that our concerns are being valued and that corrections, when needed, are possible.

We are working to build a community where People of Color feel welcome and where People of Color are involved in our congregations, and in the business of the UUA. We are working to create an environment where People of Color feel comfortable and supported in leadership positions. The messages that we receive let us know where the Association is on the journey and when parts of the institution need to be held accountable for making corrections that give us another chance at right relationship.

Susan Suchocki Brown: Transparency is crucial and critical and privacy is not the issue. And, those of us who witnessed the interchange are being forced into a conspiracy of silence, which we will not do. Accountability to and with members of the COA and to and with the GA requires transparency and a willingness to be transformed by experiences that offer opportunities however difficult for learning and changing.

When any member of our community is broken, discounted, or marginalized we are all broken. We need to model ways to own our mistakes and be transformed and open to change and to stay at the table even when things are difficult.

Paula Cole Jones: Just as we have discovered that covenanting is often the missing piece that keeps people at the table when things get difficult, accountability is the missing piece that brings us back to the community and working to make right relationships.

Susan Suchocki Brown: The COA is elected by GA and there exists a mandate to become an anti-racist, anti-oppressive, multicultural faith community. We must find ways to join together in the struggle.

Therefore we believe that the COA needs to enter into a serious process of accountability and develop a relationship with the Transformation Committee and DRUUMM in order to establish right relationship and be a model to all in demonstrating a commitment to transformation and transparency based on an initiative passed at a GA just like this one in 1997.

This was a very challenging time for those engaged in anti-racism efforts. Suchocki Brown recalled,

Through all the interactions that I had, I have changed in many ways. Specifically with the outcomes I briefly noted, I learned how to stay engaged even when the conversations were hard, hurtful or challenging. I learned not to take things personally but to function from an inner spiritual integrity based on my growing and changing anti-oppression lens, and from personal learning of my own identity development as an Anglo female who wants to be an ally [of people of color]. I learned that ambiguity is not a negative, that disagreements were not about me, but about values and fears and anxieties and hopes.

Rev. Manish Mishra, who joined the Commission on Appraisal as a seminarian the year after the incident in 2003, observed that the incident led the Commission to new commitments:

I think there was an awareness that the Commission fell short in 2002, and some of it was lack of adequate preparation, lack of adequate perspective, stepping back far enough from the plan to see how it would be perceived by the people who were slated to be doing it and all that. I mean there were just layers of not examining it deeply enough, thoughtfully enough. And again, that tends to happen in our denomination: very well-intentioned, good-hearted people who just didn't take the thinking and the logic, perhaps, as far as they needed to. That tends, in my experience, to be a common theme when our denomination has run into difficulties that have racial and cultural implications; invariably it is well-intentioned, good-hearted people who just haven't taken their analysis far enough. So that was the case then with the Commission, and coming out of that I have certainly seen greater intentionality. The Commission subsequently established an anti-racist, anti-oppressive process observer for every meeting. That was new, and that was a result of this 2002 GA.

The skit incident also re-engaged the UUA Board of Trustees. "We had folks on the Board who didn't think this was a serious problem," UUA Moderator Gini Courter, then a Board member, remembered. "Quebec City was a wake-up call." She said that the Board's discussion of the 2002 General Assembly skit rekindled its interest in anti-racism, which it had been moving away from because of concerns about the UUA trainings and how people responded to them.

After the incident with the Commission on Appraisal skit in Quebec City, the Board began to question how to equip all key leaders on the Associational committees with the skills to address issues around race and ethnicity that seemed to keep coming up. "It became crystal clear that something had to be done," said Sinkford. After several iterations of building a common language around race, the Board was ready to lead the way for other committees. "The Board put a stake in the ground," said Gini Courter, the Association's moderator. She said that the Board began to look at anti-racism awareness as a necessary skill for Associational leadership. "We don't let anyone off the hook. . . . We felt we shouldn't put anyone on any committee who hasn't had anti-racism education. We expect you to show you have some level of commitment."

The seriousness with which the Board took the incident was illustrated by a report by Rev. Tracey Robinson-Harris, director of the Congregational Services Staff Group:

> Issues arising out of the Commission on Appraisal report to the General Assembly in 2002 led the Board to pass a motion at its post-GA meeting that year in support of anti-racism, anti-oppression training for members of committees elected by the General Assembly. The motion read in part:
>
> Therefore, the Board of Trustees recommends that all members of committees elected by the General Assembly engage in anti-racism and anti-oppression training/consultation, developed in conversation with the Journey Toward Wholeness Transformation Committee.
>
> We request the administration to allocate resources to this effort, so that the elected leadership of the Association can be assisted in acquiring the skills and capacity necessary to be in right relationship with all of their constituencies. During the summer and early fall, support and follow up with the Commission on Appraisal led to a training/consultation with the Commission facilitated by [Revs.] Rosemary Bray McNatt and [Charles] Ortman in November 2002.

For several years prior to 2002, an annual training, focusing on a power analysis of racism, was held in November. Newly elected and appointed leaders were encouraged to attend. While providing individuals with an opportunity to explore and learn more, it was usually the case that any given leadership group was represented by only some of its members. Any effort, then, to focus on practices, culture, roles, mission of the leadership group as a whole suffered as a result. Furthermore, the mix of groups represented in any one training and their varying needs and expectations were often more than that one event could hold. Successfully institutionalizing anti-racism and anti oppression means finding ways to work with and support elected/appointed leader groups as groups. Having decided to make changes in our approach, we opted not to offer the annual training in November 2002 with the understanding that we would develop other leader training opportunities.

The 2002 General Assembly nearly included identity group caucusing, based on a report by Rev. Joshua Pawelek, an anti-racism trainer, which made this recommendation. That the Planning Committee would consider such a use of General Assembly resources was significant. The minutes from the January 2002 General Assembly Planning Committee report,

> Identity group caucusing differs from affinity groups in that in identity group caucusing separate groups related to one identity meet separately and discuss similar issues. The separate identity group discussions are followed by a whole group discussion in which separate discussions are shared and ways to change oppressive systems are brainstormed. For example, during racial identity group caucusing, People of Color (or separate groups, as people feel necessary), Whites, and multi-ethnic individuals would meet in separate groups to discuss their experiences within this society, and within the UU denomination. At a later point these groups would meet together and summarize, as they feel comfortable, what they

discussed and what changes individuals and the UU denomination, in general, can and need to make the church a multicultural, egalitarian community. In considering doing Identity Group Caucusing, the Planning Committee is bringing up issues that set an agenda for the denomination.

They were excited about the promise of caucusing—and wary that it be introduced in a way which would be best received. Trying it first in Boston [in 2003] seemed the best bet, as did partnering with the Faith in Action Department and the Journey Toward Wholeness in order to spread this approach. Also, it would be sensible to contact people within different affiliated organizations, such as Interweave [Unitarian Universalists for Lesbian, Gay, Bisexual, and Transgender Concerns], the Unitarian Universalist Women's Federation, and DRUUMM.

2003 General Assembly in Boston

As always, the 2003 General Assembly had many layers. For people of color, the gathering began with another painful incident, described by Joseph Santos-Lyons, then a seminarian: "[S]everal People of Color reported being asked by White GA attendees to take their bags. This happened at the curb where People of Color were spending time talking when White attendees arrived, as well as by the Front Desk and Concierge." This set a tone for the conversations within the community that continued throughout the gathering.

A new group's voice was reflected in the programming. The Asian Pacific Islander UU Caucus of DRUUMM presented its first session with sponsorship from the General Assembly Planning Committee and the Identity-Based Ministries Staff Group. More than three hundred people heard a presentation by Frank Wu, a law professor at Howard University, author of *Yellow: Race in America Beyond Black and White*, and a member of All Souls Unitarian Universalist Church in Washington, D.C. General Assembly reporter Kok-Heong McNaughton summarized it thus:

Whether we acknowledge it or not, race is one of the lenses through which we see the world. Why should we care about race? Why talk about race? Why write about race? By caring, talking, and writing about issues of race, we open up and continue to engage in dialogue to overcome institutionalized racism, some of which is subtle but insidious.

Extremists who commit hate crimes against racial minorities create sensational headlines. People think that if we can get rid of these extremists, we can get rid of racism. But they are not the villains. Stereotyping and generalizing are some of the innocent-looking villains that propagate racism. By assuming that all Chinese American children are wiz-kids and techno-geniuses, we limit their potential to be something else. By assuming that the young black man walking towards you at night is a dangerous thug so that you cross the street to avoid him, you give him the subtle message that he is not to be trusted and without your intending it or knowing it, he is driven to join those who would accept him, most likely a neighborhood gang. He becomes what he is expected to become.

Like democracy, said Wu, anti-racism work is a continuous journey—a march without a destination. The value of the march is in the walking. It is not something that is done once and for all, and never again. One doesn't vote once and forever never need to vote again. The work continues as we continually raise the bar. Fifty to a hundred years ago, racism was blatant. What was considered innocent fun then is outrageous by today's standard. What will today's innocent fun look like fifty years from now? What would our nation's face look like fifty years from now? Wu's dream is for the U.S. to cease to have a single identifiable racial majority, and for everyone to be judged not by appearance, but by character.

McNatt, after giving the Murry Lecture at General Assembly in 2003, was asked about the parallels between Unitarian Universalist anti-racism struggles and the struggles we have as a religious body informed with many theological perspectives. The dialogue was recorded thus:

What do you propose to do to "get out of the wilderness?"
—Many times you don't, replied McNatt, but instead you try to be as religious as possible while you head through the wilderness.

How can we become living, breathing embodiments of divinity when some of us deny the existence of divinity itself?
—That is a question that needs to be held among the people who are undergoing the journey.

Should we be considering a multi-sided conversation about theism, atheism, etc., as we did with racism?
—Most definitely, answered McNatt. I would love to see us evolve an open non-confrontational discussion of this.

McNatt continued by pointing out that those of us who care have a responsibility to take on a position of discussion and action, and not just whine. For example, we don't meet people where they are on anti-racism; it's hard to do and we think they should be farther along so we torture them, and they leave the conversation.

Yet, said McNatt, congregations can become communities of moral discernment, moving along by meeting people where they are, and not forcing them on the journey. . . . This is the way that we, as Unitarian Universalists, can work to change the world, and increase our place in the public realm.

Also at that General Assembly, Young Kim finished his term on the UUA Nominating Committee. As he made his final report before the plenary, he shared his assessment of where the Association was as far as diversity:

I'd like to talk to you again about diversity and how we do diversity as a religious movement.

We say we like diversity. This morning I picked three UU church web sites at random and looked at their mission statements. A 560-member church on the East Coast says that they are "committed to the value of diversity." A 273-member fellowship in the Southeast commits to offering a "diverse, welcoming, and accepting community." A 170-member church in the Southwest proclaims that it is "a compassionate liberal religious community that welcomes diversity."

And so I ask you: What is diversity? Is it allowing yourself to sit next to someone that voted for Ralph Nader five years ago? Or is it sitting down with that Republican you know at work, and trying to find some common ground like decent schools, taking care of our aging parents, and raising happy children? We say we espouse diversity, and yet we Unitarian Universalists still invite to dinner the kinds of people that look like us, talk like us, walk like us, spend money like us, and vote like us. That is not a journey toward wholeness. It's a journey to not fulfilling our promise.

One way to jumpstart diversity is to have leadership that reflects the diversity that we wish for our Association. But I ask you, when you go home to your districts and congregations and think about leadership, please don't do what I've seen happen over and over. A Nominating Committee creates a slate for their church; they stand back and look at their slate and—oh my gosh—all the nominees are European American, hetero, between fifty and fifty-five years old, and hold graduate degrees. The Committee then makes panicky eleventh-hour phone calls to other people to diversify their nomination slate. That's not the way to do it. This is cheap diversity. Do your homework. Reach out to people that don't necessarily look like you or talk like you.

My second thought on diversity is this: be very careful who you put forward into leadership positions. When Jackie Robinson broke the color barrier in professional baseball in 1946, he was not the most talented African-American baseball player of his generation. There were others that were more talented. Jackie Robinson succeeded in breaking the color barrier because he had the thickest skin. He had the strength to withstand the abuse, the racial insults. If he had retaliated, if he'd gone into the stands to confront some of his hecklers, he would have set baseball back thirty years.

And while the situations today are not as overtly violent, you can bet that in the not too distant future, when we elect the first female president of the UUA, she will come under an unprecedented level of scrutiny. The naysayers will be there to watch for her first mistake. Please. Choose your trailblazers carefully.

That other voices were entering the dialogue was clear. Mishra, a seminarian at the time, recalled,

The Boston General Assembly was the best General Assembly I've ever attended, and part of the reason for this was the in-depth, honest, and meaningful dialogue on racial diversity. I'd like to share some important snap-shots of this from a panel on which I participated.

I served on a panel, alongside Bill Sinkford and other prominent UUs of color, where we were asked to address racial diversity in the UU movement beyond the already clearly defined discourse between the white and African-American communities. Bill talked about how, as our first African-American president, he at times struggles with other people's projections onto him of what it means to be African American. Frequently "white guilt" over slavery and segregation characterizes the projections that African Americans must deal with and address.

I responded to Bill's comments by further elaborating that Asian-American UUs face similar but different projections. We Asian UUs have to deal with the projection of "permanent otherness." Even if we were born and raised in the United States we continue to be viewed as "other," as somehow permanently foreign. This reality comes to life most readily in the oft asked question, "Where are you from?" Professor Frank Wu, from Howard University, who also served on this panel, noted that his answer of "Cleveland," frequently doesn't satisfy people. His answer is frequently responded to with the question, "No, where are you *really* from?" I similarly had to deal with such attitudes while I was in the U.S. Foreign Service—white American colleagues at times questioned my loyalty to our country and questioned how truly American I was, despite the fact that

I was born and raised here. We Asians struggle with the projection that we don't really belong, that we are permanently and immutably from some other culture, some other world, and therefore, to varying degrees, also open to suspicion and doubt.

The second projection Asians have to contend with is the exact opposite of the first in terms of its mood and tenor: we are foreign, but we're COOL because we're foreign. Asians are exoticized: we are from the lands of interesting and spicy curries, lands that spawned Hinduism and Buddhism, religions that lend to UU'ism a deep sense of connection to the natural world and offer us the spiritual practices of meditation and mindfulness. The "other" is idealized with an eye towards appropriation, and we Asian UUs become the symbol for all that is good about the East. The first projection is harmful in its negative otherizing; this second projection is harmful in its positive otherizing: its idealization at the expense of a more wholistic and realistic understanding, and the desire for ownership represented by such idealization. These are some of the projections that Asian UUs face, and we had good, initial discussions around all this at GA.

I'd like to share one final thought from [this panel discussion at General Assembly]. As the discussion closed, one audience member asked Bill Sinkford what our congregations could and should be doing in order to be more racially diverse. Bill responded that we should not reach out to minorities simply as a way of increasing the number of nonwhite faces in our congregations. Such numbers-based outreach is rooted in selfishness, a desire to make ourselves feel better about diversity. True outreach to racial minorities, he offered, needs to be grounded in a spiritual understanding of what we UUs have to offer people from other cultures and races. Our outreach should be rooted in the "good news" that we have to offer, not in a desire to feel less guilty about the whiteness of our congregations. I found Bill's words both inspiring and true.

CHAPTER 24

New Resources, New Tensions

New anti-racism leadership emerged, from youth and young adults active at the Associational level, and from new identity groups such as the Asian/Pacific Islander Caucus and the Multiracial Caucus, which came onto the scene in 2002 and 2003. These new leaders provided fresh interpretations of how to look at issues of race within Unitarian Universalism. Yet with each emerging group came the possibility of tensions with other groups.

Another important new resource was *Soul Work*, the book derived from proceedings of the 2001 Consultation on Theology and Racism convened by Rev. Dr. John Buehrens, then the Association's president, and Rev. Marjorie Bowens-Wheatley. At a time when the politics of language and relationships was exhausting many anti-racism advocates, the book provided a focus on race as a theological topic, a welcome new focus.

Youth Leadership

The youth and young adults active at the continental level were looking for an outlet for their interest and enthusiasm. The Association's anti-oppression approach did not fit with their perspective. Jyaphia Christos-Rodgers, a mentor and anti-racism trainer to youth and young adults, said their experiences with diversity in school and other settings differed from those of older adults.

The UUA provided support to allow fourteen leaders from YRUU (Young Religious Unitarian Universalists) and C*UUYAN (the Continental Unitarian Universalist Young Adult Network) to gather in June 2003 in Portland, Oregon, to discuss developing anti-racism resources to support youth. Later that month, they wrote to the UUA requesting permanent structures to support the anti-racism training needs of youth and young adults, stating,

> We have consistently heard from YRUU and C*UUYAN members that the language, symbols, processes, and content of the anti-racism trainings do not speak to their cultural and social reality. More specifically the critique has been that when filtered through the experience of 'Baby Boomer' trainers, the analysis ceases to speak to communities that were born and shaped in a Post-Civil Rights Era. The issues as we understand them are relevance of content, communication/presentation styles, and the accessibility of the training process.

Christos-Rogers said the youth and young adults were seeking a less "cerebral" model of training, one more focused on community building and capable of embracing multiple identities.

Serving as anti-racism trainers provided a sanctuary for some youth of color who were often the only non-white youth in their home congregations. Rev. Hope Johnson, who served as an advisor to youth of color, observed that by changing the structure of the youth organizations at the Association level youth of color were able to take leadership positions they might not have been offered because of the marginalization that typically occurred at the congregation level.

Jesse Jaeger, director of the UUA's Youth Office, said the youth and young adults were pioneering what it meant to do anti-racism training in an intergenerational way. "We have a different experience," he said. "We didn't go through integration; we live in a pseudo-integrated world."

By 2002–03, many of the young adults had been engaged with anti-racism for five years or more, since they were youth. Elandria Williams, a founding member of the Thomas Jefferson District Anti-Racism Transformation Team, had started in 1996 when she was sixteen. Petra Aldrich, youth representative to the UUA Board of Trustees recalled,

1999 was my first GA. I was very struck by the inclusion of race as an issue when we were talking about abortion because I was not used to thinking about issues as being linked in to one another and I remember heated conversations in youth caucus about which study action issue the youth caucus would support, whether it would be race or abortion.

The youth effort harkened back to youth leadership in other eras. "A lot of the young people are committed to the notion that it's just a matter of willpower," said Rev. Clyde Grubbs. "We can eliminate racism if we just try harder. This patience stuff that they see among the older generation, they think it's capitulation. They just want to really confront it. Because of the idea that it's a matter of focusing on it and eliminating it so we can go on and become the kind of religion we should be. I talked to Bill [Sinkford] about this last summer, and he said, 'Well, didn't we believe that in '68?' Of course, we did."

The Youth Caucus deepened its anti-racism engagement, arranging for the providers of the Challenging White Supremacy workshop, an outside vendor, to provide training at their 2003 and 2004 meetings. In 2003, the Caucus worked with C*UUYAN to propose an Anti-Racism Transformation Team for Youth Council and C*UUYAN. In the resolution that created this new entity, the Youth Council explored the path that led to this step:

Long before the 1997 GA Business Resolution, Unitarian Universalists have been working to transform the culture and institution of Unitarian Universalism into a more Anti-Racist, Anti-Oppressive, Multicultural and diverse faith. Although there have been many shared joys and successes there have also been many challenges and set-backs.

People of color, young and old, have born the burden of this work disproportionately. To the detriment of our faith and community we have lost, and are losing, many youth, young adults and adults of color. Because of an overwhelming culture of racism and tokenization our leaders of color find themselves singled out, unsupported and exhausted.

MANUAL
Youth Anti-Racism Analysis

Youth active at the Associational level continued to work to build anti-racist and anti-oppressive accountability into their organizations. The transience of their membership necessitated recurrent trainings. Unsatisfied with the other models of training that presumed experience with a Civil Rights era that was simply history to them, the youth adopted a youth-friendly approach to anti-racism, described in this manner in the Chrysalis Program Manual.

Anti-Racism trainings are small working conferences designed for youth and young adults centered on building a personal anti-racism analysis, which thus leads to anti-racist organizing. The Anti-Racism Training Program is still being developed: The first Training of Trainers/Organizers happened May 2004. . . .

Possible focuses for these workshops include:

- Building blocks to an anti-racism analysis, get to know the common language and definitions
- How to create a more anti-racist youth group or campus group
- Anti-racism for white people
- And many others

As YRUU [Young Religious Unitarian Universalists] and C*UUYAN [Continental Unitarian Universalist

Young Adult Network] are committed to becoming more anti-racist organizations it is essential that the people who are part of the organizations have access to the trainings and workshops they need in order to gain experience and knowledge to help them in this struggle. These are workshops focused on supporting anti-racist identity development. As each new YRUUer or member of C*UUYAN joins in this struggle we gain more strength to take on systems that perpetuate racism within our society. These workshops and trainings are a beginning step to challenging the systems that exist around us and that we are a part of. . . .

Youth trainers were to be selected through a committee process overseen by the Youth Office and the Office of Young Adult and Campus ministry. Trainings were designed to serve:

- Youth and young adults who want to be part of the anti-racism struggle in UUism.
- Advisors who want to learn to be supportive of this work.
- Directors of Religious Education and Ministers who want to learn to support anti-racist youth and young adult programming.
- Members of Youth Adult Committees who want to support the youth they serve in their districts.
- Anyone interested in working for racial justice.

Although Anti-Racism was identified as an association priority in 1997, many youth and young adults have felt that the Journey Toward Wholeness Anti-Racism program, which grew out of the resolution, did not address their specific oppression and life experience as young people who have grown up in a post civil rights era. A youth and young adult Anti-Racism Transformation Team will address these specific youth and young adult cultural needs.

Youth and young adults have been working together towards building an Anti-Racist community since 2001. However much of the work in the youth and young adult communities has been sporadic due to the fact that it has fallen on the shoulders of already overburdened staff.

In 2001, two years after C*UUYAN and YRUU Steering Committees made intentional commitments to Anti-Racism/Anti-Oppression education and work, a collective of leaders agreed to convene a strategic planning meeting with the C*UUYAN Steering Committee, YRUU Steering Committee, DRUUMM [Diverse and Revolutionary Unitarian Universalist Ministries], UUA, and youth-young adult leaders who have worked with C*UUYAN and YRUU communities around Anti-Racism/Anti-Oppression training and organizing. At this meeting a set of Anti-Racism initiatives was created entitled the Tampa Priorities for Anti-Racism.

In 2003, two years after the Tampa meeting, a meeting was called in Portland, OR, to review and envision the direction and development of resources for Anti-Oppression and Anti-Racism education, at the initiative of the [UUA] Youth and Young Adult and Campus Ministry Office, with direct involvement by a staff-appointed ad hoc youth-young adult team. At this meeting, the idea of a youth-young adult transformation team surfaced.

The youth and the young adult offices are constantly receiving requests for education and training from all over the continent. Youth groups are requesting Anti-Racism training focused conferences, young adults are interested in

DEFINITIONS
Youth Council Trainings

White
The term white people was created by Virginia Slave owners and colonial rulers. It replaced terms like "Christians" and "Englishmen" to distinguish European colonists from African and indigenous peoples. European colonial powers established "whites" as a legal concept after Bacon's rebellion in 1676 during which indentured servants of European and African descent had united against the colonial elite.

People of Color
People of color in the U.S. share the common experience of being targeted and oppressed by racism. Unfortunately one of the ways racism operates is to keep People of Color divided. Many people only think about their specific ethnic racial group when discussing oppression or the need to keep political power. By using the term people of color, we begin to push people to think more broadly. We need to build relationships with other groups of color: the term people of color has movement building potential.

Universalizing White Experience
When "white" is presented as standard/normal/good, people with white privilege internalize this superiority and sense of being "normal," viewing the world through that lens. Images of leadership, beauty, "average Americans" in institutions like schools, the media and popular culture; presentations of history that foreground white figures and their influence; and other ways in which whiteness is made central led to an institutionalized standard of experience. . . ."

Deracialization
Deracialization is to remove an issue from its context, treating it in a way that does not recognize the impact of racism or that reduces the propriety of directly challenging those impacts. Deracialization of an issue restricts the self-determination of the people who are most impacted by that issue to be defining their hard-won struggle. In a white supremacist society, all issues intersect with racism; the privilege to reframe an issue without understanding the impact of race is not available.

Blinded by the White
Reinforced by deracialized politics, this is a blindness of white activists to seeing and understanding resistance coming from communities of color. 500+ years of liberation struggles on this continent have been led by people of color, from colonization on through today. The backwards idea of "recruiting" people of color into "the" movement, defined as white radical struggle, ignores this historical and contemporary reality. Instead of "recruiting" people of color into majority white organizations in an attempt to "diversify," white social justice activists can focus on participating in anti-racist struggle.

Contradictory Resistance
Non-ruling class white people are caught in the intersection of experiencing privilege and also oppression, and so their resistance often expresses this contradiction: protesting that which oppresses while fighting to maintain privilege. Along racial lines, this often has maintained privilege. Along racial lines, this often has manifested as white activists sacrificing long-term strength and the goals of activists of color, in order to win short-term gains for their own agenda. The resulting dynamic has historically shattered the potential of various multiracial movements, which were making real progress toward radical social change.

These definitions are used by Anti-Racism for Global Justice, a project of the Challenging White Supremacy Workshop.

implementing Anti-Racism trainings within districts and continental leaders are looking for education and implementation skills. Although this interest is an important sign of growing awareness it also challenges all of us, especially C*UUYAN and YRUU, to meet the needs of their communities of youth and young adults in a coherent, intentional and long-term way.

In doing Anti-Racism work, we acknowledge the linked nature of oppressions. While this team will be focused on racism, this work is not done to the exclusion of other Anti-Oppression work. This is one step towards creating a holistic Anti-Oppression curriculum.

The resolution itself laid out a timeline for actions and specific steps, including the development of a system of educating and apprenticing youth and young adult anti-racism trainers.

Asian Pacific Islander UU Caucus

The emergence of a broader spectrum of groups that allowed exploration of a particular racial or ethnic identity was a key development. "These [identity group] meetings provide community and relationship building and a forum to process within safe identity groups that is not available in our larger home congregations/communities," observed Kim Varney, who was active in the Asian/Pacific Islander Caucus, part of DRUUMM. "Sharing individual life stories about being on the outside and not the mainstream in a safe group is a powerful deep and binding experience."

The first formal meeting of the network bringing together Unitarian Universalists of Asian and Pacific Islander heritage was in February of 2003 in Berkeley, California. Kok-Heong McNaughton of the Unitarian Church of Los Alamos, New Mexico, one of the founding members, wrote this account:

For the first time in our denominational history, a group of 17 Asian UUs from around the country gathered in Berkeley during the weekend of February 28 to organize, network together and develop plans for giving greater visibility and representation of Asian and Pacific Islander UUs in our faith communities.

Participants presented their stories during the Sunday morning service at the Berkeley Fellowship. Their homilies wove a tapestry of religious journeys in a service entitled "Asian Unitarian Universalist Voices & Visions."

The fledgling organization came away after an energizing and intensive weekend with a name, an acting Steering Committee of seven, an organizational structure, several programs for the 2003 General Assembly in Boston, and many action items for the next year.

Each of us brought our fears and hopes to the group. Amongst our fears are:
- I may not hear and understand everyone clearly—there is not enough time for knowing each one in depth. . . .
- This is lonely work—I may not find support from my home congregation. . . .
- People of Color, especially Asian American UUs, continue to be outsiders in our "inclusive faith." . . .
- We will not be able to forge unity. . . .
- We will find differences and divisiveness. . . .
These fears are balanced by some of our hopes:
- Asian voices will speak the truth about their lives. Their stories will be told and heard. . . .
- We will find commonality and comfort. . . .
- I hope to come away with a deeper understanding of what it means to be an Asian presence in an overwhelmingly Euro-American faith tradition. . . .
- A denomination that will welcome future generations of Asian, adoptee, and "hapa" [a term for bi-racial people originating in Hawaiian culture] children, embracing them for what they are and not regarding them as "unusual" or "different" or "exotic." . . .
- People of color will be welcome and comfortable within our congregations and denomination. . . .
- More Asian UUs in my church community, for a more diverse church community. . . .

VOICE
Young Kim

Young Kim was the convenor who brought together the initial members who decided to form the Asian Pacific-Islander Caucus of DRUUMM.

The idea for a group of Asian and Pacific Islander Unitarian Universalists began to bounce around in my head in 1993, when I was a member of the First Unitarian Church of San José (CA). At that point I received exposure to the UUA's antiracism efforts, which approached the issue from a Black/White perspective. While useful, I found this Black/White-only concentration to be frustrating, as my own experiences seemed to have a unique twist. The stereotypes that I had to deal with were different. I wasn't getting the "thug" or "terrorist" label stuck to me. What I was getting was "foreigner" or "geek" or "sweatshop laborer." I also found that many UUs seemed to believe that Asian Americans didn't experience racism.

I decided to do something about it at the 2001 General Assembly in Cleveland. I told all my friends to look for any Asian faces, get their names, and forward them to me. For my first "Asian sighting," I saw Kok Heong McNaughton riding down a hotel escalator as I was going up. I ran up the escalator, ran back down, and caught up with KokHeong outside the hotel. I blurted out: "Excuse me . . . are you a UU?" My wife ran into Mark Watanabe, who told me about a charming delegate from Oakland—Karen Eng. I also traded message board messages with Vivien Hao. Our first meeting was right at the message boards at that General Assembly. Three of us sat on some rusty folding chairs by the message boards, and talked about our experiences. I didn't know Mark and Karen very well, but I felt a strong bond right from the beginning.

Later that summer I called Robette Dias, one of the founders of DRUUMM and a UUA staffer at the time. I asked her to give me the email address for every Asian or Pacific Islander UU that she knew. Armed with about 35 new email addresses, I took a deep breath and fired off an email into the internet ether. People answered (!) and Joseph [Santos-]Lyons set up the email listserve.

Our second meeting at the General Assembly in Quebec had better attendance. Twelve UUs came, and we talked about the need for a national meeting. I requested and received grant funding from the UU Funding Program and in February of 2003 the A/PIUU Caucus met for the first time in Berkeley, CA.

- That I will find a community of people who understand where I am coming from and with whom I can be comfortably honest. I hope I can contribute something to this community and that I will benefit from the love and support. . . .
- That we can interweave our wealth of goodness to inspire each other to have a true bond of love—to strengthen us. The new organization is called Asian/Pacific Islander Caucus (A/PIC) and we voted to become an affiliate of D.R.U.U.M.M. (Diverse and Revolutionary UU Multicultural Ministries).

APIC's initial Steering Committee was Kim Varney, chair; Karen Eng; Vivien Hao; Linda Hsieh; Manish Mishra; Kok-Heong McNaughton; and Jennifer Ryu. To gather in identity groups proved powerful. "Most of the time I enter UU communities that are predominantly white," noted Kim Varney. "So when I am at a DRUUMM gathering or Asian/Pacific Islander Caucus gathering I can let my guard down and relax because I am 'home.' The personal sharing that we do in these identity based groups is deeply personal and many times the first time we can talk openly about our fears and feeling of exclusion with others that happen to be UUs too."

As a meeting ground for Asian and Pacific Islanders was being formed, tensions continued between DRUUMM and the Latina/o Unitarian Universalist Networking Association. Janice Marie Johnson, then president of DRUUMM, tells of trying to reach out to LUUNA:

It pains my heart that there are, in fact, two separate organizations. When I came into the presidency I thought long and hard about it. One of my fervent goals was to help bridge that divide. Speaking personally, I'm a member of both. Most of my family is either Jamaican or Cuban. Do you know that these two countries are only ninety miles apart? Colonial and neo-colonialism have done serious disservice to my people. It's a painful, very painful divide for me,

RESOLUTIONS
of the Youth Council

It's time we did even more for Anti-Racism in YRUU!

Sponsors: Siri Larsen, Nora Lindsey, Greg Boyd, Lehna Huie, Jova Vargas, Jennifer Bell, Laurel Newton, Rick Rhoelk, Jazmin Sandos-Rosado, Paul Phillips, Lyn Conley, Al Jensen, Lydia Pelot-Hobbs

Point People: Marissa Guitierrez, Lehna Huie

Primary Aide: Lily Sparks

Specific problem being addressed: Youth of Color have not been receiving the support that they need, and that we (our organization/YRUU and the UUA/our beloved community) should be giving them, both monetarily and in other ways. Part of building a strong and beloved community is responding to the needs of all in the community. As a movement, we have not responded adequately to the needs of Youth of Color. This has kept our spiritual youth movement from being a real and authentic community. Youth of Color continuously and historically have not been given enough support from the UUA/YRUU. It is time to change that.

This resolution proposes that the YFUUD (YRUU Fund for Unitarian Universalist Development) grant money be allocated to Youth of Color programming from this point on. YFUUD grant money comes from an endowment left to us (YRUU) by LRY (YRUU's predecessor—Liberal Religious Youth). Repurposing this money would be consistent with the purposes of LRY, which cared very much about Anti-Racism/Anti-Oppression work.

Hope to Achieve: YFUUD (YRUU Fund for Unitarian Universalist Development) grant money be repurposed to go to Youth of Color programming.

How this will further the principles and visions of YRUU: Youth of Color are an essential part of the YRUU community. By continuing to not provide the support they need, we're pushing Youth of Color out of YRUU. Anti-Racism and Anti-Oppression is at the forefront of our vision. YRUU has made a commitment to work toward becoming an Anti-Racist and Anti-Oppressive organization. It is our imperative to do whatever we can to work further toward that commitment.

These are the goals of YRUU . . .
- Establish a continental community of youth.
- Provide for worship, celebration and rites of passage.
- Build the Unitarian Universalist movement: its traditions, membership and heritage.
- Develop personal growth and leadership skills.
- Develop individual social consciousness: be group agents of change and encourage members to be peaceful citizens of the world.
- Develop a communications network.
- Develop educational resources.
- Develop continuity between program levels, from younger to older.
- Foster tolerance, understanding and acceptance of diversity.
- Provide resources for identifying and training program advisors.
- Develop skills in group interaction and relationship building.
- Build a greater understanding between youth and adults.

The sponsors of this resolution believe that none of these goals can happen without a change in the way we currently support Youth of Color.

Evaluation: Each thing that's done with the money will be evaluated by its participants and the committee. Each year's Youth Council will receive a report on what the money will be used for.

personally. . . . Among some of my Cuban family it's like "You're still doing that race stuff, Janice?" Yeah, I am, family. Among some of my family members, whether light-skinned or dark-skinned, whether fair or tar-black, you're not considered to be a person of color. Here I am in my world and in the UU world living the life of a person of color—my precious life.

For others, the emerging organizations did not meet their needs the way predecessors (such as the African American Unitarian Universalist Ministry) had. Rev. Rosemary Bray McNatt of Fourth Universalist Society in New York City was frustrated because broader organizations, such as DRUUMM, which included lay persons as well as ordained clergy, did not create a forum for addressing the real needs of ministers of color:

> What happens when you go to the nursing home and people think you're the nurse's aide? I mean, for me, I learned to wear my collar *everywhere* outside of my congregation. If I've got to go somewhere and do something, I put my collar on. Now white colleagues don't wear their collar as much, if at all, and they think it's this kind of return to conservative Christianity. I explained to them where I come from it's an honor to put this collar on.

Soul Work

Many, looking back, expressed the opinion that the greatest challenge to the Journey Toward Wholeness anti-racism approach was that it lacked an articulated grounding in Unitarian theology. Rev. Susan Suchocki Brown noted this "still seems so impossible . . . to engage the work on a theological basis," adding,

> I continue to believe that inherent in our UU belief system is a basic flaw that stands in the way of transformation. . . . UU's lead from an assumption that personal experience and personal perception is the paramount and primary source of authority. When the angry reply was made that addressing

racism made "them feel guilty," we were unable to shift to a focus that spoke not of guilt but of a willingness to engage in looking at the *institution* that transcends the individual. Our UU theology and polity is constantly challenging us to maintain that fine and delicate balance between the institutional and personal, but when there are disagreements, our UU tendency is to fall back to the individual personal "felt experience" at the expense of continued institutional manifestation of oppression versus growth and transformation. This is more complex theologically than the division between personal and community, it has to do with purpose of church as institution, theology of scarcity, balance of emotion, tradition, intellect, and the scripture of institutional development and authority and rebellion against leadership.

That the book *Soul Work* deepened the discussion around theology was very important to Suchocki Brown and others, including Paula Cole Jones, president of DRUUMM at the time. She recalled,

The unfinished business of race has challenged me spiritually. Five years ago, my work with my own congregation propelled me into work with the larger Association; more recently, I found myself having to admit that race was deeply unfinished business for Unitarian Universalism and this led to a true test of my lifelong faith.

At the end of 2002, reflecting on a year of engagement with UUA anti-racism efforts, I wrote in my journal, "I am no longer willing to have my personal energy and spirit absorbed by the 'Great Inertia' around anti-racism." I considered leaving the church. I spoke with my mother about visiting other churches. She was loving and supportive—and encouraged me to not give up.

Then I left for a ten-day trip on UUA business that I figured would make my decision to stay or leave. My first meeting, in Boston, included a serendipitous encounter with a colleague on a midnight walk in the snow to the corner store; he told me about some ministers who were ready to

CONGREGATIONAL STORY
First Unitarian Society of Burlington, Vermont

In 1994, Rev. Gary Kowalski led an eight-week adult education class based on Rev. Dr. Mark Morrison-Reed's *How Open The Door?* which examined UU history and our denomination's mixed record on racial issues. Participants in that class decided they wanted to form a group to explore further how they could act to counter this history.

Since that time, for more than a decade, the congregation has been engaged in some sort of exploration around race. They have had book groups, worship services, special trainings including the Jubilee World I workshop of the Black Concerns Working Group, and a workshop based on the *Color of Fear* documentary. They have sponsored forums on local issues related to race, such as one on Native American land claims in Vermont and a community forum on the burning of black churches in the South. When a report was issued on racial harassment in the Vermont schools, they sent two carloads to Montpelier to testify. They have held fundraisers to benefit local groups serving those historically under-resourced because of race or ethnicity.

In 1997, the Congregation held a congregational meeting to consider redecorating the sanctuary and vestibule to reflect a more diverse constituency. That same year, they established an Anti-Racist Leadership Award, given annually to a community leader showing outstanding effort on behalf of racial justice.

In 2001, the Anti-Racism Action Committee organized an interfaith coalition to present four public forums at a local public library where speakers could address the impact of racism in the criminal justice system, in the schools and in religion. Each event brought 25–75 people. In the wake of the attacks of September 11, 2001, the Committee worked with the Adult Program Committee to present lectures on Islam and the Middle East.

In 2003, Kowalski and the Burlington Anti-Racism Coalition led an effort to have downtown merchants sign a pledge against racial profiling in retailing. The Unitarian Universalist Anti-Racism Action Committee followed up the following year and more than fifty merchants signed the pledge to eliminate profiling in their stores.

In 2004, the First Unitarian Universalist Society of Burlington was awarded the Martin Luther King Community Service Award for their city. "We remain active and committed to this work," Kowalski noted in 2006.

enter the conversation about anti-racism. The trip led to Chicago and back to Boston for a meeting with the leaders of YRUU, who committed to incorporate anti-racism into their long-range planning. Many things happened on that trip, and each step of the way affirmed the UUA as my community.

My moment of decision came on the airplane to Chicago, tears welling up in my eyes as I read the Skinner House book, *Soul Work*, edited by the Reverend Marjorie Bowens-Wheatley and Nancy Palmer Jones, and saw that the conversation to undo racism is authentic among ministers in the UUA. By the end of the trip, I had reconciled my own misgivings, and I had grown. . . .

Grubbs recalled, "The publication of *Soul Work* was very important, and the work of many people in helping to create 'theologies of anti racism, anti oppression.'" He also said a theological frame for anti-racism was important. "Too many of our ministers think that anti-racism is nice social justice but not a theological issue," he said.

Rev. Dr. Rebecca Parker, president of the Starr King School for the Ministry, said *Soul Work* was an important milestone in the decade of theological debates about anti-racism. "A kind of heightened engagement with critical theological issues that relate to anti-racism and counter-oppressive work has happened," she said, citing the work of Rev. Drs. William Jones, Mark Morrison-Reed, and Thandeka as critical in this.

Though work to place racism in a theological context had been ongoing throughout this period, what was also clear was that many still struggled with how to give anti-racism a unique Unitarian Universalist context.

PART 5

LEARNINGS

To adopt an anti-racist identity in 2002–03 was to stake a claim in a movement that sought to change the system and that used day-to-day incidents as teaching moments. An example was the way the Association Board and staff responded to the turmoil over the Commission on Appraisal skit at the 2002 General Assembly with a series of systematic initiatives designed to ensure a common analysis of how power is transmitted through oppressive systems.

During this period, changing relationships were seen at several levels, with ambiguous results at the congregational level and mixed results at the district level. Rev. Dr. Richard Speck, said the Joseph Priestley District had made anti-racism work a priority, sponsoring adult education workshops on the topic, though other districts had not. Reflecting on the Journey Toward Wholeness initiatives, Speck concluded, "The efforts that we have made have not always been successful. While well intentioned, they have sometimes created greater resistance to moving the Association forward toward justice."

The focus shifted from personal relationships to institutional relationships. Rev. William Sinkford, who became the Association's president in 2001, said he noted that progress had been made at the leadership levels in the UUA. "Here's where the strategy to focus on continental leadership paid dividends," he said. "Thanks in part to the trainings (what we now know as Jubilee II) and the tenacious continued advocacy of leaders like Dr. Leon Spencer, Dr. Norma Poinsett, Mel Hoover, Denise (Denny) Davidoff and others, leadership groups began to view their work through UU anti-racist lenses. It was and continues to be a struggle. But the work seated itself in the UUA Board, UUA staff, the professional organizations and some Associate and Affiliate members. The transformation in these groups, though far from complete, was near to a miracle."

The publication of the book *Soul Work* in 2002 seemed linked to discussions of race as a matter of faith. Though the dialogue that led to the publication was difficult for many participants, the existence of a resource that laid out the issues as religious ones provided sustenance for some, understanding for others, and a practical resource for some who needed that focus.

Criticism in 2002–03 led some to question past anti-racism efforts, however reluctantly. "I hate to second guess. Resources were so limited at the beginning and not everyone—surprise, surprise— agreed on how to do this work," said Rev. Keith Kron, director of the UUA's Office of Bisexual, Gay, Lesbian and Transgender Concerns. "I still remember what one African-American trainer said about doing anti-racism work. He said, 'We must go slowly. We have so little time.' I often wonder if we should have moved slower and more strategically at the beginning. . . . Other things that come to mind: We really forced this work on a lot of people who didn't want to do it. I wonder if we would have been better served working with only those folks who really wanted to do the work. Perhaps there needed to be intentional pastoral care as part of the work. Anytime someone gains consciousness around emotional pain, at least in my judgment, there needs to be some sort of pastoral care involved. There was also a fight over the strategy of doing this for future generations. Some were worried if we focused on future generations we were letting people off the hook. I wonder if doing the work for future generations would have allowed some people to put themselves on a hook. You never know with these things. You can spend a lot of time beating yourself up or being afraid to move in any direction, or you can simply try and make the present work go as well as possible. I prefer the latter."

CLOSING WORDS

ANTI-RACISM JOURNEY

Poem from youth training, 2004.

Being in the red zone
Overwhelmed
Examining why we censor ourselves (why we do it,
Feeling discouraged)

Transforming guilt into something else useful
Feeling like the blame is being placed by all the white folks
People of color—feeling like they have to justify every thing that
    they say having to do with anti-racism work
People of color—having to censor self to white people so they
    don't feel bad and feeling tokenized
People are feeling uncomfortable.

PART 6

Seeds for a New Era

Human beings have human needs, faults and frailties. We act or react depending on our particular state of mind at the time, which is often compounded by other events. Additionally, we act out of our own experiences and given how diverse we are, our challenge is to affirm the life experiences that each of us brings. Everyone has their own interpretations and often those interpretations are contradictory. That does not mean that one is right and another wrong.

—Special Review Commission Report, March 2006

2004

The Asian/Pacific Islander Caucus (APIC) votes to move under the umbrella of DRUUMM (Diverse and Revolutionary Unitarian Universalist Multicultural Ministries); APIC and DRUUMM covenant together.

Seminarians of Color begin meeting at a DRUUMM-sponsored dinner and worship at General Assembly.

The YRUU Steering Committee and the Youth Council struggle, in part over issues of race; there are many confrontations and abstentions. Some youth are sent home from Con-Con (the continental youth conference); Con-Con 2005 is canceled.

The Journey Toward Wholeness Transformation Committee budget is reduced in the UUA's fiscal year 2004–2005.

The Starr King School for the Ministry offers its first required semester-long "Educating to Counter Oppression" course in the fall of 2004.

THE COLLECTIVE VOICES OF racial and cultural groups historically marginalized in Unitarian Universalism gained volume as we entered more fully into the new millennium.

General Assemblies became the forum where Unitarian Universalists with many different views of how to approach the issue of race came into contact. In the terms of Rev. Dr. William Jones, the world could be seen as those who operated out of what he called a "pre-enlightenment" frame, meaning those unaffected by knowledge of the persistence of racism, and those who are "post-enlightenment," aware that racism remains at work in our culture and that it must be resisted with conscious and intentional efforts. So at the General Assemblies, some of those who had been wrestling for decades over the issues of how to address race relations encountered those who had rarely thought about it.

The Unitarian Universalist Association Board of Trustees had begun monitoring itself and questioning its own decisions through

2005

The "JUUST Change" consultancy program for congregations is launched.

Anti-racist advocates convene a "stakeholders' meeting" just prior to General Assembly in Fort Worth to discuss strategies and concerns about anti-racism efforts.

Participants in a General Assembly workshop on transracial adoption express their pain and frustration; parents of transracially adopted children do so as well.

Youth of Color are treated disrespectfully in incidents throughout General Assembly. The youth cancel the dance on closing night and gather in anger and sorrow.

The UUA Board appoints a Special Review Commission to investigate the events at the Fort Worth General Assembly.

DRUUMM invites the creation of a white allies group; UU Allies for Racial Equity (ARE UU) is created in November.

2006

The Final Report of the Special Review Commission is published.

The "Euro-American Anti-Racism Transformation Focus Group," a group of white anti-racist ministers, meets during Ministry Days before General Assembly.

A responsive resolution in the final minutes of General Assembly calls on congregations to do programming around race and class and report back in 2007.

an anti-oppression lens. Over her years with the Board, Moderator Gini Courter said she saw them increase their skills in questioning the status quo. "People were getting more comfortable asking questions they would have been uncomfortable asking before," she said.

The Youth and Young Adults of Color played an important role, raising issues such as the pain associated with transracial adoption, which some General Assembly participants did not wish to confront. At the same time, the cost of having a small cadre of youth from historically marginalized groups take the lead became apparent. After the 2005 General Assembly, a Special Review Commission was set up to examine the events that led to difficulties for youth at that gathering.

Youth work from this period emerged as one of the sources of inspiration and hope for those engaged in anti-racism advocacy, though the hope could be bittersweet. "A positive outcome of the UUA's anti-racism work is that it has inspired strong responses from youth and young adults," Rev. Kurt Kuhwald said. "Their work in anti-racism has shown, and continues to show, energy, insight and commitment. That our youth and young adult networks are one of the very, very few places where the work of Anti-Racism is now going on leaves me disillusioned."

In other, quieter places, other small seeds of change were growing. In the theological schools, in a number of congregations, in a number of committees and processes of the Unitarian Universalist Association, change had begun.

CHAPTER 25

Race and General Assembly 2004–05

In 1992, the Unitarian Universalist journey began at a General Assembly in Calgary. By 2004–2005, the anti-racism ideals were an intrinsic part of the largest annual gathering of Unitarian Universalists even if the ideas were recognized more through intentions than consistent actions. At the national gatherings, the number of attendees from racial and ethnic groups historically underrepresented in Unitarian Universalist congregations was significant and noticeable. Official and unofficial events allowed these Unitarian Universalists who often felt marginalized in their community to gather with others, to compare notes and to assess the state of the conversation about race.

And issues involving race shaped the agenda, official and unofficial, for all attendees at the 2005 General Assembly in Fort Worth. Through the particular advocacy by and on behalf of those youth and young adults who were active at the national level, these events came to the attention of the broader Unitarian Universalist community at these major gatherings. In many ways, General Assembly became the thermometer for seeing how hot the issue of race was in any particular year.

Seen through the lens of relationship, the challenges facing those historically marginalized in the Association were highlighted. The difficulty of navigating General Assemblies for those who identified as people of color, Latina/o, or Hispanic became clearer during this time. Janice Marie Johnson, who in 2003 became president of DRUUMM [Diverse and Revolutionary Unitarian Universalist Multicultural Ministries], reflected in 2006 that people of color and those from other historically marginalized racial and ethnic groups are a part of the public General Assembly—and that at the same time there is a private General Assembly that is just for them. Tensions between the two General Assemblies perhaps accounted for the frictions witnessed in incidents from 2002 to 2006.

"We have two different General Assemblies, at least," Moderator Gini Courter said, adding that different experiences are held by the white majority not attuned to racial tensions, those involved in people of color organizations, youth, youth of color, and those of Latina/o and Hispanic descent. "And then in the plenary sessions, we all come together and all these expectations and all these pieces come together." She said issues around age and issues around race have consistently not mixed well.

For some, the growing list of groups based on identity and affinity was a comfort and a sign of progress. For others, they were a dangerous omen. Many of the flash points continued to shoot light and sparks. Finley Campbell saw identity-group caucusing as divisive and this led to his expressed opposition to the Journey Toward Wholeness efforts. "Multiracial Unity is not the goal of our journey toward wholeness—it is the means of getting there," he observed. "It's time to start thinking about building a multiracial unity movement in our denomination, especially for youth and young adults tired of identity politics. . . . It's time to create a multiracial unity caucus in the UUA under the slogan: Asian Latin Black Native American White Arab Jew we must unite! I and an acquaintance of mine, who is a member of DRUUMM, recently conversed about a deep political disagreement between us which had emerged at the Quebec UUA General Assembly, where we had worked together on some interracial problems with some youth. A disagreement about how long would there be a need to have youth and young adults of color meet separately from their white allies. At that time he argued for a thousand years; I argued that the need was over. Later, we changed our positions: he said it would only take 500 years and I said 25. In order to shorten that time even further, we need to institute NOW a multiracial unity caucus for those who are ready for it."

General Assembly Planning Committee

In September 2004, consultant Paula Cole Jones and Rev. Dr. Tracey Robinson-Harris, director of the Unitarian Universalist Association's Office of Congregational Services, facilitated a retreat focused on anti-racism and anti-oppression for the General Assembly Planning Committee. After the meeting, the Committee covenanted to operate through an anti-racist and anti-oppressive lens.

New Language and the Transformation Committee

At its November 2004 meeting, the Journey Toward Wholeness Transformation Committee discussed narrowing its role and its part in creating a new language of anti-racism that was a focus of UUA president William Sinkford:

> Bill would like to see the creation of a language set that would be accessible to people whose language is more traditional and frankly more religious; "kingdom of God." Taquiena [Boston, director of the UUA's Identity-Based Ministries Staff Group] raised the concept of creating a language of yearning. How can these two languages be part of one language set?
>
> Bill suggested finding a writer who can take the ideas of the committee and create some language that can then go back to the committee and the larger UU community. . . .
>
> UUs are living diversity and yet we have no name for it.

The Committee had a positive response, noting that it was "delighted Bill was on same page as the Transformation Committee about the Journey Toward Wholeness and being willing to let go of words and explore new language. The Committee also discussed its work with congregational presidents, which tied into the Sinkford Administration's strategy to get more presidents to General Assembly."

Members also discussed feedback they would be giving to the UUA regarding the settlement process regarding candidates in historically marginalized groups, which contained four main points:

Nominating Committee
Winifred Norman 1973–1981
Etta Green Johnson 1983–
David Eaton, 1985–1989
Sayre Dixon, 1989–1993
Charles Yielbonzie Johnson,
  1991–1995
Daniel Aldridge, 1993–1997
Michelle Bentley, 1993–1997
Laura Spencer, 1997–2001
Hope Johnson, 2005–
James Coomes, 2003–
Leon Spencer, 2009–

- The option of identifying by race/ethnicity should be made plain for the candidates.
- Anti-racism, anti-oppressive, multicultural competency requirements should be more prominent, rather than made one of the last steps.
- A way for applicants to provide feedback on the process must be provided and in a way that ensures that the applicant remains safe in providing feedback.
- Language that is not culturally neutral must be changed.

This conversation was initiated by Rev. Ellen Brandenburg, before she retired from the Department of Ministry in 2002, because she felt the ministerial credentialing process needed an anti-racism, anti-oppressive, multicultural analysis. Her successor, Rev. David Pettee, brought the issue to the Diversity of Ministry Team, and Sinkford recommended that it be brought to the Transformation Committee.

Robinson-Harris observed about the changes at the UUA: "What is different at the Associational level because we did this work? We have institutionalized anti-racism work in ways that are incomplete and at the same time astounding." She noted the support for ministerial candidates from historically marginalized racial and ethnic groups and the increased emphasis on multicultural and anti-racism competency as part of the annual evaluation process for UUA employees. "The glass is half-full in this regard for me. . . . Today there are many places within our religious community where this work is being done. We continue to struggle to figure out how to institutionalize this so that it doesn't depend on a certain person. It needs to be the way we do things."

Stakeholders Meeting
Funds to bring "stakeholder" groups together again had been sought in vain since the 1999 Kansas City event. Eventually, a more spontaneous and unofficial one-day effort was held a day before the 2005 General Assembly in Fort Worth. Advocates Kim Varney, Adele McLean, Rev. Dr. Richard Speck, Ed Wilde, and Ian White Maher

organized the meeting and sent word out by email and other informal networks. Varney, who resigned from the Transformation
Committee the same year, said the meeting's purpose was "to address the '92 and '97 resolutions that the UUA anti-racism, anti-
oppression-multicultural efforts continue to not address and that
is to 'strategically plan, guide, and coordinate the UUA effort to
become an anti-racism, anti-oppression-multicultural denomination. . . .'" The letter of invitation stated,

> Since the passage of the resolution "Toward an Anti-Racist
> Unitarian Universalist Association" at the General Assem-
> bly in Phoenix in 1997, UU congregations, districts, com-
> mittees working for the Association, and other related
> organizations have been engaged in developing vibrant anti-
> racist identities. In addition, People of Color have organized
> new organizations to serve their constituencies like Asian
> Pacific Islander Caucus (APIC) and strengthened existing
> ones like Diverse and Revolutionary Unitarian Universalist
> Multicultural Ministries (DRUUMM).
>
> But there is still *a lot* of work to do.
>
> General Assembly is a good time to build stronger rela-
> tionships between the various stakeholder groups. By shar-
> ing our successes and concerns with one another we will
> strengthen the anti-racism and anti-oppression work within
> the Association as well as develop a voice for the future of
> the work.
>
> We anticipate this meeting at the General Assembly in
> Fort Worth will be a first step toward a larger meeting of
> stakeholder groups in 2006.

Varney saw the gathering as another attempt to bring attention
to critical issues, such as funding: "The '92 and '97 GA resolutions
provided a clear mandate to resource these efforts, but that has never
happened—I would have continued in a leadership position with
these efforts had the UUA been more committed to the identity-
based communities."

Build-Up to the 2005 General Assembly

Before the General Assembly at Fort Worth, a youth leadership development conference was held in Dallas. Because of incidents that would transpire later at the GA, the conference was the subject of an investigation of a Special Review Commission. It filed this account of the events involving youth that led up to the General Assembly, recording the experience of Christopher Donshale Sims, an advisor to the youth and a member of the DRUUMM Youth and Young Adult Steering Committee:

> I was a Youth Advisor for this particular conference. During our time there, we Youth and Young Adults of Color experienced various forms and incidents of profiling and racism.
>
> Outside of First Unitarian Church, Dallas, Texas, we received looks of a strange and challenging nature. As People of Color in a foreign environment, we were looked at with indifference. I can recall at least once when some of us took a walk through the local community where First Unitarian, Dallas, TX exists. We were looked at with curious and unfriendly eyes. Some of the people's eyes read, "Who are these people? What are they doing here?"
>
> While taking a walk, some of the young Men of Color, I learned, were stopped and harassed by the local police.
>
> During one of our break-out sessions for gender caucusing, members of the First Unitarian Church, Dallas, Texas— two women—were having a conversation near where we stood. As we tried to have a discussion about the topic, our experiences, the two women spoke loudly interrupting our discussion. One of the Youth of Color approached the women and asked them could they tone down their conversation a bit. One of the women rudely raised her hand and flagged the young man as if to say, "I am not listening to you. Go away."
>
> It was disheartening to see this incident unfold.
>
> Another time, some of the Youth were approached by a man who was also a member of the church. He had a card

that spoke to the nature of women of Color not reproducing any more children of Color to slow down or stop the population of People of Color. Saying, us inhabiting this land was not good for America.

We had to have a special meeting to discuss this incident. One of the church leaders took the initiative to come speak with us about this experience. He informed us this gentleman had done this before. He also informed us our concerns were not going to be taken lightly and he would speak to the church members about what had happened.

We left the meeting feeling good about this, but the overall experience was stressing for most of us.

A few days later, we all went on an outing to see the movie "Crash." The movie was quite the experience for all of us. It heightened our sense of awareness, connectedness, and some of us focused on the racial climate of the movie and what took place with us during the conference.

So, we move on to Fort Worth for General Assembly 2005. The rest is history. . . .

Youth, Race, Class and General Assembly

Once again, the hothouse of General Assembly led to inflammatory incidents around race, this time with the focus being on youth of color. The Special Review Commission was appointed to look into the causes of conflict, consisting of Hafidha Acuay (Portland, Oregon), Rev. José Ballester (Houston, Texas), Rachel Davis (Teaneck, New Jersey), Janice Marie Johnson (Brooklyn, New York), and Rev. Dr. Margaret Keip (Grants Pass, Oregon).

Though one of the Commission's conclusions was that the events at General Assembly grew out of the long history of tensions around race and that the events that occurred there began earlier, particularly at the Youth Leadership Development Conference the week before, the chronology of events at General Assembly they put together is revealing:

June 22–24, 2005—LDC [Youth Leadership Development Conference] participants and other youth began arriving in

Fort Worth. Due to the Youth Caucus's failure to reserve rooms and to the shortage of rooms in the immediate convention area, the youth were scattered over several hotels. At meetings for youth of color, the stories of the LDC and Dallas were shared. There were several incidents in which youth of color were mistaken for hotel employees by GA participants and asked to perform menial tasks. There were reportedly incidents in which hotel employees tended to the needs of white youth but ignored youth of color.

June 24, 2005—Workshop 2067, Transracial Adoptions, Interracial Families: Changing Faces, Changing Hearts, was co-sponsored by the Planning Committee and DRUUMM. The workshop was to examine the issues faced by transracially adopted UUs, especially youth and young adults. In addition to transracially adopted youth, young adult, and ministerial presenters, there were two outside speakers. One of the featured speakers from Pact, an adoption alliance, canceled at the last moment due to a family crisis. A white UUA staffer who has adopted a child of color replaced her. The presentation of the other featured speaker, a transracial adoption activist, was reportedly confrontational and upsetting to some adoptive parents, while the youth were gaining insight into their pain and a vocabulary to express it. Tension grew as the adoptive parents and adoptees expressed their anger and frustrations. Rumors circulated that some of the adoptive parents would protest the follow-up workshop, 5017, Transracial Adoption: Perspectives of Youth and Young Adults (sponsored by Continental UU Young Adult Network and the Family Matters Task Force). The potential for further dialogue was important to many attending.

June 25–26, 2005—Racial incidents continued to be reported at identity meetings for youth of color. Some involved harassment by the police and local residents. The youth of color felt threatened at times. These incidents and the growing tension were shared with some of the young adult leadership from DRUUMM Youth and Young Adults (YaYA), but they were not passed on to other authorities in DRUUMM, the GA Planning Committee (GAPC), or the Board of Trustees. Other incidents involving other groups were reported to the GAPC and other authorities and their concerns were addressed during GA.

June 26, 2005—The purported protest at the second Transracial Adoption workshop did not materialize. The parents and sponsors managed to discuss their concerns in an amicable manner. The youth of color and their young adult leadership gathered in a Caucus meeting. They shared with each other their stories of how they had been mistreated at the LDC and GA. They decided that the delegates at GA needed to know about their pain and brokenness and that the best course of action was to stop the GA and request that their stories be heard. Representatives of the group left to arrange for a chance to speak to the delegates. However, the Closing Ceremony had begun and the last Plenary session had ended, so there was no official way for the youth of color to address the delegates, increasing their tension and frustration. Three young men of color left the Caucus meeting and headed to the convention center. There they began to perform a non-violent protest by requesting programs from the ushers and then either throwing the programs to the ground or tearing them first and then throwing them down. They repeated these actions several times in the convention hall so that the delegates would notice. One usher was concerned about their actions and asked another usher to determine the cause. Since the youth were not visibly wearing nametags, she also asked the other usher to determine whether they were UU youth or locals who had entered the hall. Some words were exchanged between the male usher and the youth as they continued their protest. These interactions began to attract the attention of others. A Youth Office staffer tried to intervene but only increased the tension as more people became aware of the protest and reactions. A minister intervened and challenged the three young men. Harsh words were exchanged and the young men began to exit the hall. The minister followed them into the lobby.

The youth of color, having finished their Caucus meeting, arrived in the lobby of the convention center still determined to somehow address the delegates. It is reported that some youth and young adult leaders were upset that they could not address the delegates and expressed their frustrations in the lobby. Other youth of color tried to find white allies and others in positions of power to assist the youth in finding a way to address the delegates. Some of the people of color leadership either happened upon the agitated gathering in the lobby or entered the lobby from the convention hall. As they tried to determine what had happened, the three young men and the minister entered the lobby from the hall. It is reported that they exchanged harsh words loudly and that the minister appeared to be following the three young men, who appeared to be trying to distance themselves from her. In the lobby, some of the youth came to the defense of the three young men, telling the minister that they were UU youth and a part of the community. The situation continued to escalate with more and more people drawn into the crowd, including youth, young adults, adults, delegates, ministers, UUA staffers, and a member of the Board of Trustees. As some of the youth tried to disengage, one young woman made a comment that seemed to infuriate the minister. Words usually reserved for an urban street argument were exchanged at increasing volume. It is reported that both the minister and the youth had to be restrained. At that point the UUA Moderator, Gini Courter, left the Closing Ceremony and attempted to restore order in the lobby. It is reported that Gini ordered the minister to distance herself from the situation several times. The minister eventually left the lobby.

Given the agitated state of some of the youth, their requests to tell the delegates of how their world was now

The Elevator Story: A Metaphor

This story was included in the report of the Special Review Commission, issued in March 2006.

Upon reviewing more than eighty accounts of the events that took place in Fort Worth, the members of the Commission came to a common understanding: Each of us brings into every situation a personal body of experience that affects the nature of our interactions. This is exemplified by what we refer to as "the elevator story."

In this true story, a woman of African descent recalls riding in a crowded elevator with several emotionally exhausted youth and young adults of color on the final night of GA. Two of the youth had just been involved in a near-altercation with a white female minister outside of the Closing Ceremony. The elevator stopped, and as the doors opened, the woman heard a white woman yelling at the youth of color in the elevator, "If you people really want to be anti-racist, you will get off the elevator now and allow this poor man to get on." The woman of African descent peered outside the doors and observed that the man in question was an older, black hotel employee with a food cart. When she looked at him, she read shame and embarrassment on his face. Meanwhile, the white woman had boarded the elevator. The woman of African descent remembers a flood of emotion. "In his eyes," she says, "I saw me." And she wondered, "What was I doing with rude, insensitive white people so far removed from *his world, my roots*?" This episode reminded her of many of the negative, race-based encounters she'd experienced within the UU community over the past fifteen years. She questioned why she was a part of this faith community, but "I stayed on that elevator. I stood my ground. . . . I belonged on that elevator, too." Soon after she learned that the white woman was a UU minister, which increased her discomfort.

The white UU minister recounts the same event. She had heard only that the dance had been canceled due to incidents of racism and the youth community feeling "broken."

Leaving the ballroom, she came upon an older, black hotel employee waiting at the elevator doors with a food service cart. An elevator arrived and a dozen YRUU youth hurried past him to fill it. This happened twice as she watched. The man told her that he'd been waiting for some time as this scenario repeated itself. The third time the elevator arrived and youth rushed to enter, she interrupted to ask if they would step out and let the man in. She recalls that the youth "were screaming at me that their world was broken."

She told them that if they were concerned about racism, they would care about *this* man.

She reminded them that everyone at GA was privileged and urged them to look after the hotel staff. After boarding the elevator, she and the youth continued to dialogue until an adult woman of color said to her, "You need to stop now and go with your white community and talk about this." This incident left her shaken. She was accustomed to speaking out for the underdog, she said. Although she too had attended the closing ceremony, "I had no clue what had happened with the youth or what I had gotten into."

She described this incident as "one of the more unpleasant experiences of my entire life."

The story of the elevator demonstrates the vastly different lenses through which two women viewed the same event. While race played a factor, so had encounters immediately preceding this one and all the experiences associated with being an adult, a parent, a woman, a person of color, a white person, a person of authority, and so on. The Commission views the elevator story as a metaphor for many of the stories we were privy to during this investigation. It is our conclusion that a vital part of the effort to become a more whole and loving community involves listening to and sharing our honest perspectives—not to determine who is "right" and who is "wrong" but to identify where we have attempted to communicate with one another and simply failed. The good news is that we *are* reaching out and striving to connect. Let us be kind to each other and try again—and again, and again. Ours is a continuing story.

broken, and the growing tension in the lobby, Gini negotiated for meetings back in the Radisson Hotel. The youth and supporters left the lobby for the hotel meetings. As the youth and leaders attempted to use the elevators, another incident took place. This particular incident, reported elsewhere, is indicative of the tensions and misunderstandings of that evening. At the hotel, the groups broke out into separate Persons of Color and White Allies meetings. Meanwhile, the evening Intergenerational Dance, sponsored by the Youth Caucus, had started in the hotel ballroom, when some youth white allies announced that the dance was cancelled. The GAPC was unaware of and had not authorized the cancellation.

At the meetings in the Radisson, adult leadership, of color or white, learned for the first time of the particular incidents from the LDC to the Closing Ceremony. Emotions were running high and one of the youth made a video recording of people's feelings. This video was to be shared with the Board of Trustees. Plans were made to address these issues to the Board of Trustees and the GA Planning Committee.

June 28, 2005—At their meeting with the new Trustees, the entire UUA Board of Trustees learned about the incidents for the first time. The Board of Trustees acted swiftly to take responsibility and resolved to investigate the allegations, publicly apologize to those who had been hurt by the incidents, and determine what could be done to vastly reduce these types of incidents in the future. The Trustees who are ministers called upon the UUMA and the Ministerial Fellowship Committee to become involved.

Talking Out About Transracial Adoption

"[T]he complexion of our congregations is changing," Sinkford wrote in the foreword of a contemporary book on the Empowerment Controversies of the 1960s. "The change is not most evident in our pews, though I see some change there as well. The change is in our RE classrooms and youth groups. Transracial adoption, blended families, mixed marriages of many kinds are beginning to make our church schools and youth programs look more like the world. Perhaps we are ready to ask ourselves what kind of a church we will bequeath to our children—all of our children. We must learn to help our children, all of them, be proud to say, 'I am a Unitarian Universalist. This is my church.'"

Events at the 2005 General Assembly illustrated the extent of the challenge in making Sinkford's vision real. A number of transracially adopted Unitarian Universalists had been searching for materials to make sense of their difficult experiences. These experiences had been the subject of conversations among the transracially adopted youth and other youth of color and Latina/o/Hispanic youth for a number of years. At the 2005 GA, the conversation came out into the open when a panel session on transracial adoption was held, co-sponsored by DRUUMM and its Asian Pacific Islander Caucus.

In the years leading up to the Fort Worth General Assembly, the UUA's Identity-Based Ministries Staff Group had been working to organize the information from the multiracial family camps that had been tried on an experimental basis. Drawing on the wisdom of those who had provided leadership for these experimental and largely volunteer events, they interviewed key participants such as Rev. Marjorie Bowen-Wheatley, James Coomes, Young Kim, Rev. Suzelle Lynch, and Joseph Santos-Lyons to try to assess how a more systematic and sustainable approach could be organized.

Coomes, who had been a transracial adoptee, had field-tested programming on this subject in 2003 when he pulled together a General Assembly panel to speak about it. The 2005 panel included a broader spectrum of views. General Assembly reporter Kok-Heong McNaughton offered this description of the panel:

The panelists were:
- Stephanie Cho, a Korean adoptee, an activist, and co-founder of Transracial Abductees, an organization that works to educate transracial adoptees and communities of color, and expose the unequal power between the white adoption industry and children-of-color adoptees.
- Meggie Dennis, a Korean adoptee UU young adult.

- The Rev. Dr. Kristen Harper, a multi-racial UU minister who was adopted by white UU parents and currently serves the 279-member Unitarian Church of Barnstable, MA.
- The Rev. Meg Riley, a UU minister who adopted a child from China. Riley was invited to be on the panel to substitute for Beth Hall, co-author of the book *Inside Transracial Adoption*. Hall was unable to participate due to a death in the family.

Janice Marie Johnson, president of DRUUMM, and Rev. Manish Mishra, president of A/PIC, welcomed participants and thanked those who worked to create this program. Mishra reminded participants that one of the foci of General Assembly 2005 is a celebration of families in all their diverse forms and changing nature. He pointed out that there are more racial and ethnic diversity in our religious education classes across the country than is reflected in our pews. This workshop is an opportunity for us to hear some of their stories.

The Rev. Leslie Takahashi Morris, recently settled co-minister of Thomas Jefferson Memorial Church of Charlottesville, Va., introduced the panelists and led the more than 100 attendees in a moment of silence to honor Hall's loss. Harper taught and led a rousing Swahili song with energetic foot-stomping and arm-waving before everyone settled down to the next hour of emotionally-intense sharing of heart-wrenching stories, engaging in extremely difficult conversations (both as listeners and as speakers) around the complex issues of transracial adoption, institutionalized and internalized racism/oppression, and overt/covert imperialism, white privilege, the loss of culture, the search for identity, and other painful issues. There wasn't a dry eye in the room as panelists and workshop participants on both sides of the adoption system related their experiences.

More than adopted children by same-race families, transracial adoptees struggle with the additional loss of cultural identity that their adopted parents, however well-meaning, cannot fill. Many white parents bring up their adopted children of color as if they were white, but when these children go out into the wider world, reality hits. White parents cannot confer their white privileges to their adopted children of color. When asked if they thought transracial adoption is ever appropriate, most of the transracial adoptees, speaking from their personal experiences, do not think so. Harper cautioned that the parents be themselves emotionally healthy and prepared, and to choose to live in a multi-racial/cultural neighborhood where their children grow up with a supportive community. Riley is thankful for the openness with which she can communicate daily with her adopted daughter. She cannot control her child's suffering but can make sure that her child does not suffer alone by holding that pain with her.

When one white parent asked about how to help a woman whose now 29-year old adopted Korean daughter is going through a crisis of identity and is seeking professional counseling, Riley suggested that counseling is appropriate not just for the daughter, but for the parents as well.

Our beloved UU community is home to many who are otherwise homeless. This workshop and the conversation it has started will begin to change the minds, the hearts and the understanding of all who have been touched by it. This work is critical for UUs as we live out our principles and purposes as a religious community. The conversation is not new. It has been going on now for several years amongst UUs of color.

The panel discussion brought into the open a discussion that had been confined to youth and young adult circles. The closing statements of the panelists exemplify the tensions that were present at that session:

LILY SPARKS (JooYoung Choi): First, I have a comment to any of the parents of adoptees, either transracially or adopting people of the same race as yourself. I think that many times, deep down inside of many adoptees, there is a sense of inadequacy, because somebody gave you up. Which means that, inherently, there is a part of you that thinks you weren't good enough to be kept—to be taken care of—by your original parents. And then when you find yourself and say as I am, I am adopted too by a white family. Everyone would always say to me "Oh, you were so great as a little girl because you would always want to play with everybody, you'd talk with everybody, play games and share your food. You were so social." And I realized, as I got older, that I felt, as a child, that who I was, was not enough. So I had to work ten times harder than non-adopted children to be loved, because of the fear of being given up. For not being good enough. And I feel like that travels on in the lives of adopted children, to their relationships, through their adolescence, the people that they date. Trying to be good enough, because inherently, they aren't, or they feel that they aren't. And that goes all the way up into their marriages and to the schools and the jobs that they work. And how much harder too they have to work; how much harder too they have to try, to be loved. To feel chosen. . . .

And also, I wanted to make a comment/question about the racism that we talked about. We talked about cultural loss and putting cultural loss and racism as the same thing, or is it. I really feel that there is a racism, that hasn't been discussed as much and that's internalized racism. And I'll tell you that I grew up with messed up internalized racism. My family was trying to create a set: they had my biological sister, who was white, they had me, and they were saving up for another one. They wanted to adopt themselves a child from South America so they could, we could have a global family. They were very excited about it and, thankfully, they ran out of funds. And so I spent my life being objectified, eroticized, and suppressed. I was asked not to talk about it in my home and there is something about being a person of color and being in a white house where you know that the outside world is a battlefield. You get called chink, you get called gook, you get harassed. Your math teachers don't understand why you can't do math well. Your music teachers assume that the reason you can play music well is because you're Asian.

And so you grow up with all this messed up—I'm not going to swear—oppression and then you go home and you cry and your parents say, "Why are you crying? I adopted you. I love you. Don't you love me? Why are you crying? If you love me, why don't you stop crying? Aren't we just one big liberal family? Can't you just . . . ? Why are you crying? You're hurting me. Don't do that."

And so you spend a life of trying not to upset people and you internalize so much pain and you forget how to connect with communities of color. And you're isolated in your bubble with a sense of inadequacy that you are not enough of a person of color and you'll never be white. And I think that the internalized oppression issue does need to be brought up and I was wondering if you guys had any comments on that.

REV. LESLIE TAKAHASHI MORRIS: Also, in light of our time, I would ask that you comment on what Lily has so heartfeltly shared with us, but also any final closing thoughts you would like to share, and I would like to start with you, or anyone who feels so moved.

REV. DR. KRISTEN HARPER: One thing I'll say is that when you get to be thirty-five, it hurts even more than you thought it was going to be when you were a kid—it doesn't go away. And that's the one thing that you know, Lily and I, over the years, some of the transracial adoptees have talked about it and it just doesn't go away. Or you get numb. But as far as the internalized racism goes, I never hated myself because I was black; I hated myself because I wasn't black enough. I hated the white part of me. I hated the light part of me. And most of the prejudice I received— I could deal with people calling me nigger. I could deal with white people not liking me, because a lot of you don't. But I couldn't deal with the people of color not liking me. That for me has always been the hardest part. Trying to fit into communities where my hair was either too curly, not curly enough, not straight enough. "OK, you have to take off your braids because real white, real black women have straight hair, and now you straighten your hair and you're trying to be white and that stuff; that internalized part was so bad and so I helped start a Latino group in the UU movement. The hardest part for me was they asked me to be vice-president and I went in and they were speaking in Spanish and they thought I didn't know Spanish, which I do, fluently. I just don't always speak it. I don't speak it a lot actually, but I still know it. It's my first language. . . . And the people were talking about the black people and how awful they were. And it was just like, it's awful, OK, I spent all my life tanning, trying to be as dark as possible and they don't like me. And I tried to be, you know, honor the Latino part, and they don't like me. And so I think that, for me, the argument that you will never fit in that you will never have a place where you can be. I guess my final thought is that, you know, as UUs we have a lot, a long way to go. You want us to be here but you don't really want us to be here. That for me is the hardest part, because there is no other place for us, because you adopted us here. And my thing about it, I guess, for me, is that anytime everyone ever passes by or ignores me whatever, says something to me like park your car, or "here's my keys; park my car," it's like, you brought me in here. I didn't have a choice, so damn it, stop ignoring, stop thinking I am somebody other than who I am. Look at my face, look at who I am and honor the fact that you chose to no longer be white. So damn well better get ready to not be white, because we're here.

MEGGIE DENNIS: For me, a lot of internalized things that I've gone through have included realizing that I was a person of color. I had grown up with my parents telling me that I was the same as anyone else, that I was the same as the white kids; there's no difference, you know, and I'm equal to anyone, just like, I mean, every child grows up. Except what I realized as I got older is that I was not the same. I was told that I would be treated the same as all the white kids—I was raised white—and then to go out into the world and realize that I'm not white and that I don't get these privileges that white people get. To be treated differently, to have people think, to have people look at me like I'm not going to be able to speak any English. And then, when I speak English perfectly, to have them look at me so surprised. So surprised—hurts. For me to realize that I was not going to get the same white privileges that my parents—that my brother—got was hard and it hurt a lot. To realize that you have been raised, basically, been lied to was what I have felt like for a very long time. That I have been lied to by my parents, by my family, by my church, treating me like I was the same and then for me to go out in the real world and realize that I am not the same and that I do not get these privileges really hurt. And it still does hurt, because in some ways I still find myself thinking that I still get these privileges, and then when I realize . . . it kills me inside.

Stephanie Cho: I think there is a common misnomer about transracial adoptees that gets a little confusing. We were talking, we're sort of teasing out the difference between class and race. I think it's also important to talk about the difference between class and race. Too much emotion up here. Anyway, I think that happens. At times, when people are talking about "You're so lucky" that you have these white parents, because they assume that there is white privilege that goes along with that as well. And that's simply not true. A lot of times, actually, in reality, in transracial adoptee homes is that you are the first line of racism. You get it first and so straight to you, you know, that's part of the thing I think that sort of incubates the internalized racism. And one of the things that is highly controversial but I think that it is something to talk about as well I think. On the web site, there is one piece that talks a bit about racism as a form of abuse, child abuse. That's something to think about when, you know, we talk about this culture. And we have to talk about that. And racism is an abusive thing. It's oppression. And that really causes a lot of emotion and it causes a lot of problems and I think, as a community, because transracial adoptees are so different. At the same time, some are really critical, some are not very critical and I think you'll meet transracial adoptees that have a really wide perspective. This is very much a snapshot. Yet, part of it is that we are all dealing with internalized racism and we deal with it in really different ways. Some of us have had positive experiences when working with other communities of color and some of us haven't. And so, similar/like you know to any sort of culture, race or whatever, you can't just say, "Oh, they would be like this, they would be like that." We have very different views and because of the oppression, the racism, you know, like all the time, it creates really different people and we handle it really differently. I think it is important to respect where people are coming from, especially around the idea of internalized racism. My final thought would be we should just all really think about how the adoption industry is part of the systemic imperialism. But I do welcome people to look at the web site—all people—and then also to really know that transracial adoptees do not have their own history. It is not a history that has been really forged, so we're working; we're trying to create a history that we completely lost, because we transracial adoptees, or adoptees of color, have a distinct and special history in the communities of color world.

REV. MEG RILEY: I guess the one thing I would contribute about internalized racism is that obviously I can't know my daughter's reality here, but that it's really important for her to know that it's not because of her that we choose to live in a neighborhood that's multiracial; that we would pick a multiracial school for any child, that our friends, of whatever race, would also choose to live in those situations. So that she doesn't feel like—because of her—we're making different choices about life than we would otherwise, because I think that's too much to balance on a person. And I think if that is true, I would really question a white family choosing to adopt a child of color. And mostly I just wanted to say thank you, so much, for all of the courage in the room, for all of the spoken truths, which are painful, deep-in-the-heart truths for all of us and I'm really excited for the next workshop—that you will all have a chance to be together—some of you—and that, as I've said before, this work—to me—is so critical to who we are as a religious people, because many of us, for a number of reasons, are culturally homeless.

TAKAHASHI MORRIS: I want to echo what Meg said about the courage and the real, true bravery that we have seen on this panel today. And I want to thank all of you for being part of a conversation that actually is not new. This is a conversation going on among our youth of color, among our people of color, in this movement, and has been going on for a number of years. What I want to celebrate here today is that, however imperfectly we have brought this conversation into our broader understanding, into our broader whole, I hope we will be able to continue to move forward. There is a lot more that needs to be said.

The panel generated significant animosity from white adoptive parents, many of whom spoke at a subsequent panel held the closing day of General Assembly. The feedback was strong enough for the matter to be discussed at the GA Planning Committee meeting after GA, whose minutes read:

> Another problem surfaced in our discussions was in response to the Continental Young Unitarian Universalist Young Adult Network (C*UUYAN)-sponsored transracial adoption program; the plan was for a balance of perspectives, but the person presenting the positive view had to cancel participation, so there was only the negative point of view presented by an angry adoptee, and white parents felt trashed. [Moderator] Gini [Courter] suggested that we need to vet workshops, look for trouble spots, and have a process if alerted. Do we want to start doing quality assurance in relationship to programming? We may want to stipulate that if you cannot offer your workshop as described, please talk to us, you may have to cancel it. We should also include guidelines for workshop presenters re anti-racism/anti-oppression; this was done some years ago but has lapsed.

Yet for many of the youth and people of color, the conversation was not a new one. "There is a crisis of support for youth and young adults of color—especially males," observed Rev. William (Chester) McCall, minister at the Unitarian Universalist Church of the Restoration in Philadelphia. "There are too few mentors and role models. Boys are in perpetual crisis, and support is barely available. Too few people, too little money, too few resources are available."

This was not a new conversation among UUA staff either. Religious educator Jacqui James said, "More and more of our children are biracial and adopted. If we want to retain these children, we have to understand their journey. . . . At some stage, questioning his or her identity will happen." James said Unitarian Universalist congregations could provide a place for this to happen in a safe manner. "If we go on thinking that we are superior and that is not the experience of our children, then they will walk."

Another factor in the controversy may be that the leadership of the youth anti-racism movement had embraced an understanding of racism as systemic. "Youth and young adults have been inspired to develop anti-racism trainings that resonate with their constituents, and they have been vigilant in exploring structural changes that are accountable to people of color and to dismantling racism," observed Taquiena Boston of Identity-Based Ministries.

Courter, who did extensive work behind the scenes in 2005 and again in 2006 to deal with the repercussions of the transracial adoption issue, noted that this issue was under discussion in the youth caucuses though transparency was lacking that would have made it visible to all. In 2005, the parents were invited into the conversation. Courter saw open discussion as critical. "We better start having these conversations," she said, "because we have something coming in the huge number of lesbian and gay parents who have transracially adopted kids. And those kids are all going to grow up in about six or seven years."

Courter observed that "some of what plays out at General Assembly, for our youth who are transracial adoptees, is that this is the only time in their religious life where there is more racial diversity than in the white congregations where they live." She said this plays into a tension that grows and tends to climax the last night of General Assembly. "I always expect the last night of General Assembly to be a crisis management because look what they have to go back to. . . . They have been in a competent community [on this issue of race and identity] and they go back to an incompetent community. . . . We haven't found a way to make this portable for people to take back home." Courter challenged the notion that the members of the Youth Caucus at General Assembly were advanced in their anti-racism understanding. "They have no mentors and they are their own vendor," she observed, adding that they are set up to fail by being assured that they are the experts.

Responses to Incidents at General Assembly

Two weeks after General Assembly closed and as the investigation into its events moved forward, the UUA Board of Trustees published "An open letter to UU youth of color and UU people of color who attended Fort Worth General Assembly and the broader UU community" that read:

> July 6, 2005
>
> At General Assembly in Fort Worth, there were several incidents that reminded us that we have much work to do in our journey to becoming an anti-racist, anti-oppressive, and multicultural association. We, the UUA Board of Trustees, want to express deep sadness and regret that these incidents took place.
>
> Some of these incidents involved apparently disrespectful and racist treatment of our youth by Fort Worth officials. We will respond appropriately to these incidents. When we visit a city, we expect that all members of our Unitarian Universalist community should be treated with respect and hospitality. For this and future General Assemblies, our presence might provide a "teachable moment" for us to work with our host cities on issues involving race and youth.
>
> But we have work do within our own community as well. We have been disturbed by reports of other unfortunate incidents during General Assembly within our own Unitarian Universalist family, in which some UU youth of color were made to feel that they were not welcome. There was an incident outside the hall during the closing ceremonies at the Fort Worth General Assembly. Based on the reports of witnesses, the incident involved several UU youth of color, a UU adult who questioned their right to be there, provoking an angry response from the youth, a UU minister

who intervened in support of the adult, and another white youth who defended the youth of color and verbally attacked the minister, who responded in like fashion with similar inflammatory language. This was not the only incident. We have also heard that on several occasions in Fort Worth, white UUs assumed that UU youth of color were hotel service people and asked them to carry luggage or park cars. We are troubled that some UUs may have treated other UUs as if they did not belong among us. We can and must do better.

Sadly, this was not the first General Assembly to have incidents like these. After one of those past incidents, the UUA Board of Trustees committed to provide safe space to process issues and concerns around oppression and racism and chaplains who could help facilitate reflection, discussion, and learning. However, we as a Board regret that we have not done enough to provide that safe space. We cannot control the actions of individuals, but we can create venues where we can all learn and grow as a community. We apologize for failing to provide those venues and commit to remedy this at future General Assemblies.

As your UUA Board, we pledge to treat all these incidents as a wake-up call for our entire community. We understand that personal stories about individuals' experiences at Fort Worth General Assembly have been recorded and we commit to hear these stories and learn from them. Also, we will work with the General Assembly Planning Committee and other groups to ensure that General Assembly in St. Louis and all future General Assemblies are more welcoming to all members of our Unitarian Universalist family.

In Faith,
Paul Rickter
UUA Secretary

As a more immediate response, the General Assembly Planning Committee began a program of cultural competency training for volunteers, mandated that all GA chaplains be ministers in final fellowship, and agreed to work with the new Allies for Racial Equity.

At its September meeting, the General Assembly Planning Committee noted,

> The Planning Committee needs to be in relationship with persons or groups who can provide the Planning Committee with needed feedback. There were instances of racism and other kinds of oppressions in Fort Worth and the year before and the year before and the year before that as well. We live in a racist society and our General Assemblies are not safe havens. Two questions to consider:
>
> 1) How can we help well intentioned UUs behave in ways that are culturally appropriate?
> 2) How can we sensitize local officials, police et al. who will be working with us that we are bringing a diverse population to their cities?

Dr. Norma Poinsett, a long-term observer of the tensions around race and youth noted,

> It seems like UUs kind of leave their young folks off to just do like Topsy in the book *Uncle Tom's Cabin*. They just grow without any counsel and I think that's unfortunate for white and black kids. When I say kids—a lot of them are a little older than kids, but I don't think we're doing enough to get them used to the atmosphere. Some of them said, "We should have General Assembly in a place where there's no racism." Well, there is no such city. There's racism *everywhere*! It's everywhere. If it's in church, you know it's everywhere. It's in northern cities, it's in Canada, it's everywhere. But there are things that might happen and then you need to be sure that instead of storing them up, you say something to someone, so that someone can help you through the confrontation. We need some kind of counseling or something for youth before they come to GA.

Mishra observed,

> What automatically, unhesitatingly stands out for me because it was a big deal to me—it was heartbreaking to me—

was the Fort Worth GA. It caused more pain than I can verbalize. . . . It was deeply hurtful, the events that actually transpired before and at that GA, but also in fairness, for me as a leader of color within our movement, the fact that our kids didn't come to us, the People of Color leadership, until the experiences of discrimination they were struggling with had stacked up to the breaking point. That, too, was also hurtful. How were we, as adults, so out of touch with our own youth that they only came to us so late in the process? That was a source of hurt, but then the actual events that transpired, too, were incredibly disappointing and hurtful, and caused me to deeply question for many months why I am doing any of this. The institution keeps turning to me to do this type of work, and are we learning anything at all? Is the institution learning anything at all? As difficult as last summer was, and the ensuing months, it may just be the case that we inadvertently reached a crisis point that may be galvanizing the majority culture to do things differently, hear things differently, and try out some new and perhaps, for some, risky things, such as sharing their power and privilege. That crisis from last year may, in five or ten years, be the event we name as an important stepping stone or even turning point. It's too early for me to say now, but it's possible. . . .

JUUST Change

A consultancy approach to doing anti-racism work in congregations had been considered for several years by the Office of Congregational Justice-Making (OCJM), part of the Congregational Services staff group. Rev. Joshua Pawelek, who had been engaged in anti-racism efforts since 1992, noted in 2003,

The UUA administration would like to see OCJM (and the various volunteers and departments with whom we work) develop an anti-racism/anti-oppression consultation program. The consultation idea stems from the recent JTWTC recommendation that district-based consultants should be developed to effectively expand the anti-racism initiative. (It needs to be pointed out that many people have confused the intent of the JTWTC's recommendation. The JTWTC did not recommend consultation as a replacement for anti-racism training. The intent was to expand the overall program, make it more flexible and adaptable.) Anti-racism consultation is actually not a new idea in the UUA. In the early 1990s, the mid-1990s, and the late 1990s, the Faith in Action Department attempted to develop consultants who could theoretically work with congregations over an extended period of time. The rationale for this was as follows: Consultants would be in a position to listen to what congregations need. They would enable congregations to not always feel pressured into hosting workshops they weren't ready to host. They would be able to offer resources and make suggestions that fit the particularities of an individual congregation. They would be in a position to identify congregations that are ready for specific workshops, and they would be in a position to provide effective follow-up to workshops, helping congregations apply their learnings in a way that typically does not happen. None of the three early attempts to create a consultancy program were successful. However, we are poised to try again, and we are very clear that the UUA administration intends for this new approach to be successful.

The goals of the new approach were articulated by President Sinkford in 2005:

A congregational focus is the new shape of the Association's anti-racism work, with the JUUST Change Consultancy rolling out this year, a "Welcoming Congregation"-type resource well along in development, and my specific invitation to our largest congregations and their ministers to get involved. Making this shift has been one of the more controversial decisions of my presidency, at least among the relatively small group of those who became committed to the initial approach. Given that none of us has a certain path to salvation for this transformation, time will have to tell.

At this time, Sinkford met with the ministers of the Association's largest congregations and asked them to focus on the problem of race in our congregations and the pastoral needs of the people of color. He brought a number of people of color and had them share their personal stories of what it was like to be ministered to in those congregations. "It opened ministers up," Sinkford recalled, adding that it was through that meeting and the leadership of Rev. Robert Eller-Isaacs, active in leadership in the group, that he recruited the first large congregation to participate in the JUUST Change consultancy program.

Robinson-Harris observed that the need to do more work on the congregational level was clear. "I could not say congregation by congregation that the majority have done x or y," she said. "It's not that every single congregation has taken the work to heart and made some great truth. I think that a significant number have taken to heart the real need to figure out how to address racism and the shift I see taking place is a recognition of the value of doing internal work as well as external. . . . Also the connection between our justice work and our theology. There are more of our congregations that are having some conversation or conversations."

The JUUST Change Consultancy became the gate through with the Jubilee workshops were offered. "I believe it is timely and appropriate that we are focusing on meeting congregations where they are and to try to engage more of them in this work," Robinson-Harris said, "because in the end that is where the transformation needs to be." A staff report on supporting congregations in anti-racism efforts, called "Next Steps on the Journey," characterized JUUST Change as "meeting congregations where they are and taking them to the next place they want to go" and continues,

> We need to honor and support the work congregations are already doing. We need to support more than one path on the journey. Our resources need to be accessible and flexible. We need to reach out to our ministers as leaders in this work. By centering our consulting on antioppression work we will be able to offer support that is flexible, agile, tailored to fit, and able to meet congregations where they are. Our consultancy work will be grounded in institutional/power analysis

of racism, linked oppressions and wisdom about congregational change/transformation.

We know that:

- approximately 150 congregations have experienced a Jubilee One [anti-racism] workshop, in the past 8 years.
- 34 congregations have experienced a Beyond Categorical Thinking workshop [anti-oppression workshop developed for congregations in search of new ministerial leadership] in 2002–2003.
- more than 275 have participated in Beyond Categorical Thinking in the past.
- we have some 370 Welcoming Congregations.

Each of these represents an opportunity—an open door, a time of readiness, a time of need. With antioppression consulting in our repertoire, we can reach out to congregations and offer to work with them to identify their next steps, to support them in expanding their capacity to engage the work of justice.

The stated goals still included references to the "transformation teams" that had guided the anti-racism efforts in the 1990s:

The UUA still supports the building of anti-racism transformation teams in those congregations, districts, and organizations that have readiness, willingness, and commitment to transform. The workshops that have historically supported this model are the Jubilee I (introduction to anti-racism), Jubilee II (analysis of racism), Intro to Building a Transformation Team, and the Planning and Design Consultation. All these programs are still intact and still deliverable by OCJM and its volunteers. Furthermore, whereas the "Educators and Organizers" training for equipping teams with anti-racism skills was previously presented by Crossroads at a cost of $20,000 for 4 1/2 days of training, OCJM is currently piloting its own version of "Educators and Organizers" modules, with the goal of the entire team-building process being offered by UUA trainers at a total cost of approximately $5,000.

By March 2005, plans were well under way for the consultancy approach, which had become known as JUUST Change. The March JTWTC minutes noted,

> JUUST Change Consultancy Orientation is happening at the UUA in Boston this weekend. The Consultancy has evolved to bring in even more diverse expertise and experience—12 individuals have been brought in. Consultants will be going into the congregations either to introduce them to A-O [anti-oppression] work, help them get un-stuck, or help them plan next steps.

"JUUST Change emerged from the Common Ground work," said Cole Jones, adding that Sinkford's election as president of the UUA and the reorganization under his administration provided a good opportunity to step back. "The 'Common Ground' gatherings led to the understanding that we needed to have multiple ways to engage people. JUUST Change was a resource that was designed to meet the congregation and other groups wherever they were on their journey . . . understanding that some had opted out." She said the new program allowed congregations to look at anti-oppression work in the context of other social justice interests.

Cole Jones added that her background in organizational and program development guided her underlying philosophy for the consultancy-based program, which she described as grounded in:

- an understanding of what it is like to work within an existing organization and how to implement change in ways that benefit those already present in the organization;
- a commitment to meet congregations where they are;
- her background as someone raised within a Unitarian Universalist church that had a multicultural component;

Rev. Sean Dennison

In its efforts to continue to reach out, the Journey Toward Wholeness Transformation Committee established a blog as a channel for dialogue. Here Dennison, who served as chair of the Committee, shares some reflections.

If I had to summarize the purpose of my life and ministry, it would be this: to live in the middle of all the conventional dichotomies and help people see the beauty of all that lies in-between the little boxes that try and fail to categorize us.

What in the world does that mean? Let me begin by listing for you the ways my life has fallen in-between.

First in most people's minds is that I used to be a woman, but now I am a man. I was born female, in a small town in Iowa, but I grew up to be a man. About seven years ago, I began the hormone therapy that enabled me to make this shift. So when it comes to gender, I know a lot about what it's like to be a girl, a mom, and a woman. I am learning much about what it is to be a daddy and a man. And, when it comes right down to it, I am and will always be both. While I move through the world as a man, I can never forget how it was to be a woman. And so my life is enriched and made more interesting by being able to understand how it is to live on either side of the "gender line."

That part of my story is what a lot of people focus on, but it is actually not the heart of why I chose to serve on this committee. What is the heart? Well, what is closest to my heart is my thirteen-year-old son, who is African-American. Learning to parent, to love, to cherish a child whose experience of race is so different from my own has been a challenge and an amazing gift. It would take me thousands and thousands of words to even begin to explain what I mean, but I will tell you one story that I hope is illustrative.

When people ask me, "What's it like to have a black child?" (And yes, people still ask things like that all the time.) I tell them this story. Before I had my son, racism was a monster out there on the edges of my world. I disliked it, marched against it, railed at it, and even sometimes hated it. I was completely and totally against racism. It was, in my mind, an ugly and hideous monster. Then I woke up one day and my baby was in the monster's teeth. So anti-racism and anti-oppression work is no longer an abstraction for me. I live with the monster. I also live with the gift of having my world opened to cultures, experiences, and strengths I never knew existed. It is the hardest and best thing I have ever done. While I have not, perhaps, crossed the "race line," I have been able to look and love across it and begin to learn how to break down the crazy concepts that go with the "race boxes" that we've lived with for so long.

That might be enough, but it's not all. . . . For most of my teen-age years, my mom worked nights as a hotel desk clerk and we struggled to survive. When I had my son, in the middle of my college years, we lived on welfare for a few years. Now, as UU minister, I am financially stable and comfortably middle class. I've crossed the "class lines" a few times, and I believe class issues are one of the most powerful, but silent, issues of oppression in UU congregations. . . .

As you can tell, my journey has been—um—unique, but never boring. I am ever grateful for the many people who have loved and supported me along the way and kept me alive and sane through so much. I'm passionate about the work that this committee has been charged with doing because breaking through these crazy boxes and into the beautiful world between and beyond them will enrich the world so very much. If we can get a little closer to true justice, equity, and compassion, we will have made an amazing difference.

That's why I'm here.

- the anti-racism advocacy of the 1990s, which held as a basic premise that institutions constructed on racist premises needed to be challenged and adapted; and
- a recognition of the long-term nature of anti-oppression efforts and the need to build healthy communities along the way.

"Part of the premise behind JUUST Change is this is a ministry," said Cole Jones, "because at its best, we're talking about developing multicultural ministries and you can't have a multicultural ministry without anti-racism. You can't separate the two. Anti-racism is the foundation for multi-racial, multi-cultural community."

One of the first clients for the new JUUST Change program was the UUA Board, which began asking for training for incoming committee members even before the new program's programmatic structure was finalized. The Board's request hastened the program's development. "We didn't want to deliver up what we had done before," Courter recalled. Both Courter and Sinkford emphasized that the JUUST Change approach was about consultancy rather than set programming, a flexible resource they felt was more suited to congregational needs.

Transformation Committee Links Oppressions
When the JTWTC met in March 2005, several themes resurfaced, including:

- Planning for a pre-GA meeting with congregational presidents;
- The Rev. Dr. Lee Barker, president of Meadville Lombard Theological School, was looking for guidance on next steps from the Committee;
- Continued updates on revision of trainings including Beyond Categorical thinking and the traditional "JTW" trainings;
- An A-O/A-R/MC [anti-oppression/anti-racism/multiculturalism] training for newly elected and appointed leaders scheduled around General Assembly, a directive of the Board; and

- Continued availability of youth and young adult A-R trainings that happen and that members of this committee could
  attend and are encouraged to attend.
- A review of the manual used by ministerial candidates preparing for internship;
- Integrating awareness of accessibility issues and awareness
  into the Committee's work.

The extent to which the Committee had now embraced monitoring a range of oppressions was made clear several times in the
course of the meeting, including one discussion that concluded that
"the Committee needs to be clear that the focus of the work is not
just anti-racism but anti-oppression and includes ableism, ageism,
racism, heterosexism, genderism, sexism, classism, etc."

And the Committee continued its work to redefine itself and to
make itself relevant in a rapidly changing Association:

> The Journey Toward Wholeness Transformation Committee
> is excited about our recent decision to refine our mission. Over
> the past several years we have realized that our broad focus, in
> which we tried to be all things to all people, including assum-
> ing liaison responsibilities to a long list of UUA committees
> and affiliate groups, has diverted us from our original 1997
> charge to "strategically plan, coordinate, monitor, assess, and
> guide the transformation of the UUA into an authentic anti-
> racist, anti-oppressive, multi-cultural faith community." We
> believe we have not been able to provide the type of effective
> assessment the Association needs. By narrowing our focus
> and providing quality in-depth analysis, we are confident we
> can better provide a more useful and meaningful report on
> the status of our journey toward wholeness.
>
> Using a model employed by the Commission on Appraisal,
> our intention each year will now be to choose a particular area
> of Association life to explore in depth, concluding with a
> report to be published and available to the General Assembly
> and to congregations. Our first area of exploration will be the
> anti-racist, anti-oppressive multi-cultural transitioning within

the districts. We will survey district leadership, select a sample of representative districts to examine in depth, and will publish a report for the 2007 General Assembly. Our work is just beginning, and our hope is that this effort will highlight best practices as well as program gaps that will be meaningful for Association and administrative staff as they support all districts, committees, and UUA affiliates in moving towards our vision of wholeness.

VOICE
Rev. James Hobart

Hobart wrote this to counter those who argued anti-racism efforts ran counter to the Unitarian Universalist tradition of congregational polity.

Unitarian Universalist congregations, by virtue of their free choice for association one with another within the Unitarian Universalist Association, are together called to take up the work of antiracism. This inescapable conclusion is based in our theologically-based form of congregational governance, congregational polity.

Our inter-related UU liberal theology and governance are grounded in covenant. Covenant is fundamental for Unitarian Universalists: from the ancient Hebrew scriptures through the Radical Reformation of the 16th and 17th centuries, especially in the first formulation of congregational polity by the Englishman Robert Browne (1582); from the Mayflower Compact (1620), the Salem Covenant (1629) and the covenants of other early New England congregations, through the Cambridge Platform (1648); from the formation of 19th century voluntary associations (including the American Unitarian Association in 1825) through the 20th century voluntary association work of James Luther Adams, and the *Interdependence* study of the UUA's Commission on Appraisal (1997).

With due appreciation for the positive contributions to Unitarian Universalism of Thomas Jefferson (inalienable human rights and church-state separation) and Ralph Waldo Emerson (the primacy of personal religious experience), both Jeffersonian and Emersonian individualism compromise the covenantal basis of congregational polity (*see* Conrad Wright, "Individualism in Historical Perspective," *Walking Together*). Both influence our tendency toward excessive UU individualism. At least as important, both contribute to an extreme UU congregationalism, which equates self-governance with independence. Self-governance is compatible with covenantal congregational polity, independence is not. A proper understanding both of our individuality and our congregational self-governance is, first, relationally grounded, based in our covenantal theology. This position is supported by the weight of our liberal church history, our theology and our ethic, and our congregational form of church governance or polity.

We Unitarian Universalists are called by our relational/covenantal theology and polity to the work of anti-racism; each of us is called, all of us are called. What is the nature of that religious call? An answer to that question requires that a fundamental distinction must be made between racial prejudice and racism. Both are antithetical to our theology and our governance (although, to be sure, not to our historical experience). Prejudice is individual, personal and psychological. Racism is social, institutional and cultural. Even when our individual racial prejudice ends (and we should not be quick to equate our intent with reality), racism persists in our social structures. Racism permeates all our American society and our institutions, including our American UU congregations and our UUA. Quite apart from our intent or our awareness, racism abides among us. In the face of this hard truth, if we are to be faithful to our covenantal religious tradition racism must be uprooted or dismantled. The issue is not whether we should do this difficult anti-racism work. Clearly it is mandated by our covenant, grounded both in our liberal theology and our congregational polity. The issue is: how do we do this hard work?

In keeping with congregational polity, the work of anti-racism cannot be accomplished by a UUA edict issued by the President or the staff, or a directive of the UUA Board or the Moderator, or an action of the UUA General Assembly. The work will not come about from righteous and prophetic words spoken in UU pulpits, or good intentions in UU pews. Yet any or all of these ways may serve to help initiate the call to anti-racist action. The fundamental and common issue is not when and where our call appropriately originates. We can be distracted and divided by arguing that question endlessly. The call to anti-racism may arise in places we least likely expect, for the Holy Spirit will not be hemmed in or tamed. Wherever it originates, the issue is how we respond to the prophetic call to change our ways, our institutional ways, and return to ways that fulfill our solemn covenant with one another and with "the holy thing in life" (James Luther Adams). Our self-governing congregations give their free and uncoerced consent to this call through what our congregational ancestor Jonathan Mayhew termed in 1749 "the gentle method of argument and persuasion." Today we would characterize "the gentle methods" as free inquiry, discussion, tolerance, appreciation of difference, persuasion, consent. For good or for ill, this is our congregational way. Always we are free to honor our covenant or to reject it, take up the work or turn away from it.

Make no mistake; our call to take up the work of anti-racism is imperative. We stand under a twin judgment: our liberal theology and our congregational and associational covenant.

But institutional change never is easy or speedy. It is always messy and contentious. Sometimes it moves ahead and other times it falls behind. It is the work of every day, and it is the work of the generations and the ages. In this circumstance we are called, in the words of the spiritual, to "keep your eyes on the prize."

A story told by James Luther Adams illustrates what "the prize" is:

Some years ago I was a member of the Board of Trustees of the First Unitarian Church in Chicago. A member of the board often complained about the minister's preaching too many sermons on race relations. He often said that academics of course know little of the world of reality. One evening at a meeting of the board he opened up again. So the question was put to him, "Do you want the minister to preach sermons that conform to what you have been saying about Jews and Blacks?" "No," he replied, "I just want the church to be more realistic." Then the barrage opened, "Will you tell us what is the purpose of the church anyway?" "I'm no theologian, I don't know." "But you have ideas, you are a member here, a member of the Board of Trustees, and you are helping to make decisions here. Go ahead, tell us the purpose of the church. We can't go on unless we have some understanding of what we are up to here." The questioning continued, and items on the agenda for the evening were ignored.

At about one o'clock in the morning our friend became so fatigued that the Holy Spirit took charge. And our friend gave a remarkable statement regarding the nature of our fellowship. He said, "The purpose of the church is. . . . Well, the purpose of the church is to get hold of people like me and change them."

Someone, a former evangelical, suggested that we should adjourn the meeting, but not before we sang, "Amazing grace . . . how sweet the sound. I once was lost but now am found, was blind but now I see."

There is the vocation of the minister and the church to form a network of fellowship that alone is reliable because it is responsive to a sustaining, commanding, judging, and transforming power.
(James Luther Adams, *The Prophethood of All Believers*, "Fishing with Nets")

The transforming possibility of liberal theology and congregational polity is seen here for individuals and congregations, if and when we live up to the relational, covenantal requirements. In this power, again and yet again, lies the anti-racism "prize" we all seek.

CHAPTER 26

Theological Schools Engaged

The efforts to generate an anti-racism conversation among the Unitarian Universalist ministry had begun to seep down from the ordained ministers and religious educators to the seminarians preparing for the ministry. Both Unitarian Universalist Theological Schools were engaged in heated conversations around race in this period. Though both experienced tension and discord, growth and change, each school took its own distinctive path.

Another priority for the Sinkford Administration was finding a new approach to the Diversity of Ministry Team, the collection of staff members who monitored the progress of ministers and seminarians of color. In Sinkford's first term, he began efforts to make the group's process known to the people it was intended to help and he added outside representatives from DRUUMM (Diverse and Revolutionary Unitarian University Multicultural Ministries). "We began by identifying the incredible gift being offered by those in preparation for our ministry," Sinkford said, "knowing that if we didn't help them with their successful settlement, it would be another failure."

As credentialing and support groups such as the Ministerial Fellowship Committee and the Diversity of Ministry Team of the UUA staff became more vocal about the special needs of religious professionals from historically underrepresented racial and ethnic groups, these seminarians began to connect with one another in formal and informal ways, such as the formation of a group for seminarians of color, another identity-based group joining the dialogue around race and relationship within Unitarian Universalism.

Starr King's Educating to Counter Oppression

In 2005, the Journey Toward Wholeness Transformation Committee asked the Starr King School for the Ministry, in Berkeley, California, to make an anti-racism assessment of itself. The response was a process involving many individuals and conversations and a comprehensive report by a committee that reflected on some of the core tensions:

> In the Spring of 2005 the Journey Toward Wholeness Transformation Committee (JTWTC) requested a comprehensive report of the process of transformation throughout all of Unitarian Universalism. At Starr King School for the Ministry, the newly formed Educating to Counter Oppressions and Create Just and Sustainable Communities Steering Committee (ECO Steering Committee) embraced and expanded the request embarking on a complete assessment of the school in relationship to its counter-oppressive ("ECO") commitments.
>
> Throughout this assessment, we found a deep commitment to ECO on the part of individuals and the institution. Students, faculty, staff and trustees in all aspects of Starr King's programs expressed over and over again a desire to "*go deeper with the work*," to move beyond an introduction to ECO towards sustained, in-depth analysis and action. But while that intention was clear, there was no satisfactory answer to the question: How does an institution sustain a commitment to educating to create just communities that counter oppressions? How does an individual sustain a commitment to educating to create just communities that counter oppressions?
>
> Throughout this assessment, we found individuals pointing to particular events as proof of our "success." But such events also point to a "failure": they suggest moments when the community is countering oppressions, rather than suggesting a community which consistently counters oppressions.

The report spoke extensively about the complex issues of identity that surround the counter-oppression work:

> The habit of not looking at intersecting oppressions and privileges leads to several dynamics which we found present at the school. When we are talking about one oppression, we cannot forget to talk about the others. When we do, it ends up dividing us.
>
> 1) There is a dynamic of competing oppressions, such as when students say that we focus too much on racism and not enough on animal rights or environmentalism, instead of looking at how people of color, the environment, and animals are all constructed as "too natural," or examining the dynamics of environmental racism.
> 2) There is a dynamic of pitting women against transgender people, instead of looking at the whole system of sexism and genderism as having different impacts on different people.
> 3) There is a dynamic of people from privileged groups claiming that they are being oppressed as men, as whites, etc., instead of recognizing the institutional, systemic dynamics of how privilege is constructed and the internalized dynamics of how resistance to change manifests.
> 4) There is a dynamic of choosing one person from an oppressed group to hold up as the "good oppressed person," and demonizing the other members of that group for not acting like they do.
>
> We need to examine the ways that the "most talked-about oppressions" are constitutive factors in other forms of oppressions. For example, how do issues of sexism play out differently for large or small women? For large or small men? How do classism and ableism contribute to the notion of what race is "supposed" to be? . . .
>
> We believe that understanding the construction of white identity is particularly important for the school at this time.

We have found that even in those areas of ECO work where the school and the Unitarian Universalist movement have been relatively successful (i.e. women's issues, gay and lesbian issues), success has been achieved because white privilege was able to accommodate those changes within itself. In those areas where we have been less successful (race and ethnicity issues, class issues, disability issues, bisexual and transgender issues), we are finding that it is because white identity and white privilege are less able to accommodate those concerns.

The ECO work also honed in on the barriers to doing the work in predominantly white institutions:

Throughout our assessment, we found that there were a number of issues which arose over and over that tended to stop the ECO conversation and work. These statements can also be conversation starters. We see a need to encourage conversation to open up rather than shut down when statements such as the following are made. Asking questions in response might be a way to invite the conversation to unfold further.

1) *"The work is too political."* Should religious people stay out of politics? Why? Or Why not? Is there an effective way to address issues of oppression and privilege without becoming involved in politics?

2) *"The work is too emotional."* Are oppression and privilege merely rational concepts to deconstruct? Is there a place for emotion in the work? What would it take for people to allow or even welcome emotion in our educational work without trying to "fix" difficult feelings of pain, anger, shame, upset, etc.?

3) *"I don't feel safe speaking out as a person with some privilege."* How can those with some privilege take into account the life and death safety issues encountered by oppressed people? How can we encourage and support the risk-

Rev. Dr. Rebecca Parker

Parker, president of the Starr King School for the Ministry, presented these two "Habits of White Privilege in Unitarian Universalism" for discussion with the seminarians who were of color/Latina/o/Hispanic. Parker is the author of several books, including Saving Paradise: How Christianity Traded Love of This World for Crucifixion and Empire *(Beacon Press, 2008, with Rita Nakashima Brock). Seminarian Joseph Santos-Lyons captured these concepts from Parker's work. The book's analysis and these concepts were a direct result of Parker's involvement in Starr King's "Educating to Counter Oppressions and Create Just and Sustainable Community."*

1. *Benevolent Paternalism*—This habit makes the assumption that the privilege and resources enjoyed by White people need to be extended to People of Color. The habit is based on viewing People of Color as less than White people. White people are helpers, People of Color are the helpees. Whites see themselves as resourceful and the habit reinforces White identity as benevolent and good. Roots of this habit can be seen in our tradition's historical leaders. William Ellery Channing, for example, wanted to raise People of Color to the standards and norms set by White people. The unequal relationships are required for the generosity to continue. This habit limits people, especially People of Color, who are viewed as not whole, not fully developed.

An example from the 1981 UUA Institutional Racism Audit provides us with more perspective from the Black experience. . . .

During a break in a UUA meeting, two black persons were talking over coffee. A white person, also a member of the same committee which was meeting, came over to the two blacks and said, "I'm so glad you're with us." At least one of those black persons wondered about the incident: Is there some kind of paternalism—a benefactor relationship here? Is she glad that I'm here today? How welcome will I be tomorrow? Was I a "stray" or an "outsider"—invited in and officially welcomed to be "with them" on the inside?

2. *Romantic Dependence*—This habit involved White people projecting their un-integrated "dark" side or prophetic voice onto People of Color. White people need People of Color to mature, express emotions, or get in touch with their passions.

In this dominant all-White cultural environment, what is the identity, spirit and way of life for People of Color? The experience within the church is inherently rife with incidents of racism, both personal and institutional. The presence of racist attitudes and behaviors, many of which are unexamined within our congregations, takes a toll on People of Color in obvious and obscure ways. The ability for People of Color to gather a critical mass is both difficult due to the small numbers and restricted by the conduct of White privilege that fails to recognize the importance of nurturing and sponsoring community and leadership development for People of Color. There is anxiety over power and place that People of Color interested in life beyond a minimalist congregant that White Unitarian Universalism expresses in unhealthy ways. Leon Spencer, a long-time UU leader, former member of the UUA Board of Trustees and District President, comments that "what makes racism so intractable (in the UUA) is white middle-class people's fear that by coming to grips with it they might lose their identity and the privileges the culture has granted them. . . . The fear is that we might have to give something up."

taking and courage necessary for counter-oppressive work? What are the resources in and around us that allow us to be bold in our commitments to compassion and justice when it is not safe to do so? Who is at risk if those with privilege avoid doing counter-oppressive work?

4) *"I'd rather talk about creating a beloved community than countering oppressions."* Is one possible without the other?

5) *"I can't hear you when you speak in that way."* Can you listen to the content of what is being said, even if the way I'm saying it makes you uncomfortable?

6) *"I can't express myself because there is so much pressure to be politically correct." "The thought police are going to jump on me if I say this wrong, so I'd rather keep my mouth shut."* Would you be willing to see the expression of your thoughts as a way to connect to others? Is "getting it perfect" really more important than participating in the conversation?

7) *"Countering oppressions is extra work that competes with or distracts from the school's mission—preparing people for UU ministry and religious leadership."* Are there forms of ministry that truly have nothing to do with wholeness and liberation? Aren't issues of justice, equity, and compassion core to our Unitarian Universalist heritage and values?

We recognize that these issues come up on a regular basis. They can leave us in a reflective state and become excuses for not engaging in ECO work. As these discussions become repetitive "stopping places" or "stuck points," we as an institution need a plan to be better prepared to deal with these issues. The plan may be as simple as naming that these comments often lead to disengagement from going further with ECO work, and naming that we aren't going to let that happen because we have a calling and a commitment to this work as Unitarian Universalists and progressive people of faith.

At Starr King, the cost of pursuing its "Educating to Counter Oppression" approach was high. The 2005–2006 report recalled,

Faculty members . . . experienced the Educating to Counter Oppression work as an "add on" to already heavy responsibilities. Trust broke down and efforts to bridge differences among faculty members' understandings of what the work asked of us were of little avail. Faculty divisions grew, mirroring and perhaps intensifying tensions among students with differing opinions, feelings, and experiences about the ECO work. The president and dean called for greater accountability to the ECO document [laying out a plan for implementing this work], which heightened long-standing systemic issues at the school regarding the power and authority of the offices of the president and dean and expectations of the faculty.

It was somewhat difficult to separate ECO issues from other issues of morale, personnel, financial stress. The school dealt with this challenge by calling on the help of an Alban Institute consultant, who interviewed all the faculty and staff, most of the board, and many of the students and made a report to the board that was transparent about issues at the school. His report was concluded in the fall of 2004. He coached us to work on communication, conflict-avoidance, and appropriate boundaries and offered an assessment of issues the school would need to address to align itself more fully with its mission and values. He especially encouraged the president and board chair to work together to empower the board to take the lead in defining and supporting the mission and values of the school.

In the early fall of 2004, we received a hate-filled letter that threatened harm to a member of our faculty and his family in connection with his advocacy of counter-oppressive education. We met this challenge, with the help of the Berkeley police, by holding a public rally of support for the school's ECO work. UUA President Bill Sinkford spoke, as well as the President of the Graduate Theological Union. The rally was attended by UU ministers, friends and supporters from Bay Area UU congregations, the Muslim community and queer communities, University of California at

Berkeley, and the member schools of the Graduate Theological Union.

At the same time, during the fall of 2004, students were engaged in the first required semester-long ECO seminar, which raised challenging issues around the emotional and psychological effort involved in ECO work—prompting some faculty members to raise concerns that the ECO work was abusive. This became a point of contention among the faculty. The board of trustees called a new professor whose ministerial work had been among poor and marginalized communities. She embodied a mixed UU/UCC, African American, and lesbian identity. The school had given its larger constituency reason to believe that this appointment would bring a minister from one of our larger congregations to the school. A trustee resigned in protest, after an angry outburst at the board meeting in which he cited his feeling that the school's president was pushing an agenda that had no room for straight, white men. Other trustees, including several who identified as straight, white men, felt otherwise and reaffirmed their support for the school.

Meadville Lombard Theological School

At Meadville Lombard Theological School in Chicago, a number of groups tried to continue conversation around race begun at the Catalyst for Change consultation convened by President William Murry in 2003 to encourage open conversation about continued tensions around issues of race and other oppressions. Responses were mixed.

"In January 2005, I participated in Meadville's Dismantling Racism program," wrote Rev. Dr. Jerome Stone, an adjunct faculty member. "The discussion had five of us associated with Meadville sharing our experiences, followed by students' responses. I have been involved in this sort of work in one forum or another for 45 years. In one sense, there was little new in 2005. But in a deeper sense, sharing successes and failures is an ever-new, ever renewing process. The Journey Toward Wholeness is a way of keeping us at this task."

In 2006, a student, Jessica Purple Rodela, began what she called the "Kaleidoscope Initiative" to reopen the question about how racial issues were discussed at the school. In explaining how and why she started this, she wrote,

When I was in Kindergarten, I stood in line with my class-mates ready to enter the school auditorium on cue for our part in the annual Thanksgiving Pageant. My teacher bent toward me, and removing my Indian headband, said, "it's so your pilgrim bonnet will fit better."

In a society where duality is considered normative, those of us with multiple identities find difficulty in balancing. I came to Meadville Lombard, knowing that it would be my first experience working and socializing with mostly Anglos. For the first time in my life, I assumed my cultural identities might be a curiosity and a resource. Instead, I've learned all the negative ways in which my "otherness" sepa-rates me from the dominant culture.

So much of our language on campus around anti-oppression initiatives starts with the assumption that some-thing is "broken" and needs to be fixed. [Another student] reminded me today that "fixed" also means to "set" some-thing in one place. She suggested that "recentering" might prove more effective.

A kaleidoscope presents us a pattern created of myriad small pieces viewed through a multi-faceted lens with mir-rored images reflecting one another. I believe success lies not in the focusing of that lens, but in the diffusion of image we create together. What would it mean for us as religious lead-ers if we collectively abandoned the language of brokenness, and instead heralded our part in the wholeness of being?

I invite you to a series of discussions over the course of next quarter to frankly discuss our varied lenses and seek ways of moving forward by working together. I propose we begin by considering the questions posed at January's Cata-lyst for Change conference:

INITIATIVE
Sankofa Archives

"We, Unitarian Universalists' Clergy and Laity of African, Native/Indian, Asian, Latin and Hispanic, Arab/ Middle Eastern, and Multiracial/ Multiethnic descent, wish to collect, record, and share our knowledge and assist others to grasp the enduring and universal truths that lie below superficial appearances of experience. We wish to share of ourselves our information freely with other women and men to help them tell their stories of joy and of sorrow, and to also show them the metaphors and the ropes, as medicine women/men, as wise uncles/aunts, as elders who sponsor growth and devel-opment of another's child—nieces, nephews, your child, my child, and many a dog-eared seminarian.

"Elder wisdom has a discerning spirit about the importance of multicultural and anti-oppression training on the battlefield of daily life."

So began the introduction to the Sankofa Archives project. "*Sankofa* is an Akan word which means: 'to go back and reclaim the past so we can move forward; so we understand why and how we came to be who we are today.' "

The project emerged from the creative energy and dedication of Rev. Dr. Michelle Bentley, who began gathering women of color together at General Assemblies. These gatherings, usually late in the evening, created a warm and receptive space for people often tired after the interactions with the white majority culture of General Assembly. "I could call them together as one of the elders," Bentley recalled. Janice Marie Johnson, president of DRUUMM (Diverse and Revolutionary Unitarian Universalist Multicultural Ministries), had once talked about "chalice bearers"—those who came before others, clearing a path. Bentley, who was ordained in 1986, had played that role many times and had a special interest in preserving the accomplishments of others who had walked those difficult paths. "We spent so much time just trying to serve," she recalled.

The archive was housed at Meadville Lombard Theological School. Bentley served as the first director.

- What is "The Work" (of anti-oppression/anti-racism)
- What is the theological underpinning for such "Work"?
- What does "success" look like?
- What will it take to feel heeded and healed?

After holding these dialogues, Rodela wrote a summary of the suggestions and comments the dialogues generated, the first of which was: "Meadville Lombard MUST involve actual Persons of Color in order to talk ABOUT Persons of Color!!! Notice who is absent! Ask: 'Who do we represent?' 'Doing things together IS anti-racism work.'" Other points included:

- ALL students can benefit by being matched with a mentor.
- Giving the Sankofa Archives Project a higher campus "profile."
- Removing the "Portraits of Race at Meadville Lombard": Please REMOVE the dead white guy portraits from the lounge or balance with display of other photos of notable Persons of Color.
- Disband ML's "Undoing Racism Committee" since too much damage now attached to this group to be an effective voice in the non-Anglo community.
- Address classroom, workshops, and other educational gaps.
- Growth and empowerment will occur through community-building, not "analysis-building" or forcing consensus.
- Reframe the language so that we define "the work" in a positive way: Rather than "undo racism" why not "creating justice"?
- Network for communication of a broader experience base.
- Exorcise the "ghosts of Meadville." Allow for a telling of the stories; allow forgiveness; encourage letting go. We are each responsible for beginning the healing. Ask: "Can I hear your story?"
- Consensus kills conflict at the price of murdering creativity. It's messy work. Do it anyway.

In this same period, Rev. Dr. Michelle Bentley, an African-American minister, began organizing an effort to be called the Sankofa Archives for documents, photographs, and scholarly work related to people of color and Latina/o/Hispanic issues. The project's materials note that "*Sankofa* is an Akan word which means: 'to go back and reclaim the past so we can move forward; so we understand why and how we came to be who we are today.'"

Seminarians of Color

The Association was making further efforts to ensure that people of color and those of Latina/o/Hispanic background could make it through the tensions inherent in the process of preparing for the ministry. Rev. Joseph Santos-Lyons, as a seminarian, had helped convene a May 2005 meeting of several of these ministers and mentor ministers. "This has developed in response to the rapid increase in Seminarians of Color who have been ordained and the subsequent increase in the number of Ministers of Color serving UU congregations," Santos-Lyons said, adding that the meeting, facilitated by the Joseph Priestly District and the UUA Identity-Based Ministries Staff Group, provided "limited support, however, to those it seeks to support, with a low-profile, uncertain funding, and little information as to the content and long-term strategy."

Santos-Lyons was instrumental in organizing a group of seminarians who were racially and ethnically diverse. These seminarians supported one another through difficult encounters in predominantly white institutions. Santos-Lyons recalled that Parker, the Starr King president, met with the caucus to discuss several points of analysis she had developed about the attitudes and behavior of whites within the UUA and the ways white privilege was manifested. Santos-Lyons observed that this allowed the seminarians to grasp "white privilege within the Unitarian Universalist context which helps us understand better the religious environment in which People of Color are raised or welcomed into."

CHAPTER 27

In the Congregations

The Association's efforts at the congregational level focused on forming teams whose aim was to transform the congregation by creating a widespread awareness of anti-racist understanding. In an essay describing how to form such teams, Rev. William Gardiner of the Faith in Action staff noted,

> Anti-racism transformation teams have been formed in the Unitarian Society of New Haven in Hamden, Connecticut; the Unitarian Universalist Society of Greater Springfield, Massachusetts; the First Unitarian Congregational Society of Brooklyn, New York; the Unitarian Universalist Church at Washington Crossing in Titusville, New Jersey; the Unitarian Universalist Church in Long Beach, California; the Unitarian Universalist Church of Annapolis, Maryland; First Unitarian Church of Oakland, California; Unity Church [Unitarian] in St. Paul, Minnesota; and First Parish in Brewster, Massachusetts. Teams also exist in the Thomas Jefferson District and the Joseph Priestley District.

Outside official UUA-supported efforts there were other innovations. For example, with the support of Whitney Young funds that had been established in 1982 to support urban ministry, in Connecticut an interracial collaborative called "Courage" sponsored interracial community conversations in the greater Hartford area with the Unitarian Society of Hartford; the Unitarian Universalist Society: East in Manchester; the Universalist Church of West Hartford; and Bethel AME church as the leading congregations.

Congregational Anti-Racism

Congregational-level efforts could be slow, tedious, and often mundane—yet looked at from a 1990 viewpoint the congregations willing to hold the conversations were showing more awareness of how issues of race play out in Unitarian Universalism.

"There is no anti-racist congregation yet," said Rev. William (Chester) McCall. "Some are in process, or think they are."

"We do not provide the education, training, awareness, or importance/impact of the effect of racism, and oppression to our UU Communities," observed Kim Varney, a former Transformation Committee member. "The JTWTC [Journey Toward Wholeness Transformation Committee] and identity based communities like DRUUMM [Diverse and Revolutionary Unitarian Universalist Multicultural Ministries] and the DRUUMM caucuses are not resourced to address the need or demand."

Congregational-level efforts ranged from non-existent to deep and intense. Kok-Heong McNaughton, one of the leaders of the Asian Pacific Islander Caucus, noted that in her congregation, the Unitarian Church of Los Alamos, New Mexico, little had changed:

> At the UUA level, I have seen more staff and volunteers of color, but I have not seen any increase in ethnic and racial diversity (that word again!) in my own congregation. . . . I think this improvement has yet to filter down to the congregation levels. Speaking from my experience as a 29-year member of my church, I've not seen any outcome of any anti-racism work here. It's only been a year since I began slowly and cautiously introducing the idea of becoming a more diverse congregation. We now have an "official" committee called "Committee on Being Accessible and Inclusive," or CBAI, of which I'm chair.
>
> After a year of adult RE dealing with issues of diversity and inclusiveness, when I introduced the idea of studying the [UUA Commission on Appraisal's] report on *Engaging Our Theological Diversity*, one Board member rolled her eyes

and said, "Another year of diversity?" The word "diversity" has negative connotation from their work environment. This is why we use "accessible and inclusive" in the name of our committee.

Many people in my church claim racism does not exist, at least not within our church. Yes, it's out there somewhere, but not here. Surely this is true because, Kok-Heong, you are one of us! One time, when I asked my Adult RE class to write down the names of five of their friends who aren't white and UUs and then share them with everyone, one person said afterwards, "Gosh, Kok-Heong, I didn't even think of you as non-white!" Some of the grandparents who have adopted Chinese grandchildren reacted negatively to a recent article I wrote as part of my GA Report, which included transracial adoption. They told me that in their families, race and color are simply not an issue. How do we teach them about anti-racism when the very idea is so horrifying that they can't look it in the eyes?

In May of 2003, when I created a display in my church in recognition of Asian Pacific Islander Heritage month, I printed out an article about the correct usage of the word "oriental" to refer to objects and not people as part of the display. One person came up to me later and told me that he had never heard that the word could be perceived as derogatory. And when I asked how he felt now that he knew, he said that it gives him more confidence now as he interacts with Asian people. I feel that sometimes, I might get a little criticism about my being "politically correct," or being "too sensitive," . . . but that in the long run, most people are appreciative of hearing a different viewpoint.

Congregational efforts continue to be fitted to the congregations' individual situations. Some have worked to change their identity, how they present themselves to the world. The Unitarian Universalist Church of Arlington, Virginia, displayed this statement prominently in its materials:

We seek to foster and celebrate diversity;
to create a more just world and a caring community;
to share creative gifts through worship and artistic
    expressions;
to support lifelong learning;
and to nurture a spirit of generosity in all that we do.

We are an intentionally inclusive congregation that welcomes people of all races, religious backgrounds, cultural origins and sexual orientations.

Some congregations, having been through trainings and self-education, began focusing on work in the community, such as the Unitarian Universalist Fellowship of Wilmington, North Carolina, which worked with others in the city to mark the anniversary of a racial confrontation that had occurred in their city.

Others persisted with multi-faceted approaches. A few, such as Davies Memorial Church in Prince George's County, Maryland, were led by people of color.

That some good was done at the congregational level seems clear, although the extent and the aims of these efforts are hard to measure. Some congregations have almost no engagement with the UUA's anti-racism and anti-oppression efforts; in some, measuring the UUA's impact is complicated by the existence of more ministers and lay leaders from historically under-represented populations. Rev. Abhi Janamanchi, minister of the Florida congregation Unitarian Universalists of Clearwater, observed,

We did the JTW [training] in my first year, and then the second year we completely departed from the script and focused on the "Color of Fear" video [a documentary on race relations produced by David Lee] and went on to collaborate with a Muslim community that was predominantly of African-American population and African composition. . . . But what I have noticed at least, thanks to all of these efforts, is there's a more organic way of embracing diversity. Even though we are predominantly white, [the] Clearwater [congregation] has a fairly visible Latino/Latina population and

CONGREGATIONAL STORY
First UU Society of Burlington, Vermont

The First Unitarian Universalist Church in Burlington gave small grants for seven years to support efforts in the community to combat racism. For example, in 2006, the church contributed $400 to "Reading Against Racism," a program that brought volunteers from the community into schools to read to students. The goal was to help eliminate racism in schools by promoting literacy and providing community interaction.

Susan Schoenfeld, co-chairwoman of the Anti-Racism Action Committee of the First Unitarian Church, was featured in the Burlington Free Press in an article about the program and about the congregation's six anti-racism grants that year to schools in local counties. She said these were "a way to decrease or prevent racial incidents from happening."

"If you really start talking to people of color in this city and this state, you realize there are issues," she said. "As our state becomes more diverse, it has the potential to increase tensions instead of defusing them."

a South Asian population, and I wouldn't completely attribute it to my presence, because I know it's partly because of the congregational culture that pre-existed my arrival, as well as some other things that happened since my being here.

That the Association had a long way to go to realize the promise of our faith was also clear. Rev. Peter Morales cited the example of the Unitarian Universalist presence in San Antonio, Texas. "San Antonio is the largest city in the country that has a majority Hispanic population," Morales said. "If you only want to take college classes from Hispanic faculty, it's not a problem. If you only want to be seen by Latino physicians, it's not a problem. How do we end up with fewer than ten Latinos in a UU congregation? If you look at sort of [the] educational demographic [of UUs], there are probably fifty thousand [Latino/as in San Antonio]. If you look at our educational demographic who will have nothing to do with the Catholic Church, who are unchurched and disaffected, you know, you're at least at ten or fifteen thousand. Probably more. They're my cousins. We don't have to be . . . patronizing. Most of us speak pretty good English. We don't need condescending stuff in Spanish. . . . How patronizing it can be, that somehow you get ten points for an immigrant monolingual laborer, who has no use for us, but the kind of isolated social worker who speaks perfect English, you get one point for. So we ignore all these people who are the next step. Who are the people who would be perfect, who work with overeducated white people all the time, so who are quite bicultural that way. They're not put off by the language or any of the stuff in our churches."

Rev. Dr. Fredric Muir, minister of the Unitarian Universalist Church of Annapolis, Maryland, noted progress in his congregation. He saw his congregation as leading from the ground level and building knowledge that could assist other congregations:

This is the role of large institutions. This is the role of Beacon Street [the UUA staff]. Supposedly they're our best minds, they know how to do the things, they put together the groups of colleagues and lay people to do it.

I think there is a role for the minister reviewing, understanding, and suggesting to a congregation that they do this
program. It's not like it just comes out of nowhere and here,
do it. Ministers have a lot of power. You can decide what to
present and what not to present.

I guess one of the things that I get discouraged about is
how to even get ministers to talk about this. . . . I'm on the
local [Ministers Association] Executive Committee and
we're looking at the possibility of suggesting to the local
chapter that we become an anti-racist chapter. There are
several folks who are interested in pursuing that. We're not
even sure what that means, what it looks like, but pertinent
to what we're talking about, it will be really interesting to
see colleagues' reactions when this is raised. . . . I've been
here for twenty-four years going to chapter meetings and to
my knowledge, I think, this is the first time we've ever had
a program on anti-racism.

For a small handful of congregations, anti-racism and anti-
oppression efforts affected real policies and practices. At Unity
Church Unitarian in St. Paul, Minnesota, an anti-racism "audit"
was conducted at the congregational level:

In 1998, in preparation for our search for new ministers,
Unity Church did extensive surveying of the congregation,
which showed that congregants felt a spiritual need to connect in meaningful ways with the world outside of Unity's
walls.

In 2001, a large group attended General Assembly and
learned of many ways in which active engagement in the
world was being encouraged by the UUA. That summer,
a group of members went on a pilgrimage for the first time
to our partner village in Transylvania. Participants were
profoundly moved by the experience of having their hearts
opened toward people whom they had just met.

A church service in early 2002 focused on the history of
the Rondo neighborhood, the one-time African-American
neighborhood just to the north that was torn apart by the

construction of Interstate highway 94. The congregation also learned that the Twin Cities are currently one of the most segregated areas in the United States. It was after this service, and in this climate of change, that some members began to question how Unity Church might make a difference.

Working with the Minnesota Collaborative Anti-Racism Initiative (MCARI), which provides training on understanding and dismantling racism, a group of interested members created a task force to develop plans for an anti-racism initiative within Unity Church. They presented a project description and received the support of the Board of Trustees. The Anti-Racism Ministry Team of Unity Church was formally commissioned by the congregation in January 2003.

The congregation of Unity Church Unitarian commissioned the Anti-Racism Leadership Team in January 2003. The ten-member team has participated in several training sessions to learn about the power of systems and institutions with regard to race, as well as how to function as a leadership team. They have crafted vision and mission statements to guide them in their work, and in spring 2005 they completed an institutional audit of the Unity Church.

VISION STATEMENT

Unity Church Unitarian is an anti-racist community that is actively engaged in dismantling racism both internally and in the wider community in a manner that is accountable to communities of color.

MISSION STATEMENT

The mission of the Unity Church Anti-Racism Leadership Team is to lead the church in developing and living out an intentionally anti-racist identity in all aspects of church life. The team will seek opportunities to:

- promote dialogue and learning within the church community about the origins and functioning of systemic racism

- integrate an anti-racist perspective into the identity documents, religious education and member development curricula, worship service, and governance of Unity Church
- develop meaningful partner relationships between Unity Church and communities of color as we work together to dismantle racism in society.

INSTITUTIONAL AUDIT

The purpose of the institutional audit is to research an institution's identity in relationship to racism. The Anti-Racism Team examined Unity Church from the time of its earliest formation to the current day in order to provide a thorough, thoughtful analysis of the church's institutional response to race. The audit will be a guide as the church moves forward in the process of becoming an intentionally anti-racist institution.

The audit is also an invitation to the congregation to participate in work that is extremely vital for the health and future of Unity Church and Unitarian Universalists everywhere. We believe that we can create a church that is not only anti-racist in word, but has genuine acceptance, respect, and love for all people as a recognizable part of its identity. As expressed in the conclusion of the audit report:

... [W]e must have the will and determination to undertake what may at times be very painful work. We want to create a religious institution that is known throughout the neighborhood, the city, and beyond, as a place of loving, welcoming, joyous Unitarian Universalists who are not afraid to live out their values. Can we imagine a day when Unity's bell peals and the whole neighborhood takes comfort, knowing what that ringing symbolizes?

Looking for Support Outside the Congregational Context

For many people of color and those of Latina/o/Hispanic heritage, congregational participation could be marginalizing. Many were the only non-European participants in their congregations or one of just a few.

Janice Marie Johnson, who served as director of religious education for the Community Church of New York, a congregation with a greater racial diversity than most, observed,

I look at 25 Beacon Street. I look at the persons of color in positions of leadership. I don't see too many. Is it that they're not applying? I mean I have no doubt that the hiring practices are stellar. They're stellar in my congregation. . . . But if I weren't serving as DRE, there'd be no person of color in an administrative, managerial position in my congregation. . . . Would a person of color consider coming to Community Church in New York? What might they say? Well, it looks like a good place with good values, but there's no person of color minister or staff member in a position of authority—forget Community. How do we demonstrate that truth in a positive way assuming that we understand that reality? And if we cannot demonstrate that truth, we need to figure it out without compromising our integrity.

Many found community in caucuses organized around racial or ethnic groups at the Associational level. Karen Eng, who has been a leader both in the Asian/Pacific Islander Caucus and DRUUMM, expressed the longing that caucuses fill when she wrote about this 2005 experience:

I hosted the Asian Pacific Islander UU conference at my church in Oakland, California. I was sitting towards the front at the first service on Sunday, feeling very satisfied with how the weekend was going. When I looked up I saw three women from our group leading worship. So then I turned around and looked at the congregation and saw the people from the conference. I'll never forget my surprise when tears started to well up in my eyes. We were all there worshiping together in my beloved church. I could hardly believe it! I saw myself reflected in the pulpit and in the congregation—I had never imagined what that would be like, and there it was. I'm certain that we set the record

CONGREGATIONAL STORY
Unitarian Church North, Mequon, Wisconsin

At the Unitarian Church North in Mequon, Wisconsin, lay leadership interest and strong ministerial support from Rev. Elena Rigg resulted in a major Journey Toward Wholeness focus. Starting in 1999, when the congregation began active participation after Rev. Rigg's call, its work included:

- Obtaining Board approval for a congregation-wide anti-racism/anti-oppression effort
- Hosting a summer service primer on anti-racism and other speakers throughout the years
- Hosting a workshop from Milwaukee Interfaith Conference's Beyond Racism Project, entitled, "Who Am I in the Multi-Cultural World?"
- Developing the Unitarian Church North Fund for Social Justice within the Greater Milwaukee Foundation.
- Holding a congregational forum on the Indian mascot issue.
- Coordinating a trip to the Black Holocaust Museum and to the African Hut Restaurant.
- Collaborating with community activities including providing two scholarships to UNIFEST, the NAACP-sponsored retreat for suburban and city high school students and presenting a sports-mascot forum at UNIFEST.
- Developing the UCN Multi-Cultural Film Series which is on-going.
- Presenting the eight-week UU curriculum, "Weaving the Fabric of Diversity."
- Hosting a weekend "Journey Toward Wholeness" conference in March 2002, facilitated by staff.
- Participating in national efforts such as Campaign Against Racial Profiling meetings and public witness.
- Receiving a grant and presenting two screenings of the video, "What I Want My Words To Do To You," through the national Prison Reentry Program, as funded by the Annie E. Casey Foundation. Guest discussion facilitators were Jodine Deppisch, warden at the Taycheedah Correctional Facility, and Kit McNally, Director of the Benedict Center.
- Continued with the UCN Multi-Cultural Film Series, in the fall of 2003, featuring three films highlighting Indigenous People's films and issues. February '04 film, "The Hurricane," focused on issue of those wrongly-accused and incarcerated, particularly with regards to race. The Series is ongoing.
- Doing public education in the community including educational meeting about powwows, followed by field trip to winter powwow at State Fair Park.
- Engaging in various service projects, such as Guest House, Cathedral Center (both homeless shelters and rehabilitation centers), food pantry at Bethesda Church of God in Christ, and the yearly disbursement from UCN Fund for Social Justice.
- Compiling, and made available, on the occasion of groundbreaking for addition to church, a land history of the church property, with a focus on Native peoples who lived on the land before immigrant settlers.
- Continuing work on partnerships with MICAH and NAACP—how to, as a suburban church, partner, learn, and work with an urban-based community-organizing group, and how to effectively partner with the NAACP in a suburban setting.
- Beginning to advocate, legislatively, on the local and state level through the WI UU Advocacy Network (supported by UUSC), and through our own efforts. It seems that advocacy is the next step for some in the journey, keeping in mind that new members need the opportunity to benefit from an education and partnering process that must be ongoing.

What is key to the congregation's participation? Lucy Friedrichs, social justice chair for the congregation from 2000 to 2005, credits the persistence of lay leaders who kept driving it home to the membership. She also noted that ministerial support was critical: "Rev. Rigg has been our minister since 1999 and has consistently supported these efforts through her participation in events, helpful feedback, and numerous sermons dealing with anti-racism, anti-oppression, and with important figures in the history of civil and human rights."

for the number of Asian/Pacific Islander UU's worshipping together in a parish church on that Sunday morning. It was historic! And it was a profoundly spiritual moment for me. For in that moment I realized that for the first time I was present in a different way than I'd ever been: I felt like a Chinese American and a Unitarian Universalist. Now why is that such a big deal? Well for starters it's hard to make that happen when there are only one or two Asians in an entire UU congregation. But more than that, we showed that when we did make it happen, we experienced worship in a way that was rich and wonderful for both my congregation and for the Asian Pacific Islander conferees.

I believe that our faith wants me to bring my whole self to it, just as it wants my gay and lesbian sisters and brothers, my disabled co-religionists, and all of us in our many identities, to be in community with one another. As religious people, we are called to make this happen.

Let me tell you about my spiritual path. I grew up Presbyterian—in an all-Chinese church. We have many Chinese churches in Oakland. Not only are these religious communities, but they are also cultural communities. By growing up in a Chinese church I lived and learned the cultural practices of my forebears. I don't just mean that I celebrated holidays and rites of passage. Through the church community I became a Chinese American. I practiced deference and respect. I came to venerate sacrifice and hard work. I was groomed to be a model minority. My entire extended family went to that same church.

But I couldn't stay in a church that was increasingly at odds with my worldview, so I drifted away. Then quite by accident I stumbled on a Unitarian church some 23 years ago, and I knew I had found a spiritual home where I could make meaning of my life.

So I accepted a trade-off. My daughter does not have that same cultural foundation. She doesn't feel the rhythm of the cultural year or suffer the relentless reinforcement of those cultural patterns. But she is a UU down to her bones.

And I live out my faith in a context that lacks the cultural connection that I long for.

Now don't get me wrong: I made that choice, and I'm stickin' to it! This is my chosen faith. But does it have to be either/or? This is my dream: to be a UU and a Chinese American in my beloved church community.

I don't know how we make that happen. I wish I did. It's complicated; it takes work and it takes time. But things worth doing are rarely quick and easy. And as religious people I believe that we are called to figure this out. It is the work of affirming the worth and dignity of each of us.

Snapshot of Congregational Life

In the Fall of 2005 Joseph Santos-Lyons developed and distributed a short survey to three hundred Unitarian Universalist People of Color as part of his Harvard Divinity School thesis work. Santos-Lyons wrote that the survey was distributed "exclusively through email list serves and an internet website. In addition, the announcement of the survey was carried to many White UUs, who were asked to communicate the existence to any People of Color in their congregations. The survey received 91 responses in the three-month timeframe provided. There were 16 questions, including several identifying characteristics." Respondents were asked about UUA denominational involvement:

Not Involved At All 29.67%

Very Involved 26.37%

Somewhat Involved 24.18%

Limited Involvement 19.78%

This survey provided a snapshot of congregational life, with a small sample of its findings including the following:

In the Survey of Unitarian Universalist People of Color I conducted, the following are the results of the stated racial/cultural diversity of their Unitarian Universalist congregation:

LEARNINGS
From a Diversity Growth Effort

Davies Memorial member Joyce Dowling wrote this piece, "What I've Learned in the Davies UU Diversity Growth Effort."

- Excuses like "they wouldn't be interested in UUism" or "they have their own churches" are more signs of resistance to integration than truth.
- Everyone wants to be thought of as an individual, not identified by race.
- It's hard to be the first one (or close to it) to integrate a group.
- The friendlier and more sincere people are, the more likely a person is to stay.
- Sincerity can be shown by remembering names and details about a newcomer & giving personal invitations to events you think they'll enjoy due to their interests or invite them to get involved specifically due to their skills.
- If someone is ignored upon joining a work group, they might feel their invitation was tokenism.
- Photos on the web presenting a multicultural appearance are helpful.
- Photos in ads with a multicultural appearance are helpful—the UUA now has some good ones.

- Trust takes time and effort to build up—there are good reasons for many people of color to distrust white people—if we want to be trusted, we need to take extra steps to show trust-worthiness—willingness to give up some power & allow new ideas from new members of color to take hold.
- ADORE, A Dialogue on Race & Ethnicity (Paula Cole Jones creation—UUA Anti-oppression consultant) has been very useful in getting to know each other & building trust.
- "ADORE moments"—new awareness of racism in our culture.
- Learning about White Privilege is very useful to understand how we might be experiencing the world differently without knowing it.
- Learning how one might sound like a white supremacist or at least arrogant in a way that sounds like I want to be a leader without sharing leadership or letting someone else have a greater role
- Creating a Jubilee World was very useful & an exhilarating & community-building experience.
- There are numerous resources to expand your knowledge about anti-racism, including books, articles (many are free online), and online forums.

Racial/Cultural Makeup of UU Congregations Attended by People of Color:

Mostly All White 64.84%

More than average UU church 12.09%

Diverse, not majority, but significant. 15.38%

No Answer/No Place of Worship/
Unknown. 8.79%

It is important to note that of the 15% who reported the most racial/cultural diversity, nearly one-third were members of the same congregation—All Souls Washington DC. For those 9% who had no answer, were not sure or not in a congregation, several were members of the Church of the Larger Fellowship or Church of the Younger Fellowship, virtual congregations connected by mail, phone and internet, and people were unaware of any statistics or presence of other People of Color. Looking at these numbers, reported by self-identified People of Color, we can make the assertion that while all People of Color worship in congregations where they are a considerable numerical minority, the 27% who stated a higher than average racial/cultural diversity (more than 5%) is most likely higher than the percentage of White Unitarian Universalists who worship in such congregational settings.

These selected comments from respondents help to convey both their awareness and their frustrations.

Virtually All-White Congregations (64.84%)

These responses, by far a majority of the respondents, showed a sentiment of frustration at the token presence of People of Color that appeared to manifest with either matter-of-fact resignation or a sense of sharp frustration. Sample responses:

"I am the only People of Color church member in a congregation of 150 membership."

"It falls within the UUA norm, i.e., over 90% White."

CONGREGATIONAL STORY
All Souls Church, Washington, D.C.

The following is adapted from a UU World *article by Paula Cole Jones, a lifelong member of All Souls Church, Unitarian, in Washington, D.C.*

Practicing reconciliation is my personal spiritual discipline. As a management consultant, I know a lot about helping people work through their differences, but until I embraced reconciliation as a spiritual practice, I didn't realize just how transformative reconciliation can be. Practicing reconciliation means I commit to being in right relationship with people in my life and, when I'm not, caring enough to face unresolved issues and improve the relationship.

Practicing reconciliation has helped with my personal relationships but I have also been learning to practice reconciliation across divides in our broken culture, especially racial divides. I have carried reconciliation with me while working in All Souls Church in Washington, where I am a lifelong member, and increasingly, in the Unitarian Universalist Association at large. From this experience I have learned that reconciliation is a competency we can bring to four levels of conflict—in our own souls, between individuals, within groups like my congregation, and between groups such as people of color like me and the dominant white culture. Reconciliation helps us to get into right relationship.

On a sticky weekend in July 1998, seventy members of All Souls gathered to discuss reconciliation at the church. Our racially diverse congregation was staggering after a divisive crisis that ended a ministry. The meeting began a painstaking process of rebuilding our community and deciding how to move forward.

A colleague and I had been hired to facilitate the process. One of the many changes that came out of our effort was "A Dialogue on Race and Ethnicity" (ADORE). People came together to share personal stories about how race had shaped their life experiences, and it was clear that we had tapped into something deep in the community. We kept the door open for anyone who wanted to participate: Everyone has a story about race and ethnicity. Telling the stories brought a new dimension of our lives to the church community and brought us closer together. Six years later, ADORE continues to meet and welcomes new participants.

Several months after the first ADORE meeting, our assistant minister handed me a flyer and said, "You might be interested in this." It was an announcement for "Creating a Jubilee World," a UUA-sponsored weekend workshop about antiracism hosted by the Unitarian Universalist Church of Annapolis, Maryland. About eighty people from congregations in the area attended. I was deeply impressed.

In my professional life I have attended and conducted diversity trainings and hadn't seen any with the courage to approach race as directly and to delve as deeply as this UUA program does. The leaders provided a structure for this large group of people to address one of the most difficult issues in our lives; they took the conversation much deeper than I had expected. My mother and another member of our congregation attended with me, and we agreed that such a workshop would be good for our congregation.

But as we learned when the workshop came to All Souls, some people found this deeper involvement a challenge. We were fortunate to have members of the church board, search committee, ADORE, and other leaders participate in the even more challenging "Jubilee Two" workshop before the search committee reviewed applications for a new senior minister. After five years of reconciliation work, with ministerial participation and lay leadership, antiracism has been embraced widely in the congregation.

"It is very white. You can count with your fingers the People of Color in a congregation of over 800 pledgers. About 65% within a five-mile radius of the neighborhood are People of Color and about 85% are children of color."

"Only a handful of the 250 congregation members are 'People of Color.'"

"Out of congregation of 400, only 6 persons are African-American and 4 East Indian."

Predominately White Congregations (12.09%)

These responses, while attempting to describe what is clearly more racial diversity than the average congregation, still note isolated nature of People of Color in congregational life.

Several noted how the few People of Color are rapidly dispersed among multiple committees in the congregation, an admission that provides evidence of potential burnout, and others commented on the importance of anti-racism and diversity work in bringing together People of Color in the first place, including spouses and children of color who may not normally attend the predominantly White congregation. Sample responses:

"Out of about 750 members and 250 friends at First UU Church of San Diego, we have about 40 People of Color, most of whom are actually multiracial: Latino/Latina, African Diaspora, Indian, Native American, Filipino/Filipina, Japanese, Chinese, Korean, and Middle Eastern. About 7 of these People of Color are active in the church including three who are currently serving on the Board of Trustees. Our active People of Color meet once per month by themselves and once with our white allies. We have a person of color on the nominating committee, one person chairing the associate minister search committee, two on the JTW committee, and one on the worship resource team. People of color also serve as RE leaders and OWL trainers."

"My congregation of about 140 has about 10%, i.e. about 14. How do you count a Hispanic male who is married to a white woman with three kids? Is this 1, 4 or 5? Likewise we have a white man married to an Argentinean with two kids. Have a white couple who adopted a South American girl, how is she counted?"

"There is a small group of People of Color that have begun to organize in my home church. We have started with a potluck for about 50 people with the full support and participation of the church leadership, and are planning activities and events to try and institutionalize the importance of both diversity work and the value of caucusing."

Majority White Congregations, Significant Minority of People of Color (15.38%)

As discussed earlier, nearly half of these responses visibly identified All Souls [Church, Unitarian, in Washington] D.C. as their congregation (the survey did not ask for congregational name). Most voiced a sense of pride and enthusiasm for the presence of People of Color, noting their involvement in leadership, impact on the culture, and the importance to their spiritual growth. Sample comments:

"VERY DIVERSE. I attend All Souls Unitarian in Washington, DC. The racial/cultural diversity is why I am willing to attend church again."

"My church has several African-American lay leaders including me, the treasurer. However the congregation is probably only about 20% People of Color—inclusive of all non-whites."

"The only UU community or worship I participate in is DRUUMM [Diverse and Revolutionary Unitarian Universalist Multicultural Ministries], so it is very racially diverse. And diverse with People of Color, not so much with White folks, though there is the occasional worship with White Allies and family members."

CONGREGATIONAL STORY

Davies Memorial UU Church, Camp Springs, Maryland

These words are excerpted from the 2006 Davies Memorial Growth Plan.

In November 2001, John Crestwell, seminary-trained and interested in parish ministry, contacted Joseph Priestley District Executive the Rev. Dr. Richard Speck to tell him that he was an African American interested in a church; John asked many questions about how he could achieve his goals. Richard told our pastor of 11 years at the time, the Rev. Donald Cameron-Kragt, that he was very impressed with John. The Crestwell family showed up at church the next week. By January 2002, they had joined the church and become very active members.

Rev. Don provided John several preaching opportunities, and soon recognized his gifts for ministry. On May 16, 2002, the Davies Board of Trustees decided to sponsor John for the Unitarian Universalist ministry. . . . We saw that we had before us, through a unique combination of people and place, a special opportunity to build a suburban, multiracial congregation in our Association. . . . Prior to the congregation's Annual Meeting on April 6,

Rev. Don mailed a letter to members and friends to begin the process of congregational consideration of a proposal to the UUA.

We proposed that John be invited to join our staff as Director of Outreach, with the goal of being called by the congregation to join Rev. Don as Co-Minister after he is fellowshipped [as a Unitarian Universalist minister] in June at the 2005 General Assembly.

We received UUA and JPD grants totaling $65,000, which started in Jan. 2004. This amount was not enough to meet our goals. John served as Intern Minister under the direction of Rev. Don until December 2004. He has also served as Director of Outreach throughout 2004. He has shown a commitment to our goals with hard work and results, while at the same time working to support his family since our funds did not allow us to pay him more than a small salary for his efforts. . . . He is a gifted young minister and the results are obvious. In 2001, we had a total of 6 African American members. As of January 2005, we have 28 members and 10 friends as well as nearly 20 children. Our work has been successful.

Rev. John Crestwell was later called as minister of the church.

No Answer/Not Sure/No Congregation (8.79%)

These responses come from persons who live and work as People of Color within Unitarian Universalism but do not attend a congregation, or have not recently, or belong to the distance-based Church of the Larger fellowship, a congregation without a bricks-and-mortar home.

Sample responses:

"I am a member of the Church of the Larger Fellowship. I don't know the racial/ethnic/cultural diversity of this congregation. I don't believe CLF has surveyed its membership to find out our racial/cultural diversity."

"I don't attend worship on a consistent basis anymore. When I was Catholic, I was immersed in a People of Color community. Some of the most meaningful worships for me have been in People of Color communities."

VOICE

Rev. John Crestwell

This is an excerpt from "Paralysis by Analysis," a sermon delivered at the Davies Memorial Unitarian Universalist Church in Camp Springs, Maryland, on December 10, 2005.

There is a Unitarian Universalist paradox. And that is on one hand we need to be rational, analytical and thoughtful—and that's why we're here. We are thinking people, we don't "leave our brains at the door"; we love to get to the root of things and we like discussion, being argumentative—to make sure the democratic process is followed in our church. Detail is important.

But on the other hand, we know we should show and have more faith and less reason sometimes; we know we should be bolder and just throw caution to the wind sometimes but it is hard. And sometimes we know we are arguing a moot point about process, enjoying hearing ourselves talk—we're living in our head—instead of going with the flow of the meeting, when synergy emerges to take us to another plane spiritually. . . . I find that we can be the very antithesis to our wants and desires sometimes. . . .

We talk about a religion that allows us to be free mentally, where we have the space to grow; we talk about the friends we meet and have here at Davies and the love we share. But on the other hand, we never invite a friend who thinks like us to come to our church, we never express our ideals for fear that we may offend someone. That's what we tell ourselves. . . .

I've spoken at several UU churches now and I am amazed at the "coma of complacency" that exists. Even in some of the congregations that are said to be "thriving." They are warm places with wonderful people but not much is being done from my perspective to really make our religion a beacon of light in this country. . . .

Dr. King, during the end of his short career, saw liberal religion as full of many words and few deeds. He grew disenchanted and disheartened by the majority of churches that claimed to believe in justice but would not work to end injustice. Now we know many UU and protestant churches were involved in the movement, but most were not in that time. . . . Sunday after Sunday he said the preachers would preach nice "essays" about relaxing and keeping your blood pressure down and he said they would never challenge the cultural ethos—instead they apathetically "played with religion," he said. He felt liberal religion, in particular, claimed lofty values; liberal religion believed in the best of the American ideal; it believed in being open-minded, and believed in creating the world community that offers peace, liberty and justice for all. But when it came down to it, he felt they were more interested in preserving what they had than making space for those at the margins. Dr. King would quote from the book of Amos 5: 21–24: "I hate, I despise your religious feasts; I cannot stand your assemblies. Away with the noise of your songs! I will not listen to the music of your harps. But let justice roll on like a river, righteousness like a never-failing stream!"

And he would quote from Isaiah 40: "Comfort, comfort my people saith your God."

This was King's way of trying to compel Christian churches to see that their god called them to something more than just an assembly; something more than music and that something more was service to community—as a true example of living religion. . . .

[W]e've got to move past our paralysis from analysis. We've got to move past getting stuck in our metaphors and similes; we get stuck in our poetry, in our history lessons, in our scientific explanations, in our theology, psychology, biology, physiology, and anthropology, to name a few. And these are good things to know, don't get me wrong, but we've got to get out of our heads. And something tells me we stay upstairs—in our heads—as a justification for not going downstairs to the basement where the work must be done. Every now and then we've got to move from the mountaintop and into the valley. Every now and then we've got to move from hibernation and stagnation to participation.

Now, I know this from first-hand experience because I look at myself everyday and I think I am analytical and critical and not doing enough. I've told myself, "John, don't live through the history books—make history! Don't wait for change—be change! Don't wait for peace, create peace!"

CHAPTER 28

Youth Step Ahead

In 2005, the Youth Council, the governing body of the Young Religious Unitarian Universalists (YRUU), had to navigate through divisive issues posed by the Consultation to and for Youth, an effort to reexamine the UUA's youth programming. The Youth Council's concerns were many, and several centered on anti-racism, in particular that the task force overseeing the consultation did "not live out our anti-racist/anti-oppressive commitment" and that "due to a lack of representation of People of Color interested and dedicated to Youth Ministry, the approximate $150,000 [consultation] process cannot be as efficient as we need it to be." In addition, the Council voiced "concern that youth voices will not be heard when trying to explain our issues of non-representation of People of Color."

The Youth Caucus, made up of all the youth delegates to General Assembly, also passed two resolutions related to anti-oppression work, including "It's time we did even more for Anti-Racism in YRUU!" which called for the creation of an anti-racism staff person for youth.

Janice Marie Johnson and Rev. Hope Johnson, sisters both serving in the New York City area, were vocal champions of the youth. "I'm trying to imagine what would it be like if we didn't have the younger generation," Janice Marie Johnson said. "I actually think that my involvement is most purposeful because of the younger generation. And it's not because they are the leaders of tomorrow. In the UU movement, they're the leaders of today, too. . . . If we think of them and the pain that I feel, see, and know. Where are the books to help guide them? Where are the books and people to help us guide them? They are kind of far and few between."

Youth Challenges

The Spring 2005 issue of *Synapse*, the YRUU newsletter, reflected the level of energy the youth and young adults active at the national level had invested in the anti-racism efforts. Siri Larsen, a member of the YRUU Steering Committee, wrote in the Spring 2005 newsletter,

> This year's Steering Committee has gone through a lot together this year in terms of Anti-racism/Anti-Oppression work. We've stretched and grown and are energized to work hard for a truly Anti-Racism and Anti-Oppressive YRUU. There's so much exciting work going on right now!
>
> - This February, our UU Anti-racism Trainer Organizer Program (a youth-led training program) led the first-ever Regional Anti-racism Analysis Development Conferences, which were open to elected Youth and Young Adult leaders as well as others.
> - There is a Youth of Color Leadership Development Conference happening in Dallas, Texas in June. . . .
> - A website on Youth and Young Adult Anti-racism work is coming into its final stages of completion, soon to be available to you to check out for HOURS at a time!
> - A meeting of YRUUers of Color to evaluate Youth Council's People of Color leadership structure and the relationship with DRUUMM is happening soon.
> - And the Youth and Young Adult Anti-Racism Transformation Team is starting up!

Though youth active at the national level had been seen as some of the most committed advocates of anti-racism work, tensions had grown within the community of youth and young adults, some of whom found themselves at odds with their congregational culture when they returned from General Assembly or other national-level gatherings.

Megan Dowdell, who had been invited to be part of Youth Caucus staff at the 2000 General Assembly, recalled, "All I remember feeling was how my home congregation . . . was so disconnected and I had no idea how I could bring all this amazing information I had heard back to them, especially at 15."

One story illustrated the inherent challenges youth faced. Elandria Williams started out as a member of the Thomas Jefferson District Anti-racism Team when she was sixteen in 1997. She remembered doing an exercise called "The Wall of History": "We hit the 1960s and Judy Turnipseed said she had been working for Bull Connor. I realized I was sitting with people who could talk about having nannies and help and then to see them breakdown and cry. . . ." While this was shocking, the acceptance and openness to change were important. She was allowed to participate. "I felt loved," she said. "That summer I came to General Assembly and the TJD Annual conference."

After a negative experience with race at her first General Assembly, she decided to focus on local activism and connection to all anti-racism activities through the District team.

Though she was committed to addressing issues around race, she and other youth continued to find that the Crossroads model, centered as it was in a post-Civil Rights era design, did not work for youth who had other realities and other benchmarks. In 2002, Williams was tapped to become anti-oppression/anti-racism coordinator for the two major young adult conferences, OPUS and CONCENTRIC, and in 2003, began working with Jyaphia Christos-Rodgers. Sent to the airport to pick up someone, Williams had a bad encounter with the person she was to pick up: "I go to this girl and she says, 'Oh, I don't need any help with the luggage.'"

One difference she sees with youth and young adult work is the value put on staying in relationship as well as the emphasis on being "anti-oppressive" over "anti-racist." "There's no such thing as a hierarchy," she said.

"I had one guy come up to me and say, 'I don't think I agree with everything you say, but you came up to me and talked,'" Elandria Williams recalled. "That's one thing I don't think the adults do, leave room for dissent. . . . I understand we are not in a secular movement, we are in a faith movement. In a faith movement, we

VOICE

JooYoung Choi

This was sent to participants at a November 2005 youth conference held in Philadelphia. JooYoung Choi is a former member of the youth staff at General Assembly.

The one thing I wish to do is to stress to everyone to not be color blind or blind to other aspects of people's identities. I say this because I do believe it is possible for people to treat one another with respect and care AND see a person's color. . . . I hope that we can deconstruct phrases like "color blind" or "I'm just a human being" or "I will treat and expect others to treat me the same." These are phrases that I grew up with, but many of these sayings left me in an awkward place as a person of color in a primarily white town. Many of these sayings ignored my identity, didn't leave space for my identity, or ignored the systemic oppression I was affected by as a youth, and thus ignored the strength I had cultivated due to resourcefulness, faith, and the mentorship from many other young leaders and adult teachers that believed in ending racism and oppression.

The first phrase, "I am Color Blind," as a child it made me ask, What is so wrong with my color that you must be blind to it? In my youth I realized that many of the people I knew were blind to the systemic oppression that I and other people of color and queer folk battled with. . . .

As for the phrase "I'm just a human being" this was something my white family had said to me a lot, we are just human beings, but when I got older I realized that people never asked my white sister where she was from, yet, at least twice a day I was asked either "what are you?" or "where you from?" So everyday I had to explain, what I was, and although I would say I was human first a lot, it didn't work like my parents had said it would, people gave me looks, people told me I was being "fresh or smart" with them. Or that I didn't have to "give them that attitude." After a while I gave up being a "human being," I was tired of that battle and so, I patiently just told people I was Korean.

Third, there is the phrase, "I will treat and expect others to treat me the same"; this seems like a fairly basic idea, that

would make sense. But I have noticed that if people and people's experiences are different, than how can we treat them the same?

If a doctor "treated" everyone's sickness the same, then only some of the people would get better.

What if the doctor treated everyone like they had a stomach ache, then everyone with an ache would get their pepto bismol and feel better, but everyone else, who had asthma, diabetes, heart palpitations, and the flu probably wouldn't be doing okay. The same thing does with systemic oppression, which I feel is a lot like an illness that hurts our communities and hurts the people within the communities.

So if people are affected by classism, racism, homophobia, heterosexism, sexism, ageism, etc, and we give them all the "pepto-bismol treatment" it probably won't work.

I do believe being loving and caring are so important in this world, and many people believe that love is beyond all the above-listed oppressions.

And I believe that, too, but to get there, we can't ignore all those oppressions because they are very real, it is only when we start to acknowledge the oppressions that we or the people in our community have been affected by that we are able to see the struggle that ourselves or the people in our community have had to battle with, and it is only when we see the struggle that we can see the resourcefulness, the creativeness, the faith, the gifts, the love and the lives which have endured through the oppressive forces. It is only when we see all this that we can truly be able to love one another, as three dimensional, diverse, beautiful, laughing, crying, breathing, reaching, living, learning and real people.

But we must get there, and the first step is we must see each other.

If you wish to love me, do not be blind to my color, my sexuality, my abilities, my class. If you wish to love me, do not be blind to systemic oppression, and do not be blind to the oppression that has affected me. My color is beautiful.

The oppression must be identified, if we wish to destroy it. And if you do not see the systems that tried to break me down, you will never see my soul that has soared so high. Don't you see it? My soul has grown strong throughout the struggles, and if you do not see any of this, you will never know me. And if you do not know me, you cannot love me.

can't leave anybody behind. . . . [W]e need each and every one of you, because each and everyone of you is a Unitarian Universalist like I am."

She said the youth needed support: "These kids are trying to take on their school system and get people to stop using the N-word and they don't know they have adult support." She noted that she felt as if she hadn't really had real mentors because she came in and was immediately put in leadership positions.

Rev. Hope Johnson, who has served as a formal and informal advisor and mentor to the youth, said that she saw this sort of leadership development as perhaps the most significant contribution she made to anti-racism work. She also said it was "the most difficult thing I've ever taken on in Unitarian Universalist leadership."

The youth had a growing ability to understand a complexity of identities, which was a hallmark of this time. "I can say a lot about identity, because I came in with folks expecting me to be African American, and it was like, I mean, I remember being called to the carpet for daring to say that I'm culturally Caribbean," recalled Janice Marie Johnson, president of DRUUMM [Diverse and Revolutionary Unitarian Universalist Multicultural Ministries]. "African American isn't good enough? Well, that's not who I am! I can't change my life experience. This is who I am, why would I want to change? I also come at the AR work through the lens of not being American, and that's a very different experience. So there's all of that, really all of that in the grand mix, and it's an exciting time. But back to accountability. One of the things for us has been, all of us as people of color, look at how we've been able to work on our growing edges around rubbing up against, understanding, learning about each other's identities. Who we are today is a far cry from who we were as a collective twenty years ago."

CHAPTER 29

More Ideas About Identity

The emergence of an identity group for supporters of anti-racism advocacy who identify as "white" or "European-American" was greeted as positive. Many leaders from racial and ethnic groups historically under-represented in Unitarian Universalist circles saw "white allies" as a group capable of taking up some of the leadership burden that had fallen disproportionately on them.

White Allies Organize
A little-noticed event at the charged 2005 General Assembly in Fort Worth was the emergence of an organization for those who identify themselves as "white allies" in the work of anti-racism. Many saw the emergence of this group as one of the most significant achievements of the Journey Toward Wholeness. The incidents at the Fort Worth General Assembly accelerated the growth in understanding for whites in a predominantly white Association that they have particular anti-racism and anti-oppression roles to play.

"The founding of Diverse and Revolutionary Unitarian Universalist Multicultural Ministries [DRUUMM] is one of the most positive outcomes of the UUA's anti-racism efforts," Rev. Josh Pawelek, who began his anti-racism commitment as a young adult seminarian in 1992, said before the GA began. "Although DRUUMM serves many purposes, certainly one of the most critical is that of a national anti-racist accountability structure for the UUA. I have been personally impacted in a variety of ways by the existence of DRUUMM. Most recently, and perhaps most importantly for me, DRUUMM leadership called on its white allies to form an independent organization in the late winter of 2004. I and about ten other white anti-racist UU activists heeded this call,

516

planned an organizational meeting at the 2004 General Assembly in Long Beach, CA, and were voted in as the interim steering committee of the Unitarian Universalist Organization of White Anti-Racist Allies [later renamed Allies for Racial Equity]. Over the past year we've been creating the basic structures of an organization . . . and we've been planning a business meeting for General Assembly 2005. I have made this work a priority in my life, because my organized UU sisters and brothers of color have asked for it. I am very clear about the things I have given up to make room for doing this very important work. When white people make themselves accountable to people of color, it cannot help but change our lives."

Said Rev. William Gardiner, a leading UUA anti-racism trainer before he retired: "The harder I've worked on my white identity, the deeper my relationships are with people of color: not trying to fix them, not trying to fix other whites, either (that's another trap). How to wake up whites out of denial, to invite them into different ways of being?"

Added Rev. Keith Kron, director of the UUA Office of Bisexual, Gay, Lesbian, and Transgender Concerns: "This is what I look for from our white folks on this work: 1) Do they understand they do not know everything? 2) Do they know that they are still good people? 3) Do they understand that the work of unlearning oppression is lifelong work?"

The emergence of a "white allies" presence was heralded by many in DRUUMM and in the Latina/o Unitarian Universalist Networking Association (LUUNA). Said Janice Marie Johnson, DRUUMM president until 2006,

My observation is that they've asked themselves the tough questions, "Okay, who are we?" "Why are we in this work?" Truth be told, if it's about who's the better anti-racist, we need to close up shop. I see them being intentional around eyes-wide-open looking at events and situations, thinking about what their role and responsibility is or should have been, and really looking at the incredible learning of how to get up to speed, how to be an effective ally. Being an ally, whether you like the term or not. Being an effective ally means really understanding that you've got to give something up. You are not asked or expected to give up your power per se, but you're knowingly giving up your sense of entitlement. You are giving up always being in the driving seat. You are giving up distrust of persons of color to do a job less well than you think you can do it. You can only work honestly with people of color in an anti-racist context if you trust them. I can only work honestly with white people if I can consider them to be my allies in the work of anti-racism. That is a call that I am willing to trust, that the allies are making the right call and I think that they can be instrumental in helping stuckedness become unstuck. It's not going to be the people of color doing it. We're getting tired of doing it.

The creation of a "white allies" group was not met with universal enthusiasm. "I think it was very fragmented opinion as to the value of—they call them identity groups now, where you separate into individual caucuses," said Rev. Marjorie Bowens-Wheatley. "There's a lot of ambivalence about the value of that. Whether it was helpful, whether it was damaging, what it has led to is the white allies' group—and the whole notion of whites being accountable to people of color I also have some ambivalence around. On the one hand, yes; on the other hand, there's so much diversity of opinion within the people of color group, how are you going to quantify that? What does accountability really mean? I've had many conversations about this with UUA leadership. There's a lot of ambivalence. I've never been able to get a satisfactory answer as to how it really works. And so now that there's a formal white allies group. . . ." She added that initially, the group was affiliated with DRUUMM, which gave it more accountability.

Rev. Manish Mishra, elected president of DRUUMM in 2006, hailed the creation of Allies for Racial Equity:

The white culture does not turn to other white people in the culture, in the movement, to ask for help in doing the work of racial diversity. They turn to us. And there's a feeling that only *we*, as people of color, can accountably represent the

VISION
Allies for Racial Equity

This statement comes from the founding documents of Allies for Racial Equity.

Our vision: We the UU Allies for Racial Equity ground ourselves in a vision of an anti-oppressive, multicultural Unitarian Universalist faith. We will be accountable to DRUUMM [Diverse and Revolutionary Unitarian Universalist Multicultural Ministries] by building a movement among white UUs to understand white privilege and unlearn racism and white supremacy. Recognizing that we have a long journey to becoming an anti-racist, anti-oppressive, multicultural faith community, we begin with a commitment to:

- Develop an anti-racist practice
- Support DRUUMM leadership and DRUUMM initiatives
- Include diverse perspectives committed to recognizing our humanity
- Cooperatively journey together in mutuality and right relationship towards transformation and wholeness
- Support other white UU's as we struggle together to effectively use our anti-racist power to help transform the institution and Unitarian Universalist congregations
- Provide resources for a sustainable road to justice built on love, faith, hope, and courage

views of people of color. That's a dichotomy; it's a fallacy that sets the very, very small number of people of color that are first in the movement—and that, second, pass the smell test of being acceptable interlocutors—it sets us up to be burned out. If nobody else can do this work except us, then we *are* going to get burned out. . . . What I saw at this past GA was the Allies for Racial Equity (ARE), who are in my experience as a UU a group of very well-intentioned white folk, who have done a lot of work around understanding their own identity and how their identity impacts those who are different—I saw them stepping up to the plate and saying "No," this work is not just the work of people of color. We are here and we're going to do it as well. And I've been processing all of it in the weeks since GA, and one of the phrases that I found so helpful in helping me contextualize all of this is that these folks in ARE are "giving us access to their power and their privilege." They're voluntarily giving us access to their power and their privilege. It's power and privilege that we cannot recreate. Even if the institution asks us to be on seven, eight, and nine committees, my raising an issue on a committee or board that I'm on is different from a majority-culture UU on the same committee stopping the discussion and saying, "Hey, I need us to think about the impact of this on how diverse we can be or won't be."

Having a separate place for "white allies" to meet also allowed the deepening of community within communities of color. Kim Varney, chair of the Journey Toward Wholeness Transformation Committee and a founding member of the Asian Pacific Islander Caucus of DRUUUM, recalled a worship service as part of an annual DRUUMM meeting: "The comment was that the gathered community that day is the future makeup of the Unitarian Universalist Community envisioned by the General Resolution in '92 and '97 on anti-racism, anti-oppression and multiculturalism."

Operating as a white ally involved a set of skills, as Rev. Dr. Tracey Robinson-Harris, director of the Congregational Services staff group of the Unitarian Universalist Association and a long-time anti-oppression trainer reflected on in an essay:

When I walked into the room to introduce myself—being the newly settled minister and this my first Sunday of the new church year—I expected a warm welcome and an opportunity to learn. What I got from the leadership of the Black History Committee were polite introductions and a clear message. The message—in so many words—was that they did not need me there, thank you very much. I had the good sense to leave them as graciously as possible. And it finally dawned on me that it was true—they knew the church better than I and certainly knew more about Black History than I and they did not need me. What was the best relationship for me with this committee and in the service of the congregation?

Then I had no name for it—and had to figure it out as I went. The journey I was on was not really about being a good minister. It was about transforming what it means to be a "good minister." But the "good minister" wish I held so tightly was the thing that drove me, pushed me forward into unfamiliar territory time and time again; sometimes against my will.

There are numerous incidents, moments, encounters that make up the winding path I have followed. There was my march beside the Nation of Islam in a protest against the first Iraq war and conversations with Imams serving the Muslim communities in New York City. There was the confrontation that led to Dialogues in Black and White. And there was the group of white folks that gathered to explore white privilege—in a multiracial congregation where integration remained central to our identity.

Since then—then being the late 1980's to mid 1990's—there have been many more moments, with frustration, embarrassment, joy and understanding. What I eventually came to understand is that I was learning about what it means to be white—and in a particular way. I was learning about what it means to be white and to be an ally to persons of color in our faith community.

Those encounters that have become part of my identity—that have led me to reshape my self-understanding as a white woman—have become a history that can teach me about the spiritual work that I need to do to grow in my identity as a white anti-racist ally. Taken together they move in and out of familiar places, cross territory I cannot imagine before getting there, bring me up short and push me forward.

Spiritual Practice: Mapping the Terrain

I was born and grew up in the South—in a small city that like the rest of the South was segregated. My home state of Virginia has a long and stubborn history of maintaining racism at almost any cost. People of color—all of them as I remember them were African American—have been a part of my life for as long as I can remember, in the ways that segregation and racism constructed such things then (1950's and 60's).

The messages about my superiority as a white person were everywhere—racism was overt. There were the stories of the lynching tree not far from my house. And there were the "best" restaurants, the front of the bus, the cleanest water fountains, the public pools in the city parks, the "nicer" neighborhood, the "nicer" house, the front doors to every institution and the better hospitals, schools were for me. I knew about the Klan. And the black part of town. And those people.

I knew about the inferiority of people of color—captured in the simple phrase "lock your doors, honey" uttered as we approached the black part of town which we drive through regularly on the way to my grandmother's house.

I grew up Southern Baptist. Another institution made for me—created when the Baptists split into Northern and Southern branches over the support of slavery, the religious/theological support of slavery. In my church every Sunday there were two rows of pews roped off—everyone said they were saved for visitors. And everyone in this white congregation knew that they were saved just in case, by some chance, we should have some black people "visit" our church.

As Judith Levine wrote some years ago in an essay in *Ms.* magazine:

INVITATION
For White Folks Who Hate Identity Groups

When she wrote this with help from Nancy Digiovanni and Annie Abernethy, Selby was a member of the Anti-Racism Trainer Organizer Collective, a former Young Religious Unitarian Universalist staff person, and a student in Bloomington, Indiana.

Part I: The Apology

I'm writing this piece to some of my fellow White People who may have attended Identity Groups and gone away feeling angry, accused, or hurt. I'm writing to those of you who have heard that White Identity Groups are where White People get together so the facilitators can tell them they're racist and bad; I'm even writing to those of you who have attended in the years past and kept coming back. To all of you, I want to say I'm sorry.

I'm sorry because I've been a facilitator of several White identity groups, which I now believe were led very poorly. There was a lot of shaming, invalidating your experiences, broad generalizations, and unnecessary schooling involved. I'm sorry I called you out in anger or tried to shove definitions down your throat. I'm sorry I tried to tell you what your experience as a White Person was supposed to be. I'm sorry I dismissed your concerns and your pain. I did this because of my own feelings of guilt as a White Person and my own struggle with my identity and life experiences that I didn't know how to handle then. I didn't know how to deal with it all, so I took it out on other White People. I used that age-old bully tactic of pushing other people down to lift myself up, and I'm really sorry you had to experience that.

You see, Identity Groups are a fairly new thing for YRUU. We've only been doing this for five years now, and compared to the history of an organization that's a pretty short time to enact institutional change. . . .

Part II: The Invitation

With that said, I would like to invite you all back to White Identity Caucusing. As short of a time as five years is, some significant changes have been/are being made. Those of us who have been working with White Folks on Anti-Racism have learned quite a bit from our mistakes and our successes. We are beginning to listen to all of your concerns, and are starting to listen better to People of Color who are concerned about our activities and strategies in ID Groups. There is collaboration with other organizations doing Anti-Racism and Identity work, and as we have been witnessing their style they have been giving us some important critiques of our work. We have Anti-Racist elders in our faith who are working with us now giving us their support and guidance. We're doing things differently now. We're becoming a community of White Folks that support each other's struggles, validate one another's experiences, and appreciate the cultural diversity that exists in White communities.

Don't get me wrong. Some of the old problems are still present. . . . We need to reach all those people who have attended those shame-based White ID Groups of the past, say "we're sorry," and show them another way of doing AR [anti-racism] work so "the shame" isn't perpetuated. We need to be continuously critical of what we're doing in our activities, strategies, words, and principles. We still need to break down issues of elitism in the White Allies community and be more inclusive and appreciative of new folks. We need to value different ways of approaching Anti-racism, so if someone doesn't follow the YRUU precedent we can still appreciate and incorporate those sentiments and view them as steps in building an Anti-Racist community. Most importantly, we White People need to keep working on Anti-racism and the struggle to understand our identity as people who are privileged by the oppressive system of racism. It is our responsibility. . . .

Give White ID Groups another chance. See if you find truth in anything written here. See if there are changes being made. If you still don't like them, I won't blame you. I'll do my best to listen to your concerns and explore what other transformations can be made. We can work together to build our community. We need to work together.

"Whiteness purports to be nothing and everything. It is the 'race' that need not speak its name. Yet it defines itself as no less than whatever it chooses to exclude. To grow up white is to be the ground zero from which everyone else differs. . . . 'I didn't think of myself as white. I didn't think of myself as superior. I just felt *normal.*'"

To borrow Rebecca Parker's phrase from [the book] *Soul Work*—am struggling to inhabit my country. My country is the one I inhabit as defined by whiteness and race. And my country is also the one shaped by my own ethnic and cultural heritages. The latter was no easier than the former to see and learn—since the one country as defined by whiteness rendered the other invisible. And in my case, the latter has meant learning about Scots Irish immigration into and through the Shenandoah Valley of Virginia and the life of the Scots Irish before they were immigrants to the place I know as Virginia. Like a thirsty soul who finally found a well, so many things fell into place—family stories, the importance of place and land, a physical connection to the rhythms of Appalachian folk music as though I know them even though I am hearing them for the first time.

Spiritual Practice: Living in Discomfort

Given the invisibility and normativeness of being white in this society, myriad assumptions follow, unseen and unquestioned until they surface with attendant discomfort. Those that I have first-hand experience of include:

If you get what you want, I will lose what I want/have. (Either/or. Scarcity. It is either me or you; there is not enough to go around.)

Of course, I can speak and you will listen and you will take seriously what I say and probably even agree with me. (Entitlement. Of course I am in charge. I get to have my say, my way, and without challenge.)

I don't know everyone. They don't do this the way I do. I don't know where I belong. (Loss and grief—the world will not be the same and I will not have the same place I now have.)

Who are these people? What do they want? Why are they here? What do they want from me? (Fear. Of the unknown. Of the other. Of sharing my self. Of the risks of being with the stranger, or being the stranger.)

Several years ago I found this quote from Alice Walker and found in it the greatest source of discomfort I encounter. As a Minister of Religious Education, leadership was my calling. And then there was this: "I will cease trying to lead your children, for I can see I have never understood where I was going. I will agree to sit quietly for a century or so, and meditate on this."

I have moved on since then. And now the landscape of my discomfort is not so much a question of my leadership as it is a continual challenge of my capacity to discern. The experience of safety—or lack of it—for those of us Unitarian Universalists who have privilege(s) of status (as straight or white or able bodied or male) is mediated by the status we, individually and/or collectively, enjoy. Those of us with privilege(s) of status face the difficult necessity of discerning the difference between lack of safety and loss of comfort, loss of the familiar. How can we develop a fine-tuned sense of the difference between safety and comfort? As we sat together and wrestled with this issue one of my colleagues said simply: If it feels uncomfortable move towards it. If it feels unsafe, pay attention.

When we confuse safety and comfort—saying we feel unsafe when what we really feel is uncomfortable—we impact our efforts for change, too often slowing or diverting them until we regain some sense of ease with the way things are. For those with the privilege(s) of status we must learn to allow our lack of comfort with something to be a sign to pause, take stock, and move toward our discomfort. Moving toward discomfort may well be a sign that we are practicing a healthy spiritual discipline that is part of change and transformation.

**Spiritual Practice: Appropriation and the Challenge
of a Tradition that Draws from Many Sources**
I remember the General Assemblies when we debated the
addition of a source to the list of those from which we
draw—to add "earth centered traditions." For my personal
spiritual wellbeing this seemed so right. And I know that
my chosen spiritual path is one that is so often colonized—
as aspects of the religious/spiritual lives of native peoples
around the world are simply taken. Taken and used. The
challenge of a religious tradition that relies on wisdom from
peoples around the world is to connect with those whose
lives are lived according to this spiritual truth, be enriched
by what we learn, and to do no harm. I remember those
General Assemblies and my struggle with appropriation—
I wanted us to vote yes; to say yes; to make our claim. And
I wanted us to vote no, to say no until we understand more
about what we have done to the people whose lives we somehow also lay claim to in this vote. We are called to appropriate. Our sources are about the nature of truth—that it is
diverse and continually revealed. And they are also about
relationship—our relationship as Unitarian Universalists to
the sources that speak most deeply to us and our relationship as a predominantly white religious institution to religious traditions lived by peoples around the world.

Hispanic Ministry Caucus
In November 2005, the Hispanic Ministry Caucus held its first formal gathering of Hispanic, and Latino and Latina ministers and
students in the UUA. Called "Drinking From Our Own Wells:
Celebration, lamentation, community, and ministry in Latino/a
and Hispanic Unitarian Universalist theologies," it was held at
Meadville Lombard Theological School in Chicago. Its focus was a
series of papers to address questions such as "Who are we? How do
we understand ourselves? How does this affect how we do our ministry? What are the differences among us? What are the commonalities? and ultimately, What does it mean to us in our movement?"
Publishing the conference proceedings was a goal.

CHAPTER 30

A New Commitment at General Assembly 2006

After the tensions that arose from incidents at the 2005 Fort Worth General Assembly, the next year's Assembly in St. Louis had a feeling of walking on eggshells. The report of the Special Review Commission examining the issues around youth and race in Fort Worth was shared and discussed at the St. Louis gathering. The careful tone of the report was praised by some and received negatively by others.

The maturation of the anti-racism conversation was especially noticeable in a session on the multiracial experience featuring Matt Kelley, president of the MAVIN Foundation, a resource group for multiracial individuals. That his address was funded by the General Assembly Planning Committee and that he spoke openly about his experience of being from a mixed racial and ethnic background were particularly healing for those who had been present at the previous year's conflicted sessions on transracial adoption. Though controversy was generated in the question-and-answer period, the emerging "white allies" network was available to assist as were members of DRUUMM (Diverse and Revolutionary Unitarian Universalist Multicultural Ministries), who had instituted a system of General Assembly chaplains to care for those affected by distressing conversations or experiences around race or ethnicity at General Assemblies.

Special Review Commission Report

Janice Marie Johnson, who served on the Review Commission, said that one aim of the report was to help the white majority understand the experiences of people of color. "When does the reality within the people of color communities become real within the white community?" she asked. "And when I say real, I mean real and endorsed, because real without the endorsement isn't taking us too far."

Rev. Joseph Santos-Lyons offered this account in his seminary thesis:

> The commission interviewed several dozen persons in preparing the report, although little of this was made public in the 25-page report. Instead a comprehensive timeline was developed stretching back to the beginning of Unitarian and Universalist consolidation in 1961. The report concluded with a list of recommendations, focused primarily on GA structure, beginning and ending with a call for nametag wearing, and issued a vague reminder that we are responsible to "preserve and live by our covenants and to uphold and maintain the ideals of our Unitarian Universalist faith." The Special Review Commission is very unique, as there is no other record of such a high level group being called together in response to racism in the UUA. In truth, it is a testament to the growth and establishment of a collective of People of Color who were able to hold and listen to the experiences of one another that helped lead to this action. Yet this institutional response is not a complete response, notes Rev. William (Chester) McCall, a Chaplain for DRUUMM, who urges us to respond to the individuals who have been dehumanized by the experience.

A tension revealed in the Commission's report was the pressure cooker produced by the combination of anti-racism work and General Assembly youth culture. Rev. Hope Johnson, who had served as a mentor and advisor to the youth of color, said the youth needed to be accountable both to one another and to the adult participants at the General Assembly. "Every time a youth says something, the youth start clapping," she said. "I have enough faith to ask our youth to be accountable. Some adults also clap whenever a youth says or does anything—this is also problematic. Accountability is

VOICE

Janice Marie Johnson

A small number of people of color and Latina/o/Hispanics are asked to play many leadership roles. Janice Marie Johnson, who served as president of DRUUMM from 2003 to 2006, offered these thoughts in a 2006 interview.

Well, here's another request. How will I fit this into my day, my week, my year? The question immediately following for me is if I don't, who will? There are so few of us willing to work with the institution.

I think years ago I might have thought, well, we can find a person of color to take this position, but there's a way in which, if we are really trying to build beloved community and considering this as spiritual work, it's got to be in addition to POC, the *right* POC.

I'm an institutionalist, and there are ways in which I believe that the forward movement is happening because institutionalists are helping to create bonds of trust and so I think there's an added burden, if you're willing to work within the system. And it is hard, so I find that I'm always working on three levels: the congregational, the district, and the institutional. And I'm juggling the three levels. Add the institutional to the continental, to the cultural. I'm juggling all of these balls. And my friends who are not in this UU world of mine actually believe that I have a full time job working for the UUA.

I was initially thinking of the time that I spend on DRUUMM, on whatever is on the people of color agenda, but the reality is that no matter what the work, anti-racism takes up a large part of my time. You know, I served on the Commission on Appraisal for a six-year term and even there, anti-racism work crept in and took time, tenacity, and strength of character. No matter where, there's a way in which people of color step into the agenda and there's a way in which people of color work takes so much time. You're on the phone a lot. You know, the other thing is, your resources. I'm not keeping tabs on my phone bills, on my hours, but for me it is, and I think for all of us, it's whatever it takes to get the job done. So yeah, we put out the extra mile, but what is it we want in return? For me, it is not walking away from this faith community. It is, in addition to not walking away from it, having my place in it, my place at the table that I helped design, thank you very much, and helping.... There's a whole younger generation, two younger generations. They had better have an easier time than the time that we had! ...

I think about congregants, just generally speaking, and I think about my work as a Jubilee I trainer, Jubilee II trainer, and JUUST Change consultant. It's a part of the conversation where we're more adept at welcoming strangers who are racially other, we are more careful and sensitive with languaging issues, and when so that's on the positive. I believe most committees, most boards, whether congregational or district, would certainly look at a balance around race if it is humanly possible. My concern is that the wrong person is invited to participate for the wrong reason. And so it doesn't help any of us if X congregation picks a person of color to share their committee, serve on the whatever, even, well whatever. Lead in any way if it's just for the factor of the person being a person of color. I think that's a very tough question for folks to wrestle with.

omni-directional. We must all do better." She noted that the General Assembly Youth Caucus was not representative of the youth in the congregations and applauded the UUA Administration's decision to begin a process of reviewing the Association's ministry to and with UU youth.

A General Assembly session sponsored by the Multiracial Caucus of DRUUMM and funded by the GA Planning Committee looked at issues affecting multiracial individuals. To those of all races and ethnicities, the fact that another open discussion was being held on this topic was critical. Unlike the previous year, the session was scheduled for a large space and featured a speaker—Matt Kelley of the MAVIN Foundation—whose story spoke to many there:

> I think that my life being multiracial among other things has made me quite an expert at being an outsider. And I don't mean to cry myself a river in saying that growing up as a multiracial person and later identifying as a gay man was often confusing and lonely, even though I grew up with loving parents in a liberal, well-educated community outside of Seattle. . . .
>
> Now, I wanted to just give some quick stories to help elucidate what that was like, although again growing up in a liberal, somewhat diverse, well-educated, it's not really a suburb of Seattle—it's called Bainbridge Island—but there are several stories that I hope kind of highlight what it was like growing up multiracial and why race, then and now, plays such an important part of my life. And the first story I have is on my first day of kindergarten no less, when my mother told me to sit in the front of the bus. So the bus came, and I got in the front, with my lunch pail and all, and I looked across the aisle of the bus and there was a little girl who was also going to her first day of kindergarten. And she looked at me, and she pointed, and she said "You're black and you have purple eyes." Her name was Wendy and I will always remember her name and I will tell you her name in case you run into her, and you can tell her that I'm trash-

talking her all across the country, but Wendy B. was telling me that I was different. I'm going to be very petty here and fill you in on a little detail that Wendy did the first grade twice. But the fact remains that Wendy introduced me, gave me my first memory of somebody giving me my racial identity.

Fast forward a few years when we were visiting my Was-sung-chum, which is a Korean word meaning my mother's brother, in Denver, Colorado. He lives in one of those very manicured housing developments on a golf course where the cul-de-sacs conclude a very nice, meandering long boulevard. And these beautiful homes all look strangely similar and then one home will break all the rules and paint their door red or something. And my sister and I were taking a walk down one of these sad boulevards and a little boy comes out on his patio and he says, "Hello Chinese people!" He might as well have said, "Earthling!" And a couple of years later I was the beneficiary of an affluent classmate who wanted me to come to Mexico with her and after a week in the Mexican sun, and given my predilection for spicy food and probably because I was pretending I was Puerto Rican at that point in my life, I was sitting at this out-of-the-way taco stand, putting a lot of salsa on my taco, and this beet-red, sun-burnt American tourist points down at my taco and goes, "*Picante*," like he was communicating with the locals. The very next day, I'm on my flight home and when the flight attendant asks me what I'd like to drink and I say pineapple juice, the guy next to me swings around and goes, "So you're Hawaiian" because all Hawaiians drink pineapple juice.

But based on those experiences, even today, I find comfort in not fitting in completely. Among white people and the gay community, I am kind of an ambiguous person of color. I'm a gay man among heterosexuals. Among Koreans I am, unfathomably, both gay and mixed race. And I'm a half-white guy among other people of color. As a result of these experiences, I am aware of both my own and other people's discomfort with my ambiguity. I know what it is to lack a cohesive, complete community and have parts of my identity routinely denied. This familiarity, however, never alleviated my desire to find a community that affirmed my whole self, a community where I could feel the comfort, safety and intimacy of being an insider. Beyond this racial/ ethnic ambiguity, multiracial and transracially adopted people often have narratives that are different from both white people as well as people of color and I'd like to give some examples. And again, these are just generalizations that don't necessarily apply to everyone, but I hope they can provide some insight into the experience. I think the most obvious one . . . is that we don't fit into a simple box in a society that really clings to the idea that everyone can fit into one box, despite being the most diverse country on earth. And so . . . I grew up for a time being forced to choose between, essentially, my parents, on forms requesting racial data, because if I checked both Asian and white, the forms would be returned to me.

And probably the most ubiquitous experience shared by mixed heritage and many non-mixed heritage people is the infamous "What are you?" question that I would receive sometimes on a daily basis from total strangers, who somehow could not continue with their day without learning my racial recipe. And it's interesting that the "What are you?" question preceded a "Who are you?" or a fairly polite "How are you?" And then there are also the "Where are you from?" questions, the "Is that your mother?" question or the "Are you the nanny?" question.

Many of us who are multiracial or transracially adopted often have parents who cannot relate to what it is like to not necessarily have full membership in either-or racial communities. We often grow up in predominantly white communities, schools, places of worship. We often experience discrimination with people of color and communities of color. And we are often times denied access into white circles, yet our lack of cultural cues and nuances can also make it uncomfortable for us to fit into communities of color. Again, this isn't for everybody; these are just some experiences. And the last one, which I think is perhaps, for me, the most interesting is that those of us who through either our birth families or adoption have one or more white parents, have a complex relationship with white privilege. Even though, when people see me, they don't typically (unless they're Korean) they don't typically see a white man, the fact that my father is white and has access to his friends and his network does, I do benefit from that. And without parents, teachers, mentors, peers who are willing or able to give me, to help me prepare for these experiences, much less cope with them, I often times felt very alone and confused about where exactly I fit in when it came to my identity and I often felt like I was navigating the identity path alone.

When I try to explain to people what that was like, I think again, actions speak louder than words and the way I reconciled the difficulty of trying to develop my own identity was the past eight years—creating an organization that was dedicated to creating a sense of community and identity among mixed heritage people. I created that in order to fill a void—first for me—and then once that void was filled, for other people. Hopefully some of you—I don't get anything out of it, because I am not there anymore—but hopefully some of you will check out MAVIN foundation and will look into some of their resources.

Kelley also spoke directly to the challenges he saw as an outsider looking at the Unitarian Universalist Association:

So the core of what I want to talk about this afternoon is really this idea of insiders vs. outsiders and I believe that much of our identity is defined by where and with whom we feel included and where and with whom we feel excluded. I think that we are all familiar with organizations that thrive on maintaining exclusive boundaries between insiders and outsiders; organizations that literally have "members only" rosters that are kept to distinguish who belongs and who does not. Through my conversations with people, through meetings and what not, I really don't get the impression that the UUA is that type of organization, yet, looking through some of the demographics of your faith—that only 2% identify as people of color—I fear that UU insiders and outsiders alike might draw a different conclusion. Again, as someone who is familiar with feeling excluded, I'm especially sensitive to the issue. And, by most measures, your organization is significantly less diverse than your respective communities or society at large. And, by the later measure, your organization is less economically diverse and disproportionately older. Frankly, as an outsider, when I look at that fact, those facts, I recognize that there must be barriers that maintain these disproportions. . . .

[L]ast night, I had the opportunity to attend a DRUUMM meeting and it was simultaneously inspiring and gut-wrenching. I had the privilege of witnessing some remarkably strong, competent and compassionate individuals who clearly had great faith in the UUA and their role in it. I saw strong, talented and insightful women and men who demonstrated phenomenal compassion and commitment. But even as an outsider, I felt an overwhelming sadness sink in as the meeting went on, as I saw and felt that their dignity had been assaulted, their pain had been trivialized, their experience, marginalized; their identities, tokenized. I saw tears of humiliation and, though I am not a psychologist, what I saw felt like symptoms of trauma.

Two people in particular shared with me some experiences I thought were particularly salient. One young woman told me about how she had left the UUA, because she didn't feel respected and affirmed. One young man in particular, who was at the meeting last night, told me an interesting story about . . . his family is Catholic and he is Filipino and he identifies as gay, I believe. In the Catholic faith, his Filipino identity was affirmed, given that the Catholic faith is a large part of the vast majority of Filipinos' family and cultural life. However, his gay identity was not affirmed in the Catholic church. As he became part of the UU, part of a UU congregation, it flipped. His gay identity was affirmed and supported, but his identity as a Filipino-American was not. He also told me that the reason he is UU was because of DRUUMM. And I think what also really impressed me was even through these tremendous stories of pain that these different people shared with me, they still spoke about and acknowledged the support of white allies in UU congregations and also here. And my own inquiries reveal to me the institution's historic leadership around lesbian, gay, bisexual and transgender and women's suffrage issues. So it is inspiring to see that the UUA has a history of progressive leadership on social issues and it makes me hopeful that when it comes to increasing ethnic and racial diversity, there's also hope there.

Kelley took questions after his remarks. When questions by white parents began to cause agitation in the youth of color, chaplains from both DRUUMM and Allies for Racial Equity were on hand to respond. The presence of volunteers who had agreed to serve as a listening ear for people in distress was able to keep the conversation from escalating as it had in 2005 in the session on transracial adoption. Hope Johnson noted this as an example of the way leadership had deepened within the communities of those seeking more authentic race relations within the Unitarian Universalist Association.

And a New Challenge . . .
This book covers a period of time. Determining when to end the period has been a challenge. In light of the tensions that arouse around race and youth at the 2005 and 2006 General Assemblies, perhaps the last event to relate is UUA moderator Gini Courter's report to the 2006 Assembly. Here is the reporter's account for the Association web site:

Courter began addressing the delegates by making reference to a scene in the movie "A League of Their Own" where one player was leaving because "It's so hard." The coach tells her, "Of course it's hard; the hard part is what makes it great.

If it was easy, anybody would do it." Courter said we are involved in a whole lot of things with differing levels of difficulty. She knows how hard it is to build the beloved community, and yet how important it is to do so.

Earlier, she said, "I rose to talk about some instances of privilege and power, and following that conversation our youth and young adults of color and their allies wanted to bring a list of what they would like me to tell you. I realized they needed to have their own voices, because they are delegates, and they are a part of our Assembly, part of our community. Some of them are afraid to talk with you, and let me tell you why."

Courter said the youth and young adults are not afraid there will be verbal or physical violence, "that you would punch or throw them, but they are afraid that you would not hear them, and that we would hug them whether they want you to or not, and then think that this makes it okay." Courter invited delegates to listen to the words of these people "in a spirit of deep learning." She asked delegates to honor her request that, from the point where these people begin to speak until the end of her report, there be no applause. Courter introduced UUA trustee-at-large Julian Sharp to introduce the two speakers. He encouraged delegates to listen to their voices, "let them challenge and inspire us to live out our values, and let us struggle together." He asked that after the presentation we do not approach these people or others who join them on stage. "We have youth chaplains and adult chaplains who would love to talk with you, and there is lots of programming available for delegates to learn from," he said.

Hannah Eller-Isaacs, a member of the Youth Caucus of General Assembly delegates, read a list of comments gathered from her conversations with people, including:

- This is not about this year, last year, and not about name tags and specific instances.
- People who are doing anti-racism work are being shot down and criticized.

- People put their heart and soul into this work with no or next to no institutional support, without funding, and without guidance.
- This is not a youth issue, not a programming issue.
- Lots of people are accusing anti-racist, anti-oppressive youth and young adults without themselves being involved in this work.
- Adults generalize about youth, and what they say is not true; there are many of us doing this work.
- There is lack of credit to people of color and youth organizing anti-racism work.
- White adults need to turn to other adults to learn and discuss.
- There is a lack of antiracist-minded allies.
- Name tags are not the problem nor the solution, and they do not address nor solve the larger issues.
- There are scores of younger generation UUs who give their hearts and souls to anti-racism work and who have left, broken hearted and burnt out, there is lack of support and lack of credit, and there also needs to be credit given to those who are supporting youth and young adults.

Zarinah Ali then offered a separate list of concerns:

- GA volunteers are patronizing and demeaning youth of color.
- Demands are being made to stop doing anti-racism work.
- White Board members were let into events without badges, only youth of color were not let in.
- People of color, particularly youth leaders and Youth Office staff, are the most targeted.
- There is inconsistent enforcement of whether name tags are worn; this is not just a GA issue.
- The UUA is leaving a lot of anti-racism work up to youth and their officers.
- Youth are seen as troublemakers.
- Whites are learning about anti-racism at the expense of people of color too much.

- Youth are disrespected.
- The situation is being framed as being about name tags, but it's more than that.
- Young men of color are being told they don't belong.

Courter stood at the podium in silence, and then began by saying that one thing she has realized is that never in the history of the UUA has there been a Study/Action Issue or Statement of Conscience that says that we need to study racism in our congregations, and this appears to be something that is difficult for us. It is, she said, "at some level, about leadership, and this is not the moderator's report I intended to give." She went on:

One thing we learned during UU University [a pre-General Assembly series of workshops for congregational lay leaders] was that the way you change is to be very tolerant of pain. In my business life, I am an IT professional, and there is a saying that in order to build good systems, you need to put the pain in the right place. For too long, it hasn't hurt some of us very much, and we have been unknowing, and probably not caring, but being okay with being in another place. And yet, our children are in pain, and we have not taught them, as well as we wish, how to be together. Our adults of color are in pain, and we haven't taught ourselves how to be together. This is the business of this GA, the business of a movement facing a new dawn. It is about leadership, and you need to want to learn more.

Courter then told delegates that for many folks, and speaking specifically to the youth of color in the hall, "it seems often that I sprung before you a fully formed anti-racist, and nothing could be further from the truth. When I joined the Board of Trustees, one of the first things I did was rebel against the anti-racist training I received, and I led a movement to get something different." Yet her colleagues on the Board "loved me into a different way of being," she said, and she came to realize that "even though the training wasn't perfect, until we knew what perfect was, we could not be complacent. They were afraid that we would give up because the work was hard," Courter said. Yet, Courter explained, "there are many ways to do the work, to bump off the rough edges, and that's what they did for me." Continuing:

> Increasingly, the people who teach me tend to be white UUs, and that gives me great joy as we are developing the sophistication to do the work, not just lip service. This is a learning process, and a soulful process. I recommend that if you want to change your spiritual life, you give consideration to doing significant reading and having significant conversations around race and racism, age and ageism, accessibility and ableism. There is a myth that there is only one way to do this, that there is one UUA curricula and approach, but this is not true. You are inventing the way to do this in your congregations. There are videos to watch—three listed in the GA program—to watch and talk about. Have those conversations, even if everyone in the room is white. When we come together, we are gathered in one strong body as an association of congregations. Diversity is real with us, and we are a faith that speaks to all people of all ages. Part of setting the welcome table is making it real. Dealing with racism is about leadership and pain, and if you are feeling weird or funny, then that's the place where we learn.

Some, she said, "may be feeling we spend way too much time on issues of race and racism, of how to be in community together." She urged delegates to get in touch with the part of themselves that feels that way, and figure out why that is—"this might save your soul."

Courter said she is honored to serve as moderator of the UUA, of this Assembly, and as chair of the UUA Board. The reason this is true, she said, is that she could state with complete confidence,

> If there is a community that will be a beacon on this continent and in this world about how different people can be together—across ages, races, ways of being, and speaking— then we are it. We are the best hope there is, none better, and it is almost a holy trust and a sacred piece given only to us. It is time for a new revolution. The last time that we

spoke and cared deeply about what it means to be a democracy, we created the country we live in today. This is our work—to create a democracy and be with that in this hall, with these delegates, with these people.

A delegate asked for permission to present another responsive resolution to the officers' reports. She moved that each congregation carry out one program to address racism or classism in the next year, that congregations be asked to report such efforts (or lack thereof) on their annual certification form, and that the results of those reports be shared with General Assembly next year. It is, she said, "imperative to work on this process, and having a single program is a very low bar, and very serious work to do."

After Courter's remarks, which she delivered near the end of the Assembly's final plenary session, Debra Boyd, a delegate from First Unitarian Universalist Church of Columbus, Ohio, arose to offer the following "responsive resolution":

Resolved: that the delegates to the 2006 Unitarian Universalist Association's General Assembly are charged to work with their congregations to hold at least one program over the next year to address racism or classism and to report on that program to next year's General Assembly.

The resolution carried. The story continues.

FINDINGS

Racial Barriers in UU Congregations

Some people interviewed for this account of about fifteen years of the UUA's religious response to racisim and oppression said that its anti-racism and anti-oppression efforts have been positive. Others said it has been divisive. Few have said it was unnecessary. One of the challenges has been to quantify what barriers remain and how to address them. In an effort to end this account on the right note, here is data from the thesis work of Rev. Joseph Santos-Lyons, which was based on three hundred responses from people of color.

Overwhelmingly, People of Color surveyed believe there are barriers in congregations for People of Color. Many expressed the linkage to other forms of institutional oppression and cultural conditions of congregations, in particular the higher economic and educational class levels, that point to a difficulty in welcoming and authentically accepting People of Color, and others. There is also some attention to the fact that congregations, through religious professional leadership or laity, are ineffective in redressing these barriers, due to a lack of preparation, training, vision and courage. The responses shared below are meant to be representative of the total collection. Ideally these responses will help both the reader, and ultimately the institution, gain more clarity into the nature of the barriers, and from this diagnosis, determine more successful and precise initiatives to address the situation.

Do You Perceive Racial Barriers in Your Congregation?
Yes. 85.71%
No 10.99%
Unsure/No Church. 3.30%

Those Who Answered "Yes" (85.71%)
"Yes. Affluence is a serious barrier on a number of different levels. Class, education, and social mores separate the vast majority of ethnic minorities from our typically affluent congregations. People of color have a difficult time relating to everything we do. This must change."

"At first yes, because often times people speak of being accepting of blacks, gays, transgender people, etc. . . . and they talk about being liberal minded but their individual lives outside of what they profess do not reflect this so when people of color or other cultures visit they are welcomed, but not embraced if you know what I mean."

"I've seen social elitism where people socialize with their equals. We don't advertise other than in the yellow pages, there is very little community outreach."

"People in our congregation tend to socialize with people they already know, so it is difficult for new prospective members to feel welcomed on more than a superficial basis. Though our congregation is a relatively 'welcoming' congregation, most do not make any sustained effort to connect with 'newcomers' regardless of color."

"There are always barriers. UU congregations and communities may politically/religiously/culturally be more progressive than many others in the U.S., but this does not always translate into knowledge, understanding and acceptance of others. I heard about the incident at the last GA in Texas where it was assumed by some Anglo UU's that a group of youth of color were valets because of skin color . . . we have a long way to go. UUs are a part of this society, and there are a great many divisions along class and race that we are clearly not confronting. I would not expect UUs to somehow be immune to all this. Structural/institutional racism and discrimination affects all of our perspectives, actions, attitudes, and beliefs since it pervades this society."

"Absolutely, and that is one reason I believe the Journey to Wholeness is a great move on the part of the UU Church. The advent of both the People of Color and the White Alliance caucus will begin to make a difference. If UU haven't already, let's add the writings of People of Color and not only the Transcendentalists. Frederick Douglass, Harriet Tubman, Sitting Bull, Seneca and Black Elk, Lao Tzu, Ram Dass, Krishna Murtha etc.—let's revisit our history of

1840–1870—let's talk about what else was going on during the Transcendentalist Movement. Like the genocide of the Native Americans in the West, Slavery in the South, U.S. Mexican War and what it was like for 'civilized man' during Thoreau's and Emerson's time. What were the Child Labor Laws and Women's Rights during that time as well. What made the Transcendentalist Movement occur? It just didn't spontaneously generate. Personally, I believe the Unitarians were a response to the times. The white man had become divorced from Nature because of 'civilization.' The U.S. Government was doing horrible things in the name of Jesus Christ and their Christian God."

"I think that we as UUs have a very specific cultural experience in general. The majority being white, middle to upper middle class folks, with liberal political views. Because we don't have a 'let's save the whole world' attitude, we have a fairly exclusionary mindset to begin with. In practice, not on paper. I think we're rather xenophobic, across many cultural, class, racial lines, but especially race. The growth of female ministers, for instance, has highly out lapped, many, many times over the population of ministers of color."

"I think that Anti-Racism work functions to assuage White guilt in many places, and so when People of Color come into a Church, they are often asked to join several committees for which they are not qualified and do not have the capacity to sit on. No one has any real clue on how to be in community with the People of Color in a Church, so those who come often get 'burned out' and frustrated with continually being treated very differently from the mass of the community. On the other side of things, some congregations do not deal with race at all. This is just as bad, because the Person of Color feels just as excluded from the community and more unwelcome.

Those Who Answered "No" (10.99%)
"No barriers, it is one of letting those seeking a liberal religion know we exist. One of the things that came out of a recent discussion about religion is UUs are almost alone in encouraging their members to question their beliefs."

"To speak of 'barriers' presupposes a certain frame of thought. It assumes that something within UU churches prevents outsiders from coming in and that all we have to do is remove that impediment and people will flock in. But is that really the case? And to get the most use out of the barrier metaphor, should we not also be asking if any barriers exist in non-UU circles, outside of UU control, that prevent people from stepping out of their group and into a UU church?"

"The issues here are complex. It is difficult even to determine what all the issues are, and equally difficult to determine what can be done about them. We know there is a correlation between UU churches and low racial diversity, i.e., when you find the former, you're likely to also find the latter. But we do not know if one causes the other, or if it is the other way around, or even if other outside factors are causing both. In my own experience, I have always felt welcomed in my church. To be precise, I know what it feels like to be socially rejected by a group of people, and I have never experienced that feeling in my church. On the other hand, I cannot say that my church is particularly 'warm' to newcomers. Again, to be precise, in my previous religious affiliation, we were taught to go out of our way to act friendly to visitors, to find ways to draw them into our groups, and to constantly try to make them feel 'as one of us.' That is not something that spontaneously happens in my current church, despite recent efforts to behave in a more welcoming manner. How do I reconcile these two seemingly disparate conditions? I'm not sure. In part the answer lies in me. Going to new places and introducing myself to new people does not intimidate me. In part, the answer also lies with the church, because even though they're not overly open, once I introduced myself to them they were quick to accept me. Another component was the availability of alternatives, or rather the lack of them. I wanted to find a 'church community,' not a club or an interest group. But I required one that was intellectually open, one that would embrace science, rather than reject it. And I felt, rightly or wrongly, that the UU church was my best option."

PART 6

LEARNINGS

As we look at this final period, some of the themes from earlier times seem to be there as well, writ larger and more dramatic.

A disquietude existed in the first part of this time period that somehow the focus on addressing racism had been lost. "I have a feeling that the momentum is lost, to some degree, because we talk a good talk," said long-time African-American activist Dr. Norma Poinsett, "but . . . we're not after any real change. We just want to sound good, feel good."

Yet in real ways, change was happening. *Identity* continues to be a critical issue, with the youth and young adults active at the Associational level, in particular, taking the lead in helping Unitarian Universalists grapple with a variety of identities. The particular experiences of transracially adopted and multiracial youth in our movement were brought to the wider attention of General Assemblies in these years and these youth sought to forge new identities for themselves and to have those identities embraced by the larger movement.

Robette Dias, formerly of the Faith in Action Department, said, "You hear it all the time in the work, 'What should we do.' But the first thirty years of the work are not about what you do. It's about who you *be*."

Paula Cole Jones, who consulted with the Sinkford administration around anti-oppression issues, said that Sinkford's efforts to reach out to the ministers of large congregations in the Association were a turning point. "Prior to this, the large congregations were not engaged," she recalled, adding that the first activities undertaken by the new JUUST Change Consultancy were in large congregations. Among the piloting congregations were the Unitarian Universalist Church of Arlington, Virginia; the Eno River Unitarian Universalist Fellowship in Durham, North Carolina; and Unity Church-Unitarian in St. Paul, Minnesota.

Signs of institutional identity shift included the work of the Ministerial Fellowship Committee, the continuing work of the theological schools, and the Unitarian Universalist Ministers Association. Rev. Dr. Rebecca Parker, president of Starr King School for the Ministry, noted that their work could be seen as a long-term investment. "Starr King has helped educate people for ministry who are now in leadership around Journey Toward Wholeness and anti-racism work and I do need to say that we have been emphasizing the intersection of oppressions," she said, referring to a broader approach to anti-oppressive work that emphasizes the places where people experience multiple oppressions. "People are coming through Starr King and through the work we're doing here and then translating their education into leadership in various settings for our movement, including denominational leadership positions. So that's an outcome."

In terms of *relationship*, this was a time of reassessment and adjustment. "[W]e've had probably 4 or 5 years of sort of a step back from the formal Crossroads Ministry program [of anti-racism training], but there's still a lot of hurt feelings, a lot of healing and a lot of resistance based on the damage that has already been done," observed Rev. Marjorie Bowens-Wheatley. "That would be necessary and, quite frankly, a lot of people have just lost faith in the UUA's ability to lead, so I'm not saying that for myself, necessarily, but I know, I'm very aware of a lot of hurt, a lot of loss of faith."

In this sense, the annual General Assembly of Congregations became a testing ground. Moderator Gini Courter suggested that the events at General Assembly from 2004 to 2006 in particular offer some lessons, given the Association's fragility around race relations. "We actually needed a community to process whatever the trigger is and that community can't be a couple of adults who happen to see a bunch of youth moving in one direction and everybody else under twenty."

The question in this period was one of bearings—where were we on this collective journey we had undertaken? What were the critical parts of the dialogue? Rev. Mel Hoover offered this rejoinder to those who might believe the work was done. "If you looked at a thirty-year model of change [suggested in the Crossroads model], then at one level we've done, we're doing, quite well, if we understand what we're really doing and it's part of crossing the range of mountains instead of being the mountain."

If the issue was a thirty-year model of change then how to involve and support youth doing this work was critical. What emerged during this period were models that addressed the specific experience, vocabulary, and multicultural sensitivity of youth, many of whom lived in a much more diverse world than their parents and other Unitarian Universalist elders. "Crossroads was not youth friendly and it was not welcoming," noted Elandria Williams, who had been involved in anti-racism work since she joined the Thomas Jefferson District anti-racism training in 1997 at age sixteen. "Aside from [the Thomas Jefferson District] team, it was not welcoming."

This was also a time when a shift began occurring away from the idea of anti-racism as a unitary focus toward an "anti-oppression" strategy, which encompassed an array of oppressions.

Karen Eng said,

So I am here in Atlanta [at the Asian Pacific Islander Caucus] this weekend because my heart is so full when I am in my faith community and with my cultural community—at the same time! It is powerful. It renews me in a special way. And I am grateful.

Dr. Norma Poinsett's perspective is seasoned with decades of watching Unitarian Universalists wrestle with these issues. Of the nature of the Journey Toward Wholeness, she reflected,

I feel we over-organized. I think that for the JTW to be an oversight group . . . that was fine. . . .

I don't know whether people grasped what they should do. . . . Unless you just happen to run into a group who're just ready to say, "We gotta change. We got to do better," not too much is going to transpire. I think [UUA president Rev. William Sinkford] put it in the right place when he put the anti-racism work into the congregations, but they are so caught up with so many other things. There's not going to be much emphasis on racism when you are concerned with all of the other things that come under the umbrella, you know.

[The Transformation Committee] did a lot of planning, but how do they implement it? I mean who's implementing it? Who's helping with the implementation? I didn't see it. I didn't see it moving on out to the congregations, out to the other places to really get any work done. I thought it was beautiful planning. I thought it was too much planning in a way.

I think we've done some good things, but I think what we need to be sure to realize is it has not been a total immersion. Or not even a quarter immersion because no matter how many workshops we had, we still haven't had enough to affect more than, I'd say 2,000 [people].

That the focus changed after the reorganization was clear. Simona Munson, program coordinator for the Identity-Based Ministries staff group, who worked through the staffing change at the UUA, observed that efforts became less focused, especially for the Transformation Committee with a broader focus on "anti-oppression" rather than "anti-racism." The new mission could seem daunting, particularly for those who supported the Committee's work: "It is impossible to do all these things—facilitate, monitor, guide, and assess. What is [the Committee's] identity is the struggle every year." On the positive side, the changes made the staff efforts more inclusive: "We've really tried to expand our focus so we now are serving multiple constituencies and groups with multiple identities." For her personally, the underlying message has remained clear: "What I have learned here is an understanding of systemic oppression."

Rev. Dr. William Jones, author of *Is God A White Racist*, also expressed his doubts that the path taken by the Unitarian Universalist Association staff would lead to the desired destination. "The present model that they're working on may not be effective in accomplishing what they're trying to accomplish. My view is that a lot of the models we used have as a consequence, not an intended consequence but an actual one, of copping—conserving and preserving—the oppression that they are claiming to correct. That's a difficult kind of admission to make, to get people to acknowledge." He presented another framework from the training around racism he developed. "We have this little exercise that we often start with, where you're given four slots and you have to identify yourself. Pre-enlightened oppressor, pre-enlightened oppressed, post-enlightened oppressor, post-enlightened oppressed. Then we go through and show the actions, the creeds and deeds that are correlated with those four things. That's been a helpful approach to getting people simply to start thinking about the possibility of correction."

The resource level had declined since the height around 1998–1999. Moderator Gini Courter, who previously served as chair of the UUA Board's Finance Committee and as finance advisor to the Board estimated that at the highest point, expenditures on anti-racism training and related activities were about 12 percent of the budget and that this line item was down to about 6 percent in 2003–04. Unitarian Universalist Association executive vice president Kathleen Montgomery said that it was difficult to compare expenditures for anti-racism-related efforts across years because the methodologies were so different year to year. Initially, more money was spent with outside organizations such as Crossroads, she said, because the UUA lacked internal capacity, "The decision at Calgary to institutionalize our anti-racism work resulted in a search for resources to help us do that," she wrote in an email. "We knew we did not have, at that point, staff expertise in that kind of institutional change. It was then that we began working with Crossroads, using their methodology and believing that in order to make the lasting change that the General Assembly envisioned it was essential to begin with buy-in from leadership. Thus, those early trainings were aimed at the board, staff, and committees of the Association. Gradually, staff and consultants gained the expertise needed and we relied less on outside sources and adapted the Crossroads model to our own constituency. The Veatch Program at Shelter Rock provided considerable funding for our trainings during those early years, though they gradually tapered off that funding and ended it in the late '90s."

Janice Marie Johnson said that the shift began from personal relationships to institutional relationships, with an emphasis on having institutions be accountable to those who have historically been marginalized within them. "I think accountability is fascinating because I think so much headway has been made it's exciting," she said. "We do pay attention to each other, we pay attention every which way, whether it's across—an example I would give is across the caucuses. So there's very much heightened awareness across the caucuses in terms of APIUUC, respect for APIUUC, respect for this, respect for that, looking at the balance. If you do this, how will this impact that? How will we understand each other? The accountability around wrestling with urban youth versus suburban, and so on and so forth. I think it's a very exciting time around accessibilities and around the access to cultural awareness. . . . We've learned so much around the misperceptions, the jealousies, the stereotyping, the this, the that, just around different cultures. And how are we not accountable to each other. It's an exciting time. I think the accountability is not simply lip service. It's real. So that's very encouraging. . . . In terms of accountability, this has afforded us a wonderful opportunity to figure out with real intentionality that we need to be accountable to each other as people of color. It's about learning about each other's cultures, then it's about supporting each other. I think that's been another very positive piece of the hard work that we've had to do among ourselves."

Whether you had any analysis of oppression, whether your analysis took a systemic look, whether class was a factor, whether your views were sympathetic with Unitarian Universalist beliefs were all questions raised in the discussions that swirled. And because these perspectives and analyses were not, for the most part, academic, because they grew out of the life experiences—in some cases, the most searing life experiences—of the people who professed them, to have them discounted was hurtful and damaging. That individuals and relationships among individuals were damaged in this period is clear and that legacy continues.

CLOSING WORDS

WE ARE TRYING TO TELL YOU
By Marta Valentin

Rev. Marta Valentin was ordained in 2003. She identifies as a Latina.

*People of color have been trying to tell UUs how to
keep us here.*

Do you hear us? Are you listening?

*It seems we are using the same words,
but not speaking the same language.
We are telling you that your desire to create a multicultural
community, is fabulous
but requires that you make room for us
in your head
in your heart
in the room
at the table
it requires that you be willing to grow
and transform. . . .
it requires that you be willing to share a meal with me,
of what I like to eat
because I eat your food all the time
better yet, it requires that you invite me to your house for dinner
it doesn't matter if we eat your food or ours
only that you invite me into your space.*

*People of color have been trying to tell UUs how to
keep us here
for decades. . . .
We are trying to tell you that all your good efforts
without doing the analysis
have only served to maintain the status quo.*

Do you hear us? Are you listening?

And when you bring us in without doing the work of learning the
    analysis
all you accomplish is status color.
And you wonder why this multicultural world you are trying to build
isn't working
manifesting
colorizing
it reminds me of those rainbow colored plastic sheets
we used to put on the TV
before real color TV came along.

Are you listening when we tell you
that we have pulled up our socks,
grabbed the bull by the horns
carried our weight—and yours.

Do you hear us when we tell you
that we take our Seven Principles seriously.
They are our system of accountability
to the interdependent web of all humanity and
sentient beings.
If it were up to us we would make the last Principle our first
for how we are connected to each other is far more important
than who we are as individuals.
There I said it.
I went against our individualistic suit of armor
to acknowledge that we are socialized into group identities.

The people of color in the UU world
are offering you a new language, to create a new world
but you must get out of your individualistic heads
and feel us
feel that what we bring is more than words
feel that what we bring is more than trouble
understand and accept that we bring a multitude of opportunities
to create a multicultural world that has yet to be lived
we bring the delicious diversity that so many crave
we bring a notion of a world that is truly equal

we bring you
to you
in unimaginable ways
that we've only had inklings of so far.

And when you hear us, when you listen,
when you feel us . . .
you bring us
to us.

The people of color are trying to tell UUs
that all love is the same
but it must be expressed truthfully.

Messages for the Future

If there is no struggle, there is no progress. Those who profess to favor
freedom and deprecate agitation are men who want crops without
plowing up the ground, they want rain without thunder and lightning.
          —Frederick Douglass

ONE OF THE HARDER MOMENTS of the journey that began in 1992 with the General Assembly's vote to adopt the Racial and Cultural Diversity resolution was a contentious meeting in Kansas City designed to identify anti-racism "stakeholders." Minutes for that meeting noted, "The Journey Toward Wholeness struggle is that we don't have whole stories to tell yet. We have stories of incremental changes. Story is about struggle. Part of our story is how we recover from struggle and mistakes. Our story is not finished yet."

In many ways, those words could be the conclusion of this book, for indeed, this is a story not whole enough to tell. Whether we have made progress or not, whether we have crossed a mountain or a part of a mountain range, or a bay or a sea, or are still standing still, depends on who you ask and what conversations compose their frame of reference in the moment they are asked.

And yet, some truths seem apparent—that we have had thunder and lightning seemed a good sign that rain was coming. Since the 1992 vote, a dialogue resumed that had been quieted for more than a generation after the Empowerment Controversies of the 1960s and 1970s. Janice Marie Johnson, director of lifespan religious education at Community Church of New York and former president of DRUUMM (Diverse and Revolutionary Unitarian Universalist Multicultural Ministries), said of anti-racism and anti-oppression efforts,

One of the outcomes I see is that folks across the board are speaking about it. It has come into its own as a topic worthy of conversation. So I think that's really key. Folks who probably had no idea of the issue, as well as folks who have felt very uncomfortable with the issue, not knowing how to move forward, not knowing how to be "acceptably" correct, rather than politically correct, as well as folks who constantly remind us that they marched in Selma—on all levels, I think, the conversation is open and I think that there's no turning back.

She said this was positive—and that it had come at a "heavy price." What is the price of freedom, friends?

For some people, and in a few Unitarian Universalist settings, anti-oppression efforts and the specifics around anti-racism have caused a change in identity. How permanent that change is and whether it will affect mainstream Unitarian Universalism remains unclear. "There was a paradigm shift, from white liberalism 'helping' people of color to noting how whites benefit from institutionalized racism," observes Rev. William J. Gardiner, who left the Association staff after the Faith in Action Department was disbanded in a reorganization. "From expecting people of color to change, to an awakening to the need for whites to reexamine their cultural assumptions about power and privilege . . . to unpack, dismantle and reorient . . . to learn to be in equal relationship—it has changed the conversation."

This was also an era of redefining relationships, of trying to understand the ways race and ethnicity affect interchanges, even among those who embrace liberal religion. New ideas emerged, such as how to be truly accountable to one another or to hold our actions in a larger frame that acknowledges the hidden biases and unintentional messages of superiority that the dominant culture may impart.

For President Rev. William Sinkford and his administration, the focus was on finding new ways to address an old problem, new methods such as the JUUST Change consultancy. "I think we were successful in getting a significant portion of the congregation and their leaders unstuck," he said.

He was also proud of his efforts to diversify the executive staff of the Association around race, ethnicity and sexual orientation, and for the work of the Identity-Based Ministries Staff Group. "I remember Meg Riley [Director of UUA Advocacy and Witness] looking around at the Leadership Council retreat and saying, 'This is what leadership could look like in our movement.'"

Still unanswered are basic questions: How can a white majority be accountable to those historically marginalized for reasons of race or ethnicity? How can members of different, marginalized racial or cultural groups be accountable to one another? How do groups formed around a particular racial or ethnic identity structure themselves to provide a collective rather than a set of individual, and often competing, voices? How can the world of Unitarian Universalists above thirty-five years of age be accountable to those under thirty-five who are willing to take leadership on this issue, and vice versa?

The largest question confronted in workshops and trainings, in institutional structural changes, and in individual conversations around race and ethnicity was about faith. Discussions about anti-racism and race relations in general, when they began to emerge again in the 1980s, did so in the social justice language that so engaged Unitarian Universalists in the 1960s and 1970s. The leaders of these efforts wrestled with anti-oppression's theological and belief implications—yet the language that transmitted the message, particularly through the early collaborative efforts with Crossroads Ministry, did not speak to the Unitarian Universalist mainstream. In the decade and a half since the 1992 General Assembly resolution, with its mandate that we become more racially and culturally diverse, more Unitarian Universalists have become interested in matters of belief, in religious language that speaks to the difficult issues of an increasingly small and frightening world, and in understanding ourselves as a religious people rather than as a social movement. To the authors of this book, the anti-racism journey has been part of this change in ways not easily pinned down and identified and yet real all the same.

The ultimate question was whether the Principles and Sources of Unitarian Universalism compel us to address uncomfortable and messy issues that inevitably must prove costly, in terms of time, energy, and money. As authors, we would answer yes, echoing the words of UUA executive vice president Kay Montgomery, who sees a need for a "personal contribution to transforming a faith that needs more faith." What cannot be so easily answered is where this priority stands among others. Is addressing these issues more important than rapid growth with the white middle class who forms our natural constituency? This and other related questions remain in the ongoing dialogue.

As we near the end of this book, we share a collection of voices addressing the question of this era's legacy. As we compiled this history, inadequate and incomplete as it is, one thing became clear to us: that to suppress the era's lessons and to fail to wrestle with its truths would be to repeat a dysfunctional pattern that has marked our Unitarian Universalist histories around race relations. The truths of this period vary with one's vantage point and perspective—and yet some overarching themes seem important to identify. Throughout this book, we have tried as much as possible to mute our opinions in favor of the many voices heard in these pages. In this last section, we speak from our voice—from our limited perspectives as three people who have wrestled with this history, personally and through the writing of this book, and who have had the great privilege of talking to many of the wise and brave forerunners in these efforts. What follows are the touchstones from this period that guided our effort to build Unitarian Universalism's collective memory of witness and hope. We offer them here so that the next steps in this necessary collective journey will be informed by them.

1. We need to know and wrestle with our own history. As Unitarian Universalists, we have been inventors and innovators, ones to forge new paths and look to progress. Part of this heritage means that we have also tended to be ahistorical: In the era the 1992 resolution set in motion we often didn't know or value our own history. Failures to wrestle with our history in the past often meant that we had to wrestle with it in the present. An example was the way the unresolved Empowerment Controversies issues from the 1960s and 1970s played out in the black-white focus of anti-racism efforts in the 1990s. Another example, that our civil rights work was done as a matter of social imperative and not religious imperative, became visible again in the late 1980s and early 1990s as the issue of race re-emerged in Unitarian Universalism. The drift in religious identity our religion experienced in the twentieth century alienated us from our history as a religious people.

The complexities of our heritage needed mining. This includes the pride of being on the front lines in some ways in the Civil Rights and other human rights movements—as well as our shame in the ways we did not resolve our internal race controversy about how to embrace black empowerment in the 1970s.

We lost some of our most engaged youth then and we have seen this loss again as a result of the debate about anti-racism and anti-oppression. An irony exists in the fact that our innovation, which should clear the way for new voices, often alienates us from our committed youth, who live in a world much more embracing of diversity. It also alienates our youth from the history that is their heritage. The stories of youth and racial justice have long been intertwined in our movement, for youth are often the ones that see the world to come. The Special Review Commission the Association's Board appointed after the 2005 Fort Worth General Assembly noted that youth had been racial justice leaders since the Empowerment Controversies. Reading that history revealed a pattern of idealism, allied support, and eventual disillusionment. Some felt that this was what inevitably must happen with our youth while others were less sanguine. "Some youth are bailing—the older folks' agendas are too conservative, too slow," observed Rev. Kurt Kuhwald, an anti-racism trainer. "Some youth are very resistant. . . . If our young people leave, we lose their energy for this work."

"The early racial justice work empowered us as leaders to do the work," noted Paula Cole Jones. The primary architect of the JUUST Change program piloted in 2002 and implemented in 2005. She noted that the analysis of how power was shared or not shared within institutions was very strategic and important. For example, she said it allowed discussions about multicultural competencies, since such discussions are about the capacities of institutions, rather than individuals. She also spoke to the strength of the "Jubilee" trainings, adding that they were an important path into an understanding of oppression though "people needed more than one way to connect with the work."

2. As our nation grows more multiracial and multicultural, we need to find ways to embrace its complexities that are in sympathy with our purposes. If Unitarian Universalism is to remain relevant in a world where complex identities are growing more prevalent, we need to build a dialogue about racial and ethnic identities. This need grows out of the history of our movement, our continued discomfort with issues of race and class, and the expansive and iterative nature of anti-oppression efforts.

Since 1992 the link between race and class has emerged more clearly. One point of conflict became the separating of race issues from class issues and the perception that a "hierarchy of oppressions" existed. For some, these were theoretical and philosophical issues; for others they were about a validation of experience and were deeply linked to identity. Race and class were linked again as time unfolded and our understanding of oppression advanced. "The next step is class," Kuhwald said. "Our whiteness does define us. We tried to keep class out, to make sure it's known that race *is* an issue," he continued. But doing so means that "people don't get our idea of how they link."

As the demographics of our nation evolved, negotiating identity in a multicultural world became more critical. We continued to seek more effective language and actions to address a world in which dialogues around oppression are more nuanced. Understandings of oppression developed by UU youth contained more sophisticated and layered taxonomies of identity.

At the time of President Clinton's 1997 White House Initiative on Race, the Association's strategy was considered to be on the forefront of these issues. Yet since then the challenges and the awareness of the complexities of identity issues have grown.

As a justice-seeking people, failure to deal with complex issues creates a basic identity problem. "Corporate domination, classism, racism and violence are the most pressing problems facing our country," said Rev. Clyde Grubbs, a member of the Native American caucus of DRUUMM. "And we cannot become a viable religious movement without engaging these 'evils.'"

3. Efforts to identify and reduce oppression can run counter to the dominant culture of Unitarian Universalism. In some ways, the idealism of Unitarian Universalism was a barrier, for we are the people who can confuse our ideals with our faith—faith in the sense of what we do each day, what we walk with to make real. We can confuse our largest goals (i.e., a united world where all are treated with respect) with the need for intermediate strategies. A common argument against the anti-racism initiative was that it divided rather than united people in a religion whose goal is unity. Yet the paradox remains that a strongly united identity relies on people's ability to understand their own individual identity and that temporary divisions have the potential to come together as the foundation for a true commonality. In a sense, our ideals can be an unhealthy proxy for real effort.

As Rev. Manish Mishra, then president of DRUUMM (Diverse and Revolutionary Unitarian Universalist Multicultural Ministries) beginning in 2006, noted,

> As somebody who came to Unitarian Universalism in the late 90s and was not personally a part of the history from the late 60s, or the ensuing attempts at reconciliation, my biggest impression about all of it was and continues to be that in our UU heart of hearts, we are, and I'm speaking of the majority culture, and not myself as an Asian-American and person of color, I think in the broadest cultural UU sense, we believe we're committed very deeply to diversity, but we're not willing to do much about it in terms of personal effort. And what that has meant in practice is that we have had a Journey Toward Wholeness Transformation Committee that's been charged with pursuing and doing something with these GA resolutions affirming our denominational commitment to being racially and culturally diverse, but the committee itself hasn't had a lot of support, and it hasn't been taken very seriously in terms of a larger UU cultural perception.
>
> I think if you asked an ordinary UU, "What do you think about the JTW?," they're going to say, "Well, you know, it wasn't very effective; they didn't do very much."

But I say the other side of the coin is, "How seriously did you take their work, and how seriously did you attempt to engage with them?" It's kind of this self-fulfilling prophecy and self-fulfilling feedback loop of, "Oh, well, the mechanism we created to do this work wasn't effective, and we didn't get anywhere." So we get caught up as UUs in wanting to really affirm our aspirations of diversity, and then not doing much about it, and finding reasons to complain or justify or affirm that what currently is happening is just ineffective, and that's why we're not getting anywhere.

Rev. Peter Morales, minister of Jefferson Unitarian Church in Golden, Colorado, noted that we tended to overstate our commitment to diversity and in doing so, neglect foundational work essential to our future. "So now instead of being sort of less cold and off-putting, we had to be 'radically hospitable,'" Morales said, using a phrase often repeated by the Association staff. "Why don't we just try plain vanilla friendliness instead of being radical? It doesn't have to be radical. I mean, you've got to start somewhere. If you're out of shape and overweight, you don't start by running a marathon, you start by walking around the block. We didn't know how to be warm and friendly to a Ph.D. driving a Volvo station wagon, who's a microbiologist with a couple of kids, who's our mainline, down-the-middle demographic. Forget how to be welcoming to people of different class and cultural and ethnic and backgrounds. We just mostly have to stop being so awful. Do we need to work on that? Hugely."

Rev. Dr. Fredric Muir, minister of the Unitarian Universalist Church of Annapolis, Maryland, said our recent emphasis on growth might prove short-sighted. "Many of the ministers have not wanted to go toward addressing anti-racism because of a fear of losing people, and/or not attracting people, so they just haven't done it," he said. "Actually I think maybe some of the best work is being done in smaller congregations where perhaps the focus isn't as much on growth. I think some of the ministers who are in medium-sized to large program churches, there's a real push by the UUA . . . to grow. In that sense, perhaps we need to see models of congregations that have been doing the work of anti-racism, anti-oppression, multiculturalism, who have been growing and say, 'Look, if you want to grow, you need to do this work.' This is one way of growing. With anti-racism, with being a Welcoming Congregation [with a commitment to being welcoming to bisexual, gay, lesbian, and transgender people], I know there are people who come explicitly because of those."

The General Assemblies became the place where many of the tensions and triumphs of identity and relationship played out. The hothouse nature of the Assemblies and the lack of deep relationships to support difficult discussions made this problematic. "GA is the 'gathering of the clan,' a meeting of the tribe," the Special Review Commission noted in its report on tensions and incidents at the 2005 General Assembly in Fort Worth. "Even in the midst of the fun, learning, and excitement, each of us knows how difficult these occasions can be. We steel ourselves for five days in a strange city. GA is a time when our routines shift dramatically. We are in an artificial construct of a community. We eat differently, socialize more, live differently, and sleep less. One of the immediate realities at Forth Worth was that individuals were overloaded and stressed and nearly always unaware of larger contexts related to what was immediately happening in a given moment. Overtaxed, individuals kept trying to work harder, cycling toward burn-out. Can we call for help without shame, without feeling that we've failed? Can errors become teachable moments rather than judgments against us? Yes."

4. Anti-racism and anti-oppression efforts challenge implicit understandings of Unitarian Universalist core identities. The liberal tendency was to see ourselves as already "there"—we did not need to examine our cultural assumptions because we were already on the right side of issues around race. This was both true—and insufficient.

Confusion about UU identity—theological and otherwise—caused more thunder and lightning because no clear UU lens for understanding it existed. The anti-racism initiative coincided with other efforts to tease out a UU identity, resisted by many who prefer the premise that Unitarian Universalists can believe anything they wish or those who cast the identity in a narrow way that combines notions of academic freedom with radical individualism. In a more unsettling vein, some seemed to equate Unitarian Universalism with racial and class characteristics, concluding that our current demographic profile was unalterable. The 2005–2006 Starr King report outlining the institution's "Educating to Counter Oppression" efforts, noted, "We have been struck by the tendency of some in UUism to unconsciously and uncritically conflate 'UU identity' and 'White privilege.' We've grappled in our context with the extent to which counter-oppressive work can be labeled as an abandonment of or lack of commitment to 'UU identity.'"

Interpretations of congregational polity, the foundational UU commitment to the congregations' independence and ultimate authority, made dialogue more difficult. Many questioned whether the anti-racism should come from the Unitarian Universalist Association Board, staff, and other leaders, while others posited that in a decentralized system, it could never have emerged from congregations. While the initiative was girded by resolutions approved by delegates from the congregations, its vision and leadership came from key Association staff members and a small cadre of very committed volunteers; the national monitoring committee set up to oversee it was never able to find a comfortable role. Some argued that the staff's central role was a misinterpretation of congregational polity. Others said that waiting for the awareness to come from the congregational level might have meant lack of initiative on an issue fraught with inherent hardships at the congregational level. For ministers, the fact that they serve congregations as long as the congregations are willing could make it dangerous to raise an issue this difficult and potentially divisive. Others were impatient with these implications. "Congregational polity or not, it's dysfunctional," observed Rev. William (Chester) McCall, then minister of the Unitarian Universalist Church of the Restoration in Philadelphia. "We should be allowed to hold congregations accountable to the Calgary resolution, explicitly confront every congregation: 'How are you going to incorporate this in your work this year?'"

"As you begin to solve one set of problems, you actually create a new set of problems and that is success," said Paula Cole Jones, consultant to the UUA's JUUST Change program. "To not be a barrier, you have to be always assessing the barriers. The change process probably requires that you be uncomfortable."

5. An emerging theological understanding of how to address racism in a Unitarian Universalist context built a foundation for the future. Because we are a faith community, casting this as an issue of faith was important, though difficult. In the late 1980s, when racial justice concerns again took hold in our faith, theological clarity was not common in most aspects of Unitarian Universalism. People did not feel a theological imperative to address issues around race (or other oppressions) values, at least not initially. Tomas Firle, active in anti-racism efforts in First Unitarian Universalist Church of San Diego, said anti-racism was perceived as a focus on the negative "rather than as a prerequisite to build[ing] a 'beloved community.'"

Many observers saw the lack of a theological foundation for anti-racism efforts as a barrier. "I would change the [UUA's] Jubilee [anti-racism] workshops to dwell more on the theological reasons for why we do this work," said Rev. Richard Speck, district executive for the Joseph Priestley District. "If we are to honor the central premise of inherent worth and dignity for all, this calls us to not only think but act in ways that show we are honoring each individual." Proponents of the racial justice approaches dominant in the 1980s and 1990s disagreed, asserting that the work was grounded in the Unitarian Universalist Principles. At the very first meeting of the Journey Toward Wholeness Committee, its members discussed the need to reach out to Unitarian Universalist theologians such as Rev. Dr. Michelle Bentley and Dr. Elias Farajaje-Jones to discuss "the role of seminaries and theologians in addressing the issues of antiracism and JTW." Others would observe that work on race in the Unitarian Universalist Association propelled us into a larger conversation about theology.

Anti-oppression leaders from the 1980s on saw their efforts as a religious journey. Explorations of the theological implications of anti-racism began with the work of pioneers such as Rev. Anita Dr. Farber-Robertson, Rev. Dr. William Jones, Rev. Dr. Mark

Morrison-Reed, Rev. Dr. Michelle Bentley, Rev. José Ballester, and others. Airing these perspectives was risky because of UU discomfort with religious language and "God language."

Anita Farber-Robertson, who co-chaired the Racial and Cultural Diversity Task Force, said Unitarian Universalists faced a theological barrier in the fact that they are "Christian-phobic." She observed, "We are not nice to people who care about Jesus and liberation theology cares about Jesus."

Theological challenges posed by Rev. Dr. Thandeka and others led to an explicit articulation of anti-racism's faith base in efforts such as *Soul Work: Anti-Racist Theologies in Dialogue*, published in 2003. *Soul Work*, along with the theological writings of Rev. Dr. Paul Rasor, Rev. Thandeka, and others, deepened Unitarian Universalist anti-racism's theological underpinnings. One of the most tangible products of this time in our history is, in fact, work outlining the theological tenets of anti-racism in a Unitarian Universalist context.

Anti-oppression work provided another entry point for building a common theology. A common criticism of early UUA anti-racism efforts, after the 1997 General Assembly adopted the resolution entitled "Toward an Anti-Racist Unitarian Universalist Association," was that they were done outside a Unitarian Universalist theological frame. Yet these strategies were adjusted in response to the initial criticism of their Lutheran roots and were given a grounding in Unitarian Universalist theology. Debates about addressing race and maturing as a religion were intertwined. The fact that we as a movement were unclear about what we believed together and how to voice what we believed helped convolute discussions of anti-racism understandings with conversations about related issues such as the use of more traditional religious language.

Interest in reclaiming our Universalist heritage grew alongside anti-oppression efforts, with many in historically marginalized racial and cultural groups finding Universalist theological concepts compelling. What is clear is that our heritage contained a mandate that does not allow us to hide behind a resigned sense of Unitarian Universalism as a cultural religion that can save only white, middle-class intellectuals. The Universalist doctrine that all are saved was interpreted in its early twentieth century form to also profess a religious imperative to work for the kind of unity that can be found only by authentically embracing diversity.

The key was embracing something larger than the will of one individual, i.e., the "creative good" of a community or an understanding of a system. "Theologically we tend to individualism and what that can lead to is a focus on personal prejudice," Rev. Dr. Tracey Robinson-Harris, a long-time advocate of racial justice, said. "I don't think collectively we are good systemic thinkers." This made it difficult for many Unitarian Universalists to grasp such concepts as how to analyze the way race influenced who had power in systems. She added that, within Unitarian Universalism, "certain cultures are affirmed and others dismissed because they tend to think of themselves individually or in opposition to a system and resist labels and collective identities."

Our inability to articulate a theological concept of evil, a classic criticism of liberal religion, also figures into the debate. "Whether the structure we're dealing with is racism, or sexism, or heterosexism, or violence, or materialism, the evil is in the ability of the dominant worldview to make itself seem logical, even necessary," Rasor observed. "To fight them, we need an inner transformation. . . . It is not simply a matter of purifying our hearts. It is also a matter of coming to have a different sort of perception. What we need in these cases is the kind of transformation that will allow us to perceive things in a new way. We need a shift in our worldview, a new gestalt that allows us to move forward together and to resist. Social analysis by itself can't give us this. In fact, much of our social analysis is done from the perspective of the dominant worldview. Much of our social justice work makes only a political statement, not a faith statement. It can speak only to the intellect, and seeks a political response. But when we deal with the spiritual aspect, we are making a faith claim, and what we seek is a spiritual response. That's what I'm hoping to work toward in my approach to evil."

Our basic world view as liberal religionists stood in our way and made us resistant to some of the truths this work exposed. The Special Review Commission put it this way: "Unitarian Universalists hold high the premise that love can conquer every oppression that beats people down." One young adult writes,

> I believe that too, but to get there, we can't ignore all those oppressions because they are very real. It is only when we start to acknowledge the oppressions that we or the people in our community have been affected by that we are able to see the struggle that we, or the people in our community, have had to battle with.

Cole Jones suggested the questions about theology may have been a diversion. "Many Unitarian Universalists had invested energy into the debate about ideology and that is where it ended, whereas if you focus on skills, it doesn't matter where you stand on ideology."

6. Most anti-racism effort was at the Associational level; many congregations were touched—and have yet to be transformed. A number of Associational leaders have found anti-racism work transformational while the impact in congregations was mixed. Specific groups that have made real changes because of their anti-racism commitment include the Unitarian Universalist Association Board of Trustees; the Association's staff, through procedures that attempt to measure competency in this area; the Ministerial Fellowship Committee; and—with more mixed results—the two Unitarian Universalist theological schools. Sometimes the changes have been small, yet significant. "The changes in the MFC paperwork have been a concrete, positive change," Robert Gross, a member of the Journey Toward Wholeness Transformation Committee, observed in 2005.

And real affects could be seen in other areas:

The UUA Board of Trustees adopted new practices. Tamara Payne-Alex, a member of the UUA Board from 2000 to 2009, described the Board culture during the second term of the Sinkford administration as that of a "very, very loving and also confrontative group." She noted,

> The culture of the Board is particularly holistic. It viewed itself as a leadership group but it viewed itself as a religious

group also. Board members believed in holding one another accountable. . . . When people got angry, they didn't let people off the hook, they continued to say, 'We have work here.' People didn't give up on one another.

In her years on the Board, she saw it wrestle with what she called "periodic tests" around the group commitment to anti-oppression work, whether it be issues at General Assembly or other points of conflict and decision. "These things kept it real," she recalled.

The Board also moved away from an emphasis on forcing diversity during this time, recalled Payne-Alex, who grew up as a Unitarian Universalist and noted her experience was shaped by being biracial, light-skinned, and African-American. "The good news is we've moved away from a focus on having a diverse group, because you can easily have a diverse group where no one is skilled in anti-oppression."

JUUST Change consultant Cole Jones said that the hardest choice is to take on this sort of systems change at the congregational level. "I often see people at the national table who are not doing the work in their churches," she said.

Selected districts have taken the lead. The Joseph Priestley, Metro New York, Massachusetts Bay, and Thomas Jefferson Districts all devoted significant sustained attention to anti-racism. For example, the Joseph Priestley District, voted in 2002 to look at all its activities through an anti-racist lens.

Some congregations were engaged in a variety of ways. The programming of this time period touched scores of congregations and others developed their own approach to improving race relations. Rev. Abhi Janamanchi, minister of the Unitarian Universalists of Clearwater congregation in Florida, said it is hard to assess which congregational efforts were successful in that they are very diverse and their goals varied. "My struggle is what is our marker for success," he said. "Are we marking success in terms of some part having had a positive impact, you know, not only helping the congregation deal with some of those issues but also providing more diversity in their midst?"

Youth and young adults active at the Associational level have been among those taking leadership. More attention needed to be paid to the groundbreaking work done by youth and young adults engaged at the national level through YRUU (Young Religious Unitarian Universalists) and C*UUYAN (Continental Unitarian Universalist Young Adult Network). Their efforts needed to be showcased as a major contribution to anti-oppression, not as a minor tangent. They have specific needs as well—they are the ones who know the particular pains and challenges of the transracial adoption issues and are more likely to be living as multiracial people.

Despite these efforts, many individual Unitarian Universalists remain untouched by anti-racism and anti-oppression efforts. A disconnect developed between individual anti-racism and anti-oppression leaders and the dominant Unitarian Universalist congregational culture. Rev. Rebecca Parker, president of the Starr King School for the Ministry, said seminarians' biggest issue after taking positions in congregations or other ministry settings was how to apply their anti-racism and anti-oppression understanding when it generally eluded the people they were serving. "When people get into their parish internship full-time field-work things," Parker said, "it feels like it's really separated. So really, then, I think we've only made very small progress on how we get from a deeper engagement in theological education to people's own transformation and development of skills to a real application of congregational change."

Rev. Melvin Hoover, former UUA director of Faith in Action, said the efforts at the Association level fell short of their goal. "The power was really never shared," he said of the white majority. "They weren't ready to give up ultimate control."

Yet perhaps it is not realistic to be discouraged that we have not completed a task that may never be finished. As Rev. Dr. Robert Eller-Isaacs, minister of Unity Church-Unitarian in St. Paul, Minnesota, said about anti-racism and Unitarian Universalism: "This isn't about learning how people can get along; this is about changing a system."

7. The perception that the Journey Toward Wholeness was a cookie-cutter approach limited its effectiveness. In its first few years the initiative had a tight focus on the Crossroads Ministry anti-racism approach. Leaders adopted it in a search for a strategic approach to address specific, entrenched, systemic issues. Yet even from the beginning more than one approach was being explored and implemented, such as the Black Concerns Working Group's "Building a Jubilee World." Parker, the Starr King president, said the intellectual understanding of racism and white privilege deepened with time. "When you act on commitments you start to learn things," she said, "and I know just for myself as an educator and a theologian working in the UU context, at this point I'm beginning to have a much more crystallized analysis of how white privilege performs itself in UUism. . . . The resistance and objection to anti-racist work and commitments by white privilege has also shown itself more and more clearly, at least to me and to our institution. So I think one outcome is that white privilege has shown its habits and strategies in a variety of ways which have allowed for a more complex and specific analysis. . . . I think the rhetoric that led to the adoption of the 1992 resolution was almost completely about a second chance after the failure of Unitarian Universalism to move forward with its commitments and things that were emerging during the black empowerment years. It wasn't a voice—I don't remember voices in 1992 that were speaking about the importance of a multiracial understanding of anti-racism work."

In sum, the anti-racism initiative moved:

From a focus on black/white to include other ethnicities. The unresolved dilemma entering into the 1990s was how to ensure that the black issues got addressed. Now other issues remain unsolved, including how to mend the rift between some of Latina/o and Hispanic origin and other historically marginalized racial and ethnic groups. And the issue of the particular challenges of incorporating black Unitarian Universalists remains: Dr. Norma Poinsett noted that while embracing a wide spectrum of people of color and multiculturalism has been positive, it can overshadow the persistent problems of black people in this Association. "This is something you can't stop working on," she said.

From a focus on a Christian theological base to including other theologies. The Crossroads Ministry approach was based on a Christian analysis; the approach broadened after Unitarian Universalist leaders retooled it to their context. An irony here was that engagement with anti-racism provided us a path back to reclaiming parts of our own Christian heritage, particularly our Universalist roots.

From a focus on racial oppression to include other oppressions/identities. If the work of our youth is any indication, this is an important development.

From a program based on training workshops to a flexible menu that expanded to also include congregational consultancy through the UUA's JUUST Change program. This allows for a focus beyond training to organizational assessment. Rev. Marjorie Bowens-Wheatley, who designed trainings and did research to support racial justice, observed,

> My own feeling is that there is no one model that the congregation and the whole Association can and should adopt. I think it's a false expectation that all of our congregations will be involved in this work. I think we need a much more individual approach. When I say individual, I mean look at each individual congregation. . . . So when a congregation feels that it wants specific help, they can call a JUUST Change consultant who will come out just as if it were a management consultant, look at that particular congregation, say here's our recommendations based on your situation. That's the only thing that I think will work, frankly.

The complaints and "disconnects" that arose around anti-racism efforts also consumed much energy. The "disconnects" included:

That racial justice efforts could only be done one way. The Special Review Commission cited the anti-racism approaches of the National Coalition Building Institute, Crossroads Ministry, and the Industrial Areas Foundation as the three most widely known models in the UUA in 2006 and then noted,

> Each of these models is valid. We UUs expend far too much energy weighing them and judging their validity. We can ill afford to get caught up in the senseless debate. Would we not be more effective with antiracism toolkits that reflect our pluralism and draw from multiple schools of thought?

That it addressed issues already addressed by legal changes. Overcoming the federal, state, and local legal barriers to racial equality had been a clear and concrete task. Understanding the work that remained, in changing people's learned prejudices and other attitudinal constraints, was much harder. The idea that these attitudes and prejudices could be built into the fabric of systems, rendering them still unequal despite changes in the law, was harder still for those who had an inherent faith in the self-correcting balances of democratic systems.

That it was simply an extreme example of political correctness or an expression of a "culture of victimhood." Some Unitarian Universalists saw anti-oppression as nothing more than an excessive expression of liberal attitudes. These allegations were particularly difficult for the people of color whose pain was put on exhibit for a white majority during anti-racism trainings and consultations that relied heavily on personal testimonials to establish emotional validity. With the small number of individuals from racial and culturally diverse groups available within the faith movement, these people were often asked to repeat their stories of pain and humiliation again and again for the edification of a majority unaware of their realities. And for others, these personal testimonials were merely emotional outbursts that could not be proved with "rational" methods such as statistics.

That anti-racism was a trend overtaken by others in a short order. Initiatives such as the Journey Toward Wholeness were seen by some as flash-in-the-pan efforts soon to be replaced by more trendy ones. The launch of its programming phase so close to the Fulfilling the Promise effort may have overshadowed it. In a joint meeting in 1999, the Journey Toward Wholeness Transformation Committee and the Fulfilling the Promise Steering Committee asked, "Next year the two groups (JTW & FTP) should get married; right now we are engaged. How shall we get together?" Many thought Fulfilling the Promise would overshadow the Journey Toward Wholeness, but Fulfilling the Promise faded and, a decade after the 1997 resolution, the Journey Toward Wholeness was still present.

That anti-racism was against congregational polity. The perception that anti-racism was an Association-led effort allowed opponents to raise perennial issues. The Association's efforts were framed by two resolutions, adopted in 1992 and 1997 by a vote of the delegates from congregations, the highest authority under our polity. Still, the Association's Board may not have been ready to provide the leadership needed in 1992 and so that fell to the racial justice proponents, both volunteers and staff. What was lacking was an accountable structure that would have congregational input during implementation, a place for questions to be asked, rumors squashed, and consensus built.

That it was abandoned in the administration of UUA president William Sinkford. The Sinkford administration ended the Association's formal relationship with Crossroads Ministry and disbanded the Faith in Action Department in a reorganization that distributed anti-oppression responsibility to every staff group. But the administration also formed the Identify-Based Ministries staff group to support Unitarian Universalists from all marginalized groups and developed the JUUST Change program. This approach was designed to provide greater flexibility for congregations, to address their needs more specifically; it draws from a variety of approaches. Critics charged that it was soft on systemic analyses and failed to build a common vocabulary to help people understand oppression.

That it is not relevant to virtually all-white, middle-class congregations. The fact that this observation could be made illustrated perhaps as well as anything the breadth of divide anti-racism sought to overcome. The idea that Unitarian Universalism could only appeal to white and middle-class people was rife with its own assumptions.

A challenge is to understand the need for these shifts not as a sign that we have moved into some wiser time but rather as a sign that we have been willing to learn and grow. As religious educator Jacqui James observed, "It was a real learning time for us. I think it was a time when the Unitarian Universalist Association was trying to do the right thing but hadn't figured out the best way to do that." Rev. Susan Suchocki Brown, the first chair of the Journey Toward Wholeness Transformation Committee, said that even the early problems with Crossroads Ministry should be looked at in perspective. "They were one of the first educational religious groups that were looking at institutional racism and looking at what an institution is and how you make change. . . . Crossroads really helped me analyze from an institutional perspective, and they gave me a lens to do critical analysis."

8. Individuals, especially people of color and their "white allies," face a hard path. The pastoral challenge of anti-racism is significant; damaged relationships need reconciliation. The truism states that change is not easy. The anti-racism approach of Crossroads Ministry, the starting point for post-1997 efforts, and some other models tried by the Association's staff, met resistance. To many advocates, the tendency was to associate resistance with resistance to doing the necessary work and paying the costs that change imposes.

People of color or Latina/o/Hispanic origin faced special difficulties finding support in congregations. This spurred the formation of identity groups and caucuses of people from marginalized groups. Groups such as Unitarian Universalist Native and Indigenous Americans, Diverse and Revolutionary Unitarian Universalist Multicultural Ministries, and the Latina/o Unitarian Universalist Networking Association provided spaces for support and safety. This was important because the anti-racism infrastructure was built through the hard work of dedicated individuals who often paid a high cost, many of them leaving Unitarian Universalism as a result.

Communications failures and misperceptions exacerbated this friction. For many of the most engaged Unitarian Universalists, those who participate at the national level or attend General Assemblies, the Journey Toward Wholeness was just one of many initiatives undertaken by the Association—something that sounded vaguely familiar. The average congregation member most likely heard nothing of them. The sense of urgency that anti-racism advocates felt had dramatic collisions with others' desire for maintaining the status quo. People on both sides felt unheard and disrespected. While some argued that too much of an emphasis was placed on anti-racism training, a more accurate statement in our estimation would be that training needed to be supported by more pastoral care, theological exploration, and skills in conflict management. And yet, all of these required time and financial resources.

We must note that some relationships were broken before a conscious dialogue on anti-racism began. Those relationships did not cause stirs in General Assembly sessions or attract debates in the pages of *UU World*. They ended when many people with racial and ethnic backgrounds different from mainstream Unitarian Universalism, as well as many people of European descent who had experienced more inclusive communities in other settings, chose to leave quietly because they despaired that the prevailing culture could ever comprehend their reality. In writing this book, one of the heavy sadnesses we held was the realization of how many voices could not be included because they are gone from the conversation, disillusioned and injured.

People of color paid a huge tax in time and spiritual energy. Unitarian Universalism has so few people of color and of Latino/a/Hispanic heritage that they tend to be pulled in many directions and often are thrust immediately into leadership without context or support. This overextension and lack of support has led to disillusionment and burn-out. The example of Rev. Peter Morales, though extreme, was illustrative. He recalled,

> I get out of seminary. I'm on the Exec [the Unitarian Universalist Ministers Association Executive Committee], then I get out of the Exec, and then I get asked to be on the UUA Board of Trustees. So my third year in ministry, I'm on the Board of Trustees—first Latino—and then get invited to be on the senior staff of the UUA. It's been a wild ride. . . . In the UUA you never know whether they want you or whether they just want a spic on this committee.

UU professionals who are people of color or of Latino/a/Hispanic heritage face difficult challenges. "We still don't know what is necessary—what work is required—[for a congregation] to be ready to call a minister of color, or of another oppression," observed McCall. "This should be a result of the JTW, etc., work." When asked what was one thing he would change about the UUA and anti-racism, Rev. Timothy Malone, who was affiliated with the Davis, California, congregation, said, "I would demand that the UUA be more honest about who they really are."

Youth of color lack needed support. The Special Review Commission's report about incidents affecting youth at the 2005 General Assembly stated,

> The Commission found that UU antiracism work is notably lacking in support for our youth of color. So many people, including youth of color themselves, as they have told us, are still trying to figure out if and where youth of color belong within this faith. Far too much time in youth-of-color identity groups is spent discussing white people and youth and their relation to whiteness. Positive identity development for youth of color was dangerously deficient. While white youth have the title of "ally," to be earned and used responsibly, youth of color lack the same opportunity. They miss any opportunity for forward motion. Their growth tends to happen by enduring and recovering from incredibly invisible and painful experiences. At youth anti-racism workshops and conferences, the progress of the group often comes at the expense of the feelings and comfort of people of color.

"White allies"—those of white or European heritage who considered themselves advocates of anti-racism, described being marked as troublemakers. Some suffered loss of congregational community, ostracized for raising issues others would prefer they leave dormant. Those who were Unitarian Universalist professionals also reported losing collegial support, and facing narrowed job possibilities. The formation of Allies for Racial Equity in 2005–06 as a place for "white allies" to meet about their support for anti-racism work, emerged as potentially an important antidote to the problem of needing one of a small number of non-white people to be present to allow anti-oppression work to go forward.

Another issue was what has happened to early white allies who threw themselves heart-first into anti-racism only to experience the Sinkford administration's anti-oppressive programmatic focus as abandonment. "Shifting the Association's focus away from racism at this time actually represents a deep lack of spiritual, ethical and moral courage," said Rev. Kurt Kuhwald. "It chillingly mirrors the nation's abandonment of racial justice work and the derailment of

Affirmative Action, long before its full power for good could be realized. It demonstrates one of the liberal spirit's greatest vulnerabilities . . . an inability to stay strong in and to act persistently and courageously for one's values in the face of adversity and opposition; and the lack of a sustaining, life-tested, and realistic vision about humankind and its place in the cosmos that is intimate with what is sacred. My disappointment and grief are deep, though I now realize that the trust I put in the UUA as an institution was immature, unwise and overly idealistic."

Specific examples of relationships damaged include:

Seminarians toe perceived "party line"/creed related to credentialing. The efforts of the Ministerial Fellowship Committee to bring an anti-racist sensibility to the attention of seminarians was perceived by some as an attempt to limit freedom of expression. By bringing these issues to the attention of seminarians, awareness is built. How meaningful this engagement was remains to be seen.

Participants in early trainings felt mocked and criticized as unrepentant racists. As mentioned before, the challenge to their self-identities shocked liberal Unitarian Universalists. The Crossroads approach called for jolting people out of their comfort zone. The combination of these two factors created a huge amount of bad feeling for some.

Some felt it dangerous to critique the program or its trainers/proponents. The passion and commitment of advocates of the Crossroads-based approach was clear. Some perceived that the approach perceived challenges to anti-oppression efforts as resistance to the idea that inequities remain within Unitarian Universalism.

Individuals have been wounded by anti-racism efforts and it is not clear what was done or what can be done to help them heal. One of the challenges of this project was that people were often reluctant to talk, unwilling to reengage with painful memories. The reconciliation process that began with the Common Ground meetings the Sinkford Administration initiated in 2002 engaged some and yet others remain estranged and bitter. Those who are now missing from our movement—including those who entered as youth or young adults of color and a number of people whose racial or ethnic heritage propelled them into leadership roles—are a particular challenge and tragedy. The process for collecting information for this book has shown just how much relationships and trust have been damaged. Rev. José Ballester, a member of Association's Board, echoed the sentiments of others when he wrote as part of his input for this book:

> As requested, here are my replies to your inquiries. I do this with hesitation and a lack of trust in the process. As should be evident, my involvement in these efforts has often met with frustration, broken promises and vilification. There is a high level of cynicism for which I do not apologize.

A clear learning was that chaplaincy and pastoral care are central to anti-oppression efforts. Workshops that challenged people's worldviews and their most closely held assumptions shook people at the deepest levels. In recent years, as affinity groups and identity groups such as Youth and Young Adults of Color and Allies for Racial Equity have organized to "care for their own," the opportunity for chaplaincy has emerged and seems to offer promise.

9. Key stakeholders were not engaged in early anti-racism efforts, yet became so as it moved forward. The anti-racism initiatives were developed by a small cadre of committed leaders whose strategy was to start a grassroots effort at General Assembly rather than work through established channels, which they perceived to be at best unenthusiastic and at worst hostile. As a result, the 1992 and even 1997 resolutions took the ministers, religious educators, and district leadership by surprise; their lack of readiness may have contributed to resistance. The majority of congregational presidents were then so distanced from Associational work that they were also not engaged. As the strategies progressed, key stakeholders were brought in and key constituencies began to find ways to offer support and opportunities for mutual learning.

Janice Marie Johnson saw the emergence of multiple organizations based on racial and ethnic identity as an opportunity for different groups to be accountable for different pieces of the effort. "Here's an opportunity to become unstuck and to be heard. Not heard, but to be really listened to," Johnson said. "Because if you take the time to listen, you will hear with a listening heart. We can help each other, but you've got to be for real."

Within a few years, the importance of stakeholders was identified. Stakeholders could be key individuals or organizations which had the power to change the overall culture or conditions that affected historically marginalized populations. Of note, given the demonstrated importance of professional leadership, was the growing involvement of the two Unitarian Universalist theological schools—Meadville Lombard Theological School in Chicago and the Starr King School for the Ministry in Berkeley, California. A focus on race has helped some strengthen an identity they already had. Parker, the Starr King president, shared this observation about where some Starr King graduates are vis-à-vis the congregations that call them: "We did a survey of our graduates from the last five years that included a lot of questions about their education for counter-oppressive and justice work and anti-racist work," she said. "The survey included asking people to assess how the school had changed or developed their understanding. . . . To a large extent, where they had counter-oppressive and justice and anti-racism commitments, they mostly [already] had them when they came in [to Starr King]. And their theological education may have introduced them to a few areas that they hadn't known about, but that their commitment was formed before they came to the school. A lot of people said, 'You know, I came to school already having done this and done that, and then I learned about this area that I hadn't been involved in. Like I'd done a lot of gay activism but I hadn't done much economic justice work." Yet the school was raising their consciousness.

The anti-oppression efforts of the theological schools, which train the next generation, are critical because we stand in danger of neglecting and creating despair among a key part of our future membership and leadership. Multiracial identities needed exploration as well as the intersections among oppressions. This was a key finding as youth and young adults developed an approach that worked for them. The Starr King "Educating to Counter Oppressions" report also identified this, adding:

In particular, deeper theological and spiritual resources are needed to sustain us during periods of conflict and upheaval, and to help us see that our failures can be as important to our learning as our successes. These theological themes need to be drawn explicitly from the Unitarian, Universalist, and Unitarian Universalist traditions and from the articulations of faith that come out of those traditions. This will also provide resources for spiritual connection for students who are coming to terms with the roles they have played as oppressor and oppressed.

The development of the Sankofa Archive at Meadville Lombard Theological School under the leadership of Rev. Michelle Bentley was another important step toward acknowledging that the experience of all Unitarian Universalists is not the same.

10. Anti-racism efforts in the years since Calgary served as a bridge to new, emerging approaches. Each bridge led to another challenge:

From black/white to include other ethnicities. Efforts to discuss race and ethnicity were rooted in the unfinished dialogue remaining from the Associational fissures over how to respond to the black empowerment movement in the 1960s and 1970s. Yet the twenty-first century is one with much more racial and ethnic diversity and a more embracing sense of what multiculturalism should be. Challenge: How do we address the issue of those of African descent, who often have the hardest time integrating into congregations?

From a Christian-based understanding of anti-racism to one including other theologies. Challenge: How do we overcome the fact that we still lack a consistent point of theological reference in Unitarian Universalism?

From a focus on racism to one that better acknowledges other oppressions/identities. Race was the unfinished business of the 1960s and 1970s and the dialogue in the 1980s started there once more. Yet in a world more sensitized to a range of oppressions, this isolated focus could not be sustained. Challenge: How can we keep the focus on race when it seems easier for us to deal with other oppressions such as gender identity and sexual orientation?

From the perception of one anti-racism approach to a menu of approaches. Examination of the actual approaches used to educate and create dialogue about racial and cultural difference throughout the 1990s and into the twenty-first century within Unitarian Universalism reveals that the approaches were also complicated and multifaceted. For example, the Black Concerns/Jubilee Working Group continued to offer their approach to dialogue around race even after the Crossroads Ministry model gained ascendency and others were experimenting with other ways to generate conversation. Challenge: How can we maintain coherence without becoming dogmatic or creedal? How can we assure that we are developing a common vocabulary that can allow for systemic change?

From an approach focused at the national UUA level to one designed to focus at the congregational level as well. The plan for affecting Unitarian Universalist attitudes around race and culture began among those active at the Associational level, both from within the office of President William Schulz and within a group of activists focused on urban concerns. The efforts naturally focused on change at the Association and among its committees and functions. Yet the power of any change in our radical system of congregational polity, which gives power to the congregations, is that which affects the congregational leadership, which ebbs and flows with the whims of volunteerism. "One of the things we forgot to our detriment is that we were dealing with volunteers," observed Taquiena Boston, director of the Association's Identity-Based Ministries staff group. Challenge: How can we maintain progress with frequent changes in leadership?

From an approach solely based on training workshops to one that includes multiple ways of building knowledge. This was also a move toward an emphasis on accountability to people of color. Accountability was an issue for many groups, as noted by the Transformation Committee in 2004 when they noted, "There's a question about how the TC interacts with Jubilee trainers as a stakeholder group. Stakeholders identified should be organizations that speak for some membership. There's an inherent danger in dealing with individual stakeholders; it raises questions about accountability." Challenge:

Will a gentler approach be enough to overcome resistance to change and conflict and overcome real imbalances of power and privilege?

From a model that reached a section of the Association's leaders to one which was compelling to a broader cross-section of lay leaders and easier for congregations to access. The widespread use of the initial "Building a Jubilee World" workshop as conceived and delivered by the Black Concerns Working Group (later the Jubilee Working Group) suggested that congregations did respond to efforts to address racial injustices. Challenge: How do we find what works in congregations and adopt it widely?

From a loose model of intent to one with more understanding of the need for accountability. In the fifteen years between 1992 and 2007, leaders interested in finding better ways to communicate across racial and cultural difference have come to understand how important it is that these discussions address systemic change and not merely personal transformation. Yet with so few people of color or Latina/o and Hispanic origins within our midst, we struggle to devise a way to do this that is not just about anointing a small group of those who meet a demographic category to be a default conscience for a white majority. Under this system, this small group faces burnout and disillusionment and often those who have served in this sort of impossible arrangement leave the Association, further reducing the numbers. Real effort and radical imagination are needed to devise a system where decision makers can be held to a real standard of accountability linked to a democratic and replicable process. Challenge: How do we develop more clearly articulated systems of accountability and bodies that are consistent enough to which to be accountable?

From an approach centered on addressing white attitudes to one that focuses on different needs of different groups. Challenge: How can we support the range of identities and provide opportunities for those in historically marginalized groups to grow in their own awareness?

From an oppressed/oppressor understanding to one that includes multiple identities. Those who have engaged in the ongoing dialogue over race have, by necessity, developed a more nuanced understanding of identity, largely because of the growing awareness of the greater United States culture of complex identities.

All of these are small pieces and yet they add up to an intentionality that did not exist before. As Moderator Gini Courter said in one plenary at the 2006 General Assembly, "People of color have been trying to be heard in this Association for a long time, and we need to ensure that that happens more easily."

As we offered these dozen observations, we did so knowing this list to be incomplete and that each person who reads this could add their own observations to make it at least a baker's dozen. Perhaps most important to those of us who have used our time to create this list was that Unitarian Universalists take the time to engage with this history as we go forward with whatever comes next. This time period leaves a mother lode of learnings that should not go untapped. In the way that the Empowerment Controversies informed the design of the Journey Toward Wholeness, may the legacy of this time also be built into the foundation of our ongoing efforts to build toward the goal of a more inclusive, multicultural Unitarian Universalism.

That new issues will continue to come up is evidenced by the discussions on "cultural misappropriation," which came up more frequently in the 2005–2006 General Assemblies. Here one incident from the 2006 General Assembly suggests to us a new part of the journey ahead:

> Musicians appeared on the stage to lead the delegation in singing "Thula Klizeo," a South African piece found in the UUA's new *Singing the Journey* hymn book supplement. The history of the song was shared—as well as information that, in the language of the Zulu people, singers would stomp their feet to show how strong they were. It could feel like an earthquake and sound like thunder when they were together, said the leader, Jan Chamberlin. Chamberlin pointed out that under apartheid, stomping was made illegal, and the Zulu then created a "silent stomping." The creator of this style, Joseph Shabalala, went on to found the singing group Ladysmith Black Mambazo. When they left Africa to perform, they became political refugees, missed their

country, and wrote this song to say, "O God, Even here, I can be happy."

Immediately following the singing of the piece, which was offered by a "chorus line" of singers, Tamara Payne-Alex, a member of the UUA Board, was recognized at the Procedural Microphone. She voiced concern that from an anti-racist, anti-oppressive, and multicultural lens, it was important to use music in ways that feel as if it is in right relationship with the roots of the music. Acknowledgment of the history of the music helps, and yet there was no acknowledgment made of the privilege we have to perform music, and to take music from other cultures where it means something more than what we can take out of performing it.

PART 7

FINAL VOICES

The Special Review Commission, in its 2006 report on incidents at the previous summer's General Assembly in Fort Worth, noted,

> What we have learned is that none of these events happened in a vacuum and that the trajectory does not start at the Leadership Development Conference [for youth of color preceding the GA] and has not yet ended. Human beings have human needs, faults, and frailties. We act or react depending on our particular state of mind at the time, which is often compounded by other events. Additionally, we all act out of our own experiences and, given how diverse we are, our challenge is to affirm the life experiences that each of us brings. Everyone has their own interpretations and often those interpretations are contradictory. That does not mean that one is right and another wrong. We on the SRC have heard differing stories of the same experience, seen from widely varying perspectives, given what each participant brought to the moment. No story told it all; no story told truth to power. Was each story true? Yes, for the one living it. What is the factual story? That question is not ours to ask. People's truths are not.

In that spirit, we wish to end with the voices of some of those who took the time to be part of this project, assessing the UUA's efforts with anti-racism, anti-oppression, and multiculturalism—or offering their experiences to a young person some years in the future.

"I have both joys and sorrows about where we are now. I have a sense of sorrow about the fact that the anti-racism work hasn't made a bigger impact on the year-to-year, day-to-day congregational life that we see in our churches. I think that our efforts in the 90s to change congregational culture have been limited to people who have played leadership roles and to a certain kind of reflex monitoring of who we are, but I'm not sure how much our Association actually functions at the congregational level as anti-racist allies, white allies in the life of communities. I think for many churches, and I think it's true in the one I serve now, if it wasn't for a few advocates, often supported by the minister, there would be not much attention paid to anti-racist work. . . . On the other hand, I guess the joy side of it might be that I do believe that the last fifteen years have profoundly transformed a lot of individual lives and have made the UU religious practice for those who really take it seriously inseparable from an understanding of how power and oppression work in our society. Anybody who's articulate at all, anybody who goes to seminary in UUism now, cannot be trained as a UU minister without having exposure to what it means to bring an anti-racism, anti-oppression analysis into your religious life as a whole, and religious leadership. Again, I think we fail as ministers being able to effectively translate that into making the same kind of difference in our congregation members' lives."

—Rev. Wayne Arnason, co-minister, West Shore
Unitarian Universalist Church, Cleveland, Ohio

"I would hope to say that: Five years ago we finally had the courage to acknowledge our mistakes, forgive ourselves for those mistakes, and began to truly work for the elimination of racism and oppressions, but also upholding the vast multiculturalism of our society. This allowed us to establish justice instead of building systemic theories of justice and recognize and effectively deal with differences rather than acknowledging the problem of our differences. Living out the truth that justice cannot be achieved at the expense of others."

—Rev. José Ballester, minister, First Unitarian
Universalist Church of Houston, Texas

"My journey to bring my culture to bear and being fully myself was hard. . . . Some of our worship does look different. Can we be ourselves without passing?"

> —Rev. Dr. Michelle Bentley, founder of the Sankofa
> Archives, Chicago, Illinois

"We've lost a lot of people. My biggest heartache is the loss of human hearts and community. Even people who are still among us are closing their hearts."

> —Rev. Sofia Betancourt, minister, Identity-Based
> Ministries, Unitarian Universalist Association

"I think the days when ministers don't see this as part of their job are just about over. . . . People going to seminary now—they know this is their work. I mean, the biggest problem, I think, is dealing with white guys in their fifties. White guys who are my age and older. Anybody younger than that gets it or has the potential to get it."

> —Rev. Rosemary Bray McNatt, minister, Fourth
> Universalist Society, New York City, New York

"Much has happened, and it is good. It's a kind of a gradual increase. We have so many more African-American ministers, now. Empowerment really is on the denominational agenda, but more than the agenda, the consciousness. . . . We have a black [UUA] president, which would just have been unheard of. I've seen things change, but hey, I've seen the society at large change, and whether we have changed in accordance with the society's changes, or whether we have changed as a result of the society's changes—well, I think that's a toss-up. I don't see any particularly prophetic stance emerging."

> —Rev. Dr. Victor Carpenter, emeritus minister,
> The First Church in Belmont, Massachusetts

"I want people to understand that everything we have done has been important to getting us to where we are and have been. This is a redesigning of our culture and relationships. I want people to appreciate the journey that we have been on. Everybody has been an important part of it—this is not about replacing one person or program with another."

—Paula Cole Jones, lead consultant,
JUUST Change Consultancy

"It has taken all these fifteen years to get the change and so we're having authentic conversations. I do have a hope that the legacy of this past fifteen years will be transformational change across congregations in the next fifteen. And I wouldn't have thought that five years ago. We've gotten past the point of having to defend a model and in doing so letting the perfect—if that is what we thought it was—be the enemy of the good. We are off the continuum and put it in a place more authentically UU."

—Gini Courter, moderator, Unitarian Universalist
Association, 2003–2009

"We skinned our knees a lot and didn't get it right a lot and yet failure was not an option. Not doing this work is not an option. I hope that we are developing leadership that will sustain us for a long time to come. Many youth and young adults are pivotal in the work. I hope they will also be pivotal in the larger Unitarian Universalist movement, that we are developing sustainable leadership."

—Jyaphia Christos-Rodgers, trainer with youth
and young adults

"We can't be what we want to be, or what we think we are, or what we think we want to be without seriously addressing the fact that racism exists in our society. It's a major, major issue and because we have tried to get our hands around it, albeit not quite knowing what we're doing and not being sure how to be effective, and not being sure what works and what doesn't, but because we keep trying to work, if we gave up on that and said, well, actually either 'That's too hard; there's nothing we can do that will change it' or 'It's not important; we have other things we need to do,' it would absolutely betray the integrity of what we see as our religious mission, in my opinion. And I would not be interested in it. It's a religious imperative. It's what makes us more than a community of like-minded folks. It's what gives us the opportunity to try to be change agents in a way that matters. If I could say, I've kind of been mulling in the back of my mind that question about what could we have done differently."

> —Phyllis Daniel, past member of the Unitarian
> Universalist Association Board and past chair
> of the Ministerial Fellowship Committee

"People are imperfect and we do things that are wrong and foolish and embarrassing and still we need to keep at it one step at a time. You keep going. Hopefully you learn from the mistakes and the mistakes are not a reason to stop. There is progress—slower than we wish—there is progress."

> —Rev. Dr. Anita Farber-Robertson, interim minister

"We started the journey, a spiritual one, to be truly 'whole,' to accept, respect, value each person while responding to his/her behaviour on its own merits. Then we worked to change our own church institution, and finally started on all of those of American society. Sorry, we still have a long way to go. And this is where you must carry on!"

> —Tomas Firle, member, First Unitarian Universalist
> Church of San Diego, California

"We are still not 'there' yet, but we're a long way from 1990. Departments who were once resisters are now allies. That does impact the denomination."

> —Rev. William Gardiner, former staff member,
> Faith in Action Department

"I have devoted much of my ministerial career to opposing racism and other oppressions and attempting to build a more just and inclusive society. That is why I was in jail in Selma in 1965 only two weeks after I was ordained as a Unitarian Universalist minister. That is why I lived and worked in Mississippi 1969–1984, working as a Unitarian Universalist minister and as an investigator for the Equal Employment Opportunity Commission. But I have had reservations about the content of our 'Journey Toward Wholeness,' reservations that have diminished as the program has become more diverse in its approaches and as we have finally seemed to get more of our facts straight. I want the story to be factually as correct as possible so that we do not impale ourselves on the spikes of the cactus fence."

—Rev. Dr. Gordon D. Gibson, minister emeritus,
Unitarian Universalist Fellowship of Elkhart, Indiana

"Corporate domination, classism, racism and violence are the most pressing problems facing our country, and we cannot become a viable religious movement without engaging these 'evils.'"

—Rev. Clyde Grubbs, minister, Throop Memorial
Church, Pasadena, California

"My commitment to Unitarian Universalism has been my belief that this faith can become a microcosm of the Beloved Community and a model for the country, and that the dream we all talk about and which the Rev. Martin Luther King described can be made real. I'm inspired when I see some of our younger ministers who went through the anti-racism training process. That training shaped and grounded their ministries and enhanced their capacity to reach out to a wider variety of people. My hope is that more and more of our religious leaders will choose to intentionally live from an anti-racist, anti-oppressive, multicultural world view."

—Rev. Melvin Hoover, co-minister, Unitarian Universalist
Congregation of Charleston, West Virginia

"In Fort Worth, Texas, the current GA Planning Committee has supposedly been part of this JTW, Journey Toward Wholeness. They're trying to be inclusive in all this stuff. Now, look at this opening ceremony. There was an acknowledgment of the indigenous ancestors who were there. There was something about white people who came later. There was absolutely no mention, anywhere, that Texas was part of Mexico, that there are probably more people in that city who were Mexican or other Latinos, before then or even now. So—I'm sitting there thinking, 'Where are *we*?' This is Fort Worth, 2005. What have we really done?"

> —Rev. Patricia Jimenez, chaplain, Hennepin County
> Medical Center, Minneapolis, Minnesota

"You have to get over not making mistakes—we don't accept the fact that we can make mistakes. Perhaps it is our individual roots. We are still learning to be in right relation one with one another, so that we can honestly say 'I love you. I made a mistake, let's fix it.' Sometimes we just need to understand that we screwed up and yes, it is hard. For me it is wonderful for all of us to be able to stay at the table of Unitarian Universalism."

> —Rev. Hope Johnson, minister, Unitarian Universalist
> Congregation of Central Nassau, Garden City, New York

"If life were different, I wish we were as strong in our convictions as in our actions. If we had done our business a little differently, this notion of 'do your own work' would have been framed differently. My frame would look more like, 'I will support you in your work but I need to know that I am not doing the work in isolation. I need to know that I'm not doing work *for* you. Given that clarity, I will work *with* you to the best of my ability. The trains are running on different tracks. One is the slow and steady, long-haul work of JTW—Jubilee [training workshops], I would also say JUUST Change, Faith in Action, Identity-Based Ministries— all that long-haul work that is on the institutional level, that is real work. Hard work is happening, and what these incidents, these negative incidents, do, they create the sparks that allow the long-haul work to become time-sensitive. I would almost say it is invisible work. You have folks who believe in the initiatives, folks of all races, and they're plodding along doing their work making these tiny inroads that are really important. It's not about negating the inroads, but every now and then we get an incident to really fuel the work. I believe it is called 'growing pains.'"

—Janice Marie Johnson, past president, DRUUMM
(Diverse and Revolutionary Unitarian Universalist
Multicultural Ministries)

"You see in the larger culture where they will go back and still honor [Dr. Martin Luther] King and so forth—they'll acknowledge the discrimination back then—but they do not see the present with discrimination and the oppression in their present deeds. So they don't see that as oppression, they don't see themselves as culpable or causing the oppression, so they don't make a correction. For instance, most UU ministers need some kind of analysis in, for instance, Fagin's Four Types of Discrimination. They don't, they confuse the direct, institutionalized discrimination and the indirect, institutionalized discrimination, and if you don't have a proper understanding of those kinds of distinctions, you're going to come up with errors in terms of solutions to the problem."

—Rev. Dr. William Jones, professor emeritus,
Florida State University

"I sometimes wonder if Unitarian Universalism is ever going to truly understand the impact of race and racism in our society. We are the people who mean well, who think we know something, who want to do the right thing. And yet, more often than not, we don't. Or, better said, a large majority of people don't. I look at what has happened since Calgary and I wonder, Will we ever live our values? That's not to say I don't see some individuals within our movement who do incredible things. I'm just not sure we are where we say we are, and definitely where I would like us to be. I do see the youth doing many different things to work on anti-racism. There are more allies than there were in 1992 for doing this work. I hear different language from a lot of folks who are ministers, other religious professionals, and lay leaders. This gives me hope. We have a long way to go. What a grand and worthwhile journey it is. Whenever possible listen to the stories of those who have gone before. Learn from them—both what to do and what not to do. The work that UUA has done on this work, is like all of us, in process. Please risk being a part of the process for the rest of your life. Whatever the bumps, the joys, the pains, the conflict, the movement backwards, and forwards, it is a journey worthy of our faith. We must simply continue to work to be a religion where we can say that all the people who believe in our Unitarian Universalist faith can be Unitarian Universalists. Oppression may still get in our way, but it is a worthy effort for our faith."

> —Rev. Keith Kron, director, Office of Bisexual,
> Gay, Lebian and Transgender Concerns,
> Unitarian Universalist Association

"It was an effort that inspired much authentic growth and trans-formation individually and systemically. It initiated some won-derful work by youth, young adults and by the UUA Board of Trustees. But Association-wide, in the end it was undermined by the very forces that it sought to change and ultimately abandoned. My advice to youth would be: 'Pick your battles carefully, fight them fiercely and compassionately, hang together in the groups that truly give you nurture and courage, pay heed to your ancestors and wise elders, stay open and committed and stay strong. The forces of racism are deeply embedded in the human heart and mind, and in all the institutions our society has invented and sus-tains. Anti-racism is a spiritual practice and a life work that will gift you with joy and sorrow, suffering and peace. If you dare to choose it, you will go with the blessings of generations of women and men who wore at their hearts the fire's center.' Cornel West says, 'Optimistic? I've been a black man in the U.S. for 40 years. I have absolutely no optimism that the U.S. will change. But am I hopeful? Yes, I am always hopeful.' This is an activity of the holy."

> —Rev. Kurt Kuhwald, former member,
> Jubilee Working Group

"We need to remember that this is holy work."

—Rev. Kate Lore, Social Justice Minister,
First Unitarian Church, Portland, Oregon

"Look at who is in the UUA and who is not in the UUA and
ask yourself honestly if you really are a part of the UU family?
Do they accept you as you are or do you have to think like them
and be like them in order to be accepted?"

—Rev. Timothy Malone, Unitarian Universalist Campus
and Community Outreach, Davis, California

"I would tell this young person that the work that began in 1992
is important and that he/she must carry the flame when they are
ready. The UUA has only had a Web presence since about 1995/6
and this has made it possible for our religion to 'go global' so to
speak. We can become a world religion up at the top along with
Catholicism and other major Protestant denominations. We must
continue this work to reach out to those millions of would-be
UUs that aren't white and American."

—Kok-Heong McNaughton, founding member,
Asian/Pacific Islander Unitarian Universalist Caucus

"This cultural pattern of turning to the very limited number of
people of color within our movement to solve everything, to do
everything—one effect it has had is while it does grant a certain
level of institutional access, which is good, the demands and
requests are so numerous, so large, and what we are now starting
to understand is that the volume of institutional requests co-opts
the entire agenda and priority-setting of DRUUMM [Diverse
and Revolutionary Unitarian Universalist Multicultural Minis-
tries]. There hasn't been time, in recent years, for anybody in
DRUUMM leadership to focus on the internal community-
building needs, supportive needs, of the DRUUMM membership because so much of our energy and attention and time goes
to responding to the requests and needs of those outside of
DRUUMM. As we have come to be able to name this, the

new DRUUMM leadership, myself included, is very clear that we are going to be saying 'No,' and that we are not going to let the majority culture continue to define the agenda of our people of color organization, of DRUUMM. We're in the process of reclaiming our agendas, so to speak. That, too, is exciting. It's also a question of maturity, in a way, that DRUUMM's own leadership and institutional understanding is maturing to the point where we're able to understand that that is what's been happening. I don't necessarily think that we could have named that five years ago. Things are shifting. Important shifts are occurring at multiple levels. That's very interesting to me. It's making me very hopeful. I certainly was not hopeful in the way that I am now after [the] Fort Worth [General Assembly], but even a year before that, in 2004, if somebody had asked me, 'What do you see as the trajectory of cultural and racial diversity in our denomination,' I would have said, 'I'm not sure the majority of folks in our religion are very serious about this. The rhetoric and the words are right, but I never see anyone acting on those words to make the dream actually come true.' It feels like perhaps that is starting to change, and that feels good; it gives me hopefulness. It's a nice note on which to be beginning my presidency."

> —Rev. Manish Mishra, past president,
> DRUUMM (Diverse and Revolutionary Unitarian
> Universalist Multicultural Ministries)

"Any effort like this is going to have its ups and downs, its fits and starts, but I'm honestly, in my calmest moments, not convinced that we wouldn't have been better off without it. Because it was so polarizing; it was so driven by a narrow ideology that it may well have set the cause back. Happily, it had very little impact on the congregations that I know. I don't know of a Journey Toward Wholeness effort happening in [the] Mountain Desert [District of the UUA]. There may be, but it certainly has no presence at district minister meetings, and no presence at district assembly. *And* some wonderful things are happening in our congregations. Excellent work in public witness, social justice work, working on poverty, supportive of the UU Service Committee's work on human rights—there is a whole litany of wonderful, healthy things that are completely disconnected. So what is healthy—and this needs to be said—what is healthy and thriving, and honest, in congregations I know, has no connection to Journey Toward Wholeness. I don't know if other people share that perspective, but it's mine."

—Rev. Peter Morales, minister, Jefferson Unitarian
Church, Golden, Colorado

"It's almost bittersweet. The thing that I see, and the thing that I think I am beginning to understand, is that perhaps unlike what people thought in the sixties and seventies, addressing the challenges of anti-racism is going to be a multigenerational task. It's going to take a long time. It could take hundreds of years. This is not something that's going to be fixed in a decade. The concern I have as I look back is peoples' staying power with this issue. Because it's not something that you go in, and you get a certificate for doing the program, and everything's okay. Nothing's that simple, not [the UUA's] Welcoming Congregation [to prepare congregations for making gay, lesbian, bisexual, and transgender members comfortable] or anything, but I think a lot of people want to know the work is being done and they don't want to change. It's institutional cultural change—not just the way you look but the way worship is done. Most people don't want to change their worship. They don't want to change the church school. We're not only talking about change, but about change over long, long periods of time. People get frustrated and they get disheartened. While I'm really pleased with the work the Annapolis church was doing, and I'm really pleased at the direction we've been going and the way we're going about it, it's going to take a long, long time. It's just hard to get your head around something taking that long, that it's not going to happen in their lifetime."

—Rev. Dr. Fredric Muir, senior minister, Unitarian
Universalist Church of Annapolis, Maryland

"I think one thing that will be remembered will be the fact that we tried to do something, just the very fact of recognizing that we had, that the UUA as a whole had, a very bad record on race, and that we needed to address that problem and change that culture. I think that's one of the things that will be remembered, and it should be remembered. I think that the other thing that I hope will be remembered is that the students who came out of our seminaries during this period were more sensitive and aware of the need to address racial problems, to address racism. And I would hope that people would look back and be able to say that a systemic change began in 1997."

> —Rev. Dr. William Murry, president and dean emeritus,
> Meadville Lombard Theological School

"After the destruction of the World Trade Towers in NY a white UU asked me how it felt to be a Black male living under high alert. I replied that it felt normal as I have had to be on high alert my entire life. This person thought my remark was funny and I began to understand that all the antiracism workshops and programs we'd done had not made any change in the designed blindness of our church cultures."

> —Bill Norris, once an active Unitarian Universalist
> who became "inactive"

"I would say (and have said) something like this to such a young person: 'I'm glad you're interested in this history. It's a wonderful—though sometimes painful—story about a denomination with deep roots in American history trying to understand and account for its own racism. It's a challenging story about a denomination yearning for transformation, justice, and wholeness. It's a story about people believing they can change. And the best part of the story is that along the way people have changed. Not everyone. Not every congregation. But along the way there have always been moments when transformation happened. These are wonderful moments—moments of justice, moments of wholeness, moments of redemption. If you are going to get involved in this movement, learn to recognize these moments. Learn to celebrate them. Let them inspire you to keep engaging, even though the ultimate goals may seem, at times, farther away than when you first started.'"

—Rev. Josh Pawelek, minister, Unitarian Universalist Society East, Norwich, Connecticut

"Out of my experience, our youth have a totally different perspective and we don't honor their paradigm. We take our paradigm and want them to work on it. Every generation needs to invent its own. I would also like our youth to be scholars of the work that has come before, and not to allow the experts to define their starting point. I would say to them, 'Your world is a real world and you need to start with a critical eye as to what is your work in your lifetime. Figure out where you want to put your efforts, some issues will pass with time."

—Tamara Payne-Alex, member, Board of Trustees, Unitarian Universalist Association, 2000–2009

"It is my hope that a decade from now, a young person will be amazed that we had trouble first convincing people we needed to do the work in the UUA and in our congregations, and then that we encountered so much resistance and made so many mistakes. I will tell this young person that we are continually challenged to have the courage to stand with the people who have been placed in the margins, and bring them into the center. It is the heart and soul of our Living Tradition—all souls are included, universalism—for women, for gays, for children, for differently-abled, for the poor, for people of color, for immigrants, etc. And I will tell the young person to keep his/her eyes and hearts open to discover the next steps that need to be taken, even if seeing them challenges the prevailing sense of satisfaction."

—Rev. Linda Olson Peebles, minister of religious education, Unitarian Universalist Church of Arlington, Virginia

"Maya Angelou said, 'The small gains that we make have helped me to be present—in the world and in this moment.' I respect all of the religions of the world. I believe that they ultimately help people make a better world—by helping oneself, one's family, one's community, and the world become more humane. When asked, 'Why are you a Unitarian Universalist?' I explain. And if the questioner continues to question, I tell them that Unitarian Universalism is the only religion I can stand. That really seems to confuse them. I would like to see it a better place for my grandchildren; I have to work at it now so it might be a little bit better for my grandson, and better for his grandchildren. Everybody has to keep working to make it a better place. It might be just the one thing that you do. But if enough people do one thing, it might not be that much better, but at least you might influence a few people to do better. . . . I know if it's not worked at, people regress. It's sort of like in our political world. All of the stuff we had done to make the races, to make black people have voting rights and all of these things that they didn't have, and you come right along with the right president who will take some of the things from you that you thought you had.
. . . Since it is the only religion I can stand:
To be present is to serve,
To serve is to be an advocate,
In being an advocate of Unitarian Universalism I find an anchor,
A life line that gets me from Sunday to Sunday
And from January to January."

—Dr. Norma Poinsett, member,
      Black Concerns Working Group

"I have been deeply engaged in the work for twenty years. The times when the most significant opportunities have presented themselves have been the times of crisis. I keep wishing there was some other way but I haven't found it. I am not at all convinced that there was a gentle and easy way to do this. This is the time when we have been able to say out loud and do out loud a kind of transformational work we had nearly let go so far underground that we were in danger of being captive to the stories we told ourselves about the past, captive in work around race to Selma and the Black Empowerment history. And now we are not. I'll tell others who come after me that in this time we did it out loud."

—Rev. Tracey Robinson-Harris, director of congregational services, Unitarian Universalist Association

"I would tell him or her that I fought to better inform it, with as much time as I thought I could afford to give a goodhearted, sentimental, ill-informed initiative, and that I will continue to do so when the occasion arises. And I would tell him/her, believe in you. Take responsibility for your actions, and shed any feeling of responsibility for people long dead who may have been related to you. Understand how powerful you are, and recognize the responsibility that goes with that power, but do not overestimate your power, nor accept guilt for that which you have not done, and did not create."

—Dr. Jon Rice, staff, adjunct professor, Meadville Lombard Theological School

"Anti-racism work is spiritual work. Religious people are called to make the world a more just, equitable and compassionate place. We cannot fulfill that promise when the very structure of our organization and decision-making perpetuate injustice, inequity and indifference. Because Unitarian Universalists encourage and embrace diversity in our spiritual paths (or at least we understand this as a virtue to strive toward), we are especially aware of the need to celebrate and strive toward cultural diversity and to uproot racism that divides us."

—Michael Sallwasser, former "Building a Jubilee World" anti-racism trainer, and member, First Unitarian Church of Los Angeles, California

"My hope is that the young person coming to me will be someone who identifies him/herself as a person of color. That would mean some progress was made within our congregations. The UUA states that we value all people and encourages us to work to eliminate all the oppressions. The best way to counteract the '-isms' in our society is through education and interpersonal relationships. Our denomination needs to keep developing and stressing communication tools to bring youth and young families into this work. Let's make multiculturalism the norm instead of the exception. Our church families are increasingly bi-/multi-racial. We need to validate and value these families."

> —Jean Shepard, past convenor, Thomas Jefferson District Antiracism Transformation Team, and member, Thomas Jefferson Memorial Church, Unitarian Universalist, Charlottesville, Virginia.

"My hope is that I would be able to say: 'We tried and continue to try and we are having some success. More of our congregations are transforming themselves into anti-racist institutions and we are learning more about what that means every day. . . . I'm very much impressed with how much we have to do and with the reality that our world is changing so rapidly that if we don't get about it, we'll simply be left behind. Both of those things. And how this will unfold I think is going to be—I gave up my crystal ball some time ago. I think it can go either way, to be honest with you. It's similar to the issue of growth. . . . If we don't find a way to get unstuck, the chances for our becoming more and more irrelevant to the conversation are great. If we are able to get unstuck I think we have some real contributions to make and some real movement is possible.'"

> —Rev. William Sinkford, president, Unitarian Universalist Association

"I would tell them that this faith community realized that if it was to live fully the principles it espouses, it had to confront its own systems of oppression and racism and change from within. The UUA worked hard to confront and address issues so that while there is more to do, the congregations are becoming leaders in their communities in working toward reconciliation and wholeness."

> —Rev. Dr. Richard Speck, district executive, Joseph Priestly District

"We are trying to overcome the inhumanity of humans in which we all share. We are doing this by:

a) listening to and working with all kinds of people,
b) examining ourselves and asking how we can grow, and
c) learning that the dominant white culture within the UU's are not 'running the show' ourselves (the old integrationist model).

Our efforts are rooted in our faith in the creative struggling advance of life, which some of us call God, and to which we are all committed."

> —Rev. Dr. Jerome Stone, adjunct professor of theology,
> Meadville Lombard Theological School

"I would tell them that I, along with a group of very committed and energetic visionary prophetic leaders, really did try to work to disable the racist, oppressive, structures within the UUA. But that it was very hard, challenging, and sometimes painful work, and because of the inability of the institution to sustain the vision, because of the institution's lack of willingness to deeply engage in the spiritual and soul searching that is necessary to bring about the transformation, we were unable to permanently effect that change. I would tell them that I am glad that we are racially, culturally, ethnically, theologically diverse but that the institutional structure has not done the more difficult work of becoming a genuinely anti-oppressive, anti-racist faith community. I would say, 'This is now your task, youth were leaders in this in the past and you can be again.' I would offer to be available as someone to talk to about what did work, and what didn't. I definitely would ask them to let me know how it's going because I want my grandchildren's children to know a Unitarian Universalism, that I had hoped to see in my life, but that seems impossible now."

> —Rev. Susan Suchocki Brown, founding chair,
> Journey Toward Wholeness Transformation
> Committee

"We need to teach our children better. We can't sugarcoat everything."

> —Archene Turner, member, of DRUUMM
> (Diverse and Revolutionary Unitarian Universalist
> Multicultural Ministries)

"Getting to realize the UUA's work on antiracism, anti-oppression and multiculturalism is a long and winding road. It took us 500 years to get in our current predicament and it will take us a few to unravel the mess. Find your UU home in your identity—hopefully there will be a group out there with your identity to support you!!"

> —Kim Varney, founding member, Asian/Pacific Islander
> Caucus of DRUUMM (Diverse and Revolutionary
> Unitarian Universalist Multicultural Ministries)

"My hope for the future is that the adults take this work as seriously and passionately as the youth and young adults. I've met some passionate adults but most of them are not doing the work in the churches. I don't think we have a singular goal—what are we doing this for?"

> —Elandria Williams, youth and young adult anti-racism
> trainer and former member, Tennessee Valley Unitarian
> Universalist Church, Knoxville, Tennessee

A Final Word on the Inevitability of Imperfections

A project of this scope, especially one headed by amateur scholars, is inevitably incomplete and flawed. We hope that you can accept this work in the spirit offered, and in the truth noted by the Special Review Commission:

> Every one of us is human, and humans make mistakes. Every one of us will make more mistakes in the future, and this is exactly what enables change to happen. The gift of mistakes is the opportunity they provide for deep learning, so we need not replay them but can grow beyond what's happening now.

Epilogue

A vision for Unitarian Universalism in a multicultural world:

*With humility and courage born of our history, we are called as
Unitarian Universalists to build the Beloved Community where all
souls are welcome as blessings, and the human family lives whole and
reconciled.*

—UUA Leadership Council, October 1, 2008

Eᴠᴇʀʏ ʙᴏᴏᴋ ᴍᴜsᴛ ʜᴀᴠᴇ ᴀɴ ᴇɴᴅɪɴɢ ᴘᴏɪɴᴛ, yet we have struggled
to put a "period" to a history of work that by its nature is iterative
and ongoing, wishing we could use an ellipsis rather than a full
stop. The decision to end the main narrative in 2006 was practical
and necessary, and yet, by doing so, some of the seeds planted in
this era cannot be seen in full flower in this narrative—in particular, the anti-oppression and multicultural initiatives of the administration of Unitarian Universalist Association president Rev. William
Sinkford.

The purpose of this Epilogue is to capture the flavor of some of
these efforts. Unlike the other sections of this book, we did not seek
multiple viewpoints or seek comments from those who would be
proponents or critics of these efforts. Our purpose here is merely to
present a few highlights of the new approaches and their early
results.

As in other periods, anti-oppression efforts took place in the
context of other key transitions and of initiatives by the Association's Board of Trustees. Tamara Payne-Alex, who served on the
Board from 2000–2009, noted that the Board's move toward a new
governance system called policy governance required it to be clear
about its roles and lines of accountability. "It becomes critical that

there be an articulation of what you want the priorities to be," she said, adding that the Board in her experience developed a less reactive and less contentious presence. A key development, Payne-Alex said, was the Board's learning from multicultural ministry models in other denominations.

After the racially charged events at the 2005 General Assembly in Fort Worth, Texas, efforts to provide systematic ways to prevent and address conflicts between racial and ethnic groups increased. UUA moderator Gini Courter said these included mandatory training for worship leaders and other key presenters as well as addressing issues such as how to be in right relations and how to use the words and music of another culture respectfully. "There's been a lot of effort made," she said. Sinkford agreed, saying, "We've worked hard to make General Assembly serve the interests of the congregations."

As we write this, the Sinkford Administration is in its last months. New leadership and, inevitably, new approaches to addressing the perennial challenges of race relations within and throughout the Association will emerge in subsequent administrations.

And, of course, the story we tell is one that will continue, just as the events between 1992 and 2006 grew out of the times before them. Rev. Anita Farber-Robertson traced the antecedents to the Racial and Cultural Diversity Task Force she chaired in the 1980s. "All the issues of cultural misappropriation are outgrowths of our work," she said.

A key question as we write is how close the Association's anti-racism and anti-oppression efforts have moved it to the critical mass that transformation will require. By 2008, UUA consultant Paula Cole Jones said, about five hundred congregations had participated in a Beyond Categorical Thinking training as part of ministerial transition, in addition to those who had participated in other trainings such as the "Building a Jubilee World" workshops. "If we can get one-third of the congregations to be proactive, we could cause a cultural shift," Cole Jones said. "If we can get one-third of the people in a congregation to act from an understanding of racism in an institution, or one-third of our congregations to be undertaking multi-racial, multicultural ministry, we can cause a cultural change."

JUUST Change

In 2005–2006, the Association's new JUUST Change program began to accept applications from congregations. This is a consultancy program designed to meet congregations where they are in their anti-oppression understandings and tailor resources to strengthen their capacity to apply anti-oppression principles and knowledge. As a 2004 report to the Board of Trustees noted,

> The consultancy—parsed to its simplest—is about connecting and inviting, finding leverage points and choosing tools to apply the right amount of "oomph," supporting long-term transformation.
>
> One lesson—a blinding flash of the obvious—is in the power of an invitation. Can we learn from you? Can we work with you? Will you join with us? Give us a chance to
>
> - hear what the congregation is doing,
> - learn who their resource people and/or lay leaders in this work are,
> - explore congregational history around ARAOMC [anti-racism, anti-oppression, multicultural] work,
> - understand who in the congregation owns the work,
> - recommend resources, UUA and other; identifying opportunities for other programs/resources to be brought to bear,
> - strategize ways to increase participation and/or deepen the work of the congregation.

The report said that "when anti-racism and anti-oppression take the shape of something familiar . . . a book discussion group or planning a worship service become tools with enough 'oomph.'"

In a report to the Association's Board of Trustees in March 2005, Rev. Tracey Robinson-Harris, the UUA's director of congregational services, described the program's potential as helping to "identify internal leaders; facilitate group processes in developing vision and mission, dialogue, problem-solving, team development, developing capacities for building partnership in the larger community, and goal-setting/action planning."

Given the consultative nature of the program, different congregations had different experiences with JUUST Change, which collected these testimonials in 2007.

What changes in direction or in your planning do you see as a result of the consultancy?

"Empowerment to work with ministers and [the church] board more directly. Encouragement to keep going because we are not alone. Ability to bring anti-racism/anti-oppression content to congregation that we did not find a way to do before." —*Barbara Johnson, lay leader, UU Church of Arlington, Virginia*

What were your expectations for this first year?

"I've learned to try to stay open-hearted and open-minded in this work and not have too many expectations. The hope is that people will have life-changing insights, be committed to the work and join with others for cultural and congregational change. I don't have expectations as to the form that will take." —*Arvid Straube, minister, Eno River Unitarian Universalist Fellowship, Durham, North Carolina*

What did you find most useful?

"The consultant took the time to listen carefully and understand the congregation, then suggested positive actions we could take to enhance our anti-oppression work. We adapted two of the ideas almost immediately to create successful programs: a course based on [the book] *Soul Work* and a Sunday service that was very powerful. A group has emerged which is wanting to continue the consciousness raising work." —*Arvid Straube, minister, Eno River Unitarian Universalist Fellowship, Durham, North Carolina*

What changes in direction or in your planning do you see as a result of the consultancy?

"I see the identification of competency in anti-racism and multiculturalism, through the required preparation and through the interview process, coming much more clearly into focus. We are much clearer on what we want to see and hear from [ministerial] candidates in this regard, and are not willing to accept a lack of competency in the fellowshipping process. We see our role as verifying for congregations that the ministers who serve them will be competent to assist them in their own work toward becoming anti-racist, anti-oppressive congregations, in keeping with the stated goal of the UUA." —*Phyllis Daniels, chair, UUA Ministerial Fellowship Committee*

"This consultation helped the UUA Nominating Committee jump-start its conversation on diversity and its meaning in the widest sense of the word. It provided a framework for future discussions as we go about presenting a slate that reflects the diversity that we wish for our Association." —*Young Kim, chair, UUA Nominating Committee*

Embracing a Multicultural Future

In 2007, the Association's Congregational Services staff group hosted the first in a series of annual conferences focused on multicultural congregations. Entitled, "Now Is the Time: Leading Congregations in a Multiracial, Multicultural Future," the first conference, held in Arlington, Virginia, drew 146 participants from 58 congregations. The main presenter at the conferences was Rev. Dr. Jacqueline Lewis, senior minister of vision, worship, and the arts at Middle Collegiate Church in New York City. By focusing on the experience of a congregation outside Unitarian Universalism, the conference established a new way of thinking about how to tap into the growing multiculturalism of communities around the nation, shifting away from the anti-racism or even anti-oppression frame.

A resource for congregational use field-tested in this period was *Building the World We Dream About*, a curriculum designed to enable Unitarian Universalist congregations to become more welcoming of racial, ethnic, and cultural diversity, and to dismantle racism in congregations and the larger community. Using an approach similar to the "Welcoming Congregation" approach for raising awareness around bisexual, lesbian, gay, and transgender issues, the curriculum was designed to:

- Promote multicultural welcome, inclusion, and affirmation in all facets of Unitarian Universalist congregational life
- Cultivate participants' knowledge and skills in addressing issues related to race, ethnicity, and cultural identity both individually and institutionally
- Identify ways congregations can build multiracial/multicultural communities of love and justice.

Through a series of interactive seminars conducted over twelve months, *Building the World We Dream About* participants explore topics that increase their understanding of race and ethnicity, as well as systemic racism, through spiritual reflection, journaling, visual arts, poetry, music, theater tools, simulations, guest speakers, and field trips. The curriculum was designed by Mark Hicks, a member of the All Souls Church Unitarian in Washington, D.C., and a professor at George Mason University who joined the faculty at Meadville Lombard Theological School in 2008. About the curriculum, he wrote,

As is well-documented, building a multi-racial/multi-cultural spiritual community is extraordinarily complicated work, but it can be done. The curriculum gently and intentionally builds a community of learners who carve out time to explore their own racial/ethnic histories, inter/intra group dynamics, the role of power and privilege in congregational life, and most important, how to respond to what is learned through these discussions with an anti-racist/anti-oppression lens.

From September 2007 to December 2008, forty-five congregations were selected to field test *Building the World We Dream About*.

Support for Ministers

Among the focuses for the Sinkford administration was formalizing and expanding the charge of the Association's Diversity of Ministry Team into a "Diversity of Ministry Initiative." The former was a more informal effort to support ministers of color, Hispanic/Latina/o ministers, and individuals from these racial and ethnic groups preparing for the Unitarian Universalist ministry; the expanded focus had a more programmatic thrust, again with an emphasis on multicultural ministry. Goals articulated for 2008 included "a three-part approach consisting of sustaining current ministries; creating healthy new ministries; and investing in a well-funded, multicultural start-up congregation." Some important highlights:

- The creation of twelve new ministries in twelve congregations over the next five years: This process includes extensive preparatory and ongoing educational opportunities for the congregations, lay leaders, and staff; start-up funding support from the UUA; and ongoing support for the ministers.
- Similar educational and support opportunities for congregations and ministers in already existing settlements.
- The development of an in-care system available to all ministers of color and Latina/o, Hispanic, and multiracial clergy who are cleared for settlement.
- A fully funded annual retreat for ministers and ministerial candidates of color and Latina/o, Hispanic, and multiracial identities.
- Institutionalized support for a seminarians group with monthly online and conference call opportunities for community support and conversation, and annual meetings during General Assembly.
- The creation of a well funded multicultural start-up congregation.

New Vision from Congregations

Perhaps most significant was the continued work at the congregational and district level. For example, the First Unitarian Church of Oakland's Journey Towards Wholeness Transformation Team adopted the following mission statement:

> The Journey Towards Wholeness Transformation Team of the First Unitarian Church of Oakland works with the congregation, including the leadership, through organizing and training to help the church become a fully anti-racist/anti-oppressive institution.
>
> - We work to understand how racism and oppression have shaped our lives.
> - We engage in meaningful dialog about the ways we experience internalized racism and oppression.
> - We develop tools to move beyond guilt and blame.
> - We create a process to help those involved in all aspects of church life begin dismantling racism and oppression individually, organizationally, and institutionally.
> - We help the church make connections to other groups in the community making anti-racist/anti-oppressive change.

The First Unitarian Universalist Church of San Diego established its own chapter of the national Diverse and Revolutionary Unitarian Universalist Multicultural Ministries (DRUUMM), which along with its continuing Journey Towards Wholeness team worked within the other ministry teams of the church to hold an anti-oppression agenda.

Also in 2008 the Joseph Priestley District, which extends down the Atlantic coast from Pennsylvania to Northern Virginia, demonstrated a deepening commitment by hiring Rev. Om Prakash John Gilmore to serve as its first director of racial and social justice. In his introductory message to the District, Gilmore wrote,

> It is my hope that we will be working together throughout the Joseph Priestly District to knock down all the lies and stereotypes so that we can see ourselves and our sisters and brothers as authentic beings who are an expression of the

Las voces del camino

Rev. Lilia Cuervo, the first ordained female Latin American minister in the Unitarian Universalist Association, joined the ministry team at the First Unitarian Universalist Church of San Jose in 1999 as "extension minister for outreach to Latinos." In leading worship in the Latino context, one of her biggest challenges was the lack of theologically appropriate liturgical music in Spanish. While other traditions had translated hymns and while hymns popular in Latin America were available, they were not always appropriate to the Unitarian Universalist context. This was a true liability in leading meaningful worship, Cuervo noted. "To begin with, hymnals are indispensable in any church," she said. "Not having theologically correct songs was a dire situation."

Not long into her ministry in San Jose, she translated "Be Ye Lamps Unto Yourself" into Spanish despite limited musical training. Gaylord "Smitty" Smith, a member of the San Jose congregation, mentioned to Cuervo that he was about to retire and looking for new outlets for his energy. He built upon an interest in composing and began taking courses in composing while beginning to translate dozens of hymns from *Singing the Living Tradition*, the Association's hymnal. Soon the partnership expanded, with Ervin Barrios adding translation skills; Gildardo Suárez bringing his talents at classical piano and arranging. Soon the San Jose congregation had compiled their own hymn collection of more than one hundred hymns, many of which they used regularly both in their Spanish language services and the bilingual services begun by senior minister Lindi Ramsden and later continued by Cuervo and senior minister Rev. Nancy Palmer Jones.

Yet they had trouble keeping track of the copies of their hymn resource, for visitors would grow so excited, they would "borrow" them to bring home to their church so the group brought several hundred hymns to the UUA for consideration and began the conversations about producing a Spanish-language hymnal for the Association.

Palmer Jones noted the importance of the project, writing, "There are songs that we use that are Hispanic (to me this means from Spain) or Latino (from Mexico southward) in origin that bring so much to our Unitarian Universalist worship. I'm thinking of our 'anthem': 'Danos un corazón' ('Give us a great heart for loving; give us a strong heart for struggling [for justice]') and of the simple, graceful 'alleluias' of the hymn 'Gracias por el amor' ('Thanks for love') as just two of many outstanding examples."

Despite long delays in publication and other difficulties that spanned nearly a decade, Cuervo has persisted with the project because of the resources it would bring. Looking forward to the anticipated release in the summer of 2009, she said it has been very powerful to be able to bring the Unitarian Universalist hymns so meaningful to her to others. "I want Latinos and not Latinos to hear these songs so dear to my heart," she said.

Divine. It is time for us to reclaim our power to be loving, compassionate individuals, because that is really what we come to congregations for one Sunday after the other. It is our time. Our backs are against the wall. Let's take this journey together and reach our goal: a healthy world for us, our children and our children's children, where we can flow together like a mighty river healing all of those who we touch along our banks; supporting diverse forms of life within ourselves; and returning to the source of life from which we all come. This is the beauty of the Journey Toward Wholeness.

Gilmore's hiring arose through the efforts of the Baltimore/Washington-area congregations to create an anti-oppression "tipping point." The district encouraged its member congregations to be active in a variety of activities—attending the "Now Is the Time" conference, working with Allies for Racial Equity, attending the district anti-racism conference, using JUUST Change consultants, hosting Jubilee World trainings, field-testing the "Building the World We Dream About" curriculum, participating in the Diversity of Ministry Initiative, and offering the "A Dialogue on Race and Ethnicity" program. "We are building a concept of 'Tipping Point Congregations,'" a report from the Congregational Services staff group read, "those that voluntarily engage in developing skills and an institutional culture that supports racial justice and sustainable multicultural inclusion among staffs, congregation members, and community partners."

Imagining the Future

Much of the work of anti-racism, even as the first decade of the new millennium nears its end, remains elusive and focused toward a future yet unrealized. Perhaps the members of Oakland's Journey Toward Wholeness Team captured this best. They ask, "Can you imagine . . .

- Entering the sanctuary on Sunday and seeing your beloved church community as vibrantly multi-racial as all of Oakland?
- A church community in which race is discussed seriously, honestly, openly, easily, and even jokingly?
- Moving beyond guilt and blame, towards a shared understanding of racism as a social malady that damages all of our lives in the service of providing privilege for a white minority?
- Collaboration with other churches in which we make friends, pray together, learn, and work for more justice in Oakland?
- White leaders who can defer their own strongly held opinions and humbly ask leaders of color, "Here's an idea I have, what do you think?"
- A UU theology that articulates and supports us in a journey to spiritual and social wholeness?
- Being intimately involved in the lives of people of all races, not only at church, but in our personal lives and neighborhoods as well?
- A church building with art and decorations that celebrate and reflect many cultures and many people?
- Being able to think clearly about how racism operates in our society, our lives, and even our church—and being able to think about what we want to do together to change that?
- If every group in the church regularly asked, "How does what we are doing serve to perpetuate white privilege, and how can we change that?"
- Being known as the church in the heart of Oakland that welcomes everyone, and that makes a difference in the city?
- Having hope that things can change?"

Notes

Website URLs referenced in these notes were valid at the time they were accessed for this book but may have changed.

Notes on Language and Sources

xxii **to be learners**, This approach informed by the work of Valerie Batts, *Modern Racism: New Melody, Same Old Tune* (Cambridge, MA: Episcopal Divinity School Occasional Papers, 1998).

xxii **terms like multiculturalism**, minutes of DRUUMM religious professionals, May 14, 2001, Unitarian Universalist Association, recorded by Kenneth Hurto.

Introduction

xxv **affirms the self**, Mark Morrison-Reed, *Black Pioneers in a White Denomination* (Boston: Skinner House, 1980), 176–177.

Part 1

1 **and their allies**, William Sinkford, introduction to *Long Challenge: The Empowerment Controversy (1967–1977)*, by Victor Carpenter (Chicago: Meadville Lombard Theological School Press, 2004), vii–viii.

1 **civil rights activities**, Racial and Cultural Diversity Task Force, *The Journey Towards Wholeness, The Next Step: From Racial and Cultural Diversity to Anti-Oppression and Anti-Racist Multiculturalism*. Boston: Unitarian Universalist Association, 1996, 28.

1 **James Reeb is killed**, Victor Carpenter, *Long Challenge*, 38.

1 **for four years**, Black Affairs Council, "1968 Business Resolution," www.uua.org/socialjustice/socialjustice/statements/14445.shtml.

1 **the "Empowerment Controversy"**, Carpenter, *Long Challenge*, 57. The events surrounding the Unitarian Universalist Association, the Black Affairs Council, and the Black and White Alternative are often referred to as the "Black Empow-

erment Controversy." William Sinkford has suggested that these be referred to as the "Empowerment Controver*sies*" since, in his view, the issue went beyond black empowerment and extended to white views of empowerment.

2 **support urban churches**, Unitarian Universalist Association, "History of Urban Ministry," www.uua.org/urbanuu/history.html.

2 **good race relations**, Racial and Cultural Diversity Task Force, *Journey Toward Wholeness, The Next Step*, 29.

2 **in seven cities**, UUA, "History of Urban Ministry."

3 **multicultural/multiracial congregations**, Journey Toward Wholeness Transformation Committee, ed., *The Journey Toward Wholeness Sunday Handbook* (Boston: Unitarian Universalist Association, 2001), 87.

3 **Network of Black Unitarian Universalists forms**, Davies Memorial Unitarian Universalist Church, "U, U, & UU Racial Diversity History Timeline," www.dmuuc.org/about/racial_timeline.html.

3 **Common Ground II**, Special Review Commission, "Final Report of the Special Review Commission," March 2006, Unitarian Universalist Association files, Boston, 11.

3 **Commission on Appraisal is released**, Commission on Appraisal, *Empowerment: One Denomination's Quest for Racial Justice, 1967–1982*, in *Unitarian Universalism and the Quest for Racial Justice* (Boston: Unitarian Universalist Association, 1993), www25.uua.org/coa/Empowerment_1983.pdf.

3 **Commission on Appraisal's report**, Commission on Appraisal, *Empowerment*, 183.

3 **Task Force on Racism**, Special Review Commission, "Final Report," 11.

3 **the larger society**, Susan Suchocki Brown, "The Journey Toward Wholeness Transformation Committee: Vision, Charge, and History," 2003, Unitarian Universalist Association files, Boston, 2.

3 **African Americans can minister**, Charles Gaines, report of Extension Department, n.d., Unitarian Universalist Association files, Boston.

4 **Task Force on Racism's suggestions**, Special Review Commission, "Final Report," 11.

4 **first meeting in Boston**, Horace Seldon, "We Have 'No Problem' . . . Again," in *Anti-Racism Resources*, ed. Black Concerns Working Group (Boston: Unitarian Universalist Association, 1989).

4 **historically marginalized groups**, Racial and Cultural Diversity Task Force, *JTW, The Next Step*, 30.

4 **adopted and approved**, The Continental Unitarian Universalist Young Adult Network, "C*UUYAN Bylaws," www.uua.org/ya-cm/cuuyan/bylaws/CUUYAN%20bylaws%20rev_%202004.pdf.

6 **lurched and sputtered**, Commission on Appraisal, *Empowerment*, 175.

6 **entire human family**, Gordon B. McKeeman, Starr King President's Lecture, Unitarian Universalist Association General Assembly, June 27, 2004.

7 **go as a board to Selma**, Joseph Barndt, interview by Leon Spencer and Leslie Takahashi Morris, July 2006.

7 **a mixed bag**, Jerome Stone, email message to authors, April 2005.

8 **wrong against wrong**, Commission on Appraisal, *Empowerment*, 173.

8 **as "Bloody Sunday"**, Gustav Niebuhr, "A Civil Rights Martyr Remembered," *New York Times*, April 8, 2000, www.uua.org/news/reeb/nyt030800.html.

8 **the moment had come**, Victor Carpenter, telephone interview by Leslie Takahashi Morris, February 2007.

9 **white middle class**, Commission on Appraisal, *Empowerment*, 174.

9 **Yes, we did**, Carpenter, interview.

9 **on anybody's screen**, Ibid.

9 **succinct summary is difficult**, This complicated story, the events leading up to it, and the personal and organizational costs of the conflicts are covered in Carpenter, *Long Challenge*.

10 **and nothing since**, Carpenter, interview.

11 **with everyone else**, Commission on Appraisal, *Empowerment*, 11.

11 **needs for empowerment**, Anita Farber-Robertson and Leon Spencer for Racial and Cultural Diversity Task Force, grant application to Veatch Program of the Unitarian Universalist Church at Shelter Rock, Manhasset, NY, November 23, 1993, Unitarian Universalist Association files, Boston.

11 **its report noted**, Unitarian Universalist Association, "Institutional Racism Audit," April 1981, Unitarian Universalist Association files, Boston, 48.

11 **healing and transformation**, Sinkford, "Introduction," in Carpenter, *Long Challenge*, vii.

12 **of the movement**, Chester McCall, interview by Chip Roush, July 2005.

12 **'blacks and whites' approach**, Robert Nelson West, *Crisis and Change: My Years as President of the Unitarian Universalist Association 1969–1977* (Boston: Skinner House Books, 2007), 44.

12 **Black Affairs Council**, Ibid., 28.

12 **from the UUA**, Ibid., 45.

13 **feel, and be, brave**, Denise Davidoff, remarks in response to Victor Carpenter, Unitarian Universalist Association General Assembly, June 23, 2001.

13 **taking a stand and standing**, Norma Poinsett, commentary in Opening Ceremony and Plenary, Unitarian Universalist Association General Assembly, June 21, 2001, www.uua.org/ga/ga01/1026poinsett.html.

14 **anti-racist, anti-oppression history**, Wayne Arnason, telephone interview by Leslie Takahashi Morris, February 2007.

14 **Journey Toward Wholeness**, Betty Bobo Seiden, email message to authors, April 2005.

16 **can be congruent**, Melvin Hoover, "The African American Experience and Unitarian Universalism," *The World*, 1993.

17 **leave your culture at home**, Melvin Hoover, telephone interview by Leslie Takahashi Morris, September 2005.

18 **as 'verbal dentistry'**, UUA, "Institutional Racism Audit," 31.

18 **the mid-1980s**, UUA, "History of Urban Ministry."

18 **and Washington, D.C.**, Unitarian Universalist Association, "Summary of 'Results' of Urban Ministry in the UUA from 1972–1998," archive.uua.org/urbanuu/umresults.html.

19 **racial justice concerns**, Hoover, interview, September 2005.

19 **on the table**, Leon Spencer, telephone interview by Leslie Takahashi Morris, February 2007.

19 **multicultural/multiracial congregations**, JTWTC, *JTW Sunday Handbook*, 87.

19 **projects and partnerships**, Unitarian Universalist Association, "Many Paths, One Journey," www.uua.org/programs/justice/antiracism/jtwsunday/wyinfo.html.

19 **from the grass roots**, William Gardiner, telephone interview by Chip Roush, August 2005.

19 **was increasing**, Farber-Robertson and Spencer, Veatch grant application.

19 **Institutional Racism Audit**, Racial and Cultural Diversity Task Force, *Journey Toward Wholeness, The Next Step*, 29.

19 **basis of race**, UUA, "Institutional Racism Audit," 1.

20 **not for me**, Horace Seldon, quoted in *Unitarian Universalist World*, "UUA team seeks way to racial balance," November 15, 1980, 6.

21 **of its being**, UUA, "Institutional Racism Audit," 52–53.

21 **similarly equitable society**, Racial and Cultural Diversity Task Force, *Journey Toward Wholeness, The Next Step*, 44.

21 **try to implement**, Seldon, "We Have 'No Problem' . . . Again."

21 **lower the standards**, Joseph Santos-Lyons, "25 to 1: People of Color Experiences in Unitarian Universalism 1980–2005" (unpublished thesis, Harvard University), 2006, www.radicalhapa.typepad.com/my_weblog/2006/05/25_to_1_people_.html.

21 **audit's thirty-two recommendations**, Seldon, "We Have 'No Problem' . . . Again."

22 **was subsequently established**, Farber-Robertson and Spencer, Veatch grant application.

22 **note in 1993**, Ibid.

22 **at UUA headquarters**, Ibid.

22 **on the subject**, Commission on Appraisal, *Empowerment*, 157.

23 **it still hurts**, Robert Hohler, "A class-bound church," in "Religious Liberals Share Views on Black Empowerment: Review of controversy evokes powerful emotions," *Unitarian Universalist World*, March 15, 1984, 4.

23 **in Columbus, Ohio**, Suchocki Brown, "The Journey Toward Wholeness Transformation Committee," 2.

23 **frustration and failure**, Mark Morrison-Reed, "The Cultures of Religion," in "Now I Begin to Understand . . . ," *The World*, March/April 2000, 41.

25 **on the committee**, Spencer, interview, February 2007.

25 **UUA Board in 1983**, Special Review Commission, "Final Report," 11.

25 **for the UUA**, Commission on Appraisal, *Empowerment*, 183.

25 **1985 General Assembly**, Seldon, "We Have 'No Problem' . . . Again."

25 **sought new perspectives**, Ibid.

25 **denominations and organizations**, Farber-Robertson and Spencer, Veatch grant application.

26 **that was unreal**, Spencer, interview, February 2007.

27 **to go forward**, Hoover, interview, September 2005.

27 **set aside $5,000**, Ibid.

27 **hopes and wishes," Hoover said**, Ibid.

27 **need for education**, Spencer, interview, February 2007.

27 **vision for GAs," Hoover said**, Melvin Hoover, email message to Leslie Takahashi Morris, September 2006.

27 **of this resolution**, Jubilee Working Group for Anti-Racism, ed., *Creating a Jubilee World*, Second Edition (Boston: Unitarian Universalist Association, 1999), 87.

28 **All were enriched**, Ibid., 10.

29 **had some impact**, Spencer, interview, February 2007.

29 **a full position**, William Schulz, telephone interview by Leslie Takahashi Morris, December 2007.

29 **inclusion and justice**, Hoover, interview, September 2005.

30 **publications, and communications**, minutes of the Black Concerns Working Group, March 13–15, 1987, Unitarian Universalist Association files, Boston.

30 **Here we go again!** Ibid.

30 **throughout the continent**, Norma Poinsett, interview by authors, November 2005.

30 **urban church coalition**, minutes of the Black Concerns Working Group, November 6–8, 1987.

30 **in UU congregations**, Black Concerns Working Group, undated memorandum, Unitarian Universalist Association files, Boston.

31 **sister, Wendy LeWin**, "Sanctuary and Government Surveillance" (resolution passed by Unitarian Universalist Association General Assembly), 1985, www.uua.org/socialjustice/socialjustice/statements/19779.shtml

31 **remembering their names more important**, minutes of the Black Concerns Working Group, 1994–1997.

32 **Rev. Marjorie Bowens-Wheatley**, Marjorie Bowens-Wheatley and Nancy Palmer Jones, eds., *Soul Work: Anti-Racist Theologies in Dialogue* (Boston: Skinner House, 2002), 234.

32 **(DRUUMM), in 1998**, Joseph Santos-Lyons, "25 to 1: People of Color Experiences in Unitarian Universalism 1980–2005," unpublished thesis, Harvard University, 2006, www.radicalhapa.typepad.com/my_weblog/2006/05/25_to_1_people_.html.

32 **to the Association**, Arnason, interview.

32 **at this time, Sinkford said**, William Sinkford, telephone interview by Leslie Takahashi Morris, February 2007.

32 **one's own community**, Kenneth Torquil MacLean, "Translating the Spirit of Selma," *The Register-Leader of the Unitarian Universalist Association*, November 1965, 11.

33 **in the 1960s**, Laurel Hallman, telephone interview by Leslie Takahashi Morris, February 2007.

33 **in the 1940s**, First Unitarian Church of Chicago, "Our Commitments," www.firstuchicago.org/commit.html.

33 **Commission on Appraisal's *Empowerment* report**, Fredric Muir, telephone interview by Leslie Takahashi Morris, February 2007.

34   **as a congregation**, Lee Barker, telephone interview by Leslie Takahashi Morris, January 2007.

34   **African American congregations in town**, Ibid.

35   **what prompted it**, Arnason, interview.

35   **in general society**, "'Minority'—simply a half tone?" *Ethics & Action: Supplement for the UU World*, December 15, 1980.

35   **for Racial Justice"**, Ibid.

35   **understanding of it**, William Jones, telephone interview by Chip Roush and Leon Spencer, December 2005.

36   **to be together**, "In Miami: Bridges are built," *Unitarian Universalist World*, November 15, 1981, 1.

36   **greeters, and singers**, "In LA: A racial-growth unit," *Unitarian Universalist World*, November 15, 1981, 1.

36   **Department of Ministry in 1988**, Racial and Cultural Diversity Task Force, *Journey Toward Wholeness, The Next Step*, 30.

36   **that did not**, Unitarian Universalist Association Identity-Based Ministries staff group (report to the Unitarian Universalist Association Board of Trustees), December 19, 2005, Unitarian Universalist Association files, Boston, 2.

37   **might be lost**, Spencer, interview, February 2007.

38   **by existing societies**, Eugene Pickett, quoted in Lucy Hitchcock and Melvin Hoover, "Report of the Consultation on Unitarian Universalist Racial/Ethnic New Congregations with Recommendations for Future Action," September 13, 1991, Unitarian Universalist Association, Boston.

39   **in their lives**, Unitarian Universalist Association Extension Department, "Organizing Diversity Focused New Congregations in the Unitarian Universalist Association" (report to the Unitarian Universalist Association Board of Trustees), January 1995, Unitarian Universalist Association files, Boston.

39   **still be there**, Archene Turner and Kate Lore, telephone interview by Leslie Takahashi Morris, March 2005.

39   **historically marginalized economically**, Michelle Bentley, interview by Leslie Takahashi Morris, January 2006.

40   **are African American**, Unitarian Universalist Association Extension Department, planning documents, January 1995, Unitarian Universalist Association files, Boston.

40   **then do something**, Charles Johnson, quoted in Marjorie Bowens-Wheatley, "Five Congregations Started by African American Unitarian Universalist Ministers" (draft), ca. 1994.

42   **for future generations**, Unitarian Universalist Association Extension Department, "Department Evaluation of Racial/Ethnic Diversity Programs in the Department of Extension," January 5, 1994, Unitarian Universalist Association files, Boston.

41   **from other congregations?** Ibid.

41   **in other congregations**, Hoover, interview, September 2005.

41   **more traditional programs**, UUA Extension Department, "Department Evaluation."

42   **many big challenges**, Ibid.

43   **without ministerial leadership**, minutes of the Task Force on Affirmative Action for African American Ministers, October 26, 1989, Unitarian Universalist Association files, Boston.

43   **Afrocentric UU congregations**, Ibid.

44   **then held responsible**, Robert Eller-Isaacs, telephone interview by Leslie Takahashi Morris, January 2006.

46   **who we were religiously**, Sinkford, interview, February 2007.

46   **entire human family**, McKeeman, Starr King lecture.

47   **must do it**, Poinsett, interview.

47   **people of color**, Eller-Isaacs, interview, January 2006.

47   **not being told**, Ibid.

48   **from the Black Affairs Council**, Arnason, interview.

48   **incidental to it**, Henry Nelson Wieman, *Source of Human Good* (Carbondale, IL: Southern Illinois University Press, 1964), 46.

48   **not been worked out**, Carpenter, interview.

49   **how you got there**, Sinkford, interview, February 2007.

50   **become our todays**, Loretta F. Williams, "Affirmation of Hope," in *Been in the Storm So Long*, edited by Mark Morrison-Reed and Jacqui James (Boston, MA: Skinner House Books, 1991), 19.

Part 2

51   **power to control**, William Jones, in "Racial Justice for Times Like These," video (Boston: Unitarian Universalist Ministers Association, 1993).

51   **under-represented in Unitarian Universalism**, The Journey Toward Wholeness Transformation Committee, ed., *The Journey Toward Wholeness Sunday Handbook* (Boston: Unitarian Universalist Association, 2001), 3.

51   **Afro-Americans' Experience in Unitarian Universalism**, Mark Morrison-Reed, *How Open the Door?: Afro-Americans' Experience in Unitarian Universalism* (Boston: Unitarian Universalist Association, 1989).

51   **UU Ministers Association Professional Days**, Special Review Commission, "Final Report of the Special Review Commission," March 2006, Unitarian Universalist Association files, Boston, 12.

51   **to achieve diversity within ten years**, Ibid.

52   **Native American issues**, Michael Bettencourt, "On the Cutting Edge: Meadville/Lombard and Religious Education," in *The World*, March/April 1992, 25.

52   **in Unitarian Universalism**, JTWTC, "Next Steps on the Journey—Supporting Congregations in Anti-racism and Justice Making Work" (report to the Unitarian Universalist Association Board of Trustees), April 2003, Unitarian Universalist Association files, Boston, ii.

52   **for achieving diversity**, Ibid., 1.

52   **in Newton, Massachusetts**, Ibid., 48.

52   **For Such A Time As This**, Ibid., 46–47.

52   **1994, 1995, and 1996**, Susan Suchocki Brown, "The Journey Toward Wholeness Transformation Committee: Vision, Charge, and History," 2003, Unitarian Universalist Association files, Boston, 2.

52   **Charlotte, North Carolina**, Special Review Commission, "Final Report," 12.

52   **the Southwest Conference**, Davies Memorial Unitarian Universalist Church, "U, U, & UU Racial Diversity History Timeline," www.dmuuc.org/about/racial_timeline.html.

52   **the congregational level**, "Briefly Noted," *Interconnections* vol. 6, no. 4, Unitarian Universalist Association, Boston, http://archive.uua.org/interconnections/briefly/vol6-4-briefly.html.

52   **Religious Education Department**, Special Review Commission, "Final Report, 12.

53   **in Spokane, Washington**, Unitarian Universalist Association Young Adult and Campus Ministry Office website, www.uua.org/ya-cm/youngadults/ar_ao/ar_index.html.

53   **curriculum for adults**, Jacqui James and Judith A. Frediani, *Weaving the Fabric of Diversity: An Anti-Bias Program for Adults* (Boston: Unitarian Universalist Association, 2006).

53   **Anti-Oppression and Anti-Racist Multiculturalism**, Racial and Cultural Diversity Task Force, *Journey Toward Wholeness, The Next Step: From Racial and Cultural Diversity to Anti-Oppression and Anti-Racist Multiculturalism* (Boston: Unitarian Universalist Association, 1996).

53   **blacks and whites**, Special Review Commission, "Final Report," 13.

53   **to racial justice**, Christine Murphy, *A Road Map to the Journey Toward Wholeness* (Boston: Unitarian Universalist Association, ca. June 1997–September 1998), 4.

53   **people of color**, Starr King School for the Ministry, "Educating to Counter Oppression Self-Assessment Report" (draft), August 2006, Berkeley, CA.

53   **added in 2000**, Unitarian Universalist Association Ministry Department, Ministry Packet, September 2001, www.uua.org/programs/ministry/publications/fall2001.pdf.

55   **of the consultations**, Lucy Hitchcock and Melvin Hoover, "Report of the Consultation on Unitarian Universalist Racial/Ethnic New Congregations with Recommendations for Future Action," September 13, 1991, Unitarian Universalist Association files, Boston.

56   **to head it**, JTWTC, *JTW Sunday Handbook*, 3.

56   **was a priority**, William Schulz, telephone interview by Leslie Takahashi Morris, December 2007.

56   **director of international congregations**, Unitarian Universalist Association, "Summary of 'Results' of Urban Ministry in the UUA from 1972–1998," archive.uua.org/urbanuu/umresults.html.

56   **Board of Trustees had adopted in 1980**, minutes of the Task Force on Affirmative Action for African American Ministers, October 26, 1989, Unitarian Universalist Association files, Boston.

56   **Afro-Americans' Experience in Unitarian Universalism**, Morrison-Reed, *How Open the Door?*

57   **"we have no problem" . . . again!**, Horace Seldon, "We Have 'No Problem' . . . Again," in *Anti-Racism Resources*, ed. Black Concerns Working Group (Boston: Unitarian Universalist Association, 1989).

57   **presented to the Board of Trustees**, Special Review Commission, "Final Report," 12.

57   **not just individuals**, Melvin Hoover, telephone interview by Leslie Takahashi Morris, September 2005.

57   **racial diversity concerns**, Ibid.

57   **and cultural diversity**, Schulz, interview.

57   **was very supportive**, Ibid.

58   **the next incident**, Seldon, "We Have 'No Problem' . . . Again."

59   **had taken place**, Marjorie Bowens-Wheatley, Abhi Janamanchi, and Clyde Grubbs, interview by Leslie Takahashi Morris, February 2006.

59   **confluence of rivers**, Joseph Barndt, interview by Leon Spencer and Leslie Takahashi Morris, July 2006.

59   **emerging organization, Barndt said**, Ibid.

60   **teach them about racism**, Marjorie Bowens-Wheatley, "10 Reasons Why Racism Is Still With Us," *Minister's Corner*, April 21, 1996, Community Church of New York.

61   **what we were doing**, Ibid.

61   **the Jubilee trainings**, minutes of Black Concerns Working Group, January 10–12, 1992, Unitarian Universalist Association files, Boston.

62   **was not available**, Norma Poinsett, telephone interview by Leslie Takahashi Morris, October 2008.

62   **kind of ignored them**, Rosemary Bray McNatt, telephone interview by Leslie Takahashi Morris, February 2007.

62 **black and white**, minutes of Black Concerns Working Group, April 10, 1992.

63 **and resisted changes**, Anita Farber-Robertson, "Toward a Theology of Anti-Racism," in *Journey Toward Wholeness, The Next Step*, ed. Racial and Cultural Diversity Task Force, 39–40.

63 **the urban agenda**, The Benevolent Fraternity of Unitarian Churches was established in 1826 by Unitarian minister Joseph Tuckerman to work with poor people in Boston and to educate the more affluent about poverty, mental illness and injustice. See: Neil Chethik, "Outside Church Walls," *The World*, September/October 1994, 18.

64 **achieve that justice**, William Schulz, quoted in Deborah J. Weiner, "Unanimous Vote for Diversity," *The World*, September/October 1992, 59.

66 **and early 1980s**, Mark Morrison-Reed, email to Leslie Takahashi Morris in consultation with Kay Montgomery, April 2009.

67 **Susan Leslie, Lola Peters**, Unitarian Universalist Association Task Force on Racial and Cultural Diversity, "Memorandum to Congregations, Associate Organizations, District Presidents and Executives," November 22, 1993, Unitarian Universalist Association files, Boston.

67 **new anti-racist antidote**, Anita Farber-Robertson and Leon Spencer for Racial and Cultural Diversity Task Force, grant application to Veatch Program of the Unitarian Universalist Church at Shelter Rock, Manhasset, NY, November 23, 1993, Unitarian Universalist Association files, Boston.

67 **gay and lesbian issues**, Unitarian Universalist Association, "History, Welcoming Congregations Program," www.uua.org/leaders/leaderslibrary/welcomingcongregation/index.shtml.

67 **the General Assembly**, Susan Suchocki Brown, interview by Leslie Takahashi Morris, December 2007.

68 **not a curse**, Susan Suchocki Brown, "Unity and Diversity" (sermon delivered at First Church Unitarian Universalist in Leominster, MA), October 24, 1993.

69 **could be introduced**, Denise Davidoff, interview by Leslie Takahashi Morris, December 2007.

69 **race or both," Schulz recalled**, Schulz, interview.

69 **in her report as well**, Davidoff, interview.

69 **focused on politicking**, John Buehrens, interview by Chip Roush, December 2007.

69 *Racial and Cultural Diversity in Unitarian Universalism,* **which read**, Racial and Cultural Diversity Task Force, *Journey Toward Wholeness, The Next Step*. ii.

71 **address the delegates**, Davidoff, interview.

71 **Let's not blow it!**, Victor Carpenter, interview by Leslie Takahashi Morris, February 2007.

71 **had co-sponsored it**, Weiner, "Unanimous Vote."

71 **other than white men**, Poinsett, interview.

72 **my spirits were buoyed**, William Sinkford, telephone interview by Leslie Takahashi Morris, February 2007.

72 **realizing its vision**, Racial and Cultural Diversity Task Force, *Journey Toward Wholeness, The Next Step*, 1.

72 **part of my campaign**, Phyllis Daniel, telephone interview by Leslie Takahashi Morris, December 2005.

72 **in front of us**, Tracey Robinson-Harris, telephone interview by Leslie Takahashi Morris, July 2005.

73 **to be ready**, Fredric Muir, telephone interview by Leslie Takahashi Morris, February 2007.

73 **a differing opinion**, Latina/o and Hispanic Ministers Caucus, interview by Chip Roush, November 2005.

74 **to be doing**, Rebecca Parker, interview by Leslie Takahashi Morris and Chip Roush, May 2006.

74 **committed the Board**, Gini Courter, telephone interview by Leslie Takahashi Morris, August 2006.

75 **resolution in Calgary becomes important**, Wayne Arnason, telephone interview by Leslie Takahashi Morris, February 2007.

75 **a broken world**, Linda Olson Peebles, email message to authors, August 2005.

76 **blacks and whites**, Latina/o and Hispanic Ministers Caucus, interview.

76 **people of color**, Anita Farber-Robertson, telephone interview by Leslie Takahashi Morris, September 2008.

77 **within our congregations**, Leon Spencer, telephone interview by Leslie Takahashi Morris, March 2007.

77 **to doing so**, Denise Davidoff, remarks in response to Victor Carpenter, Unitarian Universalist Association General Assembly, June 23, 2001.

77 **such an initiative**, Farber-Robertson and Spencer, Veatch grant application.

77 **institutionally and structurally**, Spencer, interview, March 2007.

78 **every combination possible**, Racial and Cultural Diversity Initiative, "Exploratory Research Results" (draft), June 26, 1993, Unitarian Universalist Association files, Boston.

78 **to the next**, Spencer, interview, March 2007.

79 **all the time**, Racial Diversity Initiative, "Exploratory Research Results."

79 **their own communities**, Ibid.

80 **their own traditions**, Ibid.

82   **each General Assembly**, Commission on Appraisal, *Empowerment: One Denomination's Quest for Racial Justice, 1967–1982*, in *Unitarian Universalism and the Quest for Racial Justice* (Boston: Unitarian Universalist Association, 1993), www25.uua.org/coa/Empowerment_1983.pdf, 153–159.

84   **lack of financial resources**, minutes of Black Concerns Working Group, January 10–12, 1992.

85   **the report noted**, Hitchcock and Hoover, "Report."

85   **New Congregation Training**, Unitarian Universalist Association Extension Department, Department Evaluation of Racial/Ethnic Diversity Programs, January 5, 1994, Unitarian Universalist Association files, Boston.

85   **their professional ministers**, minutes of Black Concerns Working Group, January 1–12, 1992.

86   **more deeply, more authentically**, Ross, "Becoming Multicultural."

87   **a charter member**, Marjorie Bowens-Wheatley, "The Only Way to Go," *The World*, March/April 1993, 28.

88   **the Salvadoran movement**, Ibid.

88   **doing things**, Hitchcock and Hoover, "Report."

89   **ahead of her time**, McNatt, interview.

89   **not my intention," said Seon**, "Yvonne Seon Biography," *The History Makers*, www.thehistorymakers.com/biography/biography.asp?bioindex=611&category=educationMakers.

89   **process of politicization**, Yvonne Seon, quoted in Marjorie Bowens-Wheatley, "Five Congregations Started by African American Unitarian Universalist Ministers" (draft), ca. 1994.

90   **known and left**, Bowens-Wheatley, "Five Congregations."

90   **path to faith**, Ibid.

91   **of sexual orientation**, Ibid.

92   **for congregational growth**, Ibid.

92   **from the onset**, Ibid.

93   **has been formed**, William McCall, Bylaws of All Souls Church, Unitarian Universalist, Durham, NC, ca. 1998.

95   **San Francisco, California**, Raquel Sneed et al., "Open Letter to Unitarian Universalist Leaders," n.d., Unitarian Universalist Association files, Boston.

95   **positive and necessary step**, Bowens-Wheatley, "Five Congregations."

96   **we would like**, William Sinkford, quoted in David Whitford, "A Step Towards Racial Reconciliation," *UU World*, May/June 2002, 27.

96   **almost all of them," he recalled**, Sinkford, interview, February 2007.

96   **imitate the evangelicals**, Buehrens, interview.

96   **similar outreach," he said**, John Buehrens, email message to authors, October 2008.

97   **to feel uncomfortable**, Bill Norris, correspondence to authors, June 2005.

97   **was never published**, minutes of Black Concerns Working Group, April 2–4, 1993.

97   **on liberal religion**, Mark Morrison-Reed, quoted in "Among Ourselves: Congress Report," *The World*, March/April 1993, 37.

97   **Light and dark**, Jacqui James, "Dark and Light, Light and Dark," in Mark Morrison-Reed and Jacqui James, eds., *Been in the Storm So Long* (Boston: Skinner House Books, 1991), 8. A conversation about the use of dark-light imagery was part of the discussion of using culturally diverse worship resources.

98   **a particular race**, Jacqui James, in Robette Dias and Marjorie Bowens-Wheatley, *The Language of Race*, edited by Jacqui James (unpublished curriculum created for the Unitarian Universalist Association), 1998.

99   **every inch of progress**, Warren R. Ross, "Becoming Multicultural: How One Church Points the Way," *The World*, March/April 1993, 31.

99   **one-time event**, Sinkford, interview, February 2007.

100   **resurrecting Harper's work**, David Reich, "Inspirations: Harper Resurrected," *The World*, March/April 1993, 38.

101   **for the congregation**, David Reich, "From an Island to a Continent: A Spanish-Language Ministry," *The World*, July/August 1995, 33.

102   **never really left UUism**, Layla Rivera, "Shades of UU," *Ferment*, May 1999, Unitarian Universalist Association Young Adult and Campus Ministry Office, Boston.

104   **of anti-racism processes**, Arnason, interview.

105   **to Unitarian Universalism**, Farber-Robertson and Spencer, grant application.

105   **to be "whole"**, Jones, "Racial Justice."

107   **towards health, towards wholeness**, Mark Morrison-Reed, Introduction, in "Racial Justice."

107   **power to control**, Jones, "Racial Justice."

107   **are sent in**, Farber-Robertson and Spencer, Veatch grant application.

107   **racial justice efforts**, Ibid.

108   **be of service**, Cornel West, quoted in Alex Poinsett, "Cornel West: Extending the Public Conversation," *The World*, September/October 1993, 14.

108   **come in period costume**, Keith Kron, email message to authors, April 2005.

108   **of Unitarian Universalism?" Jones asks**, "General Assembly News," *The World*, September/October 1993, 42.

109   **honor Jefferson in period costume**, Hope Johnson, interview by Leslie Takahashi Morris, February 2007.

109 **in advance of GA**, Joseph Santos-Lyons, "25 to 1: People of Color Experiences in Unitarian Universalism 1980–2005," unpublished thesis, Harvard University, 2006, www.radicalhapa.typepad.com/my_weblog/2006/05/25_to_1_people_.html.

110 **view of history**, Hope Johnson, quoted in Unitarian Universalist Association, "The District Name—The History," www.tjd.uua.org.

110 **not to attend it**, Roger W. Comstock, "Report on Anti-Racism Activities to the UUA Board, March 10, 1998–Feb 4, 1999," Unitarian Universalist Association, Boston, 1.

111 **of her victories**, Buehrens, interview.

111 **of the ball**, Davidoff, interview.

112 **a long time**, Kron, email message.

113 **this kind of event**, Arnason, interview.

113 **brought to awareness**, Robinson-Harris, interview.

113 **to see it**, Kron, email message.

114 **people are poor**, Melvin Hoover, memorandum to Unitarian Universalist Association staff, March 24, 1993, Unitarian Universalist Association files, Boston.

114 **conversion of souls**, Poinsett, interview.

114 **professor at Emory University, and others**, Farber-Robertson and Spencer, Veatch grant application.

115 **market research organization, Trost Associates**, Davidoff, response at GA.

115 **long uphill road**, Davidoff, interview.

116 **in March 1996**, Olivia Holmes, "Racial and Cultural Diversity," 60.

117 **not very committed (41%)**, Anita Farber-Robertson and Leon Spencer, in Racial and Cultural Diversity Task Force, *Journey Toward Wholeness, The Next Step*, 58.

117 **choice of words**, Olivia Holmes, "Racial and Cultural Diversity: Where Unitarian Universalists Stand," in Racial and Cultural Diversity Task Force, *Journey Toward Wholeness, The Next Step*, 59.

118 **than factual accuracy**, Gordon D. Gibson, email message to authors, September 2005.

118 **the Anti-Racism Assessment**, Unitarian Universalist Association, "Toward an Anti-Racist Unitarian Universalist Association; 1997 Business Resolution," www.uua.org/socialjustice/socialjustice/statements/14244.shtml.

119 **my colleagues, of course**, Sinkford, interview, February 2007.

119 **to move forward**, Arnason, interview.

121 **the youth movement**, Arnason, interview.

121 **to go forward**, Davidoff, interview.

122 **gift of power, indeed**, Kurt A. Kuhwald, "Understanding Racism," in Jubilee Working Group for Anti-Racism, *Creating a Jubilee World*, Second Edition (Boston: Unitarian Universalist Association, 1999), 13.

123 **to be heard**, minutes from conference call between Barbara Bedingfield, Anita Farber-Robertson, Leon Spencer, and Susan Leslie, September 20, 1993, Unitarian Universalist Association files, Boston.

123 **nearly one hundred people**, Melvin Hoover and Susan Leslie, "Office for Racial and Cultural Diversity, 1993–1995 Evaluation and 1995–1996 Goals," March 1995, Unitarian Universalist Association files, Boston.

123 **in a Boston suburb**, Melvin Hoover, letter to anti-racism training participants for the Unitarian Universalist Association Task Force on Racial and Cultural Diversity, August 31, 1994, Unitarian Universalist Association files, Boston.

123 **essential for transformation**, Melvin Hoover, memorandum to Unitarian Universalist Association staff, March 24, 1995, Unitarian Universalist Association files, Boston.

124 **the congregational level**, Robinson-Harris, interview.

125 **was a beginning**, William Sinkford, email message to authors, May 2005.

126 **workshop date requested**, Jubilee Working Group for Anti-Racism, "Creating a Jubilee World" (undated flyer), Unitarian Universalist Association files, Boston.

127 **break my heart, too**, Daniel, interview.

127 **options for congregations**, Melvin Hoover, memorandum to Anti-racism Collective, October 25, 1994, Unitarian Universalist Association files, Boston.

127 **dead ends," he observed**, William Jones, telephone interview by Chip Roush and Leon Spencer, December 2005.

128 **programs and processes**, Hoover, memorandum to UUA Staff.

128 **honor this request**, Melvin Hoover, report to Unitarian Universalist Association Board of Trustees, March 1995, Unitarian Universalist Association files, Boston.

128 **in our congregations**, Robinson-Harris, interview.

129 **use of UUA funds**, Melvin Hoover, "UUA Efforts for Racial and Cultural Diversity," January 1993, Unitarian Universalist Association files, Boston.

129 **and local communities**, Melvin Hoover, report to UUA Board of Trustees, January 1993, Unitarian Universalist Association files, Boston.

129 **to follow suit**, Susan Leslie, memorandum to Lola Peters, December 20, 1993, Unitarian Universalist Association files, Boston.

130 **District Racial Justice Task Force**, Farber-Robertson and Spencer, Veatch grant application.

131 **committees and functions**, Jubilee Working Group, *Creating a Jubilee World*. Margaret Link is a member of the Unitarian Universalist Fellowship of Raleigh, North Carolina, and was a member of the Unitarian Universalist Association Black Concerns Working Group.

132 **to do what**, Hoover, interview, September 2005.

132 **Task Force warned**, Farber-Robertson and Spencer, Veatch grant application.

132 **ministers of color**, Melvin Hoover and Susan Leslie, annual plans for the Office of Racial and Cultural Diversity, October 1, 1995, Unitarian Universalist Association files, Boston.

132 **Unitarian Universalist groups**, Notes from Black Concerns Working Group workshop, 1993, Unitarian Universalist Association files, Boston.

133 **1995 General Assembly**, Laurel Hallman, telephone interview by Leslie Takahashi Morris, February 2007.

133 **provided institutional support**, Young Adult and Campus Ministry Office website.

134 **in Unitarian Universalism today**, Santos-Lyons, "25 to 1."

135 **have this training**, minutes of Black Concerns Working Group, October 27–28, 1995.

135 **deep into my soul**, Jean Shepard, email message to authors, June 2006.

136 **continue this path together**, Sherry Weston, quoted in minutes of Black Concerns Working Group, April 12–14, 1996.

136 **Working Group participation**, staff notes, 1996, Unitarian Universalist Association files, Boston.

136 **the congregational level**, Murphy, *Road Map*.

137 **anti-racism self-appraisal**, Ibid., 37.

137 **been very flexible**, Bowens-Wheatley, Janamanchi, and Grubbs, interview.

138 **build a bridge**, Lee Barker, telephone interview by Leslie Takahashi Morris, January 2007.

139 **the faculty handbook**, Educating to Counter Oppression Committee, "Report."

139 **being "counter-oppressive"**, Parker, interview.

139 **being one-way**, minutes of Black Concerns Working Group, January 13–16, 1994.

140 **the school's actions**, Educating to Counter Oppression Committee, "Report."

140 **for social transformation**, Unitarian Universalist Association Department for Diversity and Justice, "Faith in Action" (undated flyer), Unitarian Universalist Association files, Boston.

141 **twice a year**, minutes of Black Concerns Working Group, April 12–14, 1996.

141 **all other oppressions**, minutes of Black Concerns Working Group, October 3, 1996.

141 **the minutes noted**, Ibid.

141 **make a difference**, Shepard, email message.

141 **into the conversation**, Clyde Grubbs, email message to authors, August 2005.

141 **low-income and immigrant neighbors**, First Unitarian Church of San José, "A History of the First Unitarian Church of San José," www.sanjoseuu.org/FUCSJ_about.html.

143 **encouraged to attend**, Faith in Action Department of the Unitarian Universalist Association, "Getting Started: A Congregational Action Plan" (draft), 1995, Unitarian Universalist Association files, Boston.

144 **community of color**, Notes, Anti-Racism Organizer's Training, Chicago, IL, September 5–8, 1996, Unitarian Universalist Association files, Boston.

144 **much better received, frankly**, Bowens-Wheatley, Janamanchi, and Grubbs, interview.

145 **race and anti-racism**, Schulz, interview.

146 **risk their jobs**, Anita Farber-Robertson, interview.

146 in the 1960s, Bowens-Wheatley, Janamanchi, and Grubbs, interview.

147 **undermined our work**, Grubbs, email message to Leslie Takahashi Morris, October 2008.

147 **into our shell**, Jerome Stone, email message to authors, April 2005.

148 **what would the Unitarian Universalist answer be**, Barndt, interview.

148 **in her honor**, Farber-Robertson, interview.

149 **racial or cultural conflict**, Holmes, "Racial and Cultural Diversity," 59.

149 **name ourselves Unitarian Universalist**, Hitchcock and Hoover, "Report."

150 **the land my people we seek**, Melvin Hoover, worship document, 1996, Unitarian Universalist Association files, Boston.

Part 3

151 **heart of goodness**, Michelle Bentley, "I Am Somebody," in Jubilee Working Group for Anti-Racism, ed., *Creating a Jubilee World*, Second Edition (Boston: Unitarian Universalist Association, 1999), 53.

151 **Massachusetts Bay District**, Massachusetts Bay District of Unitarian Universalist Association, "The Interchurch

Newsletter for the Mass Bay District," October 1997, www.mbd.uua.org/link/oct97link.html.

151 **Thomas Jefferson District**, Thomas Jefferson District of Unitarian Universalist Association, "T.J. District Retains Name for Now; New anti-racism task force mandated," www.tjd.uua.org/names.html.

151 **coordinate anti-oppression efforts**, Journey Toward Wholeness Transformation Committee, ed., *The Journey Toward Wholeness Sunday Handbook* (Boston: Unitarian Universalist Association, 2001), 3.

151 **anti-racist transformation team in October**, Liberal Religious Educators Association, "LREDA Anti-Racism Initiative Time Line," www.uua.org/lreda/content/timeline.html.

151 **convenes itself, in June**, Unitarian Universalist Association Young Adult and Campus Ministry Office website, www.uua.org/ya-cm/youngadults/ar_ao/ar_index.html.

151 **to become anti-racist**, Robette Dias, "Invisible Americans: Racism and the UUA," in *JTW Sunday Handbook*, ed. JTWTC, 34.

151 **program for anti-racism**, "Toward an Anti-Racist Unitarian Universalist Association" (resolution passed at Unitarian Universalist Association General Assembly), 1997, http://www.uua.org/socialjustice/socialjustice/statements/14244.shtml.

151 **holds its first meeting in October**, minutes of Journey Toward Wholeness Transformation Committee, October 19–21, 1997, Unitarian Universalist Association files, Boston.

151 **its expanded focus**, JTWTC, *JTW Sunday Handbook*, F25

151 **Unitarian Universalist Religious Professionals of Color**, Joseph Santos-Lyons, "25 to 1: People of Color Experiences in Unitarian Universalism 1980–2005," unpublished thesis, Harvard University, 2006, www.radicalhapa.typepad.com/my_weblog/2006/05/25_to_1_people_.html.

152 **Starr King School for the Ministry co-sponsors**, "Now I Begin to Understand: Personal Race Reflections," www.uuworld.org/2000/0300feat2.html.

152 **"Theology, Faith and Action," in January**, minutes of JTWTC, October 19–21, 1997.

152 **(Diverse and Revolutionary Unitarian Universalist Multicultural Ministries)**, Joseph Santos-Lyons, "25 to 1." .

152 **and Northwest Districts**, Young Adult and Campus Ministry Office website.

152 **The Baltimore Papers**, Santos-Lyons, "25 to 1."

152 **Journey Toward Wholeness Sunday in December**, Donald E. Skinner, "Program Helps Churches Raise Anti-Racism Funds," *InterConnections*, January 1999, Unitarian Universalist Association, Boston, 7.

153 **assessment and planning meeting**, Journey Toward Wholeness Transformation Committee, "Continuing the Journey: Report and Recommendations to the 2001 General Assembly," June 2001, Unitarian Universalist Association files, Boston, 4.

153 **to Kansas City**, Ibid.

153 **and other participants walk out**, Special Review Commission, "Final Report of the Special Review Commission," March 2006, Unitarian Universalist Association files, Boston, 14.

153 **support this work**, minutes of Unitarian Universalist Association Board of Trustees, October 1999, www.uua.org/TRUS/minutes10-99.html.

153 **Crossroads/Journey Toward Wholeness approach**, Thandeka, "Why Anti-Racism Will Fail" (speech delivered to Unitarian Universalist Association General Assembly), 1999, www.uua.org/ga/ga99/238thandeka.html.

153 **of racial issues**, Special Review Commission, "Final Report," 14.

153 **its Executive Board**, Deborah Weiner, "Ministers Discuss Issues of Racism and Oppression in pre-GA Session," www.uua.org/ga/ga01/0001.html.

154 **its conference, OPUS, in July**, Young Adult and Campus Ministry Office website.

154 **into its membership**, Special Review Commission, "Final Report," 14.

154 **take anti-racism training**, minutes, UUA Board of Trustees, October 1999.

154 **undertakes anti-racism training**, LREDA, "Time Line."

154 **anti-racism trainings in November**, Young Adult and Campus Ministry Office website.

155 **in the journey**, Laurel Hallman, telephone interview by Leslie Takahashi Morris, February 2007.

157 **those who tried**, Keith Kron, email message to authors, April 2005.

157 **be grappling with**, Phyllis Daniel, telephone interview by Leslie Takahashi Morris, December 2005.

157 **That didn't happen**, Melvin Hoover, telephone interview by Leslie Takahashi Morris, September 2005.

158 **Congregational, District and Extension Services**, John Buehrens, email message to authors, October 2008.

158 **"knocking down" the structure**, Hoover, interview, September 2005.

158 **multicultural religious organization**, minutes of Anti-Racism Core Team and JTWTC joint meeting, October 21, 1997, Unitarian Universalist Association files, Boston.

158 **ad hoc group**, Kathleen Montgomery, interview by Leslie Takahashi Morris, December 2007.

158 **Cheng-Imm Tan**, minutes of Anti-Racism Core Team and JTWTC, October 21, 1997.

159 **formal and expanded entity**, Melvin Hoover and Robette Dias, interview by Leon Spencer and Leslie Takahashi Morris, September 2006.

159 **they owned anti-racism**, John Buehrens, interview by Chip Roush, December 2007.

159 **resources, funding, people, etc.**, minutes of Anti-Racism Core Team and JTWTC, October 21, 1997.

160 **incredibly staff-driven**, Robette Dias, interview by Leslie Takahashi Morris, September 2006.

160 **1997 or 1998**, Bowens-Wheatley, Abhi Janamanchi, and Clyde Grubbs, interview by Leslie Takahashi Morris, February 2006.

161 **at General Assembly**, Hoover and Dias, interview.

161 **and biracial children**, Ibid.

161 **10 percent multiracial**, minutes of JTWTC, May 14, 1998.

161 **keeping the faith**, Marjorie Bowens-Wheatley, "Nurturing Our Faith: Not By Ourselves Alone" (lecture delivered at Unitarian Universalist Church of Birmingham, AL), March 8, 2002, www.uuma.org/Documents/Convocation/Not%20By%20Ourselves%20Alone%20MBW.html.

162 **relationships with women**, Thomas Jefferson District, "The District Name."

162 **and Leon Spencer**, Leon Spencer, telephone interview by Leslie Takahashi Morris, March 2007.

163 **the larger community**, Thomas Jefferson District, "T.J. District Retains Name."

163 **and institutional oppression**, Leon Spencer, "What's In A Name?" www.tjd.uua.org/conn/summer2003/p2.html.

163 **place for reconciliation?" he asked**, Spencer, interview, March 2007.

163 **as "brilliantly aggressive"**, Denise Davidoff, interview by Leslie Takahashi Morris, December 2007.

164 **the Association staff**, Buehrens, interview.

164 **a new resolution**, Susan Suchocki Brown, interview by Leslie Takahashi Morris, December 2007.

164 **General Assembly agenda**, minutes of UUA Board of Trustees, April 19–20, 1997, Unitarian Universalist Association files, Boston.

166 **was distributed**, Anita Farber-Robertson and Leon Spencer, in Racial and Cultural Diversity Task Force, *Journey Toward Wholeness, The Next Step.*

167 **with the community**, Fredric Muir, telephone interview by Leslie Takahashi Morris, February 2007.

167 **had seventy congregants**, Laurel Hallman, interview.

167 **General Assembly resolution**, Ibid.

167 **of their congregation**, Tomas Firle, email message to authors, September 2005.

168 **in the world**, Fulfilling the Promise Committee, "Fulfilling the Promise Final Report," Unitarian Universalist Association General Assembly, 2001, archive.uua.org/ga/ga01/4015.html.

168 **and the world**, Clark Olsen, "Fulfilling the Promise: A Response to the Survey Results," www.uua.org/archive/promise/olsen.html.

168 **its June 24 meeting**, minutes of UUA Board of Trustees, June 24, 1997, Unitarian Universalist Association files, Boston.

168 **on our principles**, Clark Olsen, "Fulfilling the Promise."

169 **Multicultural faith community**, minutes of JTWTC, October 19–21, 1997.

169 **to move forward**, minutes of Black Concerns Working Group, April 9–13, 1997, Unitarian Universalist Association files, Boston.

170 **the term "oversight"**, minutes of JTWTC, October 19–21, 1997.

170 **of the resolution**, Ibid.

170 **not the same**, Ibid.

170 **to reduce racism**, Journey Toward Wholeness Committee, report to Unitarian Universalist Association General Assembly, June 1996, Unitarian Universalist Association files, Boston.

171 **Charlotte and Phoenix**, minutes of JTWTC, May 14, 1998.

171 **the UUA didn't**, Susan Suchocki Brown, email message to authors, May 2005.

171 **one racial category**, Robert Bellah, lecture delivered at Unitarian Universalist Association General Assembly, 1998, www.robertbellah.com/lectures_7.htm - 53k.

172 **meeting of GA**, Joseph Santos-Lyons, "25 to 1."

172 **the Confederate flag**, Elandria Williams, interview by Leslie Takahashi Morris, June 2006.

174 **we are power**, "A Conversation on Race and Class," *World*, July/August 1998, 18.

175 **of African descent**, Paula Cole Jones, interview by authors, May 2005.

175 **think and do**, Melvin Hoover, telephone interview by Leslie Takahashi Morris, September 2006.

175 **to the good**, William Jones, telephone interview by Chip Roush and Leon Spencer, December 2005.

176 **more appropriate venue**, Ibid.

177 **a major problem**, Ibid.

178 **minimizing side comments**, minutes of UUA Board of Trustees, October 1999, www.uua.org/TRUS/oct99ungar. html.

178 **of the JTWTC**, minutes of JTWTC, October 17–19, 1999.

178 **REs [religious educators]**, Ibid.

178 **areas of oppression**, Suchocki Brown, email message.

179 **than 50 years**, Susanne Skubik Intriligator, "Valora Washington and the UUSC: A Lifetime of Service." *The World*, January/February 2000, p. 37.

180 **reach more congregations**, Hoover and Dias, interview.

181 **all of these situations**, Danielle DiBona, email message to authors, August 2006.

181 **to other stakeholders**, Anita Farber-Robertson, telephone interview by Leslie Takahashi Morris, September 2008.

182 **that racism oppresses**, Crossroads Ministry, *Crossroads Ministry Principles of Organizing to Dismantle Institutional Racism* (handout), 1996, Crossroads Ministry, Chicago.

183 **the overall initiative**, Robette Dias, email message to Leslie Takahashi Morris, October 2008.

184 **an "old head!"** Elandria Williams, email message to Leslie Takahashi Morris, October 2008.

184 **people feeling good**, William Sinkford, telephone interview by Leslie Takahashi Morris, February 2007.

185 **in order to survive**, Jon Rice, email message to authors, April 2005.

185 **Latina/o Unitarian Universalist Networking Association**, Grubbs, email message to Leslie Takahashi Morris, October 2008.

185 **over the decade**, Jubilee Working Group for Anti-Racism, *Creating A Jubilee World*.

186 **make a change**, Ibid.

186 **those seeking training**, minutes of Black Concerns Working Group, October 10–12, 1997.

186 **for the committee**, minutes of Black Concerns Working Group, October 3–6, 1997.

186 **group was defunct**, Ibid.

186 **UU theological language**, minutes of JTWTC, 19–21 October 1997

186 **Susan Leslie, Christine Murphy**, minutes of Jubilee Working Group, 1997–1998, Unitarian Universalist Association files, Boston.

187 **the Jubilee trainings**, minutes of Black Concerns Working Group, April 9–13, 1997.

187 **any particular leader**, minutes of Jubilee Working Group for Anti-Racism, April 16–18, 1998, Unitarian Universalist Association files, Boston.

187 **new Jubilee trainers**, minutes of Jubilee Working Group, October 8–11, 1998.

187 **in leadership positions**, Ibid.

188 **no place to go," he said**, Leon Spencer, telephone interview by Leslie Takahashi Morris, February 2007.

188 **at the time**, Dias, interview.

188 **feeds my soul**, William Gardiner, interview by Chip Roush, August 2005.

189 **with a district**, Joseph Barndt, interview by Leon Spencer and Leslie Takahashi Morris, July 2006.

189 **systemic dynamics around race**, Hoover, interview, September 2005.

189 **in Baltimore, MD**, minutes of Jubilee Working Group for Anti-Racism, 1998, Unitarian Universalist Association files, Boston.

190 **some of them**, Michael J. S. Carter, email message to authors, April 2005.

190 **such an influence**, Barndt, interview.

190 **some of them aren't**, Gardiner, interview, April 2005.

190 **at each other**, Kurt Kuhwald, interview by Chip Roush, August 2005.

190 **and white complicity**, Kurt Kuhwald, email message to authors, October 2008.

191 **have an agenda**, Keith Kron, email message.

191 **clean it up . . .** , Bowens-Wheatley, Janamanchi, and Grubbs, interview.

191 **often created divisions**, Grubbs, email message to authors, August 2005.

191 **helped UUs become clear**, Clyde Grubbs, email message, October 2008.

192 **black and white**, Gini Courter, telephone interview by Leslie Takahashi Morris, August 2006.

192 **Unitarian Universalist Ministers Association**, Wayne Arnason, telephone interview by Leslie Takahashi Morris, February 2007.

193 **evaluating its work**, minutes of JTWTC, May 14, 1998.

193 **beginning to happen**, minutes of JTWTC, January 29–February 1, 1998.

194 **as well as Association funds**, Bowens-Wheatley, Janamanchi, and Grubbs, interview.

194 **model for youth**, minutes of Jubilee Working Group, April 1998.

194 **the "Jubilee" workshops**, minutes of Jubilee Working Group, October 1998.

194 **to do that**, Hoover, interview, September 2005.

195 **understand evil**, Barndt, interview.

195   **ought to have**, Bowens-Wheatley, Janamanchi, and Grubbs, interview.

196   **been like in Tucson**, leaders of Latina/o Unitarian Universalist Networking Association, group interview by Chip Roush, November 2005.

196   **these new folks**, Courter, interview.

197   **They are OUR heritage**, Rice, email message.

197   **to affirm that**, Bowens-Wheatley, Janamanchi, and Grubbs, interview.

198   **Journey Toward Wholeness**, Unitarian Universalist Association Faith in Action Department, "Journey Toward Wholeness: Path to Anti-racism," n.d., 3.

199   **seemed particularly difficult to Courter**, Courter, interview.

199   **the merit of it**, Jones, interview.

200   **of San Diego, California**, minutes of Black Concerns Working Group, June 19, 1997.

200   **bring their ideas to the table**, minutes of JTWTC, October 17–19, 1998.

200   **in Manhasset, New York**, Ibid.

201   **40 largest congregations**, minutes of Jubilee Working Group, October 8–11, 1998.

202   **tap into it**, minutes of JTWTC, April 24–27, 1999.

203   **pay for it**, minutes of JTWTC, January 29–February 1, 1998.

203   **speak on it at GA**, Ibid.

204   **not an ending**, Robette Dias and Marjorie Bowens-Wheatley, *The Language of Race*, edited by Jacqui James (unpublished curriculum created for the Unitarian Universalist Association), 1998.

204   **was several things**, Bowens-Wheatley, Janamanchi, and Grubbs, interview.

205   **the finished product**, Santos-Lyons, "25 to 1."

205   **once more toward oblivion**, Institutional Racism Audit, in Victor Carpenter, *Long Challenge: The Empowerment Controversy (1967–1977)* (Chicago: Meadville Lombard Theological School Press, 2004), 37.

206   **with interpersonal issues**, minutes, JTWTC, April 24–27, 1999.

206   **trust and power . . .** , Ibid.

206   **lateral and hierarchical relationships," they concluded**, Dias and Bowens-Wheatley, *Language of Race*.

206   **they want to**, Paula Cole Jones, interview, May 2005.

206   **the JTW Committee**, Buehrens, interview.

207   **a new culture**, Dias and Bowens-Wheatley, *Language of Race*.

208   **about that?' she said**, Hallman, interview.

209   **already have been**, Connie and Guy Loftman, in Susan Leslie, "Anti-Oppression/Anti-Racism Multicultural Mini Case Studies of UU Congregations," 2004, Unitarian Universalist Association files, Boston.

211   **of all concerned**, Grubbs, email message, October 2008.

213   **sacred, powerful beings**, Robette Dias, "Theology, Class and Race: Conference Dialogue" (speech delivered at Urban Church Conference in Chicago), March 2001.

214   **a hole in the ground. Nothing**, leaders of Latina/o Unitarian Universalist Networking Association, group interview by Chip Roush, November 2005.

215   **at each other**, Peter Morales, telephone interview by Leslie Takahashi Morris, February 2007.

215   **open to everyone**, minutes of JTWTC, January 29–February 1, 1999.

216   **the wider society**, Latino/a Unitarian Universalist Networking Association, ed., *Baltimore Papers* (Boston: La Lucha Press, 1998).

218   **Julio Noboa, Publications**, LUUNA Executive Committee, "Bringing Gifts," LUUNA files, 1999.

219   **racist multiculturalism, Latino/identity**, minutes of JTWTC, April 24–27, 1999.

219   **empowerment of white people**, Barndt, interview.

220   **of congregational life**, Commission on Appraisal, *Belonging: The Meaning of Membership*, 82–84, www.uua.org/coa/belonging/06.pdf.

221   **their own experiences**, José Ballester, email message to authors, May 2005.

221   **shape the work**, minutes of JTWTC, January 29–February 1, 1999.

221   **conversation around race**, Joseph Santos-Lyons, "Radical-Hapa is Joseph Santos-Lyons," www.radicalhapa.typepad.com.

222   **a threat to justice, everywhere**, Jose Ballester, speech at Theology, Class and Race dialogue at Urban Church Conference, March, 2001, Chicago.

223   **professionals of color**, Deborah Weiner, "UU Religious Professionals of Color form organization," www.lists.uua.org/pipermail/uua-l/Week-of-Mon-19980504/000297.html.

223   **seven years later**, William McCall, interview by Chip Roush, July 2005.

223   **who support me**, Ibid.

223   **aspect of the anti-racism work for him**, Timothy Malone, email message to authors, April 2005.

224 **upset me as much**, Santos-Lyons, "25 to 1," quoted in Leon Spencer, handout for identity workshops and trainings for identity trainers, 1990s.

225 **because of disappointments**, Paula Cole Jones, interview. May 2005.

225 **rather than supported**, minutes of JTWTC, October 13–15, 2000.

226 **to all participants**, JTWTC, "Continuing the Journey," 3–4.

226 **Faith in Action Department**, Gardiner, interview, April 2005.

227 **and economic oppression**, Taquiena Boston, email message to authors, May 2005.

227 **individuals and groups**, Journey Toward Wholeness Transformation Committee, Continuing the Conversation (report), 1991.

227 **a tense situation**, José Ballester, telephone interview by Leslie Takahashi Morris, August 2006.

228 **a bully pulpit**, Dias, interview.

229 **learned very little**, Ballester, email message.

229 **we did not**, Patricia Jimenez, interview by Chip Roush, November 2005.

230 **were being targeted**, Ballester, interview.

231 **that pain exist**, Manish Mishra, interview by Leslie Takahashi Morris, July 2006.

231 **little was resolved**, minutes of Journey Toward Wholeness Transformation Committee, June 25, 1999, Unitarian Universalist Association files, Boston.

232 **they do not**, minutes of JTWTC, June 25, 1999.

232 **by the UUA**, minutes of JTWTC, October 17–19, 1999.

232 **at Youth Council**, minutes of JTWTC, January 29–February 1, 1999.

232 **in that work**, William Gardiner, interview by Chip Roush, April 2005.

233 **mandatory and daily Anti-Racism workshops**, Santos-Lyons, "25 to 1."

234 **how to respond**, Ruth J. Alatorre, "Urban issues & Latinos," in *Baltimore Papers*.

235 **the larger culture**, Spencer, handout.

236 **social action corner of the church**, Robert Eller-Isaacs, telephone interview by Leslie Takahashi Morris, January 2006.

237 **protecting church polity**, DiBona, email message.

237 **disdain for the Association**, Eller-Isaacs, interview.

237 **had not understood before**, Gary Smith, telephone interview by Leslie Takahashi Morris, January 2007.

237 **'get it' again**, Ibid.

238 **the anti-racism work**, Ibid.

238 **served as facilitators**, Unitarian Universalist Association, "Theology, Faith and Action" (press release), 1998, Unitarian Universalist Association files, Boston.

238 **an institutional alternative**, William McCall, Preliminary Fellowship Renewal Request, October 12, 1999, Unitarian Universalist Association files, Boston.

239 **become an issue**, Rebecca Parker, interview by Leslie Takahashi Morris and Chip Roush, May 2006.

239 **a college education**, John Buehrens, email message.

240 **were not written**, Buehrens, interview.

240 **stopped giving money**, Rosemary Bray McNatt, telephone interview by Leslie Takahashi Morris, February 2007.

240 **in anti-racism workshops**, minutes of Jubilee Working Group, 1998.

241 **about our movement**, Morales, interview.

242 **then it passed**, minutes of Unitarian Universalist Ministers Association, January 1999, Unitarian Universalist Ministers Association files, Boston.

242 **kind of goofy**, Morales, interview.

243 **race and class and gender**, McNatt, interview.

245 **it just is**, Fredric Muir, "White and Anti-Racist" (sermon delivered at First Unitarian Church of Annapolis, MD), February 27, 2000.

246 **continental leadership groups**, Sinkford, email message, May 2005.

247 **have been right**, Hoover, interview, September 2005.

247 **concerns about anti-racism**, Eller-Isaacs, interview.

255 **must be stopped**, Thandeka, "Why Anti-Racism Will Fail," *Journal of Liberal Religion*, Vol. 1, No. 1, October 1999, www.meadville.edu/journal/1999_thandeka_1_1.pdf.

255 **to anti-racism analysis**, Barndt, interview.

264 **Susan Leslie, staff**, JTWTC, "Response to Rev. Thandeka's 'Why Anti-Racism Will Fail,' Workshop," www.uua.org/WRLD/jtwtcresponse.html.

266 **important, but different issue**, James T. Brown, "Antiracism Reconsidered," www.swuuc.org/resources/sermons/antiracism.html.

267 **weren't prepared enough**, Hoover, interview, September 2005.

267 **doing this work**, Muir, interview.

268 **look at ourselves**, Ibid.

269 **this is just crazy**, Morales, interview.

270 **for what ends?**, Melvin Hoover, in "A Conversation on Race and Class," *The World*, July/August 1998, 18.

270 **struggles and disagreements may emerge**, Susan Suchocki Brown, "Transcending Boundaries" (sermon delivered at

First Church Unitarian Universalist in Leominster, MA), February 6, 1994.

271 **their only interest**, McNatt, interview.

271 **the hardest time**, Norma Poinsett, telephone interview by Leslie Takahashi Morris, October 2008.

272 **in political terms . . .**, McNatt, interview.

273 **on UU values**, Tomas Firle, email message to authors, September 2005.

273 **funding from that group became available**, Dias, interview.

273 **Manhasset, New York**, Buehrens, interview.

273 **Plandome, New York**, Buehrens, email message.

273 **the lightning rod**, Davidoff, interview.

274 **weight in gold**, Buehrens, interview,

274 **got done very little**, Hallman, interview.

274 **the world with a kiss**, James Luther Adams, "Hidden Evils and Hidden Resources," *The Prophethood of All Believers* (Boston: Beacon Press, 1986), 83.

Part 4

275 **Journey Toward Wholeness Transformation Committee**, Journey Toward Wholeness Transformation Committee, *Continuing the Journey: Report and Recommendations to the 2001 General Assembly from the Journey Toward Wholeness Transformation Committee* (Boston: Unitarian Universalist Association, 2001), 10.

275 **of the UUA**, Continental Unitarian Universalist Young Adult Network, "Endorsement of Linked Identities Networking in Coalition (LINC): C*UUYAN Business Resolution 2000-C," www.uua.org/ga/ga01/uuagafri2087.html.

275 **C*UUYAN-sponsored conferences**, Unitarian Universalist Association Young Adult and Campus Ministry Office website, www.uua.org/ya-cm/youngadults/ar_ao/ar_index.html.

275 **anti-racism trainer Taquiena Boston**, Liberal Religious Educators Association, "LREDA AntiRacism Initiative Time Line, October 21, 1996," www.uua.org/lreda/content/timeline.html.

275 **One America in the 21st Century**, "Unitarian Universalist Leaders Meet with Clinton on Anniversary of Fatal Attack on UU Minister," www.uua.org/news/reeb/index.html.

275 **Diverse and Revolutionary Unitarian Universalist Multicultural Ministries**, Unitarian Universalist Association Department of Ministry Packet, Fall 2001, www.uua.org/programs/ministry/publications/fall2001.pdf.

275 **UUA anti-racism training**, Young Adult and Campus Ministry Office website.

276 **white identity groups**, Ibid.

276 **UUA anti-racism consultants**, Ibid.

276 **remain in DRUUMM**, Special Review Commission, "Final Report of the Special Review Commission," March 2006, Unitarian Universalist Association files, Boston, 15.

276 **conversation about race and ministry**, Karen Matteson et al., "Conversation About White Anti-Racism: UUA Ministry Days 2000," www.uua.org/ga/ga00/ministrydays/white-antiracists2.html.

276 **Unitarian Universalist Service Committee**, Deborah Weiner, "Ministers Discuss Issues of Anti-Racism and Oppression in pre-GA Session," www.uua.org/ga/ga01/0001.html.

276 **first conference, in Atlanta**, Diverse and Revolutionary Unitarian Universalist Multicultural Ministries website, www.druumm.org/youthcom.html.

276 **for Unitarian Universalists**, JTWTC, "Continuing the Journey," 10.

276 **anti-oppressive, multicultural stance**, LREDA, "Time Line."

276 **General Assembly in Cleveland**, Young Kim, "How We Began," www.apiuu.org/began.htm.

277 **150 religious participants**, Unitarian Universalist Association, press release, 2000, Unitarian Universalist Association files, Boston.

277 **is cutting edge**, minutes of Journey Toward Wholeness Transformation Committee, April 28–30, 2000, Unitarian Universalist Association files, Boston.

277 **its mascot, "Chief Wahoo"**, Danielle DiBona, Robert Martin, and John Millspaugh, "2001 General Assembly Vigil: Protesting the Misappropriation of Native American Terms and Images by the Cleveland Baseball Team," www.uua.org/ga/ga01/vigil.html.

277 **Cleveland General Assembly**, Deborah Weiner, "UUA 2001 Installation of New Officers: William Sinkford Installed as Seventh UUA President in General Assembly Closing Ceremonies: Diane Olson Becomes Moderator," www.uua.org/ga/ga01/installation.html.

277 **appoints a Steering Committee**, Special Review Commission, "Final Report," 15; minutes of the Unitarian Universalist Ministers Association Executive Committee, October 14–17, 2001, www.uuma.org/Exec/Documents/minutes/ECMin2001.10.htm.

277 **Diverse and Revolutionary UU Multicultural Ministries**, Weiner, "Ministers Discuss Issues."

277 **anti-racism, anti-oppression, and multiculturalism**, Ibid.

277 **and Joshua Pawelek**, Continental Unitarian Universalist Young Adult Network website, www.uuyan.org/.

277 **business meeting in August**, Ibid.

277 **for anti-oppression work**, Ibid.

277 **Racism, Racial Discrimination, Xenophobia and Related Intolerance**, Unitarian Universalist Service Committee website, www.uusc.org/news/VWter092801.html.

278 **get us there**, Melvin Hoover, telephone interview by Leslie Takahashi Morris, September 2005.

279 **all our ministers**, Norma Poinsett, telephone interview by Leslie Takahashi Morris, October 2008.

279 **General Assembly in Nashville**, Matteson et al., "Conversation about White Anti-Racism."

280 **and the same**, Linda Olson Peebles, email message to authors, August 2005.

280 **Rev. Gary Smith, UUMA President**, minutes of JTWTC, October 13–15.

280 **General Assembly in Cleveland**, minutes of UUMA Executive Committee, October 21–23, 2000.

281 **issues of oppression**, José Ballester, "Chronology of Events," undated memorandum, Unitarian Universalist Association files, Boston.

281 **to their congregations**, minutes of UUMA Executive Committee, January 23–25, 2000, Unitarian Universalist Association files, Boston.

282 **UUMA and UUA**, Ibid.

282 **accountable organization**, Danielle DiBona, interview by Leslie Takahashi Morris, March 2008.

282 **fill this position in 2001**, minutes of UUMA Executive Committee, January 23–25, 2000.

282 **hold the portfolio**, José Ballester, telephone interview by Leslie Takahashi Morris, August 2006; minutes of UUMA Executive Committee, January 23–25, 2000; Ballester, "Chronology of Events."

283 **person-of-color/Latina/o/Hispanic seat**, DiBona, interview, March 2008.

283 **the CENTER committee**, Weiner, "Ministers Discuss Issues."

283 **whole committee carry anti-racism**, minutes of JTWTC, October 13–15, 2000, Unitarian Universalist Association files, Boston.

283 **trust and process," Ballester said**, Ballester, interview.

284 **a living reality**, Jose Ballester, Patricia Jimenez, and Peter Morales, "A Latino View of the Journey Toward Wholeness" (undated memorandum), Unitarian Universalist Association files, Boston.

285 **came to be considered**, DiBona, interview, March 2008; Weiner, "Ministers Discuss Issues."

285 **such as Ministry Days**, John Gilmore and Patricia Jimenez, "Memo and 2002 Report to Unitarian Universalist Ministers Association Membership," June 2002, Unitarian Universalist Ministers Association files, Boston.

285 **their white colleagues**, DiBona, interview, 2007.

285 **in the congregations**, Ibid.

286 **able to present . . .**, minutes of JTWTC, April 28–30, 2000.

287 **call attention to resistance**, minutes of JTWTC, February 5–8, 2000.

288 **working at the UUA**, minutes of JTWTC, February 1–4, 2001.

288 **only use Crossroads**, Ibid.

288 **ongoing past start-up**, Ibid.

288 **racial and cultural groups**, John Buehrens, interview by Chip Roush, December 2007.

288 **seminarians and ministers of color**, John Buehrens, email message to authors, October 2008.

289 **work we do**, minutes of UUMA Executive Committee, October 21–23, 2000.

289 **toward education**, minutes of UUMA Executive Committee, January 21–23, 2001.

291 **Oscar Romero Congregation**, This congregation no longer exists.

291 **May we stand together**, Patricia Jimenez, "Facing the Challenge, Dreaming the Possible," in Latino/a Unitarian Universalist Networking Association, ed., *Baltimore Papers* (Boston: La Lucha Press, 1998).

293 **into racial justice**, Joseph Barndt, interview by Leon Spencer and Leslie Takahashi Morris, July 2006.

293 **with mutual respect**, minutes of JTWTC, February 5–8, 2000.

293 **needing to change**, Susan Suchocki Brown, interview by Leslie Takahashi Morris, December 2007.

294 **transformation committee should do**, Ibid.

294 **what the model is**, minutes of JTWTC, February 5–8, 2000.

294 **lacking in anti-racism responsiveness**, minutes of JTWTC, April 28–30, 2000.

294 **General Assemblies were held**, minutes of JTWTC, February 5–8, 2000.

295 **to marginalized people**, minutes of JTWTC, minutes, February 5–8, 2000.

295 **in many ways undermined it**, Hoover, interview, September 2005.

295 **to that team**, Buehrens, email message.

295 **as a competition**, Buehrens, interview.

296 **and conference centers**, Buehrens, email message.

298 **gender, class, sexual preference, and ability**, Tom Stites, "Anti-Racism Primer," *The World*, March/April 2000, www.uuworld.org/2000/0300primer.html.

299 **least five more**, Unitarian Universalist Association Faith in Action Department, report to Veatch Program of Unitarian Universalist Church at Shelter Rock, NY, January 2001, Unitarian Universalist Association files, Boston.

299 **at that time**, Taquiena Boston, interview by Leslie Takahashi Morris, December, 2007.

299 **Disciples of Christ**, Taquiena Boston, email message to authors, May 2005.

300 **Rev. Suzelle Lynch provided leadership**, Joseph Santos-Lyons, email message to authors, July 2005.

300 **rather than congregations**, minutes of JTWTC, February 1–4, 2001, Unitarian Universalist Association files, Boston.

301 **in their areas**, minutes of JTWTC, February 1–4, 2001, Unitarian Universalist Association files, Boston.

301 **health and safety**, Joseph Santos-Lyons, "Parents shouldn't take their children's race personally," www.radicalhapa.typepad.com/my_weblog/2006/07/my_angry_asian_.html.

302 **of congregational life**, minutes of JTWTC, February 1–4, 2001.

303 **journey toward wholeness**, minutes of JTWTC, April 2001.

304 **anti-racism transformation teams**, Ibid.

304 **various "stakeholders" groups**, minutes of JTWTC, April 22–24, 2001.

304 **and facilitate this?** Ibid.

306 **on the journey**, Joshua M. Pawelek, "The Racism Embedded in Our System," in "Now I Begin to Understand: Personal Race Reflections," *The World*, May/June 2000, www.uuworld.org/2000/0300feat2.html.

309 **larger UU world**, DiBona, interview, 2007.

309 **the magazine's staff**, Tom Stites, email message to the authors, October 2007.

310 **with the divine**, Tom Stites, sermon delivered at Unitarian Universalist Association chapel, November 21, 2000.

311 **freedom of the press**, minutes of JTWTC, October 17–19, 1999.

311 **key staff person**, minutes of JTWTC, October 17–19, 1999.

311 **a critical lens**, minutes of JTWTC, April 28–30, 2000.

311 **changes the magazine and publications underwent**, Susan Suchocki Brown, email message to authors, May 2005.

312 **an Anti-Racist Multicultural Institution**, "Continuum on Becoming an Anti-Racist Multicultural Institution," edited for use in the Unitarian Universalist Association by Jacqui James, adapted from original concept by Baily Jackson and Rita Hardiman and further developed by Andrea Avazian and Ronice Branding.

313 **and Lynn Bacon**, LREDA, "Time Line."

316 **of an organization**, Taquiena Boston, "LREDA Final Report (Abridged)," December 2000, www.uua.org/lreda/content/observer01.html.

316 **race and ethnicity**, Joseph Santos-Lyons, "25 to 1: People of Color Experiences in Unitarian Universalism 1980–2005" (unpublished thesis, Harvard University), 2006, www.radicalhapa.typepad.com/my_weblog/2006/05/25_to_1_people_.html.

317 **all of these situations**, Danielle DiBona, email message to authors, August 2006.

317 **anti-racism process monitoring**, minutes of JTWTC, February 5–8, 2000.

318 **talk about class**, David Reich, "To Nashville with Class," *UU World*, September/October 2000, www.uuworld.org/2000/0900feat4.html.

320 **is to love**, Jone Johnson Lewis, "Racism, Theology, and the Institutional Church: Faith in Action Dept. UUA Workshop," www.uua.org/ga/ga00/243.html.

321 **in these resources**, Youth Advisors Task Force, report to Unitarian Universalist Association Board of Trustees, June 2000, Unitarian Universalist Association files, Boston.

321 **in the minority**, minutes of Young Religious Unitarian Universalists Youth Council, July 28–August 3, 2001, Unitarian Universalist Association files, Boston.

321 **UU Women's Federation, in May**, C*UUYAN, "Endorsement of Linked Identities."

322 **Just get going!** Melanie Griffin, "Start Becoming an Actively Anti-racist Youth Group," in Unitarian Universalist Association, Religious Education Action Clearing House Packet, February 2001, http://archive.uua.org/re/reach/winter01/youth/anti_racism.html.

323 **Young Religious Unitarian Universalists (YRUU)**, Diverse and Revolutionary Unitarian Universalist Multicultural Ministries Youth and Young Adult files, June 2006, Knoxville, TN.

323 **the Cleveland Indians**, minutes of JTWTC, February 1–4, 2001, Unitarian Universalist Association files, Boston.

323 **their own faith**, Santos-Lyons, "25 to 1."

325 **minister and the congregation walk together**, Denise Davidoff, remarks in response to Victor Carpenter, Unitarian Universalist Association General Assembly, June 23, 2001.

326 **will evaporate**, Richard Trudeau, "My Racialization," in "Now I Begin to Understand: Personal Race Reflections," *World*, March/April 2000, www.uuworld.org/2000/0300/feat2.html.

326 **reputation of grown-ups**, Frank Rivas, "Moses and the UUA," in "Now I Begin to Understand."

328 **ethnic cultural pride**, Ervin Barrios, "Two Sides of the Same Coin," in "Now I Begin to Understand."

329 **have been—and are—oppressed**, Rosemary Bray McNatt, "The Problem of Theology in the Work of Anti-racism: A Meditation," in Marjorie Bowens-Wheatley and Nancy Palmer Jones, eds., *Soul Work: Anti-Racist Theologies in Dialogue* (Boston: Skinner House, 2002), 37.

329 **their own lives?**, Ibid, 32.

330 **was its convener**, Deborah Weiner, "UUA hosts invitational consultation on Theology and Racism," www.lists.uua.org/pipermail/uua-l/Week-of-Mon-20010129/000626.html.

330 **dialogue on race**, Buehrens, interview.

330 **on the journey**, John Buehrens, "Foreword," in Bowens-Wheatley and Jones, *Soul Work*, xi.

331 **strained and "nasty"**, Peter Morales, telephone interview by Leslie Takahashi Morris, February 2007.

331 **was way overdue," he said**, Buehrens, interview.

333 **lead to justice**, Marjorie Bowens-Wheatley, in Deborah Weiner, "Theology, Class, and Race: Conference Dialogue," www.uua.org/urbanuu/urbanministriesconference/tcr2.html.

334 **and within us . . .**, Cheng Imm Tan, (sermon delivered at Urban Church Conference in Chicago), March 2001, www.uua.org/urbanuu/urbanministriesconference/sunworship.html.

336 **or internal debate**, Paul Rasor, "Liberal Religion and the Problem of Evil," speech delivered at Unitarian Universalist Association General Assembly, 2001, www.archive.uua.org/ga/ga01/3088.html.

337 **it may seem**, Qiyamah Rahman, in Thomas Jefferson District of Unitarian Universalist Association, *TJD Connections*, February/March 2000, adapted by Qiyamah Rahman.

340 **safe for everybody**, Gary Smith, telephone interview by Leslie Takahashi Morris, January 2007.

341 **for our congregation**, Catalogue for Philanthropy, "Jericho Road Project," www.catalogueforphilanthropy.org/ma/2005/jericho_road_5622.htm?ref=1.

342 **continue their ministry**, David Whitford, "A Step Towards Racial Reconciliation," *UU World*, May/June 2002, 24–30.

344 **built between strangers**, Kristen Harper, "Bridges Go Both Ways" (sermon delivered at Unitarian Universalist Associa-

tion General Assembly), 2000, www.uua.org/ga/ga00/263.html.

345 **at the table**, Poinsett, interview.

345 **black empowerment movement**, Wayne Arnason, telephone interview by Leslie Takahashi Morris, February 2007.

345 **and District Staff**, Unitarian Universalist Association, "Affirmative Action Reports to the General Assembly, 2000–2005 (except 2002)," quoted in Santos-Lyons, "25 to 1."

346 **to one degree or another with Bill**, Barndt, interview.

346 **was very common**, William Sinkford, telephone interview by Leslie Takahashi Morris, February 2007.

346 **Asian Pacific Islander Caucus**, Kok-Heong McNaughton, email message to authors, October 2005.

350 **General Assembly 2002 workshop . . .**, Unitarian Universalist Ministers Association, *UUMA News*, Unitarian Universalist Association files, Boston.

350 **in our community**, Susan Leslie, "Creating Partnerships for Anti-racist Actions," in Bowens-Wheatley and Jones, *Soul Work*, 210.

351 **can't even recognize**, William Sinkford, "Deconstructing Racism" (sermon delivered at First Unitarian Church of Dallas, TX), January 28, 1996.

352 **with this lens**, Olson Peebles, email message.

352 **Phyllis Daniel, former chair**, Phyllis Daniel, telephone interview by Leslie Takahashi Morris, December 2005.

352 **far-reaching ramifications**, DiBona, email message.

353 **early [antiracism] trainings**, William Sinkford, email message to authors, May 2005.

353 **growth in numbers**, Fredric Muir, telephone interview by Leslie Takahashi Morris, February 2007.

354 **is to me**, Michael Sallwasser, email message to authors, September 2005.

354 **our whole language**, Smith, interview.

355 **make us all ponder**, Sinkford, email message, October 2008.

355 **around race and culture**, DiBona, interview, 2007.

355 **Each word is encoded**, Christopher Donshale Sims, "Word Warrior," www.bebo.com/Profile.jsp?MemberId=3171802.

Part 5

357 **the seventh generation**, Wayne Arnason, in Journey Toward Wholeness Transformation Committee, "Continuing the Journey: Report and Recommendations to the 2001 General Assembly," 2001, Unitarian Universalist Association files, Boston, 2.

357 **in Tampa, Florida**, Unitarian Universalist Association Young Adult and Campus Ministry Office website, www.uua.org/ya-cm/youngadults/ar_ao/ar_index.html.

357 **anti-oppression training/consultation**, minutes of Unitarian Universalist Association Board of Trustees, June 2002, www.uua.org/TRUS/minutes06-02.html.

357 **second annual conference in Chicago**, Young Adult and Campus Ministry Office website.

357 **YaYA conference in Chicago**, Ibid.

357 **young adult anti-racism conference**, Ibid.

357 **trainers/organizers for youth**, Unitarian Universalist Association Youth Office, "Chrysalis Program Manual: Youth Leadership Training," www.uua.org/documents/youthoffice/chrysalismanual.

357 **woman of color**, Special Review Commission, "Final Report of the Special Review Commission," March 2006, Unitarian Universalist Association files, Boston, 15.

357 **Concerns are raised**, Commission on Appraisal, "Apology to the Delegates of the 2002 General Assembly: A Statement of Accountability from the Commission on Appraisal," www.uua.org/coa/apology.html.

357 **Asian/Pacific Islander group**, Young Kim, "How We Began," www.apiuu.org/began.htm.

358 **begin to depart**, William Gardiner, memorandum, July 1, 2002, Unitarian Universalist Association files, Boston.

358 **through our community**, Deborah Weiner, "3003 Plenary III," www.uua.org/ga/ga02/3003.html.

358 **UUA anti-racism efforts**, Simona Munson, email message to authors, May 2006.

358 **in New England**, Young Adult and Campus Ministry Office website.

358 **C*UUYAN and YRUU**, Ibid.

358 **the first time**, Young Religious Unitarian Universalists website, www.uua.org/YRUU/events/pdfs/19Organizations2.pdf.

358 **the next fiscal year**, Young Adult and Campus Ministry Office website.

358 **racial and ethnic groups**, minutes of Journey Toward Wholeness Transformation Committee, October 24, 2002, Unitarian Universalist Association files, Boston.

359 **C*UUYAN-sponsored events**, Young Adult and Campus Ministry Office website.

359 **Undoing Racism at Meadville Lombard conference**, minutes of Undoing Racism Committee, Unitarian Universalist Association files, Boston.

359 **first annual meeting in Berkeley, California**, Kim, "How We Began."

359 **Chicago and Dallas**, Munson, email message.

359 **both in March**, Young Adult and Campus Ministry Office website.

359 **endorse this request in August**, Ibid.

359 **its core mission**, Tracey Robinson-Harris, "Update to UUA Board Anti-Racism Assessment & Monitoring Team," www.uua.org/TRUS/apr04/anti-racism-assessment-team-200404.pdf.

359 **Young Adult and Campus Ministry Office**, Laurel Albina, "Youth of Color Leadership Development Conference," www.lists.uuyan.org/pipermail/yacmprofessionals/2003-April/000082.html.

359 **to anti-racism training**, Special Review Commission, "Final Report," 15.

359 **explore and dismantle racism**, Unitarian Universalist Service Committee website, www.uusc.org//pdf/83040.pdf.

360 **staff member Jacqui James**, Jacqui James, telephone interview by Leslie Takahashi Morris, November 2005.

361 **range of oppressions**, William Sinkford, "Bay Area design," memorandum, 2001, Unitarian Universalist Association files, Boston.

362 **to do it**, minutes of JTWTC, October 21–23, 2001.

362 **this proposal as well**, minutes of JTWTC, February 2–4, 2002.

363 **are doing, etc**, minutes of JTWTC, April 21–23, 2002.

363 **the Transformation Committee**, William Sinkford, telephone interview by Leslie Takahashi Morris, February 2007.

364 **Board of Trustees for Anti-Oppression**, minutes of JTWTC, October 24–28, 2002.

365 **for a year**, Ibid.

366 **But they're not**, Norma Poinsett, telephone interview by Leslie Takahashi Morris, October 2008.

366 **transform the Association**, Ibid.

366 **undermine the work**, William McCall, interview by Chip Roush, July 2005.

366 **needs of the MFC were**, Phyllis Daniel, telephone interview by Leslie Takahashi Morris, December 2005.

367 **might partner with**, minutes of JTWTC, October 21–23, 2001.

368 **identity change behind that**, Joseph Barndt, interview by Leon Spencer and Leslie Takahashi Morris, May 2005.

368 **clear or consistent**, minutes of Journey Toward Wholeness Transformation Committee "Finding Common Ground" meeting, January 11, 2003, Dallas, TX, Unitarian Universalist Association files, Boston.

369 **average person could do**, Paula Cole Jones, interview by authors, May 2005.

369 **was also clear**, minutes of JTWTC, February 2–4, 2002.

370 **get any easier?**, Summary of participant evaluations at Journey Toward Wholeness Transformation Committee

"Finding Common Ground" meeting, January 11, 2003, Dallas, TX, Unitarian Universalist Association files, Boston.

370 **bright, competent, passionate individuals," she said**, Tamara Payne-Alex, interview by Leslie Takahashi Morris, September 2008.

371 **from sustained interaction**, Ibid.

371 **That was hard**, Sinkford, interview, February 2007.

372 **is currently facing**, Joshua Pawelek, "Jubilee II Trainers' Response to proposed UUA Restructuring" (memorandum), February 2003, Unitarian Universalist Association files, Boston.

372 **Faith in Action**, Ibid.

372 **the next year**, Gardiner, memorandum.

373 **redistribution of work**, Pawelek, "Jubilee II Trainers' Response."

373 **historically opposed the work**, Ibid.

374 **of Congregational Services**, Ibid.

374 **and community partnerships**, "Office of Community Justice Making Announcement," Unitarian Universalist Association files, Boston.

374 **to our expertise**, Pawelek, "Jubilee II Trainers' Response."

375 **in anti-racism staff**, Joshua Pawelek, email message to Leslie Takahashi Morris, February 2003.

376 **that organizing capacity**, William Gardiner, email message to authors, April 2005.

377 **changed a thing**, Pawelek, email message to authors, April 2005.

377 **more leader/messengers, not fewer!**, Jean Shepard, email message to authors, June 2006.

379 **is our dream?**, Kurt Kuhwald, email message to authors, May 2005.

379 **dispersed . . . devalued . . . disrespected**, McCall, interview.

379 **which affect identity**, James, interview.

380 **hard at work**, William Sinkford, undated memorandum to Journey Toward Wholeness Transformation Committee, in minutes of JTWTC.

381 **for themselves," Boston said**, Taquiena Boston, interview by Leslie Takahashi Morris, December 2007.

381 **heterosexism/homophobia, and racism**, Unitarian Universalist Association Identity-Based Ministries staff group, mission statement, www.uua.org/aboutus/professionalstaff/identity-basedministries/index.php.

382 **and the trainings," Boston said**, Boston, interview.

384 **Perhaps we're ready**, William Sinkford, "The Language of Faith" (sermon delivered at First Jefferson Unitarian Universalist Church, Fort Worth, TX), January 12, 2003, www.uua.org/president/030112.html.

385 **if the end of that ever came**, Barndt, interview.

385 **our best shot**, Kurt Kuhwald, email message, May 2005.

386 **by the UUA**, minutes of JTWTC, November 21–24, 2003.

386 **matters of anti-racism**, Susan Suchocki Brown, interview by Leslie Takahashi Morris, December 2007.

386 **to one another**, Boston, interview.

388 **we must change**, Pawelek, email message, April 2005.

389 **to educate them**, Gary Smith, telephone interview by Leslie Takahashi Morris, January 2007.

390 **to cultural competency**, Clyde Grubbs, email message to authors, August 2005.

390 **Manhasset, New York**, Rosemary Bray McNatt, telephone interview by Leslie Takahashi Morris, February 2007.

394 **after that, it's okay**, McNatt, interview.

395 **That's pretty damning**, William R. Murry, telephone interview by Leslie Takahashi Morris, May 2006.

395 **what my place would be**, Kate Lore and Archene Turner, telephone interview by Leslie Takahashi Morris, March 2005.

396 **over the just**, Jon Rice, email message to authors, April 2005.

397 **with the consultation**, Leslie Takahashi Morris was as well, though not involved in its design.

397 **until you experience this," she said**, Lore and Turner, interview.

398 **for all students**, William Murry, "President's Report to the Board of Trustees," February 11, 2003, Meadville Lombard Theological School files, Chicago.

399 **the work begins**, Murry, "President's Report."

399 **process of accountability**, minutes of Meadville Lombard Theological School Board of Trustees, March 1, 2003, Meadville Lombard Theological School files, Chicago.

399 **a summary was made available**, Ibid.

399 **the whole institution**, minutes of JTWTC, March 29–30, 2003.

399 **described the event as "pathetic"**, Patricia Jimenez, interview by Chip Roush, November 2005.

399 **about these meetings**, Patricia Jimenez, "Memo from Committee on Anti-racism, Anti-Oppression and Multiculturalism to Unitarian Universalist Ministers Association Executive Committee meeting," April 5, 2003, Unitarian Universalist Ministers Association files, Boston.

400 **as "reverse racism"**, Lee Sanchez, "Challenges to Doing Anti-racism/Anti-oppression/Multicultural Work at Meadville Lombard School of Theology" (undated memo to Meadville Lombard School of Theology students).

401 **for another generation**, Murry, interview.

401 **of Unitarian Universalism**, Lee Barker, telephone interview by Leslie Takahashi Morris, January 2007.

401 **Of course, we did**, Marjorie Bowens-Wheatley, Abhi Janamanchi, and Clyde Grubbs, interview by Leslie Takahashi Morris, February 2006.

403 **talk about that**, Daniel, interview.

403 **been very helpful**, Jerome Stone, email message to authors, April 2005.

403 **identify Latina/o students**, Jimenez, "Memo."

403 **in summer 2000**, minutes of JTWTC, October 24–28, 2002.

403 **a big shift**, minutes of JTWTC, November 21–24, 2003.

403 **begin to itch**, David Bumbaugh, "Detecting a Party Line," *Stairwell Wall*, Meadville Lombard Theological School, April 26, 2005, Meadville Lombard Theological School files, Chicago.

405 **make this journey. Come**, Peter Morales, "Anti-Anti-M," *Quest*, April 2002, Church of the Larger Fellowship, Boston, clf.uua.org/quest/archives2002.html.

407 **there's a lag**, minutes of JTWTC, February 2–4, 2002.

408 **of public libraries**, Metropolitan New York District of Unitarian Universalist Association, "Anti-Racism and Diversity Committee," www.antiracism.net/.

409 **interactions with people of color before**, "Connecting with Others."

409 **have to do with congregations**, minutes of JTWTC, October 24–28, 2002.

409 **educate ourselves away on anything**, Suchocki Brown, interview.

410 **religious education curricula**, minutes of JTWTC, March 29–30, 2003.

410 **create an identity**, Ibid.

410 **provide this function**, minutes of JTWTC, n.d.

410 **Diverse and Revolutionary UU Multicultural Ministries (DRUUMM)**, minutes of JTWTC, March 29–30, 2003.

410 **staff Core Team**, Ibid.

411 **the congregational level**, "Connecting with Others Through Anti-Racism Work," *InterConnections*, Unitarian Universalist Association, March 2002, www.uua.org/leaders/leaderslibrary/leaderslibrary/interconnections/48062.shtml

411 **feel at home**, minutes of JTWTC, November 21–24, 2003.

411 **to the table**, Ibid.

411 **various continental committees**, Ibid.

411 **in May 2003**, Ibid.

411 **Wyoming Arts Council**, "Connecting with Others.".

413 **and our congregations**, Tony Brumfield, First Unitarian Universalist Church of San Diego website.

414 **the white community?**, Janice Marie Johnson, telephone interview by Leslie Takahashi Morris, January 2006.

415 **of the Association**, minutes of Unitarian Universalist Association General Assembly Planning Committee, September 2003, Unitarian Universalist Association files, Boston.

415 **regular General Assembly**, Commission on Appraisal, "Commission on Appraisal: About Us," www.uua.org/aboutus/governance/electedcommittees/appraisalcommission/index.shtml.

416 **was taken aback**, Christopher L. Walton, "General Assembly Report: Delegates Take a Global View in Quebec," *UUWorld*, September/October 2002, www.uuworld.org/2002/05/feature3.html.

416 **was not okay**, Hope Johnson, interview by Leslie Takahashi Morris, February 2007.

418 **GA just like this one in 1997**, http://dev.uua.org/world/2002/05/druumm-jtwtc.html.

419 **values and fears and anxieties and hopes**, Susan Suchocki Brown, email message to authors, May 2005.

419 **this 2002 GA**, Manish Mishra, interview by Leslie Takahashi Morris, July 2006.

420 **level of commitment**, Gini Courter and William Sinkford, telephone interview by Leslie Takahashi Morris, September 2008.

421 **leader training opportunities**, Tracy Robinson Harris, "Update to the Board: Anti-Racism Assessment and Monitoring Team," April 2004, Unitarian Universalist Association files, Boston.

422 **Unitarian Universalist Women's Federation, and DRUUMM**, minutes of UUA General Assembly Planning Committee, January 11–14, 2002.

422 **Front Desk and Concierge**, Joseph Santos-Lyons, "25 to 1: People of Color Experiences in Unitarian Universalism 1980-2005" (unpublished thesis, Harvard University), 2006, www.radicalhapa.typepad.com/my_weblog/2006/05/25_to_1_people_.html.

423 **but by character**, Kok-Heong McNaughton, "Race in America Beyond Black and White," *UUA News & Events General Assembly 2003*, Unitarian Universalist Association.

424 **the public realm**, Rosemary Bray McNatt, in Allan Stern, "3111 John Murry Lecture: Love and Power—The Universalist Dilemma," http://archive.uua.org/ga/ga03/3111.html.

426 **Choose your trailblazers carefully**, Young Kim, report of Nominating Committee to Unitarian Universalist Association General Assembly, 2003, Unitarian Universalist Association files, Boston.

427 **both inspiring and true**, Manish Mishra, "Thinking More Expansively about Racial Diversity" (sermon delivered at Unitarian Universalist Congregation of Arlington, VA), July 6, 2003, www.apiuu.org/manishjul06.html.

428 **those of older adults**, Jyphia Christos-Rogers, telephone interview by Leslie Takahashi Morris, August 2006.

429 **the training process**, Participants in Portland Youth and Young Adult Anti-Racism Development meeting, interview by Michael Tino, Jesse Jaeger, and William Gardiner, June 2003, Unitarian Universalist Association files, Boston.

429 **embracing multiple identities**, Stern, "3111 John Murray Lecture."

429 **the congregational level**, Hope Johnson, interview.

429 **a pseudo-integrated world**, Jesse Jaeger, telephone interview by Leslie Takahashi Morris, August 2006.

430 **race or abortion**, Petra Aldrich, interview by authors, June 2004

431 **for racial justice**, Youth Office of the Unitarian Universalist Association, "Youth Leadership Training," *Chrysalis Program Manual*, updated April 2005, www.uua.org/YRUU/training/pdfs/chrysalismanual.pdf.

432 **Challenging White Supremacy Workshop**, minutes of Young Religious Unitarian Universalists Youth Council, Unitarian Universalist Association files, Boston.

433 **holistic anti-oppression curriculum**, Unitarian Universalist Association Youth Council, "2003 Concentric and Youth Council Transformation Team Resolution," www.uua.org/ya-cm/youngadults/ar_ao/ar_index.html.

433 **youth and young adult antiracism trainers**, Ibid.

433 **deep and binding experience**, Kim Varney, email message to authors, May 2005.

435 **in Berkeley, CA**, Young Kim, "How We Began," March 2005, www.apiuu.org/began.html.

435 **(Diverse and Revolutionary UU Multicultural Ministries)**, Kok-Heong McNaughton, "Asian UU Network Forums," *Hot Rice*, Spring 2003, www.apiuu.org.

435 **and Jennifer Ryu**, minutes of JTWTC, March 29–30, 2003.

435 **to be UUs too**, Varney, email message, April 2005.

436 **will be used for**, YRUU Youth Council, "Resolution to Establish a Joint YRUU-CUUYAN Anti-Racism Transformation Team," www25.uua.org/YRUU/governance/ycresolutionarchive/yc04.htm#4.

437 **my precious life**, Janice Marie Johnson, interview.

437 **put this collar on**, McNatt, interview.

438 **rebellion against leadership**, Suchocki Brown, email message.

439 **for their city**, First Unitarian Universalist Society of Burlington Anti-Racism Action Committee, "What Is Our Dream? The First Unitarian Universalist Society of Burlington and the Quest for Racial Justice (1994–2002)."

439 **I had grown . . .**, Cole Jones, interview.

439 **of anti-racism, anti oppression**, Grubbs, email message, October 2008.

439 **a theological issue," he said**, Group interview by authors at Unitarian Universalist Association General Assembly, June 2006.

439 **as critical in this**, Rebecca Parker, interview by Leslie Takahashi Morris and Chip Roush, May 2006.

439 **noted in 2006**, Gary Kowalski, email message to Leslie Takahashi Morris, June 2006.

440 **forward toward justice**, Richard Speck, email message to authors, September 2005.

440 **to a miracle**, Sinkford, interview, September 2008.

441 **prefer the latter**, Keith Kron, email message to authors, April 2005.

442 **are feeling uncomfortable**, minutes of YRUU Youth Council.

Part 6

443 **Special Review Commission Report, March 2006**, Special Review Commission, "Final Report of the Special Review Commission," March 2006, Unitarian Universalist Association files, Boston, 11. 3.

443 **APIC and DRUUMM covenant together**, Asian/Pacific Islander Caucus and Diverse Revolutionary Unitarian Universalist Multicultural Ministries, "Covenant Between the Diverse and Revolutionary Unitarian Universalist Multicultural Ministries (DRUUMM) and The Asian/Pacific Islander Caucus (A/PIC)." www.apiuu.org/covenant.pdf.

443 **at General Assembly**, *The Religious Leader*, 2004, Unitarian Universalist Association, Boston, www.uua.org/programs/ministry/publications/rlprega04.pdf.

443 **Con-Con 2005 is canceled**, Special Review Commission, "Final Report," 16.

443 **fiscal year 2004–2005**, minutes of Unitarian Universalist Association Board of Trustees, April 17–18, 2004, www.uua.org/documents/boardtrustees/040418_minutes.pdf.

443 **fall of 2004**, Starr King School for the Ministry, "Educating to Counter Oppression Self Assessment Report" (draft), 2006, Berkeley, CA, 31.

444 **Consultancy program for congregations is launched**, Unitarian Universalist Association, "JUUST Change Consul-

444 tancy," 2006, www.uua.org/leaders/leaderslibrary/leaders library/27108.shtml.

444 **do as well**, Special Review Commission, "Final Report," 17–18.

444 **anger and sorrow**, Ibid., 17–19.

444 **Fort Worth General Assembly**, Ibid., 1.

444 **created in November**, Special Review Commission, "One Event, Two Perspectives," 2006, www.uuallies.org/NameSurveyReport.pdf.

444 **Special Review Commission is published**, Special Review Commission, "Final Report."

444 **before General Assembly**, Heather Janules, email message to authors, June 2005.

445 **asking before," she said**, Gini Courter and William Sinkford, telephone interview by Leslie Takahashi Morris, September 2008.

445 **leaves me disillusioned**, Kuhwald, email message, May 2005.

447 **from 2002 to 2006**, Janice Marie Johnson, telephone interview by Leslie Takahashi Morris, January 2006.

447 **not mixed well**, Gini Courter, telephone interview by Leslie Takahashi Morris, August 2006.

447 **ready for it**, Finley C. Campbell, flyer distributed at Unitarian Universalist Association General Assembly, 2006.

448 **anti-racist and anti-oppressive lens**, minutes of Unitarian Universalist Association General Assembly Planning Committee, September 15–19, 2004, Unitarian Universalist Association files, Boston.

448 **name for it**, minutes of Journey Toward Wholeness Transformation Committee, November 12–14, 2004, Unitarian Universalist Association files, Boston.

448 **explore new language**, Ibid.

448 **Leon Spencer, 2009-**, compiled by Mark Morrison-Reed, email to authors, March 2009.

449 **must be changed**, minutes of JTWTC, November 12–14, 2004.

449 **the Transformation Committee**, Ibid.

449 **we do things**, Tracey Robinson-Harris, telephone interview by Leslie Takahashi Morris, July 2005.

450 **meeting of stakeholder groups in 2006**, Richard Speck et al., letter to colleagues, March 18, 2005, www.metrony.org/metronyminutes/april05/JPD_Anti-Racism.doc.

450 **identity-based communities**, Kim Varney, email message, May 2005.

452 **The rest is history**, Christopher Donshale Sims, email message to authors, July 2005.

456 **a continuing story**, Special Review Commission, "Final Report," March 2006, 21–22.

457 **to become involved**, Special Review Commission, 17–19.

458 **This is my church**, William Sinkford, introduction to *Long Challenge: The Empowerment Controversy (1967–1977)*, by Victor Carpenter (Chicago: Meadville Lombard Theological School Press, 2004), viii–ix.

460 **UUs of color**, Kok-Heong McNaughton, "Transracial adoptions, interracial families: changing faces, changing hearts," www.uua.org/ga/ga05/2067.html.

466 **needs to be said**, "Transracial adoptions, Interracial Families: Changing Faces, Changing Hearts," Unitarian Universalist Association General Assembly 2005, transcript by Catie Chi Olson, July 2005.

466 **but has lapsed**, Unitarian Universalist Association, "General Assembly Coverage," www.uua.org/ga/pc/pcmmjune05.pdf.

467 **too few resources are available**, William McCall, interview by Chip Roush, July 2005.

467 **they will walk**, Jacqui James, telephone interview by Leslie Takahashi Morris, November 2005.

467 **Identity-Based Ministries**, Taquiena Boston, email message to authors, May 2005.

468 **are the experts**, Courter, interview.

469 **Allies for Racial Equity**, minutes of UUA General Assembly Planning Committee, January 6, 2006.

470 **to their cities?**, minutes of UUA General Assembly Planning Committee, September 14–18, 2005.

470 **come to GA**, Norma Poinsett, telephone interview by Leslie Takahashi Morris, October 2008.

471 **but it's possible . . .**, Manish Mishra, interview by Leslie Takahashi Morris, July 2006.

472 **to be successful**, Joshua Pawelek, email message to Leslie Takahashi Morris, February 2003.

472 **have to tell**, William Sinkford, email message to authors, May 2005.

473 **JUUST Change consultancy program**, Courter and Sinkford, interview.

473 **conversation or conversations**, Robinson-Harris, interview.

473 **want to go**, Journey Toward Wholeness Transformation Committee, "Next Steps on the Journey—Supporting Congregations in Anti-racism and Justice Making Work," report to the Unitarian Universalist Association Board of Trustees, April 2003, Unitarian Universalist Association files, Boston.

474 **work of justice**, Ibid.

475 **of approximately $5,000**, Pawelek, email message, February 2003.

475   **plan next steps**, minutes of JTWTC, March 10–13, 2005.

475   **had opted out**, Paula Cole Jones, interview by authors, October 2008.

476   **why I'm here**, Sean Dennison, comments on "Step by Step" (Journey Toward Wholeness Transformation Committee blog), April 5, 2004, http://jtwtc.wordpress.com/.

477   **multi-racial, multi-cultural community**, Paula Cole Jones, interview, October 2008.

477   **to congregational needs**, Courter and Sinkford, interview.

479   **vision of wholeness**, Monica Cummings, Carolyn Cartland, Sean Dennison, Bob Gross, Julio Noboa, Charles Ortman, Taquiena Boston (president's liaison), open letter to Unitarian Universalist Association, May 25, 2006, Unitarian Universalist Association files, Boston.

481   **we all seek**, James Hobart, email message to Leslie Takahashi Morris, July 2006.

482   **be another failure**, Courter and Sinkford, interview.

483   **consistently counter oppressions**, Starr King School for the Ministry, "Report."

485   **accommodate those concerns**, Ibid.

486   **give something up**, Rebecca Parker, "Habits of White Privilege in Unitarian Universalism," in Joseph Santos-Lyons, "25 to 1: People of Color Experiences in Unitarian Universalism 1980–2005" (unpublished thesis, Harvard University), 2006, www.radicalhapa.typepad.com/my_weblog/2006/05/25_to_1_people_.html.

487   **people of faith**, Starr King School for the Ministry, "Report."

489   **for the school**, Ibid.

489   **at this task**, Jerome Stone, email message to authors, April 2005.

491   **who we are today**, Michelle Bentley and Qiyamah Rahman, "Sankofa Project Archive," www.uusankofa.org.

491   **heeded and healed**, Jessica Purple Rodela, "The Kaleidoscope Initiative," *The Stairwell Wall*, Spring 2006, Meadville Lombard Theological School.

491   **Do it anyway**, Ibid.

491   **to serve," she recalled**, Michelle Bentley, interview by Leslie Takahashi Morris, January 2006.

492   **we are today**, Qiyamah Rahman, "Sankofa Project Archive Home Page," www.uusankofa.org/tiki-index.php?PHPSESSID=49a93a989dab2b36ad828684825c2040.

492   **long-term strategy**, Joseph Santos-Lyons, "25 to 1: People of Color Experiences in Unitarian Universalism 1980–2005" (unpublished thesis, Harvard University), 2006, www.radicalhapa.typepad.com/my_weblog/2006/05/25_to_1_people_.html.

493   **Joseph Priestley District**, William Gardiner, "The Steps in Forming a Transformation Team," www.uua.org/ya-cm/youngadults/pdf/dt-pre-packet/Transformation%20Team%20Formation.pdf.

493   **the leading congregations**, Unitarian Universalist Association, "General Assembly coverage," www.uua.org/ga/ga02/5057.html.

494   **think they are**, McCall, interview.

494   **need or demand**, Varney, email message, May 2005.

495   **a different viewpoint**, Kok-Heong McNaughton, email message to authors, October 2005.

496   **and sexual orientations**, Unitarian Universalist Church of Arlington, VA, "Journey Toward Wholeness," www.uucava.org/org/vworgdet3tst.aspx?Sys_ID=392.

496   **in their city**, Group interview by authors at Unitarian Universalist Association General Assembly, June 2006.

497   **my being here**, Marjorie Bowens-Wheatley, Abhi Janamanchi, and Clyde Grubbs, interview by Leslie Takahashi Morris, February 2006.

497   **in our churches**, Peter Morales, telephone interview by Leslie Takahashi Morris, February 2007.

497   **instead of defusing them**, Bina Venkataraman, *Burlington Free Press*, June 26, 2006.

498   **program on anti-racism**, Fredric Muir, telephone interview by Leslie Takahashi Morris, February 2007.

500   **that ringing symbolizes?**, Unity Church-Unitarian, "Anti-racism Team," www.unityunitarian.org/antiracismteam.html.

501   **compromising our integrity**, Janice Marie Johnson, interview.

502   **must be ongoing**, Lucy Friedrichs, email message to authors, September 2005.

502   **and human rights**, Ibid.

505   **and online forums**, Joyce Dowling, "Anti-racism," www.drix.net/jdowling/antiracism.html.

506   **in the congregation**, Paula Cole Jones, "Reconciliation as a Spiritual Discipline," adapted, *UU World*, March/April 2004, www.uuworld.org/2004/02/feature1.html.

509   **People of Color communities**, Santos-Lyons, "25 to 1."

509   **has been successful**, Davies Memorial Unitarian Universalist Church, "Davies Memorial Growth Plan," May 14, 2006, Davies Memorial Unitarian Universalist Church files, Camp Springs, MD.

510   **Don't wait for peace, create peace!**, John Crestwell, "Paralysis from Analysis," www.dmuuc.org/minister/John/Paralysis-from-Analysis.html.

511 **People of Color,** minutes of Young Religious Unitarian Universalists Youth Council, August 21–30, 2005, Unitarian Universalist Association files, Boston.

511 **staff person for youth,** Ibid.

511 **and few between,** Janice Marie Johnson, interview.

512 **starting up!,** Siri Larsen, "From the Steering Committee," *Synapse,* Spring 2005, Unitarian Universalist Association Youth Office, www.uua.org/YRUU/synapse/2005-1/spring05.pdf.

513 **especially at 15,** Group interview with young adults by Chip Roush and Leslie Takahashi Morris, Unitarian Universalist Association General Assembly 2006.

514 **you cannot love me,** JooYoung Choi, "A Note from Joo Choi," www25.uua.org/YRUU/events/pdfs/02Note.pdf.

515 **have adult support,** Elandria Williams, interview by Leslie Takahashi Morris, June 2006.

515 **Unitarian Universalist leadership,** Hope Johnson, interview by Leslie Takahashi Morris, February 2007.

515 **twenty years ago,** Janice Marie Johnson, interview.

517 **change our lives,** Joshua Pawelek, email message to authors, April 2005.

517 **ways of being,** William Gardiner, email message to authors, April 2005.

517 **is lifelong work?** Keith Kron, email message to authors, April 2005.

518 **tired of doing it.** Janice Marie Johnson, interview.

518 **white allies group,** Bowens-Wheatley, Janamanchi, and Grubbs, interview.

519 **love, faith, hope, and courage,** Allies for Racial Equity, "Guiding documents," www.uuallies.org.

519 **or won't be,** Mishra, interview.

519 **anti-oppression and multiculturalism,** Varney, email message, May 2005.

522 **to work together,** Megan Selby, "For White Folks Who Hate Identity Groups," www25.uua.org/YRUU.

525 **around the world,** Tracey Robinson-Harris, email message to authors, April 2006.

525 **was a goal,** Flyer for "Drinking From Out Own Wells: Celebration, lamentation, community, and ministry in Latino/a and Hispanic Unitarian Universalist theologies," www.uuma.org/main/conferences.html.

527 **taking us too far,** Janice Marie Johnson, interview.

527 **by the experience,** William McCall, interview by Joseph Santos-Lyons, May 2006, in Santos-Lyons, "25 to 1."

528 **to wrestle with,** Janice Marie Johnson, interview.

529 **to and with UU youth,** Hope Johnson, interview.

534 **also hope there,** Matt Kelley, speech delivered at Unitarian Universalist Association General Assembly, 2006, transcript by Catie Chi Olson, July 2006.

534 **Unitarian Universalist Association,** Hope Johnson, interview.

539 **The story continues,** Lisa Presley, "5030 Plenary VII," www.uua.org/ga/ga06/5030.html.

541 **my best option,** Santos-Lyons, "25 to 1."

542 **sound good, feel good,** Poinsett, interview.

542 **who you** be, Group interview by authors at Unitarian Universalist Association General Assembly, June 2005.

542 **St. Paul, Minnesota,** Paula Cole Jones, interview, October 2008.

543 **that's an outcome,** Rebecca Parker, interview by Leslie Takahashi Morris and Chip Roush, May 2006.

543 **loss of faith,** Bowens-Wheatley, Janamanchi, and Grubbs, interview.

544 **being the mountain,** Melvin Hoover, telephone interview by Leslie Takahashi Morris, September 2005.

544 **array of oppressions,** minutes of JTWTC, April 2002.

544 **I am grateful,** Karen Eng, homily delivered at First Unitarian Church of Oakland, CA, February 2006.

545 **I'd say 2,000 [people],** Poinsett, interview.

545 **of systemic oppression,** Simona Munson, interview by Leslie Takahashi Morris, July 2006.

546 **possibility of correction,** William Jones, telephone interview by Chip Roush and Leon Spencer, December 2005.

546 **in 2003–04,** Courter, interview.

546 **year to year,** Kathleen Montgomery, interview by Leslie Takahashi Morris, January 2008.

546 **the late '90s,** Kathleen Montgomery, email message to Leslie Takahashi Morris, March 2008.

547 **do among ourselves,** Janice Marie Johnson, interview.

550 **be expressed truthfully,** Marta Valentin, email message to authors, July 2007.

Part 7

551 **thunder and lightning,** Frederick Douglass, "The Significance of Emancipation in the West Indies," in *The Frederick Douglass Papers.* Series One: Speeches, Debates, and Interviews, vol. 2, ed. John W. Blassingame (New Haven: Yale University Press, 1991), 204.

551 **not finished yet,** minutes of Journey Toward Wholeness Transformation Committee, June 25, 1999, Unitarian Universalist Association files, Boston.

552 **a 'heavy price'**, Janice Marie Johnson, telephone interview by Leslie Takahashi Morris, January 2006.

552 **changed the conversation**, William Gardiner, telephone interview by Chip Roush, August 2005.

553 **in our movement**, Gini Courter and William Sinkford, telephone interview by Leslie Takahashi Morris, September 2008.

554 **needs more faith**, Kathleen Montgomery, interview by Leslie Takahashi Morris, December 2007.

555 **the Empowerment Controversies**, Special Review Commission, "Final Report of the Special Review Commission," March 2006, Unitarian Universalist Association files, Boston.

555 **for this work**, Kurt Kuhwald, interview by Chip Roush, August 2005.

556 **with the work**, Paula Cole Jones, interview by Chip Roush, Leon Spencer, and Leslie Takahashi Morris, May 2005.

556 **how they link**, Kuhwald, interview.

556 **engaging these 'evils,'** Clyde Grubbs, email message to authors, August 2005.

558 **not getting anywhere**, Manish Mishra, interview by Leslie Takahashi Morris, July 2006.

558 **work on that? Hugely**, Peter Morales, telephone interview by Leslie Takahashi Morris, February 2007.

559 **because of those**, Fredric Muir, telephone interview by Leslie Takahashi Morris, February 2007.

559 **judgments against us? Yes**, Special Review Commission, "Final Report," 8.

560 **to 'UU identity'**, Starr King School for the Ministry, "Educating to Counter Oppression Self-Assessment Report" (draft), August 2006, Berkeley, CA.

560 **in your work this year?**, William McCall, interview by Chip Roush, July 2005.

561 **you be uncomfortable**, Paula Cole Jones, interview by authors, October 2008.

561 **a 'beloved community,'** Tomas Firle, email message authors, September 2005.

561 **honoring each individual**, Richard Speck, email message to authors, September 2005.

561 **antiracism and JTW**, minutes of JTWTC, October 19–21, 1997.

562 **cares about Jesus**, Anita Farber-Robertson, telephone interview by Leslie Takahashi Morris, September 2008.

563 **and collective identities**, Tracey Robinson-Harris, telephone interview by Leslie Takahashi Morris, July 2005.

563 **approach to evil**, Paul Rasor, "Liberal Religion and the Problem of Evil" (speech delivered at Unitarian Universalist Association General Assembly), 2001, www.archive.uua.org/ga/ga01/3088.html.

564 **to battle with**, Special Review Commission, "Final Report," 6.

564 **where you stand on ideology**, Paula Cole Jones, interview, October 2008.

564 **observed in 2005**, Robert Gross, interview by Chip Roush, September 2005.

565 **skilled in anti-oppression**, Tamara Payne-Alex, interview by Leslie Takahashi Morris, September 2008.

565 **in their churches," she said**, Paula Cole Jones, interview, October 2008.

565 **an anti-racist lens**, minutes of Board of Trustees of Joseph Priestley District of Unitarian Universalist Association, May 2002, www.jpduua.org/minutes/minutes0502.html.

565 **in their midst**, Marjorie Bowens-Wheatley, Abhi Janamanchi, and Clyde Grubbs, interview by Leslie Takahashi Morris, February 2006.

566 **give up ultimate control**, Melvin Hoover, telephone interview by Leslie Takahashi Morris, September 2005.

566 **changing a system**, Robert Eller-Isaacs, telephone interview by Leslie Takahashi Morris, January 2006.

567 **of anti-racism work**, Rebecca Parker, interview by Leslie Takahashi Morris and Chip Roush, May 2006.

567 **stop working on," she said**, Norma Poinsett, telephone interview by Leslie Takahashi Morris, October 2008.

568 **that I think will work, frankly**, Bowens-Wheatley, Janamanchi, and Grubbs, interview.

568 **schools of thought**, Special Review Commission, "Final Report, 6.

569 **How shall we get together**, minutes of JTWTC, June 25, 1999.

570 **to do that**, Jacqui James, telephone interview by Leslie Takahashi Morris, November 2005.

571 **do critical analysis**, Susan Suchocki Brown, interview by Leslie Takahashi Morris, December 2007.

572 **on this committee**, Morales, interview.

572 **JTW, etc., work**, McCall, interview.

572 **who they really are**, Timothy Malone, email message to authors, April 2005.

573 **people of color**, Special Review Commission, "Final Report," 6.

574 **and overly idealistic**, Kuhwald, email message, May 2005.

575 **do not apologize**, José Ballester, email message to authors, May 2005.

576 **be for real**, Janice Marie Johnson, interview.

576 **raising their consciousness**, Parker, interview.

577 **oppressor and oppressed**, Starr King School for the Ministry, "Report."

578 **Identity-Based Ministries staff group**, Taquiena Boston, interview by Leslie Takahashi Morris, December 2007.

578 **questions about accountability**, minutes of JTWTC, November 12–14, 2004.

580 **happens more easily**, Gini Courter, quoted in Lisa Presley, "5030 Plenary VII," www.uua.org/ga/ga06/5030.html.

581 **take out of performing it**, Ibid.

582 **People's truths are not**, Special Review Commission, "Final Report, 3–5.

583 **congregation members' lives**, Wayne Arnason, telephone interview by Leslie Takahashi Morris, February 2007.

583 **expense of others**, Ballester, email message.

584 **be ourselves without passing?**, Michelle Bentley, interview by Leslie Takahashi Morris, January 2006.

584 **closing their hearts**, Sofia Betancourt, interview by Leslie Takahashi Morris, March 2006.

584 **to get it**, Rosemary Bray McNatt, telephone interview by Leslie Takahashi Morris, February 2007.

584 **particularly prophetic stance emerging**, Victor Carpenter, telephone interview by Leslie Takahashi Morris, February 2007.

585 **one person or program with another**, Paula Cole Jones, interview, October 2008.

585 **more authentically UU**, Gini Courter, telephone interview by Leslie Takahashi Morris, August 2006.

585 **developing sustainable leadership**, Jyphia Christos-Rogers, telephone interview by Leslie Takahashi Morris, August 2006.

586 **have done differently**, Phyllis Daniel, telephone interview by Leslie Takahashi Morris, December 2005.

586 **there is progress**, Farber-Robertson, interview.

586 **must carry on**, Firle, email message.

586 **impact the denomination**, Gardiner, interview, August 2005.

587 **the cactus fence**, Gordon D. Gibson, email message to authors, September 2005.

587 **engaging these 'evils,'** Grubbs, email message, August 2005.

587 **multicultural world view**, Melvin Hoover, email message to authors, October 2008.

588 **What have we really done?** Group interview by Chip Roush, November 2005.

588 **of Unitarian Universalism**, Hope Johnson, interview by Leslie Takahashi Morris, February 2007.

589 **called 'growing pains'**, Janice Marie Johnson, interview.

589 **to the problem**, William Jones, telephone interview by Chip Roush and Leon Spencer, December 2005.

590 **for our faith**, Keith Kron, email message to authors, April 2005.

590 **of the holy**, Kuhwald, interview.

591 **is holy work**, Archene Turner and Kate Lore, telephone interview by Leslie Takahashi Morris, March 2005.

591 **to be accepted?** Malone, email message.

591 **white and American**, Kok-Heong McNaughton, email message to authors, October 2005.

592 **beginning my presidency**, Mishra, interview.

593 **but it's mine**, Group interview by Chip Roush, November 5, 2005.

593 **in their lifetime**, Muir, interview.

594 **began in 1997**, William Murry, telephone interview by Leslie Takahashi Morris, May 2006.

594 **our church cultures**, Bill Norris, email message to authors, 2005.

595 **you first started**, Joshua Pawelek, email message to authors, April 2005.

595 **pass with time**, Tamara Payne-Alex, interview.

595 **sense of satisfaction**, Linda Olson Peebles, email message to authors, August 2005.

596 **thought you had**, Poinsett, interview by authors, November 2005.

596 **January to January**, Norma Poinsett, "On Unitarian Universalism," March 3, 1999, www.firstuchicago.org/norma_on_uu.html.

597 **did it out loud**, Robinson-Harris, interview.

597 **did not create**, Jon Rice, email message to authors, April 2005.

597 **that divides us**, Sallwasser, email message to authors, September 2005.

598 **value these families**, Jean Shepard, email message to authors, June 2006.

598 **some real movement is possible**, William Sinkford, email message to authors, May 2005.

598 **reconciliation and wholeness**, Richard Speck, email message to authors, June 2006.

599 **are all committed**, Jerome Stone, email message to authors, April 2005.

599 **seems impossible now**, Susan Suchocki Brown, "Transcending Boundaries" (sermon delivered at First Church Unitarian Universalist in Leominster, MA), February 6, 1994.

600 **can't sugarcoat everything**, Turner and Lore, interview.

600 **to support you**, Kim Varney, email message to authors, April 2005.

600 **doing this for,** Elandria Williams, interview by Leslie Takahashi Morris, June 2006.

600 **what's happening now,** Special Review Commission, "Final Report, 8.

Epilogue

601 **whole and reconciled,** William Sinkford, email message to Leslie Takahashi Morris, October 2008.

602 **in other denominations,** Tamara Payne-Alex, interview by Leslie Takahashi Morris, September 2008.

602 **of the congregations,** Gini Courter and William Sinkford, telephone interview by Leslie Takahashi Morris, September 2008.

602 **of our work," she said,** Farber-Robertson, telephone interview by Leslie Takahashi Morris, September 2008.

602 **"Building a Jubilee World" workshops,** Paula Cole Jones, interview by authors, October 2008.

602 **a cultural change,** Cole Jones, interview, October 2008.

603 **with enough 'oomph,'** Paula Cole Jones, Susan Gore, Taquiena Boston, and Tracey Robinson-Harris, "One Journey, Many Paths: A Report to the UUA Board of Trustees," April 2004, www.archive.uua.org/programs/justice/antiracism/consultancy.html.

603 **goal-setting/action planning,** Tracey Robinson-Harris, report to Unitarian Universalist Association Board of Trustees, March 15, 2005, Unitarian Universalist Association files, Boston.

604 **collected these testimonials in 2007,** Unitarian Universalist Association, "JUUST Change Anti-Oppression Consultancy Participant Feedback, Anti-Racism and Anti-Oppression," 2007, www.archive.uua.org/programs/justice/antiracism/testimonials.html.

606 **anti-racism or even anti-oppression frame,** Tracey Robinson-Harris for Unitarian Universalist Association Congregational Services staff group, report to Unitarian Universalist Association Board of Trustees, March 2007, Unitarian Universalist Association files, Boston.

606 **love and justice,** Unitarian Universalist Association, "Building the World We Dream About," www.uua.org/aboutus/professionalstaff/identity-basedministries/110030.shtml.

607 **anti-racist/anti-oppression lens,** Mark Hicks, in Robinson-Harris, report, 2007.

607 **Building the World We Dream About,** UUA, "Building the World We Dream About."

607 **multicultural start-up congregation,** Unitarian Universalist Association, "Diversity of Ministry Initiative," 2008, www.uua.org/aboutus/professionalstaff/identity-basedministries/racialand/diversityministry/index.shtml (accessed November 2008).

608 **anti-racist/anti-oppressive change,** First Unitarian Church of Oakland, CA, "Journey Towards Wholeness," www.uuoakland.org/jtw.

608 **an anti-oppression agenda,** Ezabel Martin, "Other Teams to Know About," August 28, 2007, First Unitarian Universalist Church of San Diego, www.firstuusandiego.org/site_getinvolved/ottmstoknowabt.html.

609 **dear to my heart,' she said,** Lilia Cuervo, interview by Leslie Takahashi Morris, April 2009; Nancy Palmer Jones, email to Leslie Takahashi Morris, April 2009.

609 **Journey Toward Wholeness,** Om Prakash John Gilmore, introductory message, November 2008, Joseph Priestley District of Unitarian Universalist Association, www.jpduua.org/pages/jpd-leadership-notes.php.

609 **"A Dialogue on Race and Ethnicity" program,** Robinson-Harris, report, 2007.

609 **and community partners,** Ibid.

610 **things can change,** First Unitarian Church of Oakland, CA, "Journey Towards Wholeness."

Index

300, 302, 304, 307, 309, 311, 317, 330,
350, 350s, 358t–359t, 361–65, 367–69,
380, 385, 402–3, 406, 409–11, 416–17,
420, 443, 448, 450, 471–72, 475–76, 478,
483, 494, 519, 545, 557, 560, 564,
569–70, 599, 608, 610
Jubilee Working Group, 126s
Jubilee World Working Group for Anti-
Racism, 3, 4t, 12s, 24–30, 28s, 30s, 35,
37, 52t, 53–54, 56, 59, 61–62, 70–71, 73,
76, 84, 102s, 106–7, 120–21, 122s, 123,
126s, 127, 129–32, 132s, 134–36,
139–41, 151t, 160, 169, 173, 181, 185–88,
186s, 189s, 194, 206, 228, 240, 273, 298,
358, 358t, 377, 438, 567, 578–79, 590
Jubilee World workshops, 24, 30, 61, 73,
116s, 121, 123, 126s, 131, 135, 167, 167s,
183–85, 187–88, 188–89s, 194–95, 201,
208s, 209-10, 297, 304, 317, 322, 365–66,
371–76, 402, 406, 438, 440, 474, 506s,
528, 578, 596
JUUST Change Anti-Oppression Consultancy, 19, 444t, 472–73, 475, 477, 528s,
542, 552, 555, 561, 565, 568, 570, 585,
588, 603–5, 609

Kain, Julie, 412s
Kapuscik, Jean, 67s
Keip, Margaret, 452
Keizer, Bea de Muinck, 223
Kelley, Matt, 526, 529, 532
Kim, Hyun Hwan, 85
Kim, Young, 276t, 300, 357t, 424,
435s–436s, 458, 605
King, Martin Luther, 1t, 7–8, 16s, 39, 49,
62, 65, 142s, 197, 209, 253, 327s, 332,
340s, 350s, 387s–388s, 394, 411s, 510s,
589
King, Rodney, 64, 71, 145
Kings Chapel, Boston, 41, 416
Klaus-Li, Lucy, 313
Kowalski, Gary, 438–39s
Kron, Keith, 98, 108, 111, 113, 156, 190,
203, 381, 441, 517, 590
Krugman, Paul, 252–53

Ku Klux Klan, 28s, 210, 260, 269, 305s,
392, 521
Kuhwald, Kurt, 30s, 122s, 171, 186s, 190,
236, 264, 268, 298s, 377, 445, 556, 573,
590
Kyuchkov, Hristo, 496s

Ladysmith Black Mambazo, 580
Language of Race, 83–84, 97, 98s, 203–4,
206–7s
Larsen, Siri, 436s
Las voces del camino, 608
Latimer, Lewis, 66s
Latina/o Unitarian Universalist Network-
ing Association, 53t, 73, 134, 147,
152t–153t, 185, 195, 214–21, 220s, 225,
231–32, 232s–233s, 240, 271, 276t–277t,
282, 284s, 290s–291s, 327s, 381, 386,
400s, 404s, 435, 517, 571
Latino Professionals Network, 222s
Leadership Council, 124, 601
Leadership Development Conference for
Youth of Color, 359t, 582
Lee, David, 496
Leslie, Susan, 30s, 67s, 141, 158, 186s, 264,
350s
Levine, Judith, 521
LeWin, Wendy, 31
Lewis, Jacqueline, 605
Lewis, Pauline Warfield, 347
Liberal Religious Educators Association,
123, 151t, 154t, 275t, 276, 276t, 311–16
Liberal Religious Educators Association
Anti-Racism Task Force, 314
Liberal Religious Youth, 3t, 13–14, 35, 192
Liberal Syndrome, 20
Liberator, 15s
Lifespan Faith Development staff group,
372, 410
LINC, *see* Linked Identities Networking in
Coalition
Lindsey, Nora, 436s
Link, Margaret Ann, 30s, 130, 186s
Linked Identities Networking in Coalition,
275t, 321

Links, 35
Liuzzo, Viola, 1t, 8, 16s, 337
"Living with Jim Crow in Monroe County,"
207
Loftman, Connie, 207
Loftman, Guy, 207
*Long-Term Initiative for Racial and Cultural
Diversity,* 52t, 69
Lore, Kate, 395, 397, 591
Love and Charity, 350s
LREDA, *see* Liberal Religious Educators
Association
LRY, *see* Liberal Religious Youth
LUUNA, *see* Latina/o Unitarian Universal-
ist Networking Association
Lynch, Suzelle, 133, 285, 300, 458
Lyons, Joseph, 158, 300, 412s

MacLean, Kenneth Torquil, 32
Maher, Ian White, 449
Major, Barbara, 113
Malone, Timothy, 223, 572, 591
March on Washington, 15s
Marcuse, Herbert, 8s
Mason, Hilda H.M., 23
Massachusetts Bay District, 151t, 297, 565
Massachusetts Bay Districts Anti-Racism
Transformation Team, 96, 151t, 305s
Matteson, Karen, 281
Matthies, Kent, 321
MAVIN Foundation, 526, 529, 532
May, Samuel Jay, 15s
Mayflower Compact, 480s
Mayhew, Jonathan, 481s
McCall, William (Chester), 11, 44, 92s,
166s, 223, 238s, 283, 366–67, 379, 466,
494, 527, 560, 572
McComb, Mississippi, 32
McCoy, Olivine, 100s
McCulloch, Kevin, 321
McDonald, Michael, 301
McGavin, Judith, 67s
McGee, Michael, 210
McIntosh, Peggy, 142s
McKeeman, Gordon B., 6, 46